Simon Fietze | Wenzel Matiaske [eds.]

Dimensions and Perspectives on Financial Participation in Europe

Nomos

The Deutsche Nationalbibliothek lists this publication in the Deutsche Nationalbibliografie; detailed bibliographic data are available on the Internet at http://dnb.d-nb.de

ISBN 978-3-8487-1876-4 (Print)
978-3-8452-5941-3 (ePDF)

British Library Cataloguing-in-Publication Data
A catalogue record for this book is available from the British Library.

ISBN 978-3-8487-1876-4 (Print)
978-3-8452-5941-3 (ePDF)

Library of Congress Cataloging-in-Publication Data
Fietze, Simon / Matiaske, Wenzel
Dimensions and Perspectives on Financial Participation in Europe
Simon Fietze / Wenzel Matiaske (eds.)
507 p.
Includes bibliographic references.

ISBN 978-3-8487-1876-4 (Print)
978-3-8452-5941-3 (ePDF)

1. Edition 2016

Contents

Introduction 7
Simon Fietze & Wenzel Matiaske

The role of employee share ownership for corporate governance in the aftermath of the financial crisis – a closer look at the Central Eastern European EU Member States 13
Jens Lowitzsch, Iraj Hashi & Alban Hashani

Financial participation in Europe: Some kind of a dream 39
Jean-Michel Content

How to overcome the 'Great Divide' of the capitalist market society: Development, legal grounds and perspectives of employee capital participation in Germany and Europe 49
Herwig Roggemann

Historical perspectives on employee ownership in Germany 107
Alexander Kern

Financial participation in Germany: Management's and works councils' view 145
Simon Fietze, Wenzel Matiaske & Verena Tobsch

Works councils and profit sharing in the German metalworking industry 177
Thomas Haipeter

The corporate culture of silent partnerships – shareholding vs. participation? 205
Thomas Steger, Christina Beisiegel & Madeleine Dietrich

Profit sharing in France: Substitute or complement to wages? 241
Mathieu Floquet, Loris Guery, Patrice Laroche & Anne Stevenot

Employee financial participation: Evidence from Italian firms 263
Mirella Damiani, Fabrizio Pompei & Andrea Ricci

Employee share ownership in the Netherlands 285
Eric Kaarsemaker & Erik Poutsma

Government, union and business associations' perceptions of employee financial participation in Gipuzkoa 301
Begoña Arregi, Fred Freundlich, Mónica Gago, Maite Legarra, Nerea Lizarraga, Sylvia Gay, Jose Antonio Mendizabal & Ainhoa Larrañaga

Employee financial participation in Polish listed companies – a management approach 349
Maciej Kozłowski

Employee financial participation in Bulgaria 389
Spartak Keremidchiev

Determinants of financial participation – two decades of Croatian practice 425
Nina Pološki Vokić, Maja Klindžić & Ivana Načinović Braje

Workers' risk attitude and financial participation 459
Rahma Daly, Marc-Arthur Diaye & Jean-Max Koskievic

Cooperatives: Direct and indirect forms of employee financial participation 473
Theresia Theurl & Sandra Maria Swoboda

Introduction

Simon Fietze & Wenzel Matiaske

If one takes the first PEPPER report (Promotion of Employee Participation in Profit and Enterprise Results, Uvalic, 1991), which had been funded by the European Commission, and the subsequent eponymous Council Recommendation of 27 July 1992 as a benchmark, employee financial participation (EFP) has been on the European agenda for roughly 25 years. Since then, EFP has been extensively discussed in various quarters – not only in the realm of politics but also in the scientific community – as a means of shaping industrial relations and conseuently human resource management. These discussions had been intensified in the European Union (EU) when the search was on for capable (regulatory) tools to master the financial crisis of 2007-08. In 2013, after the above-mentioned crisis had waned to some extent, a conference in Hamburg gave scholars from various fields such as law, economics and social sciences ample opportunity to make an interim assessment of the usage of EFP in Europe. The results of this endeavour, along with some additional contributions, are provided in this edited volume.

It was and still is necessary to reflect on the socio-economic preconditions of EFP – especially with regards to the legal, economic and cultural framework and to industrial relations. Given the three, if not four distinct "EFP cultures" in Europe, namely the Anglo-Saxon, Continental, German and Scandinavian varieties, the prospects for a harmonized European approach to EFP have not particularly improved since the (early) ninety-nineties. Likewise, the experiences East European economies in transition have made in recent years inspire with confidence that EFP can indeed make a significant contribution to economic and social well-being, to socio-economic inclusion and integration.

The discussion sets out with three contributions addressing the European dimension of EFP. Drawing upon various secondary sources, *Jens Lowitzsch, Iraj Hashi* and *Alban Hashan* sketch the advancements EFP has made in the EU-15 and in the extended EU-27 since 2000. Centre stage, however, is taken by the EFP-related dynamics in Central Eastern Europe over the last decade, which have unfolded in a much more positive fashion than in the EU-15 countries. Albeit the introduction of EFP was mostly a by-product of the privatisation process, it is nevertheless crucially dependent on sustained political support and especially on a stable legal framework, in order to realise its full potential. In his contribution, *Jean-Michel Content* also focuses on the European dimension by assuming the perspective of the International Association for Financial Participation (IAFP). The author provides an up-to-date account of the debates that accompanied PEPPER I (Uvalic, 1991), PEPPER II (Commission of the European Communities, 1996) and PEPPER III (Lowitsch, 2006), as well as a number of EFP-related key studies and policies peak organizations have outlined and introduced. The reader not only gains a profound insight into the basic lines of reasoning (of EFP-proponents and -adversaries), but also into the fundamental problems and challenges on the way to the realisation of "some kind of a dream" of a harmonized approach to EFP in Europe. The European concept of a welfare state that bridges the “great divide” of capitalist market societies is the subject matter of *Herwig Roggemanns* contribution. Taking various historical and contemporary notions of social justice as a point of departure the author investigates those obstacles with impede the proliferation of Louis O. Kelso's Employee Stock Ownership Plans (ESOP) in Europe and especially in Germany. The contribution outlines initiatives and arguments that were put forward in Europe in favour as well as against EFP while paying particular attention to the developments in Germany since the revolutionary year of 1918.

Hereinafter, four contributions continue to focus on Germany, virtually a developing country in terms of EFP. *Alexander Kern* outlines the historical dimension of the issue in hand: choosing Bismarck’s social reforms as a starting point and chronologically addressing forward thinkers like Heinrich von Thünen and progressive practitioners like Ernst Abbe, the former director of the Zeiss Werke Jena in the late 19th century, the author nevertheless puts emphasis on the post-war period in Germany. Especially, the attitudes the ordoliberal founding fathers of the German “*Soziale Marktwirtschaft*” (social market economy) hold towards EFP and the evolution of the German model of industrial relations are carved out. A particularity of the German approach to industrial relations is workers' participation on the company level. *Simon Fietze, Wenzel Matiaske* and *Verena Tobsch* observe in their contribution that the attitudes both the Human Resource Management and works councils hold towards EFP are surprisingly well aligned. *Thomas Haipeter* analyses the policies and practice of works councils in implementing and regulating profit sharing in companies of the metal-working and electrical engineering industry. Based on surveys and interviews the author comes to the conclusion, that works councils not only play a pivotal role in the design and implementation of EFP-models, but in many cases also initiate the introduction of EFP-models. *Thomas Steger, Christina Beisiegel* and *Madeleine Dietrich* discuss silent partnerships, a specific mode of participation, which has so far been largely neglected in the literature. Based on two case studies on mid-tier companies (where silent partnerships are relatively more common than in small or large businesses) the authors come to emphasize the role corporate culture plays regarding EFP and the detrimental effects a paternalistic leadership style can have on such forms of participation.

The dissemination and design of EFP-models and the boundary conditions under which they are set up and maintained in the EU member states is the subject matter of the following string of contributions. It is a stylized fact that EFP is common in France. *Mathieu Floquet, Loris Guery, Patrice Laroche* and *Anne Stevenot* show however, that French companies exhibit remarkable differences with regards to the EFP-models they maintain. Large, profitable and listed firms with a relatively uncontested market position, for instance, tend to refer to EFP-models more frequently than other companies. On the basis of a standardized cross sectional study the authors furthermore show that wage levels in companies with an EFP-model are significantly higher than in companies without an EFP-model. Italy, where EFP enjoyed a steep increase in popularity in the nineteen eighties, is the subject of *Mirella Damiani, Fabrizio Pompei* and *Andrea Ricci*. The authors trace this development and show, referring to longitudinal employer survey data which had been collected from 2005-2010, the significant impact EFP has both on labour productivity and wage levels. *Eric Kaarsemaker* and *Erik Poutsma* show that in the Netherlands a largely positive attitude towards EFP prevails, although models of employee share ownership are not especially widespread. The authors shed light on the attitudes employers, unions and the state hold towards EFP, but also introduce the reader to the "Dutch model" for sustainable employee share ownership which had been developed on the basis of empirical data. The European Union is not only a union of member states, but also a union of the regions. In the context of EFP, *Begoña Arregi, Fred Freundlich, Mónica Gago, Maite Legarra, Nerea Lizarraga, Sylvia Gay, Jose Antonio Mendizabal* and *Ainhoa Larrañaga* introduce the reader to "Gipuzkoa", an autonomous community of the Basque country. Gipuzkoa is home to the cooperative "Mondragon", widely regarded as a role model for EFP. However, it is not Mondragon taking centre stage in this contribution, but the support for the cooperative idea of responsible participation in the region Gipuzkoa. Gipuzkoa, in turn, provides an example of the commons in the sense of Elinor Ostrom. First and foremost, it is the cooperation between labour unions, business associations and public institutions which allows EFP to gain a foothold, to make visible contributions to the development of the region, and, eventually, to be firmly established for the long term.

Three additional contributions shed light on recent developments in younger EU member states. In Poland EFP had been put to early use during economic transformation and is nowadays widespread and firmly established in Polish companies. Unlike in other EU member states, however, Polish EFP-models accrue to managerial personnel in the first place while blue-collar workers usually do not enjoy EFP-related benefits. Reason enough to put not only the facts under scrutiny but also the attitudes the management and staff member hold towards EFP. This has been accomplished by *Maciej Kozłowski* who outlines in his contribution the findings he has made in an online survey. The case of Bulgaria also exhibits some particularities, which *Spartak Keremidchiev* traces in his contribution. In historical terms EFP is deeply rooted in the cooperative movement, which emerged in the late 19th century and strongly drew upon the credit cooperation principles of Franz Herrmann Schulze-Delitzsch. The first Cooperative Law of 1907 gave this movement a considerable momentum, and at the end of the World War II almost a quarter of the Bulgarian population was a member of a cooperative. Although the cooperative movement ceased in the communist era its ideas nevertheless survived and inspired the process of economic transformation in Bulgaria. During this stage, the tendency to avoid risks was presumably stronger in Bulgaria than in any other East European country. Against this backdrop the author outlines the role EFP has played from the early stages of the economic transformation up to present day (when its relevance has been significantly reduced, however). Eventually, the focus is on Croatia, the youngest EU member state. *Nina Pološki Vokić, Maja Klindžić* and *Ivana Načinović Braje* outline the development over the last two decades. Starting from the Yugoslavian model of social organization, which favoured total employee participation in decision making and employee control over financial results, the authors move on to describe the post-soviet stage of economic transformation, when employee and management buy-outs were widely applied, to finally arrive at the present day state of affairs (which is characterized by low levels of EFP-use). The contribution refers to the latest CRANET survey (Cranfield Network on International Human Resource Management) in order to provide descriptive empirical data as well as a description of those determinants relevant for EFP in the Croatian economy in transition.

The final two contributions address cross-sectional research issues. By referring to the household wealth survey INSEE had carried out in France in 2010, *Rahma Daly, Marc-Arthur Diaye* and *Jean-Max Koskievic* put a fundamental assumption in standard economics under scrutiny, namely the assumption of risk averse staff members. To this end, the authors bring to bear an experimental device that measures risk attitudes by asking study participants to make choices between lotteries (where pay-offs are associated with respective probabilities of occurrence) and certain pay-offs. The results not only support the assumption of risk-averse staff members but also highlight EFP-models as an especially attractive offering to staff members with decreased risk-aversion. The question whether the cooperative is a suitable legal form to further EFP in the spirit of the PEPPER initiative is frequently discussed – not only in the literature as such but also in various instances in the contributions of this edited volume. *Theresia Theurl* and *Sandra Maria Swoboda* provide a thorough discussion of the legal form of the cooperative and the scope it offers for direct and indirect financial participation of staff members. Cooperatives facilitate collective self-help in form of an enterprise. While in the early days of the cooperative movement comrades often were cooperative workers at the same time – the term "workers' cooperatives" is frequently used in this context – cooperatives nowadays usually employ non-members (for example, the reader may call into mind housing or consumer cooperatives). The advantages of this specific legal form, its inherent participation rights, but also its independence of financial markets and its long-term orientation are also highly relevant for the design and implementation of EFP-models. The authors outline the specific design features of cooperatives which have established financial participation models and provide a number of insightful cases where cooperatives were founded in order to put EFP-models into practise, to alleviate market entry or to execute specific projects.

The idea for the conference and this volume was conceived in context of two research projects on EFP in Germany supported by the Hans Böckler Foundation (2007-2009, 2012-2015). We like to thank the members of our scientific advisory boards who have supported this plan. The meeting was held January 17-19, 2013, at Helmut-Schmidt-University in Hamburg. Expenses for the meeting, including transportation for all concerned, were covered by the Deutsche Forschungsgemeinschaft (DFG), for whose generosity we would like to express our sincere appreciation. After the conference the papers were submitted and the review process took some time. We are grateful to our authors not only for their contributions but also for patience.

June 2016, Sonderborg and Hamburg

Simon Fietze, Wenzel Matiaske

References

Commission of the European Communities (1996). *Pepper II: Promotion of participation by employed persons in profits and enterprise results (including equity participation) in Member States (COM 96, 697). Commission of the European Communities.*

Council of European Communities (1992). Council recommendation of 27 July 1992 concerning the promotion of participation by employed persons in profits and enterprise results (including equity participation). *Official Jounal of the European Communities*, 35, 53-55.

Lowitzsch, J. (Ed.) (2006). *The PEPPER III Report: Promotion of participation by employed persons in profits and enterprise results in the New Member and Candidate Countries of the European Union.* Rome, Berlin: Inter-University Centre, Freie Universität Berlin.

Uvalic, M. (1991). *The Pepper Report: Promotion of Employee Participation in Profits and Enterprise Results in the Member States of the European Community.* Commission of the European Communities.

The role of employee share ownership for corporate governance in the aftermath of the financial crisis – a closer look at the Central Eastern European EU Member States

Jens Lowitzsch, Iraj Hashi & Alban Hashani[1]

Abstract

Following a 2010 initiative opinion by the European Economic and Social Committee and a 2012 study on employee financial participation (EFP) commissioned by the European Parliament, in December 2012 the European Commission included the promotion of employee share ownership (ESO) in its Action Plan to reform European company law and corporate governance (European Commission, COM/2012/0740). This marks an extension in the perception of the issue of EFP in general and ESO in particular as a policy area that in the 1990ies had been seen predominantly as related to social policy.

As the link between better corporate governance and ESO is complex it is worthwhile to review the main arguments and findings. As will be shown, ESO is directly relevant to all three areas for action identified in the Action Plan, i.e., transparency, responsibility and competitiveness.

These related issues, i.e., information sharing, long-term shareholding and participation in decision-making are interlinked and elevate the status of employees; they are workers but also shareholders and stakeholders who can play an active role in corporate governance. Such employee shareholding is a kind of long-term investment that may help to stabilise capital markets, a welcome contrast to the destabilising effect of speculative short-term investment.

Against this background we investigate the dynamics of ESO in the Central Eastern European (CEE) countries over the last decade. Particular

1 Jens Lowitzsch (corresponding author): Kelso Professor of Comparative Law, East European Business Law and European Legal Policy, European University Viadrina, Frankfurt (Oder), Germany; Iraj Hashi: Professor of Economics, Staffordshire University, Stoke on Trent, United Kingdom; Alban Hashani: Senior Researcher, Riinvest Institute for Development Research, Prishtina, Kosovo.

attention is given to the difference in evolution of ESO in the CEE countries – as opposed to that in the old EU Member States. Finally, lessons for the support of sustainable employee ownership are drawn from the cases of Poland, Hungary and Lithuania.

1. Introduction

In 2005 in the EU-15[2], between 18 per cent (employee share ownership - ESO) and 34 per cent (profit sharing) of employees in the private sector were offered to participate financially in the enterprise for which they work (Lowitzsch, Hashi, & Woodward, 2009). These existing schemes constitute a pillar of the European Social Model. A generally favourable attitude within a given country has usually led to some supportive legislation for EFP schemes, which in turn has spread their practice. This suggests a clear link between national attitudes, legislation and diffusion.

A quite different situation exists in the emerging economies of the EU-13 and candidate countries (Lowitzsch, 2006).[3] Few laws specifically address employee financial participation (EFP), and these refer almost exclusively to ESO; legislation on profit sharing is rare. Although employees were frequently offered privileged conditions for buying shares of their employer companies, the purpose was not to motivate employees to become more efficient and productive; nor was there more than mild concern for social justice. Rather, this method was simply an expedient for privatising state-owned enterprises for which at the time there were no buyers. Essentially it was a decision made by default.

In the aftermath of the financial crisis, employee shareholding as a type of long-term investment that may help to stabilise capital markets has received attention as a welcome contrast to the destabilising effect of speculative short-term investment. Contrary to expectations[4] across the EU-27 both take-up and offer continued to rise (see Figure 1).

---

2 Member States, which had joined the European Union before 1 May 2004: Belgium, Denmark, Germany, Ireland, Spain, France, Greece, Italy, Luxembourg, Netherlands, Austria, Portugal, Finland, Sweden, United Kingdom

3 Member States, which joined the European Union after 1 May 2004: Bulgaria, Croatia, Czech Republic, Estonia, Cyprus, Latvia, Lithuania, Hungary, Malta, Poland, Romania, Slovenia, Slovakia

4 With the risk discussion in mind, one might expect employees under the current economic uncertainty to seek conventional pay systems and flee EFP schemes. Of

It is against the background of the recent discussion of ESO and its role for corporate governance that the question arises of what impact, if any, the different origins of ESO in the emerging economies of the new EU Member States had on the development of employee shareholding.

Figure 1. Dynamics of employee shareholding 2000-2013 in the EU.

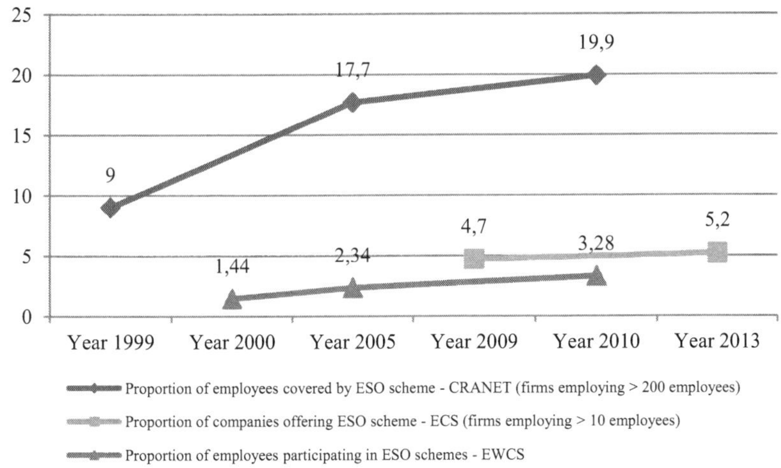

Source: Lowitzsch, Hashi et al. (2014).

Digesting three EU-wide cross country data sets, i.e., European Working Condition Survey (EWCS) and the Cranfield Network on International Human Resource Management (CRANET) from 2000, 2005 and 2010 and the European Company Survey (ECS) from 2009 and 2013, we discuss the dynamics of ESO in the ten new EU CEE Member States focusing on possible implications these may have had for the role of ESO in the aftermath of the financial crisis. Narrowing the angle to the cases of Poland, Hungary and Lithuania, and describing the circumstances for the development of ESO in these countries more in detail, lessons for the support of sustainable employee ownership are drawn.

---

course, this argument would be more relevant to share ownership schemes since market volatility affects share prices directly.

2. Background: EFP and Corporate Governance[5]

Good corporate governance improves company performance and thus benefits all of its shareholders. As the link between better corporate governance and ESO is complex it is worthwhile to review the related arguments. ESO broadens the role of employees thus elevating their status contributes to:

1. A desired change from short to long-term incentives: Companies with a significant employee shareholder base gain a bloc of demanding but loyal shareholders made up of their own employees who understand the firm more intimately than outsiders ever could. In this way employees support management in resisting the prevailing short-term policies of the financial markets and may impose some constraint on opportunistic management and short term oriented management.
2. Improving EU firms' competitiveness by productivity gains arising from increasing employees' loyalty and identification with the company: Employee share ownership can increase employee participation and reward the assumption of new responsibilities at both the shop floor and shareholder levels including issues of transparency and exchange of information.
3. Higher transparency of remuneration: Employee shareholders having a 'say on pay' contributes to making executive compensation transparent, a step toward more sustainable remuneration policies. As knowledgeable insiders they can exercise effective 'oversight'.

The related issues, i.e., information sharing, long-term shareholding and participation in decision-making are interlinked and result in employees not being regarded as just another factor of production, but as shareholders and stakeholders who can make an active contribution to good corporate governance.

5 This section is an extended version of the discussion of the relationship of ESO and corporate governance in the Final Report of the Commission's DG MARKT pilot project 'The Promotion of Employee Ownership and Participation' prepared by the Inter-University Centre (Lowitzsch, Hashi et al., 2014, p. 17 et seq.).

2.1 With regard to information sharing

Anyone with an important stake in a company such as his/her own job naturally wants full transparency on company accounts and company decisions. In this way participation based on share ownership complements participation based on information and consultation. To facilitate the development of positive attitudes and behaviours, management also needs to adopt practices such as information sharing, clarifying and strengthening the link between both individual and organisational performance, and employee participation in decision-making, as adjuncts to the incentive plan - measures which complement EFP (Pendleton & Robinson, 2010). Well-informed employees can also make a significant contribution to the operation of company boards and their important function of monitoring and overseeing management.

Financial participation and in particular ESO is also believed to enhance information sharing because of the alignment between individual employees and corporate interests, which is also likely to improve the decisions made within the company. The company should supply the employees with extensive, independent and regular information about firm performance and its determinants in order to help employees understand the financial risks and benefits associated with joining a scheme (Pérotin & Robinson, 2002). Moreover, information sharing can attract a large number of employees that might otherwise not involve themselves in company affairs.

For non-employee shareholders, it is advantageous to know that they have the company's employees as fellow shareholders pursuing the same objectives. ESO appears to benefit the firm by also increasing disclosure from the firm to *all* of its stakeholders by mitigating the firm's need to keep information opaque (Bova et al., 2013). Employee shareholders can monitor and exercise oversight on management better than any other entity. They also have an incentive to monitor their fellow employees. This can potentially lead to improved corporate governance arrangements within the company. The presence of employee shareholders should assure other long-term investors, such as institutional shareholders, that long-term interests of the company would prevail.

2.2 Related to participation in decision-making

Employee participation in the decision-making process and employee financial participation are regarded as complementary, with the potential to mutually increase each other's beneficial effects on productivity and the quality of management. While financial participation gives employees an additional incentive for involvement, participation in decision-making processes gives them a means to realise it. In this way financial participation rewards results - i.e. profits - while participation in decision-making offers employees the ways and means to actually make the firm more profitable - not necessarily by working harder but smarter, and by eliminating the organisational and other bottlenecks that impede production and increase costs.

As a concept, participation in decision-making has been so heavily weighted with ideological connotations that it is necessary to state that the term as used in this context encompasses various levels of involvement – having a say on work organisation is quite different from participating in board decisions. The extent of participation in decision-making will be influenced by the home country's history of labour relations[6], by the amount of company stock employees own, and many other factors. These are corporate governance issues relating to the future development of the firm, especially in respect to employee ownership. Concerning financial participation, however, three areas of participation have proved to be crucial: information sharing; involvement at the shop floor level, and executing voting rights as a shareholder.

- Because company performance depends on many factors, both internal and external, employees may be generally unwilling to exert more effort unless they are informed about major decisions, e.g., those investment or strategic decisions having an impact on profit and share prices. The positive impact of financial participation may depend on providing employees with all information needed to understand how firm profitability can be increased. This in turn will influence

6 E.g., the consensual continental contrasts with the Anglo-American confrontational model; likewise the strong position of the state in France contrasts with the powerful role of the German collective bargaining parties, such as trade unions and employer associations (Pendleton & Poutsma, 2004).

employees' investment decisions, i.e., the decision whether or not to acquire shares in the employer company.

- As to active involvement at the shop floor level, it is important that employees' ideas and concerns are listened to and that employee suggestions for improving work procedures and operations are put into effect. Otherwise inability to positively influence the company's financial results could lead to demoralizing frustration, undermining the positive motivational effects that financial participation was adopted to provide.
- Regarding participation via shareholder voting rights, employee shareholders represent a type of investor who is concerned with the long-term performance of the business, not short-term fluctuations, which may occur from year to year. In this respect ESO may lead to participation in decision-making processes through voting rights, which - depending on its structure - are executed individually or collectively, via an intermediary entity. Employee shareholders as the natural stewards of their companies will support them in their efforts for sustainable development.

With regard to participation via shareholder rights it is important to stress the EU trend towards using an intermediary vehicle, e.g., a trust, as custodian of employee shares, because this allows for the pooling of voting rights (EESC, SOC/371/2010). These indirect share ownership schemes use a separate intermediary entity, which manages the shares held in trust for employees (e.g., in British and Irish ESOPs) or, at the enterprise level, uses the combination of a savings plan and a mutual investment fund (e.g., in French FCPEs). Pooling voting rights and voting a trustee to execute them ensures a 'professionalization' of the management of employee's voting rights. This way employee's share of the votes may eventually be large enough to be represented on the board.

2.3 Contributing to remuneration policy reforms

Executive compensation structures are often cited as one cause of the current financial and economic crisis. The pre-crisis executive compensation structures are criticised for putting too much emphasis on short-term variable compensation and thus leading to myopic management decisions (Teichmann, 2009). Furthermore, experts note that they created *moral* hazard as taking risks and achieving a positive outcome was rewarded with high bonuses while failures due to high-risk management practices were not correspondingly punished with compensation cuts. Empirical evidence from management boards in Sweden (Oxelheim, Wihlborg & Zhang, 2010) as well as supervisory boards in Germany (Koch & Stadtmann, 2012) support these findings. Furthermore, examples from different countries have already shown that when employees control a significant proportion of shares, they make effective use of their say on pay.[7] The British ESOP Centre already refers to these series of actions as the 'shareholder spring' and notes that employee shareholders might be the protagonists of 'the most capitalist of the revolutions' (ESOP Centre, 2012).

As financial participation is promoted, it gradually facilitates a change in the orientation of the remuneration system from short-term to long-term. Even if initially limited in its extent, employee shareholding can be an element supporting transparency until it eventually becomes a factor influencing compensation systems as the employees' equity share and thus their voting rights increase. If employees have small minority shareholding, as in most cases[8], then they will act as a pressure group. If companies embrace EFP, they are more likely to be transparent, share information with employees, and therefore employees will know about executive compensation. Although, as a rule, the extent of shareholding will be too low for influencing compensation packages through votes, employee shareholders can put the issue on the agenda of the general assembly. Once employees have a significant minority of shares, they will be able to influence the compensation package as institutional shareholders sometimes can. Since employees are more concerned with long-

7 In the U.S.-based firm Wal-Mart, a group of employee shareholders placed a proxy regarding compensation (Rodgers, 2012). The employees demanded an annual analysis with which the board should ensure that Wal-Mart's compensation schemes discourage managers from making capital investments, which might lower the company's returns. Also the firm Verizon had to deal with employee concerns about the compensation topic. Other examples of shareholder (but not specifically employee shareholder) actions against certain executive pay schedules are Aviva, Trinity Mirror, Astra Zeneca as well as General Electric. In the banking sector, shareholders voted down the proposed compensation schedules of UBS and Barclays in 2012.

8 The average shareholding of employees in large listed companies in the EU-27 is around three per cent, although it may be slowly increasing (Lowitzsch, Hashi et al., 2012, p. 30, Figure 6).

term orientation than ordinary shareholders are, they will have an interest in long-term value maximisation.

Empirical evidence suggests that employee shareholders face significant incentives to reduce risk while they are able to influence decisions relating to firm risk (Bova et al., 2012). The vote of shareholders and higher transparency of remuneration schemes will bring employees closer to the decision about executive compensation. This should have an even more positive effect on the desired long-term orientation of executive compensation than the vote of the average shareholder as the following argument illustrates:

- There are two reasons why the average shareholder might be focused on short term profits rather than long term profitability, minimum level of risk and survival of the firm itself: First, in economic theory the shareholder is assumed to have a diversified position. He does not invest in one single firm only, but in several firms. With his diversified portfolio, he does not care about the performance of an individual firm, but is rather interested in an attractive relationship between risk and return (Markowitz, 1952). The second reason is that his transaction costs are low. Thus, when stocks he holds are not performing as desired, he might sell them and invest somewhere else.
- For an employee shareholder the situation is different: He has a rather non-diversified position as he works for the firm and fears losing his job. Depending on the details of the EFP scheme, employees might invest more heavily in company shares since they are often discounted and thus more attractive than shares of other firms. If given as a compensation component, there might be restrictions on the time of sale, resulting in a non-diversified portfolio. Secondly, the employee shareholder would have transaction costs and this encourages a long-term orientation. To change jobs is not so easy, while a sale of the shares might not be possible if there is a holding period. These considerations give employee shareholders a vital interest in executive compensation oriented over the long term, which fosters a balanced attitude towards risk.

It is sometimes argued that employee shareholders will not have the necessary expertise to properly execute their voting rights to have a beneficial influence as described above. However, the fact that most likely there will be a compensation expert on the remuneration committee while the remuneration committee will be present at the annual general meeting on compensation compensates for a possible lack of employees expertise. Thus, EFP can contribute to ensuring that as for remuneration a long-term view is taken. As a consequence of these issues, changes have been proposed and/or implemented by different actors.

3. EU policy initiatives embracing EFP and ESO in particular

Both employee financial participation and corporate governance have attracted rapidly growing interest in the European Union in the past two decades. However, only recently have both topics been linked to each other in a common policy approach.

3.1 With regards to ESO and corporate governance

On 21 October 2010 the European Economic and Social Committee (EESC) adopted an own-initiative opinion on *Employee financial participation in Europe* (EESC, SOC/371/2010) referring to the 1992 Council Recommendation (92/443/EEC)[9] and the 2002 European Commission Communication (COM/2002/0364) on a *Framework for the promotion of employee financial participation.* Following the EESC initiative report the EU Parliament commissioned a study on EFP released on 3 October 2012 (Lowitzsch, Hashi et al., 2012) as a prelude to an Own-Initiative Report on financial participation of employees in companies' proceeds that was adopted on 14 January 2014 (European Parliament, 2013/2127(Ini)).

In a parallel move, the EU Commission included the promotion of ESO in the action plan to reform European company law and corporate governance (European Commission, COM/2012/740). In the action plan the Commission commits to 'identify and investigate potential obstacles to trans-national employee share ownership schemes' and to 'take appro-

9 The recommendation formulated the following principles: Regular application; calculation in accordance with a predefined formula; application complementary to the traditional remuneration system; variable participation depending on company results; benefits for all employees; application to both private and public enterprises; application to enterprises of all sizes; simple models; information and training for employees on models; voluntary introduction and participation in models.

priate action to encourage employee share ownership throughout Europe.' Finally, on the basis of a budget line previously issued DG MARKT implemented a pilot project on employee ownership and participation with the final report being published in October 2014 (Lowitzsch, Hashi et al., 2014).

3.2 With regards to executive remuneration

The European Commission had already passed suggestions regarding executive director compensation in a 2004 Recommendation (European Commission, 2004/913/EC). In 2009, these were expanded as a consequence of the financial crisis by two recommendations (European Commission, C/2009/3177 and C/2009/3159), one dealing with executive director compensation across industries and the other dealing with compensation structures in the financial sectors on all hierarchical levels in special consideration of those job positions dealing with risk.[10]

Already in 2009 new supervisory and equity provisions were issued on the European level (European Union, 2010/76/EU) which now have been reworked, supplemented and heavily extended. On 27 February 2013 the European Parliament reached a compromise with the Member States putting strict limits on the bonuses paid to bankers, hoping to discourage the risk-taking behaviour that set off the financial crisis. On 5 March 2013 European finance ministers broadly agreed on these rules, which were approved by a majority of the member states and the European Parliament plenary. They comprise of equity provisions for financial service companies, which were taken from regulation 575/2013 as well as directive 2013/36/EU of the European Union – the so called Capital Requirements Directive (CRD) IV-package (Lowitzsch, Kocsis & Koch, 2013) – came into force on 17 July 2013 and have been applied since January 2014. The extensive new regulatory package contains, among others, guidelines and provisions on compensation policies and practices along

10 Two main areas can be distinguished, i.e., structure of remuneration (esp. avoiding 'pay without performance') on the one hand and remuneration committees and disclosure ('say on pay') on the other. Of course, there are also special regulations related to executive compensation in banks that were granted financial state aid during the recent crisis.

with their supervision. The deal is part of the 'Basel III' banking regulations aimed at reducing the danger of big bank failures.

The coveted bonuses that many bankers receive are now capped at no more than equal to their annual salaries. Only if a bank's shareholders approve either with a majority of 65 per cent of the votes holding half of the shares or with a 75 per cent majority can a bonus be higher - and even then it would be limited to no more than double the salary. To ensure a sustainable business strategy even with higher bonuses, in such a case pay-out is deferred over a period of at least five years. In addition, under these regulations banks have to submit more detailed data concerning turnover, profits, taxes paid and subsidies received. Also additional data on the number of employees in their respective countries of operation is requested. In 2014 these reports were only filed to the European Commission, in 2015 these accounts will have to be made public.

4. Evolution of EFP in emerging economies of Central and Eastern Europe

As to the dynamic of EFP in emerging economies, the evolution of the attitude of social partners, political parties and governments is a classic soft indicator. Furthermore, the legal framework, i.e., the presence or absence of specific regulations as well as of fiscal and other incentives is important in distinguishing conducive and *non*-conducive legal arrangements.

4.1 Governments and the social partners' attitudes

In the CEE EU-10, the general attitudes towards EFP schemes of governments and the social partners differ markedly from those in the EU-15, particularly in the Member States of Central and Eastern Europe. The prevailing attitude is general indifference. This mind set has been strongly influenced by the legacies inherited from communist times and the priorities imposed by the post-1989 transition to multi-party democracy and a market economy. The word 'participation' was frequently misinterpreted and its promotion confused with the desire to re-introduce out-dated concepts and practices, which these countries had long abandoned. Consequently, EFP has rarely appeared on a trade union policy agenda; only in a few Central and Eastern European countries have trade unions actually promoted employee ownership within the privatisation process, nor did they develop institutions to protect employee shareholders. As to employer associations in the Central and Eastern European countries, their position on EFP has been passive; in most countries, a clear official viewpoint has not developed.

However, during the past years EFP in its various forms is more frequently viewed as a complementary element to social and industrial relations. A good example is the 2009/11 initiative of the Polish Vice-Prime Minister Pawlak, which promotes employee-owned companies and regards ESO as a factor that enhances sustainability, one that can preserve the national identity of Polish companies and thus benefit the economy as a whole (Polish Ministry of Economy, 2009). Another example is the employer association in Slovenia, which recently successfully lobbied for tax concessions from the government for enterprises implementing EFP schemes (ZAVEZA, 2012).

4.2 Legal framework

There are important differences between the former socialist countries and the mature market economies of the EU-15, and, within the former group, between those in which employees had participated in the operations of their enterprise in varying degrees (e.g., the former Yugoslavia and Poland) and those where employee participation was minimal or non-existent (e.g., Czechoslovakia). The difference in legal and political priorities between Eastern and Western Europe stems from the fact that the first priority of post-socialist legislators was to transform their socialist economic systems through privatisation and re-privatisation; thus, the development of EFP schemes does not represent any intention to develop the remuneration system, as in the EU-15; it is rather an accidental consequence of the transition reforms (Uvalić & Vaughan-Whitehead, 1997).

Given the absence of general support for EFP in the Central and Eastern European countries, legislation promoting EFP schemes has been limited-aside from privatisation laws, which favoured the acquisition of shares by employees. Countries having privatisation laws and which sold shares to insiders on privileged terms are also the countries that ended up with a substantial number of firms owned by employee workers and managers (e.g., Poland and Slovenia). Privatisation laws favouring share acquisition by employees under privileged conditions have been a fundamental cause for the diffusion of ESO throughout CEE.

5. Dynamics of ESO in selected Central and Eastern European countries

Against the background of the different genesis of EFP in the EU-15 and the CEE EU-10 described above, it is interesting that the data examined in the PEPPER IV report (Lowitzsch, Hashi & Woodward, 2009) seem to indicate that a West-East divide (i.e., significant differences between the old EU-15 member states on the one hand, and at least some of the 10 post-communist states that have joined the EU since 2004) is less significant than one might have anticipated. There seems to be much more variation within those two groups than between them. The following discussion uses the same data sets as presented in the 2012 European Parliament study (Lowitzsch, Hashi et al., 2012) isolating 10 CEE emerging economies covered therein and contrasting them with the CEE EU-10 and the EU-15 averages (weighted averages[11] for all countries available in all three data sets).

5.1 General trends with regards to offer and take-up of ESO-schemes

According to CRANET[12] data shown in Figure 2, the percentage of companies offering broad-based share ownership schemes, in the old EU-15, increased from 9.52 per cent in 1999 to 16.12 per cent in 2005 while it slightly dropped to 14.61 per cent in 2010. In the new CEE

---

11 In calculating weighted averages the population of each country is used as its weight.

12 The CRANET Survey is a large-scale survey of the human resource practices of around 10,000 companies in Europe and other countries (in 2010 it covered firms over 100 employees, in 1999 and 2005 the threshold was 200). Some EU Member States were not included in all of the three rounds of the survey. The questionnaire includes a number of questions on EFP practices in thee surveyed companies. We thank partners of the CRANET Network, coordinated by Cranfield University School of Management, for the use of CRANET database. We are especially grateful to Professor Erik Poutsma and Dr Paul Ligthart, Institute of Management Research, Radboud University, who recalculated the figures of the datasets for Figure 3 and Figure 4.

Member States, the percentage of companies offering broad-based share ownership schemes increased from 9.09 per cent in 2000 to 11.54 per cent in 2005 and further extended to 19.45 per cent in 2010.[13]

Although we observe a general trend of the offer of ESO schemes increasing across the EU-27, it has somewhat halted in the old Member States recently; in the new Member States it kept increasing despite of the financial crisis.

Figure 2. Proportion of firms offering broad-based employee share ownership (ESO) schemes in selected EU Member States, 1999-2010 (in per cent)

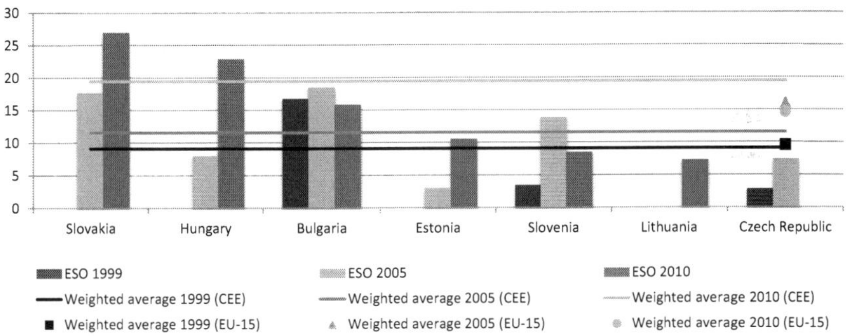

Source: CRANET 1999, 2005 and 2010. Poland, Romania and Latvia were not included in the survey.

Using the CRANET survey, it is possible to calculate the proportion of employees in the sample covered by broad-based ESO plans (or to whom the schemes are offered) as shown in Figure 3. In the old EU-15, coverage increased from 15.52 per cent in 1999 to 18.18 per cent in 2005 and slightly increased to 19.62 per cent in 2010. In the new CEE EU-10, the coverage increased from 10.55 per cent in 1999 to 13.24 per cent in 2005 and further extended to 23.62 per cent in 2010.

13 Interestingly, we observe an opposite development for the percentage of companies offering broad-based profit-sharing schemes in the new Member States: The percentage dropped continuously from 15.24 per cent in 2000 to 15.17 per cent in 2005 which was further narrowed to 7.87 per cent in 2010.

Figure 3. Proportion of employees covered by employee share ownership (ESO) schemes in selected new EU Member States, 1999-2010 (in per cent)

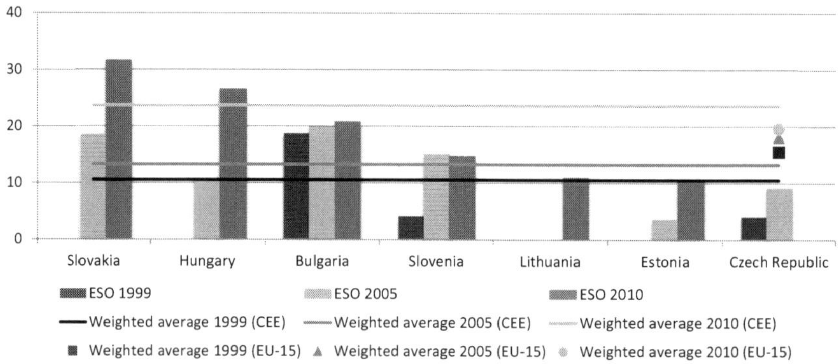

Source: CRANET 1999, 2005 and 2010. Poland, Romania and Latvia were not included in the survey.

With regard to the coverage of ESO schemes, the positive trend across EU 27 is more consistent. However, while the increase in the new Member States is smaller than that of the offer in both cases they overtook the old Member States (compare Figure s 2 and 3) in 2010.

The availability of the new European Working Conditions Survey (EWCS)[14] 2010 makes it possible to compare the take-up of ESO schemes over the entire decade, shown in Figure 4. In the old EU-15, take-up increased from 1.63 per cent in 1999 to 2.44 per cent in 2005 and further increased to 3.74 per cent in 2010. In contrast, in the new CEE EU-10, the percentage of employees participating in broad-based ESO schemes increased from 0.78 per cent in 2000 to 1.95 per cent in 2005 dropping to 1.54 per cent in 2010.

14 The EWCS is a large-scale survey of working conditions across Europe undertaken by the European Foundation for the Improvement of Working and Living Conditions (Eurofound) every four or five years to investigate a variety of factors influencing individuals working and living conditions. It covers some 30,000 people in 30 countries. The 1999 Survey was conducted in the EU-15. The EU-12 were surveyed in 2000. The data reported here refers to the employees of private sector companies only as the public sector does not lend itself to ESO (as there are no shares in these organisations).

Figure 4. Proportion of employees participating in employee share ownership (ESO) schemes in 10 new CEE EU Member States, 2000-2010 (in per cent)

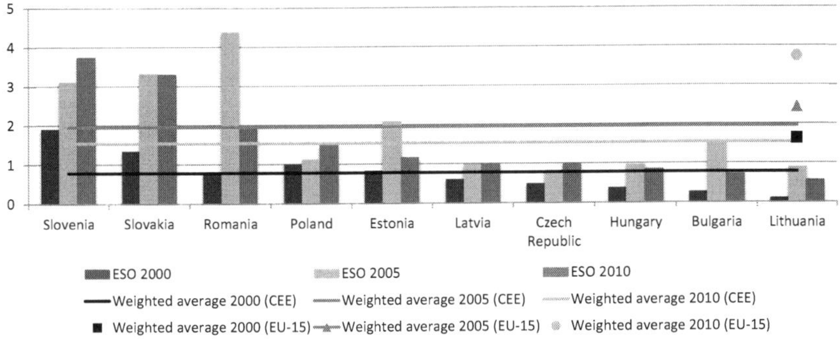

Source: EWCS 2000, 2005 and 2010.

The proportion of company employees participating in broad-based ESO schemes – which in general has been increasing though in recent years growth has slowed – shows a different pattern in the old Member States, where it kept increasing and in the new CEE Member States where it recently slightly dipped.

To summarise, in the new CEE Member States the offer of ESO schemes in companies kept increasing despite the crisis – unlike in the EU-15, where it remained stagnant; the increase in coverage was even greater; in both cases it exceeded that in the old Member States in 2010. However, – in spite of a generally positive dynamic during the last decade – the percentage of employees that actually participated in these schemes in 2010 was smaller than in the EU-15.

5.2 ESO in companies of different size

The European Company Survey (ECS)[15] contains information on company size, which can be matched against the availability of an EFP scheme. As expected, the size of the company is closely associated with

15 The ECS is a survey of all European companies conducted by the European Foundation in 2009. It covers some 30,000 companies in 30 European countries (all EU Member States and candidate countries).

the incidence of ESO. Figure 5 shows the availability and extent of ESO schemes in companies of different size groups (large, medium and small).

Figure 5. Proportion of companies of different size offering employee share ownership (ESO) schemes to their employees in 10 new CEE EU Member States, 2009 (in per cent)

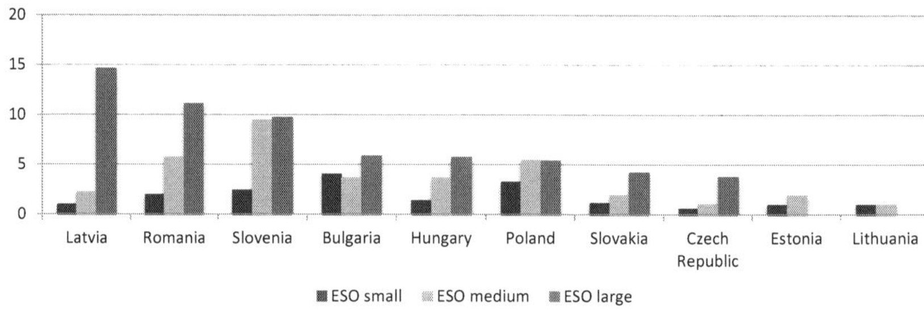

Source: based on ECS dataset, 2009, own calculations.

It indicates that large companies almost always have higher levels of employee share ownership schemes than medium and, especially, small companies. Exceptions are Poland and Bulgaria (in Estonia and Lithuania there were no large firms in the sample). Similarly, medium-sized companies exhibit higher incidence of employee share ownership than small companies (only Bulgaria is an exception to this pattern).

These findings were confirmed by a study for the European Parliament (Lowitzsch, Hashi et al., 2012), investigating the relationship between countries' degree of support for EFP and the actual offer of EFP schemes by firms.[16] Consistent with the experience in many EU Member States, it finds that profit sharing is less dependent on supportive measures than ESO, and is often introduced without them. For ESO - especially in smaller companies, as the incidence is strongly size-related - the opposite is true: Only when supportive measures are in place over a long period of time without substantial changes, is ESO likely to be sustainable.

16 For this comparison of the EU-27 (ranked according to a set of criteria – including the legal framework, fiscal and other incentives and government support – in countries clusters) with the offer of EFP schemes the ECS 2009 cross-country data (EFP in firms with more than 10 employees) was used; see p. 59-63.

5.3 Summary of the empirical findings

On the whole, there are some discrepancies between data sources with regard to certain countries; however, the overall picture is quite clear. While for most individual countries it would be rather risky to make definitive assertions about the degree of advancement of dissemination of ESO schemes on the basis of the data we have examined, we can identify what seem to be some general trends.

In the new Member States the offer of ESO schemes in companies (employing more than 200 employees) and particularly the coverage kept increasing despite the crisis. In this respect the CEE EU-10 dynamic is more positive than in the EU-15. However, the percentage of employees actually participating in these schemes in 2010 was smaller than in the EU-15.

With regards to sustainability of employee share ownership – especially in smaller companies, as incidence is strongly related to size – a key element seems to be that supportive measures are kept in place over time without substantial changes.

6. Promoting sustainable ESO – Lessons from three selected countries[17]

In general, employee financial participation needs sustainable policy support to realise its potential. Best practice from the old Member States show that a stable legal framework for EFP induces individual firms to offer these schemes and suggests that this is particularly true for share schemes, as they require a more complex setting (Lowitzsch, Hashi & Woodward, 2009). In the following we analyse three cases, i.e., Poland, Hungary and Lithuania to investigate to which extent this finding holds true for emerging economies. We conclude with policy recommendations drawn from our findings.

---

17 The authors thank in particular Gyula Kocsis, Adam Wojtkowski and Thijs Wubbels who contributed to the case studies (for a more extensive and detailed report on these countries see Lowitzsch, Hashi et al., 2012, annex 6).

6.1 SME employee buyouts in privatisation (Spółki Pracownicze, Poland)

A positive example of utilisation of employee ownership plans in the course of privatisation is the case of 'Spółki Pracownicze' (Employee Companies) from Poland. The important feature of this case is that - unlike most East European countries, which ceased to support employee ownership after the privatisation was completed - Poland introduced further supportive measures. As a result companies retained majority employee ownership and also showed good performance, even during the financial crisis.

> The most significant form of EFP in Poland today is employee ownership. Poland's privatisation programme was characterised by significant incentives for employee participation, especially in firms privatised by leasing and transformed into so-called Employee Companies (spółki pracownicze). Contrary to expectations, ownership structures in these companies have, on the whole, been relatively stable, with non-managerial employees retaining, on average, a significant portion of enterprise shares. Although all current forms of financial participation may also be used in employee compensation schemes outside of privatisation, there are no tax incentives to encourage this.
>
> By 2002, the most common way to manage a privatised enterprise was to lease it to an 'Employee Company'. From 1990 until 2010, 62.4 per cent of enterprises undergoing 'direct privatisation' were transferred into private hand through a leverage-lease buyout resulting in a total of 1,563 Employee Companies that emerged from former state enterprises. However, over time, there has been a slow but steady decline of Employee Companies, some of them going public, others going bankrupt or being liquidated.
>
> Until the end of 2010, their population decreased to 852 employing a total of 131.5 thousand workers with an average size of 150 employees. It is difficult to obtain information on the reasons for the decline of employee ownership as Employee Companies are not a specific legal form of enterprise but registered together with all other corporations. It was certainly not economic distress: In 2010, Employee Companies have achieved a positive gross profit of PLN 2,322 million (as compared to PLN 2,106.7 million in 2009) with an average gross turnover profitability rate close to five per cent.
>
> Reacting to this decline, in the end of 2009, the Polish Government launched the current programme to support Employee Companies entitled Supporting Privatisation Through Granting Sureties and Guarantees to Employee Companies and Civic Activity Companies. Beyond a system of guarantees for Employee Companies, the programme defines the Company of Civic Activity, a joint-stock company or limited liability company where 33 per cent shares belong to at least 30 per cent of the active employees of a privatised enterprise.

On the one hand, the Polish case is limited in its transferability to countries with no significant large-scale privatisations programmes. On the other hand, the case is useful especially for other Eastern European emerging economies, especially for Lithuania and Hungary, which - as their cases below will show - still have an opportunity to reactivate the support for employee ownership and thus support employee ownership in a sustainable way as in Poland.

6.2 Decline of Hungary's employee-owned firms failing long-term policies

The case from Hungary shows that the discontinuation of political support leads to a rapid decline of employee ownership. The specific feature of the Hungarian ESOP experience is that intermediary entities, which could be well used after privatisation was completed, declined steeply due to lack of political support.

In the course of transition, instruments for broad individual and collective participation of employees have been introduced. During the first stage of privatisation, the support of social partners and political parties, on the one hand, and the actual development of employee ownership, on the other, seemed to be promising. However, on the long run, the attempt of policy makers to turn a considerable proportion of Hungarians into owners, i.e., into small capitalists, and to establish an economic balance did not bring the desired outcome. In many ways it resulted in the opposite. Since then only about 300 ESOPs were established in total and less than one quarter is still functioning today.

The legal framework for the Hungarian ESOPs, which already existed in practice, was laid down in Law XLIV of 1992 on the Employee Share Ownership Programme. Deriving from the U.S. ESOP model, the Hungarian ESOP structure simulates the Anglo-American trust. It served a dual purpose: It transformed employees into owners of state-owned companies while accelerating the privatisation process. The legal framework of the ESOP today largely retains its original form, though it has been amended several times, most recently in 2003. The ESOP Act enabled employees to acquire state property under preferential conditions, which were significantly limited by Law XXXIX of 1995 on Realisation of Entrepreneurial Property in State Ownership providing (i) credit facilities of up to 50 per cent of the value of the respective property to be purchased, with a ceiling of HUF 50 million; (ii) a discount corresponding to 150 per cent of an annual minimum wage. The total equity purchased by an ESOP was not to exceed 15 per cent of the nominal value of the company. The legal incentives are based on a governmental decree of 1991 on 'Egzisztencia' credit and the amendments of the ESOP Act of 1992 still in force. The fact that no ESOP loans have been granted since 1998, although the decree is still in force, shows that these conditions need revision, in particular abolishing the link of preferential credit conditions to the nearly terminated privatisation process.

After 1996, one year after the amendment of the ESOP Act, the absolute number of ESOP organisations declined continuously. Following 1998, no more ESOPs have been established, and from 1996 on the number of ESOPs shrunk until 2010 to approximately one-fourth, which is also the lowest point.
The primary cause for the failure of the ESOP model was the lack of commitment to this idea and the lack of sufficient far-sightedness of political institutions. This is even more regretful, as companies in majority ownership of employees did not perform worse than other private economic entities. The Hungarian ESOP was a premature model because policy makers did not change the provisions early enough and thus permitted the abuse of the original concept behind it. For these reasons, ESOP schemes were not as successful as they could have been in the long run, as they lacked the necessary sustainable provisions in the post-privatisation era. Furthermore, the time window of three to four years, when SMEs were privatised, was a period too short to be able to measure the real outcomes of ESOPs and to make policy amendments to foster employee ownership.

A lack of supportive measures and inconsistent legislation led to a steep decrease in the number of ESOPs in Hungary. However, this tendency could still be changed if a comprehensive supportive legislation were developed. The European trend to implement employee financial participation schemes through an intermediary entity could give orientation to the Hungarian Government to introduce new rules. On the other hand, a European framework could contain rules for intermediary entities giving positive impulses to those still existing in Hungary.

6.3 Failing sustainable support to employee shareholding in Lithuania

Given the prevailing economic conditions in Central and Eastern Europe, the CEE EU-10 could discover that financial participation is even more important to them than to the EU-15. However, although these countries mostly introduced share ownership as a one-time incentive to employees during privatisation, they did not follow up with policies and measures that would make employee share ownership a permanent component of their new private property, free market economies. By contrast, a number of Western governments as well as the EU itself have actively promoted EFP precisely because of its beneficial long-range effects. In conjunction to the best practice of Poland presented above, the case of Lithuania, like the case of Hungary, shows that employee ownership is likely to be sustainable if political support is continuing.

> The development of employee financial participation in Lithuania started in the early 1990s in the course of privatisation. Until 1994, Lithuania was in the vanguard of economic reform. Not only economic, but also political considerations of achieving complete independence from the Soviet Union led to the concept of fast privatisation. In addition, the leading politicians favoured egalitarian forms of employee ownership also supported by the trade unions. For that reason, the most popular privatisation forms were mass privatisation on the basis of vouchers and management-employee buyout, while sale to outsiders or liquidation were hardly used at all. Irrespective of the reasons for promoting employee ownership, the policy first led to a rapid growth of employee share ownership.
>
> By 1994, more than 95 per cent of privatised firms in the programme implementing the Law on the Initial Privatisation of State-Owned Property had employee ownership, while the percentage of enterprises where employees had taken over most of the privatised assets increased from three per cent in 1991-1992, to 65 per cent in 1993 and 92 per cent in 1994-1995 (Privatisation Department at the Ministry of Economics). However, the situation completely changed during the late 1990s and early 2000s. Whereas in 1993 around 50 per cent of employees were shareholders of their enterprises, in 1999 the percentage fell to one third. According to the survey conducted in connection with the PEPPER IV Report, only four per cent of Lithuanian firms offered broad-based ownership plans in 2007, and only 1.7 per cent of employees actually participated in such scheme.

The case of Lithuania exemplifies the importance of sustainability of legal and fiscal incentives. Whereas sufficient legal incentives, even if they are not the typical tax incentives, can lead to a surprisingly rapid increase of employee ownership from nought to almost 90 per cent in only three years, the abolishment of the same incentives leads to an equally dramatic decline. Not the volume of incentives, but their stability can produce a long-term effect.

7. Policy recommendations: EFP needs sustainable political support to realise its potential, especially a stable legal framework

In the new Member States the offer of ESO schemes in companies and in particular the coverage kept increasing despite the crisis. In this respect the CEE EU-10 show a dynamic more positive than the EU-15. However, the percentage of employees that actually participated in these schemes in 2010 was smaller than in the EU-15. However, there is much variation within the CEE EU-10, especially with regard to the different policy approaches in different countries. Actually the sustainability of employee share ownership – especially in smaller companies, as incidence is strongly related to size – a key element seems to be that supportive measures stay in place for a long period of time without substantial change.

These empirical findings from our data digest are reflected in the individual case studies of Hungary and Lithuania. These clearly show that discontinuation of political support leads to a rapid decline in ESO, even when the level of ESO was previously high. By contrast, the case of Poland shows that support measures – even small ones – can have an opposite effect, helping to stabilise employee ownership. The important feature of the Polish case is that – unlike most East European countries, which ceased to support employee ownership after privatisation was completed – the government introduced further supportive measures. As a result, companies maintained majority employee ownership and also performed well, even during the financial crisis.

This confirms best practice findings in the old EU Member States, especially those from France and the UK, showing that a stable legal framework of measures in support of EFP facilitates the implementation of ESO schemes as a vehicle for strategic employee ownership in individual enterprises.

Interestingly, with regard to profit sharing the experience of Lithuania can be observed also in other Eastern European countries where the increase in employee financial participation was mostly a by-product of the privatisation process and often not considered as worthy of further support; opposite to the development for ESO the percentage of companies offering broad-based profit-sharing schemes dropped continuously between 2000 and 2010.

All three cases together indicate that the stability of political support is more important than the number of incentives and their extent.

References

Bova, F., Dou, Y., & Hope, O.-K. (2013). *Employee ownership and firm disclosure. Working paper.*

Bova, F., Kolev, K., Thomas, J., & Zhang, F. (2012). *Non-executive employee ownership and corporate risk-taking. Working paper.* Retrieved from http://faculty.som.yale.edu/jakethomas/papers/esoprisk.pdf

Employee Share Ownership Centre (ESOP Centre). (2012). 'Shareholder spring': Employees' voices can and do count. Retrieved May 24, 2012, from http://www.esopcentre.com/shareholder-sprin

European Commission (2002). *Communication from the Commission: Framework for the promotion of employee financial participation, COM(2002)0364.*

European Commission (2004). *Recommendation of 14 December 2004 fostering an appropriate regime for the remuneration of directors of listed companies (2004/913/EC).*

European Commission (2009a). *Recommendation complementing Recommendations 2004/913/EC and 2005/162/EC as regards the regime for the remuneration of directors of listed companies, C(2009) 3177.*

European Commission (2009b). *Recommendation on remuneration policies in the financial services sector C(2009) 3159.*

European Commission (2012). *Communication from the Commission: Action Plan: European company law and corporate governance - a modern legal framework for more engaged shareholders and sustainable companies, COM(2012)0740, 12 December 2012.*

European Council (1992). Council Recommendation 92/443/EEC of 27 July 1992 concerning the promotion of employee participation in profits and enterprise results, including equity participation, 26 August 1992. *Official Journal* L 245 , 26/08/1992.

European Economic and Social Committee (2010). *Own-Initiative Opinion on employee financial participation in Europe SOC-371, CESE 1375/2010, OJ C 51, 17 February 2011.*

European Parliament (2013). *Own-initiative report: Financial participation of employees in companies' proceeds, 2013/2127(INI) T7-0013/2014, 18 December 2013.*

European Union (2010). *Directive 2010/76/EU of the European Parliament and of the Council of 24 November 2010 amending Directives 2006/48/EC and 2006/49/EC as regards capital requirements for the trading book and for re-securitisations, and the supervisory review of remuneration.*

European Union (2013a). *Directive 2013/36/EU of the European Parliament and of the Council of 26 June 2013 on access to the activity of credit institutions and the prudential supervision of credit institutions and investment firms, amending Directive 2002/87/EC and repealing Dir.*

European Union (2013b). *Regulation 575/2013 of the European Parliament and of the Council of 26 June 2013 on prudential requirements for credit institutions and investment firms and amending Regulation (EU) No 648/2012.*

Koch, R., & Stadtmann, G. (2012). *Determinants of supervisory board compensation in Germany.* Working paper.

Kruse, D. L., Freeman, R. B., & Blasi, J. R. (Eds.). (2010). *Shared capitalism at work: Employee ownership, profit and gain sharing, and broad-based stock options.* Chicago: University of Chicago Press.

Lowitzsch, J. (2006). *The PEPPER III Report: Promotion of employee participation in profits and enterprise results in the New Member and Candidate Countries of the European Union.* Rome, Berlin: Inter-University Centre, Freie Universität Berlin.

Lowitzsch, J., Hashi, I. et al. (2012). *Employee financial participation in companies' proceeds*. Brussels: European Parliament.

Lowitzsch, J., Hashi, I. et al. (2014). *The promotion of employee ownership and participation*. Luxembourg: European Union.

Lowitzsch, J., Hashi, I., & Woodward, R. (Eds.). (2009). *The PEPPER IV Report: Benchmarking of employee participation in profits and enterprise results in the Member and Candidate Countries of the European Union*. Berlin.

Lowitzsch, J., Kocsis, G., & Koch, R. (2013). Die Regulierung der Vergütung von Führungskräften im Finanzdienstleistungssektor im Rahmen des CRD IV-Pakets (Compensation regulation of financial sector executives in the framework of the CRD-IV package). *Zeitschrift Für Europäisches Sozial- Und Arbeitsrecht (ZESAR)*, *10*, 343–351.

Markowitz, H. M. (1952). Portfolio selection. *The Journal of Finance*, *7*(1), 77–91.

Oxelheim, L., Wihlborg, C., & Zhang, J. (2010). *Macroeconomic fluctuations in CEO compensation. Working paper*.

Pendleton, A., & Poutsma, E. (2004). *Financial participation: The role of governments and social partners*. Dublin: European Foundation for the Improvement of Living and Working Conditions (Eurofound).

Pendleton, A., & Robinson, A. (2010). Employee stock ownership, involvement, and productivity: An interaction-based approach. *Industrial and Labor Relations Review*, *64*(1), 3–29.

Pérotin, V., & Robinson, A. (2002). *Employee participation in profit and ownership: A review of the issues and evidence. SOCI 109, European Parliament, Directorate-General for Research*. Luxembourg.

Polish Ministry of Economy. (2009). Support for Privatization through State Guarantees for Companies with Participation of Employees and Local Governments (Citizens' Activity Companies). Retrieved February 3, 2010, from http://www.mg.gov.pl/files/upload/10233/prywatyzacja.pdf

Rodgers, L. (2012). Employees starting to vote against executive pay. Retrieved May 24, 2012, from http://www.nceo.org/main/column.php/id/431

Teichmann, C. (2009). Pay without performance? Vorstandsvergütung in Deutschland und Europa [Compensation of directors in Germany and Europe]. *GPR – Zeitschrift Für Das Gemeinschaftsprivatrecht*, *7*(5), 235–239.

Uvalić, M., & Vaughan-Whitehead, D. (Eds.). (1997). *Privatization surprises In transition economies employee-ownership in Central and Eastern Europe*. Cheltenham: Edward Elgar Publishing.

ZAVEZA. (2012). Za uspesno prihodnost 15/2020.

Financial participation in Europe: Some kind of a dream

Jean-Michel Content[1]

Abstract

In Europe, for years, there has been an attempt to enlarge the implementation of financial participation in the Member States of the European Union which had not yet adopted its principles (all of them except France, the UK and Ireland). At the end of the eighties, the European Commission launched a project on the Promotion of Participation by Employed Persons in Profits and Enterprise Results (PEPPER), which resulted in a first report in 1992. The main findings of this report were the definition of the different types of financial participation schemes, the state of art in all the existing member states at that time. Since then there have been several successive initiatives coming from various European authorities (the Council of Ministers, the European Parliament, the Economic and Social Committee).

Despite the reiteration of a clear willingness to promoting the expansion of financial participation at each European summit, Europe becoming an example for the whole world, in social relationships, it remains obvious that a lot must be done before a full achievement. Even if it is widely considered that financial participation has benefits for employees, for employers and for economy in general. Some people believe that it could also play a role in two of the main challenges of our developed economies, unemployment and retirement issues.

1. Historical background

For years, some European countries (France, the UK and Ireland) have developed successful employee financial participation (EFP) schemes. In France, it resulted after the Second World War of the political willingness

1 Jean-Michel Content: International Association for Financial Participation (IAFP), email: iafp.aipf@gmail.com

of a new relationship between workers and owners, leading to a genuine association between capital and work. Since 1959, there have been a lot of laws and rules which built a quite exhaustive toolbox which offers to employers and employees an extensive range of schemes: profit sharing (in cash or in shares), employee share ownership, share options, free shares, etc.

In the UK, as in Ireland, the inspiration came from the U.S., where companies like Procter & Gamble have experienced employee share ownership for more than one century. Thus, the only financial participation schemes which have existed in these two countries are based on employee ownership.

A lot of research and studies have been carried out on this topic, and their general conclusion was that financial participation had a positive impact on the productivity, the performances and the well-being in the companies where it existed (e.g., Kruse & Blasi, 1995).

This is the reason why the European Commission decided in the late 1980ies to prepare a community instrument on the 'promotion of participation by employee persons in profits and enterprise results', in short 'PEPPER' (Uvalic, 1991). The European Commission funded a research project with the specific aim of getting a good overview of the 'state of art' regarding financial participation by employees in the EU. This resulted in the so-called PEPPER I report: It introduced a typology of financial participation schemes, reviewed the situation in each of the then Member States (Belgium, Denmark, Germany, France, Greece, Ireland, Italy, Luxembourg, Netherlands, Portugal, Spain and the United Kingdom) and made recommendations to the European Commission (Uvalic, 1991).

In July 1992, the Council of Ministers, adopted a recommendation on the promotion of financial participation for employees known as the PEPPER recommendation (Council of European Communities, 1992). In this recommendation, the European Commission undertook to present a report to the European Parliament, the Council and the Economic and Social Committee on the application of the recommendation.

On the basis of the information supplied to it by the Member States, the European Commission adopted the so-called PEPPER II report in January 1997 (Commission of the European Communities, 1996). One of the main conclusions of that report was that Member States have hardly, if at all, engaged in information exchanges regarding best practices, despite the potential positive effects of financial participation schemes on productivity, wage flexibility, unemployment and worker involvement.

During the following years (1998-2003), the European Foundation for the Improvement of Living and Working Conditions (in Dublin) published key studies:

- Recent trends in Employee Financial Participation in the EU (PEPPER III report; Lowitzsch, 2006)
- Employee Share Ownership and Profit-Sharing in the European Union (based on the Cranfield Network on Human Resource Management [CRANET] Survey; Pendleton, Poutsma, Brewster, & van Ommeren, 2001)
- Policies and views of peak organisations

All these studies are available on the Foundation's Website.[2]

In July 2002, the European Commission adopted a communication, ten years after the 1992 communication, in which it proposed a general framework for promoting financial participation in Europe (European Commission, 2002). The communication stressed, in particular, the need to reduce, through concrete measures, the obstacles to the introduction of financial participation throughout the European Union for enterprises established in several countries. It is against this background that a group of seven independent experts was set up in September 2002. Their report, issued in December 2003, provided seven conclusions, after having pointed out that it was essential for the Commission and the Member States to act to reduce the obstacles to the spread of financial participation across the European Union (Commission of the European Communities, 2003).

The shortcomings of the single market in the area of financial participation make European enterprises less competitive than enterprises in more unified economic areas such as the U.S.

'This is all the more regrettable since many studies have indicated that financial participation can improve the productivity, competitiveness and profitability of enterprises and contribute to greater social cohesion. The development of financial participation can help to achieve the ambitious objectives of the Lisbon European Council of March 2000 and must be vigorously promoted' (Commission of the European Communities, 2003).

2 http://www.eurofound.europa.eu/

The general recommendations were:

- It is necessary to improve the dialogue between Member States
- The social partners, employers and employees' representatives should attach greater importance to financial participation
- An informative website should be created
- Reducing complexities through the prospectus directive
- Introducing an EU convention on the taxation of share options
- For the other forms of financial participation, a procedure for mutual recognition between Member States should be introduced
- A European model should be developed

2. *Some developments*

It is clear that, ten years later, only a few steps have been achieved towards those aims.

In 2005, the IAFP (International Association for Financial Participation) completed a Project financially supported by the European Commission which proposed the main features of a model plan of financial participation: 'Common elements of an adaptable model plan for financial participation in the European Union' (O'Kelly & Pendleton, 2005)

In 2010, the IAFP presented another project, also with the financial support of the Commission, following the general recommendation of the experts group's report: 'Financial participation: A tool for better social dialogue and better corporate governance' (International Association for Financial Participation [IAFP]).

The IAFP which was founded in 1987 is an umbrella association for national associations dealing with financial participation in Europe (France, Germany, the UK, the Netherlands, Belgium, Latvia, Spain, Ireland, Norway, Czech Republic) as well as in the U.S., Australia, Canada and South Africa.

On the website of the association[3] the final reports of the above-mentioned projects are available. The website provides also an overview of laws (delivered and regularly updated by White & Case) regarding financial participation in 23 countries, among which the main ten European ones (available on IAFP website).

3 http://www.iafp-association.com/

There have been some local (national) initiatives at the same time, for instance:

- In the UK where an all-party commission was launched in the British Parliament to promote new developments in employee ownership in the UK, or more recently an ad hoc Ministry was created for the same purpose.
- In France, where the President asked in December 2013 for a renewal of the whole process of profit sharing.
- In Germany, where some incentives have been decided to promote shareholding, generally speaking, but they remain very few and low.

3. The lack of harmonisation

At present, because of the lack of harmonisation in the legislations of the different Member States, for enterprises working in different Member States, the only form of financial participation which can be proposed to all the employees wherever they work is employee ownership. And even in that case because of the different tax rules from a country to another, it seems almost impossible to offer the same advantages to all the beneficiaries. And of course without taking into account the cost of the implementation of such schemes, including the fees paid to the consultants and tax advisers.

When, after the Soviet Union has disappeared, the state-owned companies of the countries belonging to the Central and Eastern Europe, intended to become privatised, these states were advised by western experts who proposed to apply the same rules as those which prevailed in the UK and in France, where it was proposed to the employees of these companies to become shareholders at a discounted rate. The result was that at the first occurrence when the shares became negotiable, almost all the new employee shareholders sold their stake, and cashed the bonus which has been given to them. So, it was a failure, and for years it have been very difficult to convince the representatives of employers or/and of employees that financial participation could be worth to be considered.

Recently, there have been new initiatives, resulting in a report from the European Economic and Social Committee in 2010, as well as reports and studies by the European Parliament and a 2014 resolution on employee financial participation (European Parliament, 2014) emphasised the growing importance of EFP, particularly with respect to small and medium sized enterprises (SMEs).

Thirty years of research have confirmed that companies partly or totally owned by their employees are more profitable, create more jobs and pay more taxes than their competitors without employee ownership. On a macroeconomic point of view, EFP leads to higher productivity and, therefore, higher competitiveness and growth as well as strategic stabilisation of ownership. At the company level, it ensures a better well-being for employees, leading to a shortage in absenteeism, and in labour diseases. It can also contribute to solving other problems such as employee turnover and the retention of key workers, as well as business succession, especially in SMEs – which is a concern for the EU (in the few coming years more than 600,000 companies will face succession issues and may disappear because of a lack of solution). At a local level, EFP can prevent companies to be outsourced or taken over by hostile competitors.

The most encouraging message for the development of Employee Financial Participation was recently delivered by Michel Barnier, former Commissioner for Internal Market and Services (in the second 'Barroso Commission'). He stated:

> 'Employees' share of national wealth production in OECD countries has declined continually over the last three decades. [...] Employee shareholding schemes can contribute to tackling the rising imbalances in income distribution. They can help us rediscover the foundations of the competitive social market economy which characterises the European model, and can help put our economy on the road of more sustainable growth, starting with local initiatives. [...]
>
> Since the introduction of these schemes, decades of research have confirmed that undertakings which are partially or entirely owned by their employees are less subject to relocation, generate more profit, create more jobs and contribute more to tax revenue in the regions where they are located. Finally, their employees are generally long-term shareholders and this brings an element of stability to financial markets.
>
> These forms of employee involvement will have a crucial role to play in Europe in the coming years, as many directors or mangers of SMEs retire and must ensure that management succession in their companies is managed well. Employee buying part of the business is an efficient solution – not just for its founders and employees, but for preserving employment and innovation in Europe.
>
> And yet, in spite of their positive impact and their existence throughout Europe, employee share ownership schemes cover a significant share of economically active population in only a handful of Member States. In the EU, 68 percent of companies still do not provide employee participation schemes.

There is significant room for improvement; we have to translate policy into action at the European level. [...] On this basis, it will be for the new Commission, chaired by Jean-Claude Juncker, to support employment, growth and social cohesion through innovative measures, one of which could be to encourage employee share ownership.
Of course, any EU action should give priority to national action where it is more effective. However, it is not out of the question that we take action also at the European level, starting by encouraging Member States that have sound experience of these schemes to share their best practices. I am thinking in particular of France, but also of the UK, which has recently supported employee shareholding schemes as an important element of economic recovery.
To take it further, the Commission has recently published a study of some ideas for reducing the main obstacles and encouraging cross-border employee share ownership in the EU. These include creating a virtual information centre and developing a European voluntary system of employee shareholding schemes [...]' (Barnier, 2014).

4. *The challenges*

It remains clear that a lot must and can be done to improve the present situation.

The main issue is the gap existing between a real willingness of a lot of convinced people which is proved by the number of successful conferences organised on these subjects and the little number of real achievements.

The principal reason for this is likely the lack of information and formation of both employers and employees. Every people agree that in all countries, not only in the member states, the overall knowledge in financial matters is very poor. It can sometimes be pointed out as a reason not to launch an EFP scheme: 'It is not necessary; the workers cannot understand what that means.'

Another feature is a cultural one, which can be illustrated by the differences existing for example between France, the UK and Germany in the corporate governance: Where it is possible in France for an employee to take part in the decision making process of the company, it is quite impossible in the UK, even if he (or she) is a shareholder of the company. Conversely it is not necessary for an employee in Germany to become a shareholder to be involved in the management of the enterprise.

There are also differences regarding the role and the opinion of trade-unions regarding EFP, from a country to another. But these differences seem to become less important. As far as there is a clear distinction between the wages and the bonuses linked to financial participation, generally speaking the trade unions are no longer opposed to any kind of EFP.

Nevertheless, the prospective of a new social model for the EU, which should be taken as a kind of benchmark by other countries or group of countries, is worth to be pursued. Old Europe should so become an example for the whole world.

References

Barnier, M. (2014, October 28). Europe can only gain if we embrace employee share ownership. Retrieved September 11, 2015, from http://www.cityam.com/1414520921/europe-can-only-gain-if-we-embrace-employee-share-ownership

Commission of the European Communities (1996). *Pepper II: Promotion of participation by employed persons in profits and enterprise results (including equity participation) in Member States* (No. COM(96)697 final). Commission of the European Communities.

Commission of the European Communities (2003). *Report of the High Level Group of independent experts, on cross-border obstacles to financial participation of employees for companies having a transnational dimension*. Commission of the European Communities.

Council of European Communities (1992). Council recommendation of 27 July 1992 concerning the promotion of participation by employed persons in profits and enterprise results (including equity participation). *Official Journal of the European Communities*, *35*(L 245), 53–55.

European Commission (2002). Communication from the Commission to the Council, the European Parliament, the Economic and Social Committee and the Committee of the Regions - On a framework for the promotion of employee financial participation (COM(2002) 364 final). European Commission.

European Economic and Social Committee (2010). OPINION of the European Economic and Social Committee on Employee financial participation in Europe (Own-initiative opinion) SOC 371.

European Parliament (2014). European Parliament resolution of 14 January 2014 on financial participation of employees in companies' proceeds. European Parliament.

International Association for Financial Participation [IAFP] (2010). *Financial participation: A tool for better social dialogue and better corporate governance. Final report*. European Commission.

Kruse, D. & Blasi, J. (1995). Employee Ownership, Employee Attitudes, and Firm Performance (No. 5277). Cambridge, MA: National Bureau of Economic Research (NBER).

Lowitzsch, J. (2006). *The PEPPER III Report: Promotion of Employee Participation in Profits and Enterprise Results in the*. Commission of the European Communities.

O'Kelly, K., & Pendleton, A. (2005). *Common elements of an adaptable model plan for financial participation in the European Union (draft)*. Association Internationale pour la Participation Financière (IAFP/AIPF).

Pendleton, A. D., Poutsma, E., Brewster, C., & van Ommeren, J. (2001). *Employee share ownership and profit-sharing in the European Union*. European Foundation for the Improvement of Living and Working Conditions.

Uvalic, M. (1991). *The Pepper Report: Promotion of Employee Participation in Profits and Enterprise Results in the Member States of the European Commnity.* Commission of the European Communities.

How to overcome the 'Great Divide' of the capitalist market society: Development, legal grounds and perspectives of employee capital participation in Germany and Europe[1]

Herwig Roggemann[2]

Abstract

The breakdown of the so-called 'financial industry' and the crisis of the financial market system, which culminated in a global financial and economic crisis in 2008/2009, can be interpreted as a crisis of financial participation. This crisis of participation is caused by a highly asymmetric and deficient participation in the results of the economic value- creating process. One of the main factors of this negative distributive effect is the highly unequal access to and distribution of value-creating capital in its legal form of economic or entrepreneurial property ('*Wirtschaftseigentum*'). Ongoing deficits in adequate financial participation of all employees who contribute to the value-creating process lead to ongoing asymmetric accumulation of productive capital as property-creating property. The answer to this dysfunctional development which may threaten the democratic social consensus is not the way of the former Socialist states – following Marx's proposals – of abandoning private property in economic capital. Nor is it a bureaucratic system of partial *redistribution* of economic results via a more effective tax system (as proposed by Piketty and Stiglitz) or by means of more social subsidies (as also discussed in Germany).

From our point of view, the main answer to the crisis that is compatible with a democratic market economy based on private property is to create a

1 This article is based on and continues previous contributions to the topic by the author. (See Roggemann, 1996, 1997a, 1997b, 1999, 2010, 2011a, 2011b; Roggemann & Lowitzsch, 2008)

2 Univ.-Prof. a. D. Dr. iur. Dr. h. c., Institute for Eastern European Studies and Faculty of Law of Free University Berlin and Scientific Coordinator in the Interuniversity Centre Berlin/Frankfurt (Oder)/Split/Paris I,
e-mail: herwig.roggemann@gmx.de; herwig.roggemann@fu-berlin.de

widespread and growing system of financial participation of all employees in capital and enterprise results. This is the approach of direct participation in distributing the results of the wealth-creating process.

This *direct distributive participation* should have political priority and deserves better legal support because of its market compatibility and democratic decentralising qualities. The most sustainable social-political effect might be achieved by combining both alternative proposals.

1. Introduction: Sharing in capital – way out of structural deficits in participation – necessary political support – steps of analysis

Adequate and relevant financial participation of employees in the economic success of an enterprise both in profit sharing and in sharing of capital is in Europe and in Germany in particular probably the one great economic and social desideratum on the way from a divided post-industrial society of owners and of non-owners to a society where freedom and solidarity are no longer seen as being inevitably antagonistic but rather can co-exist peacefully within a participative working society of co-owners.

Furthermore, adequate, widespread financial participation in the form of capital participation of employees on a large scale, in relevant dimensions, and supported by both national and European legislation can give an answer to questions that have arisen and, in fact, continue to arise from the highly dysfunctional effects of over-concentrated capital, at free disposition for whatever investment, in the irresponsible hands of a so-called 'financial industry'. One main reason for the financial and economic crash of 2007/2008 et seq. as well as of similar future events can be found in the long-lasting structural lack of relevant financial, i.e. capital, participation of employees with its decentralising, power-sharing and power-limiting effects[3].

3 The genuine decentralizing effect of private property follows from the individual power of disposition, 'it is the ultimate right to use (and abuse) the object or right in question' (Smith, 2003, p. 6; for property rights and social power, see Levy, 1983 & Roggemann, 2010). Private Property had already been characterized as individual power against centralized state power by Proudhon (1963) in his famous controversy with Karl Marx.

Which ways and methods should be employed to reach these aims is a matter of controversy. Even the political priority is unclear as current party and coalition programmes in Germany show:

After months and even years of lively discussion on the highest political level of president[4] and chancellor[5] during the last two electoral periods, financial participation at present has been put aside once again and more or less forgotten as a political topic.

Income and property, and along with them the opportunities for life, health, education and professional success, are unequally distributed in every open market economic social order. Inequality is a component of the condition of liberty. Exactly how much inequality in the structure of income and property can be tolerated by a democratic society, or how much it should actually be tolerated as an incentive for development is a topic of much debate. Thus far agreement has been reached only on the fact that the stability required for the existence of the political, economic and legal order requires a certain minimum of solidarity and distributive justice.

This consensus about a certain minimum of solidarity realised in the market economy by means of social policy (for this and the following, see Scholz & Tomann, 1999) is a constituent part of the German conception of 'welfare state'. Elements of it are also contained in the European Union (EU) law[6] and can even refer back to universal legal standards[7].

But how can this minimum in concreto be defined and even be realised? In light of the fact that growing inequality in income and property produces growing dysfunctional social (mortality rate, health, wealth, rate of delinquency, standard of education and professional opportunities) and

---

4 The former President of the Federal Republic of Germany, Horst Köhler, in 2004: 'I think time is ripe to put participation in enterprise results and in economic property on the table again' (see his interview in Der Stern, 2005; also reported at the 57th Conference of the Bundesverband für Mitarbeiterbeteiligung [AGP]).

5 At the 20th Congress of the Christian Democratic Party (CDU) in Dresden on 27 November 2006 Chancellor Angela Merkel said that 'new ways for more justice through participation' should be found. A Congress resolution voted for 'social partnership in capital and more employee participation in profit and capital' (CDU-Bundesvorstand, 2006).

6 Principle of Solidarity: Art. 1 III; 2 I EUV; preamble. VI; Art. 27 ff. European Charter of Fundamental Rights 2007; Art. 4 European Social Charter 1961.

7 Art. 6;7 The International Agreement on Economic, Social, and Cultural Rights (The Social Pact) 1966, in effect since 1976.

structural economic effects (Kelso & Kelso, 1991; Lowitzsch, 2008)[8], this is no longer only an academic discussion, but should lead to political and law-making consequences.

This conclusion had already been drawn years ago in the German jurisprudential debate on how to overcome the negative effects of ongoing capital and property concentration: 'The prevention of a dysfunctional concentration of private property possibly not only requires legislation against concentration of economic property, but also an active public promotion of asset formation' (Papier, 2008).

Whether or not the European principle of solidarity and coherence and the German model of 'welfare state' ('*Sozialstaatsprinzip*')[9] give everyone who is willing and able the right to live on the financial result of his or her own working contribution is still an unresolved question. It is a fact that an increasing number of the working population in Germany is no longer able to live on the financial result of their work. Whether this structural deficit in financial participation can be compensated by additional alimentation from the state budget is doubtful. However, there is no doubt that effective financial participation on a large scale could lead to a way out of this dilemma.

More than half a century ago, the American lawyer and economist Louis Kelso showed a way out of this structural dilemma and developed a successful model to solve the problem of highly dysfunctional property distribution by giving employees the opportunity to participate in the success of their firm not only as wage-earners or profit sharers but also as shareholders (Kelso & Adler, 1958). Supported by a remarkable tax allowance in the US based on the Employee Stock Ownership Plan

---

8 Kelso & Adler (1958) describe these structural consequences starting with decreasing purchasing power on the one hand and the ongoing concentration of the ownership of capital on the other hand as 'the basic cause of depressions in a capitalist economy', and they point out why legislative taxation and other measures for transfers and redistribution of property and wealth 'to prevent the collapse of the economy' are of limited effect or even counterproductive because 'theses practices increase operating costs to a point at which they can be absorbed only by the most heavily capitalised business' (p. 190 et seq., p. 203, 208). This argumentation of Louis Kelso is renewed now in the debate on the introduction of legal minimum wages and its bureaucratic tendencies in Germany in 2015. For recent development of the ESOP system in the US and the following data, see National Center for Employee Ownership (NCEO) (2015) and also Rosen (2002).

9 See Art. 20 I German Basic Law – Constitution (GG).

(ESOP) model of Louis Kelso a banking system was created. As of 2013 there were 6,750 genuine ESOPs in the U.S., covering 13.9 million employees as well as 2,528 ESOP like plans covering 1.18 million employees; the total assets held in ESOPs are estimated to amount to $1.23 trillion at the end of 2013.

In Germany, the legislative results after years of debate led to the Law on Participation in Capital of 2009 (the German abbreviation of which is MKBG), which was obviously not well-constructed in comparison with other European countries and also with the US as it provided much too little governmental support through tax allowance. The macroeconomic effects of this and other legislative attempts in Germany are not at all satisfying. In fact, this legislation has produced nearly no measureable effect. The situation has not essentially changed during the last two-and-a-half decades, i.e. neither since the German reunification nor after the law of 2009. Not more than two to three per cent of all German enterprises offer sharing in capital to their employees. Where they do, it is the same percentage of employees who make use of the financial participation schemes for sharing in capital offered.

The following text

- Gives a survey of the recent political debate in Germany and the European framework (2.), arguments for and against the sharing of capital (3.), the legal compatibility of traditional German labour law and new regulations to be introduced on participation in capital (4.), the development in Germany 1918-2014: From the revolution in 1918 to the law on minimum wages in 2014 (5.),
- Understands the ongoing functional change of property rights as a condition for a future binding law on enlargement of financial participation by share ownership (6.),
- Finds German society breaking down into a small society of owners and a large society of non-owners (7.1),
- Takes into consideration recent fundamental critical analysis by European (Piketty, 2014a) and American (Stiglitz, 2012) authors (7.2),
- Points out deficits and practice of participation in capital in Germany (7.3),
- Gives an overview of legal sources concerning financial participation (8.),
- mentions a number of different models and examples of financial participation through the sharing of capital in practice (9.),

- examines the Law on Participation in Capital of 2009 and comes to the conclusion that a new law-making attempt is needed in Germany (10.).

2. Political and European framework

2.1 Financial participation – alternative or in addition to minimum wage system – political and legal-political implications

The aim seems to be clear: To close what is called 'The Gap of Justice'[10] with regard to income and property distribution or at least to stop this negative development, which, if nothing changes, will sooner or later threaten the social consensus. Several additional instruments have been discussed in Germany by the political parties both before and during the coalition treaty negotiations in 2013 to come closer to this aim without weakening the competitiveness of the German export industry:

- Labour market incentives,
- Minimum wages,
- Higher taxation of wealth (*'Reichensteuer'*).

These additional political instruments are expected to complement the conventional instrument: union agreements aiming at higher wages.

However, regular collective bargaining over the years did not usually result in agreements on an increase in remuneration much higher than the annual inflation rate.

There was always general political consensus with regard to the first point. The third point appeared from time to time in political party programmes[11], but without any concrete results. The second point was controversial at the beginning, was debated intensely and ended with a historic new law: the Law on Minimum Wages (*'Mindestlohngesetz'*) of 2014[12].

---

10 'Gerechtigkeitslücke' (Der Spiegel, 2007b).

11 See also the discussion in the context of the presentation of the fourth governmental report of the Federal Republic of Germany on poverty and wealth (Bundesministerium für Arbeit und Soziales, 2013) and in the context of the publication of the OECD report on income and property structure in Germany and economic and social consequences for Germany and Europe (OECD, 2014).

12 Law on Minimum Wage (*'Gesetz zur Regelung eines allgemeinen Mindestlohnes (MindestlohnG – MiloG)'*) dated 11/08/2014, BGBl. I S. 1348.

This result, laid down in the current coalition treaty of 2013 between Christian Democrats and Social Democrats (CDU Deutschland, CSU Landesleitung & SPD, 2013), is not at all a convincing step forward because all these political and law making activities may be able to alleviate the symptoms but they do not address the root cause: the dramatically growth of asymmetric participation in income and property.

Everyone who cooperates in the value-creating process has a right to adequate profit sharing as well as sharing of capital beyond what is specified by union agreements or legal minimum wages.

This is still not at all the case in Germany. At present, under what might be characterised as the current (2015) 'trade union labour and income policy', this is not even part of the political programme for the future social economic development in Germany – at least during the present electoral period from 2013 to 2017.

Final and sustainable effects can be realised neither by improving labour market incentives nor through a system of minimum wages with a new bureaucratic control mechanism. Nor can they be brought about by increasing the tax rates for the rich (*'Reichensteuer'*). Sustainable effects in a long run can only be achieved by issuing a legally-binding framework for profit and capital sharing models, to be offered by enterprises on a large scale.

This does not mean guaranteed payment 'on top' of remuneration laid out in union agreements but the opportunity for additional flexible income linked to the profit and success of the enterprise. This effect of both profit and capital sharing makes the total remuneration more flexible and thus can also help to reduce the risk of unemployment in periods of recession and promote greater employment stability (Lowitzsch, 2008; Vanek, 1965).

This aim, '*to let employees participate adequately and well-balanced in the production of wealth*' (see also Lowitzsch, 2008; Vanek, 1965) is not new nor was it new during the law making process before 2009. Ten years ago, the German Federal Government of a previous so-called 'grand coalition' ('*Große Koalition*') of Christian Democrats and Social Democrats during the electoral period from 2005 to 2009 made this political aim part of their governmental programme. The result was the inadequate law of 2009.

Now (2015), the legal-political situation is even worse. During the electoral campaign for the parliamentary elections of 2013, the Christian Democrats' electoral programme stated: 'Participation of employees in profit and in capital is a central topic for us.' (CDU-Bundesgeschäftsstelle, 2013). The Social Democrats' electoral programme underlined this aim with nearly the same words: 'Participation of employees in capital is a key to allowing them to participate in the economic success of the enterprise. We want to increase this participation.' (SPD-Parteivorstand, 2013). In the draft of their pre-election governmental programme (*'Regierungsprogramm'*), the Social Democrats no longer linked 'adequate participation of employees in the success of the enterprise' to the sharing of capital but to 'strengthening the collective bargaining system' obviously to avoid using the term 'sharing of capital' as a legal-political goal further on.

At the end of the same election year (2013), in their joint coalition programme for the current legislative period (2013 – 2017), comprising about 185 pages, there is no mention at all of the financial participation of employees through sharing capital. In short: Both governing political parties in Germany denied their pre-election announcements and promises in this central point of future social economic policy in Germany. They simply 'forgot' their own proposal which they had duly elaborated in a joint party commission in 2008 (CDU, CSU, & SPD, 2008). This happened very likely due to traditional and still prevailing objections of the German trade unions against effective forms of financial participation.

In their statement concerning the governmental draft of the Law on Tax Allowance to support financial participation of employees which was issued in 2009, the German trade unions stated: *'Sharing in capital is for employees no alternative to collective bargaining policy. The decreasing portion of remuneration in relation to employees' overall gross income demands an active collective bargaining policy right now. Only a combination of active collective bargaining policy, social tax policy and additional profit and capital sharing can lead to sustainable improvement of the distributive situation in Germany.'* (Hexel, 2008; Waas, 2014).

This traditional sceptical or antagonistic attitude of trade unions is mostly to be found in Germany and less in the rest of Europe – instead of unreserved and powerful support of financial participation combined with structural reform of labour and company law – it is probably thus far one of the decisive obstacles for more substantial participation in share ownership in Germany.

In addition to the other arguments mentioned above and contrary to the present coalition programme and the trade union statement cited above, financial participation means much more in Germany: It is the half of the

German model of immaterial co-determination or co-decision (the famous *'Mitbestimmung')* that has been missing to date.

With its integrative and conflict-managing capacity, this legal institution within the framework of collective German labour law contributed remarkably to the economic success of Germany after the catastrophe of the Nazi regime and Second World War (Gamillscheg, 1997).[13] On the other hand, it could not really help to avert the increasingly asymmetrical development of income and property structure in Germany, especially during the last two-and-a-half decades since reunification. Furthermore, a growing number of labour conflicts and strikes make it obvious that this traditional German model has lost some of its integrative capacity.

Instead, there is now a growing burden on employees as taxpayers who are bearing the major part of the steadily increasing costs for social insurance, whereas the employer's contribution to these insurance funds has been frozen by law at its current level and must not rise any further. Wages increasing not at all or at a rate only a little higher than the annual inflation rate cannot essentially change this situation. Otherwise, Germany's competitiveness and position as an industrial country with relatively high wages would be weakened.

2.2 Employee participation and European legal and political activities on the way to a new European social order

Financial participation and employee co-ownership correspond to the basic social principles of the EU (see also section 1). One of the main goals therefore should be the incorporation of financial participation into the legal framework of a developing new European social order.

On the level of the European Commission and the European Parliament, the growing political, economic and social relevance of financial participation both in profit sharing and in sharing of capital has been noted over the course of more than 35 years and with growing intensity during the last two decades. A number of initiatives, proposals and decisions have recently taken place.

---

13 'Germany would not have been able to act as motor and one of the three economic powers of the European Union without the German constitution of labour' (Gamillscheg, 1997, p. 11 et seq.) with its co-determination model.

From a German point of view, one might hope to see a stimulus to German legal policy and, as a consequence, also to the future law making process to promote financial participation in Germany.

The development within the EU has been analysed, summarised and extended by the PEPPER[14] reports (Commission of the European Communities, 1996; Lowitzsch, Hashi & Woodward, 2009; Lowitzsch, 2006; Uvalic, 1991). Basic activities of the organs of the EU elaborated and recommended further comparative European research and supporting measures to promote financial participation:

- One of the starting points has been the Council recommendation of 1992 'On the promotion of participation by employed persons in profits and enterprise results including equity participation in member states' (The Council of the European Communities, 1992).
- The European Commission issued a communication in 2002: 'On a framework for the promotion of financial participation' (European Economic and Social Committee, 2003).
- The Economic and Social Committee of the EU presented an opinion on further supporting activities in 2003 (European Economic and Social Committee, 2003).
- The European Parliament issued a resolution in 2003 on conditions for promoting financial participation of employees (European Parliament, 2003; Menrad, 2005).
- The Economic and Social Committee of the EU issued a new initiative on financial participation in the EU member states in 2010 (European Economic and Social Committee, 2010).
- A new attempt was made in 2014 by the EU conference in Brussels 'Taking action: promotion of employee share ownership'.

This EU conference published five key points in 2014:

- The need to establish a legal framework,
- Exchange of best practice schemes and experiences,
- Tax incentives and transparency of tax policy and fiscal treatment,
- Joint labour market and economic policy,
- Incorporation of employee share ownership into corporate government and investment strategies.

---

14 Promotion of Employee Participation in Profits and Enterprise Results (PEPPER)

These and other activities show that financial participation now gains more attention in European social, labour and economic policy (Lowitzsch & Hashi, 2014). However, on the other hand, in the nearly two-and-a-half decades since the beginning of the PEPPER reports, a framework law or a legal source with binding validity could not be developed – neither on the European nor on the level of the majority of the member states – except France. The criticism of the second PEPPER report of 1996 is still valid: 'Cash-based profit sharing still remains without incentives or legislation' (Commission of the European Communities, 1996). The 2009 PEPPER report reiterates this: *'Most urgent [is] the lack of a European legal framework for financial participation'* (Lowitzsch, Hashi & Woodward, 2009, p. 4).

During the last two decades, the number of enterprises offering financial participation schemes for all employees grew in the EU-27 by about five per cent from 13 per cent to 18 per cent regarding shareholding schemes and about six per cent from 29 per cent to 35 per cent regarding profit-sharing schemes. This can be deemed to be remarkable progress (Lowitzsch & Roggemann, 2014).

Germany unfortunately does not participate adequately in this development. Leading European countries in financial participation are France and the UK. In both countries, immaterial participation (co-determination) is much less developed than in Germany. Financial participation, therefore, in these countries could be interpreted partly as a compensation of this deficit. On the other hand, it is obvious that the German model of immaterial participation (*'Mitbestimmung'*) only in decisionmaking during the last century did not give employees a real opportunity to participate in their firms' increasing substantial values and profits.

This fact should be taken into consideration by the German trade unions as an argument to no longer oppose but to support immaterial as well as material participation: both are of equal relevance.

The total amount of enterprise capital held by employees via participation schemes does not yet reach an economically relevant level. In Germany, its amount is in total not more than about €11 billion (Beyer, 2014).

This – from a German point of view – rather poor result is confirmed by findings on the European level and by recent research projects (Boeri, Lucifora & Murphy, 2013; O'Kelly, 2013).

As the situation on the European level is not yet ripe for the drafting of a binding legal framework for financial participation in the form of a directive, other steps have been taken to intensify research and exchange of information and to prove the positive impact of financial participation on employment and productivity:

- A virtual centre for employee financial participation,
- A comparative tax rate calculator and
- An optional 'Common European regime on employee financial participation' has been developed (Lowitzsch & Hashi, 2014).

3. *Arguments in favour of and against financial participation through employee share ownership*

3.1 Arguments in favour of financial participation

Advantages of effective financial participation through the sharing of capital are proved by facts and examples of best practice of various enterprises in Europe and USA (Boeri et al., 2013; O'Kelly, 2013). The key arguments can be summarised as follows (Bellmann & Leber, 2007; Blasi, Kruse, Bernstein & Aaron, 2000; Leuner, 2009; Roggemann, 2010; Rosen, Case & Staubus, 2005; Schanz, 2000; Uvalić, 2008; Wagner, 2003, 2008, p. 138):

1. Legal and ethical arguments concerning the Law of Property (principle of social justice, justification of private property by labour, 'labour theory' (Gierke, 1889; Hecker, 1990; Holzhey, 1983; Roggemann, 2010; von Gierke, 1959),
2. Religious arguments (social doctrine of the Christian churches) (Kamp, 2010; Menrad, 2005),
3. Humanitarian and constitutional arguments (basic rights of equal opportunities, immaterial *and* material participation, articles 1 II, 2 I, 3 I, 12 I, 14 I 2 and II, 20 I with the principle of the welfare state as outlined in the German constitution; see also section 1),
4. Arguments under civil law (entitlement for co-ownership as the co-producer in the production process, § 950 BGB [German civil law code]; for this relationship between labour and property rights as a forgotten topic of German Civil Law, see Roggemann, 2010),
5. Arguments concerning industrial law (entitlement for [economic] co-determination (Däubler, 1991; a different view by Gamillscheg, 1997 and 'fair wages'),

6. Socio-ethical and socio-juridical arguments (basic right for a humane existence and 'distributional justice'[15]),
7. Economic arguments:
   a) Market stabilisation via more flexible reaction to market conditions and business cycles,
   b) Increasing purchasing power through additional money, thereby promoting economic growth,
   c) Complementing the standard wage system with a certain part of flexible wages (*'Entgeltflexibilisierung'*) (European Commission, 2007; Lowitzsch, 2010),
   d) Maintaining current employment levels and creating new jobs by flexibilisation of a limited percentage of income (Sinn, 1998),
   e) Compensation of previous financial contributions of the employees Compensation of employees' financial contributions in case of crisis of the enterprise (temporary pay freeze or renunciation of a percentage of wages or of holiday pay) by share of capital,
   f) Increasing productivity by three to five per cent or even more (Rosen et al., 2005)[16],
   g) Increasing income through additional profit as co-owner and higher standard of living,
   h) Increasing motivation, identification (corporate identity),
   i) Advantages for the enterprise in competition for skilled workers,
   j) Strengthening of the capital basis and credibility of the enterprise and therefore better access to loans,

---

15 On the legal-political dimension and the Hartz IV ruling by the German Constitutional Court (BVerfG, 09/02/2010 – 1 BvL 1/09; Borchert, 2010).

16 Recent research findings confirm this essential point. New studies found positive effects of two to three per cent higher productivity in France and other countries; in the Italian metal engineering industry even a rate of five to six per cent and more; overall in 20 countries in general either positive or non-negative effects (Boeri, Lucifora & Murphy, 2013). In the US the best workplaces have better financial performance and are far more likely to pay workers through incentive pay and financial participation than other firms (Boeri et al., 2013). Pendleton (2014) points out that the participation rate had a positive effect on productivity outcomes, i.e. a long-run productivity effect of 2.5 per cent in the UK (Oxera, 2007) and 2.5 per cent in the US (Kurse, Blasi & Freeman, 2011; Blasi, Conte & Kruse, 1996; Blasi & Kruse 1996).

   k) More independence of the enterprise from profit interests of external creditors (banks, international investment funds).
8. Socio-political arguments (reduction of social conflicts), and
9. Stabilisation of the ideological and legal basis of private property after transformation by (re-)privatisation (Roggemann, 1996).
10. Development of a 'new social market economy' in a 'new European social order' ('New Social Europe') (CDU-Bundesvorstand, 2006; Lowitzsch, 2008).

The justification for the Law on Participation in Capital (MKBG) takes up several of these arguments: *'All employees should get a fair share of the company's success. [...] It is also an act of economic sensibility and social justice to grant employees a fair and balanced share in the revenue of the national economy'* (Der Stern, 2005).

3.2 Positive effects of employee co-ownership in cases of crisis and conflict

Employee participation pays off if companies depend on the support of their employees (austerity measures, extension of working hours, employee loans) to overcome economic difficulties or to ward off pending insolvencies, compensating them by capital participation (Apitzsch, 2009; Beyer, 2010; Leuner, 2009; Menrad, 2005).

This also applies in case of pending hostile takeovers (for example Hochtief; see Der Tagesspiegel, 2010a, 2010b). Employee capital participation with coordinated exertion of voting rights can counteract takeovers by international investment companies or competing companies, which contradict the interests of the company and its employees, at least allowing them to play an active role in setting up their conditions: *'If we had extended employee participation as early as several years ago, we would have completely different constellations in some cases.'* (impulse, 2008). In fact, the interests of an enterprise's owner and its employees often are closer to each other than they are to external creditors like banks, investment banks, hedge funds and other transnational investment companies with no interest in sustainable development of the enterprise in the long run other than the development of the shareholder value.

'About 71,000 owners of family-owned companies are looking for a successor each year' (Wagner, 2008, p. 138). In such cases, solutions can be developed with the help of participation models, which better meet the interests of former owners and their employees than a takeover by investors not familiar with the company (Lowitzsch, 2007).

3.3 Arguments against financial participation

3.3.1 Counter-argument 'double risk'

The main counter-argument is the so-called 'double risk' of losing shares and jobs in case of the company's insolvency.[17]

Other counter-arguments concerning problems such as

- Evaluation of the capital engagement of the share owner,
- His or her (frozen) right of participation in decision making by company law,
- Holding period,
- Transferability in case of death or end of employment contract or
- Sale because of other personal reasons of the employee,

The right of the company to acquire its own shares with the intention to advance funds or sell the shares to its employees within the framework of a participation scheme have already been intensively discussed (Lowitzsch & Roggemann, 2014; Lowitzsch, 2008) and are not treated here.

The double risk argument does apply, but it can mostly, or sometimes nearly completely, be overcome by an appropriate arrangement of the participation and by means of a suitable insurance model, combined with financing the starting capital for share ownership not by the employees themselves but by external loans. In particular, the ESOP model permits participation in capital without investing the employee's own money.

However, there is no advantage without any risk. Private property combines the right and the risk of economic usage and power of disposition. Thus, the economic and legal function of property guarantees the freedom of the owner only in combination with bearing risks (Kirchhof, 2009). Property without risks would end in a faulty construction, as it had

17 According to the Scientific Advisory Council of the German Ministry of Economics in a letter to the minister dated 17/04/2008 (for a different view that shows a re-thinking of the problem of financial participation of employees by the German trade unions, see Die Welt, 2009).

been attempted – unsuccessfully – by the legal and economic orders created by socialist states under different circumstances (Kirchhof, 2010; Roggemann, 1996).

However, this does not at all justify setting up obstacles for the majority of employees in Germany, i.e. 97 per cent, to participating in the economic property with its high profitability and to marginalise them, as had been the case so far.

The legislatures of some German state governments (*'Bundesländer'*), such as in Berlin, Thuringia, Rhineland-Palatinate, Hessen have used their state banks (*'Landesbanken'*) to set up risk-relief programmes for employee capital participation (Althaus, 2007).

A new programme is offered by the Guarantee Bank of Thuringia (*'Thüringer Bürgschaftsbank – BBT'*) to minimise the insolvency risk for capital shared by employees of small and medium enterprises. In case of insolvency, 80 per cent of the employee-owned capital up to a maximum amount of € 250,000 is granted by the bank for a one-time fee of 0.75 per cent of the guaranteed capital plus an annual fee of 1.5 per cent.

In comparison with interest rates of eight per cent or more which are normally paid for employee loans or employee capital in special accounts or other saving schemes, this seems to be relatively attractive.[18]

A similar insolvency insurance programme is offered by the Guarantee Bank of Hessen ('*Hessische Bürgschaftsbank'*) (Menrad, 2005). This programme allows loans for financing employee participation in capital investment to be insured up to 80 per cent of the invested amount and to a maximum of € 750,000.

The state government of Rhineland-Palatinate created a programme called 'Financial participation of employees RLPlus' (Beck, 2010) and the Investment and Structure Bank of Rhineland-Palatinate (*'Investitions- und Strukturbank Rheinland-Pfalz – ISB'*) established a fund, financed by the state budget and additional contributions of employees. Their contributions are guaranteed in the beginning up to 100 per cent and after two years up to 90 per cent by the bank. The created capital is at the disposition of small and mid-sized enterprises in the state but not as external credit but rather as additional enterprise capital. Throughout the ten-year

18 Compared with the expected annual yield rate for capital owned by the enterprise (Renditeerwartung für Eigenkapital) of 25 per cent, this profit rate can be held rather conservatively (see for these examples Menrad, 2005; Lowitzsch & Hanish, 2014).

working period of the fund, the employees receive annual interest and bonus payments of nine to 14 per cent of their invested contribution, depending on the economic success of the enterprise. Additionally, and independently of this funds model, the state bank also runs an insolvency guarantee programme for all other capital held by employees as share owners. The guarantee covers 90 per cent of the employee's capital up to € 200,000.

Even more convincing is the participation scheme of the firm Emsa Werke, which offers its employees a share-based profit sharing model (*'Genußschein Modell'*), the capital of which is guaranteed by an insurance company to 100 per cent in case of insolvency. The insurance premium is paid by the employer.

These and other examples show that the 'double risk' argument which is often emphasised especially by opponents of participation in capital can be overcome by suitable legal and financial models and is not at all a definite obstacle to more financial participation. Useful insolvency insurance mechanisms for employee shares and other legal forms of direct sharing of capital with a minimum holding period can be and should be developed to a large extent. Further support by insolvency legislation is needed to promote the development of substantial financial participation.

The question remains: Why do not all of the 16 German states use their banking systems to develop and offer such risk relief programmes in order to promote employee capital participation on a large scale? Furthermore, why does the biggest German investment and development bank (*'Kreditanstalt für Wiederaufbau – KfW'*) not develop corresponding guarantee programmes – in line with EU competition law and in cooperation with the European Development Bank (EIB)?

The Law on Participation in Capital 2009 (MKBG) and the German Insolvency Code do not lay down any rules for a solution of this core problem but have remained silent about any relief of the insolvency risk of participating employees (Wagner, 2008). This shortcoming needs to be rectified by a future reform of the law of 2009. The above and other examples show that the insolvency risk is not an insurmountable obstacle but can, in fact, be managed.

3.3.2 Structural counter-argument: Lack of institutionalised representation of different interests of labour and capital – traditional thinking of German trade unions

The first comprehensive empirical studies in Germany on financial participation were published in 1878 (Böhmert, 1878) and again in 1901. Following the publication, there was a debate on the thesis of its author, who held that the main purpose of financial participation is 'to maintain or restore the social peace between employer and employee' (Böhmert, 1878). Earlier, Karl Marx had severely criticised trade unions because of their aim to improve the financial and social situation of employees within the capitalist system by reforming it instead of destroying and replacing it by eliminating private industrial property and 'definitely abandoning the wage system' (Marx, 1898 cited after Ahrens, 1982).

The conflict of interest between capital and labour and employer and employee in traditional socialist, social democrat and trade union thinking and theory was, and partly still is, viewed as a structural principle inherent to every capitalist society. Hence class consciousness and class conflict (*'Klassenbewußtsein und Klassenkampf'*) and the permanent struggle for strengthening trade unionist competence in collective bargaining for better wages and working conditions dominated the socialist, social democratic and trade unionist attitude towards financial and especially participation in capital ownership for decades (Brentano, 1898 cited after Steinhaus, 2011).

From this point of view, these new tendencies were criticised as 'corruptive' and a wrong attempt 'to create a compensation for the trade unionist conception of co-determination and transfer of basic industries into collective property' (Deutscher Gewerkschaftsbund (DBG), 1954 cited after Gundelach, 1982). This traditional thinking of the German trade unions being rather in favour of 'redistributive conceptions' and 'expansive wage policy' than of new forms of more flexible financial participation *'has essentially contributed to the fact that the distribution of wealth in the Federal Republic is still not regulated in favour of the employees'* (Gundelach, 1982; see also Otto, 2009).[19]

---

19 Yet in 1964 the IG Metall and the trade union for public services, transport and traffic rejected the proposal made by the chairperson of the trade union Bau-Steine-Erden, Julius Leber, for a collective agreement fixed capital formation by employees through the establishment of funds at the sectoral level as a 'hindrance

More than half a century later, things seem to have changed. Financial participation and sharing of capital are now part of the trade unionist social economic development programme (Hexel, 2007; Lowitzsch & Hanisch 2014, p. 47), although they still have no priority. Furthermore, schemes for capital sharing without participation of trade unions and the organs of immaterial co-determination are not taken into consideration at all. This is consistent insofar as immaterial co-determination and sharing in capital are two sides of the same coin: participation. However, it is narrow-sighted insofar as participation in political and in entrepreneurial decision making and also in entrepreneurial capital and risk is part of the role of citizens as co-owners in an economic market democracy based on private property. Therefore, it seems doubtful whether participation of trade unions should be made a conditio sine qua non in all cases and under all circumstances of possible financial participation in capital.

Within the *octagon of interests, power and acteurs of*

employers and entrepreneurs and their unions ↔ shareholders ↔ banks and investors ↔ managers ↔ employees sharing ownership ↔ employees without participation in ownership ↔ trade unions ↔ social and economic policymakers

the interests and approaches of these stakeholders and their representatives, agents and lobbyists are often not identical (Steinhaus, 2011). More often, it may be the case that within that complex constellation of balance of interests, influence and power the interests of entrepreneurs/employers/owners on the one side and of employees/workers on the other side are closer to each other than those of the other participants of that multi-dimensional fabric of interests.

Nevertheless, trade unions understand or should understand both now: promotion of participation in decision-making and of material participation in capital as a basic part of their programme (Hexel, 2007).[20]

Objections of that kind, such as that trade unions might loose influence and power over workers and enterprises with ongoing financial participation through the sharing of capital have not been sustained by empirical

---

of trade union collective bargaining'. To date, the trade unions prefer inter-company or even nationwide fund solutions (for the ideological conflict see Siegler, 1979).

20 *'It is one of the primary concerns of the DGB and its member unions to advocate for more participation and equal participation of workers in Germany.'* (Hexel, 2007, p. 75).

studies (Harbaugh, 1993, 2005; Mehrens, Stracke & Wilke, 2011; Ognedal, 1992; Pendleton, Robinson & Wilson, 1995). On the contrary: Studies found that a communicative or even cooperative structure of an enterprise with functioning immaterial participation (*'Mitbestimmung'*) through the legal organs of co-determination, i.e. the work council, organised with the help of the trade unions, is a precondition for better functioning of participation through the sharing of capital (Menrad, 2005).

The traditional role of trade unions themselves also has to be part of this transformation process towards more economically relevant co-ownership.

Employees as co-owners and co-entrepreneurs (*'Mitunternehmer'*) lose their former traditional position as opponents of the employer and probably thereby their independence (*'Gegnerunabhängigkeit'*) (Müller, 2000) in relation to the employer, to 'their' enterprise and also to the trade unions as their former agent. Their position within the system of collective bargaining, including labour disputes and strikes, will also change as they are influenced by a new constellation of interests where they are no longer only owners of labour but also owners of capital. This is true. However, on the other hand, this loss of power will be overcompensated because the trade unions will gain new and relevant influence as they have to play a new additional role and need new expertise as financial advisers and even co-administrators of employees, re-investing a part of their income with additional contributions of the employer in their own enterprise. The fight for better working conditions and wages is not at all obsolete under these new conditions but will remain a genuine function of the trade unions.

4. Legal compatibility of traditional German labour law and new regulations on participation in capital

Labour law and labour constitution in Germany offer a favourable opportunity for the legal introduction of mandatory financial participation also in the form of sharing of capital. In contrast to most other European countries, Germany had already established participation as a functioning system of immaterial co-determination nearly a century ago. Furthermore, the collective bargaining competence (*'Tarifautonomie'*) of trade unions is constitutionally guaranteed and concretised by law.[21]

The legal development started after the revolution of 1918 with the first Law on Work Councils of 1920 (RGBl. 1920, 147). After the Second World War, the legal reconstruction and consolidation of co-determination went on as follows:

- Law on Co-determination of Employees in Coal, Iron and Steel Industries (Montan-MitbestimmungsG) 1950 (BGBl. I, 347),
- Law on the Constitution of Enterprise (BetriebsverfassungsG) 1952 (BGBl. I, 681),
- New Law on the Constitution of Enterprise (BetriebsverfassungsG) 1972 (BGBl. I, 13),
- Law on Co-Determination of Employees in Supervisory Boards and Executive Boards of Enterprises in the Mining, Iron and Steel Producing Industry (MitbestimmungsG) 1976 (BGBL I, 1153),
- Law on Committees of Speakers of Leading Employees (SprecherausschußG) 1988 (BGBl. I, 2312).

Quality and intensity of the constant conflict of interests and struggle for power between capital and labour and the trade unions as traditional agents of labour in Germany have changed and the conflict management capacity has been improved by this legal framework.

The big and still unanswered question is: To what extent are the legal structure and existing organs, functions and function holders of co-determination and the social partners' right of collective bargaining compatible or can be successfully combined with new organs and their competencies representing the specific interests of employees as owners sharing capital of their enterprise?

The German Law on Participation in Capital of 2009 does not provide an answer; nor do any of the other aforementioned basic labour laws on immaterial participation by co-determination (*'Mitbestimmung'*) in amended versions of the previous laws issued after the law of 2009.

---

21 Art. 9 III GG; § 2 Tarifvertragsgesetz (TVG). The Federal Constitutional Court of Germany said: *'Based on the freedom of coaltition, the autonomous right of collective bargaining aims at regulating labour relations in the public interest through collective agreements as far as allowed by legislation, in particular to fix the wages for certain professions and thus create social peace in society.'* (BVerfG dated 06/05/1964, AP no. 15 on § 2 TVG; see also Preis, 2009).

This situation is, alongside the law of 2009, another vast field where legal-political and law making attempts are needed in Germany. In view of the current legislative and political priorities (of 2015) (see section 2.2), scepticism seems to be the appropriate attitude at present.

In this situation, a successful way to move ahead might be:

To produce a draft of building blocks for a legal framework, based on existing European recommendations and implementable by German enterprises and employers who want to offer participation schemes (Lowitzsch, 2008),

to produce a draft of a new law on financial participation including the necessary modification or completion of the other aforementioned collective labour laws and also company laws related to financial participation.

With regard to labour law, the following problems and options are under discussion:

- The existing, legally required work councils could act as organs with expanded competencies to also represent the special interests of employees as shared owners. This solution is already practised in enterprises (see, for example, Menrad, 2005). It seems to be preferred also by the trade unions (Hexel, 2007). Nevertheless, it could lead to conflicts of interest because the same organ would decide on obviously different interests of owners and non-owners among employees. On the other hand, it could be argued that German company and labour law already knows and accepts this sort of conflict of interests because leading employees and managers, who often but not always own shares or other capital of their enterprise, have a special organ of representation of their interests which was established in the law of 1988 (BGBl. I, 2312).
- In enterprises that practice sharing of capital, a special additional organ or at least a procedure to represent the special interests of the owner-employees must be installed. Enterprises that practice participation in Germany have created a number of different models and procedures of interest representation in enterprises with capital sharing schemes. The coordination of both organs can be defined in a collective agreement (‘*Betriebsvereinbarung*’). However, any agreement is limited by the legally-binding rights of information and participation in decision-making of the work councils (§ 87 I no. 8 and 10 BetrVG; see Waas, 2014).

- In case of employees as normal shareholders, company law provides them with the legal rights to information and participation in decision-making. These rights can be and in practice are often modified without problems by different participation schemes. Shareholders and other co-owners of capital can renounce or transfer these rights to management, to their representative in the work council or by other legal means.
- The work council has, according to § 87 I no. 8 BetrVG, a right to detailed information and co-determination with regard to the concrete design, financial dimension, who receives the offered capital transfer by the employer and organisation of financial participation schemes. However, the work council has no right to agree or disagree with the basic decision of the employer as to whether or not he or she wants to offer and adopt such schemes in the enterprise (Waas, 2014). This basic decision is excluded from co-determination.

The employer is also free to define the criteria for the potential receiver of additional payment for capital investment to be invested by the employee in the enterprise. The basic principle of equal treatment in German labour law derived from Art. 3 GG and the general obligation of fair treatment according § 75 I BetrVG (Hanau & Adomeit, 2000; Junker, 2009; Mengel, 2008; Preis, 2009; Waas, 2014) exclude arbitrary and obviously unjustified acts on the part of the employer and can be rejected by the work council.

The German Law on Participation in Capital 2009 (§ 3 Nr. 39 EStG in its version of MKBG 2010) limits the employer's free discretion insofar as further differentiation (age, personal skill, duration of cooperation) now seems to be excluded from tax allowance. It is doubtful whether this is an adequate and useful legal reduction because it curtails the employers' competence for reasonable differentiation. This is one of the legislative decisions that should be changed by a future reform of the law of 2009 (Roggemann, 2010).

Nevertheless, the above arguments show that there is a broad spectrum of interpretation and discretional options for the functional incorporation of necessary new rules on financial participation into the existing collective German labour law even without and before its renewal by legislation. This is one of the reasons why hundreds or meanwhile even thousands of decisions of courts on all levels in Germany deal with problems of financial participation in practice and find adequate solutions.

5. Development in Germany 1918-2014: From revolution in 1918 to law on minimum wages in 2014

Participation in decision-making without financial participation

The revolutionary demand for collectivising productive property was rejected in Germany in 1918. The social democratic majority within the revolutionary movement in Germany of 1918/1919 was not in favour of leading Germany into a political model similar to the Soviet-Russian model of soldiers, workers and peasants councils after the revolution of 1917. Such revolutionary initiatives for collectivisation of all relevant industrial capacity did not succeed. The German revolution of 1918 therefore has been characterised as an 'incomplete revolution' because the traditional private property system was left more or less untouched.[22]

Even a legal initiative on an alternative conception of financial participation of workers instead of total collectivisation failed in 1919 (Otto, 2009). German Social Democrats and trade unions advocated for power not by material financial participation but by participation in decision-making. Hence a law on work councils was passed and thus the German model of co-determination was founded in 1920 (RGBI 1920, 147; Gamillscheg, 1997). The legal concept of co-determination developed into a successful factor of the communicative, conflict-resolving abilities of labour constitution in Germany (Gamillscheg, 1997).

On the other hand, it is a fact that approximately one century of co-determination has not brought about any major changes in the structural deficit of immaterial participation, and this deficit does not allow employees to participate adequately in the companies' jointly-generated value increases and profits.

The total military, political, economic, social and even moral breakdown of Germany in 1945 can be characterised again as a revolutionary situation. The revolutionary demand for collectivising productive property arose again this time not only in the Soviet-Russian Zone but also in the Western Zone of occupied and divided Germany. Once more, this revolutionary initiative for nationalisation of all relevant industrial capacity did not succeed; but this time only in the Western part of Germany occupied

22 The well-known German author and political analyst Sebastian Haffner characterised this fact – political revolution without property revolution – as an 'unfinished' or 'betrayed revolution'.

by Allied forces, whereas in the Eastern Zone after 1945 and in the later in German Democratic Republic (GDR) it did, in fact, succeed.

In contrast to the GDR, the repeated demand for collectivising the industry of the Federal Republic of Germany (Zonenausschuss der CDU, 1947) was quickly abandoned in favour of concepts for the integration of dependent employees into the social market economy by other means. This aim was pursued with the help of subsidising saving programmes and *'creating equity in the hands of the employees'*. The *'people's share'* was introduced in the context of privatisation of state-owned companies to help make their purchasers *'economic citizens of a real economic democracy'* (Frankfurter Allgemeine Zeitung, 2009). The subsidy programmes[23] did their part to raise the average income approximately four-fold (Erhard, 1964).

The subsequent development, especially after the unification of the two German states in 1990, started to challenge the basis of the current financial balance of the welfare state (Bontrup, 2009; Rosinus, 2009) because the traditional trade union wage policy based on collective bargaining, together with this redistributive German welfare state concept, obviously could not and cannot prevent the dramatically growing inequality of income and property as described below (see section 6.2). Moreover, this conception will hardly be affordable in future without substantial reform – and without structural support by means of enlarging financial participation.

6. Functional change of property rights and participation by share ownership

Property rights and ownership are fundamental legal institutions in every developed economy and legal community (Roggemann & Lowitzsch, 2008; Roggemann, 1997a, 1999, 2010). Ownership has legal, economic, social and political dimensions (Roggemann, 2010).

23 Law on Housing Grants 1959; Law on Savings Grants 1959; Law on Property Formation 1961, 1965, 1970; Law on Property Participation 1982, 1986, 1998.

Four basic functions of the multi-functional institution of property/ ownership are to be distinguished:

(1) The (primary) property rights allotment function (*'Zuordnungsfunktion'*) from which follows a quadrilateral legal competence of the owner:

- The positive authority to possess,
- to use and exploit,
- to dispose and transfer,
- the negative authority to exclude all others of lesser legal position from exercising these legal authorities with regard to this property object.

This is the classical liberal definition of ownership in civil law which is embodied in § 903 of the German Civil Code, in force since 1900: 'The owner of a thing may, as long as the law and the rights of third parties do not oppose it, do with the thing whatever he desires and exclude others from any influence.' According to this traditional liberal conception, property/ownership had no inherent but only external legal limitations.

(2) The individual function (*'Individualfunktion'*) from which follows the constitutional guarantee of personal rights and freedom of the owner, enabled by his legal position as owner.

This function of ownership is guaranteed by article 14 of the German Constitution (Basic Law) of 1949 and had already been guaranteed so by article 153 of the post-revolutionary Weimar Constitution of 1919.

This constitutional protection of ownership is on the one hand much broader than under civil law because it also entails obligations and all legitimate positions of economic interest, in other words, the legal and economic status quo of wealth of an owner.

The Federal Constitutional Court of Germany – similar to the U.S. Supreme Court – derived from the nature of ownership as a fundamental and human right that ownership serves as a foundation for the personal protection of existence and the unfolding of individual freedom: *'The guarantee of ownership shall preserve – in the fields of property rights – a free sphere for the bearer of fundamental rights, and thus it shall enable the individual the unfolding and the self-responsible leading of his life.'*[24]

On the other hand, the social impact of ownership, its inherent limitations and legal restrictions are defined more clearly by the constitution and

24 See decision in the case concerning the possession of rented apartments dated 26/05/1993, BVerfGE 89, p. 1 et seq., 6.

have been elaborated during the last four decades by the Federal Constitutional Court of Germany (see for example BVerfG NJW 2000, 798).

(3) The social and integrational function of property (*'Sozial- und Integrationsfunktion'*) is laid down in the constitutional principle of welfare state (art. 20 I of the German Constitution – GG) and in the social and public interest or public wealth clauses (art. 14 II 1, 2 of the German Constitution – GG).

The Federal Constitutional Court developed – different from traditional civil law jurisdiction – a new theory of differentiating balance of the conflicts of interests arising from the different function of private property in the context of a welfare state: *'The legislature, while defining contents and limits of property, does not enjoy unlimited freedom of discretion (see BVerfGE 101, 239. 259). When performing the constitutional mandate of art. 14 I 2 GG, the constitutionally guaranteed position of the owner as well as the obligation of a socially just property order of art. 14 II GG has to be taken into consideration and, therefore, a just balance and adequate proportion of the legitimate interests of the parties must be found. A one-sided preference or discrimination is not in line with the constitutional conception of socially-limited private property.'*[25]

The application of this new conception of constitutionally guaranteed and at the same time limited private property produced a number of decisions finding compromises between individual and social interests (for an overview, see Wendt, 2009).

This approach also opens the door for further decisive legislative enlargement of financial participation. The Constitutional Court found the introduction of mandatory co-determination through elected representatives of workers and employees in the organs of companies in line with the new constitutional balance of the social and the individual function of private property owners and shareholders of an enterprise.[26] This argument would also be valid for future legislative support of material participation by introducing a mandatory procedure for offering participation schemes to employees.

The Federal Constitutional Court in its decision on co-determination also developed from this functional context of private property in the

25 See decision dated 22/02/2001 – 1 BvR 198/98; see also BVerfGE 101, 54, 74.

26 In its famous decision in the co-determination case (Mitbestimmungsurteil) dated 12/02/1979, BVerfGE 50, 290, 342; BVerfG, 01/03/1979 – 1 BvR 532, 533/77, 419/78, 1 BvL 21/78; see also Wendt (2009).

welfare state a ranking system concerning the increasing or decreasing intensity of personal relationship between owner and property. Decreasing individual and increasing social function legitimates more intensive interference of the legislation by defining limitations to private property and its application. Economic property of the owner of an enterprise or of a shareholder is at the disposition of the lawmaker for further-reaching restriction than, for example, a family-owned house. This is an additional legal argument in favour of the constitutionality of a future binding law on financial participation in capital (Roggemann, 2010; in detail, see Thormann, 1996).

Neither art. 14 I GG (guarantee of private property) nor art. 9 I GG (guarantee of freedom of profession) are decisive constitutional obstacles for such a new legislation (see also Waas, 2014).

(4) The economic function of property (*'Ökonomische Funktion'*) arises from the fact that property and ownership constitute the only fundamental right which at the same time appears as both a legal and an economic category. Property law not only provides the legal basis of a market economy and competition, it also defines other economic categories: *'Property does not exist outside the economy, but rather it gives relevance to all the terms which are meaningless in non-ownership economies. This applies especially to interest, money and credit, but also to value, price, profit and market.'* (Heinsohn & Steiger, 1994, 1996).

This is the basis and legitimation for the owner of an enterprise as well as the share owner, the employee as co-owner, but also for the worker and employee as non-owner, not only to receive – according to his or her contribution to the joint value-creating process – an adequate part of the yield but also to assume the liability and the economic risk as the owner of capital or as the owner of labour capacity (*'Arbeitskraft'*), both as productive factors.

7. Distribution of property and wealth and financial participation in Germany today

7.1 The society of owners and the society of non-owners

In Germany, the distribution of wealth as well as the financial participation of employees and sharing of capital are still a long way from an overall satisfying development.

Several recent national (see for this statement and the following facts and conclusions, Bach, Corneo & Steiner, 2009, 2011; Bach, 2013; Biewen & Juhasz, 2012; Bundesministerium für Arbeit und Soziales, 2013; Grabka & Westermeier, 2014; Institut für Angewandte Wirtschaftsforschung e.V. & Universität Tübingen, 2011) and international (OECD, 2014) research projects and reports on poverty and wealth and the structure of income and property arrive at similar results:

Since the reunification of the two German States, i.e. in the last two-and-a-half decades, the net income of workers and employees has stagnated or even dropped. The net income of owners, stakeholders, shareholders and other participants in co-ownership of enterprises and productive capital and, respectively, also their proportional participation in wealth and property, especially in productive property, grew rapidly.

This development did not take place continuously. The strongest growth of income and property inequality could be seen from 1992 until 2005. Since then, this trend could nearly be stopped but by no means substantially corrected.

In its annual report 2009/2010 (Sachverständigenrat, 2008), the Council of Experts of the Federal Government underlined that the gap between higher and the lower incomes in Germany reached its peak in 2005 and that the Gini coefficient was higher than the average across all OECD countries. The experts held that this inequality effect would be relatively equalised by the re-distributing effect of German tax legislation and social transfer systems (Sachverständigenrat, 2009). This is indeed the case, but on the other hand illuminates the basic structural deficit of original participation in value creating. In any case, the result is alarming: The inequality of distribution of wealth and property in Germany according to the Gini coefficient is currently the highest in the Euro-zone of the EU.[27]

Therefore, the general statement made earlier still stands: In Germany, in the last two-and-a-half decades since the political turnaround in Eastern

27 Gini coefficient for EU average: 0.68; for Germany: 0.76; in comparison for the U.S.: 0,87. Reduction of the Gini coefficient by means of tax and social security transfers to 0.35 gross and 0.29 net. In any case, this procedure illuminates the basic structural deficit of participation in value creating, and because social insurance payments, which make up the biggest part of transfer costs, are based on previous social contributions, there is no real material re-distributive result between people and generations but only a time-related transfer effect to temporarily mitigate the existing growing income inequality (Bach, Grabka & Tomasch, 2015).

Europe and the reunification of the two German states, the inequality of the development of incomes (Der Spiegel, 2007a, 2007b), which has been criticised as a 'gap of Justice (Gerechtigkeitslücke)', combined with an extraordinary concentration of wealth and property, has significantly increased and continues to do so (Frick, Grabka & Hauser, 2010; Grabka & Frick, 2007; Rosinus, 2009). Between 1991 and 2006, the income from paid labour dropped from 70 per cent to 59 per cent, the wage rate decreased from 73 per cent in 1993 to 65 per cent in 2007, while income from equity and entrepreneurial activities decreased nine-fold just in the period between 2003 and 2007 (MKGB, dated 07/03/2009, BGBl I 2009, 451; Deutscher Bundestag, 2008; Statistisches Bundesamt, 2009). Thus, the overall net income of employees has dropped in the last two and a half decades (Bontrup, 2009).

The disproportions between the structure of incomes and of property are closely related (Rosinus, 2009) but not identical. Concentration of wealth, which can also be defined as concentration of property, is twice as high or even higher than the concentration of income (Geissler, 2014; Schlomann, 1993). For several reasons, the discrepancy within the structure of property is significantly larger than within the structure of income.

The first reason is the fact that the inequality of primary market income is much larger than that of net income (*'Nettoeinkommen'*) per household after tax deduction and addition of social transfers. However, as the largest portion of these social benefits – and therefore of the difference of 0.5 to 0.29 according to the Gini coefficient – are not substantial benefits but are partially financed by earlier contributions made by the later recipients. This is, in fact, 'no redistribution between individuals or generations over time' (Bach, Grabka & Tomasch, 2015). This transfer system of the welfare state therefore cannot change growing inequality basically, but only mitigate it temporarily.

The second reason which causes the inequality of the property structure to grow faster is the property-producing quality of productive property and the already unequally-distributed opportunities to obtain and to participate in productive property. As early as in the 60s of the last century, about 74 per cent of the domestic productive assets (excluding state- or foreign-ownedproperty) were in the hands of 1.7 per cent of (West) German private households (Krelle, Schunk & Siebke, 1968; Roggemann, 2010). It is presumed that this high concentration of productive property has remained stable or even increased (Krelle, 1993).

According to recent research (Frick et al., 2010; Grabka & Frick, 2007; Rosinus, 2009), about ten percent of the adult German population owned more than 60 per cent of the entire net equity worth €6.6 trillion in 2007. Even if methodological grounds of these statistical conclusions are disputed and somewhat uncertain, the general statement and tendency can be assumed to be true.

Findings attained by adjusting the method and combining the income and tax statistics with the Socio-Economic Panel (SOEP) (Bach, Beznoska & Steiner, 2011; Westermeier & Grabka, 2015) reach the conclusion that the concentration of wealth and property, especially in financial and productive property, is actually much higher over a longer period of time. Controversial figures indicated that one-tenth of the population owned half of overall assets as early as 1983. In this group, one per cent of households owned 23 per cent of overall assets (Geissler, 2014). The share of the richest ten per cent of the population according to this research is between 64 and 74 per cent, while the richest one per cent owns 36 per cent of the net wealth, and 0.1 per cent of the population possesses 23 per cent of the wealth. The richest 20 per cent of the population own about 80 per cent of the equity, which means that 80 per cent of the German population share 20 per cent of the equity and 25 per cent have no equity at all but rather debts.[28]

Such an extent of uneven distribution of property is not a 'natural law' of the social market economy but a result of its increasingly insufficient or, to be more precise, unjust legal conditions and hence a key problem of the reform of the legal framework of the welfare state and its legal policy (Merz, 2009).

---

28 This highly asymmetric trend increased during the last decade. Parallel to the growing total net wealth of private households in 2012 (about €9.3 trillion), the share of the richest ten percent of the population increased from 64 per cent to 74 per cent and at the same time the rate of poverty and inequality also grew (Westermeier & Grabka, 2015). *'Problems do not arise from the creation of the public wealth but from its primary and secondary distribution. Poverty and inequality in Germany also have political reasons.'* (Der Paritätische Gesamtverband, 2015, p. 4).

7.2 *From the divided society of owners and of non-owners towards a new society of co-owners?*

The flip side of the society of owners is the society of non-owners. The property of an owner is at the same time the non-property of all other non-owners with regard to this owned object of property (Luhmann, 1994; Roggemann, 2010).

Wealth and property concentration on such a scale as reported above has several undesirable social, political and economic effects and may weaken the basic social consensus of a democratic society. On the one hand, it creates more 'security, independence and also economic and social influence' (Bach, 2013, p. 3) and personal freedom for the 'lucky owners'. On the other hand, the resulting lack of participation threatens democracy.[29]

These negative tendencies of growing capital concentration have recently been described and analysed by well-known authors in Europe (Piketty, 2014a, 2014b) and the USA (Stiglitz, 2012, 2014). Both fundamental analyses arrive at critical results. Stieglitz confirms: *'The American political system is overrun by money. Economic inequality translates into political inequality, and political inequality yields increasing economic inequality. In fact, as he recognises, Mr. Piketty's argument rests on the ability of wealth-holders to keep their after-tax rate of return high relative to economic growth. How do they do this? By designing the rules of the game to ensure this outcome; that is, through politics. [...] The problem of inequality is not so much a matter of technical economics. It's really a problem of practical politics. Ensuring that those at the top pay their fair share of taxes – ending the special privileges of speculators, corporations and the rich – is both pragmatic and fair'* (Stiglitz, 2014). Piketty finds: *'The ideal solution for this problem would be a world-wide progressive tax on individual wealth. Those who are just beginning to accumulate wealth would not pay anything whereas those who own billions would have to pay a lot. This would keep inequality under control and at the same time make it easier for individuals to come up. It would also put the dynamic of global wealth under public control. Missing financial trans-*

29 The European Federation of Employee Share Ownership (EFES) (2015) does right to render prominently this context underscoring the decrease of participation through share ownership in European economies like France and Italy and Germany should also be added (see also Kelso & Kelso, 1986).

parency and reliable wealth statistics are a main challenge for modern democracies' (Piketty, 2014b).

Both authors come to similar conclusions in this point: The current development is not caused by inevitable economic reasons but by policy and politics: *'Widening and deepening inequality is not driven by immutable economic laws, but by laws we have written ourselves.'* (Stiglitz, 2014). The solution for both authors lies in a basic reform of the present tax system which privileges the small society of owners and discriminates the large society of non-owners and thus perpetuates the growing dilemma of inequality.

What might be critically observed is the fact that both authors fail to adequately take into consideration the earlier proposals of Louis O. Kelso and of the much earlier alternative European cooperative and property debate: To step-by–step, systematically strengthen a system of widespread co-ownership through participation in enterprise capital by the employees of the enterprise. Both proposals demand a fundamental change of present national and international tax policy as well as effective legal support of financial participation in capital up to relevant economic dimensions of five to ten per cent and at least about 15 to 20 per cent of the respective enterprise capital, which could bring about the necessary democratic change of a humanised capitalist civil society.

Both proposals taken singly as well as a combination of the two might at present seem to be somewhat politically utopian, but another way out of the ongoing crisis of a market-economy-based welfare state can hardly be imagined to develop the democratic and social market economy without losing its substantial human qualities.

The social structure of non-voters at elections shows that there is a direct relationship between economic, social and political participation.

In the US, a country with an extremely high Gini coefficient of inequality of income distribution, this direct relationship between economic, social and political participation or non-participation is supported by the fact that the average turnout is extremely low.[30] The most extreme expression of social non-participation is exclusion of social

30 In the recent mid-term elections of 04/11/2014, the national overall turnout was 36.3 per cent, which was commented thus by the The Editorial Board (2014) of the New York Times): *'The abysmally low turnout in last week's mid-term elections – the lowest in more than seven decades – was bad for the Democrats, but it was even worse for democracy.'*

participation by imprisonment. The rate of incarceration in the US is also extremely high.[31]

A growing percentage of economically under-privileged citizens in Germany do not participate as voters in the democratic political process. Results of political elections can therefore 'no longer be viewed as socially representative'[32]. In Germany, the Euro-zone country with the highest Gini coefficient of inequality of income and property – not considering governmental social re-distributive measures – this percentage of non-voters is growing comparatively faster than in other developed democratic countries.[33]

From an economic point of view, the US economist and lawyer Louis O. Kelso and his co-author Patricia Hetter-Kelso had pointed out the negative long-term effects of an unequal distribution policy on the economic circulation process by weakening the purchasing power of the masses, the disposition of investment capital, the social security of the majority of non-owners as well as the democratic consensus more than half a century ago (Kelso & Kelso, 1967, 1991). Analysing this situation, he developed a successful system of employee participation in the form of ESOP (Menke & Hanisch, 2008; Wagner, 2008) which is still the current model for German and European companies as well (Lowitzsch, 2008).

One of the most relevant but not yet sufficiently discussed consequences is the fact that severe, ongoing unequal distribution structures of private property inevitably lead to a latent challenge of the constitutionally and legally guaranteed institution of private ownership as such.

The specific social but also legal relevance of private property and wealth as a condition for the unfolding of personal freedom, in other words, the essential connection of property and freedom as elaborated by

31 The incarceration rate ('*Gefangenenrate*') of 707 incarcerated persons per 100,000 of the adult population in the US is the highest of the world (except the Seychelles that are an incomparable example). In comparison, the rate in Russia is 618, France 96, Germany 83, Denmark 66, Sweden 74, Finland 67, but in the UK 154. Recent criminological research affirms the relationship between socio-economic integration, participatory culture and welfare state on the one hand and the rate of incarceration on the other hand (see Dünkel, 2010 with reference to Cavadino & Dignan, 2012 and Tapio Lappi-Seppälä, 2007).

32 Recently and concerning the election in the Federal State Hamburg 2014 with a voter turnout of only 57 per cent (Hierlemann, Wohlfahrt & Vehrkamp, 2013).

33 'We are democratically on the way from Denmark towards the U.S.' (Hierlemann et al., 2013)

the US Supreme Court and later also by German jurisprudence as well as by the jurisdiction of the Constitutional Court (see section 7.1) is to be questioned: *'The equivalent of property in things and in money is one of the basic functional elements of art. 14 GG. Money is coined freedom; it can be changed into things.'* (BVerfG NJW 1998, 1937).

What about the opportunity for freedom or at least for equal opportunity for participation among the growing society of non-owners with little or no money? And of the 25 or more per cent of the population who own negative property, i.e. only debts?

This is the point of re-thinking the future balance of capital and labour in the welfare state. As pointed out above, neither the traditional trade union income policy nor the enormous re-distributive attempts of the welfare state by means of tax and social insurance transfers in Germany can – because of their inherent limits (competitiveness of the 'German export machine', bureaucratic overkill of the 'social transfer state') – avert the ongoing asymmetric development of income and property and, in the long run, the breakdown of society.

The 'new social property' of claims to social funds by non-owners does not provide real compensation and, for many reasons, cannot make them real owners (Roggemann, 2010). The main reason is that this form of property substitution is far more at the disposition of the legislature for restrictions or reductions than other forms of property or even money.

Different consequences for legal theory and policy have been debated without any satisfying results. Future problems of the stable social consensus are obvious and have also been the subject of discussion (Papier, 2008; Rittstieg, 1975).

The most adequate and sustainable economic and social solution can be achieved through the development of a broad system of direct financial participation of all employees taking part in the value-creating process.

This approach to gaining and stabilising the new society of co-owners needs the full support of the social partners, government and legislation.

7.3 Deficits and practice of participation in capital

The number of enterprises in Germany joining new concepts of financial participation is stagnating rather than instead of increasing. So far, Germany is still a developing country.

Only two to three per cent of Germany's enterprises offer equity participation and about ten per cent offer profit-sharing models (Bellmann & Leber, 2007; Bellmann & Möller, 2006; Beyer, 2014; Boeri et al., 2013; CDU et al., 2008; O'Kelly, 2013). The number differs remarkably in relation to the number of employees. In small enterprises with one to 49 employees, profit sharing is practised by eight per cent and share ownership by two per cent; in enterprises with 50 to 500 employees, profit sharing by 25 per cent and share ownership by four per cent; in enterprises with more than 500, there is profit sharing in 34 per cent and share ownership in seven per cent. The total equity capital held by employees altogether is worth only € 11.6 billion. In relation to the aforementioned privately-owned capital of € 9.3 trillion, this real amount of participative capital is of little or nearly no relevance.

According to an estimate by the economic partnership consortium *'Arbeitsgemeinschaft Partnerschaft in der Wirtschaft (AGP)'*, in 2009, these were 4,725 companies with about 2,274,000 employees. The more recent overview from 2014 (Beyer, 2014) confirms that this number stagnated or even dropped to about 2.2 million employees and 4,500 companies. A comparative study from 2011 by the European Federation of Employee Share Ownership (EFES) comprising a sample of 221 German and 2,493 European companies shows that share ownership in Germany remains far behind the average development in Europe. 37.6 per cent of the German and 53.3 per cent of the European companies analysed had 'broad-based' financial participation schemes; in the German companies, 17.3 per cent of the whole workforce participated as employee shareholders, in Europe 28.2 per cent of the whole workforce.

The most relevant and, at the same time, the most negative result of the reported EFES study is the answer to the basic question: How much of the enterprise's capital is actually held by the employees in all the different participation models analysed?

In Germany, it is 1.66 per cent and in Europe 2.68 per cent (see also Beyer, 2014)[34] of the companies analysed by EFES. This result and its factual and methodological basis may be questioned; however, it does

34 The statistical basis of these figures may be questioned and should be made subject of further research, developing the approach of Rosinus (2009). However, the available data, given by the AGP (total amount of capital held by employee owners: € 11.7 billion) and by the DIW (total amount of capital held by private owners: € 9.3 trillion) at least show the dimensions of the problem.

correspond to other results.[35] After all, there is no doubt that the total amount of productive capital held by employees is far below five per cent.

In order to bring about any structural changes in the situation of the welfare state, it should be a political and legal political aim of governments and trade unions to increase this rather poor amount in a first step to at least five per cent and in a second step to ten to 15 per cent. Otherwise, any measurable economic and social structural effects can hardly be expected.

In January 2015, EFES reported ‘a new record’: ‘Assets held by European employees in shares of their company increased to € 301 billion in 2014’ (European Federation of Employee Share Ownership [EFES], 2015). However, the number of employee shareholders in Europe decreased for the third consecutive year. EFES finds this ‘clearly related to the regressive fiscal policies in many European countries’, except the UK, where double fiscal incentives recently led to the highest rate of employee shareholding ever. On the other hand, this development underlines the ongoing process of property concentration probably also among employees described above.

Compared to other European countries (Bellmann & Leber, 2007; Bellmann & Möller, 2006; Pendleton, Poutsma, Brewster & van Ommeren, 2001; Poutsma, 2001), employee participation in Germany is underdeveloped. 13 per cent of holding companies offer participation in profit and equity, among all companies in Germany this is only one per cent (Bellmann & Möller, 2006). About 12 per cent of all employees take part in profit participation programmes and three per cent take part in equity participation schemes (Bellmann & Leber, 2007). Recent findings corroborate these facts with some differentiating details (Beyer, 2014).

Despite all political declarations of intent (Der Stern, 2005), in Germany, obviously, the conditions are so lacking or unattractive that, in contrast to other EU member states, especially to the UK, employees see only small opportunities and even smaller incentives to adequately exercise their rights for participation in the jointly generated economic outcome.

Companies in Germany which currently carry out profit and equity participation schemes are doing so on a large scale and offer profit partici-

35 When the Hamburg Hafen und Logistik (HHLA), the largest German port company, was privatised in 2007, the employees were offered only 1.26 per cent of the shares at half of the shareholder value (Roggemann, 2010).

pation for 62 per cent of their employees and equity participation for 46 per cent of their employees. Hence, the number of employees of foreign (especially of French and British) companies participating in Germany is significantly higher than in German companies (Bispinck & Brehmer, 2008).

These facts and the recent British example can be interpreted in brief: It is economically feasible and beneficial to change the unacceptable present situation in Germany as well – if government and trade unions were ready.

These enterprises that practice capital participation successfully are to a large extent examples of competitive as well as profitable enterprises in a new social market economy.

8. Legal grounds of financial participation – overview

In addition to the aforementioned laws on labour and co-determination (see section 3.2.3), the following legal grounds are relevant for financial participation:

- Law on Participation in Capital (Mitarbeiterkapitalbeteiligungsgesetz [MKBG]) dated 07/03/2009, in force since 01/04/2009,
- Law on the Implementation of EU Tax Requirements and the Change in Tax Provisions (Gesetz zur Umsetzung steuerlicher EU-Vorgaben sowie zur Änderung steuerlicher Vorschriften [UmsetzungsG]) dated 08/04/2010, in force since 02/04/2009,
- Income Tax Law (EinkommenssteuerG) in the version publicly announced in 2002 in the version released 2008, as amended by MKBG 2009 and by UmsetzungsG released 2010,
- Fifth Capital Accumulation Law (Fünftes VermögensbildungG) in the version publicly announcedin 1994 in the version released 2008, as amended by MKBG in 2009,
- Investment Law (InvestmentG) dated 2003 in the version released 2008, as amended by MKBG in 2009,
- Investment Tax Law (InvestmentsteuerG) dated 2003 in the version released 2008, as amended by MKBG in 2009 and by UmsetzungsG in 2010,
- German Securities Prospectus Law (Wertpapierprospektgesetz) in the version released 22/06/2005, as amended by law to transpose the directive 2010/73/EU and by modification of the Stock Exchange Law

dated 26/06/2012 (BGBl. I Nr. 28 dated 26/09/2012) – extension of the scope of prospect-free employee participation programmes,

- Development of the implementation law of the directive 2011/61/EU on Alternative Investment Fund Managers (AIFM), approved by the federal government cabinet on 12/12/2012,
- Collective Investment Schemes Law (Kapitalanlagengesetzbuch [KAGB]), in force since 22/07/2013 – replacement of the Investment Act dated 2003 and annulment of employee share programme special fund (Employee Investment Funds [Arbeitnehmer-Investitionsfonds]) in MKBG dated 2009.
- *On the agenda,* there is also further improvement of tax legislation for making the partial conversion of employees' remuneration into shares of the capital of the enterprise (Lohnumwandlung). Examples: Case Opel (not realised), Case Schlecker (eliminated after insolvency), general rules for temporary conversion of part of the remuneration into employee contributions to the capital of the enterprise in order to prevent job losses or total insolvency,
- Research project of the Federal Ministry of Economy: 'Future aim of property and wealth policy to be supported by the state and evaluation of the 5th law on wealth formation in Germany',
- Desideratum: Evaluation of the current Law on Participation in Capital of 2009 and its renewal in 2010 with regard to the legal aim and the governmental motives of that law.

This short overview, leaving out a number of additional legal problems, already leads to the conclusion that this legislative approach is neither understandable by the 'normal reader' and addressee of such a law, nor is it adequate to achieve the official aims of the law (Deutscher Bundestag, 2008).

9. Models and examples of financial participation by sharing capital in practice

The situation in practice in Germany seems to be paradox and in opposition to the legal situation. Legal grounds of employee participation are – as it has been pointed out – missing, incomplete or ineffective. This is one of the reasons why Germany, in spite of being the leading economic power in Europe in this field, is far behind many other EU countries.

However, the relatively small number of 4,700, i.e. two to three per cent of all enterprises that offer participation schemes, have developed many different and flexible models for employee participation in capital that work remarkably well. Many of them have joined the economic partnership consortium *'Arbeitsgemeinschaft Partnerschaft in der Wirtschaft (AGP)'*, the newsletter and reports of which can be read as an impressive success story. What is lacking is a relevant dimension of these attempts to bring about measurable economic and social results.

Participation in capital can be practiced in legal forms by contribution to external capital (*'Fremdkapitalbeteiligung'*) (Lowitzsch & Roggemann, 2014):

- Employee loan to the enterprise (*'Mitarbeiterdarlehen'*),
- Bonds, promissory note (*'Schuldverschreibung'*),

By contribution in mixed forms (*'mezzanine Beteiligungen'*):

- Dormant equity holding (*'Stille Beteiligung'*),
- Convertible bond (*'Wandelanleihe'*),
- Profit participation rights (*'Genußrecht'*),
- Stock options (*'Aktienoptionen'*),

By sharing of capital (*'Eigenkapitalbeteiligung'*):

- Employee shares (*'Belegschaftsaktie'*),
- Share of limited liability company (*'GmbH-Anteil'*),
- Share of cooperative society (*'Genossenschaftsanteil'*),
- Share of Employee Stock Ownership Plan.

These ten different legal frameworks grant either different rights or no rights at all to participate in information and decision-making provided by labour law and, with regard to the last four cases mentioned, also by company law. In all cases, conflicts can arise between the legal organs of co-determination (*'Betriebsrat', 'Sprecherausschuß'*) whereas in the last four alternatives, additionally to the level of labour law, decision-making organs on the level of company law also exist. Both have to be coordinated with optional organs representing the interests of employees as co-investors or co-owners by the participation schemes. The different legal forms of capital investment by the employees also grant different degrees of participation in shareholder value and dividends or, instead of this, give only the right to annual provision or interest rates which also can be and normally are modified by the different participation schemes.

With regard to the aforementioned risk of loss of capital (see section 3.3.1) held by the employee, the most relevant difference exists between these legal forms of participation in capital. The risk of loss in case of insolvency can be excluded in all cases from the employee's contribution to external capital or mixed forms through insurance and special agreements. In the four last forms of direct participation in capital mentioned above, the normal risk of an owner of capital can be and should be limited or even marginalised by additional guarantee agreements (see section 3.3.1). This is one of the points where additional support by the legislature is needed in insolvency legislation.

In spite of or even because of its deficits, this broad and flexible legal framework gives room for the development of numerous contract-based participation schemes in practice. Capital share ownership in Germany is mostly practiced in stock companies (according to AGP report 2010; Lowitzsch & Neusel, 2014). In 720 of these companies, about 1.5 million employees hold about €7.5 billion. In 1,330 enterprises, about 350,000 employees hold capital of about €1.7 billion as partners (*'Stiller Gesellschafter'*). In 310 companies with limited liability, about 10,000 employees hold about €160 million.

Of the overall capital of about €11 billion held by 2.3 million employees in Germany, three-quarters of that capital is held by 1.8 million employees in these three forms of companies. This, along with the unsatisfying dimensions in comparison with other European states and the fact that most jobs in Germany are created by smaller enterprises, means that improvement cannot be expected without legislative initiative.

The list of names of enterprises with participation schemes is long and not to be laid out here. It contains small and medium-sized firms as well as global players in all industries (Lowitzsch & Hanisch, 2014; Menrad, 2005; newsletters and annual reports of Arbeitsgemeinschaft Partnerschaft in der Wirtschaft [AGP]). Worthy of mention because of their well-constructed or special schemes are, for example: Pieroth (wine agriculture and delivery), Homag-AG (wood machines, establishment of a participation limited liability company [BeteiligungsGmbH] for employee participation), Stihl (saws), Meissner (tools), Diestelhäuser (breweries), Loewe (electronics), Flachglas Wernberg GmbH (BeteiligungsGmbH), Pfalz Flugzeug Werke PFW Aerospace AG (employee buyout), Varitec AG (loans to employees for taxation reasons), Emsa Werke Wulf GmbH & Co. KG. (goods manufacturer, profit participation right for employees with an annual interest rate of five per cent to nine per cent and 100 per cent insolvency insurance), Grünberg AG (water treatment).

10. The Law on Participation in Capital of 2009 – contents and critical remarks

10.1 Not a new act of substantial legislation but only an enumerative act

The MKBG does not conform to its name (Mengel, 2008). It is not a new act of legislation, but, apart from the totally failed fund concept, it is the continuation of tax-relieving prescriptions of the Income Tax Law (EStG), the Capital Formation Law, the Investment Law and the Investment Tax Law in the form of an article law, which is barely comprehensible for the common reader. A law of such acknowledged significance (impulse, 2008; Menrad, 2005) is lacking in formulated legal targets[36], definition norms, conditions of application and clarifications relating to labour law (for example, BEtrVG, MitbestG, TVG; see Waas, 2014), corporate law and insolvency law.

The Law on Participation in Capital of 2009 is not a substantial law but only an enumerative law referring to other laws. Therefore, this 2009 law has no special legislative relevance on its own. It does not define any legislative aims or put existing normative rules into a context. Thus, it can hardly serve as argument for interpretative attempts to improve or develop the juridical basis of capital sharing of employees by jurisdiction.

Differences between the socio-political necessity for regulation, juridical-political declarations of intent and legislative measures do occur very often, but rarely have they been greater than in the case of this 2009 law, which barely deserves to be called a law: the Law on Participation in Capital (MKBG).

The following critical remarks try to clarify why this law, which could have been of far-reaching significance for the further development of the market-economic structure of welfare state and property, is not at all adequate to reach the targets set by the lawmaker, and which reform measures are required (see also the comprehensive evaluation by Lowitzsch, Spitsa, Roggemann & Waas, 2009).

---

36 Counterexample: Law on the Promotion of Labour dated 1969, BGBl I 1969, 582, since 1998 SBG III.

10.2 Limitation of supporting legal measures

The restriction to one participation model was eliminated in the implementation law of 2010 (Beyer, AGP press statement dated 10/03/2010). Now the negotiating parties are not prevented from agreeing on basic obligations when offering different participation models with the help of a collective bargaining agreement to solve the 'transfixed' and very unsatisfying situation, *'that there is still a major lack of regulations under collective bargaining law to help employees participate'* (Waas, 2014; Wagner, 2008, p. 138).

In promoting capital participation, the lawmaker has actually hit the key structural problem, i.e. the question of ownership. However, at the same time leaving out the most frequent profit-sharing model hardly contributes to the extension of participation making salaries more flexible.[37]

10.3 Elimination of the principle of voluntariness – binding effects for enterprise and employees

The requirement for voluntariness has been left out, but in many cases it is argued for, and it also meets European recommendations (European Commission, 2002; European Economic and Social Committee, 2010; Menrad, 2005; The Council of the European Communities, 1992). This does not keep national lawmakers from implementing the requirement anyway. Since 1967, for instance, French lawmakers have been forcing companies with more than 50 employees to offer participation plans (Körner, 2009). In Germany, progress can also only be expected if material participation as well as immaterial co-determination is given a compulsory framework.

A legal obligation for companies to offer appropriate participation models is to be considered a significant and crucial part of the welfare state in the property guarantee given in art. 14 I GG as is the corporate participation.

Specific restrictions are immanent to economic capital property (BVerfGE 50, 290). Among those are deadlines for the duration of participation and other restrictions on utilisation and disposition. Without an

37 This has also been criticised by the Union of Employers in their statement dated 29/10/2008 (Roggemann, 2011a).

appropriate limit on time and content, major mutual participation targets will never be achieved. In the current regulations, the holding periods vary between two and ten or more years.[38] Setting timelines and further appropriations of participation capital (on the Pieroth participation model see Menrad, 2005) would add to the legal clarity.

Opponents of the introduction of a legally binding framework which obliges the enterprise to offer its employees at least one adequate model for capital sharing sometimes argue that such a legal obligation would not be in line with the constitutional guarantee of private property (art. 14 I GG).

However, taking into consideration the legal obligation to organise co-determination by means of representation of workers or employees in the organs of all enterprises including corporations stipulated in the law on co-determination in enterprises of 1976[39] and also the legal obligation of enterprises to pay a minimum remuneration of € 8.50 arising from the law on minimum wages of 2014,[40] this argumentation cannot be considered convincing because the restrictive effect of these laws on the property right of free disposition is comparable to that of a binding law on financial participation. The German Federal Constitutional Court ruled the law of 1976 and its effects on the owner's right of making use of the property constitutional[41]. With regard to the law on minimum wages of 2014, the property question was left out of the discussion on whether or not the law was constitutional (Barczak, 2014; Zeising & Weigert, 2015).[42]

38 Privatisation of Preussag: two years, savings grants according to § 4 of the 5th Capital Accumulation Law (VermBG): six years; fund model RLPplus: ten years (see also BFHE 135, 542; BeckRS 1982, 22006139).

39 Co-Determination Law (MitbestimmungsG) dated 04/05/1976, BGBl. I S. 1153.

40 Law on Minimum Wages (Gesetz zur Regelung eines allgemeinen Mindestlohnes [MindestlohnG – MiloG]) dated 11/08/2014, BGBl. I S. 1348.

41 Co-determination decision (Mitbestimmungs-Urt.) dated 12/02/1979, BVerfGE 50, 290, 342.

42 Compatibility with art. 14 I GG was apparently regarded as largely beyond doubt. The central issue was the compatibility with art. 9 III GG (collective bargaining) and art. 12 I GG (professional freedom).

10.4 Tax allowance no longer only for payment on top of standard wages

Applicability of tax allowance is no longer limited only to forms of financial participation that an enterprise offers 'on top', i. e. in addition to normal wages based on contract or union agreements. This restrictive regulation would have excluded many other offered and accepted forms of capital sharing. The new regulation creates space for collective agreements, especially in case of financial problems or even insolvency of the enterprise. Employees now may contribute by way of loans or temporary renunciation of parts of their wages or holiday pay to be compensated by shares in capital.

Only the substantial savings achieved by payment in some sort of shares in the employing company can be considered to be an 'allocation of equity shares', which are exempt from tax and social charges.[43]

10.5 Limitation of tax allowance – limited effect of the law

The major failing of the law of 2009 is the small size of the tax allowance of € 360 per year. This is among the lowest rates in comparable EU member states and can hardly be expected to show any impact (Rosinus, 2009). This also applies for the case of utilising the possible combinations emerging from property and participation subsidies according to the Income Tax Law (EStG) and the Law on Capital Formation (Lingemann, Gotham & Marchal, 2010). Raising the allowance ten-fold to € 3,600 would offer a far better chance of success. Austria offers tax privileges for capital transfers from enterprise to employee which are to be re-invested in the enterprise are four times higher than in Germany.

The German Stock Institute (*'Deutsches Aktieninstitut'*) and the Arbeitsgemeinschaft Partnerschaft in der Wirtschaft (AGP) recently recommended a minimum tax allowance up to an annual limit of € 1,000 (Kuhn, 2015). The tax allowance in other comparable EU member states for annual transfer and investment in participation in capital is much higher than in Germany: UK € 3,500, Italy € 2,066, Austria € 1,460.

43 Letter from the Federal Ministry of Finance dated 08/12/2009 on the income tax treatment of cession of equity shares as of 2009 (BStBl I 2009, 1513; Plenker, 2009).

The major influence of taxation laws on the development of employee participation is proved by the examples from the US (Rosen et al., 2005) and the UK (Otto, 2009; Steinhaus, 2011). The recent support of the British legislature in the form of raising the tax allowance considerably to encourage participation in capital through double fiscal incentives recently led to the highest rate of employee shareholding ever in the UK (European Federation of Employee Share Ownership [EFES], 2015).

10.6 Socio-economic correlation of privatization and employee capital participation

Employee participation fulfils a balancing function in the case of transferring state- or community-owned property, i.e. actual 'state-owned property' owned by all state citizens, into private property owned by single legal entities. The economic policy was well aware of this correlation in the beginning years of social market economy, when about half a century ago, (partial) privatisation of large state-owned companies[44] began. This welfare-state context of privatisation has been abandoned. The MKGB lacks the obligation of state and community owners to offer their employees a minimum capital share (five per cent for instance in France) at a preferential price in case of privatisation. This lack of obligation, for instance in case of the privatisation of the GDR's former state economy (Geissler, 1992; Offermanns, 1994; Priewe, 1994; Roggemann, 1995) and the subsequent privatisation campaigns in the old German federal states, falls short of the constitutional mandate.

10.7 The law of 2009 – a way out or a failure?

The extension of employee participation could pave the way to an achievement-oriented society of co-owners in a market-economic welfare state whose burden is increasingly relieved by flexible participation of the employees. Neither the current legal instruments nor the MKBG 2009 can actually achieve this. This law has met criticism in many points, and it was

44 Preussag 1959, Volkswagen 1961, Veba 1965.

called 'half-hearted at most'[45] and a 'flop'[46]. Its offerings were not accepted to the extent expected (Rosinus, 2009) and soon had to be adjusted, first in 2010[47], and then again in 2013 (see section 8).

The only new feature of the MKBG, i.e. the fund model of the 'special employee participation equity', is one of the law's regulations subject to the harshest criticism[48] and in fact has never been applied. Therefore, the legislature decided to abandon[49] this collective form of financial participation which was introduced mainly at the request of the Social Democrats and the German trade unions but completely failed.

10.8 Conclusion: Need for evaluation and further basic reform of the law of 2009

'Taking as given the proposition that economic development depends on political support' (Scholz & Tomann, 1999, p. 97; for this institutionalist approach recently, see also Piketty, 2014a & Stiglitz, 2012; see section 7.2) the importance of an effective law on financial participation should be clear. Experiences from the US and recently again from the UK but also from France, Austria and other countries confirm a direct positive effect of supporting tax and other legislation on the development of financial participation, especially of sharing of capital (Steinhaus, 2011). To summarise the critical remarks on the Law on Participation in Capital of 2009: *With regard to other comparable EU member states, this law has discriminatory effects. Rather than supporting German employees in developing adequate share ownership, it actually prevents them from doing so and is therefore no longer in line with the reform program of the German model of welfare state and of a 'New Social Europe' moving towards a society of co-owners.*

45 Schneider, Institute for the future of labour, Tagesspiegel 23/04/2008.

46 Öchsner, Süddeutsche Zeitung 07/01/2010.

47 Through the law on the implementation of European taxation condition as well on the alteration of tax regulations dated 08/04/2010, BGBl I 2010, 386, art. 1.

48 Among others by the German Federation of Chambers of Commerce (DIHK), Tagesspiegel 23/04/2008.

49 By the new Law on Capital Investment (Kapitalanlagengesetzbuch [KAGB]), in force since 22/07/2013.

References

Ahrens, K.-H. (1982). Gewerkschaftliches Geschichtsverständnis. In T. Walter (Ed.), *Gewerkschaften und Demokratie: Analysen zum DGB-Grundsatzprogramm '81*. Walberberg: Institut für Gesellschaftswissenschaften Walberberg.

Althaus, D. (2007). Garantien für Arbeitnehmerbeteiligungen im Freistaat Thüringen/ Mitarbeiterbeteiligungsprogramm. *AGP-Forum. Zeitschrift Für Betriebliche Partnerschaft*, (1), 36–38.

Apitzsch, W. (2009). Mitarbeiterkapitalbeteiligung im Sanierungsfall – ein Plädoyer. *Betriebs-Berater Special*, *64*(1), 1.

Bach, S. (2013). Einkommens- und Vermögensverteilung in Deutschland. *Aus Politik und Zeitgeschichte*, (10-11), 15–19.

Bach, S., Beznoska, M., & Steiner, V. (2011). *A Wealth Tax on the Rich to Bring down Public Debt?: Revenue and Distributional Effects of a Capital Levy* (No. 1137). *Discussion Papers of DIW Berlin*. DIW Berlin, German Institute for Economic Research.

Bach, S., Corneo, G., & Steiner, V. (2009). From bottom to top: The entire income distribution in Germany, 1992-2003. *Review of Income and Wealth*, *55*(2), 303–330.

Bach, S., Corneo, G., & Steiner, V. (2011). *Effective taxation of top incomes in Germany* (No. Discussion Paper 2011/18). *Discussion Papers*. Free University Berlin, School of Business & Economics.

Bach, S., Grabka, M., & Tomasch, E. (2015). Steuer- und Transfersystem: Hohe Umverteilung vor allem über die Sozialversicherung. *DIW Wochenbericht*, *82*(8), 147–156.

Barczak, T. (2014). Mindestlohngesetz und Verfassung. *Recht Der Arbeit*, 290–298.

Beck, K. (2010). Rheinland-Pfalz startet ein Programm zur Förderung der Mitarbeiterbeteiligung in kleinen und mittleren Unternehmen. *AGP-Forum. Zeitschrift Für Betriebliche Partnerschaft*, (1), 39–40.

Bellmann, L., & Leber, U. (2007). Materielle Mitarbeiterbeteiligung. Geringe Verbreitung, aber hohe Intensität. *IAB Kurzbericht*, (13).

Bellmann, L., & Möller, I. (2006). Die Betriebe in Deutschland haben Nachholbedarf. *IAB Kurzbericht*, (13).

Beyer, H. (2010). Belegschaftskapital als Baustein einer Krisenlösung? Überlegungen des DGB zur Kapitalbeteiligung. *AGP-Mitteilungen*, (1), 3.

Beyer, H. (2014). Employee financial participation in Germany – Current developments and challenges.

Biewen, M., & Juhasz, A. (2012). Understanding Rising Income Inequality in Germany, 1999/2000-2005/2006. *Review of Income and Wealth*, *58*(4), 622–647.

Bispinck, R., & Brehmer, W. (2008). Kapitalbeteiligung und Bezahlung nach Gewinn. *WSI-Mitteilungen*, (6), 312–320.

Blasi, J., Conte, M., & Kruse, D. (1996). Employee Stock Ownership and Corporate Performance Among Public Companies. *Industrial and Labor Relations Review*, 50(1), 60-79.

Blasi, J., Kruse, D., Bernstein, & Aaron. (2000). *In the company of owners: The truth about stock options (and why every employee should have them)*. New York: Basic Books.

Boeri, T., Lucifora, C., & Murphy, K. J. (2013). *Executive remuneration and employee performance-related pay: A transatlantic perspective*. Oxford: Oxford University Press.

Bontrup, H.-J. (2009). Der Vorschlag der Bundesregierung für "Mehr Mitarbeiterkapitalbeteiligung in Deutschland." *Betriebs-Berater Special*, *64*(1), 2.

Borchert, J. (2010). Freiheit und Verantwortung gehören zusammen – Das Hartz-IV-Urteil ist in wichtigen Teilen richtungweisend. *Zeitschrift Für Rechtspolitik*, (3), 101–102.

Brentano, L. (1898). *Arbeitseinstellungen und Fortbildung des Arbeitsvertrags*. Leipzig: Duncker & Humblot.

Bundesministerium für Arbeit und Soziales (2013). *Lebenslagen in Deutschland. Der vierte Armuts- und Reichtumsbericht der Bundesregierung*. Bundesministerium für Arbeit und Soziales.

Böhmert, V. (1878). *Die Gewinnbetheiligung. Untersuchungen über Arbeitslohn und Unternehmergewinn*. Leipzig.

Cavadino, M., & Dignan, J. (2012). *Penal systems: A comparative approach*. London: SAGE Publications.

CDU, CSU, & SPD (2008). *Vorschlag der gemeinsamen Arbeitsgruppe von CDU, CSU und SPD für mehr Mitarbeiterkapitalbeteiligung in Deutschland*. CDU, CSU, SPD.

CDU Deutschland, CSU Landesleitung, & SPD (2013). *Deutschlands Zukunft gestalten. Koalitionsvertrag zwischen CDU, CSU und SPD. 18. Legislaturperiode*. CDU Deutschland, CSU Landesleitung, SPD.

CDU-Bundesgeschäftsstelle (2013). Gemeinsam erfolgreich für Deutschland. Regierungsprogramm 2013-2017. Retrieved from https://www.cdu.de/system/tdf/media/dokumente/regierungsprogramm-2013-2017-langfassung-20130911.pdf?file=1&type=field_collection_item&id=631 [Accessed 15/10/2015]

CDU-Bundesvorstand (2006). Beschluss des 20. Parteitages der CDU Deutschlands "Soziale Kapitalpartnerschaft – für mehr Arbeitnehmerbeteiligung an Gewinn und Kapital." Retrieved from http://www.cdu.de/doc/pdfc/061128_beschluss_c_end.pdf [Accessed 15/10/2015]

Commission of the European Communities (1996). *Pepper II: Promotion of Participation by Employed Persons in Profits and Enterprise Results (Including Equity Participation) in Member States*. Commission of the European Communities.

Der Paritätische Gesamtverband (2015). *Die zerklüftete Republik. Bericht zur regionalen Armutsentwicklung in Deutschland 2014*. Berlin: Der Paritätische Gesamtverband.

Der Spiegel (2007a). Arm durch Arbeit. *Der Spiegel 14/2007*.

Der Spiegel (2007b). Die Gerechtigkeitslücke. Deutschland zwischen Mindestlohn und Spitzeneinkommen. *Der Spiegel 51/2007*.

Der Stern (2005, December 28). "Kluft zwischen Arm und Reich verringern." *Der Stern*.

Der Tagesspiegel (2010a, October 15). Merkel gegen Übernahme von Hochtief. *Der Tagesspiegel*.

Der Tagesspiegel (2010b, October 16). Merkel bei Hochtief gegen Brüderle. *Der Tagesspiegel*.

Deutscher Bundestag (2008). Entwurf eines Gesetzes zur steuerlichen Förderung der Mitarbeiterkapitalbeteiligung (Mitarbeiterkapitalbeteiligungsgesetz).

Deutscher Gewerkschaftsbund (DBG). (1954). Protokoll (des) 3. Ordentlichen Bundeskongress Frankfurt 4. bis 9. Oktober 1954.

Däubler, W. (1991). *Das Grundrecht auf Mitbestimmung und seine Realisierung durch tarifvertragliche Begründung von Beteiligungsrechten*. Hamburg: Europäische Verlagsanstalt (EVA).

Die Welt (2009). SPD plant Mitarbeiterbeteiligung an Krisen-Firmen. 08.09.2009. Available at http://www.welt.de/wirtschaft/article4490142/SPD-plant-Mitarbeiter-beteiligung-an-Krisen-Firmen.html [Accessed 15/09/2015]

Dünkel, F. (2010). Gefangenenraten im internationalen und nationalen Vergleich. *Neue Kriminalpolitik. Forum Für Kriminalwissenschaften, Recht Und Praxis*, (1).

Erhard, L. (1964). *Wohlstand für alle*. Düsseldorf: Econ-Verlag.

European Commission (2002). Communication from the Commission to the Council, the European Parliament, the Economic and Social Committee and the Committee of the Regions – On a framework for the promotion of employee financial participation (COM(2002) 364 final).

European Commission (2007). Communication from the Commission to the European Parliament, the Council, the European Economic and Social Committee and the Committee of the Regions – Towards Common Principles of Flexicurity: More and better jobs through flexibility and security (SEC(2007) 861) (SEC(2007) 862) (COM(2007) 359 final).

European Economic and Social Committee (2003). Opinion of the European Economic and Social Committee on the "Communication from the Commission to the Council, the European Parliament, the Economic and Social Committee and the Committee of the Regions on a framework for the promotion of employee financial participation" (COM(2002) 364 final). *Official Journal of the European Communities*, *95*, 29–34.

European Economic and Social Committee (2010). OPINION of the European Economic and Social Committee on Employee financial participation in Europe (Own-initiative opinion) SOC 371.

European Federation of Employee Share Ownership (EFES) (2015). EFES Newsletter – Januar 2015. *EFES Newsletter*.

European Parliament (2003). European Parliament resolution on the Commission communication to the Council, the European Parliament, the Economic and Social Committee and the Committee of the Regions on a framework for the promotion of employee financial participation (COM(2002) 364 – 2002/2243(INI)).

Frankfurter Allgemeine Zeitung. (2009, March 24). Deutschen Volksaktien war kein großer Erfolg beschieden. *Frankfurter Allgemeine Zeitung.*

Frick, J. R., Grabka, M. M., & Hauser, R. (2010). *Die Verteilung der Vermögen in Deutschland. Empirische Analysen für Personen und Haushalte.* Berlin: edition sigma.

Gamillscheg, F. (1997). *Kollektives Arbeitsrecht – Ein Lehrbuch. Band I: Grundlagen, Koalitionsfreiheit, Tarifvertrag, Arbeitskampf und Schlichtung.* München: C. H. Beck.

Geissler, Rainer. (1992). *Die Sozialstruktur in Deutschland.* Bonn: Bundeszentrale für politische Bildung.

Geissler, Rainier. (2014). *Die Sozialstruktur Deutschlands.* Opladen: Westdeutscher Verlag.

Gierke, O. (1889). *Der Entwurf eines bürgerlichen Gesetzbuchs und das deutsche Recht.* Leipzig.

Grabka, M. M., & Frick, J. R. (2007). Vermögen in Deutschland wesentlich ungleicher verteilt als Einkommen. *DIW Wochenbericht, 74*(45), 665–672.

Grabka, M. M., & Westermeier, C. (2014). Anhaltend hohe Vermögensungleichheit in Deutschland. *DIW Wochenbericht,* (9), 151–164.

Gundelach, H. (1982). Die Sozialausschüsse der CDU und das neue Grundsatzprogramm des DGB. In T. Walter (Ed.), *Gewerkschaften und Demokratie: Analysen zum DGB-Grundsatzprogramm '81.* Walberberg: Institut für Gesellschaftswissenschaften Walberberg.

Hanau, P., & Adomeit, K. (2000). *Arbeitsrecht.* Neuwied: Luchterhand.

Harbaugh, R. (1993). *Equity-sharing – effects on collective bargaining position of trade unions* (No. Working Paper). CERGE EI, Prague, Charles University.

Harbaugh, R. (2005). The effect of employee stock ownership on wage and employment bargaining. *Journal of Comparative Economics, 33*(3), 565–583.

Hecker, D. (1990). *Eigentum als Sachherrschaft. Zur Genese und Kritik eines besonderen Herrschaftsanspruchs* (Vol. 57). Paderborn, München: Ferdinand Schöningh.

Heinsohn, G., & Steiger, O. (1994). Eigentum und Systemtransformation. In J. Hölscher, A. Jacobsen, H. Tomann, & H. Weisfeld (Eds.), *Bedingungen ökonomischer Entwicklung in Zentralosteuropa. Band 2: Wirtschaftliche Entwicklung und institutioneller Wandel.* Marburg: Metropolis Verlag.

Heinsohn, G., & Steiger, O. (1996). *Eigentum, Zins und Geld: Ungelöste Rätsel der Wirtschaftswissenschaft.* Reinbek: Rowohlt.

Hexel, D. (2007). Kapital in Mitarbeiterhand – ein Beitrag für mehr Mitbe-stimmung und Teilhabe. *AGP-Forum. Zeitschrift Für Betriebliche Partnerschaft,* (1), 73–74.

Hexel, D. (2008). *Stellungnahme des DGB zum Regierungsentwurf eines Gesetzes zur steuerlichen Förderung der Mitarbeiterkapitalbeteiligung.* (Deutscher Gewerkschaftsbund (DGB), Ed.). Deutscher Gewerkschaftsbund (DGB).

Hierlemann, D., Wohlfahrt, A., & Vehrkamp, R. (2013). *Inspiring democracy. New forms of public participation.* Bertelsmann Stiftung.

Holzhey, H. (1983). Lockes Begründung des Privateigentums in der Arbeit. In H. Holzhey & G. Kohler (Eds.), *Eigentum und seine Gründe. Ein philosophischer Beitrag aus Anlass der schweizerischen Verfassungsdiskussion* (Vol. 12). Stuttgart, Bern: Paul Haupt Verlag.

impulse (2008). Interview mit Bundeskanzlerin Angela Merkel: "Geist der sozialen Marktwirtschaft ändert sich" – Sorge um die Akzeptanz der Wirtschaftsordnung. *Impulse*, (2).

Institut für Angewandte Wirtschaftsforschung e.V., & Universität Tübingen (2011). *Forschungsprojekt: Aktualisierung der Berichterstattung über die Verteilung von Einkommen und Vermögen in Deutschland.* Institut für Angewandte Wirtschaftsforschung e.V., Universität Tübingen.

Junker, A. (2009). *Grundkurs Arbeitsrecht*. München: C. H. Beck.

Kamp, M. (2010). Der Ball liegt auf dem Elfmeter-Punkt – Michael Lezius zum Abschied. *AGP-Forum. Zeitschrift Für Betriebliche Partnerschaft*, (1), 9.

Kelso, L. O., & Adler, M. J. (1958). *The capitalist manifesto*. New York: Random House.

Kelso, L. O., & Kelso, P. H. (1967). *Two-factor theory: The economics of reality*. Vintage Books.

Kelso, L. O., & Kelso, P. H. (1991). *Democracy and economic power: Extending the ESOP revolution through binary economics*. Lanham, Maryland: University Press of America.

Kelso, L. O., & Kelso, P. H. (1986). Democracy and Economic Power: Extending the Employee Stock Ownership Plan Revolution. HarperBusiness.

Kirchhof, P. (2009). Rückbesinnung auf ein Grundrecht – Eigentum als Schule von Freiheit und Risiko. In O. Depenheuer (Ed.), *Eigentumsverfassung und Finanzkrise* (pp. 7–18). Heidelberg: Springer.

Kirchhof, P. (2010). Der Schaden der anderen. In F. Schirrmacher & T. Strobl (Eds.), *Die Zukunft des Kapitalismus* (pp. 44–51). Berlin: Suhrkamp Verlag.

Krelle, W, Schunk, J., & Siebke, J. (1968). *Überbetriebliche Ertragsbeteiligung der Arbeitnehmer*. Tübingen.

Krelle, W. (1993). Wirtschaftswachstum und Vermögensbeteiligung. Wie ist eine gleichmäßigere Vermögensverteilung zu erreichen? In Kirchenamt & Deutsche Bischofskonferenz (Eds.), *Beteiligung am Produktiveigentum* (pp. 33–56). Hannover, Bonn.

Kruse, D., Blasi, J., & Freeman, R. (2011). Does Shared Capitalism Help the Best Firms Do Even Better? Paper presented at the British Academy Seminar 'The Economics of Share Ownership and Gainsharing: Findings and Policy Implications', Centre for Economic Performance, London School of Economics, 26.05.2011.

Kuhn, N. (2015). Zeit zum Handeln – Mitarbeiterkapitalbeteiligung und Belegschaftsaktien endlich fördern.

Körner, M. (2009). Das französische Modell der Mitarbeiterbeteiligung. *Betriebs-Berater Special*, *64*(1), 8–11.

Leuner, R. (2009). *Mitarbeiterbeteiligung: Recht, Steuern, Beratung*. Wiesbaden: Gabler Verlag.

Levy, R. (1983). Eigentum und Macht in der modernen Industriegesellschaft. In H. Holzhey & G. Kohler (Eds.), *Eigentum und seine Gründe. Ein philosophischer Beitrag aus Anlass der schweizerischen Verfassungsdiskussion* (Vol. 12, pp. 145–160). Stuttgart, Bern: Paul Haupt Verlag.

Lingemann, S., Gotham, M., & Marchal, H. (2010). Arbeitsrechtliche Fallstricke im neuen Mitarbeiterkapitalbeteiligungsgesetz. *Der Betrieb*, (8), 446–451.

Lowitzsch, J. (2006). *The PEPPER III Report : Promotion of Employee Participation in Profits and Enterprise Results in the*. Commission of the European Communities.

Lowitzsch, J. (2007). Der Employee Stock Ownership Plan (ESOP) als Vehikel der Unternehmensnachfolge. *AGP-Forum. Zeitschrift Für Betriebliche Partnerschaft*, (1), 21–23.

Lowitzsch, J. (2008). *Financial participation for a new social Europe: A building block approach*. Rome, Berlin: Inter-University Centre Split/Berlin, Institute for Eastern European Studies, Free University of Berlin.

Lowitzsch, J. (2010). Neuausrichtung der Sozialpolitik im Europäischen Reformvertrag. Umsetzungsproblme am Beispiel der Mitarbeiterbeteiligung. *Zeitschrift Für Europäisches Sozial- Und Arbeitsrecht*, (5-6), 217.

Lowitzsch, J., & Hanisch, S. (Eds.) (2014). *Mitarbeiterkapitalbeteiligung unter Verwendung einer Beteiligungsgesellschaft – Gestaltung und Finanzierungsansätze* (Vol. 279). Düsseldorf: Hans-Böckler-Stiftung.

Lowitzsch, J., Hashi, I., & Woodward, R. (Eds.) (2009). *The PEPPER IV Report: Benchmarking of Employee Participation in Profits and Enterprise Results in the Member and Candidate Countries of the European Union*. Inter-University Centre Berlin/Split.

Lowitzsch, J., & Hashi, I. (Eds.) (2014). *The promotion of employee ownership and participation. Study prepared by the Inter-University Centre for European Commission's DG MARKT (Contract MARKT/2013/0191F2/ST/OP)*. Bruxelles: European Union.

Lowitzsch, J., & Neusel, T. (2014). Entwicklung eines Mitarbeiterkapitalbeteiligungsmodells unter Verwendung einer Beteiligungsgesellschaft. In J. Lowitzsch & S. Hanisch (Eds.), *Mitarbeiterkapitalbeteiligung unter Verwendung einer Beteiligungsgesellschaft – Gestaltung und Finanzierungsansätze* (Vol. 279, pp. 115–133). Düsseldorf: Hans-Böckler-Stiftung.

Lowitzsch, J., & Roggemann, H. (2014). Einführung. In J. Lowitzsch & S. Hanisch (Eds.), *Mitarbeiterkapitalbeteiligung unter Verwendung einer Beteiligungsgesellschaft – Gestaltung und Finanzierungsansätze* (Vol. 279, pp. 23–40). Düsseldorf: Hans-Böckler-Stiftung.

Lowitzsch, J., Spitsa, N., Roggemann, H., & Waas, B. (2009). Gesetz zur steuerlichen Förderung der Mitarbeiterkapitalbeteiligung.

Luhmann, N. (1994). *Die Wirtschaft der Gesellschaft*. Berlin: Suhrkamp Verlag.

Marx, K. (1898). Lohn, Preis, Profit. Vortrag gehalten im Generalrath der "Internationale" am 26. Juni 1865 von Karl Marx. *Die Neue Zeit. Revue Des Geistigen Und Öffentlichen Lebens*, *2*(27), 4–13.

Mehrens, K., Stracke, S., & Wilke, P. (2011). *Die finanzielle Mitarbeiterbeteiligung praxistauglich weiterentwickeln.* (Friedrich-Ebert-Stiftung, Ed.). Bonn: Friedrich-Ebert-Stiftung.

Mengel, A. (2008). *Erfolgs- und leistungsorientierte Vergütung*. Berlin: Erich Schmidt Verlag.

Menke, J. D., & Hanisch, S. (2008). The U.S. ESOP as an example of an advanced model. In J. Lowitzsch (Ed.), *Financial participation for a new social Europe. A building block approach* (pp. 51–88). Rome, Berlin: Inter-University Centre Split/Berlin, Institute for Eastern European Studies, Free University of Berlin.

Menrad, W. (2005). *Manifest für Vermögensbildung und Eigentum in Arbeitnehmerhand.* Berlin.

Merz, F. (2009). "Sozial ist, was Bürger zu Eigentümern macht." In O. Depenheuer (Ed.), *Eigentumsverfassung und Finanzkrise* (pp. 19–26). Heidelberg: Springer.

Müller, U. (2000). *Die vermögens- und verteilungspolitischen Aspekte einer Mitarbeiterbeteiligung*. Frankfurt am Main: Peter Lang.

National Center For Employee Ownership (NCEO) (2015). *A Statistical Profile of Employee Ownership.* Retrieved from http://www.nceo.org/articles/statistical-profile-employee-ownership [Accessed 15/09/2015]

OECD. (2014). *Society at a glance 2014: OECD social indicators*. OECD Publishing.

Offermanns, M. (1994). Das Renten-Überleitungsgesetz und seine Konsequenzen. In I. Krieger & J. Zerche (Eds.), *Vom sozialistischen Versorgungsstaat zum Sozialstaat Bundesrepublik: Ausbau oder Abbau der sozialen Lage in den neuen Bundesländern?* (Vol. 25, pp. 120–147). Regensburg: Transfer-Verlag.

Ognedal, T. (1992). The effects of union owned shares on the outcome of wage bargaining. *Journal of Economic Behavior & Organization*, *18*(2), 185–200.

Otto, B. (2009). *Mitarbeiterbeteiligung in Deutschland, Österreich und Grossbritanien*. Freie Universität Berlin.

O'Kelly, K. (2013). Policies and attitudes to financial participation in the EU.

Oxera (2007). Oxera Agenda – Advancing economics in business – Sharing the wealth: can employee share schemes improve the company performance? Agenda – Advancing economics in business, October 2007. Available at http://www.oxera.com/Oxera/media/Oxera/downloads/Agenda/Sharing-the-wealth.pdf?ext=.pdf [Accessed 15.09.2015]

Papier, H.-J. (2008). Art. 14 Rdn. 16. In T. Maunz, G. Düring, R. Herzog, & R. Scholz (Eds.), *Grundgesetz. Loseblatt-Kommentar* (p. 132). München: C. H. Beck.

Pendleton A. (2014). *Employee Ownership: Research and Practice.* Presentation at the Expert Conference of IAFP and AGP: Employee Financial Participation in Europe and Germany, Frankfurt/M., Germany, 23.10.2014

Pendleton, A., Poutsma, E., Brewster, C., & van Ommeren, J. (2001). *Employee share ownership and profit-sharing in the European Union*. European Foundation for the Improvement of Living and Working Conditions.

Pendleton, A., Robinson, A., & Wilson, N. (1995). Does Employee Ownership Weaken Trade Unions? Recent Evidence from the UK Bus Industry. *Economic and Industrial Democracy*, *16*(4), 577–605.

Piketty, T. (2014a). *Capital in the Twenty-First Century*. The Belknap Press.

Piketty, T. (2014b). Globale Ungleichheit Weshalb wir eine globale Vermögenssteuer brauchen. Retrieved April 25, 2015, from http://www.ipg-online.de

Plenker, J. (2009). Wesentliche Gesetzesänderungen aus Arbeitgeber- und Arbeitnehmersicht 2008 bis 2010. *Zeitschrift Für Bilanzierung Und Rechnungswesen*, *33*(1), 34–37.

Poutsma, E. (2001). *Recent Trends in Employee Financial Participation in the European Union*. Luxembourgh: Office for Official Publications of the European Communities.

Preis, U. (2009). *Arbeitsrecht: Individualarbeitsrecht. Lehrbuch für Studium und Praxis*. Köln: Verlag Dr. Otto Schmidt.

Priewe, J. (1994). Die Folgen der schnellen Privatisierung der Treuhandanstalt: Eine vorläufige Schlußbilanz. *Aus Politik Und Zeitgeschichte*, *44*(43), 21–30.

Proudhon, P.-J. (1963). *Ausgewählte Texte*. (T. Ramm, Ed.). Stuttgart: Koehler.

Rittstieg, H. (1975). *Eigentum als Verfassungsproblem: Zu Geschichte und Gegenwart des bürgerlichen Verfassungsstaates*. Darmstadt: Wissenschaftliche Buchgesellschaft.

Roggemann, H. (1995). *Fragen und Wege zur Rechtseinheit in Deutschland*. Berlin: Berliner Wissenschafts-Verlag.

Roggemann, H. (1996). *Eigentum in Osteuropa*. Berlin: Verlag Arno Spitz.

Roggemann, H. (1997a). *Functional changes in property rights in East and West: Some comparative remarks concerning post-socialist transformation in eastern and Western Europe* (No. IGS Discussion Papers Series 97/20). University of Birmingham, Institute for German Studies,.

Roggemann, H. (1997b). Funktionswandel des Eigentums in Ost und West – vergleichende Anmerkungen zur postsozialistischen Transformation in Ost- und Westeuropa. *Recht in Ost Und West*, *41*, 189 ff..

Roggemann, H. (1999). Functional change in property rights in the welfare state: Lessons from the Federal Republic of Germany. In I. Collier, H. Roggemann, O. Scholz, & H. Tomann (Eds.), *Welfare states in transition: East and west. Studies in economic tranistion* (pp. 25–40). Basingstoke, London: Palgrave Macmillian.

Roggemann, H. (2010). *Mitarbeiterbeteiligung und Eigentum. Ein Diskussionsbeitrag zur Wirtschaftskrise* (Vol. 65). Berlin: Berliner Wissenschafts-Verlag (BWV).

Roggemann, H. (2011a). Das Mitarbeiterkapitalbeteiligungsgesetz von 2009 – Eine rechtspolitische Kritik, Zeitschrift für Rechtspolitik (ZRP) 2011, S. 49 ff., München C.H.Beck,

Roggemann, H. (2011b). Arbeiterselbstverwaltung in Jugoslawien und Mitarbeiterbeteiligung in Europa – Systemtranszendierende Aspekte eines sozialölkonomischen Partizipationsgrundrechts auf dem Wege in eine europäische Sozialordnung. In H. Küpper (Ed.), *Von Kontinuitäten und Brüchen: Ostrecht im Wandel der Zeiten, Festschrift für Friedrich-Christian Schroeder zum 75. Geburtstag* (pp. 367–409). Frankfurt am Main, Berlin, Bern: Peter Lang.

Roggemann, H., & Lowitzsch, J. (2008). The challenge: Functional changes in property rights in Europe. In J. Lowitzsch (Ed.), *Financial participation for a new social Europe. A building block approach* (pp. 101–109). Rome, Berlin: Inter-University Centre Split/Berlin, Institute for Eastern European Studies, Free University of Berlin.

Rosen, C. (2002). Observations on Employee Ownership. United Airlines, ESOPs, and Employee Ownership. Available at https://www.nceo.org/observations-employee-ownership/c/united-airlines-esops-employee-ownership [Accessed 15.09.2015]

Rosen, C., Case, J., & Staubus, M. (2005). *Equity: Why employee ownership is good for business*. Boston, MA: Harvard Business Review Press.

Rosinus, A. (2009). *Vermögenskonzentration und Mitarbeiterkapitalbeteiligungsgesetz* (Vol. 38). Frankfurt am Main: Peter Lang.

Sachverständigenrat (2008). *Die Finanzkrise meistern – Wachstumskräfte stärken. Jahresgutachten 2008/09*. Sachverständigenrat zur Begutachtung der gesamtwirtschaftlichen Entwicklung, Statistisches Bundesamt.

Sachverständigenrat (2009). *Die Zukunft nicht aufs Spiel setzen. Jahresgutachten 2009/10*. Sachverständigenrat zur Begutachtung der gesamtwirtschaftlichen Entwicklung, Statistisches Bundesamt.

Schanz, K.-M. (2000). Mitarbeiterbeteiligungsprogramme. *Neue Zeitschrift Für Arbeitsrecht*, (12), 626–634.

Schlomann, H. (1993). Die Entwicklung der Vermögensverteilung in Westdeutschland. In E.-U. Huster (Ed.), *Reichtum in Deutschland. Der diskrete Charme der sozialen Distanz* (pp. 54–83). Frankfurt am Main, New York.

Scholz, O., & Tomann, H. (1999). The role of social policy during the transformation in Central Europe. In I. Collier, H. Roggemann, O. Scholz, & H. Tomann (Eds.), *Welfare states in transition: East and west. Studies in economic tranistion* (p. 93). Basingstoke, London: Palgrave Macmillian.

Siegler, A. (1979). Der Beteiligungsgedanke im 19. und frühen 20. Jahrhundert und seine Beurteilung durch die organisierte Arbeitnehmerschaft: Parallelen zur Entwicklung der Gegenwart? *Die Betriebswirtschaft*, *39*(1b), 143–153.

Sinn, H.-W. (1998). Kapitalbeteiligung und Lohndifferenzierung: Ein Vorschlag zur Lösung der Beschäftigungskrise. In H.-J. Arentz & H.-P. Stihl (Eds.), *Vermögensbildung in Arbeitnehmerhand: Wege zu einer Gesellschaft von Teilhabern* (pp. 9–24). Sankt-Augustin: Konrad-Adenauer-Stiftung.

Smith, R. J. (2003). *Property Law* (4th Edition). Harlow: Pearson Education.

SPD-Parteivorstand (2013). Das Wir entscheidet. Das Regierungsprogramm 2013-2017. Bonn: SPD-Parteivorstand. Retrieved from http://www.spd.de/linkableblob/96686/data/20130415_regierungsprogramm_2013_2017.pdf [Accessed 15/10/2015]

Statistisches Bundesamt. (2009). *Volkswirtschaftliche Gesamtrechnungen.Inlandsproduktsberechnung. Detaillierte Jahresergebnisse*. Statistisches Bundesamt.

Steinhaus, H. (2011). *Mitarbeiterbeteiligung als Krisenbewältigungsinstrument aus akteurtheoretischer Sicht*. Wiesbaden: Gabler.

Stiglitz, J. E. (2012). *Price of inequality*. Norton & Company.

Stiglitz, J. E. (2014). Inequality is not inevitable. Retrieved from http://opinionator.blogs.nytimes.com/ [Accessed 25/05/2015]

Tapio Lappi-Seppälä. (2007). Penal Policy in Scandinavia. *Crime and Justice*, *36*(1), 217–295.

The Council of the European Communities. (1992). 92/443/EEC: Council recommendation of 27 July 1992 concerning the promotion of participation by employed persons in profits and enterprise results (including equity participation). *Official Journal of the European Communities*, *35*, 53–55.

The Editorial Board. (2014, November 11). The Worst Voter Turnout in 72 Years. *The New York Times*.

Thormann, M. (1996). *Abstufungen in der Sozialbindung des Eigentums: Zur Bestimmung von Inhalt und Schranken des Eigentums nach Art. 14 Absatz 1 Satz 2 GG im Spannungsfeld von Eigentumsfreiheit und Gemeinwohl*. München: Boorberg Verlag.

Uvalic, M. (1991). The Pepper Report: Promotion of Employee Participation in Profits and Enterprise Results in the Member States of the European Commnity. Bruxelles: Commission of the European Communities.

Uvalić, M. (2008). Lessons from PEPPER I to PEPPER IV. In J. Lowitzsch, I. Hashi, & R. Woodward (Eds.), *Industrial relations* (pp. 179–189). Inter-University Centre Berlin/Split, Institute for Eastern European Studies, Free University of Berlin.

Vanek, J. (1965). Workers' Profit Participation, Unemployment and the Keynesian Equilibrium. *Weltwirtschaftliches Archiv*, *94*, 206–214.

Von Gierke, J. (1959). *Das Sachenrecht des bürgerlichen Rechts*. Berlin, Frankfurt am Main.

Waas, B. (2014). Mitarbeiterkapitalbeteiligung und Arbeitsrecht. In J. Lowitzsch & S. Hanisch (Eds.), *Mitarbeiterkapitalbeteiligung unter Verwendung einer Beteiligungsgesellschaft – Gestaltung und Finanzierungsansätze* (Vol. 279, pp. 67–114). Düsseldorf: Hans-Böckler-Stiftung.

Wagner, K. R. (2003). Mitarbeiterbeteiligung in Deutschland – ein Überblick. *Neue Juristische Wochenschrift*, (43), 3081–3086.

Wagner, K.-R. (2008). *Kapitalbeteiligung von Mitarbeitern und Führungskräften: Möglichkeiten, Chancen Visionen*. Frankfurt am Main: Verlag Recht und Wirtschaft.

Wendt, R. (2009). Art. 14 Eigentum, Erbrecht und Enteignung. In M. Sachs (Ed.), *Grundgesetz: GG. Kommentar* (pp. 602–667). München: C. H. Beck.

Westermeier, C., & Grabka, M. M. (2015). Große statistische Unsicherheit beim Anteil der Top-Vermögenden in Deutschland. *DIW Wochenbericht*, *82*(7), 123–133.

Zeising, P., & Weigert, D.-R. (2015). Verfassungsmäßigkeit des Mindestlohngesetzes. *Neue Zeitschrift Für Arbeitsrecht*, (1), 15–22.

Zonenausschuss der CDU (1947). Ahlener Programm.

Historical perspectives on employee ownership in Germany

Alexander Kern[1]

Abstract

This research examines shared capitalism, the theoretical and historical development of employee participation, and ownership rights in Germany.

A period from the 19th century until the beginning of the 21st century is researched. We attempt to answer the question: 'Did policy makers in Germany want to create a society of owners?' Hence, we determine the steps taken starting from Bismarck, over von Thünen and the founding fathers of the Federal Republic of Germany such as Adenauer and Erhard, to developments after the millennium. During the research we prove the hypothesis *'Employee ownership was a criterion of Germany's founding fathers in order to stabilize Germany socio-economically after the Second World War.'* We confirm it through a qualitative study of historical archive researches. In Germany, there is clear evidence that founding fathers under the leadership of Erhard pursued 'Wohlstand für Alle' through citizen's shares.

1. Introduction

This research's introduction presents the research topic: 'Historical perspectives on employee ownership in Germany.'

This topic is of great relevance in the current business world. Kruse et al. (2010) defined shared capitalism as payment systems related to a diversified set of reward practices through which employee's financial income depends on the performance of his/her corporation. Employee stock

1 Dr. Alexander Kern: Professor of Corporate Finance and Corporate Governance at the International University of Monaco, Director of Business Development and Investor Relations at Yonderbound.com, Advisor and Consultant to Startups and Venture Capital firms for the implementation of ESOP systems. PhD dissertation at the Aix-Marseille Université in 2014. Email: akern@monaco.edu

ownership (ESO from now on) is one form of this. The National Center of Employee Ownership (NCEO) in the USA estimated for the year 2012 that among the companies which offer shares, 36 percent of their employees own shares of their employer through one of the different forms of shared capitalism, which is an enormous amount. According to Kruse et al. (2010) 'almost half of US employees participate in some form of shared capitalism [...] Based on these figures, shared capitalism covered 53.4 million American workers" (Kruse et al., 2010, p. 13). In Europe employee participation is of great relevance, since 34.6 million employees hold shares of their employers, which represents roughly 20 percent of Europe's work force. The capital held in ESO systems rose by 32 percent in Europe in 2013 (European Federation of Employee Share Ownership, 2013).

ESO is a very particular form of capitalism, since multiple internal and external consequences arise through such a system. It impacts *inter alia* businesses' performance, cost of capital, corporate governance, and institutional context. Hence, to understand this system is of great relevance to academics and business practitioners.

In the introduction, we outline the study documented by the dissertation. Therefore, we commence with a general overview which includes broader information about the subject and explains the topic's relevance. We define more specifically in the introduction shared capitalism and employee ownership.

We refer to employee participation to describe two different phenomena. The first is ESO where employees hold shares of the company they work for. The second is shared decision making at the corporate level. This often involves employee representation on the board of directors. Recently, Kruse et al. (2010) defined shared capitalism as all practices associating the employees to the performance of the company they work for. Shared capitalism includes all the forms of financial participation; ESO is one of them.

We conduct in-depth historical research on employee participation and shared capitalism in Germany. The following case study contrasts the empirical research cases because Germany's ESO system is poorly developed and placed in a particular institutional context which we examine from a historical perspective as Blasi et al. (2013) did in their famous book *The Citizen's Share*.

The historical reserach on Germany was developed to give an in-depth knowledge and a qualitative argument for shared capitalism. Germany is a country which already during the Industrial Revolution pursued citizens' financial and decision making participation. Several streams are defined and examined in this chapter. We start at ESO's roots in Germany and successively develop its chronological improvement.

'Both thorns and thistles it shall grow for you; and you shall eat the plants of the field.' This curse in the Bible from God to Adam doesn't curse humans or labor, but the land and capital of production on which prosperity and wealth is built. We don't want to get too deep into the meaning of this phrase; however, it demonstrates that ownership of capital is significant for human beings. We introduce this chapter with this phrase since also the Church and Christian beliefs enhanced this development in Germany, which we study. Nonetheless, in this document we will take a secularized approach to the research.

The theologian and socio-economist Oswald von Nell-Breuning opposed already at the start of the 20th century the Marxist view of a class-less proletarian society without means *versus* a class-free society of capital owners. We could say he promoted a culture in which the entire population is able to participate in the total assets of a national economy (Solms, 2002). In this chapter, we analyze the distribution of capital throughout German society from a historical perspective and in order to expand the system for a higher economic benefit in the future.

According to Blasi et al. (2013) the system of employees owning businesses in which they work is not novel. Already in the early development of the U.S., Washington, Adams, Jefferson, and Madison believed that the optimal economic system for a republic has to include citizens' ownership of land, which was at this time a major source of productive capital.

Therefore we hypothesize: 'Employee ownership was a criterion of Germany's founding fathers in order to stabilize Germany socio-economically after the Second World War.' To test this hypothesis we conduct an empirical study.

Blasi et al.'s (2013) extensive research in the U.S. determined that the U.S. founders' original citizens' ownership system of sharing ownership and profits helped to restore a stable middle class. They demonstrate that stock ownership in a business inspires, promotes, and grow employees' loyalty, productivity, and innovation. Therefore, their book shows history-, economics-, and evidence-based policy innovations and relates it to today's world, in which ownership in productive capital of a corporation replaced traditional land as the source of wealth creation. With the intention of researching this phenomenon in Germany we conduct our research based on the *Citizens' Shares* book approach (Blasi et al., 2013).

The core of this study is the collection and analysis of secondary data such as political speeches, protocols, and conference memoranda. Moreover, historical papers, documents, and books are used. Additionally, we conduct primary data collection through in-depth interviews with politicians, economists, employees, and management in Germany to expand the knowledge in this field.

First, the sub-chapter examines the development of employee ownership in Germany starting in the early 19th century until the first decade of the 21st century.

In the second sub-chapter, we define the research methodology and actions during this study.

The following third sub-chapter starts with a broad description and definition of employee involvement, which can be through capital participation and/or through decision making systems. However, the focus is on capital participation. We determine the development of these systems in the 19th century from a political movement by Otto von Bismarck, to a socio-economic and industrial movement by Johann Heinrich von Thünen. Furthermore, we study the post-World War 2 period under Chancellor Adenauer and Economics Minister Erhard as well as the founding fathers of social market economy (soziale Marktwirtschaft) in the Federal Republic of Germany (BRD - Bundesrepublik Deutschland). Also, the development of Germany's basic rights (Grundrechte) is discussed; more precisely, the right of property.

In the fourth sub-chapter, we discuss our findings. We determine the current situation of ESO in the 21st century and its socio-economic *status quo* in Germany and Europe, before we discuss and draw final conclusions of this study in the fifth section.

2. *Research methodology perspectives on employee ownership in Germany*

In this sub-chapter, we summarize the steps of our research and how we collect our historical materials. For this chapter, we follow strictly the methodology and approach of Blasi et al. (2013) in their book *Citizen's Share*. Therefore, we want determine the historical factors which lead to

'Volksaktien' in Germany. Astonishingly, Volksaktie means 'citizen share'. We highlight the economic and political steps during this research.

In order to conduct this research on the historical development of ESO in Germany, we developed an analytical strategy. First of all, we consult the current German academic literature about ESO and Mitbestimmung. This helps us to understand the actual situation. However, more important is to determine how this *status quo* of ESO in Germany developed. In a second step, we consult historical and current German, but also international, literature. This leads us to the third step; the analysis of biographies of actors at this time. Fourth, we conduct archive research about these persons and their operations. Therefore, we collected *inter alia* data from AGP Bundesverband für Mitarbeiterbeteiligung, Der Spiegel Archive, Die Welt Archive, Die Zeit Archive, DigiZeitschriften, Frankfurter Allgemeine Zeitung Archive, Harvard Widner Library, IFO Center of Economic Studies, Institute für Arbeit und Berufsforschung, Konrad Adenauer Stiftung, Ludwig Erhard Stiftung, and Süddeutsche Zeitung Archive. Fifth, we researched the archives of all German major journals and newspapers about the current trends at the time. Hence, we searched for special and defined terms and words in German related to ESO and Mitbestimmung. These words and definitions are summarized in Appendix 1.[2] In Appendix 2 we give a list of all the newspaper archives, and databases of foundations and institutions which we consulted to develop this chapter.[3]

In a last step, we conducted several in-depth interviews, which should enhance and confirm our conclusions. We conducted six interviews.

- Dr. Heinrich Beyer, Director, AGP
- Professor Dr. Joseph Blasi, J. Robert Beyster Professor, Rutgers University
- Professor Dr. Douglas Kruse, Rutgers University
- Professor Dr. Richard Freeman, Herbert Ascherman Chair in Economics, Harvard University
- Professor Dr. Jens Lowitzsch, Europa Universität Viadrina

Based on the research, we develop policy suggestions before we conclude this section.

2 See Appendix 1: Employee ownership and Mitbestimmung research terms and translation.

3 See Appendix 2: List of Archives, Databases, Collections and Institutions

3. Literature review perspectives on employee ownership in Germany

In this section we develop the historical background of ESO based on secondary data, speeches, obituaries, biographies, and literature about ESO in Germany in order to develop a chronological base to postulate as to the purpose of ESO and the interest of the founders of Germany in such a system. In this course of action we also include primary data, which we collected through in-depth interviews.

It is complex to give a general definition for ESO and shared capitalism, particularly looking back at more than 200 years of development of ESO systems in Germany. During this time, the sense of employee ownership and participation has changed several times and with it also its name and definition.

Therefore, we use a broader definition for this research. Kruse et al. (2010) defined shared capitalism as payment systems related to a diversified set of reward practices through which the employee's financial income depends on the performance of his or her corporation. Therefore, we will analyze the historical development of ESO in this section starting in the 19th century.

3.1 Employee participation in the 19th century

In Germany the development of ESO is a parallel stream of political motivation and transformations as well as industrial and social changes caused by revolutions and wars. We analyze and compare these streams in the following paragraphs.

3.1.1 Political movement

According to Gaugler (2011), especially during the second half of the 19th century during, industrialization and the continuous fighting between on the one side capitalists and liberals and on the other socialists and communists are significant for the development of employee ownership during this time. Those class conflicts caused struggles to economic development and for citizens. However, this led in the late 19th and beginning of the 20th century in dependence on the German Reich constitution to the so called 'constitutional firm'.

Bismarck was significantly involved in the development of the first German Reich. He created Germany's first social laws which are not directly involved in the employee ownership process; however, it is important to understand the socio-political environment at this time. These social laws are still active until today; thus, they have been a base on which other legislations were developed. We summarize in this section the laws under Bismarck during the Kaiser Reich and develop how these laws indirectly impacted the development of ESO still in the 21st century.

Otto von Bismarck became the first chancellor under the emperor Kaiser Wilhelm II. During this period in the 1880s, Bismarck was the driving politician developing the social insurance system in Germany (Harbutt Dawson, 1890). The first two decades of the so-called Wilhelminian period was marked by a significant agricultural and industrial economic upswing, together with French reparation payments caused the industrial revolution. However, mainly a small wealthy society benefited from this boom, while poverty of the majority of citizens increased.

Therefore, Bismarck had to develop his laws against strong resistance towards them. He called the political system 'State Socialism'. However, he used this term and those insurances to keep the social movement and party under control (Castelli & Dieckmann, 2010). Later Bismarck said about his laws: *'My thought was, to win the working class, or should I say bribe them, to see the state as a social institution, which exists and maintains their well-being.'* (von Bismarck, 1924/1935, p. 195-196). This shows his real intentions for those laws, which became very important in the past centuries to German citizens.

Even though Bismarck had to fight criticism of his plans, on 15th June 1883 the health insurance law passed parliament. Employees up to an income of 2000 Reichs Mark (RM), which was almost everyone, got health insurance through this law. A year later, on 6th July 1884, Bismarck's casualty insurance came into place. For our research the most important law was created on 22nd June 1889, the invalidity and retirement insurance. Every person above 16 years with an income below 2000 RM had to be insured in this system (Bundesministerium für Arbeit und Soziales, 2013). This moderated social discrepancy for a while during the First World War.

However, after the First World War (1914-1918), social struggles occurred related to events such as the massive capital losses due to inflation in 1923 and the world economic crisis with extremely high unemployment rates. The collapse of the German Republic of Weimar in 1933 fuelled the conflict between capitalists and employees again. Nevertheless, the perception changed in the period of the Second World War towards a stronger solidarity, in particular in 1942/43 during the allied air attacks. However, when the economy started to recover, the tensions within labor forces and employers rose again (Gaugler, 2011). This period was marked with several social and political changes about the perception of employee ownership at that time. We will discuss the after Second World War occurrences in a more detailed way in the sub-chapter on 'Employee ownership in the post-war period'.

3.1.2 Industrial movement

Parallel to the political movement of social insurances and retirement protection, an industrial movement in the 19th century evolved, which we discuss in this section.

According to Gaugler (1987), the development of employee participation, involvement, and contribution rights evolved out of several roots, starting already in the 18th century. A main root is located in the Anglo-Saxon countries, mainly in Great Britain. During this period, the first systems of employee ownership were developed and anticipated.

At this early period of industrialization, the capabilities and knowledge of employees increased dramatically. They had a basic education which made it possible to actively shape their work and social environment. Therefore, they could participate in social movements and economic developments. As a result of this advancement, these educated employees were capable of communicating on a par with employers and politicians. Hence, the time when employees were seen as objects ended and they took an active role in the social order (Wallraff, 1960).

Therefore, this discussion of ESO and its newly developed compensation scheme spread out quickly from the United Kingdom all over Europe. In German speaking areas (which was not yet Germany), the participation of employees was tremendously discussed and practiced for the first time in the 1840s, when Heinrich von Thünen appeared and set in place one of the first corporations – a farm – which allowed employees to participate financially and generate capital for their work (Gaugler, 1987). Von Thünen purchased the farm 'Gut Tellow' in 1810. There he started his employee ownership system in 1847/1848. At Gut Tellow, he initiated a day-laborer system which was supposed to fulfill three overall goals (von

Thünen, 1850, § 8 p. 282). His first aim was the integration and identification of the employee with the farm. Therefore, he wanted to create a strong local community around the farm and allow the villagers to become family of the farm's landlord. Second, he wanted to increase the purchasing power of the employees through the accumulation of dividends and interest, and provide financial stability after their retirement. Third, he required that his retired employees still participate in capital creation, and have the possibility to bequeath capital to the next generation. Hence, von Thünen did not want that the man who worked for him depended on the arbitrariness or pity of his family after he loses his strength to work. On the contrary, he wanted a society which can leave means of production and capital to their children.

Therefore, the identification led to the investment in the own firm and the protection of their savings was done through the Werksparkassen (a company internal savings bank). Von Thünen's system paid *per capita* the same amount of interest and dividends to their employees for their retirement. Here we have to mention that it was a medium-sized farm in the 19th century, where education and quality was very similar within the workforce at a farm (Gaugler, 2002).

The contribution programs developed by von Thünen were financial and participation ownership concepts. His motivation for improvements was based on socio-political developments (Wunderer, 2002). Von Thünen was an economist, politician, and entrepreneur. Therefore, the system of employee participation was not only very smartly structured, it also included structures which are still valid and applied nowadays. Interestingly, the agricultural organization existed over von Thünen's lifetime until it was sold at the end of the 19th century. Furthermore, several documents and analyses confirm that his system was economically stable and his corporation was doing financially very well (Gaugler, 1999). According to Wunderer (2002), von Thünen's ambitions were similar to today's socio-economic goals. On the one hand, he wanted to increase the purchasing power and capital gains of the employees. On the other, he desired more integration and identification of the employee with his/her corporation.

According to Böhmert (1902), the Gut Tellow was sold by von Thünen's grandchildren and the new owner stopped this system; nonetheless in the literature there are several examples of farms which followed von Thünen's model in the 19th century.

Towards the end of the same century, industrialized corporations also started to participate in employee ownership systems on a wider scale. An excellent example is the Zeiss Werke in Jena which developed employee shares in 1897. Ernst Abbe, the Director of Zeiss at this time, argued that the income of an employee has to be split in two parts (Abbe, 1961). First was the salary which should not be subject to change, therefore it should not be adjusted to economic fluctuations; it should only be measured at the average business performance. Therefore, employees could participate stably in a prosperous company, with planning reliability for their side. Second, the other part should be adjusted to the portion of improvement of employees' performance. This made the income more elastic and able to adjust to current demands and economic situations (Gaugler, 2002).

According to him, still nowadays at least 70 corporations are known which developed at this time such systems in Germany. In the period from 1867 to 1874, five smelting plants and weaving mills created workers' shares. Also a stone producing factory in 1901 created such a system. But then, because of the First World War, it took several years until 1919-1922 for ten further chemical and textile companies to join such an ESO model.

According to the chief executive director of the Arbeitsgemeinschaft Partnerschaft in der Wirtschaft e.V. (Federal Association for Employee Participation - AGP) in Germany Dr. Heinrich Beyer (2013), whom we interviewed for this research, further initial steps were taken in the 19th century by firms such as Siemens and Bosch. They developed a financial Christmas bonus arrangement during the same period.

However, first political steps towards capital ownership were taken almost 70 years later in the 1970s, which we discuss in the following sub-chapter.

3.2 Employee ownership in the post-war period in Germany

This sub-chapter analyses one of the driving forces of employee ownership in German history, namely the social market economy and its founders after the Second World War, when Germany was destroyed and was in the process of reconstruction.

The end of the Second World War left Germany's industry, infrastructure, and social system destroyed. However, what was shared by all major political parties – the Liberals, the Christian Democrats and the Social Democrats – was the belief in freedom and the will to defend it (Kunz,

1960). During the post-war period, dignity of human rights and overcoming the class conflict were core to these ambitions. Therefore, also the conception of employee participation changed from employee to joint partner.

There were two main driving political streams for employee capital participation after the Second World War to enhance social improvement. On the one hand, the first movement, which already dated back to the 19th century, was influenced by the Catholic Church because the Church believed that capital participation would decrease tensions throughout the population. On the other hand, the bourgeois movement was initiated in the middle class of society. Their beliefs became the foundation of the ordo-liberal political movement, which was a driving force after the Second World War, shaping and developing economic and political actions in the German government (Buchstab, 2000).

3.2.1 Founding fathers of the social market economy in Germany

After the Second World War, there were still different political streams in Germany from capitalist to communist. However, the founding fathers wanted freedom through balance of power, with as little participation of the state as possible (Ludwig Erhard Stiftung, 1971).

Marx probably also wanted to enhance the dignity of humans. Nevertheless, the belief of collective ownership is the opposite of wide-ranging ownership distribution throughout a society. The employee should have a home and own land in Europe. The ESO system should be based on achievement of the worker and compensate for loses during the war (Kunz, 1960). Therefore, social market economy is the preferred political and economic system for the BRD. It is a structure in which performance is rewarded, while low performing people are supported. This was the foundation to the reconstruction and economic improvements in Germany. Therefore, the target was 'Wohlstand für alle' (prosperity for everybody). Ludwig Erhard, the first economics minister and second chancellor after Adenauer of the CDU in the BRD, was one of the most influential politicians at this time. He was one of the founding fathers of the social market economy and was the politician who most facilitated its implementation in Germany (Koch, 2002). Moreover, Ludwig Erhard's goal was to create a society of owners, in order to develop a stable middle class and a balance of power in Germany through employee ownership according to Nahrendorf (2002). Erhard's slogan was: 'Vermögen für Alle' (Ludwig Erhard Stiftung, 1971). His slogan can be translated to: power, wealth, property, (and/or) capability, for everybody. We believe, based on this study, he meant all of them. We justify this assumption through his interpretation of Germany's fundamental rights.

Accordingly, freedom is a fundamental right of the German constitution. Ownership was seen by the founders of the BRD as a key element to secure freedom and spread out wealth through Germany. Erhard promoted a society of joint partners. Erhard's social market economy's goal was to give everybody the possibility to participate in the capital of their company. The generated capital is therefore protected by the fundamental rights of Germany (Benda, 1984).

One of the driving politicians was Fritz Burgbacher, a member of the German parliament, who advocated a European Union with ESO. He argued that socio-political civilization does not only include ethical aspects but further educational, fiscal, financial and economic characteristics, which are fundamental values of a democratic society (Buchstab, 2000).

After the currency reform and during the reconstruction, capital was not equally distributed, therefore under the 'soziale Marktwirtschaft' the demand of shared capitalism increased in Germany. The CDU formulated the postulate for broad based ownership for the first time in 1953 during their election campaign in Hamburg. Therefore, the member of the German parliament for the CDU, Neuburger introduced a legislative proposal to the German Bundestag to create a form of trust which managed the purchasing, storage, and selling process of shares. Employees would be able to get shares of the trust. These shares should be able to be purchased for only 10 DM (Deutsche Mark). The dividends of the shares held by the trust would be given out as dividends to the trusts' shareholders (Der Spiegel, 1953).

However, this plan was not supported by Ludwig Erhard, the economically-oriented part of the CDU, and the liberal party. They demanded a voluntary saving system and denied a collective investment plan. Since they did not want to dictate to the individual what to do and kept freedom as their main goal, these politicians still had the bitter memory of the German dictatorship and Nazi regime. Consequently, every retrenchment of freedom was seen as an enemy of the social market economy.

However, at the Frankfurter Wirtschaftstag conference in 1957 the conflict was overcome through the liberalization of the capital market and the termination of tax discrimination of shares (Buchstab, 2000). We illustrate this process at the Volksaktie case of Volkswagen and Preussag in Germany.

3.2.2 The Volksaktie case

Towards the end of the first and the beginning of the second legislation period of Chancellor Adenauer, the topic of ESO came in focus, around 1957/58. The driving politician was his minister Ludwig Erhard, who proclaimed 'Jedem Deutschen seine Aktie', which means 'Every citizen his shares'. So, Adenauer was a promoter of privatization of state owned firms to give every citizen the chance to generate capital (Erhard, 1957).

Der Spiegel (1957) illustrated this in the following caricature, which shows Erhard as the prince who wants to liberalize the princess 'shares' for the German citizens. Hence, he wanted to broaden the ownership base to make it possible also for 'small investors', the average German population, to become a production capital owner (Der Spiegel, 1957).

Der Spiegel (1957) cited Erhard's thesis about citizen's share: 'Ohne Konsumverzicht kein Sparen, ohne Sparen keine Kapitalbildung, ohne Kapitalbildung keine Investitionen und ohne Investitionen kein "Brot" in der Zukunft, das heißt kein wirtschaftlicher Fortschritt.' The meaning of his statement is: Without saving, there won't be capital generation; without capital no investments; and without investments no 'bread' for the future, which means no economic development.

Moreover, Erhard's Volksaktie was clearly dedicated to a broad ownership for lower and middle class citizens, since he wanted to strengthen the 'small man' and give him productive capital and ownership rights. He argues that then the class conflict will end and unions have to realize that their members are not workers anymore, that they became advanced entrepreneurs (Erhard, 1957).

Therefore, the Volksaktie (Citizen Share) was planned to be created through initial public offering of state-owned corporations such as Volkswagen. This case should have built a role model for further privatizations and give a kick-start to the spread to other companies in Germany. As a result, this would lead to a broader ownership and to an increase in economic development. Erhard's focus was to attract small investors to invest in shares which did not have ownership in production capital (Erhard, 1957).

Erhard planned to incentivize these savings and investments through two systems. On the one hand, the privatization should have created excessive liquidity to the state; hence tax could have been reduced, which would increase the purchasing power of the German population. This increase in liquidity could have been then invested into shares.

On the other hand, in order to promote the Volksaktie, he wanted to abolish the double taxations for shareholders. At this time companies were taxed thirty percent on their profits and shareholders were taxed twenty-five percent on dividends.

Furthermore, Erhard wanted to establish a share ownership system, closely related to the American system. During the same period, almost 40 percent of the shares held in the U.S. were owned by small and medium savers, since this system allowed them to invest their savings there, which was claimed by German policy makers. A share outstanding was already available for one to five dollars, while in Germany a share was at least 100-1000 DM (approx. 50-500 Dollar). Moreover, in the U.S., active participation policies and public relations management were used to inform small investors. This would have been also an anticipated method for Germany to alleviate the fear of German small investors towards share ownership. Therefore, the goal was to reach broad citizen's ownership based on the Anglo-Saxon model (Der Spiegel, 1953; Erhard, 1957; Der Spiegel, 1957).

In order to make it really possible for employees to purchase shares, meaning no big investor will get the shares and voting rights, the citizen shares should be given out to workers with an income only up to 16,000 DM per annum. Therefore, the interest of strong investors would be balanced out. Further, they would not even get the chance to get more shares to become too strong. Therefore, the 'small man on the street' would have privileges to subscribe to shares. This united the views of Erhard 'Wohlstand für Alle' (prosperity for everybody) and the conservative-left wing 'Ein Volk von Eigentümern' (a nation of owners). This should have finally ended the class fight between 'factors of production' labor and capital (Erhard, 1957; Der Spiegel, 1959).

While Erhard was relatively broad in the process of development of the Volksaktie, the national treasurer of Germany Hermann Lindrath under the Adenauer government was the person who pushed for the execution of the citizen share at Volkswagen and Preussag, also as a role-model for the privatization for other companies and the improvement of citizen shares. This plan was consistent with Erhard's and the CDU's belief in a social market economy.

The goal of Lindrath was to create at Volkswagen 60,000 employees who held the Volksaktie of their company. Therefore, on 22nd January 1958, the government presented a law in the German Bundestag, which justified the privatization, with the argument that it would create a broad based ownership of capital through the privatization of corporations. The law included five main criteria to acquire citizen share. Firstly, the buyer had to have an income below 16,000 DM per year. Secondly, each citizen was allowed to buy a maximum of five shares so that every buyer could get shares. Thirdly, the face value of the share was only 50 DM, which made the shares more affordable. Fourthly, a social discount was given to employees who made less than 9,000 DM or less than 15,000 DM of 20 percent and ten percent respectively. Fifthly, the Volksaktien were to have been given out as personal shares, which needed the permission of the company to be sold and thus should have increased the holding time. However, the attempt to privatize Volkswagen first failed because of ownership issues between the BRD and the state Lower Saxony in November 1958. So Preussag, which had at this time 22,000 employees, became the first firm which was privatized to their employees. In the same year in December, the process passed parliament (Der Spiegel, 1959).

As a result of the privatization through the government of Preussag, Volkswagen, and Veba, millions of German's became owners of the Volksaktie; 9.6 million shares were distributed to 4.3 million citizens. Therefore, a broad based ownership was created through citizen shares. Someone might criticize that too few workers got shares; however most of the employees of these firms received employee shares (Die Zeit, 1966). At Preussag, 216,119 German employees as well as middle class citizens became small shareholders, which reflected 79 percent of the shares (Der Spiegel, 1959).

However, during the first shareholder meeting, the cultures of banks, board members, and 'the man on the street' clashed. On the one hand for example, a citizen representative demanded beer during this conference for everybody instead of water. The board accepted it, but was not convinced that this was a good idea. Furthermore, another new shareholder who had a farm demanded to keep prices of chemical products low, otherwise the prices for fertilizer would increase, which would harm farmers' revenues. On the other hand, the board and bankers did not take the shareholder base seriously enough and did not give up their board seats for employees and small owner representatives, which created dissatisfaction among the new owners. This demonstrates the Volksaktie was not marketed well enough, as well as showing that shareholders and board members were not well-educated (Der Spiegel, 1959).

During this process, Erhard faced hard opposition from unions. The director of the union Industriegewerkschaft Metall, Otto Brenner, argued that employees should not be encouraged to save under reduction of consume to invest in their firm to become a co-owner. The employee should rather have codetermination rights and key industries should be transferred into commonly owned public institutions (Der Spiegel, 1957).

Nevertheless, the SPD and its programmatic head Eichler (1959) still demanded to transfer firms in key industries; if necessary, into publicly owned institutions. The SPD was in favor of an economy in which the state competes with the private sector. Nevertheless, Eichler admitted that the SPD did not have a plan of how employees could become owners, but they also did not want employee ownership because they do not want to give the employee the right to decide. Hence, the SPD would support a fund or trust to which the capitalist's shares would be transferred and through the trust, wealth should be redistributed. Moreover, this trust would take the employee's representation rights, so that the employee would not become a capitalist.

Erhard did not accept this objection, so he hired an external research institute to determine if employees would like the Volksaktie and the result was on his side. A strong majority of employees were interested in citizen share no matter what union lobbyists claim. *'Die Arbeitnehmer sind - da können die Gewerkschaftsfunktionäre reden was sie wollen - durchaus an Volksaktien interessiert.'* (Der Spiegel, 1957). Erhard further wanted to give employees ownership rights such as representation on the board. 'Ich stelle mir vor, daß wirklich die Schicht der kleinen Sparer mit eigener Repräsentanz im Aufsichtsrat erscheint, und zwar mit dem Stimmrecht, das ihrem Aktienanteil entspricht.' (Erhard, 1957).

A reason for this reluctance of unions was caused by their experience of the Spindler Werke. When the Spindler Werke introduced employee participation, the company owners and employees could solve the class fight. As a result, employees felt as if they were owners and the majority of employees left their union (Der Spiegel, 1957). According to Burgbacher (1968), employee ownership is more important than codetermination.

According to Erhard (1957), this system of citizen shares through the privatization of state owned firms, which gives employees the chance to purchase shares, should give Germany a sustainable economic system and facilitate the reunion and the reconstruction and incorporation of Eastern Germany. Therefore, his goal was 'Volkskapitalismus' (Citizen Capitalism).

In the following years, Hans Katzer was the minister for employment and social affairs in the 1960s. He was a founding member of the CDU and the German union (DGB). During his time as a minister, he promoted the ESO idea throughout unions. Furthermore, he had in common with Ludwig Erhard the belief that the core of the social market economy is the spreading out of power. Therefore, the most efficient way to prevent people from abusing their power is to create a balance. Therefore, civil barriers have to be abandoned while codetermination, participation, and responsibility should be facilitated. Even though ESO is a core ingredient of the social market economy, Erhard and Katzer could not implement it entirely; hence it remains as the missing component of the social market economy in Germany (Blüm, 1996).

According to Solms (2002) since the creation of the BRD, the Free Democratic Party (FDP) in Germany has been one of the strongest political promoters of employee ownership. They believe that only a strong democratic and social society can be created if capital is spread out through society. Furthermore, politics should facilitate ownership thoughts, because ownership is the engine for responsible behavior and economic benefits throughout Germany. Ever since, a main goal of their politics was to broadly spread capital through society to secure freedom. Moreover, they saw it as a means to reconstruct Germany after the Second World War. Nevertheless, the first time that the FDP articulated employee ownership as their key focus was 1971 in their 'Freiburger Thesen'.

According to Buchstab (2000), the Social Democratic Party (SPD) under the government of Chancellor Schröder initiated a campaign of promoting partnership and participation as a social democratic goal. Nevertheless, the CDU recommended already in the 1970s a law which was aimed at more capital participation, the so-called 'Burgbacher Plan'. The CDU politicians and board members of the Rhenag argued that a democratic society, human dignity, and the possibility to generate ownership are indispensable. In power at this period was the SPD in coalition with the FDP under Chancellor Brand, who preferred a profit sharing system. Hence, they blocked the Burgbacher Plan system. The importance and discussion of capital participation diminished after the 1950s and 1960s because of rising oil prices which caused the Energy and Economic Crisis in 1974. In 1984, when the CDU in coalition with the FDP came into power, the discussion blossomed up again. Nevertheless, because of many conflicts of interest, the strong legislation initiatives became diluted laws.

According to Gaugler (2007), ESO came again into the political picture in 1989/90 during and after the reunification of Germany. The DDR had several national companies. In the process towards privatization, several politicians and the AGP promoted ESO as a solution for privatization. Also, Erhard saw the privatization of firms and ESO as a solution to increase the social and economic reunification of Germany (Erhard, 1957). Hence, at several firms in Eastern Germany, management buy outs were executed and employees became owners of their firm. Nevertheless, the 'Aufbau Ost', an economic increase, was achieved also through low salaries which attracted national and international firms to invest in the development of infrastructure and factories there. Therefore, a way to keep salaries affordable while creating ownership was through ESO and the privatization of state owned properties – still ten years after the reunification of the BRD (Sinn, 1999).

3.2.3 Industry developments towards joint venturer

In the post-war period, the term 'ESO' changed to 'Mitunternehmer' – joint venturer or co-entrepreneur. Contrary to the models of the 19th century, these systems did not focus only on material participation. The upcoming employee structures included contribution and involvement rights as well as joint responsibilities. Hence in the 1950s and 1960s, several company concepts were expanded and industry initiatives were also a driving force for ESO in the post-war period. In January 1951, a pioneer in this field were the Spindler Werke, which applied several components of the joint venturer concept such as co-partnership of the labor force, joint knowledge, and shared responsibility (Wunderer, 2002; Gaugler, 2009).

According to Gaugler (2009), the Spindler Werke offered every employee who worked for the company more than one year ESO rights at this time. Almost all 1,878 employees accepted the offer and participated in the program. In their contract, they wrote that employees should be able to participate in the capital gain of the company; in return, employees should also bear responsibility. Hence employees could get capital increases on their shares, but also engage in loss sharing. In order to be able to actively participate, employees were informed quarterly in a detailed way about the firm's activities and plans, and encouraged to take action. Already before the German government created the German code-termination laws in 1952, the Spindler Werke applied systems through which employees had co-decision rights.

Not only had the Spindler Werke created ESO plans independently from legal regulations, also the Karl Kübel Werke in Worms and the Union-Werke Dr. Naegele in Aalen developed such systems. Kübel's motto was 'partnership instead of class conflict' and Dr. Naegele put in contrast the employer-employee relationship to entrepreneur and joint venturer (Unternehmer und Arbeitunternehmer) (Gaugler, 2009).

According to Heintzeler (1968), who was an executive board member of BASF since 1952 and member at the Max Planck Institute, small and mid-size firms are important for ownership, since there a family and a small group of employees can directly impact the business actions. However, in order to stay competitive in a globalizing market, corporations need to develop a competitive advantage which many organizations reach through growth and the resulting economies of scale. However, a problem would be if those firms are held by a small amount of owning society. Therefore, he concludes that small firms and big firms are very important for a stable society. Moreover, economies of scale are a key to success and the solution to develop a stable socio-political and economic environment in which citizens have to become owners in the form of shares in the corporation. Concluding, he has in common with Erhard that he promotes the idea of a balanced free society, which can only be built through the balance of power between small and big corporations and between a balanced ownership in multinational corporations through 'Publikums Aktien' (employee shares) and their rights which create an equilibrium of power.

Therefore, legislators had been forced to react. In the next section we discuss the approach of politicians towards ESO in Germany.

3.2.4 Development of asset policies in Germany

In order to protect employees from unnecessary risk or despotism, the state had to react to the industrial drive, demand, and increasing interest in participation and ownership rights. Hence, the government had to establish suitable framework requirements.

Notwithstanding, political parties and unions had an ongoing conflict about the form of participation in Germany; under the guidance of Finance Minster Franz Etzel the so-called Volksaktien were released during the privatization of Preussag in 1959 and in 1961 during the privatization of Volkswagen (Buchstab, 2000).

This led in the same year to the first asset formation law (Vermögensbildungsgesetz). This law had the purpose of encouraging employees to save capital for their retirement. These so-called vermögenswirksamen Leistungen of maximum 312 DM were taxed only eight percent, further no social security tax had to be paid on top. In 1965, the second asset formation law passed the parliament. This law included collective agreement work contracts and increased the subsidized saving amount to a maximum of 486 DM. Again in 1970, the law was improved, hence tax benefits were abandoned, but an employee savings allowance of 612 DM was included. Moreover, a catalog of possible saving opportunities for employees was developed too. Nevertheless, employees over a certain income were excluded (Geiger, 1986; Buchstab, 2000; Solms, 2002; Wagner, 2007).

Beyer (2013) argued that the first real steps towards capital ownership happened in the 1970s with those laws in order to give a wider access to a broad population. Since then, these laws made it possible for employees to participate not only in listed corporations, but also in small firms through 'Mitarbeiteraktien' (employee stock ownership – ESO) or 'Stille Beteiligungen' (silent partnership) respectively.

We can say the three laws were a first step towards financial participation; nonetheless they failed to spread capital through society. Therefore, in the 1980's the law was revised. In 1983 a fourth law was voted. The subsidized amount was raised to 936 DM of which 312 DM had to be invested in equities or derivatives. Consequently, the catalogue was again modified to offer employees a better variety of investments for their capital (Geiger, 1986; Solms, 2002).

According to Solms (2002), the breakthrough was the § 19aEStG of this law, since it included changes in the taxation law. Ever since, employee shares of their company up to the allowances are tax free and no social charges have to be paid if the shares were given out for free or undervalued. This enhancement made it possible for companies, no matter the size or type of legal form, to give out employee shares in a savings plan.

In 1987, the fifth asset formation law passed the German Parliament (Bundestag). This law improved the catalogue of unlisted firms and derivatives in order to make it easier for small firms which do not give out shares to their employees to participate in this system.

From 1998, the last development occurred. The tax free allowance was increased form 27,000 DM to €17,900 annual income. Furthermore, two baskets were created: a home savings plan and a shares plan. The state increased the bonus from overall about 300 million to 920 million for savers.

To conclude, derived from this development, the German government tries to facilitate savings and capital participation for lower income employees. Initially, this system was expected to change the German capital structure to higher ESO. Nevertheless, employees get any company's shares, so it is not a 'real' form of ESO, since it does not give employee participation rights, neither do they become an active part of a corporation. Usually, for the employee it looks more like a savings plan from a bank or insurance company. Furthermore, usually these capital saving plans facilitate the development of private property, which ties up capital which could have been invested proactively. Hence, in Germany the population invests very little in company shares compared to the Anglo-Saxon countries. Therefore, this system helps people to prepare for their retirement but fails to increase productivity in their corporation. So the system has failed to fulfill the expectations of higher ESO involvement (Beyer, 2013).

The following table shows the developed capital ownership system in Germany. This table shows that the focus of Germany's policy makers was dedicated to property ownership first, which is logical since the aim was to develop real estate investment first because most properties got destroyed during the Second World War. Nevertheless, Tables 1 and 2 show that politicians wanted to facilitate clearly broad based capital ownership in a second step.

Table 1. Types of capital ownership systems

Capital Types in Germany		
Property Ownership	Money Ownership	Productive Capital Ownership
24.4.1950 Property Law (Wohnbaugesetz)	17.12.1952 First law to enhance the capital market from	Privatization of state owned corporations
17.3.1952 Property Bonus Law (Wohnbauprämiengesetz)	5.5.1959 Saving Bonus Law (Sparprämiengesetz)	1959 Preussag
27.6.1956 Property Building Law (Wohnbaugesetz)	5.2.1963 Development of the Saving Bonus Law	*1961* Volkswagenwerk
24.8.1965 Wohnbauänderungs-gesetz		1961 VTG
		1965 VEBA

Table 2. Capital law systems

Systematic merger of the capital laws	
12.7.1961 Law of enhancement of capital generation of employees (Gesetz zur Förderung der Vermögensbildung der Arbeitnehmer)	Labor agreement was accepted
1.7.1965 Law of enhancement of capital generation of employees	Increase of the subsidized capital amount from 312DM to 624DM Development of employee savings allowance
27.6.1970 Law of enhancement of capital generation of employees	

3.2.5 Last employee ownership attempt

Toward the end of the 20th century, two parallel movements toward ESO were fostered from the political and industrial sides. This trend was fueled by the booming stock market at the time.

From a political side, the Chancellor Gerhard Schröder of the SPD at this time realized as one of the first social democrats that capital and labor are not two opposing factors, as Marx claimed. Even though Erhard's dream of 'Wohlstand für Alle' was almost achieved, the psychological gap between the opposing groups still existed. So, Schröder developed the 'Bündnis für Arbeit', which should increase the development of the bonus system and ESO. He wanted to decrease the influence of unions and decrease labor disputes (Arbeitskämpfe) (Wintermann, 2000).

From an industrial side, in 1996 a last big attempt to spread out shares through the German society and its employees was made when a part of the at this time state owned company, 'Deutsche Post', went public and Deutsche Telecom to which T-Mobile and T-Com belong was created. The initial public offering price should have made the investment in its shares accessible for the wider German population. So shares had a nominal value of five DM and employee shares had a discount of 40 percent. These characteristics should have made the investment in it achievable for the 'man on the street' (Die Welt, 1995).

According to Beyer (2013), unfortunately this attempt failed when shortly after the 'Dot-Com Bubble' burst and again German society lost money on the capital market. Also, the bad example of the Enron case where employees had lost their savings and salary was a setback for ESO development in Germany, fuelling criticisms of ESO systems again (Schmitt, 2002). However, this is in our study one example which shows the developing collaborations between state and industry, which occurred before two movements merged at this time for a common interest in Germany.

Burgbacher's belief of creating a society of owners which earn capital shares politically is still not fulfilled according to Buchstab (2000) because of the blocking attitude of unions, which do not accept capital risk. Further, employees fear giving away decision making rights, which led to the development of codetermination, in return for ownership rights (Heintzeler, 1968). We discuss this in more detail in the next sub-chapter.

3.2.6 Codetermination in Germany

One of the major corporate governance distinctions of the German employee participation system is codetermination. In this form of organization, boards are two tiered with half of the directors representing employees. Often this system is said to be based on 'German culture'. However, this tradition is rather the result of an intense fight in the late 1940s between various interest groups such as political actors, industrialists, and trade unions in Germany (Heintzeler, 1968; Jackson, 2001; Gomez and Wirtz, 2008).

In the first decades of the 20th century, the development of codetermination started. We cover only briefly this subject, to give a holistic view of employee participation in Germany, since a common misunderstanding in the literature is that codetermination is a part of ESO and 'German culture'. ESO and codetermination are two separate movements (Heintzeler, 1968; Beyer, 2013).

Moreover, according to Müller Jentsch (2008), codetermination might have facilitated several economic developments; however, the purpose of it was not to develop a new economic system in Germany. Rather, it was a political tool to moderate economic advancement after the Second World War. Also, this system was supposed to prepare for a socialist Germany under the cover of 'social democracy'. In order to analyze and draw a parallel with ESO, we look at codetermination in a historical perspective.

According to Wallraff (1960) and Heintzeler (1968), the demand for codetermination was raised in 1918 already when the 'Rätesystem' was arising. This was a political system built of a board of elected employees ruling the country. This system was supported by the communist movement after the end of the First World War. While moderate activists wanted to keep production facilities in the entrepreneur's hands, nevertheless democratic regulation systems of employees' representatives on the board of directors were developed.

According to Müller Jentsch (2008), this 'Räte'-system became very powerful during the Weimar Republic and in order to regulate it § 165 came in place which gave employees the right to participate in salary, business, and economic negotiations within their firm. However, for the extreme left this was not enough and led to protests which caused 40 deaths and 100 persons injured when soldiers protected the parliament. In the following years, riots and conflicts of interest did not allow the system to fully develop. Nevertheless, the 'Betriebsrat' was not supposed to be a lobbying institution, rather a base to develop relationships in order to moderate, mediate, and communicate within an organization. However, both sides, labor and employer, perceived it as a political institution for the fight between employee and capital (Müller Jentsch, 2008).

However, the idea of employee codetermination was lost when German society was hit by mass unemployment before the Second World War broke out. Nevertheless, after 1945 the discussion blossomed up, again.

Unions claimed that the codetermination and democratization of corporations would have made it difficult for a regime to grow (Wallraff, 1960).

During the Nazi regime, unions were forbidden and corporations were state organized. Therefore, Germany was left without institutions and destroyed after the Second World War. Moreover, Germany was split into four parts after the war; three parts were ruled by the western allies which became the BRD and the fourth part in Eastern Germany was governed by the Soviet Union and became the Deutsche Democratic Republic (DDR). Therefore, the western allies wanted to give Germany a stable but balanced economic system. The Rhein-Ruhr area where mines were located was very important for the reconstruction. In 1948, already before a law was developed, 23 firms had to implement such a system. After this, it was impossible to take away from the unions the employee's right to be represented on the board of directors. Therefore, the western allies facilitated the Montan-Mitbestimmungsgesetz in 1951 for the mining and smelting industry in Germany which was the first case of 'Mitbestimmung' in Germany (Heintzeler, 1968; Müller Jentsch, 2008).

Based on the American and British military government's law Nr. 75 and the allied law Nr. 27, firms in the carbon and steel industry were given a corporate governance system which included owners, unions, and state representatives on their boards. Therefore, in the 1950s the government created the first constitution law[4] followed in 1976 by the codetermination law[5], which allocated half of the board seats to employees if the company has more than 2,000 employees. However, the board's director is usually elected by the owners. In the case of a 'pat situation' the 'quasi-parity' comes into place which gives the director of the board a double voting right (Renaud, 2006). Therefore, the governance system in German firms is split between the executives, the board of directors, the employee representatives, and shareholder representatives (Müller Jentsch, 2008; Gomez & Wirtz, 2008).

However, the government of Adenauer was against this system and wanted to stop these laws; nevertheless the power to strike of the unions IG Metal und IG Bergbau was too strong. So they forced Adenauer and his government to give up their plans. However, it was not yet an entire success for the unions since the law was only dedicated to the steel and

---

4 Betriebsverfassungsgesetz (BetrVG)
5 Mitbestimmungsgesetz (MitbestG)

mining industries (Heintzeler, 1968; Müller Jentsch, 2008). Further, he warned that codetermination would be against the equality principle of German fundamental rights since it causes an unbalance within the organization. However, the unions' victory came in 1972 when this law was expanded to all industries in the BRD (Müller Jentsch, 2008).

Remarkable in this process is that the German Catholic Church was capable of bringing together all involved parties to find a solution. The role of the Church is usually not recognized. Nonetheless, its efforts made the compromise of board codetermination in Germany achievable (Gomez & Wirtz, 2008).

Following this development, Pope Pius XII and the Catholic Church became involved in this discussion. Pius XII said that no matter which type of board rules the organization, it has to be in charge and responsible for its decisions. Hence in 1949, the Church published a decision document which stated that employee codetermination is a social right for everyone. However, Pius XII warned that this might lead to strong influences by external interests within the organization. This conflict of interest shows the critical view of this young system. This discrepancy leads to the question of whether ownership rights could diminish this conflict of interest within the organization (Mitchelle, 2006).

The call for action was raised and employee shares came into the big picture. Although the amount of ESO might be smaller than the Christian believe for land German populations started to recognize the value of capital because of two big inflationary periods, its related depreciation of money and savings, and the following two currency reforms (Wallraff, 1960).

3.2.7 Employee ownership today

According to Heintzeler (1968), from the times of Erhard after the Second World War, the situation has altered again. However, we have to point out that the social and political system in Germany and overall in Europe has changed to a stable and sustainable social market economy. Moreover, Europe has never been a peaceful region for such a long period in history. Society was able to gain property and ownership during this period and proletarians became middle class as Erhard predicted. This perception of Heintzeler (1968) is still accurate in the 21st century, even though disasters such Eurocrisis happened (Arbeitsgemeinschaft Partnerschaft in der Wirtschaft e.V., 2013).

According to Koch (2002), during times of crisis and globalization, citizens are scared to get lost in a faster moving society. Moreover, they are worried that they will not be capable of keeping up with current economic developments and thus lose their savings. The wealth within German society has been growing in the past three decades; nevertheless, savings were not invested in productive capital such as shares. Only about six percent of savings are used for productive capital investments. According to him, three factors facilitated this system:

1. Germany's strong social state principle introduced by von Bismarck, which is more extremely developed than in the Anglo-Saxon countries.
2. The experiences of world economic crises, which had dramatic impacts on the German economy, savings, and political system.
3. Germany's corporate growth depends strongly on debt and rather less on equity investments.

According to Reuter (1994), the former CEO of Daimler AG, his task was to increase the internal investment motivation and capability of his employees. He wanted to create an active entrepreneurial spirit within the organization for a sustainable future. The implementation of lean-management strategies in thc 1990s caused a recovery and improvement of ESO in Germany. Firms could implement strategies which incorporate better employees in their processes (Schneider, 1996). Hence the employee became an active part of the value added process of an organization (Wunderer, 1995).

We identify two aspects. First, we evaluate the current situation of ESO and second we ask the question: Why did Germany come out as the winner of the Eurocrisis? It is obviously very complex to answer this question. Nevertheless, we can say that the result of employee participation and codetermination put Germany in a better initial situation than other European countries.

To determine the current ESO situation in the 21st century, we can say that there is still the ongoing competition between ESO and the savings and retirement systems. In the governmental elections of 1998 and 2002, the SPD had employee capital participation in their program. Also the CDU/CSU formulated this goal during the election campaigns. They wanted to develop the 'We-society' in which employees are active shareholders. Moreover, they wanted to finalize Erhard's dream of a social market economy. They proclaimed the system as a means to create balance of power within citizens. Also the Liberals – FDP demand that employees should become co-owners of their firms. In their 'Wiesbadener Grundsätze' position paper they develop an Employee Stock Ownership Plan (ESOP) strategy which includes tax benefits if a firm is transferred to its employees. Also, Bündnis 90/Die Grünen, Germany's green party, demanded during the new market boom higher participation in tech firms (Nahrendorf, 2002). Nevertheless, during the 2013 campaign, employee ownership was not a publically discussed topic. However, the AGP did an 'election check' about employee ownership strategy before the 2013 election. Still all these parties answered to AGP's request and reinforced their commitment to the goal of broad based employee ownership in Germany (Arbeitsgemeinschaft Partnerschaft in der Wirtschaft e.V., 2013).

It seems to us hypocritical that all major political parties seem to be in favor of ESO, but no holistic or finalized law passed the government and became legislation in the BRD. So someone might wonder why there is so little improvement in this field. An answer to this was formulated by Heintzeler as early as 1968. He argued that the power of unions in Germany is too high. Unions are in favor of codetermination, but they reject ownership and the related ownership risks. Further, he claims that Germany's society shifted into the unbalance the German founding fathers wanted to prevent because unions have such strong bargaining power and tools such as strikes to corrupt decision making processes. Moreover, unions want to prevent employees from sharing ownership rights since they do not want their members to feel like a capital owner as they would lose their power. However, unions claim to be a pillar of the German social environment; but legally they are only an interest group which got over-proportional influence in the BRD.

A more recent answer to this question was given by Beyer (2013). He argued that the parties want ESO, but they do not want to change the historically developed system of cost allocated retirement plans, corporate retirement plans, the Riester Retirement system, and the social security system. Those systems leave very little liquidity to the market; hence, the citizens cannot invest in shares. Furthermore, unions in Germany view ESO very critically due to the double exposure of the employee towards risk. In case of a bankruptcy of the employee's firm, the employee would lose his/her salary and the shares of the firm would dilute. Also, still nowadays owners of midsize firms seem to be reluctant to give away shares to their employees because they fear loss of their power. In traded firms due to codetermination, corporations do not want to give employees too many shares because of an increasing unbalance of power due to the commutation of voting power of employees' shares and their codetermination rights. Nevertheless, the amount given out is usually far below a blocking minority.

Based on the discussion, which we focused on employees, politician, and executives during this research, we can conclude that the combination of the previous two arguments hinders the development of ESO.

We discuss briefly the case of Schlecker, which was a German drugstore chain. Schlecker got into financial troubles during the Eurocrisis in 2009. Hence, ESO was considered as a tool to rescue the company. Unions discussed in this case to save jobs through salary cuts, which would be invested into capital savings plans. However, it is unethical, unaccountable, and irresponsible to expose employees to such a risk if a firm is already in financial troubles because of their business model and the economic situation. Beyer (2013) argued that ESO systems have to be put in place before a crisis. It is too late to shut the stable door after the horse has bolted. Therefore, the politics and unions need to be open to discussions since they failed to establish adequate ESO systems in Germany for such cases (AGP Mitteilung, 2012). Therefore, the former liberal economics minister Rösler (2012) under Chancellor Merkel argued that ESO systems need to be revised; investment systems need to be expanded and improved to prevent such cases.

However, the developments during the Eurocrisis also show positive results. When the economy went down and factories had to stop producing, missing demand meant that employers were put into the situation to cut costs in order not to go out of business entirely and to prevent bankruptcies. Therefore, they had two options: lay off employees or cut the weekly amount of paid work hours so employees would get extra unpaid days off per week. Since employees are represented on boards and able to discuss with the employers, they were able to communicate effectively with each other so they chose option two. Therefore, they were able to constructively communicate with their workforce. As a result of this, employees were satisfied not to be laid off, which was good for the work climate inside the corporation. On the contrary, most companies in Europe chose option one and fired employees to reduce their costs.

More importantly for the German economy was that organizations kept running. First, they did not have the cost of layoffs and compensation for canceling contracts, which would have caused extra economic cost in times of recession. Second, it is a very time and cost expensive process to hire and train new employees. Third, when the economy starts recovering or booming it would take a while until firms will be fully efficient, which can be seen as indirect loss of income. Fourth, these expenses were minimized in the German economy. Corporations were able, when the market and demand started to pick up, to get immediately into full production capacity. Fifth, domestic demand increased rapidly too since employees went back to their regular income. This facilitated recovery in the domestic economy.

Therefore, German companies were in a better starting position and capable to outperform their international competitors.

Based on this economic success, the interest in ESO by firms is growing tremendously. Germany has a low unemployment rate. Therefore, corporations compete strongly for skilled employees, especially firms which are located in unattractive regions. Hence, these firms are looking for ways to have the long-term commitment of their employees (Beyer, 2013), similar to the Silicon Valley case by Blasi et al. (2003) where technology firms had to attract employees in a very competitive labor market.

4. Discussion and perspectives on employee ownership in Germany

This study should be useful for company managers and politicians in order to accomplish the core need of ESO, to create the founding fathers' social market economy.

We see as a limitation of this study the translation of the word: 'Eigentum' in the German literature. The concept of Eigentum is promoted, however this word can be translated into English as 'property' or 'ownership'. After the Second World War, property was promoted and properties savings plans were subsidized. Therefore, German politicians might not have had ESO always in mind when they spoke about participation and capital ownership.

Further, there is a strong contradiction in the German political arena. All major parties in Germany, the CDU, SPD, FDP, and the Green party are in favor of ESO. So someone might wonder why it is underdeveloped compared to the Anglo-Saxon nations. One of the answers is that German political interest groups don't want to give up the current social health and unemployment system (Beyer, 2013).

Already in 1968, Heintzeler argued that Mitbestimmung as the German unions demand it would create an unstable economy and cause an unequal distribution of power among certain population groups, which was not the core idea of the founding fathers such as Adenauer and Erhard. Heintzeler predicted that German citizens would have to soon work less, which means longer vacations and less work hours per month through economic growth and economies of scale. The only way to achieve this is through employee capital ownership. Hence, he thought Germany's economic scheme was at the edge of a breakthrough and would move to a system such as U.S. employee ownership in the 1970s. Therefore, employees would have gotten ownership rights, which would have made Mitbestimmung unnecessary. Unfortunately, this breakthrough did not come because of hindering interest groups, such as unions and politicians, which did not want to give up on Mitbestimmung and retirement saving plans (Solms, 2002; Beyer, 2013).

We do not disagree that codetermination has positive effects on companies and their employees. According to Fauver und Fuerst (2006), board representation enhances information sharing which has a positive impact on organizations as well as increasing productivity. Moreover, these positive effects are more efficient in human capital intense industries such as information technology, pharmaceuticals, and trade. Nonetheless, through real ownership rights which include financial and decision making rights the positive effects of codetermination could be enhanced. This is a subject for further research in Germany.

Based on this study, it seems to be impossible to replace the codetermination system with employee ownership. The capitalist side does not want to give up more rights to employees and the employees' side rejects ownership risk. However, we suggest the development of a governmental policy which gives a framework in which employee ownership can be developed. Such a system could be similar to an ESOP in the US. This legal structure would allow a group of employee to borrow money from a bank in order to buy out the company stocks. Such systems would be most appropriate for medium size enterprises. When such frameworks exist, employees would be stronger in their participation and execution of an ESOP transaction. A further possibility would be to develop an employee owned company insurances or guaranty in the case of bankruptcy which would serve the employee owners first in case of a liquidation of their firm and thus reduce their risk.

We can conclude that ESO was a core ingredient for a stable social market economy and that it is still the missing piece. Several systems have been implemented, but ESO is still a goal for the future.

We compared the historic roots with the current norms of employee participation. Therefore, we start by examining the 19th century when von Thünen developed his socio-economic persuasion which aimed for an economic system that needs employees to financially participate in an organization for a wider social benefit and which increases their purchasing power. During the post-war period, the dignity of human rights and overcoming the class conflict were core to the former ambitions. We can conclude that current systems aim to make employees joint partners in an organization. These concepts seek a co-entrepreneurial spirit in performance. Therefore, employees should actively contribute to their firm's action (Loritz, 2002).

Employees in Germany can participate in savings in many different ways such as life insurance, retirement plans, building society contracts, and many other investment possibilities. Employees can also participate in their firm through codetermination. However, Erhard's goal of developing a social market economy with a society of joint partners fell by the wayside, even though this is one of the core requirements of a stable and successful social, political, and economic system. This variety of support systems grew historically. This is an explanation but not a justification (Jungblut, 2002; Loritz, 2002). Moreover, if we compare the way ESO was structured by, for example, Spindler Werke in the 1950s with the applied systems in the 21st century, the previous systems were more defined and contours were stronger than the current 'wishy-washy' schemes (Gaugler, 2009).

In order to live up to Erhard's expectations and fulfill his goal of a social market economy, the social systems in the social market economy needs to be revised. Hence, only if common public interest is the same as self-interest will this system work more efficiently. Therefore, a system needs to be constructed in which Erhard's goal can be achieved (Jungblut, 2002).

According to Wunderer (2002), the responsibility to develop ESO systems is with the employee himself/herself. The employee needs to have the entrepreneurial spirit and motivation to produce such a system. Nevertheless, managers have to support their employees in this process and top executives must provide a framework in which the employee can use his/her creativity to build an ESO framework. Therefore, the belief in such a manner the freedom of Erhard's social market economy with the opportunity of joint partnerships is treated with care.

Based on our study we cannot say if employee ownership was in competition with Mitbestimmung, neither we can determine if codetermination was a compromise between the negotiation powers. Some sources claim it was, others say it was not. However, what seems to be clear and consistent throughout our historical research in Germany is that Mitbestimmung is a hindering and blocking factor to the development of employee ownership and citizen share systems in Germany. Hence, unions pursue the Marxist view and advertise redistribution of income, while ESO followers demand equity participation (Heintzeler, 1968). Therefore, employees become owners as Adenauer and Erhard demanded as a pillar of Germany's social market economy, and for Europe.

Concluding, we can say that the aim for employee ownership was there, but the execution was poorly done and that there is space for improvements based on the stable social market economy system in order to achieve a balance of power, and a society of owners.

References

Abbe, E. (1961). Über Gewinnbeteiligung der Arbeiter in der Großindustrie. In A. Kippenberg, & F. von der Leyen. *Deutsche Reden und Rufe. Von Martin Luther bis Ricarda Huch.* München: dtv.

AGP Mitteilung (2012). Rettung durch Mittarbeiterbeteiligung. *AGP Mitteilung*, 16.

Arbeitsgemeinschaft Partnerschaft in der Wirtschaft e.V. (2013). *AGP Wahlcheck 2013.* Kassel: Arbeitsgemeinschaft Partnerschaft in der Wirtschaft e.V.

Benda, E. (1984). Eigentum als Grundrecht. In Ludwig-Erhard-Stiftung, *Eigentum als Grundrecht und Element der Ordnungspolitik* (pp. 3-21). Stuttgart, New York: Gustav Fischer Verlag.

Beyer, H. (2013, November 12). Mitarbeiterbeteiligung in Deutschland aus Sicht der Arbeitsgemeinschaft Partnerschaft in der Wirtschaft e.V. (A. Kern, Interviewer)

Blasi, J., Freeman, R., & Kruse, D. (2013). *The citizen's share.* New Haven: Yale University Press.

Blasi, J., & Kruse, D. (2014, January). Board Representation and Codetermination in the US. (A. Kern, Interviewer)

Blasi, J., Kruse, D., & Bernstein, A. (2003). *In the company of owners – The truth about stock options and why every employee should have them.* New York: Basic Books.

Blüm, N. (1996). Mitbestimmung und Miteigentum. In *Nachruf Hans Katzer* (pp. 527-529). Bonn.

Böhmert, V. (1902). Gewinnbeteiligung der Arbeitnehmer in Deutschland, Österreich und der Schweiz. Dresden.

Buchstab, G. (2000). Historisch Politische Mitteilung Heft 7/2000. In G. Buchstab, H. Kleinmann, & H. Küsters, *Vom Mitarbeiter zu Miteigentümer. Der Burgbacher Plan von 1969* (pp. 269-288). Sankt Augustin: Böhlau Verlag.

Bundesministerium für Arbeit und Soziales (2013). *Bismarcks Sozialgesetzgebung (1881-1889)*. Retrieved from In die Zukunft Gedacht: https://www.in-die-zukunft-gedacht.de/de/page/68/epoche/129/epochen.html [Accessed 23.11.2014]

Burgbacher, F. (1968, June 15). Vermögensbildung Schiefe Ordnung. (Spiegel, Interviewer)

Castelli, N., & Dieckmann, R. (2010). Gesundheistsystem im Vergleich. In H. Rebscher, & S. Kaufmann, *Gesundheitssystem im Wandel* (pp. 9-29). Heidelberg: Economica Verlag.

Der Spiegel (1953). Sparen Das unmoralische Wertpapier. *Der Spiegel*, 8-9.

Der Spiegel (1957). Miteigentum Entlassung möglich. *Der Spiegel*, 32.

Der Spiegel (1957). Volksaktien Erhards Wahlschlager. *Der Spiegel*, 12-14.

Der Spiegel (1959). Volksaktien Bonbon des Jahrhunderts. *Der Spiegel*, 16-25.

Der Spiegel (1959). Volksaktionäre Vereinigt euch. *Der Spiegel*, 16-18.

Die Welt (1995). Telekom baut auf Mitarbeiterbeteiligung. Beschäftigte können Aktien im Wert von 750 Mark erwerben und Investmentgesellschaft beitreten.

Die Zeit (1966). Arbeiter noch keine Kapitalisten. *Die Zeit*, Nr. 34.

Eicheler, W. (1959, October 7). Der Geheimnisvolle Weg. (C. Ahlers, & E. Böhme, Interviewer)

Erhard, L. (1957, February 20). Vom Volkswagen zum Volkskapitalismus. (C. L. Brawand, & H. D. Becker, Interviewer)

European Federation of Employee Share Ownership (2013). *European Survey*. EFES.

Fauver, L., & Fuerst, M. E. (2006). Does good corporate governance include employee representation? Evidence from German corporate boards. *Journal of Financial Economics*, 673-710.

Gaugler, E. (1987). Mitarbeiterbeteiligung am Unternehmenserfolg. In F. R. FritzRoy, & K. Karft, *Mitarbeiter-Beteiligung und Mitbestimmung im Unternehmen* (pp. 11-12). Berlin, New York: Walter de Gruyter.

Gaugler, E. (1999). Mitarbeiter als Mitunternehmer Die historischen Wurzelneines Führungskonzepts und seine Gestaltungsperspectiven in der Gegenwart. In R. Wunderer, *Mitarbeiter als Mitunternehmer. Grundlagen, Föderinstrumente, Praxisbeispiele* (pp. 3-21). Neuwied: Kriftel.

Gaugler, E. (2002). Anfänge der Mitarbeiterbeteiligung. In K. R. Wagner, *Mitarbeiterbeteiligung Visionen für eine gesellschaft von Teilhabern* (pp. 17-27). Wiesbaden: Gabler.

Gaugler, E. (2007). Mr. AGP geht in Ruhestand. AGP.

Gaugler, E. (2009). Mitarbeiter als Mitunternehmer - eine personalpolitische Strategie. In T. Wrona, *Mitarbeiter als Mitunternehmer – Eine personalpolitische Strategie* (pp. 225-237). Wiesbaden: Gabler.

Gaugler, E. (2011). *Partnerschaft in Wirtschaft und Betrieb.* Mannheim: Forschungsstelle für Betriebswirtschaftund Sozialpraxis e.V.

Geiger, W. (1986). Mitarbeiterbeteiligung Ein Instrument der Staatlichen Vermögensbildung. In H.-G. Schottler, *Modelle und Perspektiven der Mitarbeiterbeteiligung* (pp. 42-50). Krefeld: Dr. Günter Marchal und Dr. Hans Jochen Matzenbacher Wissenschaftsverlag.

Gomez, P.-Y., & Wirtz, P. (2008). Institutionnalisation des regime de gouvernance et role des institutions socles: le cas dela cogestion allemande. *FARGO*, 1-40.

Harrbutt Dawson, W. (1890). *Bismarck and State Socialism.* London: Swan Sonnenschein.

Heintzeler, W. (1968). *Volkskapitalismus.* Düsseldorf: Econ Verlag.

Jackson, G. (2001). The origins of non-liberal corporate governance in Germany and Japan. In W. Y. Dtreeck, *The origins of non-liberal capitalism: Germany and Japan compared* (pp. 121-170). Ithaca: Cornell University Press.

Jungblut, M. (2002). Wie viel „sozial" verträgt die Marktwirtschaft? Martwirtschaft und Sozialwirtschaft bilden (noch) keine Einheit. In K. R. Wagner, *Mitarbeiter-beteiligungVisionen für eine Gesellschaft von Teilhabern* (pp. 185-190). Wiesbaden: Gabler.

Koch, R. (2002). „Die Gesellschaft von Teilhabern (Ludwig Erhard) wird Realität" Mitarbeiterbeteiligung zu Beginn des 21. Jahrhundert. In K. R. Wagner, *Mitarbeiterbeteiligung Visionen für eine Gesellschaft von Teilhabern* (pp. 105-110). Wiesbaden: Gabler.

Kruse, D. L. (1996). Why do firms adopt profit-sharing and employee ownership plans? *British Journal of Industrial Relations*, 515-538.

Kruse, D., Blasi, J., & Bernstein, A. (1997). Employee ownership, employee attitudes, and firm performance: A review of the evidence. In D. Lewin, D. Mitchell, & M. Zaidi, *The Human Resources Management Handbook.* Greenwich: JAI Press.

Kruse, L. D., Freeman, R. B., & Blasi, J. R. (2010). Shared capitalism at work: Employee ownership, profit and gain sharing, and broad-based stock options. Chicago: University of Chicago Press.

Kunz, W. (1960). *Mitbestimmung und Miteigentum in Europa.* Freiburg: Rombach Verlag.

Loritz, K. G. (2002). Mitarbeiterbeteiligung, Vermögens- und Altersvorsorge. Überlegungen zum aktuellen Stand und zu den Zukunftsperspektiven. In K. R. Wagner, *Mitarbeiterbeteiligung Visionen für eine Gesellsvchaft von Teilhabern* (pp. 111-118). Wiesbaden: Gabler.

Ludwig Erhard Stiftung. (1971). *Vermögen für alle.* Düsseldorf: Econ Verlag.

Müller Jentsch, W. (2008). 1918-1952: Mitbestimmung für eine neue Wirtschaftsordnung. *Magazin Mitbestimmung.*

Mitchell, M. (2006). Moderate conservatism in the Federal Republic: The Christian Democratic Union. Mimeo: Franklin & Marshall College.

Nahrendorf, R. (2002). Der lange Weg zur Teilhaber-Gesellschaft. In K. R. Wagner, *Mitarbeiterbeteiligung Visionen für eine Gesellschaft von Teilhabern* (pp. 27-31). Wiesbaden: Gabler.

Park, R., Kruse, D., & Sesil, J. (2004). Does employee ownership enhance firm survival. In P. V., & A. Robinson, *Advances in the economic analysis of participatory and self-managed firms* (pp. 3-33). Greenwich: JAI Press.

Renaud, S. (2006). *Dynamic efficiency of supervisory-board-codetermination in Germany.* Jena: Industrial Relation and Social Standard in an Internationalized Economy.

Reuter, E. (1994). Technologiemanagement. Strategien, Prozesse, Instrumente im integrierten Technologie Konzern. In E. Zahn, *Technologiemanagement und Technologien für das Management* (pp. 251-258). Stuttgart.

Rösler, P. (2012, Janury 21). Interview mit der Rheinischen Post: Wir schicken Beamte nach Athen. (RheinischePost, Interviewer)

Schmitt, U. (2002). Enron eine Pleite mit System. *Die Welt.*

Schneider, H. J. (1996). Mitarbeiter als Mitgesellschafter. *Personal*, 112-116.

Sinn, H. W. (1999). *IFO Standpunkt Nr. 3: Zehn Jahre Aufschwung Ost.* Munich: Information und Forschungs Institut.

Solms, H. O. (2002). Mitarbeiterbeteiligung aus der Sicht der FDP. In K. R. Wagner, *Mitarbeiterbeteiligung Visionen für eine Gesellschaft von Teilhabern* (pp. 192-195). Wiesbaden: Gabler.

von Bismarck, O. (1924/1935). *Gesammelte Werke (Friedrichsruher Ausgabe)*, Band 9. O. Stollberg & Co.

von Thünen, J. H. (1850). *Der isolierte Staat in Beziehung auf Landwirtschaft und Nationalökonomie, Zweiter Teil: Der naturgemäße Arbeitslohn und dessen Verhältnis zum Zinsfuß und zur Landrente.* Rostock.

Wallraff, S. J. (1960). Mitbestimmung und Eigentumsbildung der Arbeitnehmer. In W. Kunz, *Mitbestimmung und Miteigentum in Europa* (pp. 14-35). Freiburg: Romcah Verlag.

Wintermann, J. (2000). Das Modell Bertelsmann. Wie derGütersloher Medienkonzern deine Beschäftigten mittels Genussscheinen an den Gewinnen beteiligt. *Die Welt.*

Wunderer, R. (1995). Entwicklung von Arbeitnehmern zu Mitunternehmern. In E. Elschen, *Unternehmenssicherung und Unternehmensentwicklung* (pp. 32-52). Stuttgart.

Wunderer, R. (2002). HistorischeWurzeln und alternative Ansätze des Mitunternehmertums. In K. R. Wagner, *Mitarbeiterbeteiligung Visionen für eine Gesellschaft von Teilhabern* (pp. 17-27). Wiesbaden: Gabler.

Appendices

Appendix 1: Employee ownership and Mitbestimmung research terms and translation

Belegschaftsaktie	Employee Ownership
Eigentum	Ownership
Eigentumsbeteiligung	Ownership Share
Investitionslohn	Investment Salary
Investivlohn	Investment Salary
Mitarbeiter	Employee
Mitarbeiteraktie	Employee's Share
Mitarbeiterbeteiligung	Employee Participation
Mitbestimmung	Codetermination
Miteigentum	Co-Ownership
Miteigentümber	Co-Owner
Mitunternehmer	Joint Venturer
Volksaktie	Citizen Share
Volkskapitalismus	Citizen Capitalism
Volksbeteiligung	Citizen Participation

Appendix 2: List of archives, databases, collections, and institutions

This is a list of the main databases and collections we consulted to collect our qualitative data in Germany.

AGP Budesverband für Mitarbeiterbeteiligung
Der Spiegel Archive
Die Welt Archive
Die Zeit Archive
DigiZeitschriften
Frankfurter Allgemeine Zeitung Archive
Harvard Widener Library
IFO Center of Economic Studies
Institute für Arbeit und Berufsforschung
Konard Adenauerstiftung
Ludwig Erhard Stiftung
Süddeutsche Zeitung Archive

Financial participation in Germany: Management's and works councils' view

Simon Fietze, Wenzel Matiaske & Verena Tobsch[1]

Abstract

In Germany forms of financial participation are still not very common among firms. Whereas financial participation in Anglo-American and in some European countries is standard for human resource management since many years, it has been implemented hesitantly in Germany last but not least due to scepticism of labour unions. By means of a large-scale representative survey conducted in 1,200 firms between 2007/2008 within a project for the German Hans-Boeckler-Stiftung we investigate the prevalence, intensity, motives, and experiences of profit sharing and share ownership in Germany. Based on the organisational concept known as resource dependence approach we analyse determinants of implementing financial participation for all private sector companies in Germany. Furthermore, we explore the influence of several firm specific variables and motives for establishing at least one form of financial participation on the participation rate of employees. The second step of our analysis is focused on the assessment of financial participation by employers (management) and by employees (work councils). We show how strong work councils were involved during implementation of plans for profit sharing or share ownership and which problems are seen for employees.

---

1 Simon Fietze (corresponding author): Assistant Professor at the Department of Marketing and Management, University of Southern Denmark, Campus Sønderborg, Denmark, email: simonf@sam.sdu.dk
Wenzel Matiaske: Full professor at the Institute for Personnel and Employment, Helmut Schmidt University/University of the Federal Armed Forces Hamburg, Germany and Research Professor at the German Institute for Economic Research (DIW Berlin), email: matiaske@hsu-hh.de
Verena Tobsch: Senior Researcher and Partner of the Institute for Empirical Social Sciences and Economic Research (INES Berlin), Germany, email: vtobsch@ines-berlin.de

1. Introduction

The German market economy is based on the understanding that the state intervenes to create a social equilibrium. It is an important basic principle of such a regulated market economy (social market economy) that employees are entitled to a fair share of the company's profit to which they give their manpower. This is also the focus of the German law on tax incentives for employee share ownership (Law on Employee Share Ownership in the version of 7 March 2009, BGBl. I: 451. Bundesministerium für Arbeit und Soziales, 2008). However, the employees' fair share in the company's profit that is demanded can be defined and realised in different ways: e.g. as a share of the employees' remuneration in national income and respective wage agreements, or as a financial participation scheme combined with state incentives. Regarding the use of 'quasi-corporate remuneration schemes', i.e. profit sharing as well as employee share ownership, Germany can be considered as an rather underdeveloped country.

In Anglo-Saxon countries and especially in the U.S., models of financial participation have been regarded as an immanent part of human resource management since the 1980s. The concepts of strategic human resource management that were developed in those days (Beer et al., 1985; Devanna et al., 1981; Fombrun et al., 1984) emphasize the relevance of strategic incentives (appraisal, remuneration and participation schemes) with regard to achieving long-term strategic aims. However, due to different labour market setups, the human resource management of U.S. companies is faced with other problems in terms of motivating and retaining staff compared to German companies. A comparison of fluctuation rates between these countries (Weller, 2007) underpins this argument. Yet, in the U.S. the increasing implementation of financial participation can rather be traced back to state incentives than attributed to a 'participation philosophy' of human resource management. Koch (1993) reports that the number of companies with employee participation in company assets increased dramatically in the U.S. since tax breaks were introduced in 1975, from 1,601 to 9,800 in 1992. While roughly 11.3 million or 10 per cent of U.S. employees were already equity shareholders and received part of their remuneration in the form of shares in 1992, it raised to, according to a study of the U.S. Global Social Survey from 2006, 20 million or 17 per cent of all U.S. employees who own shares of the company they work for via employee share ownership. Moreover, 10.6 million or 9.3 per cent hold employee stock options (NCEO, 2007).

Thus, quasi-entrepreneurial remuneration systems are not only of interest from an human resource policy perspective. State subsidies – like in the U.S. – can be a crucial external variable, stimulating the utilisation of quasi-entrepreneurial instruments. Against this background, it is of theoretical, as well as practical interest, which forms of financial participation are practised in Germany and which reasons and obstacles companies find therein.

This study is based on a representative survey in businesses. We outline the methodology in section 2 and report our findings regarding the spread, intensity and reasons for financial participation in Germany. Furthermore we contrast the views of management and works councils (section 3). Following this descriptive outline, we show the results of multivariate estimations of the determinants for the implementation of financial participation schemes, as well as the influence of these parameters on the intensity of utilising these instruments (section 4). The final discussion (section 5) summarises the empirical findings and gives a brief outlook for future research.

2. Aim and design of the study

The aim of the study that is summarised here was a representative capture of the utilisation and intensity of financial participation on a corporate level in order to give a comprehensive overview of the current situation in Germany. This covers information regarding concrete forms and arrangements of quasi-entrepreneurial remuneration schemes, the motivation behind them, experience and reasons to refrain from them, as well as questions regarding interlinking with non-financial forms of employee participation. To realise these aims, a survey was initially carried out among staff managers of businesses based in Germany (business survey). That was followed by a second survey in those businesses with works council or other employee representation. In this second survey (works council survey) a member of the works council or the employee interest group respectively was interviewed. The works council survey was mainly conducted in order to contrast the employees' and their representatives' views and experience with the aims and motives of the employers. This should yield more information about the role of works councils and employee representatives during the implementation process of financial participation, also with respect to their overall exertion of influence.[2]

Population of the business survey are all companies[3] in Germany with a minimum of 150 staff members. The sampling procedure was carried out by simple random selection by means of an industrial premises directory. A total of 1,201 interviews were conducted with staff managers, managing directors or senior executives. The standardised interviews were conducted via telephone in November 2007 (CATI – computer assisted telephone interview).[4]

Out of all private-sector businesses with a completed interview those who utilise financial participation schemes and have a works council or some other form of employee interest group were contacted again for the second survey. In that survey, which was conducted roughly six months later, we managed to interview a member of the works council or an employee representative via CATI from a total of 121 businesses.

Since the market research institute that carried out the interviews provided a unique (anonymous) identifier of the data, it is possible to link both surveys directly on company level.

The following evaluations are limited to private sector companies, i.e. public services enterprises and institutions were excluded from the analysis, because they don't have any form of employee financial partici-

---

2 The survey took place within the scope of the project 'Entrepreneurial elements in the new remuneration policy' supported by the Hans-Boeckler-Foundation, project no. S-2006-874-3 B and was carried out by the market research institute Produkt +Markt.

3 The term 'business' refers to industrial premises, i.e. it can also be a branch office or a subsidiary of a corporation. This definition is in accordance with the differentiation of the IAB Establishment Panel or the WSI Works Council Survey. Moreover, taking the Establishment History Panel of the Federal Employment Agency (BA) as our population, this definition yields comparative figures that were used to verify the representativeness of the sample.

4 The target population comprises 24,933 businesses with a minimum of 150 employees (according to a special analysis of the Establishment History Panel of the Federal Employment Agency (BA) from 30 June 2007). Due to fluctuations the sampling procedure of our business survey contained businesses with at least 100 employees. By means of a screening question we verified whether at least 150 people were currently (November 2007) employed. We targeted 1,200 interviews (net sample). Based on the adjusted gross sample (6,589 businesses) this is equivalent to a response rate of 18.2 per cent. 13.5 per cent of the companies or respondents, respectively, could not be reached. 68.3 per cent refused to participate or cancelled the interview.

pation. The results are weighted and projected for all private-sector companies located in Germany with a minimum of 150 employees.

3. Financial participation in Germany – prevalence, intensity, motives and obstacles

Up to now only a few quantitative studies have examined the occurrence of financial participation in Germany. That is mainly due to the fact that data sources regarding financial participation in Germany are lacking. Data sources accessible for research are the IAB (German Institute for Employment Research) Establishment Panel and the WSI (Economic and Social Science Institute) Works Council Survey – both are survey data on business level. On individual level the Socio-economic Panel Study (SOEP), the Microcensus and the European Working Condition Survey (EWCS) are possible alternatives. However, the accessible information with regard to use, design and impact of quasi-entrepreneurial remuneration concepts is not very comprehensive, as the topic of financial participation is only covered marginally and not the main focus of these surveys. The WSI Works Council Survey of 2007 is the only exception (Bispinck & Brehmer, 2008; Bispinck, 2008). Based on these data, though, we can only make statements for businesses with a works council; information about businesses with other forms of employee representation or none remains hidden.

However studies on financial participation in Germany show, that there has been no significant increase of importance over the past years. There only have been shifts in the number of employees participating, between East and West Germany and in different industries (Bellmann & Leber, 2007). According to results of the EPOC (Employee Direct Participation in Organisational Change) study 1996 and the Cranet (Cranfield Network on Comparative Human Resource Management) study 1996/2000, Germany belongs to the middle-ranking countries with respect to the utilisation of quasi-entrepreneurial remuneration schemes, such as Sweden, Denmark, Austria and Belgium (Hofmann & Holzner, 2002; Pendleton et al., 2001; Poutsma, 2001). Yet, the most cited studies only analyse the prevalence and intensity of quasi-entrepreneurial remuneration schemes and are based on out-dated data. The study presented here will close the gap and provides both a description of the current situation in Germany and a more comprehensive insight into the design and implementation of financial participation as well as subsequent experiences.

3.1 Prevalence and intensity of financial participation

There are no legal incentives for performance-related remuneration in Germany. This however is not the case when looking at employee share ownership, even if it is not yet widespread: legislation provides regulations to promote share ownership and capital acquisition (via tax reduction). Nevertheless, (moderate) changes can be observed over a longer period of time based on the studies quoted in the previous section and by means of our business survey. We asked the management of businesses which use some form of financial participation when it was introduced. As a result there is a clear increase for both forms of quasi-entrepreneurial remuneration schemes – i.e. profit sharing and share ownership – over the years (Figure 1).

Figure 1. Implementation of financial participation in private enterprise companies in Germany (cumulative number).

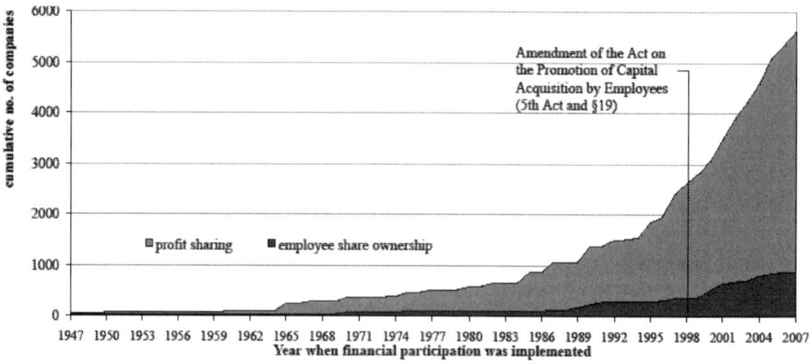

Note. Based on all private sector businesses in Germany with a minimum of 150 employees and financial participation scheme, own calculations.

While employee share ownership was just a marginal phenomenon for a long time, a first increase can be noted in the mid-1980s, which is probably due to a wider spread of target agreement schemes and staff appraisals as a means of assessing remuneration (cf. for example Heiden 2007). The increase of businesses with employee share ownership schemes after 1998 partly can be ascribed, among other things, to an extensive revision of tax incentives in Germany. However, this did not have the desired effect, as is indicated by the continuously low spread later on and the implementation of the new law on the expansion of tax incentives for employee share ownership ten years later (Bundesministerium für Arbeit und Soziales, 2008).

Based on our survey it can be stated that currently nearly one third of all private sector companies with 150 employees or more have implemented some form of profit sharing (Table 1). 5.8 per cent are planning to introduce a profit sharing scheme in the near future whereas share ownership can only be found in 4.9 per cent of the companies, while nearly one per cent is planning to introduce an employee share ownership scheme.

Table 1. Use of financial participation (in percentage)

	Profit sharing	Share ownership
Existent	31.2	4.9
Planned	5.8	0.9
Abandoned	1.3	0.6
Non-existent	61.7	93.5

Note. Based on all private-sector businesses in Germany with a minimum of 150 employees and financial participation scheme, own calculations.

Table 2. Share of companies with financial participation by legal form (in percentage)

	Profit sharing	Share ownership
Sole proprietorship	(-)	(-)
Partnership	(-)	(-)
GmbH/GmbH & Co. KG[a]	31.2	3.5
AG/KGaA[b]	57.0	23.4
Other	15.3	3.4

Note. Based on all private sector businesses in Germany with a minimum of 150 employees and financial participation scheme, own calculations.
(-) case number too small.
[a] Ltd./Limited partnership with a limited liability company as general partner.
[b] plc/partnerships limited by shares.

Financial participation is widespread especially among joint stock companies and partnerships limited by shares (Table 2). More than half of the businesses (57 per cent) use some form of profit sharing and almost one quarter (23.4 per cent) use some form of share ownership. In addition, a good third of all limited liability companies share their profits with employees while employee share ownership plays rather a minor role with a share of only 3.5 per cent.

There are also differences with respect to the size of enterprise as expected. More than every fourth company with 150 to 249 employees and every third company with 250 to 499 employees has a profit sharing scheme (Table 3).

Table 3. Share of companies with profit sharing according by business size, industry sector and region (in percentage)

	Location of industrial premises		Company headquarters		Total
	West	East	Germany	Abroad	
Business size					
150-249 employees	32.3	7.4	25.1	50.0	27.5
250-499 employees	33.1	32.2	32.3	41.8	32.9
500 and more employees	39.5	36.0	37.6	53.3	39.0
Industry sector					
Agriculture and forestry, fishery	(-)	(-)	(-)	(-)	(-)
Energy, mining and water supply	(-)	(-)	52.3	(-)	51.8
Processing industries	38.0	35.5	37.1	40.4	37.8
Consumer goods	22.8	(-)	18.3	(-)	20.1
Raw material processing	36.0	(-)	35.0	(-)	37.0
Capital goods	44.7	(-)	46.8	37.5	45.1
Building	(-)	(-)	(-)	(-)	(-)
Service industries	31.9	13.3	26.1	(-)	28.1
Trade and repair	40.2	(-)	36.3	(-)	37.9
Transport and communications	33.4	(-)	27.1	(-)	29.0
Credit and insurance industries	50.7	(-)	49.9	(-)	49.9
Services mainly for businesses	33.1	(-)	22.9	(-)	25.4
Other services	19.1	(-)	16.9	(-)	19.5
Other	(-)	(-)	(-)	(-)	(-)
Total	33.8	18.3	29.5	47.6	31.2

Note. Based on all private sector businesses in Germany with a minimum of 150 employees and financial participation scheme, own calculations.
(-) case number too small.

The situation is different for employee share ownership (Table 4). Only 3.8 per cent and 6.1 per cent, respectively, of the businesses of the above mentioned sizes let their employees have a share in their assets. It is not surprising that mostly large enterprises with 500 or more employees make use of financial participation schemes. They usually have a personnel department that practises professional human resource management and that also includes financial participation schemes. Smaller businesses (with 150 to 249 employees) use these quasi-entrepreneurial remuneration practices less frequently, possibly due to the high costs and the considerable effort involved. A comparison between West and East Germany shows only a small difference with respect to the connection between company size and the use of employee financial participation, with a slightly larger number of companies willing to share in West Germany.

Table 4. Share of companies with employee share ownership by business size, industry sector and region (in percentage)

	Location of industrial premises		Company headquarters		Total
	West	East	Germany	Abroad	
Business size					
150-249 employees	3.7	3.9	3.0	10.6	3.8
250-499 employees	6.9	1.6	6.0	8.6	6.1
500 and more employees	6.4	5.9	5.4	15.2	6.3
Industry sector					
Agriculture and forestry, fishery	(-)	(-)	(-)	(-)	(-)
Energy, mining and water supply	(-)	(-)	2.3	(-)	2.9
Processing industries	5.7	3.4	5.5	5.6	5.5
Consumer goods	2.6	(-)	1.6	(-)	2.3
Raw material processing	6.0	(-)	5.7	(-)	5.9
Capital goods	6.7	(-)	7.0	4.4	6.4
Building	(-)	(-)	(-)	(-)	(-)
Service industries	5.3	2.1	3.7	(-)	4.6
Trade and repair	4.5	(-)	3.8	(-)	6.0
Transport and communications	4.0	(-)	4.2	(-)	3.9
Credit and insurance industries	6.1	(-)	6.0	(-)	6.0
Services mainly for businesses	10.3	(-)	6.0	(-)	6.9
Other services	2.0	(-)	0.8	(-)	1.5
Other	(-)	(-)	(-)	(-)	(-)
Total	5.2	3.5	4.4	10.7	4.9

Note. Based on all private sector businesses in Germany with a minimum of 150 employees and financial participation scheme, own calculations.
(-) case number too small.

In terms of location of the respective headquarters, it was found that financial participation schemes occur more frequently in companies with foreign headquarters (Table 3 and 4). One reason for that could be the fact that financial participation is more widespread in other European countries (e.g. France, Great Britain) and in the U.S., where this kind of additional remuneration already has a longer tradition (Kabst et al., 2006). It can be assumed that foreign companies transfer their human resource strategies and instruments to their German subsidiaries because of positive experiences gained in their home countries.

Due to a large share of small businesses in Germany further differences in the spread of financial participation can be found in the various industry sectors (Bellmann & Leber, 2007). Profit sharing is widespread in the mining industry, energy and water supply, as well as in financial services and insurances, where it is implemented by half of all businesses (Table 3). Equally willing to share are companies from the capital goods industry, from commerce and repair, and raw material processing. The distribution across industry sectors is similar when looking at employee share ownership (Table 4). 5.5 per cent of businesses in the manufacturing industry and 4.6 per cent of service enterprises offer their employees some form of share ownership.

Another indicator to estimate the importance of financial participation in businesses is the average number of employees who share the company's success (intensity)[5]. In businesses with profit sharing an average of two thirds of all employees can participate in the success (Table 5), whereby this figure with an average of 77.7 per cent is slightly higher in East Germany than in West Germany (65.7 per cent).

That means that although less businesses offer their employees profit-sharing schemes in East Germany, the participation rate is significantly higher than in West German businesses. This is caused by the unequal development of small and large businesses in East and West Germany (Bellmann & Möller 2006). Comparing the intensity of financial participation according to business size classes, size has again a positive effect for businesses with profit sharing: The bigger the size of a company, the more employees can have their financial share in the company's success. Not only do larger businesses implement some form of profit sharing more frequently, but they also do this on a larger scale by offering it to the vast majority of their staff (e.g. on average 71.5 per cent in businesses with 500

5 Business representatives were asked: 'Which groups of employees does your business allow to partake in the business' profit (respectively assets) or allow profit sharing (respectively share ownership)?' It is therefore the maximum possible, and not the actual number of employees who participate actively.

or more employees). With regard to the location of headquarters there is only a small difference for businesses with profit sharing. Looking at employee share ownership the rate is on a very high level with an average of 85.9 per cent of employees per company.

Table 5. Intensity of financial participation by size, industry sector and region (average percentage of employees participating per company)

	Participation rate Profit sharing	Share ownership
Business size		
150-249 employees	64.5	(-)
250-499 employees	67.0	(-)
500 and more employees	71.5	(-)
Industry sector		
Agriculture and forestry, fishery	(-)	(-)
Energy, mining and water supply	(-)	(-)
Processing industries	69.9	(-)
Consumer goods	(-)	(-)
Raw material processing	72.4	(-)
Capital goods	67.5	(-)
Building	(-)	(-)
Service industries	64.6	(-)
Trade and repair	59.4	(-)
Transport and communications	(-)	(-)
Credit and insurance industries	(-)	(-)
Services mainly for businesses	(-)	(-)
Other services	(-)	(-)
Other	(-)	(-)
Region		
Location of industrial premises		
West Germany	65.7	84.7
East Germany	77.7	(-)
Company headquarters		
Germany	66.6	92.1
Abroad	67.8	(-)
Total	66.8	85.9

Note. Based on all private sector businesses in Germany with a minimum of 150 employees and financial participation scheme, own calculations.

3.2 Motives for introducing financial participation schemes

Motives and reasons for introducing financial participation schemes in businesses have already been found in other studies (Kronberger et al., 2006; Schwarb et al., 2001, amongst others). We therefore asked our interview partners from those businesses with financial participation to rate the given motives with regard to the importance at the time of introduction of financial participation schemes in their companies. They were also requested to assess the same aspects with regard to the company's satisfaction (from the point of view of the interviewees) after the participation schemes had been implemented. Therefore the difference between importance and satisfaction can be considered to act as an indicator for the achievement of these objectives.

Motives for introducing financial participation schemes are multifaceted and refer, according to the executives, usually to aspects of work efficiency, initiative and staff retention as well as the company's image and climate. On average our interview partners mentioned an increase in motivation, better performance, a distinct entrepreneurial attitude, as well as improving staff retention as the most important motives for launching a profit sharing scheme (Table 6). Introducing a more flexible remuneration scheme and improving the corporate climate still played an important role, while improving chances in staff recruitment, enhancing corporate image and decreasing staff turnover were considered only partly important. The latter aspect and also a reduction of absenteeism are frequently mentioned as an effect of introducing financial participation in the literature (Schwarb et al., 2001; Strotmann, 2002, amongst others). Business representatives did not assess these as important motives, though.

Looking at the average satisfaction rated by companies with profit sharing schemes we receive an almost identical image (Table 6). The satisfaction with an increase in motivation, better performance, a distinct entrepreneurial attitude and improved staff retention are top priority, while the reduction of absenteeism ranks last. All in all, the 'aims' mentioned have been met satisfactorily on average from the surveyed businesses' point of view.

Individual deviations between the ratings of importance and satisfaction (difference) indicate whether expectations were exceeded (positive difference) or missed (negative difference). Even if the business representatives stated that they were satisfied with the increase in motivation and improved performance, entrepreneurial attitude and better staff retention, the differences show that the expectations with regard to theses aspects could not be fully met. In contrast, expectations regarding the motives of a reduction of absenteeism and lower staff turnover were exceeded.

For businesses with employee share ownership schemes we surveyed three additional motives regarding share ownership, of which only the aspect 'employees become co-entrepreneurs' was rated as important (Table 6). Moreover, the rating of the aspects is analogous to the assessment of those businesses with profit sharing schemes. Improved motivation and better performance, improved staff retention and employees' distinct entrepreneurial attitude were also rated the most important motives by the interviewees. Having more flexible remuneration schemes and reducing absenteeism are equally assessed as less important by business representatives. The other motives – amongst others those related to company assets like increase of liquidity and equity capital, respectively – were only rated partly important.

The average answers from companies with employee share schemes show a similar order as in the expected values with regard to satisfaction (Table 6). Business representatives were most satisfied with the improved retention of staff, the increase in motivation, better employee performance and that co-workers become co-entrepreneurs. Aspects like 'more flexible remuneration schemes' and 'reduction of absenteeism' were less satisfactory for the businesses we surveyed, but these objectives also played a minor role for the introduction of a profit-sharing scheme (were less important).

Looking at the degree to which objectives were achieved (difference), businesses with employee share ownership schemes also have a close match with expectations, whereby the satisfaction with the objectives mentioned was generally a little less than in businesses with profit-sharing schemes (Table 6). Even if those companies that had a higher retention of staff were on average most satisfied, this objective – compared with the importance when introducing the employee share scheme – was just barely achieved, but not fully.

Table 6. Importance of motives for financial participation, satisfaction and achievement (means)

	Profit sharing Importance	Satisfaction	Diff.
Increasing motivation and performance	1.54	1.94	-0.40***
Distinct entrepreneurial attitude	1.77	2.08	-0.31***
Higher staff retention	2.02	2.19	-0.17***
Higher flexibility of staff remuneration	2.29	2.20	0.09
Improving business climate	2.53	2.52	0.01
Improving chances in recruitment	2.74	2.63	0.11
Improving business image	2.82	2.64	0.18
Reducing staff turnover	2.88	2.55	0.33***
Reducing absenteeism	3.27	2.89	0.38***
	Employee share ownership		
Increasing motivation and performance	1.95	2.25	-0.30
Distinct entrepreneurial attitude	2.14	2.43	-0.29
Higher staff retention	1.97	2.18	-0.21**
Higher flexibility of staff remuneration	3.72	3.39	0.33
Improving business climate	2.72	2.77	-0.05
Improving chances in recruitment	3.16	2.85	0.31
Improving business image	2.60	2.46	0.14
Reducing staff turnover	2.98	3.04	-0.06
Reducing absenteeism	3.84	3.78	0.06
Employees become co-entrepreneurs (#)	2.14	2.37	-0.23
Increasing company's liquidity (#)	3.28	3.07	0.21
Increasing company's equity capital (#)	3.33	3.09	0.24

Note. Based on all private sector businesses in Germany with a minimum of 150 employees and financial participation scheme, own calculations.
Scale importance: (1) very important, (2) important (3) partly important, (4) less important, (5) not important.
Scale satisfaction: (1) very satisfied, (2) satisfied (3) partly satisfied, (4) less satisfied, (5) not satisfied.
(#) These motives were only asked in businesses with employee share ownership.
Significance level: <0.01(***), <0.05(**), <0.1(*).

3.3 Management's motives and target achievement from the works council's perspective – contrasting two views

The WSI Works Council Survey 2007 (Bispinck & Brehmer, 2008; Bispinck, 2008) provides first results about an assessment of financial participation from the employees' view. In contrast, our study includes a broader spectrum of financial participation – profit sharing as well as share ownership – and allows a direct link of managements' and works councils' view. Respondents of our works council survey were therefore asked to assess the same motives as the company representatives. Members of the works council first rated the motives from their own point of view, according to their importance for the company and for management, respectively, at the time of introducing financial participation schemes. It was of particular interest to what extent the statements of company representatives deviated from those of the works councils. These deviations might indicate some potential for conflict between management and works council. Generally the works councils believe that the motives mentioned were less important to management than what company representatives estimated in the first survey (Table 7).

Table 7. Importance of motives and satisfaction - two views (means)

	Importance of management's motives according to views (means[a])		
	MGMT	WCEIG	Diff.
Increasing motivation and performance	1.46	1.83	-0.37***
Improving business climate	2.40	2.45	-0.05
Improving business image	2.78	2.38	0.40
Improving chances in recruitment	2.61	2.62	-0.01
Distinct entrepreneurial attitude	1.75	2.36	-0.61***
Reducing absenteeism	3.12	3.31	-0.19
Reducing staff turnover	2.82	2.72	0.10
Higher staff retention	1.93	2.20	-0.27*
Higher flexibility of staff remuneration	2.18	2.79	-0.61***
	Satisfaction with motives according to views (means[b])		
Increasing motivation and performance	1.82	2.41	-0.59***
Improving business climate	2.32	2.89	-0.57
Improving business image	2.50	2.42	0.08
Improving chances in recruitment	2.49	2.65	-0.16
Distinct entrepreneurial attitude	1.94	2.70	-0.76***
Reducing absenteeism	2.70	3.22	-0.52***
Reducing staff turnover	2.41	2.74	-0.33*
Higher staff retention	2.04	2.47	-0.43***
Higher flexibility of staff remuneration	1.90	3.00	-1.10***

Note. Based on all private sector businesses in Germany with a minimum of 150 employees, financial participation scheme and works council or other form of employee representation, own calculations.

[a] scale from 1 'very important' to 5 'not important'.

[b] scale from 1 'very important' (MGMT)/'fully met' (WCEIG) to 5 'not satisfied'/'not met'; MGMT = management; WCEIG = works council/employee interest group.

Significance level: <0.01(***), <0.05(**), <0.1(*).

Differences between the two views are, however, only statistically significant for some motives. The increase in employees' motivation and performance was most important from management's point of view. Works councils agree with that, even though they evaluate the importance slightly lower on the scale. Promoting a distinct entrepreneurial attitude among employees was important to very important for management, while it was only important to partly important to the works councils. There is a similar picture as far as more flexible remuneration schemes and staff retention is concerned. It needs to be mentioned, though, that on average the ranking of motives in the works councils' assessment matches roughly with the ranking of the company representatives. This also indicates that company representatives communicated their motives to staff in order to prevent possible potential for conflict. Differences in the rating of individual motives suggest either an overestimation of the motivation by the companies or a diverging assessment of the degree of importance by the works councils.

In the general assessment, however, objectives were only partly achieved from the point of view of works councils and employee representatives. Comparison with the company representatives' satisfaction shows particular differences with regard to a more flexible remuneration. While company representatives are rather satisfied, it has only been partly achieved from the works councils' point of view. The same applies to the promotion of an entrepreneurial attitude among employees, reduction of absenteeism, an increase in motivation and performance as well as improved staff retention. Although these objectives were only partly met from the works councils' point of view, the ranking (even if only partly) corresponds with the satisfaction ranking of the company representatives. Works councils and employee representatives consider increased motivation and better staff performance as most likely achieved, while reduction of absenteeism was considered least achieved (Table 7). Like the other results this outcome shows that the motives behind the introduction of profit sharing in a company were well communicated among staff. The varying assessment of the degree of fulfilment might indicate that company representatives are anxious to assess their motivation positively.

3.4 Obstacles for financial participation

Besides motives, objectives and experiences with quasi-entrepreneurial remuneration schemes, the low prevalence of financial participation schemes among businesses in Germany raises the question, which obsta-

Table 8. Obstacles for financial participation according to use of participation (median)

	Profit sharing				
	Existent	Planned	Abandoned	Non-existent	Total
Costs too high	3.17	3.30	3.03	3.14	3.16
Too complicated	3.23	3.23	4.57	3.37	3.33
Effort too high	3.19	3.17	4.31	3.45	3.36
No direct benefit noticeable	3.63	3.59	3.30	3.42	3.50
Employees get too much insight into financial data	3.53	3.72	4.64	3.46	3.51
Legal uncertainty	3.55	3.38	4.60	3.68	3.63
Loss of company's authority	3.85	4.03	4.01	3.77	3.82
Employees not interested	3.96	3.67	4.79	3.86	3.89
Resistance of works council/ employee representatives	3.56	3.21	4.75	4.16	3.93
Staff resistance	3.92	3.91	4.95	4.28	4.15
	Employee share ownership				
Costs too high	3.00	3.19	2.96	3.23	3.22
Too complicated	2.78	2.19	4.40	3.25	3.22
Effort too high	3.62	3.78	4.96	3.24	3.27
No direct benefit noticeable	2.77	2.82	2.54	3.33	3.30
Employees get too much insight into finances	3.28	2.98	4.42	3.36	3.36
Legal uncertainty	3.17	3.41	3.57	3.51	3.49
Loss of company's authority	3.74	4.31	4.50	3.52	3.54
Employees not interested	3.64	3.53	4.15	3.82	3.81
Resistance of works council/ employee representatives	4.24	3.30	4.96	4.08	4.08
Staff resistance	4.21	3.74	4.96	4.21	4.21

Note. Based on all private sector businesses in Germany with a minimum of 150 employees, own calculations.
Scale: (1) applies fully, (2) applies mostly, (3) applies partly, (4) applies less, (5) does not apply.

cles were perceived from the businesses' perspective. In our business survey we therefore asked the interviewees of all participating companies to rate possible reasons that speak against the introduction of financial participation schemes from their point of view. The statements are fairly clear, irrespective of whether a company has had experience with financial participation schemes or not. Most companies assess the introduction of a scheme as too costly, too laborious and too complicated (Table 8). Moreover, some of the interviewees did not see a recognisable benefit and they were afraid of a loss of the company's independence, partly due to the increased insight of employees into the company's financial data when deciding for a financial participation scheme. On the other hand, potential resistance of staff and trade unions or employee interest groups, as well as a lack of interest from staff, were not seen as obstacles for introducing financial participation schemes (Table 8).

Comparing the statements of those businesses with financial participation schemes and those without experience in this field there is only little difference. The trade union's or works council's potential resistance is, all in all, hardly seen as an obstacle for the introduction of a participation schemes, though more from businesses with profit sharing schemes than from businesses without experience in this field.

3.5 Problems from the works council's and employee representatives' perspective

A core factor for a successful implementation of financial participation is the relationship between staff and management (executive board and superiors). A cooperative collaboration and a spirit of trust ensure not only a higher identification of staff with their company and its aims, an increased motivation and a higher commitment, but also make it more likely that a financial participation scheme is used. Bispinck & Brehmer (2008) and Bispinck (2008) state in their evaluation of the WSI Works Council Survey that 'companies where there is a certain amount of friction between management and works council have significantly less likely employee share ownership schemes'. The results of our study can also be seen against this background.

It is noteworthy that 44.5 per cent of the interviewed works councils from companies with profit share schemes and 32.2 per cent of the interviewees from companies with share ownership schemes gave no answer to the question about changes and potential problems that the introduction of financial participation might entail. This might suggest that one third to almost half of the works councils did not want to answer this question or really had no problems – no specific interpretation is possible here. The remaining valid statements show that most works councils see problems for profit sharing in the fact that employees have little influence on the company's success, that an inequality is created between staff and superiors, that potential for conflict increases due to strong competition and

Table 9. Problems of financial participation seen by works councils (in percentage)

	Profit sharing	Share ownership
Lack of transparency/ comprehensibility	9.1	5.3
Determination of key indicators	5.0	8.2
Competition/ potential for conflict	10.0	3.5
Expected effects fail to appear (long-term)	1.4	3.7
Employee risk	6.5	4.2
Inequality between staff and supervisors	10.2	9.0
Abuse of financial participation from entrepreneurial point of view	5.1	(-)
Staff has little influence on success	11.2	15.6
Decrease in quality	2.2	(-)
Performance pressure/ responsibility	4.1	(-)
Share amount not sufficient	2.2	8.2
Other	7.4	18.4
No answer	44.5	32.2

Note. Based on all private sector businesses in Germany with a minimum of 150 employees, financial participation scheme and works council, own calculations. A maximum of three problems was asked.
(-) case number too small.
[a] For businesses with both profit sharing and employee share ownership solely problems with profit sharing were used.

that there is a lack of transparency and traceability (Table 9). The latter is of vital importance in connection with productivity: exchange of information, agreement processes and trust building between works council and board of management (Heywood et al. 1998). In businesses with share ownership works councils perceive similar problems, though here the potential for conflict is more in the background, but interviewees see problems in determining key indicators.

From the works councils' perspective the relationship among staff members changed only in approximately 30 per cent of the businesses, whereby 20 per cent of the interviewees reported that cohesion and support among colleagues increased – greatly to moderately (Table 10). In eight per cent of the businesses with financial participation and existing works council the works councils reported that cohesion had decreased – also greatly to moderately. The number of conflicts between staff and superiors changed only in one fourth of the businesses surveyed according to the works councils' assessment. The number of conflicts increased and decreased more or less equally and on average rather moderately (Table

Table 10. Changes in cohesion, support and conflicts between staff and management/supervisors seen by works councils (in percentage)

	Cohesion and support among colleagues		Conflicts between staff and mgmt./supervisors	
Increased	20.4		13.4	
No change noticeable	71.6		75.2	
Decreased	8.0		11.4	
	Increased	Decreased	Increased	Decreased
Very strong	3.4	14.5	3.6	0.0
Strong	54.1	22.4	25.4	19.1
Average	31.6	63.1	49.6	57.6
Low	10.9	0.0	21.4	23.3
Very low	0.0	0.0	0.0	0.0

Note. Based on all private sector businesses in Germany with a minimum of 150 employees, financial participation scheme and works council, own calculations.

10). Cohesion among colleagues changed hardly with the introduction of financial participation – if it did, it changed positively. New conflicts between staff and management hardly arose either. Green & Heywood (2008) analysed the connection between profit sharing and job satisfaction and were able to show that employees tend to be less satisfied with their superior if the company has a profit sharing scheme.

3.6 Linkage of financial and organisational participation

There has been a lively discussion within the field of research on financial participation about the connection between quasi-entrepreneurial remuneration schemes and nonfinancial participation of employees in the company (Backes-Gellner et al., 2002; Poutsma et al., 2006, amongst others). The positive interrelation between financial and direct participation of employees was confirmed by, amongst others, Poutsma (2001), based on the EPOC data, and Pendleton et al. (2001), based on the Cranet data. Bearing this in mind, all companies surveyed in our study were asked which forms of organisational employee participation they use.

Table 11. Share of businesses with organisational employee participation by financial participation (in percentage)

	Without	With
	Financial participation	
Organization participation		
None	31.9	29.0
At least one form	68.1	71.0
Amongst that:		
Staff appraisal/ target agreements***	57.3	66.8
Downward shift of responsibility/decision*	50.8	56.4
Introduction of team work[a]	46.8	52.1
User participation[b]	45.1	48.1
Quality circle	45.0	45.9
(Regular) staff survey	38.0	42.5

Note. Based on all private sector businesses in Germany with a minimum of 150 employees, own calculations.
[a] or independent work groups.
[b] e.g. introduction of new techniques.
Significance level: <0.01(***), <0.05(**), <0.1(*).

The results show, for most forms of participation, that on average more companies with financial participation also involve their staff in organisational decisions than companies without a financial participation scheme (Table 11). Looking at the use of staff appraisals and target agreements, respectively, and at the downward shift of responsibilities and decisions, this clearly becomes evident. It indicates that these forms of participation in decision-making are implemented in order to accompany and to complement financial participation.

Table 12. Agreement to statements regarding financial participation (in percentage and means)

	1	2	3	4	5	Means
It is an appropriate way to let employees participate in the company's favourable economic situation.	44.8	33.6	19.3	1.1	1.1	1.80
Employees are more interested in the company's economic situation.	18.4	41.0	24.8	12.7	3.1	2.41
Employees would like to participate more in important decisions of the company.	16.6	42.4	27.5	10.3	3.2	2.41
Security of employment increases.	11.9	24.9	33.7	17.0	12.4	2.93
Financial participation leads to fairer remuneration.	5.6	26.4	26.9	25.9	15.2	3.19
Financial participation has a negative effect on income security (e.g. employees have to accept loss of income in case of a negative economic situation of the company).	13.7	20.4	19.6	19.9	26.3	3.25
Financial participation limits room for salary negotiations.	8.3	13.1	26.2	27.8	24.5	3.47
Only minor fixed salary increases can be achieved.	6.6	13.5	30.5	21.2	28.2	3.51
Employees are burdened by taking over entrepreneurial risks.	3.4	17.5	26.4	18.6	34.1	3.63
Employees went on trainings to understand key business indicators.	6.0	13.9	12.6	28.5	39.0	3.81

Note. Based on all private sector businesses in Germany with a minimum of 150 employees and financial participation scheme, own calculations.
Scale: (1) fully agree, (2) agree, (3) partly agree, (4) partly disagree, (5) disagree.

3.7 Assessment of financial participation from the works councils' and employee representatives' perspective

For their assessment of financial participation interviewees were asked whether they agree or disagree to individual statements (Table 12). Works councils and employee representatives consider financial participation as an appropriate way to let employees partake in the company's good economic situation. They also confirm that due to financial participation employees are more interested in the company's economic situation and more interested in taking part in important decisions. According to the interviewees' assessment, taking over entrepreneurial risk does not or only partly burden employees. Regarding an increase in employment security the interviewees' assessment is rather mixed: one third of the interviewees agreed to this statement, one third disagrees and one third decided on 'applies partly'. Roughly one third of the interviewees confirm that financial participation leads to fairer remuneration or has a negative effect on employment security. The vast majority, however, does not agree. A majority of the works councils and employee representatives also consider it less applicable that the room for salary negotiations is limited through financial participation and that only little salary increases can be pushed through.

22 per cent of the businesses we surveyed stated that fixed remuneration components were changed into variable ones. According to the assessment of the interviewed works councils ten per cent of the remuneration was transformed on average, which corresponds to just more than a monthly wage or salary. According to the interviewees there was no change in three quarters of the businesses, though.

Finally, works councils were asked about a general assessment of financial participation. Both participation schemes were rated 2.5 on average by the interviewees – 58 per cent rated financial participation as good to very good, 28 per cent as satisfactory, and nearly ten per cent as sufficient and only just under four per cent as poor.

4. Multivariate estimation

In the previous section we presented the results of the business survey by some characteristics but without controlling for multiple effects. Therefore we use multivariate estimation techniques and discuss the results comprehensively. Following Poutsma et al. (2006), we will first look at the influence that different business characteristics might have on the probability of introducing a financial participation scheme in a company – separately for profit sharing and share ownership. We expect several effects according to legal form, size, industry, location of industrial premises and headquarters of the company and therefore treat these as our independent variables. We will also control for the fact that employees are offered profit sharing and share ownership at the same time or as a supplement. Ultimately, we want to check the interrelation between financial and organisational participation. Following Poutsma et al. (2006), we again distinguish between indirect organisational participation (existence of a works council or other forms of staff representation) and direct participation as the sum score of the forms of participation presented in the previous section. Table 13 shows the results (marginal effects[6]) of a logit model estimate for profit sharing and share ownership, respectively.

The statistically significant factors influencing the probability that a business will introduce financial participation are hardly surprising and confirm the findings of previous studies. Business with profit-sharing schemes are more likely to be found in the credit or insurance industry; they also have employee share ownership and are rather incorporated companies (public companies [German: AG], associations limited by shares [German: KGaA] or limited liability companies [German: GmbH]). Furthermore, business size and direct organisational participation have a positive, though small, influence on the probability whether a business has a profit-sharing scheme or not. Results for employee share ownership are less clear. Statistically significant results can only be found for existing profit sharing schemes and foreign headquarters of the company, as well as for the parameters business size and incorporated company (public company [AG], associations limited by shares [KGaA]). Contrary to expectations, there are no significant effects for industry or organisational participation. Considering the legal form, business size and location of businesses there are no differences among industries regarding the implementation of employee share ownership. Also there is no statistically verifiable relationship between organisational and financial participation (share ownership schemes).

Factors influencing the intensity of the use of financial participation were estimated by means of OLS regression, also following Poutsma et al. (2006). Now the dependent variable is the percentage of employees who participate in profit sharing or share ownership schemes. As the participation rate equals zero in businesses that do not have financial participation,

6 In this case a marginal effect indicates by how many percentage points the probability that a business will introduce profit sharing or share ownership changes if the respective independent variable (e.g. company size) increases by one unit. With dummy variables (almost all here, because of nominal scales) the marginal effect is the change in probability (in percentage points) in relation to the respective reference group. Marginal effects can be compared with each other within the estimation – similar to standardised beta values in a basic OLS regression, provided that scales correspond.

we considered only those businesses that have implemented these schemes. The explanatory variables are the same as in our first analysis.

Table 13. Determinants of financial participation – prevalence (logit – marginal effects)

	Probability	
	Profit sharing	Share ownership
Financial participation		
Employee share ownership (ref No)	0.324***	
Profit sharing (ref. No)		0.048***
Organisational participation		
Indirect: works council (ref. None)	0.030	-0.006
Direct: sum score(+)	0.007**	-0.001
Industry sector (ref. building, trade, transport, communications)		
Processing industries		
Raw material processing	0.006	-0.017
Capital goods	0.033	-0.011
Consumer goods	-0.147***	-0.007
Energy and mining	-0.009	0.013
Services		
Credit and insurance industries	0.375***	-0.008
Other services	-0.105*	-0.011
Region		
Location of premises (ref. West Germany)	-0.020	-0.002
Foreign headquarter (ref. Germany)	0.077	0.037***
Business size (logarithmized)	0.046**	0.008*
Legal form (ref. other)		
GmbH/GmbH & Co. KG[a]	0.186***	-0.008
Corporation (AG, KGaA)[b]	0.289***	0.041*
Constant	-0.628***	-0.163***
Case number	992	992
Log likelihood	-592.260	-180.130
LR	84.12**	54.27***
Pseudo R^2	0.079	0.164

Note. Based on all private sector businesses in Germany with a minimum of 150 employees, own calculations.
[a] Ltd./limited partnership with a limited liability company as general partner.
[b] plc/associations limited by shares.
(+) sum of standardized individual variables for the existence of: team work, quality circle, staff survey, target agreements, downward shift of decision making, other (e.g. suggestion system).
Significance level: <0.01(***), <0.05(**), <0.1(*).

Table 14. Determinants of financial participation – intensity (OLS – Beta-Coefficient)

	Participation rate	
	Profit sharing	Share ownership
Financial participation		
Employee share ownership (ref No)	17.38**	
Profit sharing (ref. No)		-10.33
Organisational participation		
Indirect: works council (ref. None)	4.14	-1.57
Direct: sum score(+)	0.76	-1.77
Industry sector (ref. building, trade, transport, communications)		
Processing industries		
Raw material processing	18.42**	-8.65
Capital goods	6.65	18.32
Consumer goods	12.16	38.20
Energy and mining	26.08**	42.82
Services		
Credit and insurance industries	11.18	38.60
Other services	10.35	10.91
Region		
Location of premises (ref. West Germany)	12.93*	29.90
Foreign headquarter (ref. Germany)	-4.80	-8.04
Business size (logarithmized)	-1.30	-3.32
Legal form (ref. other)		
GmbH/GmbH & Co. KG[a]	-9.64	0.00
Corporation (AG, KGaA)[b]	-4.44	24.01
Constant	66.47***	89.28*
Case number	330	50
Adj. R^2	0.097	0.277

Note. Based on all private sector businesses in Germany with a minimum of 150 employees and financial participation scheme, own calculations.
[a] Ltd./limited partnership with a limited liability company as general partner.
[b] plc/associations limited by shares.
(+) sum of standardized individual variables for the existence of: team work, quality circle, staff survey, target agreements, downward shift of decision making, other (e.g. suggestion system).
Significance level: <0.01(***), <0.05(**), <0.1(*).

There are no significant differences for the intensity of share ownership regarding the business characteristics we considered (Table 14). It should be noted here that, on the one hand, the underlying number of cases is very small. On the other hand, the descriptive results of the previous section already show a high level and low variance of participation rates. This means that businesses with share ownership offer this form of financial participation to a vast majority of employees – none of the parameters that we took into account here were essential for the extent. In contrast, several statistically significant determinants could be found for the intensity of profit sharing. For example, the rate of employees participating in profit sharing schemes was 26 percentage points higher in businesses in energy and mining industries in comparison to the reference group (building, trade, transport, communication). For businesses in raw material processing, this value is 18 percentage points higher. Moreover, businesses that not only have a profit sharing, but also an employee share ownership scheme and which are based in East Germany, have a higher participation rate.

5. Conclusion

With these analyses we have presented first results of what is so far the only representative study in Germany that solely and comprehensively investigates the use and spread of quasi-entrepreneurial remuneration schemes in companies – from the point of view of management and works councils. Even if participation schemes are a popular topic in current public and scientific debates, we have evidence that quasi-entrepreneurial remuneration schemes still play a rather insignificant role among German businesses. The business survey confirms, amongst others, the results of the IAB Establishment Panel (Bellmann & Leber, 2007).

The spread of financial participation in Germany is low, yet the average share of employees per company who are involved in a participation scheme is very high. At the same time there is an interrelation between profit sharing and employee share ownership. Companies that have experience with profit sharing schemes will also rather use employee share ownership and vice versa.

The main motives for businesses to introduce financial participation refer primarily, directly or indirectly, to positive effects in productivity. For example, the objective might be that employee motivation increases and performance improves. In addition to that, it is expected from the business representatives' point of view that employees act more like co-entrepreneurs in their company as a result of profit sharing or share ownership and that ultimately staff retention is increased. The latter is probably the critical point when it comes to retaining highly qualified staff in the company and avoiding migration of human capital. Therefore, it is primarily the highly qualified members of staff who participate in the company's success (Bispinck, 2007).

From their point of view works councils assessed the company's motives similarly, though less important. On average the ranking of motives, according to the works councils' assessment roughly corresponds with the ranking of company representatives. There are differences in the assessment of target achievement. A more flexible remuneration has only partly been accomplished from the works councils' perspective, while management boards are rather satisfied.

Obstacles are clearly rated by the companies, whether they have implemented profit sharing or employees share ownership or not, whether they are planning to do so or have even abandoned it again. Most companies feel that introducing a financial participation scheme is too expensive, too complicated and too laborious. Based on the WSI Works Council Survey, Bispinck & Brehmer (2008) and Bispinck (2008) studied the views of works councils on profit sharing, amongst others. They emphasized this form of remuneration as an important point. Ultimately, the implementation of financial participation instruments can only work out if there is a good partnership and climate between company, works council and employees. That should also be clear to companies. From the view of business representatives, neither trade unions nor employee representatives or staff members are considered as obstacles.

Works councils consider the problem that employees have little influence on the company's success, that inequalities are created between staff and superiors and that the potential for conflict increases. However, works councils confirm that financial participation may increase rather than decrease support and cohesion among staff members. They also report that the number of conflicts between superiors and staff members only changed moderately but still on a small scale. Works councils generally consider financial participation as an appropriate way of letting employees partake in the company's success and would rather not agree that salary negotiations are limited or employment security is jeopardized. This is confirmed by a study based on the IAB Establishment Panel 1998. Ugarkovic (2007) concludes that financial participation does not lead lower base salaries but that companies see it as an additional salary component.

Overall the level of utilisation (spread and intensity) is determined the regulatory framework. In Germany the principle of voluntariness between labour and management prevails, following the industrial relations systems. It is obvious that both parties pursue different interests. The bill for the law on tax incentives for employee share ownership came into force in 2009. The German Association of Trade Unions (DGB) welcomed the presented draft and law as 'a step in the right direction' but sees a need for improvement. They criticized, among other things, the low scope (Hexel, 2008). It is likely that it will not have a particular effect on the spread. Furthermore the DGB considers it an essential necessity to provide security for employee share ownership schemes making them low-risk. Employees will not be interested in shifting part of the corporate risk over to their side.

Other countries, e.g. the U.S. and France, have shown that it is possible to increase the spread of financial participation via consistent tax incentive schemes and legal intervention. The reform pursued by the government focuses mainly on adjusting and raising tax deductibles and takes only one form of financial participation into account. Support and promotion of profit sharing schemes remains excluded.

References

Backes-Gellner, U., Kay, R., Schröer, S. & Wolff, K. (2002). Mitarbeiterbeteiligung in kleinen und mittleren Unternehmen. Verbreitung, Effekte, Voraussetzungen. Schriften zur Mittelstandsforschung, 92NF, Bonn, Institut für Mittelstands-forschung.

Beer, M., Spector, B., Lawrence, P. R., Miles, D. Q. & Walton, R. E. (1985). *Human resource management: A general manager's perspective.* New York, London: The Free Press.

Bellmann, L. & Leber, U. (2007). Materielle Mitarbeiterbeteiligung. Geringe Verbreitung, aber hohe Intensität. IAB-Kurzbericht, 13/2007, Nürnberg: Institut für Arbeitsmarkt- und Berufsforschung (IAB).

Bellmann, L. & Möller, I. (2006). Die Betriebe in Deutschland haben Nachholbedarf. IAB-Kurzbericht, 13, Nürnberg: Institut für Arbeitsmarkt- und Berufsforschung (IAB).

Bispinck, R. (2007). Bezahlung nach Erfolg und Gewinn. In: Bispinck, R. (Ed.): *WSI-Tarifarchiv. WSI-Tarifhandbuch 2007.* 57–81.

Bispinck, R. (2008). Gewinnabhängige Bezahlung und Kapitalbeteiligung. Ergebnisse aus der WSI-Betriebsrätebefragung 2007. Vortrag auf der Expertentagung des Projektes 'Quasiunternehmerische Entgeltkonzepte' (11. Juni 2008, Berlin).

Bispinck, R. & Brehmer, W. (2008). Kapitalbeteiligung und Bezahlung nach Gewinn. *WSI-Mitteilungen*, 6, 312–320.

Bundesministerium für Arbeit und Soziales (2008). Regierungsentwurf – Gesetz zur steuerlichen Förderung der Mitarbeiterkapitalbeteiligung. Stand: 18.08.2008.

Devanna, M. A., Fombrun, C. & Tichy, N. M. (1981). Human resources management: A strategie perspective. *Organizational Dynamics*, 51–67.

Fombrun, C., Tichy, N. M. & Devanna, M. A. (Eds.) (1984). *Strategic human resource management*. New York: John Wiley & Sons.

Green, C. & Heywood, J. S. (2008). Profit sharing and the quality of relations with the boss. Working Paper 2008/013, Lancaster: Lancaster University Management School.

Heiden, R. (2007). Entgeltrelevante Zielvereinbarungen aus arbeitsrechtlicher Sicht, *Der Betrieb*, 32, 1705-1709.

Hexel, D. (2008). Stellungnahme des DGB zum Regierungsentwurf eines Gesetzes zur steuerlichen Förderung der Mitarbeiterkapitalbeteiligung. Berlin: Deutscher Gewerkschaftsbund (DGB).

Heywood, J. S., Hubler, O. & Jirjahn, U. (1998). Variable payment schemes and industrial relations: Evidence from Germany. *Kyklos*, 51(2), 237–257.

Hofmann, H. & Holzner, C. (2002). Mitarbeiterkapitalbeteiligung – Ein internationaler Vergleich. *ifo Schnelldienst*, 55(12), 7–13.

Kabst, R., Matiaske, W. & Schmelter, A. (2006). Financial participation in British, French and German organizations: A neoinstitutionalist perspective. *Economic and Industrial Democracy*, 27(4), 565–585.

Koch, T. (1993). *Employee Stock Ownership Plans in den Vereinigten Staaten von Amerika*. München, Mering: Rainer Hampp Verlag.

Kronberger, R., Rauner, A. & Past, H. (2006). Mitarbeiterkapitalbeteiligung aus Sicht der Arbeitgeber. Wien: Wirtschaftskammer Österreich, Abteilung für Finanz und Handelspolitik.

NCEO (2007). New data show widespread employee ownership in U.S. http://www.nceo.org/library/widespread.html (23.10.2008).

Pendleton, A. D., Poutsma, E., Ommeren, J. von & Brewster, C. (2001). Employee share ownership and profit-sharing in the European Union. Luxembourg: European Foundation for the Improvement of Living and Working Conditions.

Poutsma, E. (2001). Recent trends in employee financial participation in the European Union. Luxembourg: European Foundation for the Improvement of Living and Working Conditions.

Poutsma, E., Kalmi, P. & Pendleton, A. D. (2006). The relationship between financial participation and other forms of employee participation: New survey evidence from Europe. *Economic and Industrial Democracy*, 27(4), 637–667.

Schwarb, T. M., Greiwe, S. & Niederer, R. (2001). Erfolgs- und Kapitalbeteiligung von Mitarbeitenden in der Schweiz. Repräsentative Unternehmensbefragung. Schlussbericht. Reihe b: Sonderdruck 2001-w03, Fachhochschule Solothurn Nordwestschweiz.

Strotmann, H. (2002). Zur Bedeutung materieller Mitarbeiterbeteiligung in Baden-Württemberg - Eeine empirische Analyse mit dem IAB-Betriebspanel. Gutachten Gutachten für das Wirtschaftsministerium. Baden-Württemberg. Tübingen: Institut für angewandte Wirtschaftsforschung.

Ugarkovic, M. (2007). *Profit sharing and company performance.* Wiesbaden: DUV (Gabler Edition Wissenschaft)

Weller, I. (2007). *Fluktuationsmodelle. Ereignisanalysen mit dem Sozio-oekonomischen Panel.* München, Mering: Rainer Hampp Verlag.

Works councils and profit sharing in the German metalworking industry

Thomas Haipeter[1]

Abstract

This chapter aims to analyse policy and practice of the works councils in implementing and regulating profit sharing in companies of the metalworking and electrical engineering industry. It will be discussed how the main patterns of regulation of profit sharing in the plants look like, in how far profit sharing is coupled with the broader trend of financialisation of corporate governance in the companies, what the positions and strategies developed by works councils with respect to profit sharing are and, finally what the effects of profit sharing both on the development of wages and on the position of works councils in plant-level labour relations are. The findings are that profit sharing is in many cases initiated by the works councils who negotiate the issue as a compensation for concessions or as an instrument to safe fringe benefits. Whereas profit sharing seems to strengthen the legitimacy of the works councils, it is not part of an encompassing management strategy of financialisation. However, it reflects a changing redistribution of profits between capital and labour and between companies along the value chain.

1. Introduction

The importance of profit sharing is growing in the German economy. For some years now, press and television reports in Germany on high profit sharing bonuses for employees covered by collective agreements have been a regular feature of the spring months. Besides large companies in the chemical industry and banking, these reports tend to focus particularly

---

1 Thomas Haipeter: Prof. Dr., University of Duisburg-Essen, Institute Work, Skills and Training, email: thomas.haipeter@uni-due.de

on the large German car manufacturers and other big and mostly multinational companies. However, little is known about the way profit sharing schemes are regulated in the plants and about the role they play for plant level labour relations and, in particular, the works councils.

In the German system of labour relations, profit sharing can be regulated in two ways: Either as a form of company level fringe benefits or in the form of, mainly, industry level collective bargaining agreements. In both forms codetermination of works councils plays a crucial role. Fringe benefits are the most important issue of works councils' wage policy in the German system of labour relations. Works councils have rights of codetermination according to the Works Constitution Act in case the company wants to change given standards of fringe benefits and wages paid by the companies above the level of the collective bargaining agreements. So works council cannot codetermine if a company pays fringe benefits, but they can codetermine how and to whom they are paid in case they are paid. If profit sharing schemes are based on fringe benefits and not on collective bargaining agreements, they are an issue of codetermination; in the other case it would be the unions to negotiate about profit sharing as an issue of collective bargaining agreements.

But even in case profit sharing is an issue of collective bargaining, it is at the same time an issue of codetermination of works councils. This is the case in some industries like the chemical industry, the banking industry and the energy sector. In the collective bargaining agreements of these industries, profit sharing is dealt with mainly in the way that the Christmas bonus is opened in a certain range for variable payments in the plants, e.g. to depend up on a maximum range from 80 per cent to 120 per cent of the Christmas bonus on the development of profits. This is a framework that usually can and has to be adopted by the plant level actors, management and works councils. They have to decide if and how profit sharing is regulated in the plants. This is why works councils play an important role in the implementation of profit sharing schemes, even if profit sharing is regulated in collective bargaining agreements. However, in most of the industries, among them the metalworking and electrical engineering industry, profit sharing is paid on top of agreed wages in collective bargaining. If not agreed in collective bargaining agreements it is a form of fringe benefits and therefore subject to codetermination in the way it is defined in the Work Constitutions Act.

This chapter aims to analyse policy and practice of the works councils in implementing and regulating profit sharing in companies of the metalworking and electrical engineering industry. It will be discussed how the main patterns of regulation of profit sharing in the plants look like, in how far profit sharing is coupled with the broader trend of financialisation of corporate governance in the companies, what the positions and strategies developed by works councils with respect to profit sharing are and, finally what the effects of profit sharing both on the development of wages and on the position of works councils in plant-level labour relations are.

Figure 1. Incidence of profit-sharing by employee and industry (percentage).

Source: SOEP, own calculations (weighted data)

The spread of profit sharing in the metalworking industry is booming and far above the average both of the German economy as a whole and the manufacturing sector including the chemical or energy industries (Figure 1), where regulations about profit sharing in collective bargaining agreements exist.

The analysis is based on the results of a research project financed by the Hans-Böckler-Foundation in the years 2012 and 2013 in the course of which we made use of three methods. First, we evaluated various sources of data on profit sharing like the Socio-economic Panel (SOEP), a representative and yearly survey among 12.000 households, and the IAB Company Panel, a representative company survey among around 16.000 companies, in order to get an impression of the spread and dynamics of profit sharing. Second, we surveyed and analysed the agreements on profit sharing in the forty largest firms of the metalworking industry as far as they exist. In this way, we could identify patterns of plant level regulation of profit sharing with respect to the definition of profits, the entitlements of employees or procedures of codetermination. In addition, third, nine case studies in large companies of the metalworking industry were undertaken. The cases have been selected in accordance with the metalworkers' union IG Metall and were to represent practices of profit sharing, mainly along the value chains of the automotive industry where profit sharing is most widespread. They are based on expert interviews with works councils, local or regional union secretaries and representatives of HR management. The case study analysis sheds light on the patterns of strategies and interactions in the plants or the effects of profit sharing in terms of money (for the employees) or legitimacy (for the works councils). However, before presenting the empirical findings, a glance will be thrown at the sociological discussion about financialisation, profit sharing and works councils.

2. Financialisation and profit sharing

Profit sharing can be regarded as an important aspect of financialisation of companies (Breisig, 2009). There is a common sense that financialisation or financial market capitalism has become a dominant frame of reference in the German industrial relations literature (Minssen, 2011). There are three characteristics of financialisation stressed in this respect. Financialisation is marked, first, by excess savings based on the redistribution between profits and wages (in favour of the former), the reduction of economic growth rates and the privatisation of old-age pensions (Huffschmid, 2007); second, by the emergence of a new 'service class' of financial market capitalism composed of institutional investors and other financial agents (Windolf, 2008); and third, by the changes of corporate governance and control towards the model of shareholder value and the implementation of financial concepts of control, in which enterprises are regarded as a portfolio of assets in form of decentralised business units with operative autonomy (Fligstein, 1990).

Financialisation in the third sense is going hand in hand with a new form of justification to rationalise and legitimise management action (Kädtler, 2009). Top-management is constructing and inventing tales to convince investors and other financial actors of the coherency of management strategy (Froud et al., 2006). At the same time, financial justifications pave the way for posing demands on works councils and unions and for interpreting financial targets as inherent necessities of the markets. Creating value (Stern et al., 2002) is becoming the core goal of economic action (Kädtler, 2009).

By defining capital costs as a threshold for the creation of value (Bontrup & Springop, 2002; Chahed et al., 2004), the value oriented management has severe impacts on wages. On the one hand, capital costs define a minimum profit rate and thereby seem to guarantee the incomes of the investors and shareholders – at least as far as it is possible in a market economy. However, taking the interests of these groups as given means that profits are re-defined from a residual to a contractual income (Chahed et al., 2004). On the other hand, wages are, at least according to the logic of the concept, transformed in residual incomes by shifting the entrepreneurial risks towards the employees (Deutschmann, 2008). Wages are regarded as an expense factor – and not as a factor of innovation – which has to be reduced or at least kept at a level compatible with the threshold of the capital costs. Profit sharing is the adequate wage component to fulfill the requirements of the capital costs, for wages and profit margins are directly coupled and ensure that the wage development is in line with the profit targets set by management. In this way, it is the financial performance and the financial output of the company and not the individual performance or the input in form of quality or volume of work by the employees which is assessed by profit sharing wages (Voswinkel, 2005; Bahnmüller, 2001). Legitimising economic action by creating value corresponds to a sense of performance in terms of financial results assessed by the markets.

However, contrary to the concept it can be said that profit sharing wage components are still by far too little widespread among workers to transform wages in residual incomes (Faust et al., 2011). Profit sharing is only one – and a minor – wage component amongst others which are still fixed by industry collective bargaining agreements, although most of them allow derogations on plant level (Haipeter, 2009). However, these caveats do not contradict the fact that the spread and significance of profit sharing wages is increasing. First, there are many hints that profit sharing wages more and more substitute other wage components paid by the companies above the general wage scale, especially in companies that are strongly exposed to the capital markets (Faust et al., 2011). Second, profit sharing wages could be implemented in the plants in form of a trickle-down effect by transferring wage systems from the area of management, where profit sharing is widespread, to the employees covered by the collective bargaining agreements. The goal of this transfer would be to create a coherent wage system covering all groups of employees (Faust et al., 2011). Third, profit sharing wages are introduced on plant level because they are regarded as a model of good human resource management and as a proven good practice in the organisational field, creating legitimacy for the personnel departments by isomorphism (Di Maggio & Powell, 1983).

In the literature, the view on the general effects of financialisation on works councils is rather sceptical. There are at least five negative consequences of financialisation that can be concluded from literature (Deutschmann, 2008; Dörre 2009; Kädtler 2009; Sauer 2013). The first is the short-termism of management. Investments have to create short-term value and to convince external investors. Short-term horizons go along with a reluctance to finance long-term projects of innovation or organisational development. In both cases, works councils have to fight for long-term investments or projects.

Long-term investments, second, are calculated with reference to the interest rates given by alternative investments. Investments that do not meet these targets will not be made, or will be made only if the profitability of the investment can be increased respectively. If works councils demand investments, they have to show at the same time how the profitability of investments can be raised. In this way, works councils can be forced to agree on measures to improve profitability or even to develop them on their own.

Third, concessions on wages or working times can be part of these measures. Profitability can be raised by innovative forms of work organisation; however, their development and implementation usually is a long-term process with little support by management. Short-term cost-cutting of personnel costs by wage reductions seems to be the much more probable solution. In this case, works councils and workers might have to pay for investments with material concessions.

Fourth, outsourcing or offshoring of activities as an important element of financialised management strategies have become usual business for companies and works councils as well, who might be, if at all, able to safeguard jobs or to make agreements for a business transfer of employees to another company only at the price of concessions.

Fifth, wage differentials might be used within the company by making use of precarious forms of work. An important example in this respect is the strategic usage of temp agency work characterised by cutting personnel costs and the replacement of core workers by flexible workers (Holst et al., 2010). Works councils try to prevent the expansion of precarious work by agreeing on quotas or other instruments with management; however, they use to have to make concessions in these agreements. Moreover, the wage differentials between core and precarious workers might put pressure on the works councils to agree on material concessions for core workers in order to prevent further replacements of the core workforce by precarious workers.

Taken as a whole, the financialisation of corporate governance seems to have severe impacts on works councils' policy and power resources. Even though the formal and institutionalised rights of codetermination the works councils can build on have not been changed, the bargaining context has a lot, forcing the works councils to give political priority to the safeguarding of jobs and the preservation of labour standards which are both endangered by financialised management strategies.

3. *Regulation of profit sharing wages in collective agreements*

Given the growing defensive of works councils in a financialised environment, how does profit sharing fit in this picture? How is profit sharing regulated on plant level by means of collective agreements? Among the 40 largest companies of the metalworking and electrical engineering industries only six enterprises have no profit sharing scheme. Thus, the majority of large firms operate such schemes. Of these, a collective agreement on the topic has been negotiated in 26 companies. Agreements on profit sharing use to include the area of coverage, the period of validity, the indicators for defining profit, the forms of calculating profit sharing wages and connections to other topics or procedural rules to cope with problems of controlling or with conflicts. Concerning the period of validity of the agreements it is interesting to note that quite a lot of the agreements have been implemented recently. 16 of the 26 agreements have been implemented since 2000, and six agreements have their origins in the three years before 2009. Only three agreements are valid for ten years or longer. This observation leads to the conclusion that a wave of modernisation in regulating profit sharing wages took place in the companies in the last years.

The area of coverage of the agreements in most of the cases is the whole company, whereas it is in a minor number of cases either only the parent company or defined subsidiary companies. All employees paid according to the collective bargaining agreements are covered by profit sharing wages. In some cases, also the employees in wage groups above those of the collective bargaining agreements are included. In the bigger number of cases there are different agreements made for this group of employees. However, the main line of segmentation is drawn elsewhere. The provisions governing the application of the collectively agreed arrangements to the various occupational categories are characterised by clear fault lines between core and peripheral employees. Workers with temporary contracts are entitled in about two thirds of the agreement. Temp agency workers, however, are covered in none of them. Profit sharing wages are fragmented along the employment status of the workers. Thereby, they are aggravating wage fragmentations that already exist because the temp agency workers use to get much lower basic wages.

The level of profit sharing pay-outs is determined first and foremost on the basis of *financial indicators*. The majority of firms use just one indicator for this purpose. However, in eight of the 26 firms with collective agreements, several indicators are used. In these cases, indicators for the company as a whole and for individual business units or subsidiaries are combined. The indicators most frequently used are operating profit (EBIT), economic value added (EVA) and return on sales (ROS). Four firms use return on capital employed (ROCE) and three earnings before tax (EBT). In two agreements, the annual surplus and/or dividends were used. Earnings before interest, tax and amortisation (EBITA), earnings before income, tax, depreciation and amortisation (EBITDA) and free cash flow were mentioned only once (Figure 2).

In business economics, a distinction is made between traditional and value-oriented indicators (Meyer, 2011). The principal characteristic of value-based indicators is that they take account of capital costs. The capital costs for borrowed and own capital, which are reported as the minimum interest return on capital used, define the claims of creditors and

Figure 2. Distribution of profit indicators in the collective agreements (absolute figures).

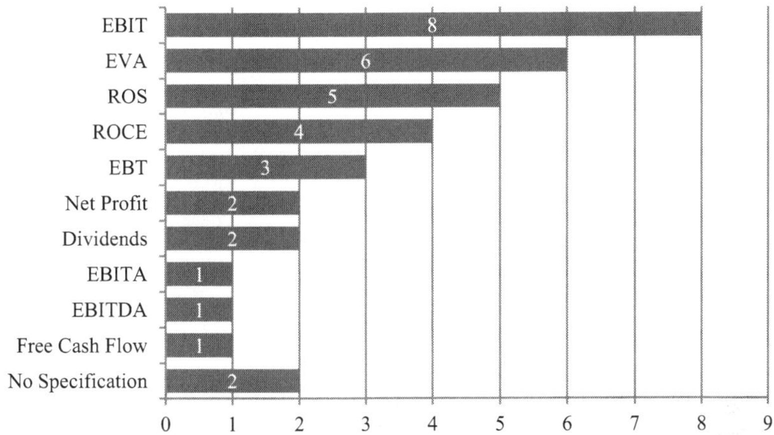

Source: own survey, multiple counts possible.

shareholders on company profits. Company value is not created until these claims have been met, which means that they are taken as given and fixed. Because they are geared to the interests of actors in the capital markets, value-oriented indicators are a manifestation of the financialisation of corporate management. Of the total of 33 indicators in use, value-oriented indicators (EVA, ROCE, Free Cash Flow) are used eleven times to calculate profit sharing. In two agreements, the level of dividends is used for this purpose. Since this indicator also relates to investors, it can be classified as value-oriented financial indicator. It is true that, overall, value-oriented indicators are still in the minority. However, value-oriented indicators are on the rise as means of calculating profit sharing. A high share of the agreements (16) were negotiated in the last four years and virtually all these more recent agreements stipulate the use of value-oriented indicators exclusively.

Two forms of calculating profit sharing wages can be distinguished. On the one hand, individual profit sharing wages are directly connected to the indicators, either in form of thresholds defined or to the development of the indicators. In this case, which can be found in 18 of the 26 agreements analysed, the level of profit determines directly the wage level. On the other hand, the level of profit can also be connected to a profit sharing payroll which is distributed among the employees entitled to get profit sharing wages. The second form of calculation corresponds to the famous model of profit sharing by Weitzman (1984). It implies that the individual payment varies with the number of entitled workers, whereas in the first form of calculation the payment is determined directly by the profit level. Within these two forms, profit sharing wages can be influenced by intervals, thresholds and limits. In a minor number of agreements, profit intervals are defined and levels of profit sharing are assigned to them. In the other cases the payments vary continuously with the profit level. Profit sharing wages can as well be based on a profit threshold, as it is the case in 19 agreements. In these cases profit wages will only be paid after a certain minimum profit level larger than zero is achieved. Finally, profit sharing wages can also be limited from above by a threshold. In 16 of the 26 agreements such a threshold is defined beyond which the wages remain on a constant level.

The agreements also can contain procedural rules concerning controlling or conflicts. Such rules are defined in roughly half of the agreements. Seven agreements contain separate rights of continuous information and consultation of the works councils about the development of the profit sharing wages; five agreements define certain rules for coping with conflicts in case the works councils do not agree with the level or the calculation of the wages. And in two agreements it is explicitly said that beyond the technical calculation the concrete level of profit sharing wages has to be negotiated between management and works councils afterwards.

In eleven of the agreements, finally, profit sharing wages are connected in the one way or the other to other topics of collective regulation. In all of these cases, profit sharing wages are part of local alliances for work, dealing with concessions by employees and counter-concessions by management. Profit sharing wages are concessions made by management to compensate concessions made by the workers on issues like the extension of working times, the variabilisation of the Christmas bonus, changes in the wage framework – especially concerning the implementation of the new framework agreement on wage groups that was negotiated in the metalworking industry in 2003 – or the suspension of collectively agreed wage increases. The connection to other topics in local alliances of work gives first hints of the origins of profit sharing wages in the companies.

4. The regulation of profit sharing at company level and the works councils' policy

The analysis of the regulatory texts gives little information about the origins and the practice of profit sharing or the role of the works councils. These aspects will be analysed in this chapter based on nine case studies on plant level. The cases have been selected according to two criteria: first, that above-average high profit sharing has been paid out in the plants, and second that the metalworkers union has identified them as important plants within their respective local administrative units. The studies were based on guided expert interviews with works councils, trade union officials and management representatives. In total we conducted 29 interviews, among them 13 with works councils, eleven with trade union officials and five with HR managers.

Not by chance, eight of our nine case studies are taken from the automotive industry, the most dynamic sector of manufacturing in Germany in the last years with many big companies at the head of the value chain, either being OEMs or big first-tier suppliers (for an overview of the case see Table 1). *Car*, *Vehicle*, *Limousine* and *Automobile* are big OEMs. *Limousine* and *Automobile* are belonging to the same company holding; *Limousine*, *Vehicle* and *Car* are mainly producing luxury cars for the upper segments of the market. *Automobile* has a traditional focus on the mass segment of the market and is the by far most highly internationalised among the German OEMs. *Power Train*, *Electronics*, *Gears*, *Bearings* are big suppliers with dominating business activities in the automotive industry; the names of the abbreviations are indicating some of their core business, like electronics, which is producing mainly electronic based systems for brakes or steering systems. The automotive sector is without doubt forming the booming core of the development of profit sharing wages in the metalworking industry. The remaining case study (*Jet*) is a big producer of the aircraft industry which is the only case of a European agreement on profit sharing.

The analysis of the social patterns of action and the role of the works councils in regulating profit sharing wages is structured along three topics: the origins of the regulations and the initiative to negotiate them, the indicators and the determination and level of payments and, finally, the interpretation schemes of the employees and the effects on the legitimacy of the works council (both from the point of the works' councils, because we could not make interviews with employees in the research project). The main findings of the analysis are summarised in Table 1 and will be explained in this chapter.

Table 1. Summary of findings

Cases	Origins and Initiatives	Indicators, Determination and Payment 2011	Interpretations of Employees and Legitimacy of Works Councils
Power train	Compensation Works Council and Union	EVA By Calculation 1,040 Euro	Approval and Critique Legitimacy Improved
Car	Tradition and Compensation Works Council and Management	ROS By Calculation 9,000 Euro	Approval and Critique Legitimacy Improved
Electronics	Tradition and Safeguarding Works Council and Management	EVA By Negotiation 1,600 Euro	Approval and Critique Legitimacy Improved
Vehicle	Safeguarding Management	EBIT By Negotiation 4,100 Euro	Approval and Critique Legitimacy Improved
Gears	Tradition and Safeguarding Works Council and Management	EBIT By Calculation 1,850 Euro	Approval and Critique Legitimacy Improved
Jet	Tradition Works Council	EBIT and EVA By Negotiation 1,800 Euro	Approval and Critique Legitimacy Improved
Limousine	Compensation Works Council	EBT By Calculation 9,300 Euro	Approval and Critique Legitimacy Improved
Bearings	Tradition and Safeguarding Works Council and Union	EBIT By Calculation 1,000 Euro	Approval Legitimacy Improved
Automobile	Compensation Works Council and Union	EBIT By Negotiation 7,500 Euro	Approval and Critique Legitimacy Improved

4.1 Profit sharing - origins and initiatives

What are the *origins* of profit sharing in the plants? Among the nine case-study companies investigated, the origins can be divided into three types. The first type is characterised by a long tradition of profit sharing as an additional company benefit. In the cases of *Car, Electronics, Gears, Jet* and *Bearings,* the history of profit sharing goes back to the time of the 'economic miracle' of the 1950s and 60s. In the case of *Electronics* for example, the 'performance and profit sharing bonuses' were part of a comprehensive range of additional company benefits that were regarded within the company as a key element of an employee-oriented corporate culture. The same motives of implementation were found at *Gears* and *Bearings*. At *Car*, profit sharing was introduced after a deep company crisis at the end of the 1960s and as an expression of a high sense of social partnership between management, works council and union. With the exception of *Car*, there was no formula in these cases for calculating profit sharing pay-outs. What constituted profits and to what extent employees should participate in them was negotiated anew each year by the negotiating parties at company level. In this first type, the works councils had a minor role with respect to the creation of profit sharing; it was management which had the initiative. However, works councils played an important role in the yearly negotiations about concrete pay-outs.

The initiatives are distributed quite differently in the second type of origins, which is made up of those cases in which profit sharing was introduced as compensation for material concessions made by employees in job safeguarding agreements. Here the works councils played a leading role in the implementation of profit sharing schemes. *Power train, Limousine* and *Automobile* belong in this category. In the case of *Limousine*, for example, the company management had demanded reductions in wage levels in the course of the introduction of the new framework agreement on wages (*Engeltrahmentarifabkommen* or ERA) in 2005 by threatening to make investments for new products not at the German locations but at locations abroad. Works councils and the union had to accept a reduction of the level of the basic wages in the company of about four per cent, which originally has been above the levels of the collective bargaining and after the reduction is more or less on par. Besides production decisions in favour of the company's German sites, the most important reciprocal measure was the expansion and reorganisation of the profit sharing scheme. At *Automobile*, the company management linked product and investment decisions to working time increases without pay compensation, albeit the weekly working times here have been much lower and still are below the level laid down in the regional collective agreements. Automobile is the most internationalised among the sample companies and threats of relocation are easy to fulfil. Here too, profit sharing was a key component of the reciprocal measures that were negotiated by the employee representative bodies in return for the longer working hours.

In the third and final type, previously fixed wage components paid in addition to the collectively agreed rates have been converted into profit sharing bonuses. This is the case at *Vehicle, Electronics, Gears* and *Bearings*. Partly, at *Electronics*, *Gears* and *Bearings*, they have been combined with older forms of profit sharing wages and regulated anew in this way. At *Electronics*, for instance, an extra payment on the performance based pay component which was traditionally paid by the enterprise was converted to profit sharing by adding its financial volume to the profit sharing scheme. In most of these cases, the works councils were the drivers of the conversion. One key motivation of the employee representative bodies to accept and even demand such a conversion of wages above the general pay scale was to safeguard additional company benefits. The works councils' explicit aim was to protect additional company benefits from the companies' cost-cutting drive. The employee representative bodies clearly feared that fixed wage components paid in addition to the collectively agreed rates would sooner or later be called into question in negotiations on job protection. This was not expected to apply to profit sharing arrangements, firstly because they are valued on the employer's side as a feature of modern management and secondly because they do not appear on balance sheets as cost factors (since they are deductions from profits).

Thus, the use of profit sharing arrangements as a *quid pro quo* for concessions on other issues and as a means of safeguarding additional company benefits marks a fundamental shift in the *bargaining context* for profit sharing. It is no longer participation in a company's success but rather locational competition, the threat of outsourcing and profit targets that determine the conditions under which profit sharing is negotiated and regulated. Not by chance, it is usually the works councils who call for profit sharing bonuses as compensation or protection, firstly because profit sharing bonuses are one of the few material company benefits on which consensus can still be reached with employers and, secondly, they are following the examples set by other works councils in other companies. Especially among the companies of the automotive sector, the works councils stressed that they wanted to imitate the positive experiences with profit sharing wages which were made in their eyes in other companies. So the growing spread of profit sharing to a certain extent also is an effect of mutual learning and isomorphism between works councils.

However, it is important to stress that in many cases it is not the company management, who is initiating and demanding profit sharing wages as part of a strategy of (shareholder) value orientation or to strengthen financial governance of the companies. Rather, it is the works councils who take the lead. Only in the case of *Vehicle* it was the management who has opted for profit sharing wages, and it did so explicitly with reference to a strategy of shareholder value it was willing to pursue. In most of the other cases, like at *Electronics* or *Gears*, management regarded profit sharing wages with favour as a model of a modern human resource wage police and as an instrument to increase the motivation and performance of workers, to strengthen entrepreneurship among employees, to make the company more attractive for workers or to flexibilise wages (see also Matiaske, Tobsch, & Fietze, 2009). However, management did not take the initiative and was reluctant to initiatives from the works councils for the reason that profit sharing wages are payments on top of the collectively agreed wages. Therefore, the only way to make profit sharing acceptable for the management of most of our sample companies was to transform other wage components like it has been done by wage concessions or the conversion of additional wage components.

This can be regarded as an indicator of the fact that the context of profit sharing today is completely different from the one in former days. In former times, in the 1960s and 1970s when profit sharing for the first time became more widespread in Germany, it has been an expression of the material participation of the employees in the well-being of the firms. And it is in this manner that profit sharing wages in some companies have become an issue of the wage policies of works councils. Today, profit sharing wages have returned as an important issue of works councils' wage policy. However, they are not an expression of material participation but of material concessions the employees have to make in the wake of local alliances for work.

4.2 Profit indicators and profit sharing payments

Among the indicators used in the plants to define profits, only at *Power Train, Electronics* and *Jet* value oriented indicators (EVA) are used to calculate profit and profit sharing wages. Therefore, the level of financialisation of profit sharing among the sample cases seems to be rather low.

However, the indicators themselves are only one aspect of financialisation of wages by profit sharing. Another aspect is whether there is a connection between the indicators used to determine profit sharing pay-outs and those used in corporate management. The first thing to note is that all companies in our sample have introduced *a financial control system.* Decentralised units have been established and endowed with operational independence. Depending on the company in question, these units may be brands, product areas or divisions. In all cases, however, they are managed by means of financial targets. Business areas that lie outside the core business and are unable to demonstrate any long-term prospect of achieving the targets set are doubtful cases and run the risk of being closed down or sold off. And investments that cannot be shown to produce a return on capital used to match the targets set simply do not go ahead or, if they do, with conditions attached.

Nevertheless, the companies do differ in how strictly the system of management by indicators is actually operated. In this regard, there is a fairly wide spectrum of practices, which are determined not least by *exposure to the capital markets. Vehicle* is one of the companies that operates its financial control system very strictly, with shares owned by diverse shareholders. At the beginning of the 1990s, the company embarked on the process of dividing itself up into business units and divisions to which responsibility for profits was devolved. Management of these divisions is based on financial targets and investments are linked to requirements for return on capital that are derived from the interest yields that might be obtained in the capital markets. At the other end of the spectrum are *Gears* and *Electronics*, both of which have a low level of capital market exposure. Both are owned by foundations and the negotiating parties in both firms emphasise that this fact is accompanied by long-term investment and planning horizons. Nevertheless, even here fundamental changes in organisational structures took place, such as decentralisation and the subjection of the decentralised business units to financial scrutiny. The other firms in our sample lie somewhere between these two extremes. At *Automobile*, for example, capital market exposure is low because of the prominent role played by private and public anchor investors. The company is pursuing an explicit growth strategy. However, this strategy is linked to ambitious yield targets, which are measured by the returns on capital used and on sales.

Only at *Power Train, Electronics,* and *Jet*, the indicators used for corporate management purposes are at the same time used to calculate profit sharing. In the other companies investigated, profit sharing is not linked directly with the indicators used in corporate management. At *Power Train, Electronics* and *Jet*, value-oriented indicators (economic value added at the first two and cash flow at *Jet*) have been introduced for the purpose to create a homogeneous system of management by indicator, each of which takes account of capital costs. However, in these companies the financial indicators are not actively used either in company management or in personnel policy to reinforce the notion of 'company value' among employees. This adds to the former observations that the companies lack a coherent strategy of financialisation that includes human resource management.

Indicators give little rise to *disputes* in the companies investigated. In most cases, there was no disagreement on the matter between the negotiating parties. The creation of indicators usually followed the same pattern, with a proposal being made by management that was subsequently accepted in the ensuing negotiations. The decisive factors for the works councils are that the indicators should be transparent and readily comprehensible. They regard this as ensured if the parameters used also occur in the company's financial statements and hence can be proved to be correct by both themselves and the company's auditors.

However, the *determination of profit sharing pay-outs* can be contested in the plants. The cases in our sample fall into two categories: those in which the level of such pay-outs is clearly determined on the basis of defined indicators and the associated calculations and those in which the basis for calculation is indeed set out through a series of indicators and formulae but the actual level of any pay-outs is not determined until follow-up negotiations have taken place between the relevant parties at company level. In the second category, works councils again have a leading role in defining the wage level, because it is usually the works councils who demand for higher profit sharing wages than calculated with reference to the financial indicators.

In five cases (*Power Train, Car, Gears, Bearings* and *Limousine*), on the one hand, the level of profit sharing pay-outs is calculated automatically by using profit indicators and mathematical formulae. This practice is generally perceived by the works councils as an easing of their burden. At *Car*, for example, the negotiating parties in the company emphasise that this method avoids conflict. A similar argument is made by the works council at *Limousine*. In that company, the volume of the profit sharing pay-outs is calculated as a share of the operating profit. In the works council's view, there is no need for negotiations; there is a clear mathematical relationship between indicator and pay-out that requires no subsequent processing for political purposes.

At *Electronics*, *Vehicle*, *Jet* and *Automobile*, on the other hand, profit sharing pay-outs are determined not only by indicators and mathematical formulae but also by negotiations. These take the form of follow-up negotiations on the pay-outs, which are calculated initially on the basis of indicators and mathematical formulae. In all these cases, the driving force behind the negotiations is the works council. At *Jet*, these follow-up negotiations are enshrined in the agreements on profit sharing and hence are formally safeguarded. At *Automobile*, the follow-up negotiations are based not on official rules but rather on informal patterns of behaviour that are shared by the negotiating parties. At *Vehicle*, finally, the company profit sharing agreement expired a long time ago and is now used only as a starting point for annual negotiations. Whatever form they take, the works councils take the view that follow-up negotiations facilitate the *politicisation* of profit sharing and offer an opportunity to increase the level of pay-outs beyond that calculated by means of mathematical formulae alone, thereby strengthening the legitimacy of profit sharing arrangements among the workforce.

A comparison of the companies in our sample shows that the *level of profit sharing pay-outs* in 2011 varied considerably. They ranged from around €1,000 at *Bearings* to an average of €9,300 at *Limousine.* In fact, the figure for *Limousine* is a conservative estimate, since up to ten per cent of the pay-out can be paid voluntarily into the company's pension scheme and does not appear in the published figures. These differences in pay-outs reflect to a large extent the different positions the companies occupy in the *automotive value added chain*. It is the large end producers *Limousine*, *Car, Automobile* and *Vehicle* that make the biggest average pay-outs. Of these four, *Vehicle,* with a pay-out of €4,100, lags a considerable way behind the others, which is why the works council there is pushing for a new agreement to be concluded that makes provision for possible higher pay-outs. The component suppliers, *Power Train, Electronics, Gears* and *Bearings*, pay out between €1,000 and €2,000 a year. The gap between them and the end producers is not attributable to the fact that the works councils at component suppliers have less negotiating power. The calculation methods and shares of profits paid out to employees are very similar. Thus at *Automobile* and *Limousine*, the profit sharing pay-outs represent ten per cent of the companies' operating profits, while at *Gears* the figure is as high as eleven per cent. In 2011, however, this led to pay-outs at *Limousine* and *Automobile* of €9,300 and €7,500 respectively, while the average pay-out to employees at *Gears* was €1,850.

These developments reflect the power structures that have emerged in the automotive value added chains in the last two decades (Banyuls & Haipeter, 2010). The end producers have increasingly succeeded in shifting price pressures on to component suppliers. The large component suppliers can still escape these pressures to some extent, firstly by passing cost reductions on to their own suppliers and secondly by competing increasingly on the basis of innovation and quality. However, even for the small number of technology leaders among the suppliers, their ability to generate profits has declined compared to the final producers. This applies all the more to suppliers at the bottom end of the value-added chain. These firms are usually able to pay just the collective agreed rates and indeed may have to negotiate derogations from those rates because they would otherwise be unable to meet their customers' cost targets. This is how the financial gap between firms in the value added chains widens. The differences in profit sharing pay-outs reflect this evolution and aggravate its effects on employee remuneration.

4.3 Interpretation patterns of the employees and legitimacy of the works councils

Based on the methods used in this particular investigation the employees' attitudes to profit sharing can be analysed only indirectly through the statements made by work councillors and management representatives. Even with this constraint, however, there are some interesting findings to be made. Firstly, in all the companies in our sample profit sharing is described as being very popular among employees. As an additional component of pay it seems to meet with high levels of acceptance everywhere. The reasons put forward combine considerations of distribution and performance. On the one hand, profit sharing pay-outs are regarded as a welcome addition to their regular wages; on the other hand, they are also seen as recognition of their work effort.

In the eyes of the works councils, employees' assessments of the profit sharing schemes in the companies investigated depend essentially on three factors: experience, comparison and the origins of each scheme. *Experience* refers primarily to the development of profit sharing within the companies. In those companies in which profit sharing did not initially exist but has been introduced as a new pay component, or where the rate of increase has been high, acceptance is also high. *Limousine* is a case in point. Since they were introduced in 2007, profit sharing pay-outs in this company have increased continuously and are the highest among the companies in our sample. The new profit sharing scheme has proved to be a wellspring of legitimation for the works councils. Pay-outs at *Car* have reached similarly high levels, but the reactions of employees there have been considerably more sceptical, since they have enjoyed relatively high pay-outs for a long time.

A second source of critical assessment is to be found in comparisons with the *pay-outs* made at other companies. In all the component supplier companies, the lower pay-outs compared to the end producers were perceived as unfair because the employees judged their performance in terms of effort and physical output to be equal in value to that of workers at the end producers. The works councils at each company tried to make employees understand and accept the situation by explaining the structure and position of their companies in the automotive value-added chain and to deflect the criticism on to the distribution of power within the value-added chain and the end producers' sourcing strategies. However, critical assessments also exist at the end producers themselves. At *Vehicle*, the annoyance was caused by the low level of the pay-outs relative to those made by the other manufacturers of prestige cars. In this situation, the works council reacted by explaining and defending the company's arrangements to the workforce. Its most important argument was the company's low level of transfer and outsourcing of production, which meant that the company had lower profit margins.

A third source of evaluation in addition to experience and comparison is the initial situation with regard to material concessions. At *Limousine,* employees' experience of material concessions gave rise to some severe criticism, but it was soon drowned out by the increasing demand for cars and the company's high profit levels. At *Automobile*, on the other hand, the wounds inflicted by the agreement on job security were not so quick to heal. The unpaid increase in working time conceded in exchange for job security had plunged both the works council and the trade union into a profound crisis of legitimacy. The works councils tried to bring the work-force on side by holding information events at which they sought to justify the increase in working time. However, their efforts met with little success. The works council's crisis of legitimacy was eventually overcome, primarily because the provisions on job security proved their value in the crisis of 2008 and 2009 and because the works council was able at that time to negotiate a profit sharing pay-out of €1,200, even though employees were not actually entitled to any payment at all (or at best a sum of €14 only). Nevertheless, the profit sharing scheme's origin as part of the compensation for material concessions cast a long shadow and made its acceptance more difficult.

However, pay gaps with regard to profit sharing were also described as critical between members of the core workforce and temporary agency workers. In none of the companies in our sample are temporary agency workers included in the profit sharing scheme. As a result, profit sharing pay-outs further intensify the pay fragmentation that already exists between the core workforce and workers whose pay and employment status are precarious. Most of the companies in our sample make considerable and strategic use of temporary agency workers, since they are used not only to deal with fluctuations in staffing needs but also to replace core workers, reduce costs and increase profitability (Holst, et al. 2010). However, only in a minority of cases are temporary agency workers critical of their exclusion from the profit sharing schemes. In most of the companies in our sample, they accept this additional unequal treatment. Two factors are cited by works councillors in explanation of this attitude. The first is the high basic rates of pay offered by large companies in the metalworking and electrical engineering industries relative to the collectively agreed rates in the temporary agency sector (in some of the companies in our sample separate agreements have been concluded that guarantee temporary agency workers are paid the rate of basic pay stipulated in the collective agreement for the metalworking industry). Secondly, many temporary agency workers hope to be offered a permanent job in the company. In three of the sample companies, however, critical reactions on the part of temporary agency workers are reported. In these cases, the agency workers raise the question of equity and ask the works councils why they are not entitled to a pay-out when their colleagues doing the same work are. At *Jet*, the works council has taken up this feeling of injustice and is demanding that agency workers are also included in the profit sharing scheme. This makes it an exception in our sample in this respect.

What effects does the existence of profit sharing schemes have on works councils' codetermination practices? The findings on this issue could not be more unanimous. Despite the critiques of the employees mentioned by the works councils and the problems of wage segmentation along the value chains, all the employee representative bodies regard profit sharing schemes as an instrument that strengthens their legitimacy among the workforce and therefore also consolidates their position in the workplace industrial relations system. Profit sharing schemes enable works councils to further employees' material interests and to present themselves as assertive champions of their interests. What is more, they can point to concrete results and figures in evidence. In favourable economic circumstances, the works council can present the profit sharing pay-outs as a success for their interest representation policy, while in times of economic crisis they can point to external circumstances that are preventing the company from making higher pay-outs. In comparison, the legitimacy problems caused by discontent among the workforce do not matter a great deal in the eyes of the works councils.

For all the works councillors surveyed, however, one important precondition is that they should be able to control and micromanage the flow of information about profit sharing pay-outs. For all the works councillors, this includes being the first to announce the level of pay-outs, giving high-profile presentations at workplace meetings and declaring them to be a success for their interest representation policy. The works councils want to be regarded as the originators of the profit sharing schemes, the more frequently the better. At *Limousine*, the works council was able to obtain agreement that the profit sharing pay-out in its several variants would take the form of three special payments distributed over the year. This ensures that profit sharing becomes a long-running issue that the works council can address repeatedly at workplace meetings.

The positive effects on legitimacy profit sharing has according to the works council is one explanation for the willingness of works councils to introduce profit sharing schemes as a compensation for concessions they have to make or as an instrument to safeguard fringe benefits which otherwise would be disputed in conflicts about labour standards, employment and local alliances for work. Like the ups and downs of management concepts, profit sharing at the moment is regarded as a success model by works councils to regulate wages on plant level, and its growing spread can be explained as a process of mimesis and isomorphism (Di Maggio & Powell, 1983).

However, there are three caveats that should not be forgotten in this respect. First, profit sharing is not part of a new and long-term strategy of wage policy that the works councils have developed and that they try to enforce in their companies. Even in their strongholds of the big automotive companies, works councils are threatened by their companies' plans to relocate production or to source out other activities, which enforces works councils to make concessions and to lower labour standards, being it wages or working times. In this new bargaining context profit sharing seems to be an opportunity to re-compensate the losses, at least partially, that the works councils negotiate and they have to take the responsibility for vis-à-vis the employees. Therefore it is a short term instrument to regain legitimacy. Second, this instrument is viable not for all works councils; its opportunities and effects depend on the position of the company in the value chain. The higher the position in the value chain, the more the instrument can provide positive material results and legitimacy – and vice versa. And finally, it has to be noted that the aspect of financialisation is not part of the considerations of the works councils. In none of the cases studied works councils have really called into question financialised concepts of control or profit targets defined by top management. Nor do they reflect the possible role profit sharing can play as a driver of financialisation of their companies which is contributing a great deal to the problematic bargaining contexts works councils are facing these days.

5. Concluding remarks

Profit sharing schemes reflect the financialisation of companies and the change in performance norms. The main parameter used to determine performance in profit sharing schemes is the company's economic success expressed in financial indicators. And within these indicators, there is a trend in the more recent agreements towards the use of value-oriented indicators that take account of capital costs and thus reveal the 'value added' that is being achieved for investors, i.e. shareholders. In this way, profit sharing schemes are reinforcing the financial mode of control that can be observed in all our case study firms and that is based on the use of financial indicators and targets to manage operationally independent business units. However, the indicators used in profit sharing schemes are not universally linked to those used in corporate management. Moreover, they are not being used for rigorous financialisation in the sense of establishing a new rationale for economic action or the development of a coherent strategy of a financialised human resource management.

The lack of a coherent strategy of financialised human resource management is one of the reasons why it is in most of the cases the works councils and not management who demand for profit sharing wages in the companies, in many of the cases as a compensation for employee concessions. First, works councils think that profit sharing wages are a comparatively 'safe' wage component because they will not be called into question in employment pacts by management as easily as other wages paid above the levels of the collective bargaining agreements. And second, regarding profit sharing the works councils of the automotive companies are learning from each other in the way that they are mutually imitating practices they observe in other companies and that they regard as successful.

By taking the lead in demanding and regulating profit sharing the works councils tie in with older practices they have developed in cases where profit sharing has a long tradition in the companies. And yet the circumstances under which this is taking place have changed fundamentally compared with the 1960s and 1970s. Today, profit sharing at company level is no longer the product of a broadly based process of growth, in which a small number of above-averagely successful firms stand out. Rather, it is the product of redistribution within the automotive value added chain, concessions made by employees in the negotiation of employment packages, which have resulted in increasing corporate profits, and pay fragmentation between the core workforce and temporary agency workers. Obviously the payment of profit sharing bonuses still requires economic success, but in those companies that are able to make such payments, they are increasingly the product of redistribution between companies and employees and between different categories of employees.

This change in the context in which profit sharing schemes are implemented has considerable implications for workplace representative bodies. In the 1960s and 1970s, such bodies had the upper hand and were in a position to negotiate benefits that were paid in addition to the collectively agreed rates. Today, their aim is much more to use profit sharing as a means of safeguarding those additional benefits that still exist or to demand employee participation in profits in exchange for material concessions. It is true that employee representative bodies have often taken the initiative in the introduction of profit sharing schemes, but they have done so from a defensive position. Globalisation and financial forms of control have permanently shifted power relations in the workplace in favour of employers and changed the context in which negotiations are conducted. Safeguarding jobs has become the principal concern of employee representative bodies and they are constantly faced with the real or potential threat of business areas, production sites or areas of activity being transferred or outsourced.

Against this background, profit sharing has developed into a new compromise position on pay policy between the negotiating parties at company level. For works councils, it has opened up opportunities for safeguarding additional benefits or demanding compensation for concessions; for employers, it appears to have the cachet of a modern remuneration policy and fits very well with the financial forms of control that have now been widely adopted by companies. Profit sharing pay-outs fluctuate with profits and do not appear on balance sheets as labour costs but rather as deductions from profits. This makes them attractive to both sides of the workplace industrial relations system. Profit sharing schemes are a wellspring of legitimacy for works councils in the eyes of those they represent, while for companies they are a bountiful source of returns. However, although based on a compromise, in many cases profit sharing is a political issue. The politisation of profit sharing is, besides the sheer level of wages paid, an important instrument to increase the legitimacy of the works councils. Although financialisation of corporate governance in general can be expected – and with good reasons – to weaken the power position of the works councils, financialised wages have proven to be one of the power resources of works councils in financialised companies.

At the same time, however, it should be noted that the successful profit sharing schemes are well-known exceptions to the general rule. The dividing line in the metalworking and electrical engineering industries runs between the successful end producers in the automotive industry and their component suppliers. The scope for distribution at firm level is very unequal, which further reinforces existing wage differentials. Further research on profit sharing in other sectors of the economy would be necessary to show if the lines of wage segmentation along the value chains and groups of employees found in the metalworking industry also exist in other industries or not and what the sources of profit sharing wages are. However, with respect to the metalworking industry it can be said that profit sharing is full of ambivalence for works councils and trade unions. On the one hand, it is an effective instrument for exploiting the scope for distribution that exists at company level; on the other hand, it is a manifestation of a process of redistribution and increasing wage differentiation. In the current contexts of negotiation, these ambivalences are unlikely to be resolved.

References

Ackermann, K. F., Bahner J., & Festerling S. (2005). Kennzahlen der Unternehmensführung und variable Vergütung. In E. Zander & D. Wagner (Eds.), *Handbuch des Entgeltmanagements* (pp. 115-138). München: Vahlen.

Bahnmüller, R. (2001). *Stabilität und Wandel der Entlohnungsformen. Entgeltsysteme und Entgeltpolitik in der Metallindustrie, in der Textil- und Bekleidungsindustrie und im Bankgewerbe*. München: Rainer Hampp Verlag.

Banyuls, J., & Haipeter, T. (2010). Against erosion of labour standards: global reorganisation of value chains and industrial relations in the European motor industry. *Work Organisation, Labour and Globalisation, 4*(1), 57-70.

Bontrup, H. J., & Springob, K. (2002). *Gewinn- und Kapitalbeteiligung. Eine mikro- und makroökonomische Analyse*. Wiesbaden: Gabler.

Breisig, T. (2009). *Leistung und Erfolg als Basis für Entgelte. Betriebs- und Dienstvereinbarungen – Analyse und Handlungsempfehlungen*. Frankfurt: Bund-Verlag.

Chahed, Y., Kaub, M., & Müller, H. (2004). *Konzernsteuerung börsennotierter Aktiengesellschaften in Deutschland. Edition der Hans-Böckler-Stiftung 109*. Düsseldorf: Hans-Böckler-Stiftung.

Deutschmann, C. (2008). Die Finanzmärkte und die Mittelschichten: Der kollektive Buddenbrooks-Effekt. *Leviathan, 36*(4), 501-517.

DiMaggio, P. D., & Powell, W. W. (1983). The iron cage revisited: Institutional isomorphism and collective rationality in organizational fields. *American Sociological Review, 48*(3), 147-60.

Dörre, K. (2009). Die neue Landnahme. Dynamiken und Grenzen des Finanzmarktkapitalismus. In K. Dörre, S. Lessenich & H. Rosa (Eds.), *Soziologie - Kapitalismus – Kritik. Eine Debatte* (pp. 21-86). Frankfurt am Main: Suhrkamp.

European Commission. (1991). *Social Europe: The PEPPER report: Promotion of employee participation in profits and enterprise results*. Supplement 3/91. Luxemburg: Office for the Official Publications of the European Communities. Retrieved from https://www.eurofound.europa.eu//sites/default/files/ef_files/docs/areas/participationatwork/pepper1.pdf

Faust, M., Bahnmüller, R., & Fisecker, C. (2011). *Das kapitalmarktorientierte Unternehmen: Externe Erwartungen, Unternehmenspolitik, Personalwesen und Mitbestimmung*. Berlin: Edition Sigma.

Fligstein, N. (1990). *The transformation of corporate control*. Cambridge, London: Harvard University Press.

Froud, J., Johal, S., Leaver A., & Williams, K. (2006). *Financialization and strategy. Narrative and numbers*. London: Routledge.

Haipeter, T. (2009). *Tarifabweichungen und Flächentarifverträge: Eine Analyse der Regulierungspraxis in der Metall- und Elektroindustrie*. Wiesbaden: VS Verlag für Sozialwissenschaften.

Hall, P. A., & Soskice, D. (2001). An introduction to varieties of capitalism. In P. A. Hall & D. Soskice (Eds.), *Varieties of capitalism: The institutional foundations of comparative advantage* (pp. 1-71). Oxford: Oxford University Press.

Holst, H., Nachtwey, O., & Dörre, K. (2010). The strategic use of temporary agency work - Functional change of a non-standard form of employment. *International Journal of Action Research*, *6*(1), 108-138.

Huber, B., & Hofmann, J. (2003). Ist die solidarische Lohnpolitik am Ende? Perspektiven gewerkschaftlicher Lohnpolitik. In H. Wagner & A. Schild (Eds.), *Der Flächentarifvertrag unter Druck. Die Folgen von Verbetrieblichung und Vermarktlichung* (pp. 185-200). Hamburg: VSA.

Huffschmid, J. (2007). Internationale Finanzmärkte: Funktionen, Entwicklungen, Akteure. In J. Huffschmid, M. Köppen & W. Rhode (Eds.), *Finanzinvestoren: Retter oder Raubritter?. Neue Herausforderungen durch die Internationalisierung der Kapitalmärkte* (pp. 10-50). Hamburg: VSA.

IG Metall. (1999). *Erfolgsabhängige Entgelte. Grüne Reihe Nr. 3*. Frankfurt am Main: self-publishing.

Kädtler, J. (2009). *Finanzialisierung und Finanzmarktrationalität. Zur Bedeutung konventioneller Handlungsorientierungen im gegenwärtigen Kapitalismus*. SOFI-Arbeitspapier 5. Göttingen: Soziologisches Forschungsinstitut. Retrieved from http://www.sofi-goettingen.de/fileadmin/Working_paper/SOFI_WorkingPaper5.pdf

Matiaske, W., Tobsch, V., & Fietze S. (2009). *Erfolgs- und Kapitalbeteiligung in Deutschland. Ergebnisse einer repräsentativen Befragung. Berichte der Werkstatt für Organisations- und Personalforschung 18*. Berlin: Werkstatt für Organisations- und Personalforschung.

Meyer, C. (2011). *Betriebswirtschaftliche Kennzahlen und Kennzahlen-Systeme*. Sternenfels: Wissenschaft & Praxis.

Minssen, H. (2011). *Arbeit in der modernen Gesellschaft. Eine Einführung*. Wiesbaden: VS Verlag für Sozialwissenschaften.

Ramsay, H. (1977). Cycles of control: Worker participation in sociological and in historical perspective. *Sociology*, *11*(3), 481–506.

Rehder, B. (2006). Legitimitätsdefizite des Co-Managements. Betriebliche Bündnisse für Arbeit als Konfliktfeld zwischen Arbeitnehmern und betrieblicher Interessenvertretung. *Zeitschrift für Soziologie, 35*(3), 227-242.

Sauer, D. (2013). *Die organisatorische Revolution. Umbrüche in der Arbeitswelt – Ursachen, Auswirkungen und arbeitspolitische Antworten*. Hamburg: VSA.

Stern, J. M., Shiely, J. S., & Ross, I. (2002). *Wertorientierte Unternehmensführung mit E(conomic V(alue) A(dded). Strategie, Umsetzung, Praxisbeispiele*. München: Econ-Verlag.

Voswinkel, S. (2005). Die Organisation der Vermarktlichung von Organisationen: Das Beispiel erfolgsbezogenen Entgelts. In W. Jäger & U. Schimank (Eds.), *Organisationsgesellschaft: Facetten und Perspektiven* (pp. 287-312). Wiesbaden: VS Verlag für Sozialwissenschaften.

Weitzmann, M. L. (1984). *The share economy. Conquering stagflation*. Cambridge, Mass.: Harvard University Press.

Windolf, P. (2008). Eigentümer ohne Risiko. Die Dienstklasse des Finanzmarkt-Kapitalismus. *Zeitschrift für Soziologie, 37*(6), 516-535.

The corporate culture of silent partnerships – shareholding vs. participation?

Thomas Steger, Christina Beisiegel & Madeleine Dietrich[1]

Abstract

Although the financial participation of employees within their employing companies is increasingly receiving attention in politics and business in Germany, most authors still focus on employee shares and often ignore that particularly among small and medium sized enterprises silent partnerships are the dominant form of employee ownership (EO). Against the background of this deficit we present two case studies of medium-sized companies with silent partnerships located in Southern Germany. Herein, we particularly examine the role played by a partnership-oriented corporate culture. We found that, firstly, silent partnerships can support the development of partnership-oriented corporate cultures, although this effect should not be considered an automatism and occurs, rather, in the middle and long run. Secondly, we could find that the interplay between corporate culture and silent partnership results in some influences in both directions, though the effects remain to a limited degree. Thirdly, major obstacles on the way to partnership-oriented corporate cultures are a (traditional) 'master in house' attitude on the part of leading managers, a still limited information policy, also with respect to EO, and an insufficient involvement of employees in decision-making processes. The implications of these findings both for theory and for practice are critically discussed.

1 Thomas Steger (corresponding author): Professor of Leadership and Organization, University of Regensburg, email: thomas.steger@ur.de
Christina Beisiegel, M.Sc.: Research Assistant, Chair of Leadership and Organization, University of Regensburg, email: christina.beisiegel@ur.de
Madeleine Dietrich, Dipl.-Soz.: Research Assistant, Chair of Leadership and Organization, University of Regensburg, email: madeleine.dietrich@ur.de

1. Introduction

The financial participation of employees within their employing companies is increasingly receiving attention in politics and business in Germany (Hartz, Kranz & Steger, 2009; Frankfurter Allgemeine Zeitung, 2012). In the public discussion, diverse expectations are associated with employee ownership (EO), e.g., an increase in employee motivation, employee identification, and loyalty to the company; an improvement in the financial position and liquidity of the company; or a strengthening of the retirement arrangement system (Nerdinger, Horsmann & Pundt, 2003; Schneider & Fritz, 2013).

German companies have a variety of alternatives at their disposal for the design of EO models (Mielke, 2006). Usually, given the amount of capital accumulated, most authors focus on employee shares. However, they often ignore that this dominance just mirrors the impact of large corporations and that particularly among small and medium sized enterprises silent partnerships are the dominant form of EO (Sieg, 2015). This is mostly due to the large freedom of design and the non-bureaucratic administration afforded by this form (AGP, 2011; Brezski, Böge, Lübbehüsen, Rohde & Tomat, 2006; Schneider & Fritz, 2013; Werner, 2007). Silent partnerships offer the opportunity to promote the co-entrepreneurial commitment of the employees without granting them a higher level of co-determination. The silent partnership is thus an undisclosed partnership that is not visible outside of the company. The share-ownership ratio, for instance, does not need to be entered into the commercial register.

Nevertheless, a partnership-oriented corporate culture may play a considerable role for silent partnerships as well. It was found to be a prerequisite for the development of employee performance since only under these conditions will employees contribute their knowledge, their skills, and their commitment to the success of the company (Kruse, Freeman & Blasi, 2008; Martins, Pundt, Horsmann & Nerdinger, 2008; Pierce & Rodgers, 2004). Participation in the company, accordingly, can only be achieved when employees are adequately informed, when they are given the opportunity to act responsibly and entrepreneurially in their field of work, and when they are empowered to participate in decision making (AGP 2011; Kaarsemaker 2006; Martins et al. 2008).

This is the starting point of our chapter. On the basis of two case studies of companies with silent partnerships, we will examine a) to what extent silent partnerships are combined with a partnership-oriented corporate culture, b) what the outcomes of the interplay between corporate culture and silent ownership are, and c) which obstacles still exist in this respect. Both case study companies are of a medium size, engaged in the printing industry, located in southern Germany, and organised as a GmbH & Co. KG. Moreover, both companies offer their employees a silent partnership and have an almost identical employee participation quota of approximately 50 percent.

2. *State of the Art*

The tradition of EO in Germany dates back to the mid-19th century (Gaugler, 2002). In the late 19th century, EO became a subject of scholarly attention, but it was not until the 1970s that a particular increase of interest in the topic could be identified, first of all in the U.S.

Two streams of research on EO can be distinguished; one concentrates on the international dissemination of the different models against the specific country and cultural backgrounds while the other focuses on the effects and outcomes of EO.

Back in 1977, Guski and Schneider were the first to provide some robust quantitative figures on EO in Germany. They identified some 698 companies with a total of 773,664 participating employees. Most recently, Bellmann and Möller (2011) calculated that about 1 percent of all German companies practice a model of EO. For the subsample of companies with more than 150 employees, Matiaske, Fietze, and Tobsch (2011) found 4.9 percent were practicing companies.

In international comparisons of EO, Germany lags somewhat behind, in particular behind most Anglo-American countries (e.g., U.S.: 8 percent – NCEO, 2014; EU: 5.2 percent – Lowitzsch & Hashi, 2014). Nevertheless, EO in Germany can be considered to be rather intensive as about half of the employees in companies with any kind of EO really do participate in it (Bellmann & Leber, 2007).

Three groups of targets pointing to the effects of EO can be identified: a) political targets, such as 'to secure a free economic and societal order' (Guski & Schneider, 1977, p. 31) or to fight communism, socialism, or the union movement, particularly in the U.S. (Blasi, Kruse, Sesil & Kroumova, 2003), b) macroeconomic targets, such as the reduction of the labour market, distribution and retirement provision problems (e.g.,

Kühlewind, 2000; Risser, 2005), and c) company-level targets, such as financial and liquidity effects (e.g., Scholand, 2001; Backes-Gellner & Kay, 2002), increases in productivity, and changes in attitudes and behavior, particularly on the part of the employees.

For the last group of targets, a large number of national and international studies have demonstrated a positive (or at least not negative) relationship between EO and productivity (e.g., Blasi et al., 2008; Fakhfakh et al., 2009; Kruse, 2002; Lampel et al., 2010; Swagel & Carroll, 2010; and specifically for the German context: Möller, 2000; Strotmann, 2002; Wolf & Zwick, 2002). However, some scholars also found a negative relationship in this respect (Faleye et al., 2006; Heinfelt & Curcio, 1997; Livingston & Henry, 1980). Wolf and Zwick (2000) argue that this inconsistency of the findings is due to unobserved heterogeneity between the examined companies with and without EO and to different production functions. Guedri and Hollandts (2008) generally consider the assumption of a linear relationship to be false. In conclusion, given the rather different research designs of the studies in question, any causality between EO and company performance could not be proved up to now.

Another important topic widely discussed is the (potential) impact of EO on the attitudes and behaviours of employees. Here too, we face a rather inconsistent picture. Although a majority of studies could observe some positive effects of material EO on, for instance, work satisfaction, commitment, identification, or motivation, a clear causality could not be demonstrated. Rather the same can be said of multiple studies that have examined the influence of EO on different kinds of employee behaviour such as turnover (Sengupta, Whitfield & McNabb, 2007), absenteeism (Hammer, Landau & Stern, 1981; Rooney 1992), voice (Rhodes & Steers 1981), punctuality (Rhodes & Steers 1981), or labour protection (Grunberg, Moore & Greenberg, 1996; Kardas 1997). Furthermore, the role played by different potential moderators, such as procedural justice (Kuvaas, 2003), perceived participation opportunities (Nerdinger et al., 2003), or corporate culture (Nerdinger & Wilke, 2009) is still disputed.

Moreover, the relationship between material and immaterial participation remains open (Poutsma, Kalmi & Pendleton, 2006). This holds particularly true for the role of the organisational culture. Several scholars argue that EO would definitively have an impact on the company's culture (e.g., Aubert, 2008; Martins et al., 2008). This, though, does not mean that EO necessarily increases participation or even creates a kind of participation culture but may rather consolidate the existing power structures (Steger &

Hartz, 2008). Thompson et al. (2013) suggested that organisational culture should be considered a moderator between EO and firm performance. This idea was also similarly promoted by further scholars (Bartkus, 1997; Sauser, 2009; Soupata, 2005). On the other hand though, a participative and partnership-oriented organisational culture may promote and facilitate the introduction of EO (Goic, 1999).

Finally, there seems to be a lack of research on EO in the form of silent partnerships. Although this form can be considered dominant among SMEs (Mielke, 2006; Sieg, 2015), we could not identify any study dedicated to it. Several authors mention silent partnerships but fail to address the model in more depth (e.g., Schneider & Fritz, 2013; Witt, 2001). Most recent large international studies (e.g., Lowitzsch & Hashi, 2014; Mathieu, 2015) completely ignore the silent partnership model. Meanwhile the literature about silent partnership concentrates on tax problems (e.g., Segat, 2000) or addresses banks or financial investors as silent partners (e.g. Dunlap, 2012). So, the great need to explore the topic more closely seems to be obvious.

3. Methods

This case study research follows the approach developed by Eisenhardt (1989). On the basis of two company case studies, we examine a) to what extent the companies possess a partnership-oriented corporate culture, b) what the outcomes of the interplay between corporate culture and silent partnership are, and c) which obstacles must still be overcome in this respect.

The two case studies were taken from the results of a theoretical sampling. Both companies are of a medium size, engaged in the printing industry, located in southern Germany, and organised as a GmbH & Co. KG. Moreover, both companies offer their employees a silent partnership and have an almost identical employee participation quota of approximately 50 percent. In contrast, the companies differ in the age of their silent partnership; Company A established the silent partnership in 1981 while Company B started it in 2010.

The exploration of the two case studies used multiple data collection methods, namely exploratory interviews with managers, observations during company visits, employee questionnaires, and semi-standardised in-depth interviews (to verify the findings). Field notes in the form of diaries and company documents, e.g., contracts from the EO model, completed these methods. Thus qualitative and quantitative data have been combined. Because of the overlap of data collection and analysis, the interview questions were partially adjusted during the survey process. Data collection was performed by two co-authors during 2012 and 2013. Each of them was assigned one company to cover. Since each researcher is then intimately familiar with his/her case, a deep knowledge of the individual case studies is guaranteed. The case studies were first analysed separately (i.e., within-case analysis). Then, the cross-case patterns, similarities, and differences between the two cases were explored (i.e., cross-case analysis). This resulted in a number of concluding propositions.

4. Within-Case Analysis: Company Alpha

4.1 Economic overview

Alpha was founded in 1888. It is a family enterprise, employs 120 employees, and has an annual turnover of about €28 million. Alpha's economic development in recent decades was positive. Although there were some crises in the printing industry, Alpha was not hit hard by them. Collective bargaining agreements between employer and employees do not exist since Alpha opted out of this in 2000. The aim was to simplify the complex collective bargaining agreement of the printing industry and to modernise wage and salary determination. Accordingly, holiday pay was abolished and target bonuses as well as a premium for attendance were introduced. Alpha's staff currently comprises seven apprentices and a considerable number of young employees. Many skilled workers and only a small number of non-skilled workers are employed.[2]

4.2 The silent partnership

Alpha established a silent partnership in 1981. An ideological motive was behind this as the managing director states that '*basically we wanted to somehow eliminate this distinction between capital and labor.*'[3] Alpha's

2 Interview with the managing director: 1ff.
3 Interview with the managing director: 7.

management held the assumption that all employees should contribute to the success of Alpha and, if successful, the employees should also be able to benefit from the success. Other motives were financial asset building for the employees and the identification of employees with the company.[4]

The initiative and decision to introduce employee financial participation was taken by Alpha's management. The main initiator was the former managing director (and owner), who is the father of the current managing director. He was a powerful entrepreneur with strong feelings of responsibility towards his employees. The idea of employee financial participation corresponded with his idea of how a company should work. At that time, a model of financial participation (with bonus shares for employees) also already existed at Bertelsmann and was viewed as a model for the printing industry. The project of implementing the financial participation was passed on from father to son. A committee of about 15 people was formed in which employees from each department were represented. This committee, together with a management consultant, developed a financial participation model that has remained and been preserved in this form since then.[5]

Alpha has an employee financial participation quota of approximately 50 percent (i.e., 50 percent of employees participate in the model). Each year, Alpha offers all employees some new company certificates with which they become silent partners.[6] Accordingly, the employees may share in the profits of Alpha, depending on its business situation. The holding period for the shares is at least ten years. None of the employees, however, have sold his/her shares to this day. The employees also participate in company losses as there is a 'loss scale' that works in a similar way to the 'profit scale'. The resulting loss of shares is used to offset future profit shares.[7] In the case of insolvency of Alpha, the liability of the employees, however, is limited to the amount of their shares. If an employee leaves the company, he/she receives the shareholders' deposit, even if this occurs before ten years have passed. There are two general meetings per year in which the management explains the company's balance sheet to all silent partners.[8]

4 Interview with the managing director: 7f.
5 Interview with the managing director: 1ff.
6 Interview with the managing director: 8ff.
7 Alpha Company brochure.
8 Interview with the managing director: 8ff.

4.3 The corporate culture

After an initial reading of the case study materials, five categories were derived to describe the corporate culture and the silent partnership: (a) the personality of the managing director, (b) the role of traditions and values, (c) the employee information, (d) the communication and relationship between management and employees, and (e) the employee participation and influence.

(a) The personality of the managing director

During the plant visit, the managing director gave the impression of being very proud of the company. First, he showed the reception area with all the certificates and prizes Alpha has won in the past. It was obvious that he enjoyed showing the visitor his company, his as well as the employees' offices, and the production facilities, which are very large, bright, and clean. Furthermore, he seemed to be particularly proud that his company has practiced the silent partnership for such a long time. The managing director gave the impression that he feels like a father to his employees, which was clearly visible during the plant visit. For instance, he corrected an employee who was sorting paper sheets and demonstrated that he had made one move too many when laying down the paper sheet and thus slowed down the work process.

(b) The role of traditions and values

Traditions seem to play a major role at Alpha. The initiator of the introduction of the silent partnership was the father of the current managing director. Accordingly, the managing director emphasises the long tradition of financial participation and partnership. Like his father, he feels a high degree of responsibility towards his employees and wants them to financially participate in the success of Alpha. So, alongside his role of responsibility, the managing director aims to live out the value of 'partnership'.

For instance, he describes the department heads as fair and a major reason for the good corporate climate.[9]

(c) The employee information

The financially participating employees are informed about Alpha's balance sheet at two general meetings per year.[10] Certain business ratios from the balance sheet are explained to the employees. In these meetings, the management even discusses some investment decisions with the employees.[11] The employees work in offices that are partially separated from each other by a glass wall, and there is a small canteen in which the employees also cook for themselves. So, the facilities at Alpha support communication and information exchange between the employees. Nevertheless, in the employee survey, only about one-third of the employees feel well informed about the economic development of the company and all important processes in the company.[12]

(d) The communication and relationship between management and employees

The managing director perceives the relationship between management and employees as good; the employees are team-oriented and the departments cooperated well with each other.[13] An indication of the good communication is that the managing director spoke with many employees during his plant visit. The small size of the company and the company's success lead to a good relationship between management and employees, which is confirmed by the managing director.[14] The employees themselves describe the atmosphere in Alpha as good and state that there were only a

---

9 Interview with the managing director: 5.

10 Interview with the managing director: 8ff.

11 Interview with the managing director: 11.

12 Questionnaire statement '*I feel well informed about the economic development of the company.* ' – agreement 37 percent, neutral 47 percent, rejection 16 percent; Questionnaire statement '*I feel well informed about all important processes in the company.*' – agreement 39 percent, neutral 41 percent, rejection 20 percent.

13 Interview with the managing director: 5.

14 Interview with the managing director: 5.

few people who do not identify with Alpha.[15] As both the managing director and an interviewed employee said, Alpha has an open communication climate.[16] The employees rate both their relationship with their superiors and with their colleagues as good.[17] Moreover, the majority of them would be happy to spend their future working life at the company.[18]

(e) The employee participation and influence

The father of the managing director used to include the employees as much as possible in decision-making processes of all kind. For instance, he always passed the decision about which printing machine should be bought to the printers.[19] The current managing director has kept this leadership principle.[20] In sharp contrast to these impressions given by the managing director, however, many employees feel they are limited in their freedom to contribute their own ideas.[21] The employees also evaluate their influence on the distribution of work,[22] the design of their own work,[23] and the success of the company[24] as being little.

15 Interview with an employee: 1f.
16 Interview with the managing director: 5; interview with an employee: 1f.
17 Questionnaire *statement 'I have a very good relationship with my superiors.'* – agreement 83 percent, neutral 17 percent, rejection 0 percent; Questionnaire statement '*I have a very good relationship with my colleagues.'* – agreement 98 percent, neutral 2 percent, rejection 0 percent.
18 Questionnaire statement: '*I would be happy to spend my future working life in the company.'* – agreement 95 percent, neutral 5 percent, rejection 0 percent.
19 Interview with the managing director: 15.
20 Interview with the managing director: 15f.
21 Questionnaire statement: '*The company offers me enough freedom to contribute my ideas.'* – agreement 37 percent, neutral 32 percent, rejection 32 percent.
22 Questionnaire statement: '*Influence on the distribution of the work packages in the team.'* – agreement 29 percent, neutral 31 percent, rejection 40 percent.
23 Questionnaire statement: '*Influence on the design of my own work.'* – agreement 55 percent, neutral 22 percent, rejection 23 percent.
24 Questionnaire statement: '*Influence on the success of the company.'* – agreement 39 percent, neutral 34 percent, rejection 27 percent.

4.4 The interplay between corporate culture and silent partnership

(a) The personality of the managing director

The managing director is very proud of the silent partnership. He believes the financial aspect is the main reason behind employees participating financially. The main reason not to participate would be too little capital available.[25] Indeed, this is exactly what the employees report in the questionnaire survey.[26] Like the managing director, the employees are proud of the capital accumulation of the silent partnership. Obviously, the silent partnership mainly constitutes an investment topic, both from the perspective of the employees as well as from the managing director.

The managing director does not see any risk for Alpha in the employee financial participation, which shows that the employees are real 'silent' partners for him. A disadvantage on the part of the employees is, in his view, the financial risk if Alpha goes bankrupt. However, he states that this would be a slow process and the employees would have enough time to dispense with their financial participation in this case.[27] The managing director obviously overlooks the mandatory holding period of at least ten years here. In fact, the risk of losing the money in the case of insolvency was also reported by the employee interviewed[28] and was (partly) reflected in thc employee survey.[29]

(b) The role of traditions and values

Financial participation has a long tradition at Alpha. Accordingly about 50 percent of the employees participate in this model.[30] Moreover, the employee survey indicates that there are also employees who are not yet participating financially, but want to do so next year. Due to the favorable

---

25 Interview with the managing director: 13.

26 Questionnaire statement: '*Attractive capital investment*' – agreement 97 percent, neutral 3 percent, rejection 0 percent; Questionnaire statement: '*Too little capital*' – agreement 22 percent, neutral 22 percent, rejection 56 percent.

27 Interview with the managing director: 10f.

28 Interview with an employee: 4f.

29 Questionnaire statement: '*The participation model in our company is risk-free for me.*' – agreement 60 percent, neutral 33 percent, rejection 7 percent.

30 Interview with the managing director: 12.

interest rate connected with the silent partnership in recent years, many employees who left Alpha would have liked to continue investing their money in the company;[31] this is, however, not possible since all employees leaving the company are reimbursed.[32] Obviously, the employees are highly satisfied with their financial reward from the silent partnership. Furthermore they consider their increased commitment to Alpha to be a strong effect of financial participation.[33] Other effects of the silent partnership, according to the employee survey, are an increase in the capital base of the company,[34] a stronger focus on success,[35] and a stronger growth of the company,[36] which once more stress the financial reward character of the silent partnership for the employees.

(c) The employee information

The financially participating employees are informed about the company's balance sheet at two general meetings per year.[37] The communication climate in these meetings is said to be very open.[38] Accordingly, the managing director views this knowledge advantage about Alpha as a reason for financial participation.[39] The employees, though, do not view too little information about the silent partnership model as a reason to not

31 Interview with an employee: 3f.

32 Interview with the managing director: 8f.

33 Questionnaire statement: '*The employee financial participation leads to an increased commitment to the company on the part of the employees.*' – agreement 82 percent, neutral 16 percent, rejection 2 percent.

34 Questionnaire statement: '*The employee financial participation leads to an increase of the capital base of the company.*' – agreement 66 percent, neutral 26 percent, rejection 9 percent.

35 Questionnaire statement: '*The employee financial participation leads to a stronger focus on the success of the company.*' – agreement 55 percent, neutral 29 percent, rejection 16 percent.

36 Questionnaire statement: '*The employee financial participation leads to a stronger growth of the company.*' – agreement 52 percent, neutral 30 percent, rejection 18 percent.

37 Interview with the managing director: 8ff.

38 Interview with the managing director: 10f.

39 Interview with the managing director: 13.

participate.[40] The employees also consider the information about the company to be one main effect of the silent partnership.[41] Because of the financial participation, they feel better informed about the economic development of the company[42] as well as about important processes in the company.[43] This may be an indication that the silent partnership contributes to a partnership-based corporate culture because although the partners remain 'silent' and the managing director is still free in his decisions, the financially-participating employees are better informed about these decisions than the employees not participating financially. When we presented the results of the employee survey to the company (i.e., the management and four employees), the managing director felt validated in his open information policy. The fact that not all employees feel well-informed about the economic development of the company and about all important processes in the company[44] remained undisputed.

(d) The communication and relationship between management and employees

The relationship between management and employees is perceived by the managing director to be good.[45] Alpha practices open communication, and the management openly communicates the benefits of financial participation to the employees.[46] The employees agree with the corporate manage-

---

40 Questionnaire statement: '*Too little information*' – agreement 0 percent, neutral 14 percent, rejection 86 percent.

41 Questionnaire statement: '*Because of the participation I feel better informed about the important processes in the company.*' – agreement 70 percent, neutral 19 percent, rejection 11 percent.

42 Questionnaire statement: '*Through financial participation I am better informed about the economic development of the company.*' – agreement 75 percent, neutral 14 percent, rejection 11 percent.

43 Questionnaire statement: '*Through financial participation I am better informed about all important processes in the company.*' – agreement 70 percent, neutral 18 percent, rejection 12 percent.

44 Questionnaire statement '*I feel well informed about the economic development of the company.*' – agreement 37 percent, neutral 47 percent, rejection 16 percent; Questionnaire statement '*I feel well informed about all important processes in the company.*' – agreement 39 percent, neutral 41 percent, rejection 20 percent.

45 Interview with the managing director: 5.

46 Interview with the managing director: 5; interview with an employee: 1f.

ment about what objectives are crucial for the silent partnership, namely capital formation and the commitment to Alpha.[47]

The silent partnership model is rated by the employees as very good. They evaluate the model as fair, modern, easy to understand, and not resulting in a great amount of work for investing employees.[48] All financially-participating employees surveyed would participate in the model again and are satisfied with the silent partnership model as well as with the performance of their investment.[49] The employees perceive the financial participation as being of great benefit to Alpha but also estimate the amount of work for the company and the silent partnership model as being not very cost-efficient for Alpha.[50]

According to the managing director, the employees who stand in close contact with the management, e.g., the heads of the departments or the employees from the accounting department, are more likely to participate in the silent partnership.[51] Accordingly, the relationship between management and employees may be an important antecedent of the financial participation of the employees. Furthermore, in the managing director's opinion, the employees with a low commitment to Alpha are less likely to participate in the model,[52] because they *'are just too far away'*[53] and thus might not feel like partners of the company. All this seems to demonstrate that the silent partnership bears many advantages for both the employees as well as the company and is not detrimental to the relationship between management and employees.

---

47 Questionnaire statement: *'The employee financial participation leads to an improvement in the investments of the employees.'* – agreement 63 percent, neutral 34 percent, rejection 3 percent.

48 Questionnaire statement: *'The participation model in our company doesn't involve a great amount of work on my part.'* – agreement 95 percent, neutral 5 percent, rejection 0 percent.

49 Questionnaire statement: *'I am satisfied with the performance of the financial participation.'* – agreement 97 percent, neutral 3 percent, rejection 0 percent.

50 Questionnaire statement: *'The participation model in our company is very cost-efficient for the company.'* – agreement 8 percent, neutral 84 percent, rejection 8 percent. However, one employee from accounting rates the administrative burden and the costs of financial participation from the company's perspective as low (Interview with an employee: 3).

51 Interview with the managing director: 14.

52 Interview with the managing director: 13.

53 Interview with the managing director: 13.

(e) The employee participation and influence

The managing director aims to integrate the employees in the decision-making process.[54] It must be noted that the employees who financially participate perceive a higher influence on the design of their own work compared to employees who do not participate.[55] Moreover, not all employees consider the involvement and influence of the employees on Alpha to be positive since financial participation is also offered to the temporary employees after one year of membership in the company, which runs counter to the intent of financial participation.[56]

Another important finding is that the employees evaluate their influence as being little. This stands in contrast to the statement made by the managing director about his father passing the decision about which printing machine should be bought on to the printers and that he has kept this leadership principle and integrates the employees in decision-making processes. The ideas from the employees are only discussed; the implementation occurs based on the decision of the management. This shows that the employees are real silent partners who are not really integrated into decision-making processes.

4.5 Problems and challenges

One problem relates to the quality of information. The perceived open information policy of the managing director is in contradiction to the fact that not all employees feel well informed about the company. Also, the silent partnership seems to introduce a two-class-society in this respect since those employees who participate financially feel significantly better informed about the economic development of the company and important processes in the company than the employees who do not participate.

The finding that the employees with closer contact to the management might feel more as partners of the company and participate more often in the silent partnership also sheds light on a certain deficit. Those

54 Interview with the managing director: 5.

55 Questionnaire statement: *'Influence on the design of my own work.'* – mean participants 3.66, mean non-participants 2.00 on a five-point Likert scale.

56 Interview with an employee: 3.

employees with less contact to the management might participate financially less because they do not feel like partners.

Another problem may lie in the little influence the employees have, which stands in contrast to the perception of the managing director, who states that he integrates the employees in decision-making processes. But he claims that the advantage of the silent partnership could be found in the fact that he *'remains free in his business decisions'*.[57] This statement supports the perception of the employees of their superficial decision-making-participation. Based on the perceived little influence of the employees, the corporate culture of Alpha seems non-participatory.

A problem of the silent partnership is the insolvency risk. The managing director only sees a risk for the employees if Alpha goes bankrupt. He states that in such a case, the employees would have enough time to dispense with their financial participation, but he overlooks the mandatory holding period of at least ten years.

Ultimately, the silent partnership with Alpha is primarily an investment topic and only makes a small contribution to the strengthening of a partnership-based corporate culture. There are some obvious deficits in the implementation of a corporate culture based on partnership, mainly in the area of employee information and involvement in decision-making processes.

5. Within-Case Analysis: Company Beta

5.1 Economic overview

Beta was founded in 1980 and is still wholly-owned by the founder and his wife. Beta's current economic situation is described by the managing directors[58] as being back *'on very solid footing'*[59] and its prospects for the future as *'cautiously optimistic'*.[60] These estimates are mainly due to the downturn in 2008/2009. In these two years, the company's revenues had

57 Interview with the managing director: 9.

58 Beta is led by two managing directors, namely the founder and, since 2003, another employed managing director.

59 Interview with the managing director: 2.

60 Interview with the managing director: 2.

fallen by about 20 percent.[61] Both managing directors perceive the crisis in the industrial sector in which the company group[62] operates as being the reason for this loss in revenue. Beta makes 95 percent of sales in the field of advertising products. The company mainly serves large customers who cut their marketing budgets at the onset of the crisis. This had an immediate impact on the company. The company has in the meantime recovered, but lost three years of growth. With some additional customer acquisitions, the company has returned to a moderate annual growth of 3 to 4 percent. Nevertheless, Beta remains highly dependent on the overall economic environment because its products are waived first by customers in times of crisis.[63] In the survey year, the company had 85 employees and a turnover of €12 million.[64]

5.2 The silent partnership

Although Beta has existed for over thirty years, the EO was not introduced in the form of a silent partnership until 2010 as an additional tool to increase employer attractiveness and employee loyalty.[65] The initiator of the introduction was the founder himself: *'...that was many years ago ... a goal of mine ... it was delayed by the whole crisis situation, otherwise we would have certainly introduced it five years earlier.'*[66] He combined the introduction of the EO with the desire for a change in his employees' state of consciousness: *'Why do I work in a company? Do I work along the lines of: here's just ... the employee-, employer function, which is clearly separated ... or do I work in a company working towards a community, i.e. a joint success.'*[67] Both managing directors justify the decision for a silent partnership, stating that there was no other reasonable model for the company and based on consideration of the evidence at the time, the silent partnership was the optimal model.[68] The employees were initially

61 Interview with the founder: 3; interview with the managing director: 2.
62 The production company holds a subsidiary which is a pure distributor. Together they form a company group.
63 Interview with the founder: 3; interview with the managing director: 2.
64 Interview with the founder: 2.
65 Invitation AGP-Treffpunkt Beta: 2.
66 Interview with the founder: 8.
67 Interview with the founder: 10.
68 Interview with the founder: 12f.; interview with the managing director: 6.

informed about the model as well as about the offer for EO in two employee meetings in late February and early March 2010.[69] The objectives of the EO were formulated by the management as follows:

- 'to further strengthen the partnership-oriented corporate culture
- to recognize and encourage the dedication of the employees
- to involve the employees in the company's success
- to create an additional opportunity for the accumulation of capital
- to further improve the financial structure of the company.'[70]

In the context of a savings plan, the model enables each employee who has been working for the company for at least one year to make a monthly deposit (minimum €25). In addition, one-off payments can be made (minimum €500) on two dates during the year. Depending on the level of the personal contribution of the employee, the company grants an additional sum of between €120 and €360 per year, which is tax-free and free of social charges. Each year, the company offers all eligible employees a new investment offer. Thus, employees can decide each year whether or not and to what extent they want to join the savings plan or whether they want to make a lump-sum payment. The silent partners receive a base interest rate and a dividend. The interest is paid annually. After four years, the paid capital can be terminated with six months' notice to the year-end. The employee capital only has a share in the profits and not in the losses. In the case of company insolvency, there is no obligation to make an additional contribution. However, the employee capital can be partially or completely lost.[71]

---

69 Letter - offer for employee share ownership 16/03/2010.

70 Guideline at employee share ownership - employees meeting 26/02/2010.

71 Offer for employee share ownership 2010; contract of the silent partnership; guideline at employee share ownership - employees meeting 26/02/2010; notations speech from 06/03/2012.

5.3 Corporate culture

(a) The personality of the founder

The company is led by two managing directors. Since the *'purchased'* managing director[72] views his remit as only being in the operating of businesses and cares little about cultural issues,[73] these issues fall under the jurisdiction of the founder. He usually works with his door open, thereby allowing his employees continuous entry. This relates well with the statement of the managing director who speaks of a patriarchal-caring culture.[74] In the interview, the founder gives the impression that his employees are important to him and that he wants to be open and collegial with them, and provide them with the greatest support possible. For him, working independently, freedom at work, and few hierarchical levels in the company are essential elements of partnership-oriented employee participation. He doesn't view his employees as a cost factor but rather as effective employees who earn the generated surplus in collaboration with him.[75]

(b) The role of traditions and values

The patriarchal-caring corporate and leadership culture and the statement made by the managing director where he speaks of a typical owner-managed, founder-managed company[76] lead us to conclude that traditions and values are of great importance to the company. However, as can also be seen in the interview, the founder strives to maintain the balance – despite the traditions and values carried along since the foundation of the company. He reports *'...that ... structures ... are not rigidly predefined, but that an individual has the opportunity to change something.'*[77] The traditional values in the company are increasingly flanked by partnership-oriented values. The employees are given space for an active exchange

---

72 Interview with the managing director: 1.
73 Interview with the managing director: 2.
74 Interview with the managing director: 4.
75 Interview with the founder: 5; notations speech from 06/03/2012.
76 Interview with the managing director: 4.
77 Interview with the founder: 22.

amongst themselves in the company: *'...we foster it by ... creating appropriate opportunities, e.g. our glass hall, with levels of communication and we believe that overall we have a spirited workforce, a vibrant workforce, who are capable of grappling with the company's problems and duties and prepared to make a contribution.'*[78]

(c) The employee information

The information culture, which constitutes a significant part of a partnership-oriented corporate culture, was illuminated in the employee survey and in the interviews with the managing directors and the employees. The employee survey showed that the general information about important processes in the company[79] and about the economic development of the company[80] is perceived as being problematic. During the in-depth interviews, the employees also report of rather poor information in these fields.[81] The founder, however, does not see a lack of information concerning the general information about the company: *'...the employee sees every day ... what the company is about, where the company stands, we inform regularly.'*[82] In this context, the managing director questions the obligation to collect and the obligation to deliver: *'Most probably, the employees will say, I would like to know much more and would like to have much more information, on the other hand, we do not withhold this information greatly, but of course we do not spread the information greatly ... who wants it and asks for it definitely gets information.'*[83]

78 Interview with the founder: 22.

79 Questionnaire statement *'I feel well informed about all important processes in the company.'* - agreement 24 percent, neutral 24 percent, rejection 52 percent.

80 Questionnaire statement *'I feel well informed about the economic development of the company.'* - agreement 10 percent, neutral 48 percent, rejection 43 percent.

81 In-depth interview 1 with an employee: 5; notes in-depth interview 2 with an employee: 2.

82 Interview with the founder: 16.

83 Interview with the managing director: 13.

(d) The communication and relationship between management and employees

The short conversations with the employees during a plant visit suggest that a culture of open communication is maintained in the company. The founder supported this philosophy in the interview, too. However, these observations stand in contrast to the deficient information culture described above and the organisational climate perceived by the employees.[84] In the employee survey, moreover, the relationship with colleagues[85] was assessed more positively than the relationship with the superiors.[86] This is also highlighted by the respondents in the in-depth interviews. The mood among the workforce is described as very good and there are reports of great collegiality. In opposition to this, a discrepancy is lamented between the executive level and the employees.[87]

(e) The employee participation and influence

Evaluating the influence of the respondents on various hierarchical levels also provides some insights of how partnership-oriented the corporate culture of Beta is. Only the influence on the design of the own work is positively rated.[88] This finding supports to some extent the statements of the founder, who particularly stressed the freedom of his employees at work and working independently in his speech as well as in the interview.[89] In areas beyond their own work, the employees rate their participa-

---

84 Questionnaire statement *'The general climate in the company is good.'* - agreement 29 percent, neutral 48 percent, rejection 24 percent.

85 Questionnaire statement *'I have a very good relationship with my colleagues.'* - agreement 95 percent, neutral 5 percent, rejection 0 percent.

86 Questionnaire statement *'I have a very good relationship with my superiors.'* - agreement 76 percent, neutral 19 percent, rejection 5 percent.

87 In-depth interview 1 with an employee: 3; notes in-depth interview 2 with an employee: 2; in-depth interview 3 with an employee: 4.

88 Questionnaire statement *'Influence on the design of my own work.'* - high 55 percent, neutral 20 percent, low 25 percent.

89 Interview with the founder: 5; notations speech from 06/03/2012.

tion and their influence as rather low. This was found both in the employee survey[90] as well as in the in-depth interviews.[91]

5.4 Interplay between corporate culture and silent partnership

(a) The personality of the founder

The founder is strongly interested in the development of a partnership-oriented corporate culture. He states that the introduction of the EO was his target many years ago, and he reports of the combined desire to achieve a change in the state of consciousness among his employees.[92] With the introduction of the silent partnership, he wanted to break the clear separation between the employer function and the employee function in order to pursue joint success on a partnership-oriented basis in the future[93] – *'but of course not under socialist conditions'*.[94] The crucial point for him is *'...that everybody has the feeling ... [of being] co-involved ... in what is achieved.'*[95] But he also seems to be grateful that the silent partnership by nature doesn't grant too many rights to employees: *'It must be clear ... who ... has to make the business decisions.'*[96] All this leads to the conclusion that he seems to be ambiguous in this matter. He wants to give his employees share ownership and immaterial participation in the company, but only within a framework that does not restrict his decision-making power.

---

90 Questionnaire statement *'Influence on the distribution of the work packages in the team.'* - high 21 percent, neutral 32 percent, low 47 percent; questionnaire statement *'Influence on the corporate strategy'*- high 10 percent, neutral 15 percent, low 75 percent; questionnaire statement *'Influence on the success of the entire company'* - high 26 percent, neutral 47 percent, low 26 percent.
91 In-depth interview 1 with an employee: 2.
92 Interview with the founder: 8ff.
93 Interview with the founder: 10.
94 Interview with the founder: 10.
95 Interview with the founder: 10.
96 Interview with the founder: 9.

(b) The role of traditions and values

The aim of the founder is to complement traditional values with partnership values. The employees have the opportunity to initiate change. This approach is consistent with the objectives of the EO model. The silent partnership was introduced in the company, inter alia, to *'recognize and promote the dedication of the employees'*.[97] The silent partnership is to therefore play a supporting role in the development of partnership values. Employees who initiate changes and dedicate themselves to resolving business problems and completing tasks should have the opportunity to benefit financially. Nevertheless, the founder considers the aspired change in values to be a long process. In the interview, he reports that at the moment, there is no recognisable difference between shareholding and non-shareholding employees. For the purpose of comparison, the silent partnership is not yet anchored long enough in the company: *'...maybe in ten years ... you can ... see, yes, employees' state of consciousness ... has changed a little bit, but I do not have any illusions that we will suddenly now have very different basic attitudes in our employees.'*[98]

(c) The employee information

There are contrary opinions about the information culture of the company. The managing directors do not see any lack of information for employees in the company. However, the employees themselves see a large deficit on the part of the company in this area. As the employee survey clearly shows, however, EO has so far been unable to improve on the level of general information known to the employee about important procedures in the company or the economic development of the company.[99] The information policy about the silent partnership is perceived controversially by the respondents. While the founder reports a deficit in the specific infor-

---

97 Guideline at employee share ownership - employees meeting 26/02/2010.

98 Interview with the founder: 22.

99 Questionnaire statement *'Because of the employee share ownership, I am better informed about all important processes in the company.'* - agreement 0 percent, neutral 17 percent, rejection 83 percent; questionnaire statement *'Because of the employee share ownership, I am better informed about the economic development of the company.'* - agreement 6 percent, neutral 11 percent, rejection 83 percent.

mation about the silent partnership and openly admits that information sessions take place very sparsely,[100] half of the employees feel well-informed about the silent partnership.[101] The information that was given at the beginning of the introduction of the silent partnership in 2010 and the information received by each employee when making a purchase of silent partnership shares was reported to be sufficient for the employees. The employees, rather, see a deficit in information about the current state of the silent partnership:[102]

> *'...what good has it ultimately done, also for the company, we do not know at all ... maybe they have already done something with that money? Where is it at the moment? Has the money been invested somewhere else? No idea!'*[103]

(d) The communication and relationship between management and employees

The employees perceive the distinction between the executive level and themselves as being too rigid.[104] The silent partnership in the company could not help to reduce this either. No surveyed employee agrees with the statement that the relationship to his superiors has been improved by the EO.[105] Moreover, no interviewee agrees that it has led to a reduction of conflicts between employees and the management[106] or to an improvement in the general climate in the company.[107]

---

100 More concretely, once per year (Interview with the founder: 13).

101 Questionnaire statement *'How well informed do you feel about employee share ownership in your company?'* - well informed 52 percent, neutral 35 percent, not well informed 13 percent.

102 In-depth interview 1 with an employee: 4, 6; notes in-depth interview 2 with an employee: 2; in-depth interview 3 with an employee: 5f.

103 In-depth interview 1 with an employee: 4.

104 In-depth interview 1 with an employee: 3.

105 Questionnaire statement *'The relationship with my superiors has been improved by the employee share ownership.'* - agreement 0 percent, neutral 24 percent, rejection 76 percent.

106 Questionnaire statement *'Because of the employee share ownership, there was a reduction in conflicts between the employees and the management.'* - agreement 0 percent, neutral 17 percent, rejection 83 percent.

107 Questionnaire statement *'The general climate in the company has been improved by the employee share ownership.'* - agreement 0 percent, neutral 22 percent, rejection 78 percent.

(e) The employee participation and influence

The employees of Beta mainly find freedom and influence through the design of their own work. According to the evaluation of the interviewed employees, the financial participation of the employees did not lead to an expansion in participation and joint decision possibilities on the part of the employees.[108] In the opinion of the employees, neither the influence on the design of the own work,[109] nor the influence on the distribution of the work packages in the team,[110] the influence on the corporate strategy,[111] and the influence on the success of the entire company[112] could be improved by the silent partnership. Employees expect more, especially in areas that go beyond their own work: it '*...sometimes would be important to involve the employees.*'[113]

5.5 Problems and challenges

Some problems and challenges can be derived for Beta. These problems and challenges particularly loom for the silent partnership with respect to a partnership-oriented corporate culture.

The silent partnership was, inter alia, introduced with the objective of '*recognizing and encouraging the dedication of the employees*'.[114] The founder wants to make clear that new partnership-oriented values are to

---

108 Questionnaire statement '*The involvement of the employees in the capital leads/led to an expansion of participation and joint decision possibilities for employees.*' - agreement 0 percent, neutral 14 percent, rejection 86 percent.

109 Questionnaire statement '*My influence on the design of my own work has been improved by the employee share ownership.*' - agreement 11 percent, neutral 11 percent, rejection 78 percent.

110 Questionnaire statement '*My influence on the distribution of the work packages in the team has been improved by the employee share ownership.*' - agreement 0 percent, neutral 11 percent, rejection 89 percent.

111 Questionnaire statement '*My influence on the corporate strategy has been improved by the employee share ownership.*' - agreement 0 percent, neutral 11 percent, rejection 89 percent.

112 Questionnaire statement '*My influence on the success of the entire company has been improved by the employee share ownership.*' - agreement 0 percent, neutral 11 percent, rejection 89 percent.

113 In-depth interview 1 with an employee: 3.

114 Guideline at employee share ownership - employees meeting 26.02.2010.

make their way into the company. Therefore, participation and dedication in the company should be rewarded through the opportunity to access company shares. Whether or not the silent partnership will succeed in this, however, cannot be recognized now but will become apparent during the years to come because at the time of data collection, the silent partnership at Beta was slightly more than two years old.

With the introduction of the silent partnership, the founder formulated the aim of further strengthening the partnership-oriented corporate culture.[115] His ideas, desires, and aims are promising. Certainly, the short time since the introduction of the silent partnership may be seen as a factor that has prevented or hindered the stringent implementation of relevant issues in this area so far. Two years may not be enough for results to be visible. In this context, three main problem areas can be described:

A large problem is the information culture. The employees testify that the company and the management in charge exhibit large deficits in this area. The answers in the in-depth interviews indicate that there is a great desire for information on the current state of the silent partnership in the company and that there is still considerable room for improvement on the part of the management.[116] The employees demand information about the company and, in particular, about the current state of the EO model.

Another problem directly related to the information problem is the relationship between the management and the employees. As long as the employees sense a discrepancy between the executive level and the employee level, no partnership-oriented corporate culture can be achieved in the company. In an in-depth interview, an employee summed the problem up: *'...in my opinion more should come from the management level'*.[117] The problem is that too little communication is initiated by the management and therefore the relationship between the management and the employees is not consolidated.

Another problem is the fact that employees are not involved in decisions.[118] Of course, with the silent partnership, Beta has selected an EO model in which decision-making structures remain untouched. Neverthe-

115 Guideline at employee share ownership - employees meeting 26/02/2010.

116 In-depth interview 1 with an employee: 4, 6; notes in-depth interview 2 with an employee: 2; in-depth interview 3 with an employee: 5f.

117 In-depth interview 1 with an employee: 4.

118 In-depth interview 1 with an employee: 3.

less, the employees themselves want more participation and influence, particularly in areas that go beyond their own work.

6. Cross-Case Analysis: Company Alpha vs. Company Beta

In order to complete the picture drawn in the previous sections, a cross-case analysis will provide a comparative view of the two cases. Similarities and differences in line with the five categories introduced above are the focus of consideration and result in four propositions.

(a) The personality of the managing director

It is noteworthy that the managing director of Alpha is proud of his company and his own achievements bring him much pleasure. These achievements, however, would not have been possible if the managing director could not rely on good workers who stand behind him. Consequently, the pride also applies to the performances of his employees. It manifests itself in the impression that the managing director feels like a father to his employees. He lives out his paternal role in the sense of a 'protector' of his employees and feels a high level of responsibility towards them.

Beta is also dominated by a patriarchal-caring culture very similar to the one at Alpha, though the founder does not understand his caring role like the managing director of Alpha as a 'protector' but rather as a 'supporter' of his employees, i.e. his employees are important to him and he wants to be open and collegial with them and provide them with the greatest support possible. Thus, he mostly works with his door open, thereby allowing his employees continuous entry.

At Alpha, EO was introduced by the management of the company. The introduction of the silent partnership is based on the target to mitigate the distinction between capital and labor. This approach produces a partnership-oriented basic direction. Employees are not only seen as workforce, but as employees whose performance is appreciated. The same can also be seen at Beta. EO was introduced by the management in order to break down the barrier between employer and employee in order to pursue joint success on a partnership-oriented basis. In sum, in both companies the introduction of the silent partnership is based on the awareness on the part of the top management that an EO can help to strengthen a corporate culture based on partnership.

However, both managing directors seem to be grateful that the silent partnership does not grant too many decision-making powers to employees. Both emphasize the advantage of business decisions remaining widely in their hands.[119] In both companies, a corporate culture based on partnership is aspired to by the management, but in the end, the silent partnership seems to remain foremost an investment topic. As part of their patriarchal leadership, they both see the monetary advantages for their employees: to create an additional opportunity for the accumulation of capital and to involve them in the company's success.

> *Proposition 1: Managing directors with a patriarchal leadership style introduce a silent partnership primarily to recognise the performance of their employees and to give them a financial benefit. At the same time, they interpret their patriarchal role in such a way that they still do not fully move the decision-making power out of their hands, which results in the problem that a corporate culture based on partnership can only be achieved to a limited extent in the company.*

(b) The role of traditions and values

At Alpha, traditions play a major role. Particularly noticeable is that references are often made to the father of the managing director. The managing director wants to continue living out the values espoused by his father. This also includes a major responsibility towards the employees. These values were also established by the father through the introduction of the silent partnership. The managing director tries to give these values more space in the company through various measures. For example, offices being separated from each other only by a glass wall, or a small canteen that encourages the employees to continuously exchange with each other in order to develop and produce new ideas together.

Traditions and values play a similar role at Beta. Since Beta was founded just about 100 years after Alpha, the founder is still working in

---

119 *'It must already be clear ... who ... has to make the business decisions.'* - Interview with the founder: 9; *'...remains free in the business decisions.'* - Interview with the managing director: 9.

the company. He makes sure the values that were important to him at the foundation are still lived out in the company. Furthermore he continuously aims to foster partnership-oriented values. For example, the employees have space for an active exchange amongst themselves in the new glass hall at the company in order to discuss problems and duties together and to contribute positively.

EO in both companies is to play a supporting role towards partnership values. At Alpha, the silent partnership was introduced by the father of the current managing director with the intention of letting employees participate in the success. The father already wanted to give employees the additional opportunity to financially benefit from the company success. The same applies for Beta. The founder introduced the silent partnership with the intention of *'recognizing and encouraging the dedication of the employees'*.[120] Employees who initiate changes and are committed to the company should have the opportunity to benefit financially. Thus, the goal of partnership led the management of both companies to introduce the EO.

At Alpha the EO seems to serve its purpose. Due to the long tradition of the silent partnership, the EO positively affects the corporate culture. The employees have a high level of commitment to the company. At Beta, however, a clear impact cannot yet be identified. This may be due to the fact that the EO was only introduced recently and, thus, is not yet well anchored in the company.

> *Proposition 2: In companies that respect the traditions and appreciate values, a corporate culture based on partnership can only be achieved by granting the employees the opportunity to discuss problems and develop solutions together. This effect, however, will only appear in the middle and long run.*

(c) The employee information

The information culture is problematic in both companies: the employees do not feel well informed about the economic development of the company or about important processes in the company.

At Alpha, at least, the silent partnership leads to a somewhat higher perceived information level for the participating employees, whereas at

120 Guideline at employee share ownership - employees meeting 26/02/2010.

Beta this phenomenon could not be identified. The employees participating financially at Alpha are informed about the company's balance sheet in two general meetings per year, while at Beta the management doesn't generally practice an open information policy about the current state of the participation model and the company.

However, in the case of Alpha, the silent partnership does not just improve the perceived information level but also seems to introduce a two-class-society since the employees perceive that those employees who participate financially are better informed about the company than the employees who do not participate.

(d) The communication and relationship between management and employees

Both companies practice open communication and, accordingly, the employees generally rate their relationship with their colleagues as good. The employees of both companies rate their relationship with their superiors as good. The employees at Alpha describe the atmosphere in the company as good, while the climate in Beta is perceived only as neutral.

At Alpha, those employees standing in close contact with the management are more likely to participate in the silent partnership because they feel more like partners of the company. Thus, the relationship between management and employees may be an antecedent of the financial participation of the employees. But this can also lead to a 'two-class-society' because the employees with less contact to the management do not feel like partners and might financially participate less.

This two-class-society does not exist at Beta, but the employees of Beta perceive a discrepancy between the executive level and the employee level, and this relationship is not improved by the financial participation. Thus at Beta the relationship between management and employees may hinder any further positive effects of the silent partnership.

Proposition 3: A silent partnership can lead to a 'two-class-society'. Firstly the employees who participate financially feel better informed than the employees who do not participate. Secondly, the employees with close contact to the management feel more like partners of the company and are more likely to participate in the silent partnership.

(e) The employee participation and influence

At both companies, the employees generally evaluate their participation and their influence, e.g., their influence on the success of the company and on the distribution of work, as being little. At Beta, the employees only rate their influence on the design of their own work as good, while at Alpha even this is rated as little.

The situation of the financially participating employees looks somewhat different, at least at Alpha. They perceive a higher influence on the design of their own work than the employees who do not participate. Other than this, the employees of Alpha are not very integrated in decision-making processes because they evaluate their influence as being little. The employees at Beta have not noticed an improvement in the employee's influence as a result of the financial participation

At Alpha the employees perceive little influence, especially in the area of their involvement in decision-making processes. This is in contrast to the perception of the managing director who states that the employees are integrated in decision-making processes. At Beta the employees want more participation and influence because they perceive, like the employees at Alpha, that they are not involved in decision-making processes. The little influence perceived by the employees of Alpha and Beta shows that they arc rcal silent partners.

Proposition 4: A silent partnership does not necessarily improve the employee's immaterial participation and influence. This confirms the commonly held assumptions about the characteristics of this model.

7. Conclusions

This paper, to the best of our knowledge, presents one of the first in-depth studies of SMEs with EO in the form of silent partnerships. Therefore, we can claim to have innovatively contributed to the field of EO research. In particular, this study has examined the interrelationship of material and immaterial participation and the respective (partnership oriented) corporate culture. With regards to the questions raised at the beginning of our paper, we can state that, firstly, silent partnerships can support the development of partnership-oriented corporate cultures, although this effect should not be considered an automatism and occurs, rather, in the middle and long run (Question a). Secondly, we could find that the interplay between corporate culture and silent partnership results in some influences in both directions, though the effects remain to a limited degree (Question b). Thirdly, major obstacles on the way to partnership-oriented corporate cultures are a (traditional) "master in house" attitude on the part of leading managers, a still limited information policy, also with respect to EO, and an insufficient involvement of employees in decision-making processes (Question c).

From this point, we can derive several implications, both for theory and practice: Academic scholars need to consider silent partnerships as a particular form and concept of EO more sincerely in the future. This may help in gaining further insights about the functionalities of these companies. Moreover, EO studies ought to better respect the monetary motives of employees regarding their participation in these models and, at the same time, not overestimate the power of immaterial arguments. Practitioners, meanwhile, are generally well advised not to expect too much from EO in the form of silent partnerships. At the same time, they may acknowledge the importance of soft factors, such as information policy and, in particular, employee involvement in decision-making, for the development of a partnership-oriented corporate culture in this context.

Finally, we have to admit that our study also comprises several limitations. Firstly, notwithstanding the power of qualitative studies, we have only examined two SME cases here. This, of course, limits the generalizability of our findings; we therefore consider it an important first step. Secondly, the transferability of our findings to other forms of EO also has to remain open and, hopefully, will be subject to further studies. Thirdly, as already pointed out earlier (e.g., Steger, Schubert, Beisiegel & Dietrich, 2014), we still face a clear theoretical deficit that we were unable to close here and that requires considerable academic work in the future.

References

AGP – Arbeitsgemeinschaft Partnerschaft in der Wirtschaft e.V. (Ed.) (2011). *Mitarbeiterbeteiligung. Führungskonzept für den Mittelstand.* Kassel, Germany.

Aubert, N. (2008). Developing an ownership culture wih employee share purchase plans. *Zeitschrift für Personalforschung, 22*, 130–151.

Backes-Gellner, U. & Kay, R. (2002). Materielle Mitarbeiterbeteiligung. Eine Option für den Mittelstand? In Institut für Mittelstandsforschung (Ed.), *Jahrbuch zur Mittelstandsforschung*, Nr. 96 (pp. 1–17). Wiesbaden, Germany.

Bartkus, B. R. (1997). Employee ownership as catalyst of organizational change. *Journal of Organizational Change Management, 10*, 331–344.

Bellmann, L. & Leber, U. (2007). *Materielle Mitarbeiterbeteiligung. Geringe Verbreitung, aber hohe Intensität.* IAB-Kurzbericht, No. 13. Nuremberg, Germany: Institut für Arbeitsmarkt- und Berufsforschung.

Bellmann, L. & Möller, I. (2011). *Finanzielle Mitarbeiterbeteiligung: Selbst die Finanzkrise sorgt nicht für stärkere Verbreitung.* IAB-Kurzbericht, No. 17. Nuremberg, Germany: Institut für Arbeitsmarkt- und Berufsforschung.

Blasi, J. R., Freeman, R. B., Mackin, C., & Kruse, D. L. (2008). Creating a bigger pie? The effects of employee ownership, profit sharing, and stock options on workplace performance. NBER Working paper Nr. 14320.

Blasi, J., Kruse, D. L., Sesil, J., & Kroumova, M. (2003). An assessment of employee ownership in the United States with implications for the EU. *International Journal of Human Resource Management, 14*, 893–919.

Brezski, E., Böge, H., Lübbehüsen, T., Rohde, T., & Tomat, O. (2006). *Mezzanine-Kapital für den Mittelstand. Finanzierungsinstrumente, Prozesse, Rating, Bilanzierung, Recht.* Stuttgart, Germany: Schäffer-Poeschel.

Dunlap, N. A. (2012). When **silent** partners attack. *Journal of Property Management, 77*(2), 26.

Eisenhardt, K. M. (1989). Building theories from case study research. *Academy of Management Review, 14*, 532–550.

Fakhfakh, F., Perotin, V., & Gago, M. (2009). *Productivity, capital and labor in labor-managed and conventional firms.* http://digitalcommons.ilr.cornell.edu/ilrreviewhttp://digitalcommons.ilr.cornell.edu/ilrreview/vol65/iss4/4/ (retrieved: 26.02.2014).

Faleye, O., Mehrotra, V., & Morck, R. (2006). When labor has a voice in corporate governance. *Journal of Financial and Quantitative Analysis, 41*, 489–510.

Frankfurter Allgemeine Zeitung (Ed.) (2012). *Mitarbeiterbeteiligung. Interview mit Philipp Rösler. „Wir müssen besser informieren".*URL: https://www.bmwi.de/BMWi/Redaktion/PDF/I/interview-roesler-frankfurter-allgemeine-20120913,property=pdf,bereich=bmwi2012,sprache=de,rwb=true.pdf. (retrieved 19.06.2014).

Gaugler, E. (2002). Die Anfänge der Mitarbeiterbeteiligung im 19. Jahrhundert. In K.-R. Wagner (ed.), *Mitarbeiterbeteiligung. Visionen für eine Gesellschaft von Teilhabern* (pp. 17–26). Wiesbaden, Germany: Gabler.

Goic, S. (1999). Employees' attitudes towards employee ownership and financial participation in Croatia: Experiences and cases. *Journal of Business Ethics, 21*, 145–155.

Grunberg, L., Moore, S., & Greenberg, E. (1996). The relationship of employee ownership and participation to workplace safety. *Economic and Industrial Democracy, 17*, 221–241.

Guedri, Z. & Hollandts, X. (2008). Beyond dichotomy: The curvilinear impact of employee ownership on firm performance. *Corporate Governance – An international Review, 16*, 460–473.

Guski, H.-G. & Schneider, H. J (1977). *Betriebliche Vermögensbeteiligung in der Bundesrepublik Deutschland.* Cologne, Germany: Deutscher Instituts-Verlag.

Hammer, T. H., Landau, J. C., & Stern, R. N. (1981). Absenteeism. When workers have a voice: The case of employee ownership. *Journal of Applied Psychology, 66*, 561–573.

Hartz, R., Kranz, O., & Steger, T. (2009). Der Arbeitnehmer im Diskurs der Mitarbeiterkapitalbeteiligung – eine semantische Sekundäranalyse. *Industrielle Beziehungen, 16*, 327–348.

Heinfeldt, J. & Curcio, R. (1997). Employee management strategy, stakeholder-agency theory, and the value of the firm. *Journal of Financial and Strategic Decisions, 10*, 67–75.

Kaarsemaker, E. C. (2006). Employee ownership and human resource management: a theoretical and empirical treatise with a digression on the Dutch context. Dissertation, Radboud University Nijmegen.

Kardas, P. A. (1997). Employee ownership, participation and workplace safety: A response to Grunberg, Moore and Greenberg. *Economic and Industrial Democracy, 18*, 621–633.

Kruse, D. (2002). Research evidence on prevalence and effects of employee ownership. Testimony before the Subcommitee on Employer-Employee Relations. Committee on Education and the Workforce. U.S. House of Representatives, February 13.

Kruse, D., Freeman, R., & Blasi, J. (2008). Do workers gain by sharing? Employee outcomes under employee ownership, profit sharing, and broad-based stock options. National Bureau of Economic Research, Working Paper, No. 14233.

Kühlewind, G. (2000): *Vermögensbeteiligung – Drei auf einen Streich.* IAB-Kurzbericht, No. 8. Nuremberg, Germany: Institut für Arbeitsmarkt- und Berufsforschung.

Kuvaas, B. (2003). Employee ownership and affective organizational commitment: Employees' perceptions of fairness and their preference for company shares over cash. *Scandinavian Journal of Management, 19*, 193–212.

Lampel, J., Bhalla, A., & Jha P. (2010). *Model Growth: Do employee-owned businesses deliver sustainable performance?* http://www.johnlewispartnership.co.uk/content/dam/cws/pdfs/Resources/Model_Growth_Employee_Ownership_Report.pdf (retrieved: 26.02.2014).

Livingston, D. T. & Henry, J. B. (1980). The effect of employee stock ownership plans on corporate profits. *Journal of Risk and Insurance, 47*, 491–505.

Lowitzsch, J. & Hashi, I. (2014). *The promotion of employee ownership and participation.* Study prepared for the European Commission General Directorate MARKT, Brussels, Belgium.

Martins, E., Pundt, A., Horsmann, C. S., & Nerdinger, F. W. (2008). Organizational culture of participation: Development and validation of a measure. *Zeitschrift für Personalforschung, 22,* 195–215.

Mathieu, M. (2015). Annual economic survey of employee ownership in European countries 2014. Brussels, Belgium: EFES.

Matiaske, W., Fietze, S., & Tobsch, V. (2011). *Erfolgs- und Kapitalbeteiligung von Beschäftigten in Deutschland.* Berlin, Germany: Organisations- und Personalforschung e.V.

Mielke, B. (2006). Mitarbeiterkapitalbeteiligung. Von Aktien bis Darlehen – ein Überblick. *BöcklerImpuls,* No. 8, 4–5.

Möller, I. (2000). Produktivitätswirkung von Mitarbeiterbeteiligung. *Mitteilungen aus der Arbeitsmarkt- und Berufsforschung, 33*, 565–582.

National Center for Employee Ownership (NCEO) (2014): *ESOP (Employee Stock Ownership Plan) Facts*. URL: http://www.nceo.org (retrieved 20.02.2014).

Nerdinger, F. W., Horsmann, C., & Pundt, A. (2003). Materielle und immaterielle Beteiligung in der Wahrnehmung der Beschäftigten: Ergebnisse der Mitarbeiterbefragungen. In E. Voß & P. Wilke (Eds.), *Mitarbeiterbeteiligung in deutschen Unternehmen. Auswirkungen auf Unternehmensorganisation und Arbeitsgestaltung* (pp. 147–169). Wiesbaden, Germany: Deutscher Universitäts-Verlag.

Nerdinger, F. W. & Wilke, P. (2009). *Beteiligungsorientierte Unternehmenskultur. Erfolgsfaktoren, Praxisbeispiele und Handlungskonzepte*. http://dx.doi.org/10.1007/978-3-8349-8064-9 (retrieved: 02.01.2014).

Pierce, J. L. & Rodgers, L. (2004). The psychology of ownership and worker-owner productivity. *Group & Organization Management, 29,* 588–613.

Poutsma, E., Kalmi, P., & Pendleton, A. D. (2006). The relationship between financial participation and other forms of employee participation: New survey evidence from Europe. *Economic and Industrial Democracy, 27*, 637–667.

Rhodes, S. R. & Steers, R. M. (1981). Conventional vs. worker-owned organizations. *Human Relations, 34*, 1013–1035.

Risser, D. (2005). *Anlageverhalten von Arbeitnehmern bei betrieblicher Kapitalbeteiligung. Eine empirische Analyse der Beteiligungsbereitschaft.* Hamburg, Germany: Verlag Dr. Kovač.

Rooney, M. P. (1992). Employee ownership and worker participation: Effects on health and safety. *Economic Letters, 39*, 323–328.

Sauser, W. I. (2009). Sustaining employee owned companies: Seven recommendations, *Journal of Business Ethics, 84*, 151–164.

Schneider, H. J. & Fritz, S. (Eds.) (2013). *Erfolgs- und Kapitalbeteiligung. Vom Mitarbeiter zum Mitunternehmer*. 7th ed. Dusseldorf, Germany: Symposion Publishing GmbH.

Scholand, M. (2001). *Mitarbeiterbeteiligung auf neuen Wegen? Moderne Formen der Kapitalbeteiligung von Arbeitnehmern durch Aktien.* Munich, Germany: Hampp.

Segat, G. (2000). The tax implications of Italian silent partnerships with non-resident partners. *European Taxation, 40*, 499–510.

Sengupta, S., Whitfield, K., McNabb, B. (2007). Employee share ownership and performance: golden path or golden handcuffs? *International Journal of Human Resource Management, 18*, 1507–1538.

Sieg, R. (2015). Renaissance der Mitarbeiter-Kapitalbeteiligung. *Neue Zeitschrift für Arbeitsrecht, 32*, 784–788.

Soupata, L. (2005). Engaging employees in company success: The UPS approach to a winning team. *Human Resource Management, 44*, 95–98.

Steger, T. & Hartz, R. (2008). The power of participation? *Zeitschrift für Personalforschung, 22*, 152–170.

Steger, T., Schubert, C., Beisiegel, C., & Dietrich, M. (2014). *Mitarbeiterkapitalbeteiligung in KMU – Die Perspektive der Mitarbeiter/innen.* Abschlussbericht des Forschungsprojekts zu Händen der Hans-Böckler-Stiftung. University of Regensburg, Germany, Chair of Leadership and Organization.

Strotmann, H. (2002). *Zur Bedeutung materieller Mitarbeiterbeteiligung in Baden-Württemberg – eine empirische Analyse mit dem IAB-Betriebspanel.* Gutachten für das Wirtschaftsministerium Baden-Württemberg. Institut für angewandte Wirtschaftsforschung.

Swagel, P. & Carroll, R. (2010). *Resilience and retirement security. Performance of S-ESOP firms in the recession.* Georgetown University, McDonough School of Business.

Thompson, P. B., Shanley, M., McWilliams, A. (2013). Ownership culture and strategic adaptability, *Journal of Business Strategies, 30*, 145-179.

Werner, H. S. (2007). *Mezzanine-Kapital. Mit Mezzanine-Finanzierung die Eigenkapitalquote erhöhen.* 2nd ed. Cologne, Germany: Bank-Verlag Medien GmbH.

Witt, P. (2001). Nutzen und Kosten einer Beteiligung der Mitarbeiter am Eigenkapital von Gründungsunternehmen, *Zeitschrift für Personalforschung, 15*, 113–131.

Wolf, E. & Zwick, T. (2002). Produktivitätswirkung von Mitarbeiterbeteiligung: Der Einfluss von unbeobachteter Heterogenität. *Mitteilungen aus der Arbeitsmarkt- und Berufsforschung, 35*, 123–132.

Profit sharing in France: Substitute or complement to wages?

Mathieu Floquet, Loris Guery, Patrice Laroche & Anne Stevenot[1]

Abstract

Compared to many other European countries, profit sharing is more developed in France. This can be partly explained by a legislative and fiscal framework that promotes financial participation. Nevertheless, not all companies use profit sharing mechanisms to the same extent. Using the French Workplace Employment Relations Survey (REPONSE, 2011), we investigate the determinants of profit sharing and its impact on wage levels. Our results show that profit sharing is more developed in large, profitable and listed firms with growing activity and no particularly difficulty in forecasting. Moreover, wage levels are higher in firms with profit sharing plans. Finally, profit sharing in France may be considered as a way to motivate and retain highly qualified employees rather than a mechanism of wage flexibility or cost reduction.

1. Introduction

Many researchers in different countries and international comparative studies (Bryson, Pendleton & Whitfield, 2012; Pendleton, Poutsma, Van Ommeren & Brewster, 2003; Poutsma, 2001) show that contingent-pay systems and profit sharing are important issues for managers. According to Bryson et al. (2012, p. 3), *'[The] widespread decline of collective industrial relations, the rise of human resources management and other*

1 Mathieu Floquet: ISAM-IAE Nancy, Centre Européen de Recherche en Économie Financière et Gestion des Entreprises (CEREFIGE) - Université de Lorraine
Loris Guery: ISAM-IAE Nancy, Centre Européen de Recherche en Économie Financière et Gestion des Entreprises (CEREFIGE) - Université de Lorraine
Patrice Laroche (corresponding author): ESCP Europe, CEREFIGE - Université de Lorraine, email: patrice.laroche@univ-lorraine.fr
Anne Stevenot: Université de Technologie Belfort Montbéliard, CEREFIGE - Université de Lorraine

approaches to the management process, the intensification of product market competition, the globalization of production and changes in the political landscape over the last quarter century all seem to have promoted interest in the increase use of various forms of contingent pay.' Contexts of profit sharing development differ significantly between countries. Poutsma (2001) noted that profit sharing since 2000 was low everywhere in Europe, particularly in comparison with the US, except in France and in UK, which have a tradition of encouraging financial participation through a legal framework and tax benefits. Poutsma, Blasi & Kruse (2012) later study confirms this analysis. Differences in national business systems are translated into differences in firm practices, which depend on government intervention in labour issues, the power of the various stakeholders in the ownership of employment and the development of a market relative to international competition (Djelic, Nooteboom & Whitley, 2003). Institutional and competitive pressures play an important role in any given national context (Poutsma et al., 2012). The French context is particularly interesting because of the country's legal and tax policies, as well as its employment policy (Marsden & Belfield, 2010). Different forms of profit sharing have been developed, leading to a complex system (see Figure 1), which we will describe further. Moreover, previous studies (Poutsma, 2001) show that profit sharing is a widespread practice in France: In 2011, 56.5 per cent of private sector employees participated in profit sharing schemes (Pauron, 2013).

The first aim of this chapter is to identify the determinants of profit sharing in the French context in order to describe and better understand the reasons why some firms set them up. Indeed, profit sharing is more developed in France than in other OECD countries (Kraft & Ugarkovic, 2005) and profit sharing plans (PSPs) are still being extended (Pauron, 2013).

Profit sharing has three main objectives: (1) to stimulate worker effort; (2) to improve labour-management cooperation; and/or (3) to implement wage flexibility and moderation (Poutsma et al. 2003). These objectives are not obviously coherent. Wage flexibility and moderation can conflict with stimulating worker effort or labour-management cooperation. This is why researchers have largely concentrated on the relationship between profit sharing and wages (Black & Lynch, 2004; Burritt, Dennison, Gay, Heilman & Kendall, 1918; Chaput, Delahaie & Diaye, 2010; Coutrot, 1992; Kraft & Ugarkovic, 2005; Kruse, 1993; Kruse, Freeman & Blasi, 2010; Mabile, 1998; Ugarkovic, 2007; Wadhwani & Wall, 1990;

Weitzman, 1984). The second aim of this chapter is to study this relationship in the French context.

This chapter is structured as follows. After some theoretical considerations and a literature review (section 1), we examine our empirical data and methods (section 2). In sections 3 and 4, we describe and discuss our results.

2. Theoretical considerations and literature review

2.1 Profit sharing in French firms: Common and specific determinants

The origins of PSPs in France can be found in voluntary profit sharing schemes (1959) and mandatory employee participation in corporate results (1967) implemented by public authorities as part of an approach based on the convergence of employee and corporate interests, and designed to develop positive dynamics around labour and business. Profit sharing premiums can be invested, partially or fully, in various forms of savings plans (PEE, PEI, PERCO). An additional allowance from the firm is possible when an employee decides to invest his profit sharing premium in these plans. PSPs are strictly regulated under French law but still offer significant room for negotiation between management and employees.

Figure 1 describes the different provisions.

The mandatory adoption of *participation légale* for companies with 50 employees and more, the obligation to negotiate profit sharing and savings plans each year, and the tax benefits for both firms and employees explain why profit sharing is much more widespread in France than in other European countries. In spite of the legislative and fiscal incentives, there are still differences between small enterprises (with fewer than 50 employees) and others. For example, 81.1 per cent of employees in the largest firms (those with more than 500 employees) received a profit sharing premium in 2011; in contrast, only 11.2 per cent of the smallest firms' employees (those with fewer than 50 employees) received such a premium. Only 0.9 per cent of employees in these firms is covered simultaneously by all the provisions, as opposed to 30.4 per cent in large firms (more than 500 employees) (Pauron 2013).

Pauron (2013) also points out that firms prefer a voluntary profit sharing plan (*intéressement*) to *participation légale* when given the choice. Indeed *intéressement* distribution rules are less constraining and more

Figure 1. Profit-sharing in France

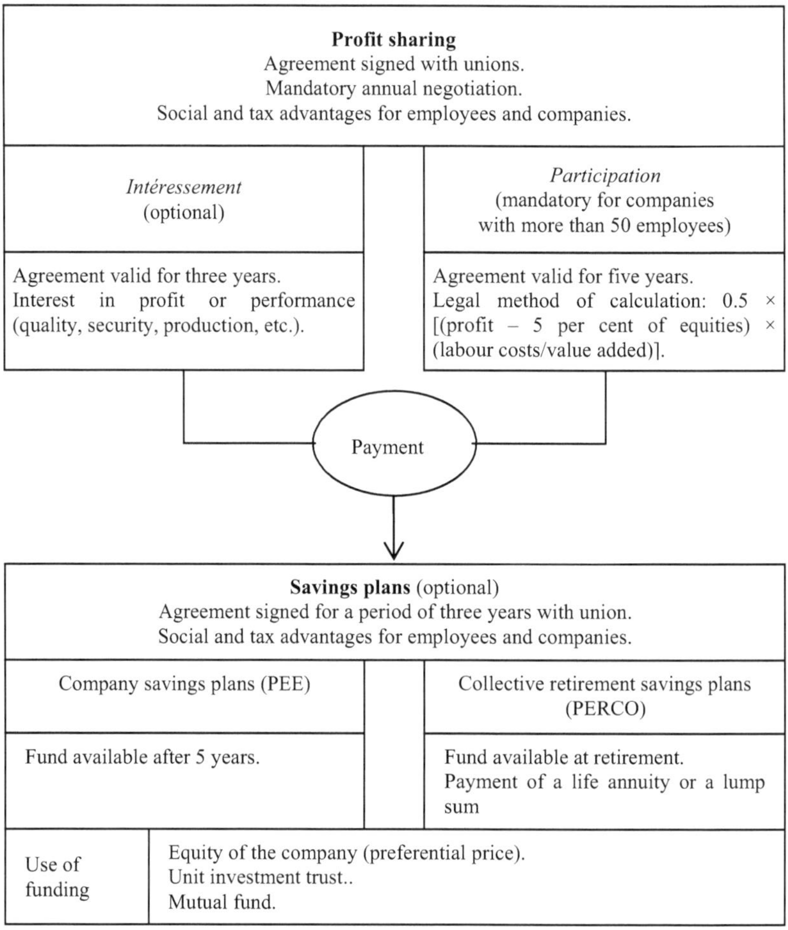

flexible: In particular, firms can choose the variables on which profit sharing depends (quality rates, productivity, customer satisfaction, etc.), whereas mandatory participation depends exclusively on global profit, which is far removed from employees' day-to-day work.

A second major feature of profit sharing practice should be taken into account: in France, profit sharing and savings plans must be available to all employees in order to qualify for tax incentives. This explains why Marsden & Belfield (2010) find that profit sharing for non-managerial employees is practiced by 21 per cent of British establishments, while *intéressement* is practiced by 42 per cent of those in France, highlighting Britain's comparative concentration of profit sharing by managers, a practice that does not exist in France.

The legislative and fiscal framework makes size more determinant of profit sharing practices in France (Cahuc & Dormont, 1992) than elsewhere (Pendleton et al., 2003). However, according to existing literature, other common determinants explain profit sharing practices. The age of the firm is another determinant (Kruse, 1996), as are the industry (Gregg & Machin, 1988; Kruse, 1991) and capital intensity (Kruse, 1996). Risky and sensitive markets, and economic and financial results, have also been identified as determinants (Kruse, 1991, 1996), as well as the structure of ownership (Brochard, 2008). Complex and interdependent work organisation (Dube & Freeman, 2010; Pendleton et al., 2003), workforce composition (Heywood, Huebler & Jirjahn,. 1998), direct and indirect employee participation (Kalmi, Pendleton & Poutsma,2005), and the influence of trade unions (Pendleton et al., 2003) are other major factors that have an influence on profit sharing practices. The first purpose of this chapter is therefore to study the determinants of profit sharing in France.

2.2 Profit sharing and wages in French firms

The French Ministry of Labour (DARES, 2015) shows that profit sharing schemes are more frequent in firms paying high wages: 70 per cent of the employees in firms with an average annual wage of over €27,065 (7th decile) are covered, compared to only 28 per cent of employees in firms with an average wage below €15,930 (3rd decile). The relationship between profit sharing and wages has attracted particular interest since Weitzman's theory of profit sharing appeared in 1984. According to Weitzman (1984), profit sharing adoption leads to lower marginal cost of labour than in the case of fixed wages. Indeed, hiring an additional worker does not change the total share of the profits allocated to the workers, which is independent of employment. Following this assumption, profit sharing should substitute to wages, inducing therefore lower wages.

Conversely, several other authors consider that profit sharing should be a supplement to wages, not a substitute for them (Kraft & Ugarkovic, 2005; Kruse et al., 2010). If the objective of profit sharing is to improve work effort, efficiency and cooperation, its objective cannot be achieved unless rewards can be guaranteed to exceed regular wages (Burritt et al.,

1918). Besides, the profit sharing incentive should lead to improved employee involvement and productivity, so employees should be rewarded with a pay rise. Furthermore, according to some authors (Kraft & Ugarkovic, 2005; Lazear, 2000), a profit sharing premium might lead to higher stress levels and higher work rates because of closer monitoring (to guard against free riding) and higher requirements. The result might be that workers who are not performance-oriented will leave the organisation and be substituted systematically with performance-oriented workers. This could have an influence on wage levels. Another argument tackles the substitution approach. Profit sharing implies sharing risk; consequently, employees should be compensated for this through higher remuneration (Delahaie & Diaye, 2008; Kraft & Ugarkovic, 2005; Kruse et al., 2010).

The French case is quite specific on this point. Indeed, according to French law, substituting part of a basic wage with a proportion of variable profit sharing is forbidden (the 'principle of non-substitution'). Cahuc & Dormont (1992) found wage levels and wage increases evolved independently whether or not a firm had a profit sharing scheme. However, recent studies have come to more nuanced conclusions. Coutrot (1992) and Chaput et al. (2010) show profit sharing would be more likely to moderate basic wages. But Chaput et al. (2010) find profit sharing has no significant effect on overall remuneration (base wage, bonuses and other forms of remuneration excluding bonuses based on profit sharing). Coutrot (1992) and Mabile (1998) find a positive effect on overall remuneration. However, these effects can vary according to the size of the bonuses paid out, the size of the organisation and how long the profit sharing systems have been in place (Coutrot, 1992; Mabile, 1998). For example, according to Mabile's (1998) results, substitution is more frequent in SMEs and appears some years after the implementation of profit sharing.

The discussion about substitution or supplementation is still controversial in France. The French Labour Ministry is still commissioning research to understand better the effect of profit sharing on wages. In this study we use recent data to analyse the relationship between various PSPs and wages in French firms.

Figure 2 summarises the determinants of profit sharing and its impact on wages level.

Figure 2. Profit sharing: Its determinants and its impact on wage levels

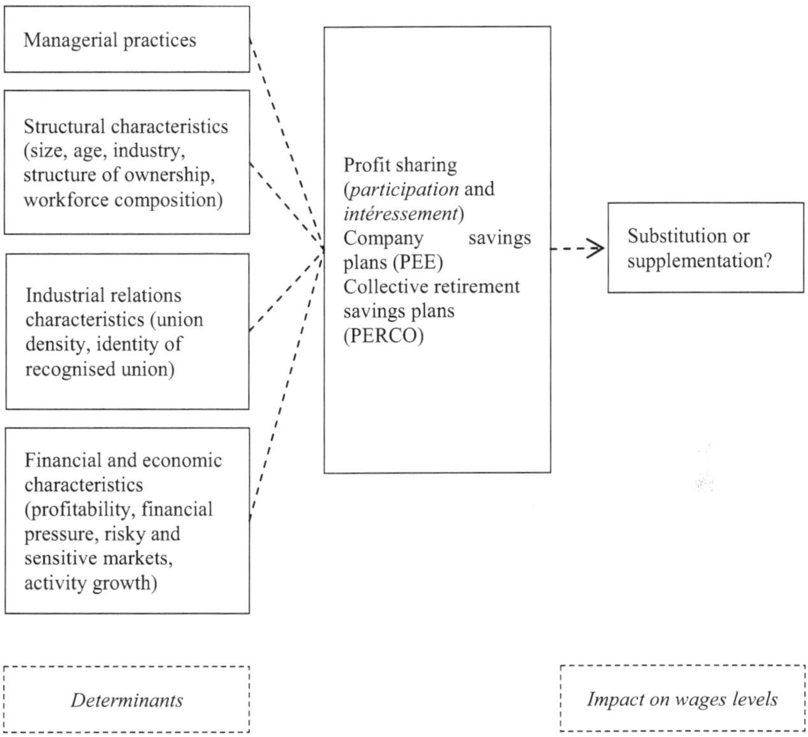

3. Data set and methodology

The data we use for this study derived from the French Workplace Employment Relations Survey (REPONSE)[2] 2010-2011. The main sample covers workplaces with 10 or more employees and was randomly selected from the register of companies maintained by the French Ministry of Labour (DARES), after stratification by location, industry and size. In total, the sample consisted of 4,023 observations. At each workplace surveyed, a questionnaire was administered to general or HR managers.

2 The REPONSE (Relations Professionnelles et Négociations d'Entreprise) Survey is modelled in large part on the British WERS (Workplace Employment Relations Survey).

The dependent variables for this analysis are several dummies indicating whether the workplace has (1) a collective agreement on a profit sharing plan (*participation* agreement, *intéressement* agreement); (2) an effective payment of a profit sharing premium for *participation* and *intéressement*; (3) a company savings plan (PEE); (4) a collective retirement savings plan (PERCO); and (5) no profit sharing mechanism at all. We distinguish between agreement and payment because payment depends on results. Thus an agreement does not necessarily lead to a payment. Table 1 shows descriptive statistics for these profit sharing practices in our sample.

Table 1. Profit sharing practices (percentage)

Profit sharing plan				Savings plans	
Participation (mandatory)		*Intéressement* (optional)		Company savings plans (PEE)	Collective retirement savings plans (PERCO)
Agreement	Payment	Agreement	Payment		
29	24	32	26	34	22

To explain profit sharing, we use a set of independent variables. Structural characteristics are measured by size (number of employees), listing, shareholding, workforce composition and industry. Two variables measure managerial practices. One is linked to involvement practices (quality circle, direct expression group and employee workshop) and a second depends on expenditure on training. Industrial relations characteristics are explained by union density (measured by unionisation rates) and identity of recognised union. Finally, we consider the financial and economic characteristics of firms in terms of profitability, growth in activity and difficulty in forecasting.

Table 2 shows descriptive statistics for a set of workplace characteristics that are correlated to profit sharing practices (all bivariate associations are significant at one per cent level).

Table 2. Some characteristics of companies with profit sharing practices

	Profit sharing plan				Savings plans			
	Participation (mandatory)		*Intéressement* (optional)				No mech-anisms	Whole sample
	Agree-ment	Payme nt	Agree-ment	Payme nt	PEE	PERCO		
Employee repre-sentatives	0.82	0.82	0.75	0.75	0.72	0.65	0.47	0.59
High expenditure on training	0.19	0.20	0.19	0.20	0.19	0.21	0.10	0.14
Forecasting diffi-culties	0.13	0.10	0.12	0.11	0.14	0.12	0.19	0.17
Activity growth	0.42	0.46	0.46	0.50	0.43	0.46	0.36	0.40
Average wages (€000s)	18.7	18.6	18.7	18.9	19.5	18.3	14.2	16.4

Note. Correlation coefficients not reported. All associations significant at the one per cent level. Reading: 82 per cent of establishments with a participation agreement have employee representatives.

Companies with profit sharing schemes and savings plans operate on less risky markets (forecasting difficulties variable) and are sensitive to the economic cycle (activity growth variable). They invest more in training. In terms of industrial relations, we observe that the presence of employee representatives is a decisive factor in profit sharing schemes. Furthermore, average salaries are higher with profit sharing.

To establish the independent association between profit-related pay schemes, characteristics and wages, we run a regression. As a first step, we investigate the determinants of profit sharing practices. Since dependent variables are dichotomous, we use logit regression to study the effect of multiple independent variables simultaneously. Separate models are estimated for the different types of profit sharing practices:

$$\ln\left(\frac{p_{jk}}{1-p_{jk}}\right) = \alpha + X_j B$$

P_{jk} is the probability of an establishment *j* has a type of profit sharing plan or savings plan *k*. X_j is a vector of independent variables (*B*).

As a second step, we investigate the effect of profit sharing on wage levels. The dependent variables are the average workplace monthly wage (per employee) and the median workplace monthly average (per employee), specified in logarithmic form. For independent variables, we use dummies to indicate whether PSPs and savings plans are present in the workplace. There are as many models (7) as there are variables relative to profit sharing and savings plans. All regressions include a large set of control variables, such as firm size, firm age, ownership, union density, and workforce characteristics (occupation, age and gender). Finally, Log wage average/median (W) in firm j is given by:

$$Log\, W_j = a + \delta PS_{jk} + \varepsilon_j$$

4. Results

As expected, structural characteristics (size, publicly owned companies and workforce composition) determine profit sharing and saving practices. The smaller the firms, the less likely they are to have *participation* or *intéressement* agreements; and the less they pay, the less likely they are to have savings plans, compared to large firms. Because of the legal threshold, firms with fewer than 50 employees are more likely to have no PSP mechanism at all. In relation to size, independent firms, which do not have to answer to a headquarters organisation, are less likely to have profit sharing plans (*participation* as well as *intéressement*). The results also confirm that the type of industry determines profit sharing and saving practices. Contrary to expectations, profit sharing is not significantly related to firm age. Although there is no significant relationship between ownership structure and profit sharing, employees on listed companies are more likely to be covered by a profit sharing agreement, all else being equal. This can be a matter of image – profit sharing is considered one of the best management practices, and is highlighted in the institutional communication of listed/publicly owned firms. Finally, workforce composition can be considered another structural determinant. Firms with a high proportion of middle managers are more likely to implement *intéressement* agreements and a company savings plan, and to pay profit sharing premiums. Firms with a high proportion of senior managers are also more likely to have a company savings plan.

Financial and economic characteristics have an impact on profit sharing policy. Profitable firms, or firms with growing activity, tend to make higher *participation* or *intéressement* payments and put in place more *intéressement* agreements. While the literature suggests that risky and sensitive markets should be more interested in profit sharing, as a way to ensure cost flexibility and to adapt wages automatically to variations in activity, according to our results, there is little evidence for the association between profit sharing agreements and difficulties in forecasting. Furthermore the payment of *intéressement* is lower when the level of activity is difficult to forecast, all else being equal. Firms that experience difficulty in forecasting are less likely to put an *intéressement* agreement in place (only 25 per cent of them have one, compared to 33 per cent of less risky and sensitive firms). The difference is significant at the 1 per cent level (Fischer's exact test). Moreover, the likelihood of paying a profit sharing premium is lower for risky and sensitive firms. This can be explained by the objectives set out in the *intéressement* agreement, which may be more complex in firms that experience difficulties in forecasting due to risk aversion.

It is interesting to note that some profit sharing and savings plans are related to managerial practices. *Participation* is the only mechanism that is not related to managerial practices, perhaps because of its legal dimension. But *intéressement* agreements and payments, as well as company savings plans, are significantly more frequent when there are high-involvement work practices (quality circles, direct expression groups, employees' workshop, etc.). Similarly, pension company savings plans are associated with higher expenditure on training. *Intéressement* and savings plans can be considered to complement high-involvement work practices.

Industrial relations characteristics and profit sharing are also related. Indeed, firms that have no employee representatives have fewer *intéressement* agreements, lower payments and fewer company savings plans than any other modes of industrial relations. The identity of the recognised union can also be significant. The French union *Confédération générale du travail* (CGT) is associated with fewer savings plans, particularly collective retirement savings plans. Indeed, as an ex-communist union, the CGT considers that profit sharing induces risk and variability in wages and upholds overall wage increases. The CGT also sees collective retirement savings plans as a way to introduce a weak and risky pay-as-you-go retirement system in France, compared to share-out pension systems.

Table 3. Determinants of profit sharing practices

			Profit sharing				Savings plans		
			Participation		*Intéressement*				
			Agreement Model 1	Payment Model 2	Agreement Model 3	Payment Model 4	Company savings plans (PEE) Model 5	Collective retirement savings plans (PERCO) Model 6	No mechanisms Model 7
Managerial practices	Involvement practices (quality circle, direct expression group, employees workshop)		-0.01	0,01	0.07*	0.08**	0.08*	0,03	-0.05
	High expenditures in training		0,02	0,03	0,04	0,05	0,01	0.06*	-0.08*
	Size	less than 50	-0.36***	-0.28***	-0.31***	-0.27***	-0.30***	-0.08*	0.32***
		between 50 and 100	-0.11***	-0.08***	-0.19***	-0.15***	-0.13***	-0.09***	0.18**
		between 100 and 500	-0,05	-0.06***	-0.16***	-0.14***	-0.12***	-0.06**	0,06
		between 500 and 1000	-0,04	-0.04*	0,01	-0.06*	-0,08	-0,03	-0,12
		more than 1000	Reference				Reference		Reference
Structural characteristics	Listed companies		0.16***	0.10***	0.19***	0.16***	0.17***	0.14***	-0.24***
	Workforce composition	artisan	0,5	0,49	0,84	0,55	0,14	-0.14	-1.01
		senior manager	-0.12	-0.08	0,04	0,01	0.37***	0,1	-0.40***
		middle manager	0,04	0,05	0.16*	0.12*	0.24***	0,07	-0.16
		clerk	-0.05	-0.03	-0.05	-0.09	0	-0.04	0,04
		labourer	Reference				Reference		Reference
	Independent companies		-0.08***	-0.06***	-0.08**	-0.06**	-0,04	-0,02	0,06
Industrial relations characteristics	Identity of recognised union	no staff representatives	-0.29***	-0.22***	-0.22***	-0.14***	-0.18***	-0.02	0.38***
		non-unionised	Reference				Reference		Reference
		CGT (ex-communist)	-0.08**	-0.07***	0,02	0,03	-0.08*	-0.10***	0.19**

		Profit sharing				Savings plans		
		Participation		*Intéressement*				
		Agreement Model 1	Payment Model 2	Agree-ment Model 3	Payment Model 4	Company savings plans (PEE) Model 5	Collective retirement savings plans (PERCO) Model 6	No mechan-isms Model 7
	CFDT (centrist)	-0.03	-0.03	-0.02	0,02	0	-0.07	0.17***
	CGC (white collars, middle managers)	-0.10	-0.09***	-0.08	-0.03	-0.08	0.02	0,25
	FO (centre left)	-0.02	-0.04	0	-0.01	-0.07	-0.04	0,1
	others unions	0.16*	0,06	-0.02	0,06	0.20**	0,06	-0.12
Financial and economic characteristics	High profitability	0,02	0.04*	0.07**	0.06**	0,03	0,01	-0.08**
	Difficulty of forecasting	-0.04	-0.06***	-0.04	0.05*	-0.05	-0.03	0,06
	Activity growth	0,01	0.04**	0.09***	0.11***	0,03	0,03	-0.09***
N		2859	2853	2858	2852	2859	2847	2831
Wald (χ^2)		569.43***	515.49***	428.02***	386.68***	443.70***	235.70***	373.75***

Note. Parameter estimates as marginal effects on probabilities. Logit models including industry, age of the firm, shareholding, union density, empowerment practices, financial pressure, workforce composition (gender and age), single-establishment employers. Full specifications for the models are available from the authors.
Significance level: <0.01(***), <0.05(**), <0.1(*).

The second part of the research model deals with the relationship between profit sharing and savings practices and salaries. There is a consistent finding that profit sharing and savings plans in French firms are significantly related to higher wage levels (average and median wage). Average wage is higher in firms that have a *participation* or an *intéressement* agreement, all else being equal. The higher the likelihood of paying a profit sharing premium, the higher the average wage. The similar findings on average and median wage suggest there is no impact on the dispersion of employees' salaries. Moreover, firms that set up company savings plans and collective retirement savings plans offer more generous salaries. These results are consistent with the theory that profit sharing supplements rather than substitutes for fixed wages (see Table 4).

Table 4. Impact of profit sharing on wage levels

			Log of average wages				Log of median wages			
			B	N	Fisher's Test	R^2	B	N	Fisher's Test	R^2
Profit sharing	*Participation*	Agreement	0.05*	2859	42.34***	0,53	0,06	2859	21.40***	0,34
		Payment	0.05*	2853	41.91***	0,53	0.07*	2853	21.24***	0,35
	Intéressement	Agreement	0.06**	2858	42.57***	0,53	0.09*	2858	21.50***	0,35
		Payment	0.07**	2852	42.49***	0,53	0.10*	2852	21.50***	0,35
Savings plan	Company savings plans (PEE)		0.12***	2859	43.10***	0,53	0.20***	2859	21.84***	0,35
	Collective retirement savings plans (PERCO)		0.05**	2847	41.68***	0,53	0,06	2847	21.35***	0,35
No mechanism			-0.10***	2831	42.28***	0,53	-0.12**	2831	21.14***	0,35

Note. Models including a large set of control variables: industry, size and age of the firm, shareholding, listing, industrial relations characteristics, HRM practices, financial and economic characteristics, workforce composition (occupation, gender and age), single-establishment employers. Full specifications for the models are available from the authors.
Significance level: <0.01(***), <0.05(**), <0.1(*).

5. Discussion

Contrary to Weitzman's anticipation, profit sharing does not seem to be considered as a response to the quest for flexibility in a risky and sensitive context that will lead to solving unemployment. Indeed, according to our results, profit sharing plans are significantly more developed in large, profitable and high-growth listed firms that have no particular difficulty in forecasting. Moreover, profit sharing plans supplement rather than substitute for fixed wages. Average and median wages are more important in firms with profit sharing agreements and payments. These results are consistent with other anticipations (Kraft & Ugarkovic, 2005; Kruse et al., 2010) and there are at least three explanations for them.

First, profit sharing incentives would lead to an improvement in employees' involvement and productivity, so that employees would be rewarded with pay rises (Burritt et al., 1918), particularly in large firms (Pedace, 2010). Profit sharing falls within the efficiency wages theory (Leibenstein, 1987). According to this approach, firms are induced to offer higher wages than the market level in order to attract the best employees and stimulate their productivity. This is all the more important as investments in human capital are high and strategic for the firm. That is why we observe in this study that firms with higher spending on training are more likely to make *intéressement* payments and to put collective retirement savings plans in place. Subscribing to the efficiency wage theory, this complement to remuneration can be used as a means to retain highly qualified employees for whom firms have invested in training (Green & Heywood, 2011; Gielen, 2011). Besides, efficiency wages respond to agency problems (Shapiro & Stiglitz, 1984). As individual productivity is difficult to observe, employers develop global remuneration contracts to attract and retain best employees and motivate them to do their best. They send out a signal to employees by offering higher wages and supplementary advantages, such as profit sharing plans, and make the threat of termination credible (Shapiro & Stiglitz, 1984) because of the risk of losing all these advantages on leaving the firm. Profit sharing that rewards collective performance is particularly suitable for situations where it is difficult to observe individual performance and where agency problems are particularly important. Pedace (2010) underlines that moral hazard is more prevalent in large firms because individual productivity becomes increasingly difficult to observe when more workers are involved in the production process. Although it is not impossible, it is difficult and costly to monitor workers in these firms. Consequently large firms offer wages above the average market level (Pedace, 2010) and develop more collective performance-based remuneration through profit sharing schemes. The difficulties of control, as well as the cost of losing workers (Ehrenberg & Smith, 2008), are compounded when employees are encouraged to work together. According to this view, it is no surprise to find that collective involvement practices, such as quality circles, direct expression groups or employees' workshops, are linked to more *intéressement* agreements and payments.

Second, firms that offer efficiency wages, including profit sharing (Kraft & Ugarkovic, 2005), substitute non-performance-oriented workers with performance-oriented workers. On the one hand, this can be explained by an adverse selection effect (Akerlof, 1970; Akerlof & Yellen,, 1986); on the other, people who are unwilling to accept higher requirements, higher stress level and increased work pace due to the increase in global productivity leave the firm. 'Worker sorting' also leads to higher productivity, creating a virtuous circle (Lazear 1986, 2000) and might influence wage levels in order to reward higher productivity (Kraft & Ugarkovic, 2005; Lazear, 2000).

Third, wages are higher when profit sharing plans are more developed because employees should be compensated for sharing risk with the firm, according to the compensation approach (Delahaie & Diaye, 2008; Kraft & Ugarkovic, 2005; Kruse et al., 2010). Listed firms are used to sharing risks with their employees by improving the funding of employee shareholdings from savings plans.

Finally, it is a way to stabilise the ownership structure when faced with the rising power of institutional funds on the French listed market (Delahaie & Diaye, 2008). Higher wages can also compensate employees for their willingness to invest in the firm and for their loyalty, particularly in listed firms.

Beyond these theoretical explanations, the French context provides some justification for both the determinants of profit sharing and the impact of profit sharing on wage levels. First, French labour law forbids the substitution of basic pay by profit sharing. Nevertheless, this rule is difficult to enforce. For example, Mabile (1998) shows that in small companies, non-substitution is rarely applied. Our results, based on a representative sample, assume a supplementation effect of profit sharing on wage levels that suggests the non-substitution principle is respected.

Second, tax regulation also plays a role. To encourage the spread of profit sharing, French tax regulations offer tax advantages for this type of compensation. For employers, profit sharing is exempted from social contributions. For employees, profit sharing premium is not taxable if invested in company saving plans or collective retirement savings plans. For these reasons, profit sharing offers the possibility of paying a salary supplement without taxes. In a system of tax progression, as in France, the higher the wage, the higher the tax saving with profit sharing will be.

Companies paying a higher level of wages will be encouraged to develop this form of compensation. Similarly, tax advantages will be higher for senior and middle managers (this is certainly why we notice a link between profit sharing and workforce composition). This is accentuated by the fact that the distribution of the overall premium between employees depends, in most cases, on the wage level of each employee. Additionally, senior and middle managers with a large capacity for saving (they can save more because they earn more) can use profit sharing schemes to build up personal savings by depositing an additional amount in the company savings plans (a *versement volontaire* or voluntary contribution) which benefits from an additional contribution by the company (*abondement*). So French labour law and tax regulation may explain why profit sharing is related to higher wage levels.

Finally, the fact that profit sharing is more developed in large, profitable and listed firms can also be explain by the French context and especially by the specificity of the labour market. In the late 1970s, Piore (1978) applied the notion of dualism[3] to the French labour market. Despite some evolution, recent studies still confirm the presence of a clear segmentation between employment policies (Lemière et al., 2001; Petit, 2003; Cour des Comptes, 2013). The distinction in French labour law between permanent and temporary contracts strengthens this segmentation. Some large companies need to build long-term employment relationships; in this way, these companies develop significant wage differentials between their workers (Pedace, 2010). This long-term relationship, which characterises the internal market, improves employees' bargaining capacity to obtain compensation advantages. These companies use profit sharing schemes to reward workers for increased productivity and to create a wage differential. Rather than being used as a flexibility instrument, profit sharing seems to be a practice deployed by large, profitable and listed firms in the primary sector to attract and retain skilled employees, according to the efficiency wage theory, as seen above.

---

3 Doeringer and Piore (1971) propose to segment the market labour in two parts. A first one (primary sector) brings together the internal markets; a second one (secondary sectors) is characterised by short-term employment relationship.

6. Conclusion

Our study aimed to analyse, in the French context, the relationship between a) profit sharing and savings plans and b) wage levels, controlling the internal and external characteristics of firms. Contrary to some expectations, profit sharing plans (*participation* and *intéressement*) and savings plans are not developed for reasons of flexibility or cost reduction but to complement managerial practices related to structural and organisational characteristics. The analyses of the determinants of profit sharing, as well as the relationship between profit sharing and wage levels, are converging. Profit sharing is more developed in large, profitable and listed companies with a growing activity and no particularly difficulty in forecasting. Wage levels are higher in firms with profit sharing and savings plans. These mechanisms depend on workforce composition and seem to be mostly related to managerial practices, especially training. Profit sharing and savings plans can be considered as ways of retaining highly qualified employees in whom firms have invested money in training. This leads us to question whether higher wage levels are the cause or the consequence of profit sharing. Indeed, according to a compensation approach (Kraft & Ugarkovic, 2005; Kruse et al., 2010; Lazear, 2000), profit sharing leads to increased wages. Conversely, however, profit sharing can be seen as a complement to remuneration to retain qualified and high-quality employees who also earn higher wages. In France, the tax benefits of profit sharing are higher for well-paid employees. Profit sharing would be a part of an efficiency global compensation package.

This study has three major implications. First, compensation and benefits managers often wonder why and how others perform profit sharing, particularly when they intend to develop or change their plans. These results can provide a benchmark. They also provide a response to unions that suspect profit sharing plans may substitute for fixed wages and increase risks for employees. This may encourage the drawing up of profit sharing agreements. Finally, as tax advantages are often challenged by the French government, this study shows that there is no competition between basic wage and profit sharing. The deadweight effect feared by the legislator is disproved. Nevertheless some mechanisms, like *abondement*, mainly benefit to senior managers even though the initial objective was collective compensation.

As a follow-up to this research, longitudinal studies could form part of further research to observe the evolution of profit sharing and savings practices following the 2012 reduction in tax benefits in France. Further research could also deal not only with the relationship between profit sharing and wage levels but also between profit sharing and compensation structure (overall pay increase, individual pay rises, collective or individual bonuses, for senior managers and for lower level employees). Profit sharing could be better understood as a component of a consistent compensation strategy.

References

Akerlof, G. (1970). The Market for Lemons: Quality Uncertainty and the Market Mechanism. *The Quarterly Journal of Economics*, *84*(3), 488-500.

Akerlof, G. & Yellen, J. (1986). *Efficiency Wage Models of the Labour Market.* Cambridge: Cambridge University Press.

Black, S. E. & Lynch, L. M. (2004). What's driving the new economy? The benefits of workplace innovation. *The Economic Journal*, *114*(493), 97-116.

Brochard, D. (2008). Logiques de gestion du travail, environnements conventionnel et concurrentiel : des politiques de rémunération sous influences, *in* Amossé, T., Bloch-London, C. & Wolff, L. (Eds) *Les relations sociales en entreprise*. Paris: La Découverte, collection Recherche, 376-398.

Bryson, A., Pendleton, A. & Whitfield, K. (2012). The changing use of contingent pay at the modern British workplace. *National Institute of Economic and Social Research*, discussion paper n° 319.

Burritt, A.W., Dennison, H.S., Gay, E.F., Heilman, R.E. & Kendall, H.P. (1918). *Profit Sharing, Its Principles and Practice: A Collaboration*. New York: Harper & Brothers.

Cahuc, P. & Dormont, B. (1992). L'intéressement en France: allègement du coût salarial ou incitation à l'effort?. *Economie et Statistiques*, *257*, 35-44.

Chaput, H., Delahaie, N. & Diaye, M.A. (2010). L'épargne salariale en France: quels enjeux pour les politiques de rémunération et les performances des entreprises ?. Miméo.

Green, C. P. & Heywood, J. S. (2011). Profit sharing, separation and training. *British Journal of Industrial Relations*, *49*(4), 623-642.

Cour des Comptes (2013). *Le marché du travail face à un chômage élevé.* Rapport public thématique.

Coutrot, T. (1992). L'intéressement: vers une nouvelle convention salariale?. *Travail et Emploi, 53*, 22-39.

DARES (2015), « Participation, intéressement et épargne salariale en 2013 », Dares Analyses, n°055

Delahaie, N. & Diaye, M.-A. (2008). Comment les entreprises construisent-elles une politique de rémunération fondée sur l'épargne salariale ?, *Congrès de l'AFSE*, Paris.

Djelic, M.-L., Nooteboom, B. & Whitley, R. (2003). Organisation studies: special issue on institutions, markets and organisations. *Organisation Studies*, *24*(9), 1579–1580.

Doeringer, P. & Piore, M. (1971). *Internal Labour Market and Manpower Analysis*, New-York: Sharp.

Dube, A. & Freeman, R. (2010). Complementarity of shared compensation and decision making systems, in Kruse, D., Freeman, R. & Blasi, R. (eds), *Shared Capitalism at Work: Employee Ownership, Profit and Gain Sharing, and Broad-based Stock Options*. National Bureau of Economic Research, 167-199.

Ehrenberg, R. G. & Smith, R. (2008). *Modern Labour Economics: Theory and Public Policy*, 9th edition. Upper Saddle River, NJ: Pearson Addison-Wesley.

Gielen, A. C. (2011). Profit sharing for increased training investments. *British Journal of Industrial Relations*, *49*(4), 643-665.

Green, C. P. & Heywood, J. S. (2011). Profit sharing, separation and training. *British Journal of Industrial Relations*, *49*(4), 623-642.

Gregg, P. A. & Machin, S. J. (1988). Unions and the incidence of performance linked pay schemes in Britain. *International Journal of Industrial Organisation*. *6*(1), 91-107.

Heywood, J. S., Huebler, O. & Jirjahn, U. (1998). Variable payment schemes and industrial relations: evidence from Germany. *Kyklos*, 51: 2, 237-257.

Kalmi, P., Pendleton, A. & Poutsma, E. (2005). Financial participation and performance in Europe. *Human Resource Management Journal*, *15*(4), 54-67.

Kraft, K. & Ugarkovic, M. (2005). Profit sharing: supplement or substitute?. Working Paper, Dortmund University, Department of Economics.

Kruse, D. L., Freeman, R. B., & Blasi, J. R. (Eds.). (2010). Shared capitalism at work: Employee ownership, profit and gain sharing, and broad-based stock options. University of Chicago Press.

Kruse, D. L. (1991). Profit sharing and employment variability: Microeconomic evidence on the Weitzman theory. *Industrial and Labour Relations Review*, *44*(3), 437-453.

Kruse, D.L. (1996). Why do firms adopt profit sharing and employee ownership plans? *British Journal of Industrial Relations*, *34*(4), 515-538.

Lazear, E. P. (1986). Salaries and piece rates. *Journal of Business*, *59*(3), 405-431.

Lazear, E. P. (2000). Performance pay and productivity. *American Economic Review*, *90*(5), 1346-1361.

Leibenstein, H. (1987), Inside the Firm. The Inefficiencies of Hierarchy. Harvard University Press.

Lemière, S., Perraudin, C. & Petit, H. (2001). Régimes d'emploi et de rémunération des établissements français en 1998. Construction d'une typologie à partir de l'enquête REPONSE. Report for DARES, French Ministry of Labour.

Mabile, S. (1998), Intéressement et salaires: complémentarité ou substitution? *Economie et Statistique*, *316-317*, 45-61.

Marsden, D. & Belfield, R. (2010). Institutions and the management of human resources: incentive pay systems in France and Great Britain. *British Journal of Industrial Relations*, *48*(2), 235-283.

Pauron A. (2013). "Participation, intéressement et épargne salariale en 2011", *Dares Analyses*, *068*.

Pedace, R. (2010). Firm size-wage premiums: using employer data to unravel the mystery. *Journal of Economic Issues*, *54*(1), 163-181.

Pendleton, A., Poutsma, E., Van Ommeren, J. and Brewster, C. (2003). The incidence and determinants of employee share ownership and profit sharing in Europe. *Advances in the Economic Analysis of Participation & Labour-Managed Firms*, 7, 141-172.

Petit, H. (2003). Les déterminants de la mise en œuvre d'un mode de gestion de l'emploi. *Economie et Statistique*, *361*, 53-70.

Piore, M. (1978). Dualism in the labour market: a response to uncertainty and flux; the case of France. *Revue Economique*, *1*, 26-48.

Poutsma, E. (2001). *Recent Trends in Employee Financial Participation in the European Union*. Luxembourg: Office for Official Publications of the European Communities.

Poutsma, E., Blasi, J. R. & Kruse, D. L. (2012). Employee share ownership and profit sharing in different institutional contexts. *International Journal of Human Resource Management*, *23*(8), 1513-1518.

Shapiro, C. & Stiglitz, J.E. (1984). Equilibrium unemployment as a worker discipline device. *American Economic Review, 74*(3), 433-444.

Ugarkovic, M. (2007). *Profit Sharing and Company Performance.* Wiesbaden: Deutscher Universitäts-Verlag.

Wadhwani, S. & Wall, M. (1990). The effects of profit sharing on employment, wages, stock returns and productivity: evidence from UK micro-data. *The Economic Journal*, *100*(399), 1-17.

Weitzman, M. (1984). *The Share Economy. Conquering the Stagflation.* Cambridge: Harvard University Press.

Employee financial participation: Evidence from Italian firms

Mirella Damiani, Fabrizio Pompei & Andrea Ricci[1]

Abstract

In the last few years, in a number of countries a trend towards decentralisation of wage setting has been associated with the increasing use of variable pays and employee financial participation (EFP) schemes to provide an important element of flexibility and more closely links to individual or collective performance. However, this trend has shown great variability across EU economies and, after the adoption of these decentralised agreements, wage settlements have often lagged behind increases in productivity. This chapter explores the Italian case and the experience gained with EFP. Particularly, by using a unique dataset obtained from the ISFOL (Institute for the Development of Workers Professional Training) Employer and Employee Surveys (2005, 2007, 2010), it investigates the effects of EFP in Italian firms comparing its impacts on productivity and wages.

1. Introduction

Over the last years, some European countries, and particularly Italy, have introduced 'far-reaching reforms of their wage setting systems in the direction of higher wage responsiveness to economic conditions at firm level' (European Commission, 2013, p. 6). However, in the same years the efficiency performance of the Italian economy has been disappointing,

1 Mirella Damiani (corresponding author): Department of Economics, University of Perugia, Italy, e-mail: mirelladamiani@libero.it
Fabrizio Pompei: Department of Economics, University of Perugia, Italy, e-mail: fabrizio.pompei@unipg.it
Andrea Ricci: The Italian Institute for the Development of Vocational Training for Workers, Ministry of Labour, Health and Social Policies, ISFOL, Rome, Italy, email: andr.ricci@gmail.com

even in comparison to other European economies (Daveri & Jona-Lasinio 2005). Furthermore, in these same years, real compensation per employee expanded at a rate below that of productivity (European Commission, 2011, 2013) and the share of national income accruing to employees has recorded large falls, as documented by OECD (2012). This chapter examines the drivers of both productivity and wages, by testing whether the insufficient room given to employee financial participation (EFP) in the form of performance related payments (PRP) has affected efficiency and distributive patterns recorded in the Italian economy. Thus, our chapter investigates the effects of payment by results, such as PRP, on both dimensions, i.e. labour productivity and wages.

We use a unique dataset for the Italian economy obtained from the ISFOL Employer and Employee Surveys (2005, 2007, 2010). This rich dataset permits to explore the role of PRP on labour productivity and to provide estimates for the effects of PRP on wages, also controlling for an ample set of covariates[2].

In the econometric analysis, various robustness checks have been performed and the main results have been validated by instrumental variable estimates. Furthermore, additional checks have been carried out by the treatments of three-stage least square (3SLS), assuming that the same instrument is valid for both labour productivity and wages. The chapter is organised as follows. Section 2 briefly discusses the related literature. Section 3 presents data and offers descriptive statistics. Section 4 illustrates the econometric framework and estimation results. Section 5 concludes.

2. *Discussion*

2.1 *Related literature*

The theoretical and empirical literature has traditionally indicated three main reasons for implementing EFP and performance related pays (PRP): risk-sharing, productivity improvement, and rent division (Prendergast, 1999; Pérotin & Robinson, 2003; Uvalic, 1991, 2006; Kruse, Freeman &

2 The determinants of decentralised bargaining and of bargaining covering PRP have been estimated on the basis of the ISFOL surveys for 2005 and 2007 by Damiani & Ricci (2014).

Blasi, 2010). The first reason, offered by agency theories, emphasises that, in conditions of imperfect competition, company agreements allow redistribution of rents and may favour cooperative behaviour between management and employees.

The second reason is that PRP schemes are risk-sharing instruments, which would arise from the outset of risk situations for firms (erratic sales, volatility of profits, high level of indebtedness). This reason has been important in the past Italian experience, especially from the second half of the 1980s: firms offering financial participation, often more labour intensive, invested more than others and implemented innovative plans which needed cooperative relationships to deal with those organizational changes.

The third aspect of productivity enhancement is *motivation*. EFP and PRP schemes offer efficiency wages to improve production quality and productivity. Employees who participate in enterprise results 'will become more committed to the goals of that enterprise, leading to improvements in individual and organisational performance. At a wider societal level, financial participation may be seen as a tool for redistribution of income and wealth, and may, therefore, serve as a broader instrument for social integration' (Pendleton, Poutsma, van Ommeren & Brewster, 2001, p.1).

However, collective bonuses may be offered when total output is the result of the efforts of many agents and individual contributions cannot easily be identified (Holmstrom, 1979; Fitzroy & Kraft, 1992). However, these group bonuses may induce employees to free ride on the efforts of others and cut productivity. In such circumstances, group incentives may lead to decentralised monitoring due to peer pressure and shame norms (Kandel & Lazear, 1992), thus mitigating opportunistic behaviour.

The positive productivity effects of collective wage variable bonuses have been tested in a number of recent studies (Ichniowski, Shaw & Prennushi 1997; Gielen, Kerkhofs & Van Ours, 2009; Kruse, et al. 2010; Kato, Lee & Ryu, 2012). What deserve closer attention are the main impacts of EFP and PRP on wage setting. In decentralised wage-bargaining, workers, through PRP, can appropriate a large part of the rents generated by their firms. One interpretation of the positive wage premium negotiated in firm-level contracts is that of rent-sharing. This phenomenon may be relevant when specific human capital is important and there is 'a match-specific surplus (rent), created by the costs of finding new partners, and this surplus will have to be shared by bargaining' (Acemoglu & Piscke, 1999, p. F121). Some authors, by using firm-level data, show a robust positive association between wages and profitability (see, among others, Blanchflower, Oswald & Sanfey, 1996). This evidence has been confirmed by introducing controls for unobserved worker heterogeneities (Gürtzgen, 2009; Martins, 2009). For the Italian firms we will address these issues in the econometric section by estimating whether employee financial participation in the form of PRP schemes has played also a redistributive function.

2.2 The Italian institutional setting

Italy recorded a substantial increase in EFP and performance-related pay (PRP) schemes only in the late 1980s, at a time when companies were involved in the process of deep restructuring and were oriented towards implementing more collaborative labour relations. Before 1988, only a small number of workers were involved in PRP. Available studies also indicated that the variable part of employee remuneration had a small incidence on total pay and suggested that the rationale behind the adoption of PRP was mainly that of enhancing labour productivity, rather than achieving wage flexibility (see Uvalic, 1991). A few other studies, available for similar periods, confirm that in the 1980s Italian enterprises had implemented PRP only on a limited scale. What is remarkable is that the adoption of PRP schemes was done on a completely voluntary basis, since until 1996 legislative provisions and tax concessions to encourage the diffusion of wage participatory schemes were totally absent in Italy.

A new phase was opened by the July 1993 Agreement which provided a new institutional setting for wage determination. Indeed, in 1993 a structural reform was undertaken in Italy to reduce the inflationary gap with respect to the other European countries and to obtain better performance in terms of productivity targets; this was necessary in order to fulfil some of the conditions for entering the European Monetary Union.

To achieve these macroeconomic goals, the July 1993 Agreement set up a new multilevel bargaining structure. The scope of the Agreement was to introduce the corporatist features of a centralised system and to impose macroeconomic consistency of industry level wage increases with the projected inflation rate. With the promotion of company level arrangements, the Agreement was also intended to amplify the incentive effects of the relative wage structure. Concerning EFP, the July 1993 agreement specifically stated that individual companies may determine wage increases only in accordance with profit and productivity gains at the firm level. This is the first time that such a provision was included in Italian legislation on wages. Employees and management were expected to co-operate to acquire all the specific and detailed information needed to evaluate the firm's economic performance and its perspective competitiveness.

The 1993 Agreement changed pay settings in three main ways:

(i) It eliminated wage indexation to the cost of living;
(ii) It assigned to national sectoral bargaining the maintenance of 'economic effects coherent with the planned inflation rate assumed as a common objective';
(iii) It encouraged the diffusion of company level agreements 'correlated with the achievement of a target jointly set by the parties and geared to improvements in productivity, quality and other elements of international competitiveness, [...] as well as to the company economic performance' (The Protocol of Incomes and Employment Policy, 23 July 1993).

It should be stressed that up to 1997, Italy had no legislative measures designed to encourage the adoption of EFP. The first measure to stimulate adoption of employee participation in enterprise results was introduced in 1997, with the Decree Law n. 67 of 25 March 1997, later converted into Law n.135 of 23 May 1997. With the law approved in 2007 (Law of 24 December 2007 no. 247) and subsequent decrees, which introduced new provisions for the 2008-10 period, the employer benefits from a reduction on social security contributions on the wage component linked to enterprise results; the tax exemption for the employer's contribution initially was a maximum of five per cent of the total annual individual wage, but in 2008 it was reduced to three per cent and in 2009 to 2.25 per cent. The firms could apply by a certain date for the tax relief within available financial resources allocated for this measure (€650 million per year) and this amount determined the number of eligible firms. In sum, in the last years, the first important issue in wage setting is the reform of the bargaining system and the implementation of company level negotiations to enhance the importance of PRP schemes (Damiani & Uvalic, 2010). The need for additional stimulus and new encouragement of EFP has inspired the reform proposals of 22 January 2009, incorporated in the agreement which was signed by the government, national employers' associations and the trade unions, with the exception of CGIL (one of three main national representative organisations of employees). The agreement designs new rules for wage setting in order to amplify the importance of the variable component, and is currently a matter of political debate. The new elements proposed are discussed further below.

First, the new agreement explicitly envisages that a production bonus is negotiated in every enterprise. In this way, the trade unions and workers will have the right to the opening of negotiations on the introduction of production bonuses in all enterprises where the new system is applied. Second, the trade unions will renounce to national level negotiations regarding increases in remuneration linked to productivity (as was done in the old system), with the aim of leaving more room to enterprise-level negotiations. However, the agreement also envisaged that national sectoral agreements include a 'guaranteed element of remuneration', intended to be effective in those enterprises where enterprise-level negotiations do not take place. This type of additional remuneration, recently used in the renewal of wage agreements of the metalworking sector, has the aim of both benefiting workers and counterbalancing local negotiations focused on individual (and not collective) bonuses, based on remuneration *ad personam* (ISAE, 2009). Third, the duration of agreements, which in the past used to be valid, for the normative part, for four years, and for the economic part for two years, will now be for three years. Fourth, enterprise agreements will be able to define procedures and conditions for modifying, entirely or partly, also temporarily, specific elements (economic and normative) of sectoral collective agreements on wages (Accordo Quadro Riforma degli Assetti Contrattuali, 22 January 2009). In this way it becomes possible to set up levels of remuneration below those determined by national wage bargaining agreements. Fifth, wage increases are anchored to anticipated inflation, determined on the basis of the estimated inflation index (the EU harmonized consumer prices index), with the exclusion of prices of imported energy products. The main points of disagreement regard points three, four and five. This is because these elements proposed in the new 2009 agreement allow the reduction in workers' real wages. Such a possibility has been stressed by the CGIL and is the main reason why it has not signed the Agreement. Moreover, the risk is even greater if we consider that Italy is one of the few European countries that still does not have legislation on minimum wages; in fact, the minimum wages categories are established through national sectoral negotiations.

Finally, notice that in 2012 the social partners agreement acknowledged 'the need to link wages set in national contracts not only to expected inflation, but also to the economic and competitive conditions of the country and concerned sectors, and promotes further decentralisation of collective bargaining by strengthening second tier bargaining'. (European Commission, 2013, p. 7).

In the following analysis we consider evidence on EFP on a national scale made available from the ISFOL surveys.

3. Data and descriptive statistics

3.1 Data

Our empirical analysis is based on a nationally representative sample of manufacturing and non-manufacturing firms, obtained from information on flexible compensation and other workplace practices collected by the ISFOL *Employer Survey* for 2005, 2007 and 2010. The survey provides information on a nationally representative sample of all the industries, leaving out only the primary sector. The information collected by ISFOL is very rich and includes not only the spread of financial participation schemes, but also information on business activities (training, innovation, foreign exposure, use of fixed-term contracts) and workforce composition (by gender and employment status). In particular, the RIL (Employer and Employee Surveys) questionnaire provides information about the adoption of decentralised bargaining and PRP. Each RIL cross-section for the years 2005, 2007 and 2010 counts about 25,000 firms, whereas its longitudinal component, over the period 2005-2007-2010, counts about 12,000 firms.

As far as PRP is concerned, each firm is asked whether or not such a scheme is adopted. Therefore, our PRP-variable is a dummy variable indicating the existence or not of a PRP scheme of some kind[3]. Dummy variables are also inserted to take into account if firms export and innovate. (see the Appendix, Table A1, for detailed definitions of all variables).

In order to link information concerning workers' characteristics to indicators of firm performance and accounting variables, a sub-sample of the RIL dataset was merged with balance-sheet information from the AIDA

3 Unfortunately, we do not know whether the different types of schemes are based on firm-, group- or individual- performance (this information is available only for 2010). Besides, the dataset does not provide statistics on how many workers in the firm receive PRP.

(Analisi Informatizzata delle Aziende Italiane) archive. The AIDA archive contains comprehensive information on companies in Italy, with up to five years of history.

Then, the longitudinal RIL-AIDA merged sample was restricted to those limited liability companies which operated in the Italian private sector over the period 2005-2010. Furthermore, we excluded firms with less than five employees to retain only those firms characterized by a minimum level of organisational structure.

3.2 Descriptive statistics

The ISFOL database reveals two main results. The first is the limited spread of PRP agreements, which are still not a common practice since they involve only a minor proportion of Italian firms. The second concerns the existence of ample differentials by region, sector and firm size.

As shown by Table 1 (that reports means for the key variables used in the econometric analysis), in 2005, 2007 and 2010, only 15 per cent, 12 per cent and 14 per cent of firms, respectively, had decentralised agreements that include payments by results, thus confirming the limited spread of these PRP schemes, and no significant changes over the observed period. The merged RIL-AIDA sample also reveals a rather slight increase in the two dependent variables (labour productivity and wages), and in the physical capital per employees between 2005 and 2010.

With respect to workforce composition, Table 1 shows that the share of blue-collar workers increased over time, from 46 per cent in 2005 to 55 per cent in 2010, while, symmetrically, the proportion of white collars decreased from 45 per cent in 2005 to 39 per cent in 2010. Concerning the percentage of women, workers with fixed-term contracts and immigrants (workers coming from other countries), a slight decrease over time was recorded, indicating a tendency in our sampled period, towards the reduction of 'peripheral' employment; on average, the proportion of women decreased from 39 per cent to 35 per cent from 2005 to 2010; analogously, the stock of workers with fixed-term contracts over the total employment is declined from eleven per cent in 2005 to ten per cent in 2010, and the share of immigrants, on total employees, reduced from nine per cent to five per cent.

Table 1. Descriptive statistics: RIL-AIDA merged sample

	2005		2007		2010	
	N.	Mean	N.	Mean	N.	Mean
Performance Related Pay	8064	0.15	8362	0.12	10136	0.14
Accounting variables						
ln (value added per capita)	5291	10.66	7512	10.73	9069	10.69
ln (wage per capita)	5241	9.93	7451	9.99	9060	10.01
ln (physical capital per capita)	5294	9.80	7507	9.85	9054	9.90
Workforce characteristics						
% executives	8064	0.09	8551	0.05	10136	0.05
% white collar workers	8064	0.45	8551	0.38	10136	0.39
% blue-collar workers	8064	0.46	8551	0.57	10136	0.55
% women	8064	0.39	8580	0.34	10136	0.35
% fixed-term contracts	8064	0.11	8580	0.1	10136	0.10
% immigrant workers	8064	0.09	8301	0.06	9955	0.05
Firm characteristics						
Age	5261	22.45	6585	24.13	4870	26.70
Process Innovation	7775	0.47	8169	0.43	9920	0.39
Product Innovation	7820	0.55	8184	0.56	9926	0.45
Export	8064	0.41	8360	0.30	9944	0.31
ln (Sales volatility)_1999-2001	3924	12.63	4940	12.56	3431	12.55
ln (Sales volatility)_2002-2004	2887	12.87	3600	12.82	2416	12.90
Firm Size						
5 < n of employees<15	8064	0.38	8551	0.42	10136	0.43
15 ≦ n employees < 50	8064	0.35	8551	0.34	10136	0.33
50 ≦ n employees < 250	8064	0.21	8551	0.19	10136	0.19
n of employees ≧ 250	8064	0.07	8551	0.05	10136	0.05
NUTS1_Macro-regions	8064				10136	
North- West	8064	0.35	8580	0.34	10136	0.33
North-East	8064	0.25	8580	0.26	10136	0.25
Centre	8064	0.2	8580	0.2	10136	0.21
South	8064	0.21	8580	0.21	10136	0.21
Sectors						
Textile, Wearing Apparel, Food Industry	8064	0.14	8580	0.14	10136	0.14
Other Manufacturing, Mining, Utilities	8064	0.28	8580	0.31	10136	0.31
Constructions	8064	0.11	8580	0.1	10136	0.1
Trade, hotels, restaurants	8064	0.13	8580	0.16	10136	0.16
Transportation and communication	8064	0.07	8580	0.05	10136	0.05
Finance	8064	0.14	8580	0.1	10136	0.1
Education and personal services	8064	0.12	8580	0.14	10136	0.14

Notes. For binary variables and dummies the mean corresponds to the relative frequency.

The overall weakness in productivity and wage growth of sampled firms may be related to the decreasing share of innovative and exporter units: Firms that originated new products declined from 55 per cent to 45 per cent, whereas the proportion of exporters slumped from 41 per cent to 31 per cent, from 2005 to 2010.

Information on lagged sales' volatility, that we used as an instrument for PRP as explained below, is available only for a restricted sub-sample of firms (about 4,000 observations per year). From the available data, it is possible to see that this volatility is remarkable (for the 2010 sampled firms, the log values of this variable ranged from 12.55 to 12.90).

According to expectations, small-size firms prevail and the largest share of firms is mainly located in Northern Italy. In particular, firms with less than 50 employees are more than 80 per cent while those with more than 250 employees, in each year considered, are about five per cent of the total sample. The RIL-AIDA data indicate that firms were mainly specialised in manufacturing sectors and less present in services, with the exception of the trade sector. These differentials in sector and territorial localisation of PRP Italian firms, as well as in various characteristics of workforce composition, show the importance of our unique data and of its wide coverage. Finally, notice that PRP firms, that are scarcely widespread, exhibited better performances and paid higher wages.

4. Estimates

The econometric strategy

In this section we present the empirical strategy aimed at estimating the effect of PRP on labour productivity and wages.

The following equation is estimated:

$$(1) \ln\left(\tfrac{P}{L}\right) = \alpha \ln\left(\tfrac{K}{L}\right) + \beta\, PRP_{it} + \delta\, X_{it} + \mu_s + \gamma_j + \eta_t + \varepsilon_{it}$$

$t = 2005, 2007, 2010$

where $\ln\left(\tfrac{P}{L}\right)_{it}$ is the (log of) valued added per employee, $\ln\left(\tfrac{K}{L}\right)_{it}$ is the (log of) physical capital per employee, PRP represents a dummy variable indicating the presence of PRP and the vector X_{it} denotes other controls for workforce composition and firm characteristics. Finally, the parameter μ_s

denotes sector specific fixed effects, γ_j regional (NUTS1_level[4]) fixed effects for macro-areas, η_t represents year fixed effects and ε_{it} is the error term capturing the idiosyncratic component of labour productivity.

The wage equation parallels the productivity equation (1). Thus, we estimate the following equation:

$$(2)\ln\left(\tfrac{W}{L}\right)_{it} = \alpha \ln\left(\tfrac{K}{L}\right)_{it} + \beta\, PRP_{it} + \delta X_{it} + \mu_s + \gamma_j + \eta_t + \varepsilon_{it}$$

$t = 2005, 2007, 2010$

where the dependent variable represents the (log of) the average annual wages (*W*) per employee (L), while the explanatory variables are the same included in equation (1).

We started with a pooled cross section analysis of equations (1) and (2), controlling for time dummies. Notice, however, that pooled regressions do not allow us to distinguish between casual effects *and* spurious correlation between PRP and productivity or wages, that will typically arise if more productive firms or firms that pay higher wages more likely adopt PRP schemes. Thus, if there are unobserved factors influencing the adoption of PRP, the estimated effect on productivity and wages will be biased. To avoid that these relationships remain obscured, the issue of endogeneity has to be taken into account.

We address this issue by investigating thc factors that influence the introduction of PRP in Italian enterprises. We use the feasible two step IV-GMM estimator on the pooled data 2005-2007-2010 for equation (1) and (2). This GMM estimator, as shown by Baum, Schaffer & Stillman (2003; 2007), is more efficient and emerges as useful alternative to the standard fixed IV estimator when the disturbance covariance matrix is affected by heteroskedasticity and observations are clustered (we have firms in a three-year period)[5]. As regards instruments, we use firm-level values of the volatility of sales recorded in two previous periods: i) 1999-2001, and ii) 2002-2004.

Furthermore, we use 3SLS estimates and the two dependent variables (labour productivity and wages) are explicitly taken to be endogenous to the system and treated as correlated through disturbances in the system of

4 NUTS is the Nomenclature of Territorial Units for Statistics, Level-1.

5 To save space we do not show the results of tests that prove the presence of heteroscedasticity in our estimated equations; however these results are available upon request.

equations. In this context, also our key variable PRP is treated as endogenous and correlated with disturbances, while other control variables, included in the right-hand side of the system of equations (1)-(2), are considered to be exogenous. Then, we perform a 3SLS-IV regression to estimate a Seemingly Unrelated Regressions model (SUR) of equations (1) and (2), using the same instruments for PRP introduced before.

5. Results

5.2 OLS estimates

The OLS estimates are presented in Table 2.

The first two columns report the estimates obtained for productivity and wages, respectively. Our findings indicate that the effect of PRP is positive and significant on labour productivity (column *a*) and wages (column *b)*. Most of the control variables show the expected sign. We find the significant and positive role of the capital stock per capita in both labour productivity and wage equations, whereas, concerning workforce characteristics, we obtain a strong negative coefficient associated with the percentage of women. The negative coefficient associated with the female component is likely to be related to the gender wage gap. Indeed, our wage estimates seem to confirm that lower productivity increases, obtained when the proportion of women is higher, are at least partially related to less generous remunerations offered to women (see also Zwick, 2004). Another interesting finding is the negative coefficient of fixed-term workers on labour productivity (columns *a* and *b*), accompanied by a parallel penalisation of these precarious workers in terms of lower chances of obtaining PRP bonuses. Other workers' characteristics, such as employment positions, play a role; the coefficients associated to white- and blue-collar workers are negative and significant, with respect to the omitted category, the executives. A plausible explanation is that managerial employees have a higher influence on productivity and more likely receive performance related pay.

Finally, the propensity to export has a positive and significant influence on both productivity and wages, and probably it also works as a good proxy of medium and large sized firms.

Table 2. Effects of Performance Related Pay on Labour Productivity and Wages (OLS Estimates)

Dependent Variable	ln (value added per capita)		ln (wage per capita)	
Explanatory Variables	*a*		*b*	
Performance Related Pay	0.069***	(0.017)	0.088***	(0.011)
ln (physical capital per capita)	0.144***	(0.005)	0.061***	(0.003)
Fixed-term contracts_Share	-0.416***	(0.039)	-0.430***	(0.035)
White Collars_share	-0.452***	(0.087)	-0.390***	(0.077)
Blue Collars_share	-0.756***	(0.086)	-0.626***	(0.075)
Women_share	-0.374***	(0.026)	-0.378***	(0.021)
Immigrants	-0.128***	(0.045)	-0.131***	(0.040)
Firm's Age	0.001	(0.000)	0.002***	(0.000)
Process Innovation	0.005	(0.012)	-0.014	(0.009)
Product Innovation	0.002	(0.012)	0.014	(0.009)
Export	0.071***	(0.012)	0.061***	(0.009)
Constant	9.974***	(0.098)	9.952***	(0.086)
Time Dummies	Yes		Yes	
Sector Dummies	Yes		Yes	
NUTS1_level Dummies	Yes		Yes	
R_Squared	0.250		0.230	
Observations	13178		13186	

Note. OLS estimates. Robust standard errors in parentheses are clustered at firm level Significance level: <0.01(***), <0.05(**), <0.1(*).

5.2 IV and 3SLS estimates

The possible endogeneity of PRP deserves further attention. The exogeneity assumption of PRP might be violated if firms adopt this reward system on the basis of productivity performance. The Instrumental Variable (IV) method requires finding instruments that can predict PRP, without directly affecting our dependent variables, labour productivity and wages. The volatility of sales at the firm level, recorded in past years before 2005 (over the periods 1999-2001 and 2002-2004) may be a valid instrument because it is not correlated with our dependent variables, but at the same time, may influence our key regressor PRP. The volatility of sales is not available for all firms; hence the robustness checks have been performed on a restricted sample.

Lagged values of volatility of sales is a proxy of uncertainty faced by firms, and it is expected not to be correlated with current values of labour productivity and wages[6], but correlated with the probability that firms introduce PRP schemes as incentive device. Indeed, in the Italian two-tiered bargaining regime, at the second level of bargaining, firms may distribute PRP wage premiums linked to firm results. This wage component is *added* to the base wage, set in the first level, and could be zero when firms do not gain positive results. Thus, also risk-averse employees will not be reluctant to accept these agreements, because these variable pays add on in years of success, but do not cause any reduction in the (first level) base pay during unsuccessful years. Employees do not take any extra-risks, whereas firms, on their part, especially in environments characterised by high volatility of demand and sales, would be more willing to adopt PRP schemes as a strategy to obtain higher employee performance and successful outcomes.

This hypothesis is confirmed by our results, as shown by *IV-GMM* estimates reported in Table 3, which prove that both our external instruments positively influence the adoption of the PRP scheme (see Table A.2, in the Appendix, for the first-stage results).

The coefficients of PRP, instrumented with the volatility of sales, show the expected sign and are significantly different from 0 at the one per cent level. The validity of the external instruments is signalled by three different tests: under-identification, weak-identification and over-identification tests (Baum, 2003; 2007).

6 Among rationales behind the choice of our instrument, one may recall some results of the strategic management and sales management literatures (Menguc & Barkers, 2003; Burke & Hsieh, 2006).

Table 3. Effects of Performance Related Pay on Labour Productivity and Wages (IV Estimates)

Dependent Variable	ln (value added per capita)		ln (wage per capita)	
Explanatory Variables	*a*		*b*	
Performance Related Pay	**1.231*****	(0.158)	**0.830*****	(0.106)
ln (physical capital per capita)	0.135***	(0.008)	0.050***	(0.005)
Fixed-term contracts_Share	-0.134*	(0.077)	-0.171***	(0.061)
Executives_share	-0.863***	(0.164)	-0.848***	(0.128)
White Collars_share	-1.225***	(0.159)	-1.120***	(0.124)
Women_share	-0.151***	(0.053)	-0.223***	(0.038)
Immigrants	-0.001	(0.089)	0.001	(0.071)
Firm's Age	-0.004***	(0.001)	-0.001**	(0.001)
Process Innov.	-0.051	(0.044)	-0.060***	(0.016)
Product Innov.	-0.021	(0.022)	-0.007	(0.014)
Export	-0.055	(0.051)	-0.022	(0.015)
Constant	10.485***	(0.177)	10.525***	(0.140)
Time Dummies	Yes		Yes	
Sector Dummies	Yes		Yes	
NUTS1_level Dummies	Yes		Yes	
Underidentification Test _ p value	0.000		0.000	
Weak Identification Test _ Wald F Stat.	76.105		74.695	
Overidentification Test _ p value (Hansen J Statistic)	0.256		0.165	
Observations	6579		6570	

Note. All IV estimations are based on the two-step efficient GMM estimator and a variance-covariance estimator that is robust to heteroscedasticity (robust standard errors in parentheses). The external instruments of the Performance Related Pay that have been used in the first stage are: i) volatility of sales at firm level over period 1999-2001; ii) volatility of sales at firm level over the period 2002-2004. Significance level: <0.01(***), <0.05(**), <0.1(*).

Table 4. Effects of Performance Related Pay on Labour Productivity and Wages (3Stages-Estimation for Systems of Simultaneous Equations)

	All Firms			
Dependent Variable	ln (value added per capita)		ln (wage per capita)	
Explanatory Variables	*a*		*b*	
Performance Related Pay	1.289***	(0.119)	0.864***	(0.081)
ln (physical capital per capita)	0.137***	(0.006)	0.049***	(0.004)
Fixed-term contracts_Share	-0.125**	(0.064)	-0.154***	(0.043)
White Collars_share	-0.890***	(0.111)	-0.814***	(0.075)
Blue Collars_share	-1.241***	(0.105)	-1.101***	(0.072)
Women_share	-0.134***	(0.041)	-0.219***	(0.028)
Immigrants	-0.002	(0.074)	0	(0.051)
Firm's Age	-0.005***	(0.001)	-0.002***	(0.000)
Process Innov.	-0.055	(0.051)	-0.062***	(0.014)
Product Innov.	-0.026	(0.020)	-0.007	(0.013)
Export	-0.053	(0.050)	-0.025	(0.020)
Constant	10.488***	(0.127)	10.509***	(0.087)
Time Dummies	Yes		Yes	
Sector Dummies	Yes		Yes	
NUTS1_level Dummies	Yes		Yes	
Observations	6531			
Correlation between equations	Corr(a,b)=0.806			
Wald Test for the coefficient of Perform. Related Pay	Diff.=0.425 p_value = 0.000			

Note. H0 in Wald Test assumes that the differences between the coefficients of Performance Related Pay in the productivity and wage equations (0.425) is not significantly different from zero. The p_value of this test shows that this H0 is rejected. Significance level: <0.01(***), <0.05(**), <0.1(*).

To confirm our results, an additional robustness check was performed by the treatment of the three-stage least squares estimator (3SLS) (see Table 4). This method combines two-stage least squares with the seemingly unrelated regressions (SUR), originally introduced by Zellner & Theil (1962). It is used when the dependent variables are correlated with each other, as in our case, and the variance-covariance matrix of error terms has to be controlled for by estimating simultaneous equations. Thus, the IV procedure deals with endogeneity problems, whereas the SUR method deals with error terms correlated across the equations. Thus, in the first stage we introduce the instruments of PRP shown above and in the second-stage we obtain consistent estimates for the covariance matrix of the equation disturbances. Finally, in the third-stage, by using this covariance matrix, we perform a GLS estimation, where instrumented values of PRP are inserted.

The last row shows the total correlation between each pair of equations that justifies the use of the covariance matrix of the disturbances, performed with the seemingly unrelated regression method. In addition, we can make a proper comparison of the PRP coefficients of the productivity and wage equations, respectively. In any case, what is worth noting in Table 4 is that our previous findings still hold and suggest the positive link of PRP with performances and pays.

6. Conclusions

Contrary to practices adopted during the late 1980s and the 1990s, over the last ten years Italian enterprises have to a much lesser degree been implemented innovative policies, including those which integrate low wages with performance-related bonuses. Most recent evidence from the mid-2000s points to some interesting results, namely positive effects of EFP schemes, higher incidence of these participatory schemes in larger firms. However, for thc whole economy, company compensation systems have failed to keep pace with (decreasing) productivity gains (Tronti, 2010), so wage moderation and favourable profitable periods have not provided the basis for the promotion of company performance related pay (PRP) arrangements.

This study has analysed the role of the implementation of these arrangements in decentralised bargaining, with a particular focus on the role played by the diffusion of EFP agreements on labour productivity. We found that PRP may significantly stimulate efficiency gains.

The chapter has also addressed distributive concerns exploring how PRP schemes bargained in local wage setting contributed to explain wages, and thus influenced the distributive patterns recorded in the Italian economy in the last few years.

All estimates were performed for a large sample of Italian manufacturing and service firms by controlling for a rich set of covariates. Furthermore, to validate our OLS results, various robustness checks were performed, by *IV-GMM* estimates and the treatments of 3SLS, testing that the same instrument is valid for both equations, labour productivity and wages. From the comparison of productivity and wage estimates, we obtained that PRP firms are more efficient and pay higher bonuses to their employees. Furthermore, the positive and significant difference of labour productivity and wage coefficients, associated with PRP, confirms that workers do not fully appropriate all returns of this provision.

The weaknesses implementation of the Italian bargaining rules originated by the 1993 reform calls for new political measures aimed at encouraging greater use of EFP systems. The recent political debate in Italy shows how participatory forms have again attracted increasing attention. After the severe effects of the global financial and economic crisis of 2008-09, employee participation in enterprise results and in decision-making is seen, also in Italy, a valid response, as shown by this study, for improving both enterprise performance and the system of industrial relations.

References

Abowd, J. M. & Lemieux T. (1993). The Effects of Product Market Competition on Collective Bargaining Agreements: The Case of Foreign Competition in Canada. *Quarterly Journal of Economics*, 108 (4), 983–1014.

Acemoglu, D. & Pischke, J.M. (1999). Beyond Becker: Training in Imperfect Labour Markets. *The Economic Journal*, 109 (453), F112-F142.

Baum, C.F., Schaffer, M. E. S. & Stillman, S. (2003). Instrumental variables and GMM: Estimation and testing. *The Stata Journal*, 3(1), 1-31.

Baum, C.F., Schaffer, M. E. S. & Stillman, S. (2007). Enhanced routines for instrumental variables/generalized method of moments estimation and testing. *The Stata Journal*, 7(4), 465-506.

Blanchflower, D.G., Oswald, A. & Sanfey, P. (1996). Wages, Profits and Rent-sharing. *Quarterly Journal of Economics*, 111(1) , 227–251.

Burke, L. A. & Hsieh, C. (2006). Optimizing fixed and variable compensation costs for employee Productivity. *International Journal of Productivity and Performance Management*, 55(2), 155-162

Damiani M. & Ricci, A. (2014). Decentralised Bargaining and Performance Related Pay. Evidence from a Panel of Italian Firms. *International Journal of Manpower*, 35(7), 1038-1058.

Damiani, M. & Uvalic, M. (2010). *Employee Participation for Good Firm Governance* . Paper presented at the 15th World Conference of the International Association for the Economics of Participation (IAFEP), Université Panthéon-Assas, Paris II, Paris, 8-10 July 2010.

Daveri, F. & Jona-Lasinio, C. (2005). Italy's decline: getting the facts right. *Giornale degli Economisti e Annali di Economia*, 64(4), 365-410.

European Commission (2011). *Wage setting: Institutional features*. Commission Note, Bruxelles: ADHOC/11/030511/EN.

European Commission (2013). *Wage Setting Systems and Wage Developments*, Bruxelles, http://ec.europa.eu /europe2020 /pdf /themes /wage_ settings.pdf.

FitzRoy, F. R. & Kraft, K. (1992). Forms of Profit-Sharing and Firm Performance: Theoretical Foundations and Empirical Problems. *Kyklos*, 45(2), 209-225.

Gielen, A. C, Kerkhofs M. J. M. & van Ours, J. C. (2009). How performance related pay affects productivity and employment. *Journal of Population Economics*, 23(1), 291-301.

Gürtzgen, N. (2009). Rent-sharing and collective bargaining coverage - evidence from linked employer-employee data. *Scandinavian Journal of Economics*, 111(2), 323-349.

Ichniowski, C., Shaw, K. and Prennushi, G. (1997), The Effects of Human Resource Management Practices on Productivity: A Study of Steel Finishing Lines. *The American Economic Review*, 87(3), 291-313.

ISAE (2009). La contrattazione collettiva di secondo livello in Italia a 15 anni dall'Accordo del '93: i risultati dell'Inchiesta ISAE", in Le previsioni per l'economia italiana, Rapporto ISAE, Istituto di Studi ed Analisi Economica, Rome.

Holmstrom, B. (1979). Moral Hazard and Observability. *Bell Journal of Economics*, 10(1), 74-91.

Kandel, E. & Lazear E. P. (1992). Peer Pressure and Partnership. *Journal of Political Economy*, l00(4), 801-817.

Kato, T., L. & Ryu, J. H. (2012). The productivity effects of profit sharing, employee ownership, stock option and team incentive plans: Evidence from Korean panel data. In Eriksson, T. (Ed.) *Advances in the Economic Analysis of Participatory & Labor-Managed Firms*, 111-135, Emerald Group.

Kruse, D.L.; Freeman, R. & Blasi, J.R. (2010). *Shared Capitalism at Work: Employee Ownership, Profit and Gain Sharing, and Broad-based Stock Options*, Chicago: University of Chicago Press.

Martins, P. S. (2009). Rent sharing before and after the wage bill. *Applied Economics*, 41(17), 2133-2151.

Menguc, B. & Barker, A.T. (2003). The Performance effects of Output-based Incentive Plans on Sales Organizations. *The Journal of Personal Selling and Sales Management*, 23(4), 341-358.

OECD (2012). *Employment Outlook*, Paris.

Pendleton, A. Poutsma, E. van Ommeren, J. & Brewster, C. (2001). *Employee share ownership and profit-sharing in the European Union.* European Foundation for the Improvement of Living and Working Conditions, Dublin.

Pérotin V. & Robinson A. (2003). *Employee Participation in Profit and Ownership: A Review of the Issues and Evidence*, Working paper, Social Affairs Series, SOCI 109 EN, Luxembourg Parliament, Directorate- General for Research.

Prendergast, C. (1999). The Provision of Incentives in Firms. *Journal of Economic Literature*, 37(1), 7-63.

Tronti L. (2010). The Italian productivity slow-down: the role of the bargaining model. *International Journal of Manpower*, 31(7), 770-792.

Uvalic M. (1991). *The PEPPER Report: Promotion of Employee Participation in Profits and Enterprise Results in the Member States of the European Community*, Social Europe Supplement No. 3/91, Luxembourg: Office for Official Publications of the European Communities.

Uvalic, M. (2006). Employee ownership - Western lessons for the Eastern New Member States, in Lowitzsch J. (Ed.) (2006) *PEPPER III Report*, 46-68, Dublin, European Foundation for the Improvement of Living and Working Conditions and Institute for Eastern European Studies, Free University of Berlin,.

Zellner, A. & Theil, H. (1962). Three-stage least squares: simultaneous estimation of simultaneous equations. *Econometrica*, 30(1), 54–78.

Zwick, T. (2004). Employee participation and productivity. *Labour Economics*, 11(6), 715– 740.

Appendix

Table A.1

Variable definition

Variable	Definition
Performance Related Pay	Dummy variable that equals 1 if the firm adopts PRP payments of any kind, 0 otherwise.
ln (value added per capita)	Log of value-added per employee (source AIDA) deflated by the value added deflator (source ISTAT)
ln (wage per capita)	Log of wage bill per employee (source AIDA) deflated by the consumer price index for blue and white collar workers (source ISTAT)
ln (physical capital per capita)	Log of capital stock per employee (source AIDA) deflated by the investment deflator (source ISTAT)
% executives	Percentage of managers and supervisors
% white collar workers	Percentage of white collar workers
% blue-collar workers	Percentage of manual workers
% women	Percentage of women among total workers
% fixed-term contracts	Percentage of fixed-term workers
% immigrant workers	Percentage of workers coming from other countries
Age	Age of firms
Process Innovation	Dummy variable that equals 1 if the firm adopted process innovations in the last three years, 0 otherwise
Product Innovation	Dummy variable that equals 1 if the firm originated new products in the last three years, 0 otherwise
Export	Dummy variable that equals 1 if the firm exported in the last three years, 0 otherwise
ln (Sales volatility)_1999-2001	Logarithm of the standard deviation of sales over the period 1999-2001
ln (Sales volatility)_2002-2004	Logarithm of the standard deviation of sales over the period 2002-2004
Firm Size	Logarithm of the number of employees at firm level
North- West	Dummy variable that equals 1 if the firm is localised in North-Western regions, 0 otherwise
North-East	Dummy variable that equals 1 if the firm is localised in North-Eastern regions, 0 otherwise
Centre	Dummy variable that equals 1 if the firm is localised in Central regions, 0 otherwise
South	Dummy variable that equals 1 if the firm is localised in Southern regions, 0 otherwise
Sectors	Dummy variable that equals 1 if the firm is localised in sector shown in table1, 0 otherwise

Note. Source: RIL Survey, ISFOL

Table A.2

Effects of Performance Related Pay on Labour Productivity and Wages (IV Estimates, First Stage)

Dependent Variable 2d Stage	ln (value added per capita)		ln (wage per capita)	
Dependent Variable 1st Stage	Performance Related Pay			
Explanatory Variables	*a*		*b*	
Sales Volatility 2002_2004	0.023***	(0.009)	0.019***	(0.004)
Sales Volatility 1999_2001	0.033***	(0.010)	0.037***	(0.004)
ln (physical capital per capita)	0.003	(0.009)	-0.002	(0.003)
Fixed-term contracts_Share	0.052	(0.111)	-0.052	(0.033)
White Collars_share	-0.316*	(0.174)	-0.134**	(0.062)
Blue Collars_share	-0.273	(0.169)	-0.061	(0.061)
Women_share	-0.193***	(0.056)	-0.100***	(0.023)
Immigrants	-0.293*	(0.103)	-0.082**	(0.038)
Firm's Age	0.002**	(0.001)	0.003***	(0.000)
Process Innov.	0.050**	(0.025)	0.043***	(0.011)
Product Innov.	0.022	(0.025)	0.018*	(0.011)
Export	0.061**	(0.025)	0.033***	(0.011)
Constant	-0.136	(0.234)	-0.517***	(0.092)
Time Dummies	Yes		Yes	
Sector Dummies	Yes		Yes	
NUTS1_level Dummies	Yes		Yes	
Observations	6579		6570	

Note. Significance level: <0.01(***), <0.05(**), <0.1(*).

Employee share ownership in the Netherlands

Eric Kaarsemaker & Erik Poutsma[1]

Abstract

This chapter investigates employee share ownership in the Netherlands: its frequency, characteristics of companies with employee share ownership, motives to adopt employee share ownership, and scheme characteristics. Incidence is generally low (3.6 per cent of companies with 10 or more employees have a broad-based share scheme) but is growing. Otherwise, employee share ownership in the Netherlands is not deviating so much from patterns seen in other countries. To explain the findings, the chapter further describes a number of Dutch contextual particularities: government measures and taxation (largely absent), attitudes of government, trade unions, employers' organisations, and financial institutions (not negative per se, but critical and slightly superficial, and broad-based share ownership's potency as a strong incentive is generally not well recognised), and a number of other relevant aspects such as attitudes towards participation and entrepreneurship more generally. The chapter concludes with a 'Dutch model' that was developed, which provides clarity for companies about what is involved with setting up a sustainable and responsible employee share ownership scheme. Also, this model might help employee share ownership to 'break through' the relatively strong industrial relations system in the Netherlands.

1. Introduction

In this chapter, we focus on financial participation in the Netherlands. We limit ourselves to employee share ownership. Generally speaking, the Netherlands traditionally score low on measures of social inequality. Its

---

1 Eric Kaarsemaker (corresponding author), email: ekaars@gmail.com
Erik Poutsma: Institute for Management Research, Radboud University Nijmegen, Netherlands, email: e.poutsma@ru.nl

industrial relations have been built on consensus; it is not a country of extremes. It is therefore not surprising that the Netherlands have not been at the forefront with employee share ownership: it has a relatively low incidence in the Netherlands, there are no fiscal incentives (anymore), and it has generally played no part in industrial and employee relations debates.

Having said that, Piketty's (2013) recent research has opened some eyes. Wealth is not spread that equally in the Netherlands after all (WRR, 2014), and a sense of urgency has been growing among at least a number of politicians. Employee share ownership might be a means to distribute wealth more equally. Apart from that, the incidence of employee share ownership in the Netherlands is low but has been increasing, and the consensus-based industrial relations system is under some pressure for example due to trends towards more flexible work arrangements (e.g. Nauta, 2015). This possibly gives employee share ownership a further boost.

As said, we investigate employee share ownership in the Netherlands. We focus on shares in particular, not share options. We focus on what is most likely hardly or not known among the readers of this book, which means that we will barely refer to 'mainstream' employee share ownership research. Where relevant, we will assume a certain level of knowledge of this research. We start with a discussion of descriptive data on employee share ownership in the Netherlands. We then give a qualitative analysis of the Dutch context. We conclude with scenarios for future developments.

2. Descriptive data on employee share ownership in the Netherlands

This section describes employee share ownership schemes in the Netherlands: their frequency, characteristics of companies with employee share ownership, managerial motives to introduce employee share ownership, employee motives to invest, and data on what the schemes themselves look like.

2.1 Frequency and company characteristics

Research in 2008 and 2009 (Kaarsemaker, 2009) showed that 3.6 per cent of companies with at least 10 employees had some form of share ownership scheme for which at least half the workforce is eligible. This amounts to roughly 2,460 companies and 400,000 employees, of whom 150,000 have actually invested in company shares. This study is based on a telephone survey amongst a random sample of 2,500 Dutch companies with 10 or more employees. The survey was carried out in October and November 2008. CEOs or HR directors were the respondents. The actual sample size was 669 companies, for a response rate of 27 per cent. The nonresponse was investigated but showed no deviating patterns.

The percentage of 3.6 companies with broad-based employee share ownership is almost double the percentage found in the previous in-depth study, in 1996 (Poutsma & Van den Tillaart, 1996). The 2009 percentage does not include share options: another 1.0 per cent had a company-wide share option programme in place. Interestingly, another 3.7 per cent said that they considered introducing a broad-based employee share (option) scheme.

These percentages have never been higher. Much earlier, back in the 20th century, employee share ownership did occur in the Netherlands, but at the time mostly in the appearance of producer cooperatives. However, these were of very little importance (*'randverschijnsel'*) (Becker & Frieswijk, 1976). Interesting to note is that SNPI, a non-profit Dutch center that promotes (financial) participation, is founded with an endowment from one of these 20th century producer cooperatives: De Ploeg in Bergeijk. Despite the minor importance of producer cooperatives and employee share ownership in the Netherlands, there is the odd but longstanding and well-publicised case of economic democracy. Examples are Sligro Food Group, ARCADIS, and Breman Group, a medium-sized construction and engineering firm (De Jong & Van Witteloostuijn, 2004). To go back to the 2009 study: Other recent (but more limited) datasets show slightly higher percentages than the 2009 study found: The 2010 European Working Conditions Survey (EWCS) dataset showed that 4.9 per cent of companies operates a broad-based employee share ownership scheme, the 2010 Cranfield Network on International Human Resource Management (CRANET) dataset showed a percentage of 4.6, and the 2013 European Company Survey (ECS) dataset showed a percentage of 6.7 (see Lowitzsch et al., 2014).

What kinds of companies have employee share ownership? Over half of the companies with broad-based employee share ownership – broad based: eligible to all or most employees – turned out to have a *listing* on the stock exchange (Kaarsemaker, 2009). Related to this, Braam & Poutsma (2015) found that 13 per cent of companies listed at the Amsterdam stock exchange have a broad-based employee share ownership scheme (a percentage that has been growing). Half of the companies with employee share ownership appeared to have a *foreign parent company*, 21 per cent had a Dutch parent, and 29 per cent was independent at the time of the research (Kaarsemaker, 2009).

Size-wise, 63 per cent of the companies with employee share ownership had more than 200 employees in the 2009 study, whereas only 12 per cent had less than 50. Of the companies with more than 200 employees, 13 per cent had broad-based employee share ownership, against only 1.5 per cent of those with less than 50. The category in between (50 to 200 employees) had an average close to the overall average: 3.5 per cent.

Above average, companies with employee share ownership had their operations in the trading and services *sectors* (both 38 per cent), and less so in production (25 per cent). In trading, 7.0 per cent of companies had broad-based employee share ownership. In services and production, these percentages turned out to be 6.4 and 2.8, respectively. In sum, the company characteristics show no deviations from the wider research on employee share ownership and some of the data have been roughly confirmed in different studies and datasets (Braam & Poutsma, 2015; Kaarsemaker, 2009; Poutsma, Ligthart & Schouteten, 2005; Welz & Fernández-Macías, 2008).

2.2 Motives

Why do companies introduce broad-based employee share ownership, and why do employees invest? The 2009 study showed that almost half the companies intend to stimulate the workforce to think and act like owners. It is expected that this, in turn, will lead to positive results for the company. Retention is also a motive for 29 per cent of the companies with employee share ownership, and 13 per cent said they introduced it to offer their employees something new, something extra. The research also showed, interestingly, that for 21 per cent of the companies it was unclear why they have broad-based employee share ownership. Unfortunately, the reasons for this have not been investigated more deeply.

In the Netherlands, many employees derive rights from collective labour agreements. These are usually negotiated sector-wide between employers' organisations and trade unions, or between (typically larger) individual companies and unions. The 2009 study showed that employee share ownership is generally not part of collective labour agreements. Of the companies with both a collective labour agreement and employee share ownership, only 13 per cent include employee share ownership in the collective labour agreement. This is a sign of the lack of attention for employee share ownership in the industrial relations discourse in the Netherlands.

In the Netherlands, employee share ownership is not per se open to all employees, or obligatory for employees. There is usually at least some choice. Often, though, companies require employees to have a permanent contract (42 per cent of the companies with employee share ownership) or at least to have been with the company for a minimum amount of time, commonly 1 year (38 per cent). Only 8 per cent of the companies with employee share ownership appeared not to apply any conditions at all for employees to participate.

Employees, on the other hand, are not necessarily required to invest in the scheme. The 2009 research showed that in only 25 per cent of the companies with employee share ownership more than half of the eligible workforce in fact invested in the scheme. On average, the percentage of eligible employees investing in the scheme is estimated to be 20 per cent, with a lot of companies scoring relatively low and a few companies scoring close to 100 per cent of eligible employees. Next to the voluntary investments, companies pass on shares to employees as part of profit sharing (8 per cent) or as part of a save-as-you-earn-scheme (another 8 per cent; these schemes do no longer exist as of 1 January 2012) (Kaarsemaker, 2009).

2.3 What does the typical employee share ownership scheme look like?

In listed companies, the employee share investment is usually linked with a personal investment account with a bank. The bank or the company itself administers the plan. In companies that are not listed, an employee share ownership trust is normally set up that administers the employee share ownership. Formally, the trust remains the owner of the shares and keeps the voting rights. The employees receive share certificates and are entitled to any pay-outs related to the shares. The employees are represented on the board of the trust and have a say in how the voting rights are applied at for instance the annual meeting.

Other particulars are described here. Only in 4 per cent of cases was employee share ownership found to be accompanied by a *reduction in wages* (Kaarsemaker, 2009). Commonly, there is no *loan* related to the investment in employee shares, neither by the trust nor by the employees (63 per cent). In 8 per cent of cases, employees took loans themselves to buy shares. The remaining 29 per cent was unsure probably because the company does not know whether individual employees took out a loan to buy shares or not. In only 17 per cent of cases appeared the *volumes* of employee share purchases or sales to be left completely to individual discretion. Another 17 per cent of companies gave every eligible employee equal rights, another 17 per cent based volumes on tenure, 13 per cent on individual performance, 8 per cent on company performance, and another 8 per cent on wage levels.

A final differentiating characteristic was *rules applied to selling* company shares. 42 per cent applied a lock-up period during which the shares had to be kept. In 25 per cent of the companies, any rights would be cancelled after leaving the firm, retiring, or being fired. Only 8 per cent allowed selling freely immediately after the transfer of shares. No company applied any limitations relating to performance.

To put the above into perspective: The average investment in company shares amounts from several hundred euros to several thousand at the most (Kaarsemaker, 2009). All in all, the above does not create the feeling that employee share ownership is deeply rooted in the history and culture of the Netherlands and its businesses. The next section elaborates on the Dutch context, which will help to understand why that might be.

3. Analysis of the Dutch employee share ownership context

In this section, we discuss the Dutch employee share ownership context. This might help to understand the relatively low incidence of employee share ownership in the Netherlands, and the relatively superficial ways in which it has generally been implemented in companies that do have a broad-based scheme in place.

3.1 Government measures and taxation

The low incidence is not consistent with the fact that the Dutch government has been stimulating the accumulation of property (*'bezitsvorming'*) since at least the 1960s. Employee share ownership is one variety of property. Accumulation of property has received government support due to its supposedly positive consequences: It will 'turn man into a fully-fledged participant in society' (Albeda & Schmelzer, 1963). Government measures, however, have been focusing particularly on pensions and home ownership. By the end of the 1990s, between 14 and 17 per cent of Dutch households held shares directly, and including mutual investment funds and pension funds the percentage was about 33 per cent (Alessie & Hochguertel, 2003). There is no reason to believe that the development towards more (indirect and direct) share ownership by households has come to a halt since.

Nonetheless, employee share ownership has hardly been part of government measures to stimulate property accumulation. Since the 1990s until 2012 there was a save-as-you-earn scheme that allowed workers to save several hundred euros a year out of their gross wages. This money would be locked in a special savings account during a number of years, usually 4 years. After this lock-in period, the money would be freely available as a net amount. The maximum annual amount could be doubled in size if invested in company shares, which on average added up to a maximum of over € 1,200. The same lock-in period would apply. This has been the only straightforward scheme in place to stimulate workers to invest in employee share ownership. As per 2012, the save-as-you-earn programme has been abolished completely. For companies, no overall measures have been in place, but companies could and can agree an individual fiscal arrangement with the revenue service.

This general lack of government support is significant, as several Dutch experts have referred to the importance of tax measures. Back in the 1960s, Albeda and Schmelzer (1963) said that it would be 'irresponsible' for government to wait for 'things to happen coincidentally'. Experts such Mr. Allard Voûte (former lawyer who wrote a PhD dissertation on employee share ownership in 1991 and was on the board of SNPI; he has unfortunately passed away) and Mr. Kees Vos (honorary president of the European Federation of Employee Share ownership, EFES) in interviews have argued that tax measures, or the lack thereof, 'explain everything'. Tax incentives help overcome cold feet. Having to pay full income tax and having to organise a special fiscal arrangement regarding deductible expenses with the revenue service is generally regarded as yet another difficulty when considering the introduction of employee share ownership in the company (Kaarsemaker, 2006).

Mr. Voûte further claimed that employee share ownership is about 'innovation'. It should therefore be stimulated in a similar manner as government has supported other innovative developments. Dutch parliament, however, could not get its head around this, as support measures for employee share ownership would create inequalities between private and public sector workers. As another expert, Mr. Mark van Beusekom, former director of SNPI, expressed it: 'in the Netherlands, everything must be equal.' See also our introduction to this chapter.

Finally, Mr. Vos contended that it would be naïve to think that for example the US employee share ownership legislation could be introduced easily in the Netherlands. This legislation has come into being over a long period of time and is very complex, with a myriad of rules. It is very particular of the US context. This legislation is therefore not at all easy to transfer to the Dutch context, at least not in ways that are immediately effective. Let alone that these complex regulations would not make it any easier for, particularly, small- and medium-sized companies to adopt employee share ownership (Kaarsemaker, 2006).

3.2 Government, trade unions, employers' organisations

Generally, the social partners are not against employee share ownership (Lowitzsch et al., 2014; Soppe et al., 2014). Their perspectives on employee share ownership, however, do differ considerably (Poutsma & Voets, 2002; Pendleton & Poutsma, 2004). *Government*'s approach has mainly been macroeconomic. Employee share ownership has been regarded as helpful for keeping wage increases in control in times of economic growth. Wage control is an important policy goal in the Netherlands. It supports the long-term competitiveness of the small and open Dutch economy. However, government involvement with employee share ownership has generally been low as was clear from our discussion of taxation. It has been left to the discretion of employers, employees and their organisations. Only risk issues have received some government attention, particularly individual risks as a consequence of corporate governance issues such as earnings management. In the current discussion on wealth distribution, employee share ownership has hardly been included as yet.

The *trade unions* have been passive, perhaps even slightly suspicious of employers' and employees' motives and worried about their power position. Unions in the Netherlands play a central role in collective labour agreement negotiations and other consultations. Works councils regularly discuss important matters with employers, for which they sometimes need advice from union experts. This might for example happen with employee share ownership and succession issues. The unions, if necessary, make an appeal to outside experts. This is one way in which participation in decision-making and consultation, the 'polder model', works out. This is also how unions can influence outcomes. Having said that, union expertise has hardly been called upon in matters of employee share ownership (Kaarsemaker, 2006).

Employee share ownership has been a topic of discussion within the unions only rarely. The unions' perspective has been mainly focused on the levels of the firm and the individual, particularly on social issues and related policies. Wage substitution – employee share ownership replacing a part of wages – has been opposed. Trade unions do see employee share ownership as a useful addition to the elaborate Dutch system of direct and indirect participation (via works councils, which companies with more than 50 employees are legally obliged to have) but in no way as a replacement thereof. Despite the decreasing levels of union membership (currently at 20 per cent of all workers), approximately 80 per cent of all workers are still covered by collective labour agreements. These, however, do not normally mention employee share ownership, as we mentioned above. Nevertheless, there is a growing need for flexibility, and working arrangements increasingly become customized according to individual companies' specific needs (Poutsma & Voets, 2002; Soppe et al., 2014).

The *employers' organisations* have perceived employee share ownership as an instrument to make wages more flexible, and to enhance organisational commitment and responsibility. It should therefore be part of performance-related pay schemes, which have become more and more acceptable to trade unions as well. Employee share ownership has not been much of an issue in small- and medium-sized companies and is unlikely to become one because of the administrative burden. There have been no policies on employee share ownership; it has been within employers' own discretion. Like trade unions, employers' organisations prefer to keep employee share ownership separated from works council arrangements and codetermination (Poutsma & Voets, 2002; Soppe et al., 2014).

3.3 Financial institutions

Banks and other financial institutions have seen no clear market for employee share ownership in the Netherlands. They have mostly had broad-based profit-sharing and share option schemes in place themselves. Banks consider employee share ownership mainly to be an employee benefit with positive effects for organisational commitment. However, they see a number of problems with this kind of benefit: For example, the indirect link between the company's share price and individual performance, and the typical scheme is difficult to understand for the average worker. Another downside mentioned is the risk of negative attitudes during economic downturns.

Fund managers have not directly considered employee share ownership schemes in their valuations. They have, however, included human resource management, organisational commitment, and corporate social responsibility in their ratings of companies. Financial institutions share trade unions' and employers' organisations' views that employee share ownership should not substitute normal wages, but be a complementary benefit. Some banks also emphasised the macroeconomic importance of employee share ownership, as it encourages savings (Poutsma & Voets, 2002; Pendleton & Poutsma, 2004; Kaarsemaker, 2006).

3.4 Developments, participation, entrepreneurship

A number of developments are relevant when analysing employee share ownership in the context of the Netherlands. As Mr. Vos mentioned in his interview, the character of the workforce has changed significantly. People are more highly qualified and demand influence. Mr. Henk Kool, another former director of SNPI, added that as a consequence, the Dutch 'polder model' – the consensus-based industrial relations system – has been changing in nature. Mr. Van Beusekom simultaneously saw an increase in the importance of the services sector, where human capital is more important than machines, and where employee share ownership is more commonly used to attract and retain people than in other sectors.

Workers want more influence, but Mr. Van Beusekom's experience is that many of the small- and medium-sized firms that he worked with were not very sympathetic to that. Those companies were in favour of employee share ownership, but they did not want the involvement of the works council and of too many other people in the organisation. However, a company that implements employee share ownership cannot avoid opening its books. Mr. Arie de Ruijter, a former board-member of producer cooperative De Ploeg and of SNPI, pointed out the importance of countervailing powers in organisations and the ability to exercise real influence. Employee share ownership needs embedding in participation in decision-making processes. In the Netherlands, many companies have works councils for that. The position of the works council could, however, become ambiguous in the case of employee share ownership due to possibly conflicting interests of participants and nonparticipants. Mr. De Ruijter could imagine the formation of a combined representative body of organised employee shareholders and the works council.

Mr. Vos, Mr. Van Beusekom, and Mr. De Ruijter further contended that the Dutch are more risk-averse than people in other countries. In the Netherlands, entrepreneurship has not been 'fashionable' and people have been less inclined to start their own businesses. As Mr. Van Beusekom said, 'entrepreneurship is not in our blood'. Nevertheless, Mr. Van Beusekom had generally encountered much willingness to invest, provided that the employee share ownership scheme had been well prepared. Also, the general attitude with regard to entrepreneurship has been changing. According to Mr. De Ruijter, the Netherlands is in many respects an exemplary country. However, the predominating ethos is not that people take care of themselves, but that they should be taken care of. Mr. Kool added that the Dutch are rather impassive, and only become active when their interests are at stake. That is when they demand influence. Obviously, this is much more easily arranged in smaller companies. Related to this, Mr. De Ruijter believed that companies with 150 employees at the most are best suited for employee share ownership (Kaarsemaker, 2006).

4. Scenarios and the 'Dutch model'

The industrial relations context of the Netherlands suggests strong support for democratic initiatives in companies. This is an important condition for further developments relating to industrial democracy (Foley, 2014), and, likewise, economic democracy. Above, however, we have seen that the Dutch context is not necessarily supportive of employee share ownership. One could say that perhaps the industrial relations system is too strong – particularly on indirect participation and the 'polder model', with regular consultations between trade unions, employers' organisations, and government – to allow for an instrument that possibly gives one group of actors a new power base: the employee shareholders. It also appeared that experts generally regard supportive tax measures as a necessary condition for employee share ownership to 'break through'. If the situation remains as is, a scenario without much change is likely to unfold.

We also described how the Dutch context is not static. A new discourse on wealth distribution has been started, the character of the workforce and of work itself has been changing, people have been demanding more influence, they have been given more responsibility over their own lives, the 'polder model' is evolving, working arrangements become more flexible, etc. Apart from that, there is the increasing adoption of employee share ownership in the countries around the Netherlands. These are all pressures that might naturally give employee share ownership a boost. The descriptive data showed signs of this picture, with 3.7 per cent of companies saying that they were considering adopting a broad-based employee share (option) scheme, and with the higher percentages of employee share ownership incidence in the other (later) datasets. This does, however, not make supportive tax measures less important. But these pressures might actually help tax measures to come about more quickly. This seems a more likely 'growth scenario'.

On the basis of earlier advice (Kaarsemaker, 2009), SNPI developed a 'Dutch model' for sustainable employee share ownership (SNPI, 2010). This model contains a number of principles and conditions for sustainable employee share ownership in the Netherlands:

- The main objective is organisational commitment (and not financial profit);
- Participation is voluntary (and not at the expense of normal wages);
- The scheme is eligible to all employees (at the minimum 75 per cent of all employees with a permanent contract);
- Principles of good governance apply;
- Shares are distributed in a balanced way (maximum annual individual investment of 10 per cent of wages, with an overall maximum indi-

vidual stake of 4.99 per cent; a lock-in period of at the minimum 2 years, at the maximum 4 years);

- Employee shareholders' voice is warranted, also in case of share certificates;
- The company communicates clearly and frequently about the (implementation of the) scheme and about the business;
- The employee share ownership is strongly linked with HR policies and practices;
- The scheme is evaluated regularly.

Some of these principles and conditions are elaborated further, for example regarding dividend policies, company valuation, trading (for companies without listing), buy-back, demand and supply, and financing of the employee shares (SNPI, 2010). Purpose of the 'Dutch model' is to create clarity for companies – in particular small- and medium-sized companies – about what is involved with setting up a sustainable and responsible employee share ownership scheme in the Netherlands. Another purpose is to create a clear model that would be eligible for fiscal incentives. It is hoped that it might help to base tax measures on, aimed both at companies and employees.

5. *Summary and conclusions*

In the Netherlands, many people seem to have a favourable attitude towards employee share ownership, but hardly anybody seems to make a move. Hence, the incidence of employee share ownership in the Netherlands has been relatively low (a study in 2009 showed that 3.6 per cent of companies with at least 10 employees has a broad-based scheme, although this percentage is growing). This is slightly surprising as the accumulation of property has been a policy issue for the Dutch government since at least the 1960s. The Dutch government, however, has mainly had a macroeconomic take on this, centred on wage control. For the remainder, employee share ownership has been left to the discretion of employers and employees, and their organisations.

Employers' organisations and trade unions, however, have not been straightforward supporters of employee share ownership. Unions may have felt threatened by employee share ownership, possibly because of their pivotal role in various consultation and codetermination bodies, and their relationship with works councils, which are so prominent in the Dutch industrial relations system. A new interest group of employee shareholders might undermine the position of the unions. This has not helped employee share ownership to appear on relevant agendas.

Nevertheless, fundamental trends cannot be ignored. The services sector has become increasingly important, and with that human capital. People have overall grown in knowledge, skills, and abilities. They demand flexible working arrangements and influence. As a consequence, the 'polder model' has been changing in nature. Also, a debate on wealth distribution has been started. All in all, under these pressures, a further increase in the incidence of employee share ownership is likely, and the descriptive data we have presented show signs of this scenario. Companies will use their individual discretion in order to find new ways to attract, retain, and motivate people, whether the industrial relations system is ready or not.

Taxation turned out to be an important factor in order to influence the development of employee share ownership in the Netherlands. There have hardly been any fiscal incentives promoting employee share ownership in the past, apart from a limited save-as-you-earn programme until 2012. As there is as yet little support to be expected from the social partners, lack of tax measures mean a further and significant disadvantage as compared to neighbouring countries, in particular for small- and medium-sized companies. Many companies are not familiar with employee share ownership, and may be overwhelmed by its apparent complexity, particularly with regard to tax regulations. SNPI has therefore developed a simple, sustainable and responsible 'Dutch model' that gives insight in Dutch employee share ownership basics. Tax measures could be based on this model. This would fit within the Dutch tradition to promote the accumulation of property. In current times, it seems a small but logical and important step to shift government support for home ownership – which had logic at the time, but nowadays is particularly profitable for wealthy people – towards support for employee share ownership.

References

Albeda, W. & W. Schmelzer (1963). *Bezitsvorming*. Utrecht/Antwerpen: Het Spectrum.

Alessie, R. & S. Hochguertel (2003). Stockholding in the Netherlands. In L. Guiso et al. (Eds.), *Stockholding in Europe*. Basingstoke: Palgrave Macmillan.

Becker, F. & J. Frieswijk (1976). Bedrijven in eigen beheer: kolonies en produktieve associaties in Nederland 1901-1958. Nijmegen: SUN.

Braam, G. & E. Poutsma (2015). Broad-Based Financial Participation Plans and Their Impact on Financial Performance: Evidence from a Dutch Longitudinal Panel. *De Economist*, forthcoming 2015.

De Jong, G. & A. van Witteloostuijn (2004). Successful corporate democracy: sustainable cooperation of capital and labor in the Dutch Breman Group. *Academy of Management Executive*, 18(3), pp. 54-66.

Foley, J. (2014). Industrial democracy in the twenty-first century. In: A. Wilkinson et al. (Eds.). *Handbook of Research on Employee Voice*, Elgar, pp. 66-80.

Kaarsemaker, E. (2006). Employee ownership and human resource management: A theoretical and empirical treatise with a digression on the Dutch context (PhD dissertation, Radboud University Nijmegen).

Kaarsemaker, E. (2009). Werknemersaandeelhouderschap in Nederland: frequentie, kenmerken, ondersteunende praktijken en gevolgen. Assen: Van Gorcum.

Lowitzsch, J. et al. (2014). *The Promotion of Employee Ownership and Participatio*n (Study prepared by the Inter-University Centre for European Commission's DG MARKT).

Nauta, A. (2015). Industrial Relations and Works Councils in the Netherlands—Results from Interviews and a Survey among HR Managers. In: M. Euwema et al. (Eds.). *Promoting Social Dialogue in European Organizations*, Springer, pp. 105-121.

Pendleton, A. & E. Poutsma (2004). *Financial participation: the role of governments and social partners* (No. EF0440). Dublin: European Foundation for the Improvement of Living and Working Conditions.

Piketty, T. (2013). *Le capital au XXIe siècle*. Paris: Seuil.

Poutsma, E., P. Ligthart & R. Schouteten (2005). Employee Share Ownership in Europe: the Influence of US Multinationals. *Management Revue*, 16(1), pp. 99-122.

Poutsma, E. & H. van den Tillaart (1996). *Tijd voor beleid! Financiële werknemersparticipatie in Nederland*. Den Haag: Nederlands Participatie Instituut.

Poutsma, E. & H. Voets (2002). *The policies and views of peak organisations to financial participation. National report: the Netherlands* (Research report). Nijmegen: IT-WORCS/Nijmegen School of Management/European Foundation for the Improvement of Living and Working Conditions.

SNPI (2010). Duurzaam aandeelhouderschap door werknemers: 'een Nederlands model'. Utrecht: SNPI.

Soppe, A. et al. (2014) (Eds.). *Delen in modern ondernemen: financiële werknemersparticipatie in Nederland* (Research report). IvO Center for Financial Law & Governance, Erasmus University Rotterdam.

Voûte, A. (1991). *Aandelen voor werknemers: motivatie door participatie*. Deventer: Kluwer (PhD dissertation, Radboud University Nijmegen).

Welz, C. & E. Fernández-Macías (2008). Financial Participation of Employees in the European Union: Much Ado about Nothing? *European Journal of Industrial Relations*, 14(4), pp. 479-496.

WRR (2014). Hoe ongelijk is Nederland? Een verkenning van de ontwikkeling en gevolgen van economische ongelijkheid (Research report). Amsterdam University Press.

Government, union and business associations' perceptions of employee financial participation in Gipuzkoa[1]

Begoña Arregi, Fred Freundlich, Mónica Gago, Maite Legarra, Nerea Lizarraga, Sylvia Gay, Jose Antonio Mendizabal & Ainhoa Larrañaga[2]

Abstract

Much research and practise have shown the benefits of employee financial participation (EFP) in the enterprise for workers, companies and communities. As a result, the Provincial Government of Gipuzkoa defined a clear policy aimed at promoting financial participation in companies in the province. In this context, the authors conduct a qualitative study that seeks to identify the different perceptions of EFP held by representatives of the three key actors in the Gipuzkoan economy: labour unions, business associations and public institutions. As discussed in the results, although there is quite a distance still to travel towards achieving common views and strategy, significant progress has been made and all agents agree that the issue must be included in future debates.

1. Introduction

New technological, financial and scientific paradigms have transformed labour and production processes and, in recent years, contributed to an

---

1 The authors wish to thank the Provincial Government of Gipuzkoa's Department of Innovation, Rural Development and Tourism for the funding it provided for this research. We also want to thank the participants in the CIRIEC 2012 (Donostia-San Sebastián), EMES 2013 (Liege) and IAFEP 2014 (Montevideo) conferences for their observations.

2 Begoña Arregi, Fred Freundlich, Mónica Gago (corresponding author email: mgago@mondragon.edu), Maite Legarra Nerea Lizarraga: MIK (Mondragon Innovation and Knowledge), Mondragon Unibertsitatea
Sylvia Gay, Jose Antonio Mendizabal, Ainhoa Larrañaga: GEZKI (Gizarte-Ekonomia eta Zuzenbide Kooperatiboaren Institutua), University of the Basque Country

acute crisis that has seriously threatened the long-term health of the real economy. In this context, the issue of employee participation – in production decisions, in company ownership and in business management – has taken on fundamental importance. This has been recognised by many of the most advanced companies in the world which apply systems of knowledge management requiring broad-based participation and other high-involvement practises. It has also been recognised by theorists who have identified the emergence in industrialised countries of a new phase of production, 'cognitive capitalism', which is as different from industrial capitalism as industrial capitalism was from the merchant capitalism that preceded it for over three centuries.

This chapter describes the current situation in Gipuzkoa, examining the issue of employee participation in general in the province and employee financial participation (EFP) in particular. Specifically, we set out the conclusions of a collaborative study carried out among MIK[3] (Mondragon University), GEZKI[4] (University of the Basque Country) and the Provincial Government of Gipuzkoa entitled, *Project Impetus: Promoting employee financial participation in collabouration with business associations, unions and government in the Province of Gipuzkoa.*

Gipuzkoa is a province in the autonomous community of the Basque Country in northern Spain. In 2013, Gipuzkoa had a GDP per capita of €30,828 (EUSTAT, 2015a). This is above the average of €25,700 reported by EUROSTAT for the 28 member states of the European Union. More information about Gipuzkoa can be found in section 3.

The territory has a single legislative chamber, the Provincial Assembly [*Juntas Generales de Gipuzkoa*]. The Department of Innovation, Rural Development and Tourism - one of the Provincial Government's several executive departments - through specific, action plans, seeks to contribute to building a society based on multidimensional sustainability – social sustainability (social cohesion), economic sustainability (innovation and competitiveness) and environmental sustainability. In particular, the department encourages any and all actions that will promote the kinds of

3 MIK (Mondragon Innovation and Knowledge - Centro de Investigación en Gestión) is a business management research centre at the Faculty of Business, Mondragon University, www.mik.es.

4 GEZKI (Instituto de Derecho Cooperativo y Economía Social) is the Institute of cooperative law and social economy of the University of the Basque Country (UPV-EHU).

employee participation that contribute to stronger bonds between employees and the overall project in the enterprise where they work. Extensive research has shown (see section 2) that this type of worker participation leads to stronger economic results for companies, better psycho-social outcomes for workers and greater territorial development.

Employee financial participation (EFP) is well established in the province. In addition to numerous worker cooperatives and worker-owned societies [*sociedades laborales*], figures published by IKEI (2011) show EFP in a significant percentage of firms sampled (see detail in section 3.2).

Previous research into employee participation shows that key issues have not been fully addressed. There is division and disagreement in the attitudes and policies of trade unions, business associations and public authorities and these divisions are not systematically addressed. Further, EFP is promoted in varying ways in different countries.

In this regard, the various conclusions reached by authors in a number of studies conducted in recent years (see Arregi, Freundlich, Gay, Mendizabal, & Lizarraga, 2012; García et al., 2013, for references) show the complexity of the subject and the profound differences of opinion among different economic agents with regard to this issue. This is also true in the province of Gipuzkoa, in the Basque Country more broadly and in other European countries. It is also important to bear in mind, in connection to promoting EFP, the territorial development strategy defined by the Provincial Government and the strategies and action plans of the various agents in the province explored in this study.

Under these circumstances, the authors felt it necessary to examine this subject in greater detail, encouraging analysis and debate with and among these three key constituencies: trade union organisations, business associations and government in the province. As a result, we conducted the research reported here, a preliminary effort to examine the perceptions of representatives of these three actors with regard to employee participation in general and EFP in particular. To the best of the authors' knowledge, this is the first time an analysis has been carried out of the perceptions of economic agents by organising and facilitating a series of debate amongst them. That is to say, this is the first study in which the three social partners have interacted around this issue in an organised way and they found this approach to be both innovative and enriching.

As regards the structure of the chapter, we have devoted the second section to the theoretical framework, analysing the perception of the different organisations on employee participation. The methodology used is set out in the third section. This is followed by the results and a discussion of the study, arranged into four categories (section 4). Finally we offer conclusions and possible future lines of research (section 5).

2. Theoretical framework

The research here, as described, focuses on an analysis of the perceptions of EFP amongst trade union, business associations and public authorities in Gipuzkoa. This section starts with a short definition of EFP, with some general information on the extent to which it has been implemented and on literature on the implications of financial participation for firms, employees and society. We also discuss the scientific literature on the perceptions of the socio-economic agents on this participation. Finally, we review the position of several European institutions on this participation.

2.1 Financial participation: definition and current situation

Employee participation in companies, described as ‘a standard label encompassing a very wide range of historical models and utopias, even when we discard the tendentious interpretation it acquires when used as a policy for opposing worker and/or trade union action’ (Villa, 1980), involves a great deal of conceptual and ideological ambiguity, as is also the case with related concepts of ‘industrial democracy’ and ‘economic democracy’. Since the early twentieth century, these concepts have been integrated into systems of labour relations with the idea of allowing or fomenting employee participation in company decisions, beyond standard collective bargaining, and in firms’ economic results, beyond standard wages and benefits. Although sometimes used as synonyms, participation takes different forms in varying mechanisms and instruments, at root, related to the collective area of employee' rights as pursed through their formally elected workplace representatives (Royo, 1990).

On the one hand, ‘industrial democracy’ encompasses a broad spectrum of concepts, ranging from defence of labour through the typical mechanisms of employee representation and trade union activity (embracing the concept of adversarial participation or countervailing-power) to different forms of employee participation in the governance and/or advisory bodies of corporate entities, referred to as institutionalised participation or participation in decision-making bodies (Baylos, 1992). 'Economic democracy' relates to fair distribution, not only of the gross domestic product, but also of other social goods, including, naturally, the satisfactory and well-paid jobs. We may therefore conclude that there is continuity between economic and industrial democracy whereby any participation in the company's economic outcomes requires participation in the decisions of the business management.

In any case, the formula of economic democracy clearly synthesises the fundamental terms of democracy, employees and firm, thus recognising that participation in decision-making and financial participation are complementary. The European Economic and Social Committee considers that EFP offers an opportunity for businesses, employees and society as a whole to participate more, and more effectively, in the success of the increasing Europeanization of economic activity and encourages Europe to draw up a framework concept which promotes Europe's economic and social cohesion by facilitating the application of EFP at various levels (Graf von Schwerin & Sharma, 2010).

The expression *employee financial participation* (EFP) was coined in the first PEPPER *(Promotion of Employee Participation in Profits and Enterprise Results*) Report, sponsored by the European Commission nearly 25 years ago (Uvalic, 1991). EFP refers to an explicit company-wide policy in a firm that involves a significant majority of the firm's staff, regardless of their organisational level or type of work, in the economic results generated through the firm's normal business activity[5]. As we shall see, this economic participation may also have implications for corporate control and/or governance[6].

The expression EFP encompasses some very different forms of participation. The three most significant are: (1) Employee participation in the firm's capital *('employee ownership')*; (2) widespread distribution of stock options among employees (more common in the English-speaking world); and (3) employee participation in company profits (*'profit sharing'*). In the second and third of these types, the significance for the firm's employees is entirely economic, and does not necessarily have any legal

5 One criticism levelled against this practice by trade unions is that participation does not ultimately add to employees' wages, but instead is used as a mechanism for replacing part of their fixed salary with a variable remuneration.

6 This has been the subject of considerable debate since the inception of EFP.

or *de facto* impact on the control/governance or management of the organisation. However, Type 1 – ownership - is in many cases different. In principle, the significance of employees' owning part of the firm's capital is not merely economic, since as co-owners, it affords them the opportunity to influence fundamental issues facing the company through their governance bodies, the general meeting of shareholders or partners and the board of directors (or corresponding representative body)[7]. However, it is important to bear in mind that the specific circumstances of capital participation vary greatly from one firm - or type of firm - to another (as does legislative treatment of these issues among countries), and by extension, the relationship between this participation and the employees' capacity to affect company governance also varies to a similar degree. The principal reason for the difference in circumstances is the legal structure used in the firm to define and channel financial participation. A detailed analysis of these circumstances can be found in Arregi et al. (2012).

If we examine the current incidence of EFP, we can see that financial participation is well established in Western economies. Each year the *European Federation for Employee Share Ownership* (EFES) measures the extent of EFP implementation in Europe, based on figures for the 2,483 largest companies in Europe. According to its website, in 2013, the capital held by employees in European companies increased by 32% to €267 billion. The stake held by employees now stands, overall, at 2.99%. According to Lowitzsch and Hashi (2014) in 2013, approximately 1.65 million employees working in companies with over ten employees had a financial stake in these firms while figures from the European Company Survey (ECS) suggest that in the same year, 5.2% of private companies in Europe offer their employees stock options (Lowitzsch & Hashi, 2014). The figures for the US are more striking still. Kruse, Blasi and Park (2010) looked at the extent of EFP using the most representative and reliable figures available to them at the time of their study, comparing the situation in 2002 and 2006. They reported that more than 40% of the population working in the private sector just before the crisis had some type of financial participation and the trend was upward. They estimated that approximately 20% of *capital* was held by employee shareholders. Figures for

7 According to many observers, participation in company capital should also mean that the company's management policies and practices (apart from the activities of its control and governance bodies) are different to those generally found in conventional non-participatory firms.

2006 and 2008 from the *National Center for Employee Ownership* (NCEO) show, that more than 13.7 million employees have a stake in roughly 11,400 American companies (Rosen, 2012a).

However, our interest in this study is not in measuring the extent of EFP in Gipuzkoa[8], but in exploring the perceptions of the EFP of its main economic agents.

2.2 Impact of financial participation

There is extensive economic literature on the firm-level economic effects of EFP. Studies consistently show that companies with EFP tend to create more favourable social and economic outcomes, positively affecting firms, people working in them and the territories in which they are located.

The more important arguments presented in these studies are summarised below and are organised in terms of the main interest of the agents studied in this chapter: the impact the EFP on businesses, for the business associations; the impact on employees, for the trade unions; and, finally, the impact on society/territory, for the public authorities.

2.2.1 Impact on businesses

A variety of EFP effects has been examined over the decades. Only a few of the dozens of studies are cited here. Several authors have founded a positive relation between EFP and productivity. Addison (2005), Arando, Gago, Jones, and Kato (2015), Ben-Ner and Jones (1995), Conte and Svejnar (1990), Craig and Pencavel (1995), Fakhfakh, Perotin, and Gago (2012), Levine and Tyson (1990) and Pencavel (2001) have studied this relation inside worker cooperatives. Fakhfakh et al. (2012), for example, found, with large representative samples of firms in France, that worker cooperatives are not less productive than conventional firms. Arando et al. (2015), using an extensive dataset of one firm with different levels of ownership, show that in some cases the cooperatives perform better. Craig and Pencavel (1995) using data for cooperatives and conventional firms in

8 As mentioned in the introduction, some introductory figures on the EFP implementation in Gipuzkoa can be found in IKEI (2011).

the Pacific Northwest in the plywood industry found that cooperatives are more efficient than the conventional firms.

Other studies have compared the survival rates of employee-owned and conventional companies. While few studies have been conducted on this specific issue, the figures that do exist indicate that employee participation is beneficial (Blair & Kochan, 2002; Estrin & Jones, 1991; Park et al., 2004; Pérotin, 2004; Quarrey & Rosen, 1991).

2.2.2 Impact on employees:

Employee ownership also has positive psycho-social effects for workers which are of key importance in a firm; for example, job satisfaction, satisfaction with capital ownership, trust, identification with the company, perceptions of cooperation and mutual help, participation in decision-making and management style (Carberry, 2011; Dong, Bowles, & Ho, 2002; French & Rosenstein, 1984; Freundlich, 2009; Gamble, Culpepper, & Blubaugh, 2002; Höckertin & Härenstam, 2006; Höckertin, 2008; Klein, 1987; Kruse, 2002; Kruse, Freeman, & Blasi, 2008; Kruse et al, 2010; Kuvaas, 2003; McQuaid, Hollywood, Bond, Canduela, Richard, & Blackledge, 2012; Oliver, 1990, 1984; Rhodes & Steers, 1981). For example, Klein (1987) found high average satisfaction with ownership in her study of American companies with employee-ownership. The same result can be seen in French and Rosenstein (1984), where 75% of the respondents were highly satisfied with ownership. Freundlich (2009) uncovered similar results in the Mondragon cooperatives. Höckertin and Härenstam (2006) found that cooperative members consider that they have better opportunities to influence in their work and that their psycho-social climate is better compared with workers in the public sector.

It is important to emphasize, however, that a not inconsiderable number of studies find either no relation or mixed relations between ownership and psycho-social results (Cheney, 2002; Hammer & Stern, 1980; Kasmir, 1996; Long, 1978; Pendleton, Wilson, & Wright, 1998; Steger & Hartz, 2008; Winther, 1999). In these cases, authors theorize that while companies have formal employee ownership arrangements, company practises do not conform to employees' expectations of shared ownership (Freundlich, 2009). Formal joint ownership does not guarantee the practises necessary for employees to perceive themselves as co-owners.

Other studies conclude that companies with employee ownership tend to generate more jobs and to protect them more effectively in times of difficulty than conventional firms (Arando, Freundlich, Gago, Jones & Kato, 2011; Blair & Kochan, 2002; Burdin & Dean, 2009; Craig & Pencavel, 1995; Estrin & Jones, 1991; Kruse & Blasi, 2001; Kruse, 2002; Kruse et al., 2010; Park, Kruse, & Sesil, 2004; Pérotin & Robinson, 2004; Quarrey & Rosen, 1991; Winther & Marens, 1997). For example, Winther & Marens (1997) compare employment growth before and after the adoption of ESOP (the most used structure in US for EFP) and they found faster employment growth after the adoption, particularly in those companies with higher levels of participation in decision making. Craig & Pencavel (2001) for US plywood firms (cooperatives) and Burdin & Dean (2009) for co-ops in Uruguay find that producer cooperatives have more stable employment.

Still other researchers have discovered a positive relationship between ownership and the employees' levels of income and/or wealth (Blasi, Kruse, & Bernstein, 2003; Buchele, Kruse, Rodgers, & Scharf, 2010; D'Art, 2002; Kruse, 2002; Freeman, & Blasi, 2008; Pencavel, Pistaferri, & Schivardi, 2006; Rosen, Case, & Staubus, 2005).

2.2.3 Impact on society

The positive consequences generated by employee-owned companies can also be seen in the territory as a whole. Some studies relate the social capital of territories to business models that foster participation. Although the theoretical and empirical evidence is not as extensive in this area as in others, there are a number of books and articles relating the two aspects through cooperativism (Burdin and Dean, 2009; Cooke & Morgan; 1998; Erdal, 1999; Irizar & Lizarralde; 2005; Mugarra, 2005; Putman, 1993).

2.3 Scientific literature on the perceptions of the different socio-economic agents with regard to financial participation

As we have mentioned, the aim of this research is to determine the territory's principal economic agents perceptions of financial participation: business associations, labour union organisations and public institutions.

Here we briefly examine the most relevant literature on the relationship between trade unionism and EFP. The theoretical literature regarding trade union opinions on financial participation is limited (see, for example, Arregi et al, 2012; Lynd, 1985; McCarthy, Voss, Eaton, Kruse, & Blasi, 2011; McElrath & Rowan, 1992; Meyers, 2011; Pendleton, Wilson, & Wright, 1995; Rothschild, 1985, 2009; Slott, 1985; Toscano, 1984; among others). The subject has been dealt with relatively little in comparison to others[9] in the area of financial participation (McCarthy et al., 2011). However limited, though, it is still greater than the literature on the opinions of business associations with regard to EFP. As far as we can ascertain, business associations' views of EFP have not been the subject of either theoretical or empirical analysis in the academic world. More literature can be found on the interest in EFP shown by public institutions, although it is also limited, less frequent than research on trade unions.

In the following sub-section, we set out a number of scientific arguments regarding financial participation published by trade union organisations. As mentioned, the scientific literature on the perceptions of trade union organisations is modest. As we shall see, it reflects a broad spectrum of experiences and opinions, ranging from very favourable to very critical.

2.3.1 Trade union positions critical of EFP

Many trade unions and labour scholars are opposed to employee participation in the capital of their companies. They argue that this type of participation and, very often, EFP in general, is a mistake from a philosophical and strategic trade union perspective. They give various theoretical reasons for their opposition. In later sections we shall see whether there is any systematic empirical data backing their arguments. Given the limited scientific literature in this field, it is important to note that the degree of empirical support (or lack of support) for certain ideological positions does not necessarily mean that they are more or less true. Our view is that the issue has not been studied in sufficient depth to allow general scientific conclusions to be drawn.

9 We have already discussed the extensive literature on the benefits of financial participation in various businesses, psycho-social and territorial aspects.

The principal argument from the trade unions against financial participation and, above all, against substantial participation by employees in company capital, is that it necessarily involves a weakening of the trade union in the company in question (McCarthy et al., 2011; McElrath & Rowan, 1992; Pendleton et al., 1995; Slott, 1985; Toscano, 1984). Trade union thinkers firmly believe that the role of the trade union continues to be crucial in a firm with EFP. They argue, however, that the social and psychological dynamics generated in the organisation when employees share in capital ownership leads a substantial proportion of them to think, erroneously, that the trade union is no longer necessary. Many managers and union members tend to believe that, in a new situation of co-ownership, the most significant sources of tension and disagreement within the company would disappear, since relations between all parties would in general be more fluid and more positive. While it is possible that relations may change in companies implementing EFP - even to an important degree - these writers stress that the root causes of many problems do not simply vanish just because all members of the company are co-owners (Ellerman, 1988; Long, 1980; Mackin & Freundlich, 1995). There continues to be a detailed division of labour and a formal hierarchy of authority with its possible abuses of power; differences in access to relevant information continue to exist and other discrepancies also continue to arise for different reasons, discrepancies in which the party with least information and authority often needs a system of guarantees and explicit and formal protection (AFL-CIO, 1986; Ellerman, 1988; Graf von Schwerin & Sharma, 2010; McCarthy et al., 2011; Pendleton et al., 1995; Toscano, 1984; Whyte & Blasi, 1984). Using a similar logic, some trade unions further maintain that certain company executives introduce employee ownership specifically to initiate this dynamic of rapprochement between employees and management and thus weaken the position of the unions (McElrath & Rowan, 1992; Redmon, Mueller, & Daniels, 1985; Toscano, 1984). The problem here is that not enough systematic empirical data exists to draw well-founded conclusions on these questions.

Another criticism levelled by the trade unions against employee ownership refers to control of the company and to the extent of real participation in governance which this type of participation provides. Here, the critics argue that such control is more or less illusory (Lynd, 1985; Meyers, 2011; Rothschild, 1985 and 2009; Slott, 1985; Toscano, 1984). Even when employees control 100% of the capital, they argue, there will always be a managing class in the company with an essentially business-oriented focus. In other words, there will always be a group dominating the organisation's management that tends to prioritise the pursuit of the organisation's interests as a business institution over and above the specific social and economic interests of the majority of its employees. Company management tends to justify this stance by arguing that it is essential to take a given decision (which may appear harmful to the interests of many employee-owners) in order to ensure competitiveness and thus protect the company and its jobs in the long term. Trade union critics, however, consider that this argument often turns into an essentially permanent position, with the result being that the interests of the majority are constantly undermined. They conclude that financial participation ends up being, to a greater or lesser degree, deceptive for employees (McHugh, Cutcher-Gershenfeld, & Polzin, 1999; Slott, 1985; Toscano, 1984).

Another criticism, linked to some extent the previous one, is that employee ownership separates employees from union priorities. Employees can end up prioritising the profitability of their financial investment and the payment of dividends while the trade unions prioritise improvements in employment and working conditions (Arregi et al., 2012).

There are other arguments against EFP from a trade union perspective. These may be summarised as follows:

1. One is related to the financial abuses that can occur in the make-up and management of financial participation (Brown, Landau, Mitchell, O ′Connell, & Ramsay, 2008; McCarthy et al., 2011; McElrath & Rowan, 1992; McHugh et al., 1999);
2. Another criticism is related to the economic risk assumed by employees, who tend not to have high levels of income or wealth, (Brown et al., 2008; McCarthy et al., 2011; McElrath and Rowan, 1995; McHugh et al., 1999);
3. A third criticism is that EFP divides the working class; employees taking a share in their company's capital can end up identifying more with their firm and the managing class than with the worker-trade union movement and the working class (McElrath & Rowan, 1992; McCarthy et al., 2011; Slott, 1985).

2.3.2 Trade union positions in favour of EFP

We have seen the most important trade union arguments against employee ownership. In this sub-section, we shall examine some of the arguments from union writers in favour of the practise. There are two chief arguments:

1. EFP is an important tool for saving jobs in two separate situations – the first (very common) is that of SMEs in good financial condition facing problems of generational transfer[10] and the second (less common) is that of business facing major economic crisis;
2. EFP offers employees the right to participate to an important degree in the strategic control of companies.

With regard to saving jobs, there is probably ultimately little disagreement in trade union circles. The literature, albeit limited, suggests that nearly all strands of trade union thinking support partial or total purchase of a company by its employees if it saves jobs and if the majority of employees are in favour (Arregi et al, 2012; Haynes, 2011; Livingston, 1985; McCarthy et al., 2011; McElrath & Rowan, 1992). This position is essentially the same for SMEs in good health facing generational transfer[11] and for companies undergoing a profound economic crisis. Nonetheless, trade union writers warn that it is important to supervise the specific legal and financial conditions in each case, with expert assistance (AFL-CIO, 1986; Livingston, 1985; McCarthy et al., 2011).

The second principal argument in favour of EFP offered by other authors refers to the control or governance of the company. Some writers do not agree with the position that participation in company control is necessarily illusory. While recognising that ownership in itself is not a guarantee of a proportional level of participation in control and that the degree of control will depend on the circumstances of the purchase, the

---

10 The issue of 'generational transfer' occurs when the existing owners are approaching retirement and plan to leave the company. A very large percentage of such companies end up being forced to close down.

11 Here we should stress (1) the importance of generational transfer in SMEs and the opportunity and threat it poses for trade unions and EFP; (2) the potential importance of ownership as a solution in situations of business succession tends to be ignored in more general discussions on EFP referring to other very different circumstances, especially in large firms and in the privatisation of publicly-owned companies.

union's negotiating strength, the union's management capacity, the legal framework of employee ownership, etc., they believe that control can be real and significant. While accepting that in some cases EFP has not led to participation in governance, they point to other cases in which it did (Meyers, 2011; McHugh et al., 1999; Arregi et al, 2012) and argue that the degree of success depends on the aforementioned factors. Even more importantly for them is the theoretical argument that ownership is a *key strategy for the future* for the trade union movement precisely for this reason, i.e., because it opens the doors to trade union participation in the control of companies (Ellerman, 1988; Gates, 1998; Mackin, 1991, 1997, 2002; McHugh et al., 1999; Swinney, 2012a, 2012b; Whyte & Blasi, 1984).

Other authors argue that one of the most difficult challenges in EFP lies within the trade unions themselves. On many occasions, they argue, the trade unions have not been active enough in studying new strategies and in accumulating the necessary specialised knowledge to put them into practice (Erdal, 2011; Gates, 1998; Mackin, 1991, 1997, 2002; Swinney, 2012a, 2012b; Whyte & Blasi, 1984).

Other authors also point to another series of advantages: Arregi et al., (2012) show that EFP leads to improved transparency of economic information for employees – another issue of interest to trade unions. Moreover, Kruse (2002) and Kruse et al. (2010) consider that financial participation is in the interests of many employees; if the trade unions were to develop explicit strategies to promote EFP, employees would feel greater attachment to the unions (Erdal, 2011; Gates, 1998; Kroumova et al., 2002; Mackin, 1991, 2002; Swinney, 2012a, 2012b).

We only know of only four empirical studies in this field, three in the United States and one in the United Kingdom, dating from the 1980s and 1990s (Long, 1980; McElrath & Rowan, 1992; Pendleton et al., 1995; Toscano, 1984). Bearing these limitations in mind, the four studies clearly conclude that EFP, rather than weakening the unions' position, in some cases, actually extends and reinforces their role.

To sum up, the scientific literature is scarce and authors in this field conclude that there are many unanswered questions with regard to the relationship between trade unions and EFP that await future scientific research.

We set out below the current positions of the different trade union organisations and public institutions in Europe on EFP, while noting, the clear lack of literature and public statements of business associations on this issue.

2.4 Review of the positions of European socio-economic institutions on EFP

In 2013, the European Parliament approved a report setting out a series of recommendations to the Commission and to the Member States to encourage financial participation. Specifically, it called on the Commission and Member States 'to engage social partners, in accordance with national law and practices, employee ownership organisations and stakeholders more closely in dialogue between policy makers, employers and workers' representatives, at the respective levels while respecting the autonomy of social partners in collective bargaining, so that existing examples of best practice can be taken into account in the development of policies to facilitate the implementation of EFP by businesses.' (European Parliament, 2013).

In turn, the European Commission, through the European Economic and Social Committee argued that EFP is key to firm resilience in times of crisis and should be promoted by member governments. It also discussed the benefits of financial participation both for business (increase in productivity, competitiveness, solvency, security, etc.) and for employees (supplementary remuneration, a voice in company strategy, job security, etc.) (Graf von Schwerin & Sharma, 2010).

Several European governments have also chosen to encourage financial participation. The British government, for example, has shown a notable interest in spreading and strengthening financial participation, sponsoring an extensive study by Graeme Nuttall (Nuttall, 2012) on ways to foment participation through public policy.

European trade union organisations, for their part, have addressed the issue of EFP at various levels, according to the legal systems of the countries in which they operate. Their positions are as diverse as the different formulas of participation practised in the European Union member states.

In 2013 the European Trade Union Confederation (ETUC/CES, 2013) adopted a resolution on EFP setting out in detail the conditions, principles and basic demands that must be taken into account in establishing a system of participation. These include the following:

- EFP has to be embedded in a whole system of worker involvement at all levels.
- The different participation models should complement each other as in the triangle of information-consultation-participation, each being beneficial for effective corporate governance.
- EFP should always provide additional income and not be a substitute for fair pay.
- EFP should not be considered as an alternative to collective bargaining and to wage increases.
- Financial participation, similarly, is not an alternative to public pensions or to collectively bargained pension schemes. Negative effects of the fiscal or para-fiscal status of financial participation on social security systems should be compensated.
- Under no circumstances should EFP worsen inequalities of income inside a company or in the broader society.
- The introduction and design of EFP should be the subject of prior consultation and agreement with worker representatives and trade unions. The details of EFP must be introduced through negotiations between social partners and collective agreements should set the framework for EFP.
- Participation in any such scheme must be always voluntary.
- EFP schemes must be open to all workers within the company, including part-time workers.

The ETUC considers that only with these conditions fulfilled can EFP have a positive effect.

As in our review of the scientific literature, when we turn to European business associations, the paucity of information on participation is striking. At a European level, the business association of Gipuzkoa, ADEGI, is represented by Business Europe. None of its policies or strategies include mention of the encouragement of EFP, or participation in management more generally, as a priority theme.

Given the antecedents and the literature analysed, the aim of this chapter, as mentioned, is to analyse the perceptions of representatives of the three economic agents in Gipuzkoa (business associations, trade unions and public institutions) on financial participation. The following section describes the methodology, context, participants, data collection methods and plan of analysis used to meet this aim.

3. Methodological design

3.1 Methodological approach

This study is essentially based on qualitative methods, with the research team seeking to ascertain social partners' views on the keys to employee participation in the business and how these have evolved.

We have opted for a qualitative approach for three reasons:

1. The study forms part of a series of interventions by the research team *in tandem with* the social partners of Gipuzkoa over a period of years, intended to encourage exploration of concepts and practices related to financial participation through dialogue; it is not a study carried out by the research team *on* or *about* the social partners in the role of 'subjects' or mere suppliers of 'data';
2. It is a flexible and open approach; the research tactics and actions can vary depending on the participants, the situations that arise, the initial results obtained and on the ways events evolve (Hernández, Fernández, & Baptista, 2010). The purpose is to observe and interact with the participants, facilitating dialogue, and not simply recording 'facts' (Williams, Unrau, Grinnell, & Epstein, 2005).
3. The purpose is to establish ties with the participants, in order to understand their internal perspective on the issues raised, their experiences and the significance of these experiences for them (Creswell, 2002; Hernández et al., 2010).

3.2 Context

As mentioned in the introduction, Gipuzkoa is a province in the Basque Country in northern Spain. It is also a 'historical territory', a territorial entity with its own, semi-autonomous internal legal systems. The provincial capital is Donostia - San Sebastian. Gipuzkoa is a territory with a land area of close to 1,900 square kilometres and a population of about 700,000 (the smallest province in Spain). In economic terms, the province's GDP per capita is above the European average and it is among the 30 most developed regions in the European Union. Economic forecasts in 2014 were optimistic, predicting slow but steady economic recovery for this and subsequent years. Despite recent events, industry in the province has weathered the current financial crisis somewhat better than the Basque

Country as a whole, suffering a more moderate downturn. Trends in foreign trade have remained favourable (better than the Basque Country as a whole) with a favourable impact on GDP, which began to see growth in mid-2013, according to a report by the Gipuzkoa Chamber of Commerce (La Cámara de Gipuzkoa, 2014).

Gipuzkoa's economic structure is as follows: agro-fishing industry has all but disappeared (0.6% of GDP); there is an important, larger than average, industrial sector (28.2%) and a fairly small construction industry (6.5%). As in most of Europe, the services sector dominates the economic structure (64.7% of GDP) (EUSTAT, 2015a).

Finally, according to EUSTAT data published in the survey of occupation (EUSTAT, 2015b), in the second quarter of 2014, Gipuzkoa had an unemployment rate of 12.6% (12.1% among men, 13.0% among women). The activity rate has fallen to 58.2% (62.8% for men and 53.8% for women).

Consider, briefly, its political-adminstrative structure. The territory has a single legislative chamber, the Provincial Assembly [Juntas Generales de Gipuzkoa]. Members are elected by direct universal suffrage every four years (coinciding with elections to municipal councils). Executive power lies with the General Deputy [*Diputado General*], elected by the provincial assembly. The General Deputy in turn appoints the deputies [*diputados*], who exercise quasi-ministerial/executive functions in the province. In addition to the ordinary powers exercised by all provincial governments in Spain, the Provincial Government of Gipuzkoa also has certain special jurisdiction as a *historical territory* of the Basque Country, under the region's statute of autonomy. For example, the provincial government has jurisdiction in matters of taxation, an important arena of authority that can be used to restrict or promote EFP (Lowitzsch, Hashi, & Woodward, 2008).

The Department of Innovation, Rural Development and Tourism – one of the Provincial Government of Gipuzkoa's several departments – through specific action plans, seeks to contribute to building a society based on social sustainability (social cohesion), economic sustainability (innovation or competitiveness) and environmental sustainability. This department firmly believes in the need to establish 'a new model of economic and social development based on a dynamic of collective learning and interaction (innovation, organisations/companies and institutions) that will ensure social cohesion, economic competitiveness; and environmental sustainability'. This is a 'social model in which the initiative lies with an actively learning and enterprising citizenry, engaging in hard work and solidarity, in a context of relationships bsed on trust.' (Departamento de Innovación, Desarrollo Rural y Turismo de la DFG, 2013). As part of this model, the Department encourages actions and funds projects that promote employee participation.

Information on EFP is sparse; there are no official statistics on employee participation in management, profits or capital in the province. According to IKEI (2011), 25% of a sample group of 230 companies analysed in Gipuzkoa allow employee share ownership, 21.1% in limited form and 4.8% with participation open to all members of the organisation. The study also analyses employees' participation in different areas within the firm: internal communication, characterisation of training, participation in management, flexible working hours and time management, and involvement and motivation in working environment. The study notes that companies in the province consider the role of employees in the five domains under consideration to be quite relevant in achieving their corporate objectives (7.1/10). They rate their organisations as being fairly advanced in this regard (6.6/10), although they give a slightly lower score for implementation of actions related to such participation (5.0). These results are positive, showing that there is a group of companies with a proactive attitude towards participation.

There are also data on the social economy in Gipuzkoa, covering the two legal structures with broad worker ownership: worker cooperatives and worker-owned societies [*sociedades laborales*]. The latest available data are for 2012. According to the Basque Observatory of Social Economy (OVES/GEEB, 2015), there are a total of 614 cooperatives in Gipuzkoa, accounting for 40% of the total for the Basque Country; there are 248 worked-owned societies, 35% of the total for the Basque Country. Altogether, in 2012 30,312 people were working in cooperatives, 10.11% of the total work force of Gipuzkoa and 3,102 in worker-owned companies, 1.03% of the total.

3.3 Participants

Participants in the study included representatives from the three social partners, business associations, trade unions and public authorities. Of the public institutions, the most important was the Provincial Government of Gipuzkoa. For some years, its Department of Innovation, Rural Development and Tourism has been working to encourage employee participation, including EFP.

There are also eleven local development agencies operating at a district [*comarca*] level within the territory. Their mission is to promote the socio-economic development of their specific districts/municipalities. These eleven agencies are: Andoaingo Udala, Debagoieneko Mankomunitatea, Debegesa, S.A., Fomento de San Sebastián, S.A., Goieki, S.A., Iraurgi Lantzen, S.A., Oarsoaldea, S.A., Tolosaldea Garatzen, S.A., Urola Garaiko Garapenerako Agentzia, S.A. (UGGASA), Urola Kostako Udal Elkartea and Bidasoa Activa.

In Spain, the most important sectoral employer associations are affiliated with the CEOE (Confederación Española de Organisaciones Empresariales). These business associations include CONFEBASK (the Basque Business Confederation) which is made up, *inter alia*, of ADEGI, the Association of Employers of Gipuzkoa, with more than 1,000 member companies (to date the organisation that has chiefly represented employers in collective bargaining[12]). In addition to ADEGI, there are also other business associations in Gipuzkoa of interest for this research. These include ASPEGI, the Association of Women Professionals and Employers of Gipuzkoa; the Gipuzkoa Chamber of Commerce, a non-profit organisation, representing all companies in Gipuzkoa; ASLE, the Basque Association of Worker-Owned Societies[13] and KONFEKOOP, the Basque Confederation of Cooperatives.

In the Basque Country, approximately 22% of salaried workers are members of a trade union (2010). In Gipuzkoa, at 31 January 2014, according to data from the Basque Government's Department of Employment and Social Policy, the four trade unions with most members were

12 In Spain the trade unions that negotiate collective wage agreements are those that have the greatest number of members in companies, as determined in trade union elections. The business associations involved in such collective bargaining are also the most representative, but there is no rule stipulating how such representation is calculated. In recent years, collective wage agreements in Gipuzkoa have been signed with ADEGI. However, in the current financial crisis and against the backdrop of instability in labour relations in Spain in general and Gipuzkoa in particular, most collective wage negotiations with ADEGI have been halted and remain unsigned. However, other employer associations have begun signing collective agreements.

13 A worker-owned society is a special business society that is majority owned by employees with a long-term contract (see Lowitzsch et al., 2009).

ELA, Eusko Langileen Alkartasuna, representing 43.74% of union members; LAB, Langile Abertzaleen Batzordeak at 27.28%; CCOO, Comisiones Obreras at 15.12% and UGT, Unión General de Trabajadores, at 6.34%; the first two are Basque regional unions and the second two are Spanish and operate state-wide.

3.4 Data collection

In keeping with the qualitative methods approach, the following techniques were used for data gathering: (1) focus groups, (2) document analysis and (3) semi-structured interviews. Although this is not a widespread technique, data were also gathered from a 'Symposium of Reflection' organised in the area affected by the project. This allowed the authors to triangulate their data, reinforcing its validity, reliability and the general rigor of the analysis (Hernández et al., 2010). The various techniques are described below:

(1) Focus groups. The focus groups formed the main pillar of the project. Several authors have described focus groups as a sort of group interview. The technique consists of organising meetings of small or medium-sized groups, at which participants discuss one or various subjects in an informal environment, with guidance from the researchers (Hernández et al., 2010).

Several meetings were held with each group of agents – two sessions with the trade union organisations, two with the business associations and two with the public authorities.

The first individual forums were held in April 2014, and lasted between two and three hours each. The second forum took place in May 2014, also with an approximate duration of two to three hours. The forums with trade union organisations were attended by representatives of LAB and CCOO. The forums with business associations were attended by representatives of ADEGI, ASPEGI, ASLE and the Gipuzkoa Chamber of Commerce. The forums of public institutions were attended by representatives of the Provincial Government of Gipuzkoa, Andoaingo Udala, Debegesa, Ugassa and Oarsoaldea.

The joint focus group was held in July 2014 and lasted 1.5 hours. This meeting was attended by representatives of LAB, CCOO and ELA for trade unions; ADEGI, ASPEGI, ASLE and the Gipuzkoa Chamber of Commerce for the business associations; and representatives of the

Provincial Government of Gipuzkoa, Debagoiena, Goieki, Iraurgi Lantzen, Oarsoaldea and Ugassa for the government organisations.

Finally, in October 2014, the different organisations were invited to a forum over a day and half. This 'Forum of Reflection' was held in Donostia-San Sebastián (Gipuzkoa) under the title 'Jointly developing participation in Gipuzkoa: People, Companies, Territory'. It was organised in tandem with the Department of Innovation, Rural Development and Tourism of the Provincial Government of Gipuzkoa. All the business associations and trade unions attended the event, either as participants or audience members. Once again, as with the focus groups, the attendance from the government agencies was irregular.

To encourage debate among the different agents, various aspects related to participation were raised at a theoretical level at these focus groups; these ranged from very general aspects - such as possible changes in the business paradigm and culture - to very specific ones, such as new systems of work organisation, employee involvement in production process innovation and new forms of worker participation. The conclusions of a study by the research team on labour relations in Sweden and Germany were also presented[14]. In addition, in the final forums and the final symposium of reflection, the results of the previous forums were presented, so that each agent could hear the other organisations' comments on the subject and offer its own opinions.

(2) Documentation. We analysed public documents of the three social partners in Gipuzkoa to determine their strategies and position on employee participation. The documentation was used to prepare the focus groups and the results of this study. Given that part of one of the focus groups was based on the presentation by the research team of two interna-

---

14 There are various alternatives for achieving employee involvement. One of these is to create channels of dialogue between employees and management. One such channel is the works council, where a clear example of co-management is to be found in Germany. Another of those channels involves employee participation in the company's organs of governance, also found in Germany (in large companies) and in Sweden. A bibliographical review was presented (Alzaga, 2003; Eriksson, 2010; Fulton, 2011; Gerum, 2007; Greifenstein, 2011; Greifenstein & Kissler, 2010; Köhler & Jiménez, 2014; Medlingsinstitutet, 2012; Michel, 2007; OIT, 2014a,b; Werner & Zimmermann, 2005) to offer a better overview of these two options. It was for this reason that we included the study of the two countries and presented it to the focus groups.

tional experiences on employee participation, in Germany and Sweden, an exhaustive study was also made of the two experiences.

(3) Semi-structured interviews. In the case of the development agencies, we were unable to locate any documents setting out their position and strategy on employee participation. To obtain this information, therefore, we conducted semi-structured interviews with a script of general questions which could be modified during the interview. This type of interview is used widely to extend questioning from issues of 'what' and 'how many' to the issues of 'why' and 'how' (Saunders, Saunders, Lewis, & Thornhill, 2009) with a view to explaining possible cause-and-effect processes in specific situations - local causality - and their significance for the parties involved (Maxwell, 2012). For this study, six interviews were held of approximately two hours duration in the six development agencies that agreed to participate: Debegesa, Oarsoaldea, Andoaingo Udala, Ugassa, Iraurgi Lantzen and Goieki. The interviewees were managers from these agencies and technical staff involved in these specific areas.

In addition, in order to gain an in-depth understanding of the situation in Germany and Sweden, various interviews were organised with trade unionists and university lecturers[15].

3.5 Data analysis

We began our analysis by preparing a preliminary list of analytical categories. These were used to develop the subjects to be raised in the focus groups and interview protocols. The categories were reviewed and modified after the first focus groups and at the end of the data-gathering process. Both the semi-structured interviews and the focus groups were recorded and then transcribed in order to carry out the analysis presented below. In designing these categories, documents from European political and trade union bodies were also used. Firstly, for some years, the European Parliament and European Commission have published recommendations on ways of encouraging EFP (e.g., the latest report from the European Parliament, 2013). Secondly, as a result of the trend towards EFP, the European Trade Union Confederation (ETUC/CES) has issued a public

15 As we do not intend to elaborate on this aspect here, we shall not list the interviewees.

policy document, arguing that social partners and member states have a key role to play in promoting EFP. The ETUC recognises that forms of EFP vary according to national circumstances and industrial relations in each country and that employee attitudes and preferences also vary. It recalls that the ETUC puts wage negotiations at the top of the agenda, together with secure and transparent income for workers and it states that it can only subscribe to EFP if six prerequisites are met (ETUC/ETUC, 2013). We considered it helpful to use these two documents as a reference point in creating the different categories.

At the end of the process, the four categories selected for analysis were as follows: the agents' strategies on EFP, comprehensive participation, ways of encouraging EFP and objectives of EFP.

4. Results and discussion

This section sets out the results of the research and analysis. The information is organised on the basis of the four categories of analysis identified above, i.e. (1) agents' strategies with regard to EFP, (2) comprehensive participation, (3) strategies for promoting EFP, (4) objectives of EFP.

4.1 Category: Agents' strategies on financial participation

In this category, we analysed the main strategies of the three groups of agents in Gipuzkoa – government, business associations and trade unions - based on the European Parliament's recommendations on strategies for encouraging EFP.

In its report on EFP in company profits (European Parliament, 2013), the parliament calls on the Commission and Member States to 'consider appropriate measures to encourage companies, acting voluntarily, to develop and offer EFP schemes, [and] to step up exchanges of best practice in this regard'. It also calls on them to 'engage social partners, in accordance with national law and practices, employee ownership organisations and stakeholders more closely in dialogue between policy makers, employers and workers' representatives [...] while respecting the autonomy of social partners in collective bargaining'.

Starting with the public institutions, the Provincial Government of Gipuzkoa and more specifically, the Department of Innovation, Rural

Development and Tourism promotes a wide range of actions intended to promote employee participation on the grounds that this promotes greater worker involvement with the business project as a whole and greater firm commitment to its social surroundings (bringing decision-making closer to the immediate environs). It also takes measures to facilitate better business management (Departamento de Innovación, Desarrollo Rural y Turismo de la DFG, 2014). Specifically, one of the concepts the Department seeks to promote is innovation in the workplace. This is defined as the integration of people, competences and technology in order to turn work places into a source of productivity and quality employment. To this end, one of its priorities is to 'develop new models of human relations in companies based on participation' (Departamento de Innovación, Desarrollo Rural y Turismo de la DFG, 2013).

As for the development agencies, after a series of individual interviews with technical staff from some of these organisations, we concluded that, while, the provincial government has a clear strategy on favouring participation, it has yet to be incorporated by the agencies into their own strategies. In the focus group, one development agency mentioned that in order to incorporate employee participation into their strategies or working axes, it would first be necessary to increase awareness of the issue among politicians, who ultimately establish the general strategies of the development agencies.

> 'We realised that as an agency we could not respond; that was up to the political officials.' (AD1)

For their part, the trade unions (with one exception) do not have a strategy on EFP. Generally speaking, to judge from our analysis papers and resolutions from the different union congresses[16], employee participation does not appear to be a priority issue. Indeed, none of these documents contains any reference to the subject whatsoever. Nor have we found any reports discussing employee participation in more general terms, except for one presented by LAB to the Basque Government's Department of Employment in May 2014 proposing a new model of labour relations. The bases for the new model discussed in the document include, 'a model that offers formulas for employee participation'. The report stresses the need for a debate on the concept of participation and its aims (LAB, 2014).

16 ELA (2008, 2013a, 2013b); LAB (2012); CCOO (2009, 2013); UGT (2009, 2013).

This absence of public documentation on the issue is significant but, as the trade unions themselves stated in the Forum of Reflection in October 2014, it does not mean that they have no interest in the subject. As we shall see in other categories, they do have an interest, but they also have a number of concerns. Although they see possibilities in financial participation, to date it has not formed part of union strategy.

> 'It is not a priority, but we are willing to discuss it.' (OS2)

As for the business associations, both ASLE and Konfekoop act for companies with broad EFP: ASLE represents worker-owned societies and Konfekoop represents cooperative companies. Naturally, therefore, they both conduct activities to encourage the creation of this type of company. ASLE heads and coordinates a work team whose participants include the Basque Government, the three provincial governments, ADEGI and Cebek[17], which seeks to encourage and foster employee participation (ASLE, 2013). It also contributes capital to the LANPAR venture capital fund (which helps employees buy stock in their companies); it participates in European projects promoting financial participation and has collaborated in academic studies intended to give greater visibility to EFP (ALSE, 2013).

ADEGI represents conventional, private companies in Gipuzkoa. It is the largest business association in the province. Its position on participation has evolved significantly over the last four years. Its 2010 report only mentions the need to encourage an organisational culture based on trust (ADEGI, 2010). In 2011, ADEGI signed an agreement on employee participation (ADEGI, 2011) and the 2012 report contains the first references to the importance of encouraging employee participation in management as a contributor to business performance. Following a strategic reflection and based on the present and future socio-economic situation, ADEGI then determined that one of its priorities for the next three years should be 'to promote styles of organisation in companies that encourage communication and involvement with the aim of developing employee engagement with the company and thus create more innovative and competitive companies' (ADEGI, 2012). In 2014 it published a 'Guide to New Business Culture' to help companies advance towards 'an approach to company-building whose key elements are transparency, communica-

17 Business Confederation of Bizkaia; the counterpart of ADEGI in Bizkaia, another of the provinces in the Basque Country.

tion, participation in management and profit-sharing' (ADEGI, 2014). The guide expressly states that 'it is necessary to promote increased employee participation in the company. Nonetheless, ADEGI does not identify a particular system of participation in management and profits: each firm has to find its own path, sharing the business project it seeks for the future'. The report specifically mentions profit-sharing, but does not discuss employee participation in company capital (ADEGI, 2014). Summing up, there has been a clear evolution in ADEGI's strategy on encouraging employee participation, from a position of making no mention at all to the issue in its 2010 report to strongly encouraging participation in its 2014 guide. However, although it discusses *profit-sharing*, it is significant that it makes no mention to employee ownership in these documents.

In the case of the Gipuzkoa Chamber of Commerce, we have been unable to find any documents that mention employee participation. The chamber's website offers members training in 'people management', but makes no specific mention of participation.

Similarly, we were unable to locate any documents from ASPEGI (the Association of Women Professionals and Employers) dealing with participation. The association's strategy currently focuses on supporting women entrepreneurs, with support from ADEGI and the Gipuzkoa Chamber of Commerce in matters of training, challenges and obstacles.

Likewise, in the focus groups, we received no significant information on this issue from these two business associations. Nonetheless, in most areas, they do appear to be aligned with ADEGI's position.

In summary, strategies on the encouragement of EFP vary greatly: (1) The provincial government has a clear and developed strategy in favour of EFP, whereas the development agencies, even though they have a territorial strategy, do not include participation in it; (2) the trade unions currently do not include the subject of EFP in their strategic themes, but they are open to discussion on the subject; (3) some evolution can be seen in the position of the business associations, although there are still many differences among them. Conditions therefore exist for developing EFP in Gipuzkoa, but there is still a long way to go and - as we shall see in subsequent sections - progress is necessary in several different areas. Each agent, first individually, and then collectively, needs to encourage dialogue to advance the implementation and consolidation of EFP in Gipuzkoa.

4.2 Category: Comprehensive participation

This category of analysis is covered very specifically in one of the prerequisites for EFP laid down by the ETUC/CES (2013): 'EFP has to be embedded in a whole system of worker involvement at all levels. […] The different participation models should complement each other as in the 'information-consultation-participation triangle', each contributing to good corporate governance. Schemes should include the possibility, in those countries where these systems exists, of employee representatives in company decision making, preferably through seats on the board'. We set out below the perceptions of the three groups of agents with regard to levels of participation (in management, results and capital ownership), presence on governance bodies and the triangle mentioned above.

With regard to the levels of participation, on reviewing the documentation of the trade union organisations, we found that the report presented by LAB to the Department of Employment in May 2014 proposing a New Model of Labour Relations contains the same idea: 'participation in the company can take place in different ways and at different levels: in management and in decision-making, in company capital and in profits. […] But it must be a model that guarantees authentic employee participation' (LAB, 2014). In other words, they call for comprehensive and effective participation. The other trade union organisations did not position themselves on this issue in the focus groups and as already mentioned, we found no mention of it in their public documents.

ASLE also advocates comprehensive participation. At its annual conference in 2012, it identified one of its key challenges as the need to encourage employee participation in management by implementing a 'people-based' management model. It considers that financial participation is not sufficient, since all its member companies already have EFP (ASLE, 2012). For ASLE, financial participation must be accompanied by participation in management. It makes no specific reference to participation in governance bodies, but this can be seen to be part of ASLE's position given the contents of its documents and its interventions in the focus groups.

ADEGI, however, is more cautious in this regard. In its 'Guide to New Business Culture' published in 2014 (cited above), it speaks of levels but makes no express reference to comprehensive participation or ownership: 'It is necessary to promote increased employee participation in the company. Nonetheless, there is no single system of participation in management and profits: Each firm has to find its own path, sharing the business project it wants for the future' (ADEGI, 2014).

These same attitudes were seen in the focus groups. The two trade union organisations participating felt that financial participation made no sense without participation in management and decision-making:

> 'We are not in favour of financial participation alone, if it is does not have other solid supports. In other words, participating in strategic decision-making, with real votes included. That is the only way of transmitting trust. There will be areas in which the decision to be made lies with a specific individual, but there will be areas in which the decisions affect all employees and we should be involved. Financial participation should take place within the framework of a much more comprehensive participation.' (OS1)

> 'In order for participation to be real and decisive, it has to take place at all levels.' (OS2)

As for the business associations, the differences discussed above regarding comprehensive participation are evident. One of the groups discussed the need for employee participation in management, going beyond ownership:

> 'One very important area is the issue of employee representation in companies. We debated this on an internal basis and then conveyed our conclusions to the companies. Because for us, this is a fundamental issue. One thing is a share in capital and another thing is representation at a workplace level.' (OE2)

In this context, this business association sees representation at a workplace level as a form of participation in management.

The other business associations spoke of taking gradual steps at different levels:

> 'One of the legs is employee participation. We have divided it into three areas, participation in management, profits and capital. [...] And we think that those three areas of participation need to be staggered; you can't start with ownership without previously having begun with participation in management or profit-sharing.' (OE1)

We may therefore conclude that the trade union organisations participants agree with the prerequisites established by ETUC/CES (2013) for accepting EFP. However, not all business associations share this requirement; the majority are in favour of a staggered approach.

Nonetheless, many cases of companies with EFP are documented and, in a significant proportion, the transition towards the paradigm of participation began with employee ownership and not with information-sharing and participation in management (Blasi, 1988; EFES, 2014; EOA, 2014;

NCEO, 2014, Oakeshott, 2000; Quarrey, Blasi, & Rosen, 1986). However, science cannot at present determine whether the strategy proposed by the business associations - gradual transition towards financial participation starting with transparency and participation in management - is the most suitable option or not. What science can do is show that the opposite path can work, since many successful cases of participation began with EFP. In other words, in many companies financial participation itself was the catalyst that led to participation in management and in governance bodies. One reason for this is the large proportion of cases of EFP which initially arose in situations of generational transfer. In such cases, the companies' initial interest was not necessarily in providing full participation, but rather in finding an exit plan for the capital of an owner approaching retirement. In such circumstances, the first move is the sale of part of this owner's stock to the employees; in other words, financial participation happens first; other forms of transparency and participation in management are only introduced as a later consequence to create a culture of co-ownership.

With regard to employee representation in the governance bodies, one of the ETUC/CES's prerequisites is that EFP must allow employees to participate in governance. This subject is not covered in the internal documentation analysed but it was raised in the focus groups.

Trade union organisations are in favour of participating in governance bodies, but only if they can have effective participation.

> 'We're not going to be somewhere where we can't achieve anything.' (OS1)

> 'If we're there to defend the rights of the workers, of course we will; if we're there to defend the shared project of course we will. But if we're there for quite the opposite reasons, to be there just for the sake of being there, then we won't.' (OS2)

These results mirror the arguments of Ellerman (1988), Gates (1998), Mackin (1991, 1997, 2002), McHugh et al. (1999), Swinney (2012a, 2012b) and Whyte and Blasi (1984); for trade unions, EFP can open the door to greater strategic influence in companies, including in important sectors. There has been considerable debate as to the advantages and disadvantages of EFP amongst the trade unions and their federations and confederations. Trade unionists who favour EFP often argue that it offers the possibility of extending their strategic influence and going beyond the current situation in which they are limited *reaction*, i.e. reacting to strategies developed and implemented by employers.

ASLE did not express an opinion, since as company owners, the employees of its member companies sit on the decision-making bodies. Of the other organisations, one took a stance on the issue, arguing against participation by employee representatives in the governing bodies, in answer to the direct question 'How far should we take the presence of the employees' representatives in the organs of governance?'

> 'It is important to choose between two ideas: In this firm, do we co-decide or participate? Co-decision goes even further than participation. That co-decision has to be accepted by the owner. [...] We encourage participation. We have not reached that moment of co-decision. Participating is not the same as co-deciding.' (OE1)

The public administration and development agencies did not express an opinion or take a position in the focus groups on employee participation in governance.

Finally in this category, we need to analyse the information-consultation-participation triangle mentioned above.

All business associations agree on the need to provide adequate information to company employees in order to advance towards participation. For example, ADEGI's 'Guide to New Business Culture' (2014) seeks to encourage 'a form of company-building whose key features are transparency, communication and participation'. Moreover, from the focus groups it was clear that information is seen as the start of participation:

> 'How is a firm going to be able to even consider, much less accept, participation in ownership, in profits for example, if it has not previously been transparent, if it has not given transparent, simple, credible information; if it has not communicated.' (OE1)

However, they are aware that the information provided is not always adequate, and there are even occasions when no information is provided.

> 'There are companies that have begun to give information and they say they're transparent, but sometimes [...] the employees know that behind the official figures there's always a "B" set of accounts. They should report what they really make. [...] as regards the obligation to provide information, Article 64 of the Statute of Workers' Rights [Estatuto de los Trabajadores] makes it obligatory to report. But we encounter situations in which the information does not reach the employees or does not reach them in an appropriate form[...] and on occasions there is also too much information, unhelpful information which often leads to confusion. The important thing is to provide the information that is closest to the worker.' (OE1)

> 'We often have to work hard to persuade managers that they have to give information. The legal obligation is to give information to the trade union delegates. When there aren't any it's difficult.'(OE2)

The trade unions agree:

> 'The trade unions can't be held responsible for non-compliance by the employers. And moreover, in cases where we ask for information, they don't give it to us in adequate form. And in the end you get another culture. […] If they never give you information when you ask for it, when they conceal information. […] There are plenty of companies that do not register their accounts.' (OS2)

At the same time, the trade unions also recognise that the unions themselves sometimes do little to ensure compliance with the rights and functions established in Article 64 of the Statute of Workers' Rights Act (SWRA) on information:

> 'We should do more, there are things we're not doing.' (OS1)

Here the provincial government mentioned the role government should play by making it a requirement for companies applying for grants or aid to report the legally required information;

> 'The Government can help to encourage this too. By forcing companies to comply with that article of the SWRA. For example, they could include clauses on compliance in the eligibility criteria for receiving grants.'

The development agencies did not express an opinion in this regard in the focus groups.

However, the trade union organisations also feel that the value of compliance with the Statute of Workers' Rights (with regard to information provision) should not be overstated, as it does not necessarily guarantee employee participation:

> 'The Statute can be helpful but it shouldn't be overstated or given more importance than it actually has. At the end of the day, that's not what participation is about. It improves information but it doesn't improve participation. These days we're supposed to collaborate in providing information, transparency and communication. There's a prevailing culture of "being nice".' (OS1;OS2)

In short, trade unions and business associations representing companies where employees are owners want to see comprehensive participation, whereas other business associations are more cautious and prefer to take small gradual steps, differentiating between participation and the presence of employees representatives on governance bodies. When it comes to information-sharing, all agents consider it to be of key importance. However, the trade unions insist that the provision of information does not in itself denote the existence of employee participation in a company.

4.3 Category: Strategies for Promoting EFP

This category is also covered in the ETUC/CES's list of prerequisites (2013): 'The introduction and design of EFP should be the subject of prior consultation and agreement with worker representatives and trade unions. The details of EFP have to be introduced through negotiations between social partners and collective agreements should set the framework for EFP [...]'. They also add that 'EFP schemes must be open to all workers within the company, including part-time workers'. In this category, we shall examine the different paths for encouraging EFP proposed by the agents.

A clear example of negotiation among the social partners to encourage participation is the agreement signed between CONFESAL (the Spanish confederation of worker-owned societies to which ASLE belongs), CCOO and UGT, aimed at 'establishing a scenario of collaboration that will favour the creation of stable employment, employee participation in the company and consequently, dissemination of the business model represented by employee-owned companies and encouragement and support for business initiatives promoted by employees' (CONFESAL, CCOO and UGT, 2014).

In 2014 ADEGI also discussed this issue in its 'Guide to New Business Culture': 'promoting direct interlocution with people in our companies without neglecting compliance with obligations to the employees' legal representatives'. This phrase has been interpreted in different ways by the different agents: the trade union organisations consider that it is indirectly saying that ADEGI wants to promote the individual company-employee relationship, side-lining trade union representatives, but ADEGI itself insists that this interpretation is incorrect; in no case is it telling members to neglect to comply with their legal obligations to the trade unions.

In the focus groups, the two trade unions agree on the need to involve all social partners in encouraging EFP:

> 'This is still a social dialogue. How do we do that in specific terms? From my point of view, by involving everyone with control or impact over the issue. Employers, trade unions and government and public authorities.' (OS1).

As for the way in which employee participation should be channelled, the trade unions were adamant that EFP must be promoted in collective bargaining. However, some business associations insisted that it should be the individual companies that choose the particular channel for encouraging participation, rather than business associations.

> 'Each firm has to cut its cloth to suit its measure.' (OE1)

As to which employees should be eligible for EFP, the trade unions believe it must be open to all, as established by the ETUC/CES (2013):

> 'The criterion must be one of free availability for all employees. [...] Participation should be open to the entire group.' (OS1)

The public institutions did not express an opinion on this issue, considering that it is entirely up to the business in question. Their public documentation does not provide any relevant information in this regard either.

Summing up, the trade unions opt for including encouragement of EFP in collective bargaining, whereas the business associations believe that the decision should lie with the individual company. However, it is important to stress that these stances are not entirely opposed, since, at present, some issues of collective bargaining are resolved at the company level and in the future, EFP might be one of those. It is even possible that collective bargaining might determine that the issue should be dealt with on a company-by-company basis. It remains to be seen how this issue will be dealt with in future rounds of collective bargaining in the province.

4.4 Category: The objective of EFP

The ETUC/CES (2013) also insists that 'EFP should always provide additional income and not be a substitute for fair pay. EFP should not be considered as an alternative to collective bargaining and to wage increases. Financial participation is equally not an alternative to public pensions or to collectively negotiated pension schemes.' It further argues that 'Employees have the right to get their fair share of the results of a company and their income must represent a fair share of the national income.' However, it adds the qualification that '[...] Under no circumstances should EFP worsen inequalities of income inside a company or in society.' In this last category, we shall examine what the different agents in the province of Gipuzkoa are (and are not) looking for in EFP.

The trade union representatives in the focus groups were in complete agreement with the ETUC position.

> 'If we have financial participation, any wage elements should not replace existing ones.' (OS1)

> 'It should never be an alternative or substitute for public pension schemes. Nor [...] should it be an alternative to a salary. And no measures taken with regard to profit-sharing should ever result in [greater]wage inequality in the company, based on either category or gender. Under no circumstances. For us, that's essential. And those are the terms on which we can sit down and negotiate.' (OS1)

> 'We hear a lot about profit-sharing these days and it's no coincidence. During the economic boom years, nobody would ever have dreamt of suggesting it. Of course, it's being seen as a way of avoiding pay rises. Naturally, discussing profit-sharing when the company's performing badly.' (OS2)

> 'Having a stake in the company stock if the employees are only going to have a 5% stake and if that's going to mean extra funding for the company. [...] I don't think that's valid.' (OS2)

As for the objectives sought through encouragement of the EFP, the trade unions mention employment, better distribution of wealth and greater power on the company's decision-making bodies:

> 'If there are plenty of capital gains, they should be shared out. We're not saying the company shouldn't make money, because that would be absurd. But it's not so difficult to have social objectives. If you make employment an objective, you also guarantee that everyone is more engaged with the company. The aim is for 200 families to have a decent living; that is a worthwhile objective.' (OS1)

> 'We say yes to financial participation, provided that there is a counter-power in the decision-making capacities.' (OS1)

Business associations seek improved competitiveness:

> 'We are working to achieve competitiveness in companies. In this regard, we see employee participation as a concept that favours competitiveness.' (OE4)

> 'When you talk about profit-sharing and presuming that financial participation does favour competitiveness, and it's also good because making employees feel part of the organisation encourages engagement. And we consider variable payment models to be positive.' (OE4)

In general, the trade unions accept the benefits of participation for the variables that affect employees most directly – employment and income. With regard to employment, they anticipate that EFP will have a positive impact, as various authors have shown, including Arando et al (2011),

Blair and Kochan (2002), Estrin and Jones (1991), Kruse and Blasi (2001), Kruse (2002), Kruse et al. (2010), Park et al. (2004), Pérotin and Robinson (2004), Quarrey and Rosen (1991) and Winther and Marens (1997). The trade union participants also saw EFP as being beneficial for income, as indicated by Blasi et al. (2003), Buchele et al. (2010), D'Art (1992), Kruse (2002), Kruse et al. (2008), Pencavel et al. (2006) and Rosen et al. (2005).

However, it is important to note that at no point do they speak of the positive effects on psycho-social aspects affecting employees, such as job satisfaction (Carberry, 2011; Dong et al, 2002; French and Rosenstein, 1984; Freundlich, 2009; Gamble et al., 2002; Höckertin & Härenstam, 2006; Höckertin, 2008; Klein, 1987; Kruse, 2002; Kruse et al., 2008, 2010; Kuvaas, 2003; McQuaid et al., 2000; Oliver, 1990, 1984; Rhodes and Steers, 1981) or of possible social and economic benefits for the territory (Burdin & Dean, 2009; Erdal, 2000; Pérotin, 2006; Whyte & Blasi, 1984). These are seem to the authors to be equally important.

Moreover, the trade union organisations see participation in governing bodies as an objective associated with EFP. In other words, through EFP they seek open participation in the governance, allowing them to influence strategic company decisions more directly, as discussed by Ellerman, 1988; Gates, 1998; Mackin, 1991, 1997, 2002; McHugh et al., 1999; Swinney, 2012a, 2012b; Whyte and Blasi, 1984.

The business associations are more interested in the benefits associated with company effectiveness and competitiveness, seeing in EFP some of the benefits identified in many studies related to different economic criteria (productivity, growth, profitability and others, e.g., Addison, 2005; Arando et al., 2015; Ben-Ner & Jones, 1995; Fakhfakh et al., 2012; Kruse et al., 2010; Levine & Tyson, 1990; Pencavel, 2001).

The Provincial Government of Gipuzkoa did not express an opinion in the focus groups on the objective of financial participation in particular, or participation in general. However, after analysing their documentation we can see that they view EFP as a way of involving employees in the overall company project and as a tool for engaging the company with its local environment (Departamento de Innovación, Desarrollo Rural y Turismo de la DFG, 2014). The development agencies did not express an opinion in the focus groups and we lack enough evidence to state what they consider to be the objective of EFP.

As we can see, the trade union and business associations differ over the goals of EFP. These differences are not surprising, but it is important to emphasize that they are not incompatible. The same business dynamics caused by EFP that lead to employment and income, the benefits that interest the trade unions, are also those that generate the competitive advantages that business associations seek. Furthermore, the objectives of the two agents clearly match those of government. It is therefore necessary to extend and strengthen dialogue between business associations and trade unions on the importance of each one's objectives and ways in which they can be reconciled and implemented in companies. Their goals are not contradictory goals - far from it. It remains to be seen whether the two groups, with the interlocution of the Provincial Government, can build EFP into their strategic reflections and continue with a process of constructive communication.

5. Conclusions

The following are the most important conclusions drawn from our research.

The trade union organisations do not include participation amongst their main strategic themes, although they agree that it is an important issue and one which needs to be addressed in the short-to-medium term. With regard to EFP, they are in favour of extending it within companies provided that participation is open to all employees and involves greater control in the decision-making bodies.

The business associations see financial participation as a desirable option, but argue in favour of encouraging the more initial levels of participation in management first – i.e. information, transparency and communication. The trade unions, however, argue that those initial levels should already have been incorporated in all companies by law. They consider that more work is required in this regard (including by the unions themselves), but that it should only be seen a support for real participation. Transparency and communication do not equal participation, however important they are. Both agents must advance in this connection.

Significantly, there are two basic discrepancies between the trade unions and business associations. First, the unions are committed to including participation in collective bargaining, whereas the business associations believe the decision should lie with company owners. These positions are not necessarily at odds, but it does raise an important difference that will have to be addressed over time. The business associations view participation as a strategy to help improve competitiveness, while unions, by contrast, see it as one of a number of ways of increasing their presence on firms' decision-making bodies, as well as creating employment and increasing employees' income. These are not incompatible aims either, but continued dialogue and commitment by these organisations will be needed to integrate and elaborate on the two objectives in terms of business policies.

As regards the public administration, we can identify two variants. The Provincial Government of Gipuzkoa advocates a model that promotes employee participation; however, most of the development agencies, although they consider it to be an important issue to be addressed, do not see it as a strategic issue.

Despite the difficulties we have identified in leading Gipuzkoa towards a new social and economic model based on commitment to the territory and its people, and although there is still much work to be done, it is important to recognise the advances observed over recent months in the discourse of the agents involved in the project, especially among the business associations and trade unions.

Finally, further scientific studies and compilations of practical experiences are clearly needed to provide the agents with a larger knowledge base. This will enable continued debate and will help promote employee participation in companies, allowing small steps to be taken to develop and transform the business world, generating intelligent companies and building an intelligent, cohesive and socially responsible territory.

References

Addison, J. T. (2005). The determinants of firm performance: unions, works councils, and employee involvement/high-performance work practices. *Scottish Journal of Political Economy*, *52*(3), 406-450.

ADEGI (2010). Memoria Anual 2010. Availabe at http://www.adegi.es/download.php?arc=85y78rvgf8/Memorias%20y%20magazine/Memoria-ADEGI.pdf

ADEGI (2011). Memoria Anual 2011. Available at http://www.adegi.es/download.php?arc=85y78rvgf8/memoria_cast.pdf

ADEGI (2012). Memoria Anual 2012. Available at http://www.adegi.es/memoria2012/es/

ADEGI (2014). Guía Nueva Cultura de Empresa. Available at https://www.google.es/webhp?sourceid=chrome-instant&ion=1&espv=2&ie=UTF-8#

AFL-CIO Industrial Union Department (1986). Guidelines on Employee Stock Ownership Plans. *Labour and Investments* 6(4 - May).

Alzaga Ruiz, I. (2003). La reforma de la Ley Alemana de Comités de Empresa. *Revista del Ministerio de Trabajo y Asuntos Sociales*, (43), 65-85.

Arando, S., Gago, M., Jones, D., & Kato, T. (2015). Efficiency in employee-owned enterprises: an econometric case study of Mondragon. *Industrial and Labour Relations Review,* 68(2), 398-425.

Arando, S., Freundlich, F., Gago, M., Jones, D., & Kato, T. (2011) Assessing Mondragon: Stability and Managed Change in the Face of Globalization. In Carberry E.J. (Ed.), *Employee Ownership and Shared Capitalism: New Directions and Debates for the 21st Century*. Cornell University ILR Press. Ithaca, New York (USA)

Arregi, B., Freundlich, F., Gay, S., Mendizabal, A., & Lizarraga, N. (2012). *La participación de los trabajadores en el capital social de las empresas*. Paper presented at the XIV Jornadas de investigadores en Economía Social y Cooperativa de Ciriec, 20-22 junio, Oñati. Spain.

ASLE (2012). *Memoria 2012.* Available at http://asle.es/pdf/ASLE_Memoria_2012.pdf

ASLE (2013). Tiempo de crisis, tiempo de oportunidades. La Sociedad Laboural del Siglo XXI. III Congreso de ASLE. 10 de Febrero, 15 de Marzo 2012. Available at http://www.aemta.es/wp-content/uploads/2014/01/Tiempo_de_crisis_tiempo_de_oportunidades.pdf

Baylos, A. (1992). Control obrero, democracia industrial, participación: contenidos posibles. *Autoridad y democracia en la empresa.*

BEN-NER, A. & Jones, D. C. (1995). Employee participation, ownership, and productivity: A theoretical framework. *Industrial Relations: A Journal of Economy and Society*, *34*(4), 532-554.

Blair, M. M., & Kochan, T. A. (Eds.). (2002). *The new relationship: Human capital in the American corporation*. Brookings Institution Press.

Blasi, J. R. (1988). *Employee ownership: revolution or ripoff?* Cambridge, MA: Ballinger.

Blasi, J. R., Kruse, D., & Bernstein, A. (2003). *In the company of owners: The truth about stock options (and why every employee should have them).* Basic Books.

Brown, M., Landau, I., Mitchell, R., O'Connell, A., & Ramsay, I. (2008). Why do employees participate in employee share plans? A conceptual framework. *Labour & Industry: A journal of the social and economic relations of work*, *18*(3), 45-72.

Buchele, R., Kruse, D. L., Rodgers, L., & Scharf, A. (2010). Show me the money: Does shared capitalism share the wealth? In Douglas L. Kruse, Richard B. Freeman and Joseph R. Blasi (Eds.), *Shared capitalism at work: Employee ownership, profit and gain sharing, and broad-based stock options* (351-375). University of Chicago Press.

Burdin, G., & Dean, A. (2009). New evidence on wages and employment in worker cooperatives compared with capitalist firms. *Journal of Comparative Economics*, *37*(4), 517-533.

Cámara de Gipuzkoa (2014). Informe coyuntura económica y perspectivas 2014. Análisis del ciclo económico. Gipuzkoa.

Carberry, E. J., ed. (2011). Employee Ownership and Shared Capitalism: New Directions in Research. Champaign, Illinois: Labour and Employment Relations Association, University of Illinois Urbana-Champaign

CCOO (2009). 9º Congreso confederal. Julio 2009. Bilbao. Available at http://www.ccoo-euskadi.net/comunes/recursos/9/doc18957_9_CONGRESO_CONFEDERAL_CCOO_EUSKADI.pdf

CCOO (2013). Ponencia 10º Congreso. Available at http://www.ccoo-euskadi.net/comunes/recursos/9/doc114339_Ponencia_X_Congreso_de_CCOO_de_Euskadi.pdf

Cheney, G. (2002). Values at work: Employee participation meets market pressure at Mondragon. Cornell University Press.

Confesal, U. & CCOO (2014). *Convenio de colabouración.* 17 de Marzo de 2014.

Conte, M. A. and Svejnar, J. (1990). The performance effects of employee share ownership plans. In A. S. Blinder (Ed.), Paying for Productivity. Washington, DC: Brookings Institute, pp. 143-181.

Cooke, P. & Morgan, K. (1988). *The Associational Economy*. Oxford, UK: Oxford University Press.

Craig, B., & Pencavel J. (1995). Participation and productivity: A comparison of worker cooperatives and conventional firms in the plywood industry. *Brookings Papers on Economic Activity*, 121–160.

Creswell, J. W. (2002). Educational research: Planning, conducting, and evaluating quantitative.

D'Art, D. (2002). *Economic democracy and financial participation: A comparative study.* Routledge.

Departamento de Innovación, Desarrollo Rural y Turismo de la DFG (2013). *Programa para la Promoción de una Gipuzkoa un Territorio que Emprende.* Nº 140 de 23 de julio de 2013. BOG. Donostia-San Sebastian.

Departamento de Innovación, Desarrollo Rural y Turismo de la DFG (2014). *Programa para la Promoción de un Territorio socialmente responsable.* Nº 131 de 11 de julio de 2014. BOG. Donostia-San Sebastian.

Dong, X. Y., Bowles, P., & Ho, S. P. (2002). Share ownership and employee attitudes: Some evidence from China's postprivatization rural industry. *Journal of Comparative Economics*, 30(4), 812-835.

EFES – European Federation for Employee Share Ownership (2014), Brussels, Belgium. Web page, cases studies section: http://www.efesonline.org/fasuk231.htm. Accessed 9 December, 2014.

ELA (2008). Resoluciones. XII Congreso del 26-27 Noviembre 2008. Bilbao. Available at http://www.mrafundazioa.eus/es/centro-de-documentacion/congresos/distribuir-la-riqueza-mas-rentas-de-trabajo-mas-gasto-social-y-mas-justicia-fiscal-propuesta-de-resolucion

ELA (2013a). Resoluciones. XIII Congreso del 23-24 Enero 2013. Available at http://www.mrafundazioa.eus/es/centro-de-documentacion/congresos/resoluciones

ELA (2013b). Ponencia y Resoluciones aprobladas. XIII Congreso del 23-24 Enero 2013. Available at http://www.mrafundazioa.eus/es/centro-de-documentacion/congresos/xiii-cogreso-ponencia-y-resoluciones-aprobadas

Ellerman, D. P. (1988). The Legitimate Opposition at Work: The Union's Role in Large Democratic Firms. Economic and Industrial Democracy, 9(4), 437-453.

Emplpoyee Ownership Association EOA (2014). Case studies. Disponible en http://employeeownership.co.uk/case-studies/. (06.12.2014).

EOA – Employee Ownership Association (2014), Yorkshire, UK. Web page, case studies section: http://employeeownership.co.uk/case-studies/. Accessed 6 December, 2014.

Erdal, D. (2011). Beyond the corporation: Humanity working. Random House.

Erdal, D. E. (2000). *The psychology of sharing: an evolutionary approach* (Doctoral dissertation, University of St Andrews).

Eriksson, Kurt (2010). *The Swedish rules on Negotiation and Mediation – a brief summary*, Medlingsinstitutet (National Mediation Office), Stockholm.

Estrin, S., & Jones, D. C. (1991). Viability of Emplyee-Owned Firms: Evidence from France, *Industrial and Labour Relations Review*, *45*, 323.

ETUC/CES (2013). *ETUC position on conditions for employee financial participation (EFP).* Comité Ejecutivo de 5 y 6 de Marzo del 2013. Brussels.

European Federation for Employee Share Ownership (EFES) (2014), Employee Ownership: real cases. Available at http://www.efesonline.org/fasuk231.htm. (09.12.2014).

European Parliament (2013), Report on financial participation of employees in companies' proceeds, (2013/2127(INI)). Available at http://www.europarl.europa.eu/sides/getDoc.do?pubRef=-//EP//NONSGML+REPORT+A7-2013-0465+0+DOC+PDF+V0//EN

EUSTAT (2015a), Instituto Vasco de Estadística. Web page, GDP and its distribution section: http://en.eustat.eus/estadisticas/tema_477/opt_0/temas.html#axzz3kZ5z42TW Accesed 15 July 2015.

EUSTAT (2015b), Instituto Vasco de Estadística. Web page, Population with relation to activity (PRA) section: http://en.eustat.eus/estadisticas/tema_37/opt_0/temas.html#axzz3kZ5z42TW Accesed 15 July 2015.

Fakhfakh, F., Pérotin, V., & Gago, M. (2012). Productivity, capital, and labour in labour-managed and conventional firms: An investigation on French data. *Indus. & Lab. Rel. Rev.*, *65*, 847.

French, J. L., & Rosenstein, J. (1984). Employee ownership work attitudes, and power relationships. *Academy of Management Journal*, *27*(4), 861-869.

Freundlich, F. M. (2009). Generational perspectives on employee ownership: The relationship between age and satisfaction with cooperative ownership in Mondragon. Doctoral Thesis, Graduate School of Education, Harvard University; Cambridge, MA (UMI Dissertation Publishing number 3385017).

Fulton, L. (2011). Worker representation in Europe. *Labour Research Department and ETUI*, *1*.

Gamble, J. E., Culpepper, R., & Blubaugh, M. G. (2002). ESOPs and employee attitudes: The importance of empowerment and financial value. *Personnel Review, 31*(1), 9-26.

García B., Aguilar M., Gago M., Arregi B., Lizarraga N., Gay S., & Mendizabal A. (2013, July). *Key factors that foster employee financial participation in firms in European Union.* Paper presented at the EMES Conference, Belgium.

Gates, J. R. (1999). The ownership solution: Toward a shared capitalism for the twenty-first century. Basic Books.

Gerum, E. (2007). *Das Deutsche Corporate Governance-System.* Eine empirische Untersuchung, Stuttgart.

Graf von Schwerin, A., & Sharma, M. (2010). *Employee Financial Participation in Europe.* Opinion of the European Economic and Social Committee, SOC/371, 21 October 2010. Brussels.

Greifenstein, R. & Kissler, L. (2010). *Mitbestimmung im Spiegel der Forschung.* Eine Bilanz der empirischen Untersuchungen 1952-2010, Berlin.

Greifenstein, R. (2011). *Perspectivas de la cogestión empresarial en Alemania ¿Paralización injustificada de la obra política?.* Instituto Latinoamericano de Investigaciones Sociales, Fundación Friedrich Ebert, Bonn.

Hammer, T. H., & Stern, R. N. (1980). Employee ownership: Implications for the organisational distribution of power. *Academy of Management Journal,23*(1), 78-100.

Haynes, R., Massachusetts AFL-CIO (2011, 15 September). *Supporting Employee Ownership of Business to Promote Job Creation and Security.* Testimoy before the Joint Committee on Labour and Workforce Development, Legislature of the Commonwealth of Massachusetts, BostonBoston.

Hernández Sampieri, R., Fernández Collado, C., & Baptista Lucio, P. (2010). Metodología de la investigación. *México: Editorial Mc Graw Hill.*

Höckertin, C. (2008). Control and participation for employees within geriatric care: Does ownership make a difference?. *Work: A Journal of Prevention, Assessment and Rehabilitation*, *30*(2), 137-147.

Höckertin, C., & Härenstam, A. (2006). The impact of ownership on psychosocial working conditions: a multilevel analysis of 60 workplaces.*Economic and Industrial Democracy*, *27*(2), 245-284.

IKEI (2011). Modelos de organisación de las empresas gipuzcoanas, implicación de las personas y competitividad y excelencia empresarial. Programa SENDOTUZ. Financiado por la Diputación Foral de Gipuzkoa. Gipuzkoa.

Irizar, I. & Lizarralde, I. (2005). Desarrollo Regional y Emprendizaje Cooperativo. *Ekonomiaz 59*, 284-305.

Kasmir, S. (1996). The myth of Mondragon: Cooperatives, politics, and working class life in a Basque town. SUNY Press.

Klein, K. J. (1987). Employee stock ownership and employee attitudes: a test of three models. *Journal of Applied Psychology*, *72*(2), 319.

Köhler, H. D., & Jiménez, J. P. C. (2014). Logros y derrotas sindicales como motor del progreso social en Alemania. In *Trabajo y ciudadanía en la Europa contemporánea: el sindicalismo y la construcción de los derechos* (pp. 17-37). Fundación 1° de Mayo.

Kroumova, M. K., Sesil, J. C., Kruse, D. L., & Blasi, J. R. (2002). Broad-based employee stock options—A union-nonunion comparison. *Advances in Industrial & Labour Relations*, *11*, 69-94.

Kruse, D. (2002). Research evidence on prevalence and effects of employee ownership. *Journal of Employee Ownership Law and Finance*, *14*(4), 65-90.

Kruse, D., & Blasi, J. (2001). A population study of the performance of ESOP and non-ESOP privately-held companies.

Kruse, D., Freeman, R., & Blasi, J. (2008). Do workers gain by sharing? Employee outcomes under employee ownership, profit sharing, and broad-based stock options (No. w14233). National Bureau of Economic Research.

Kruse, D.L., Blasi, J.R. & Park, R. (2010). Shared Capitalism in the U.S. Economy: Prevalence, Characteristics, and Employee Views of Financial Participation in Enterprises. In Kruse, D.L., Freeman R.B. & Blasi, J.R. (Eds.), *Shared Capitalism at Work: Employee Ownership, Profit and Gain Sharing, and Broad-based Stock Options (*pp. 41-75). University of Chicago Press.

Kuvaas, B. (2003). Employee ownership and affective organisational commitment: Employees' perceptions of fairness and their preference for company shares over cash. *Scandinavian Journal of Management*, *19*(2), 193-212.

La Cámara de Gipuzkoa (2014). *Informe coyuntura económica y perspectivas 2014. Análisis del ciclo económico*. Available at http://www.camaragipuzkoa.com/images/productos/Informe_de_Coynuntura_Econ%C3%B3mica_y_Perspectivas_2014.pdf

LAB (2012). *Resoluciones. 8. Biltzar Nagusia*. 21-22 de junio 2012. Nafarroa. Available at http://www.labsindikatua.org/es/lab-sindikatua/8o-congreso-nacional/ponencias

LAB (2014). Nuevo Modelo de Relaciones Labourales: propuesta de LAB al departamento de empleo. Mayo 2014. Available at http://www.labsindikatua.org/materiala/argazkiak/ekintzaSindikala/NegoziazioKolektiboa/14_05_16LanHarremanEreduBerria/NuevoModeloDeRelacionesLabourales.pdf

Levine, D. I., & Tyson L. (1990). Participation, productivity and the firm's environment. In A. S. Blinder (Ed.), *Paying for Productivity: A Look at the Evidence*, pp. 183–243. Washington (DC): Brookings Institution Press.

Livingston, C. (1985). Lessons from Three UAW Locals. *Labour Research Review*, *1*(6), 8.

Long, R. J. (1978). Employee Ownership and Attitudes Toward the Union: An Empirical Study. *Relations Industrielles/Industrial Relations*, 237-254

Lowitzsch, J. and Hashi, I. (2014). *The Promotion of Employee Ownership and Participation Study.* Prepared by the Inter University Centre for European Commission's DG MARKT (Contract MARKT/ 2013/0191F2/ST/OP). Final report October 2014.

Lowitzsch, J., Hashi, I., & Woodward, R. (2008). The PEPPER IV Report: Benchmarking of Employee Participation in Profits and Enterprise Results in the Member and Candidate Countries of the European Union. *Institute fro Eastern European Studies, Free University of Berlin.*

Lynd, S. (1985). Why we Opposed the Buy-Out at Weirton Steel. *Labour Research Review* 1(6) 41-54.

Mackin C. & Freundlich F. (1995). Representative Structures in Employee-Owned Firms. *Journal of Employee Ownership Law and Finance* 7, 2 (Spring), 1-25.

Mackin, C. (1991). Beyond the Contract: Taking on Ownership. *Workplace Topics*, *2*, 34-48.

Mackin, C. (1997). Employee ownership and industrial relations. *Perspectives on Work*, 66-69.

Mackin, C. (2002). Employee Ownership in America: A Primer for Industrial Relations. *Perspectives on Work*, 5-9.

Maxwell, J. A. (2012). Qualitative Research Design: An Interactive Approach: An Interactive Approach. Sage.

McCarthy, J. E., Voos, P. B., Eaton, A. E., Kruse, D., & Blasi, J. (2011). Solidarity and sharing: unions and shared capitalism. *Employee Ownership and Shared Capitalism: New Directions in Research, Champaign, Illinois, Labour and employment relations assocation: University of Illinois at Urbana-Champaign*, 27-58.

McElrath, R. G., & Rowan, R. L. (1992). The American labour movement and employee ownership: objections to and uses of employee stock ownership plans. *Journal of Labour Research*, *13*(1), 99-119.

Mchugh, P. P., Cutcher-Gershenfeld, J., & Polzin, M. (1999). Employee stock ownership plans: union influence and stakeholder interests. *Economic and Industrial Democracy*, *20*(4), 535-560.

McQuaid, R., Hollywood, E., Bond, S., Canduela, J., Richard, A., & Blackledge, G. (2012). Fit for work? Health and Wellbeing of Employees in Employee Owned Business. *London: Employee Ownership Association.*

Medlingsinstitutet, (2012). *The Swedish Mode.* Available at http://www.mi.se/other-languages/in-english/the-swedish-model/.

Meyers, J. S. (2011). Employee ownership, democratic control, and working-class empowerment. *Employee Ownership and Shared Capitalism: New Directions in Research*, 113-145.

Michel, H. (2007). Co-determination in Germany: The recent debate. *Johann Wolfgang Goethe-Universität Frankfurt Working Paper.*

Mugarra, A. (2005). Capital Social y Cooperativas: La Experiencia En El País Vasco, *Ekonomiaz 59*, 306-329.

National Center for Employee Ownership NCEO (2014), Employee Ownership Report. Case studies section, disponible en http://www.nceo.org/Employee-Ownership-Report/id/46/. (09.12.2014).

NCEO – National Center for Employee Ownership (2014), Oakland, USA. Web page, "Employee Ownership Report", case studies section: http://www.nceo.org/Employee-Ownership-Report/id/46/. Accessed 9 December, 2014. See also "Case Study Resources" in "Supplemental Newsletter Resources".

Nuttall, G. (2012). Sharing Success: The Nuttall review of employee ownership.

Oakeshott, R. (2000). Jobs and fairness: the logic and experience of employee ownership. Michael Russell.

OIT, Organisación Internacional del Trabajo (2014a). *Act (1976:580) on Co-determination in the Workplace.* SWE-1976-L-13980, NATLEX.

OIT, Organisación Internacional del Trabajo (2014b). *Board Representation (Private Sector Employees) Act (1987:1245).* SWE-1987-L-4662, NATLEX.

Oliver, N. (1984). An examination of organisational commitment in six workers' cooperatives in Scotland. *Human Relations*, *37*(1), 29-45.

Oliver, N. (1990). Work rewards, work values, and organisational commitment in an employee-owned firm: Evidence from the UK. Human relations, 43(6), 513-526.

OVES/GEEB (2015), Observatorio Vasco de Economía Social, Gizarte Ekonomiako Euskal Behatokia. Web page, área socio-económica section: http://www.oves-geeb.com/es/area-socio-economica Accesed 15 July 2015.

Park, R., Kruse, D., & Sesil, J. (2004). Does employee ownership enhance firm survival?. Advances in the Economic Analysis of Participatory & Labour-Managed Firms, 8, 3-33.

Parlamento Europeo (2013). *Report on financial participation of employees in companies' proceeds.* (2013/2127(INI)) Committee on Employment and Social Affairs. A7-0465/2013. Avaliable at http://www.europarl.europa.eu/sides/getDoc.do?pubRef=-//EP//NONSGML+REPORT+A7-2013-0465+0+DOC+PDF+V0//EN

Pencavel, J. (2001). Worker Participation: Lessons from the Worker Co-ops of the Pacific Northwest. New York (NY): Russell Sage Foundation.

Pencavel, J. H., Pistaferri, L., & Schivardi, F. (2006). Wages, employment, and capital in capitalist and worker-owned firms.

Pendleton, A., Robinson, A., & Wilson, N. (1995). Does employee ownership weaken trade unions? Recent evidence from the UK bus industry. *Economic and Industrial Democracy*, *16*(4), 577-605.

Pendleton, A., Wilson, N., & Wright, M. (1998). The Perception and Effects of Share Ownership: Empirical Evidence from Employee Buy-Outs. *British Journal of Industrial Relations*, *36*(1), 99-123.

Pérotin, V. (2004). Early cooperative survival: The liability of adolescence.*Advances in the Economic Analysis of Participatory & Labour-Managed Firms*,*8*, 67-86.

Pérotin, V. (2006). Entry, exit, and the business cycle: Are cooperatives different?. *Journal of Comparative Economics*, *34*(2), 295-316.

Pérotin, V., & Robinson, A. (Eds.). (2004). *Employee participation, firm performance and survival.* Elsevier.

Putnam, R. D. (1993). Making Democracy Work. Civic Traditions in Modern Italy. Princeton University Press.

Quarrey, M., & Rosen, C. M. (1991). *Employee ownership and corporate performance*. National Center for Employee Ownership.

Quarrey, M., Blasi, J. R., & Rosen, C. M. (1986). *Taking stock: Employee ownership at work*. Ballinger Publishing Company.

Redmon, G., Mueller, C., & Daniels, G. (1985). A Lost Dream: Worker Control at Rath Packing. *Labour Research Review*, *1*(6), 10.

Rhodes, S. R., & Steers, R. M. (1981). Conventional vs. worker-owned organisations. *Human Relations*, *34*(12), 1013-1035.

Rosen, C. (2012a). *The State of Broad-Based Employee Ownership Plans 2012*. National Center for Employee Ownership. Oakland, California.

Rosen, C. (2012b). A Short History of of S Corporation ESOP Scams. Retrieved April 23 2012. Available at http://www.nceo.org/articles/s-corporation-esop-scams

Rosen, C. M., Case, J., & Staubus, M. (2005). *Equity: Why employee ownership is good for business*. Harvard Business Press.

Rothschild, J. (2009). Workers' Cooperatives and Social Enterprise A Forgotten Route to Social Equity and Democracy. *American behavioral scientist*, *52*(7), 1023-1041.

Rothschild-Whitt, J. (1985). Who Will Benefit from ESOPs?. *Labour Research Review*, *1*(6), 4.

Royo, M. C. R. P. (1990). Derechos de información del sindicato y paga de beneficios. *Relaciones labourales: Revista crítica de teoría y práctica*, (2), 53-61.

Royo, M. C. R. P. (1990). Derechos de información del sindicato y paga de beneficios. *Relaciones labourales: Revista crítica de teoría y práctica*, (2), 53-61.

Saunders, M. N., Saunders, M., Lewis, P., & Thornhill, A. (2011). *Research methods for business students, 5/e*. Pearson Education India.

Slott, M. (1985). The Case Against Worker Ownership. *Labour research review,1*.

Steger, T., & Hartz, R. (2008). The power of participation? Power relations and processes in employee-owned companies. *Zeitschrift für Personalforschung/ German Journal of Research in Human Resource Management*, 152-170.

Swinney, Dan. (2012a). *Response to New Year's Questions*. Retrieved April 24, 2012 (http://www.clcr.org/resources).

Swinney, Dan. (2012b). *Review of 'America Beyond Capitalism by Gar Alperovitz*. Retrieved April 24, 2012 (http://www.clcr.org/resources).

Toscano, D. (1984). Employee Ownership and Its Effects on Attitudes Toward Trade Unions. *Labour Studies Journal*, *9*(1), 80-7.

UGT Euskadi (2009). *X Congreso*.

UGT Euskadi (2013): *XI Congreso*. 23-24 de mayo 2013.

Uvalic, M. (1991). The PEPPER Report: Promotion of Employee Participation in Profits and Enterprise Results in the Member States of the European Community: 1991 Edition. Office for Official Publications of the European Communities.

Villa, L. E. (1980). La participación de los trabajadores en la empresa. Editorial IEE.

Werner, J. R., & Zimmermann, J. (2005). Unternehmerische Mitbestimmung in Deutschland: Eine empirische Analyse der Auswirkungen von Gewerkschaftsmacht in Aufsichtsräten. *Industrielle Beziehungen/The German Journal of Industrial Relations*, 339-354.

Whyte, W. F., & Blasi, J. R. (1984). Employee ownership and the future of unions. *The Annals of The American Academy of Political and Social Science*, 128-140.

Williams, M., Unrau, Y. A., Grinnell, R. M., & Epstein, I. (2005). The qualitative research approach. *Social work research and evaluation: Quantitative and qualitative approaches*, *7*, 75-87.

Winther, G. (1999). Theory O-Is the case closed?. *Economic and Industrial Democracy*, *20*(2), 269-293.

Winther, G., & Marens, R. (1997). Participatory democracy may go a long way: comparative growth performance of employee ownership firms in New York and Washington states. *Economic and Industrial Democracy*, *18*(3), 393-422.

Employee financial participation in Polish listed companies – a management approach

Maciej Kozłowski[1]

Abstract

The major purpose of this chapter is to analyse the most important employee financial participation (EFP) programs in Poland in order to show the occurring relations between the programs applied and the socioeconomic results of enterprises. In this chapter the focus lies on collecting data and information about financial participation programs among Polish listed companies.

The choice was made due to the data availability on listed companies. Through the collected data, the multidimensional relationships between employee financial ownership and economic results are illustrated, as well as indicating that the relationship mechanisms of employee ownership on productivity are complex interactions by nature. Additionally, it has also helped to separate crucial characteristic features of the applied forms of EFP. This empirical approach concentrates on quantitative research.

The results of the empirical study conducted in the period of 2010-2011 indicate the existence of some particular regularity. In Polish public companies the vast majority of schemes are aimed at participation of the management personnel. These programs are narrow-based and rather hermetic with a high concentration of stocks or shares in the hands of the management. This is something completely different from the situation in other European countries, where the formula of EFP assumes a broad-based access of employees from other groups to participate in these schemes. The reasons behind such a situation may be different, starting from the broadly defined external conditions of company functioning, through the factors existing within all enterprises, and finishing off with a mental barrier.

---

1 Maciej Kozłowski: Ph.D., Associate Professor at the University of Lodz, Lodz, Poland, email: maciejka@uni.lodz.pl

1. Introduction

The study focused on the analysis of EFP programs in Polish listed companies in order to increase knowledge on the subject and demonstrate relations between the programs applied and the socioeconomic effects of enterprises. Efforts have been made to systematise the forms of participation presented here; although, due to their multitude, occasional lack of clear dividing criteria, and their different interpretation, the results appear dissatisfactory. Nevertheless, due to the shortage of literature concerning EFP issues, this chapter attempts to fill in the gap to some extent and aims to increase interest in the above solutions. Additionally, some crucial characteristic features of the applied forms of EFP have been separated.

It may be surprising that large[2] listed companies have been chosen as objects of analysis. Some are privatised and domestic, while foreign private firms represent the rest. Therefore, one could expect some significant remains of employee ownership after the privatisation process. The intention of the author was to deal with existing large companies, regardless of their origin, and to check if they offer EFP programs. In addition, the choice was on the availability of information on listed companies.

The aim of the detailed analysis was to provide answers to the following questions:

- Does the personnel structure decide the type of employee participation program? Four groups of employees were included: managerial, white-collar, blue-collar and administrative personnel.
- What type of personnel structure exerts influence on opinions concerning the effects of participation? Predominance of one group over another group of employees yields different results according to financial effects.
- What factors (considered as barriers and facilitations) influence the percentage of employees covered by a participation program, allowing for the employee structure and the type of program? The crucial factors were: tax incentives, costs of social insurance, company culture, accountancy regulations, the level of knowledge of the program, etc.
- Does participation in profit sharing have an advantage over share ownership, especially cash based or not? It should be noted that profit-

2 It is assumed that listed companies are large companies, whose market capitalization was €200 million or more.

sharing schemes seem to have a short-time effect, whereas share ownership schemes, such as those that produce effects in the long run, supposedly have a longer lasting nature.

Due to a significant number of variables, it is reasonable to explicitly explain some. Generally, there are independent variables that have an influence on financial programs implemented in the companies, including size of the company, sector of activity and the employee structure, ownership structure, job seniority, etc. Some of the dependent variables are: share of employees covered by the program, company financial indicators (productivity), willingness for higher involvement, efficiency of work, better profits, and social benefits.

2. Theoretical background

Participation schemes based on company profits and employee share ownership are immensely popular in the European Union. In the four largest countries (France, UK, Germany, Spain), these schemes have covered around 17 million workers (19 percent of the employees from the private sector) (Pérotin & Robinson, 2002). This is due to earlier experience and traditions with blue-collar worker ownership in France and the UK, cooperatives in Spain or widespread decision-making processes in Germany as a source of EFP. The most popular financial programs are: profit sharing and share ownership in France, varieties of profit sharing in the UK and share ownership in Germany. Countries with a significant number of EFP schemes are Italy, France, Ireland, Spain and Austria; however, post-Soviet states have a less significant number (Mathieu, 2013).

It is officially acknowledged that EFP is in accordance with state policy (in the European Union in general) because it has positive influence on efficiency and employment and accelerates fulfilment of other goals of state policy, such as redistribution of wealth or broader participation in creating welfare and overcoming in-company conflicts (Pérotin & Robinson, 2002). The mechanism of a relationship may be as follows: Participation in shares or profits subliminally leads to increased willingness and involvement to better work performance, and at the same time highly contributes to the success of the parent company. Additionally, the efficiency of work increases because there is no overtime. To some extent the employees become more connected with the company, which in turn helps to achieve more profits.

It should be noted that from the national point of view only some types of EFP schemes will be preferred, mainly those which to a great extent will contribute to the achievement of macroeconomic goals. Activities promoting implementation of participatory solutions are conducted in different countries in a varied manner and with a diverse intensity; therefore, one should bear in mind that their spread in particular countries will differ. Nevertheless, there is a constant, yet undynamic growth in the number of employees taking part in EFP schemes. Research conducted by specialists in the EU and US provides us with a large amount of significant information on the nature of these schemes and their achieved results (Caramelli, 2010; Fakhfakh & Pérotin, 2000; Freeman, Blasi, Kruse, & Mackin, 2010; Frye, 2004; Gregoric & Ivanjko, 2006; Hashi, Lowitzsch, Uvalic, & Vaughan-Whitehead, 2006; Kalmi, Pendleton, & Poutsma, 2004; Lowitzsch, Hashi, & Woodward, 2009; McCartney 2004; Pendleton & Poutsma, 2004; Robinson & Wilson, 2006). In the EU there are organizations involved in EFP, such as the European Federation of Employee Share Ownership (EFES), International Association for the Economics of Participation (IAFEP) and others. Their reports and books are extremely valuable in finding new ways to implement EFP programs.

The data is obtained from, for example, surveys sent to enterprises listed on the stock exchange and to other large companies whose capital is estimated to be at least €200 million (Mathieu, 2009).

However, gaining information and finding convincing arguments and straightforward evidence about the schemes and their effectiveness is troublesome for companies that want to implement EFP schemes. The commonly shared belief is that through implementation of participatory solutions, companies want to motivate their staff to work better and more efficiently and to convince them to stay with the company. However, the evidence suggests that in companies operating employee participation schemes, work efficiency does not radically change (Pérotin & Robinson, 2002). Therefore, it can be assumed this is not a direct reason for their implementation and the schemes are simply part of a set of employee participation tools (Jirjahn, 2002; Kato, 2002; Kruse & Blasi, 1997; Long, 2002; Pendleton, 1997; Robinson & Wilson, 2001; Shields, 2002).

In turn, the analyses conducted in over 20 EU countries, comprising several thousand enterprises, shows evidence that EFP has had a positive or at least neutral impact on efficiency. The achieved results are in favour of the higher influence of participation in profit sharing on work efficiency over the influence arising from employee share ownership (Braam & Poutsma, 2010; Fakhfakh & Pérotin, 2002; Kruse & Blasi, 1997; Mathieu, 2009; Mathieu, 2010). This might be a result of the differences in conditions in which those schemes are implemented, which in turn cause trouble with measuring the absolute effects achieved in different studies in various countries.

Presently, the most prominent form of employee EFP in Poland is share ownership. The restructuring program in Poland was characterised by crucial incentives for employee participation, especially in firms privatised by leasing and those transformed into so-called employee-owned companies. The ownership structure in these companies, in general, is relatively stable and employees who do not hold executive posts maintain a small number of shares. This was caused by a lack of interest from political and trade unions. The buyout was also hindered due to a clause included in the Transformation Law as of 1996, which stated that at least 20 percent of shares of a leased company must be purchased by people who are not employed in the company. Over the last few years the matter of employee-owned companies and EFP schemes has been dealt with again, due to extension of studies and increased interest by EU institutions.

It can be said that the structure of law in Poland provides the opportunity to implement different forms of financial participation schemes, including share ownership, profit sharing and the creation of employee-owned companies through transformation processes. However, politicians have not provided incentives for development of such schemes and have not given proper support yet. The most widespread EFP schemes embrace share ownership and profit-sharing programs, although the latter is considered to be a broad-based type of scheme related to company results and in Poland is described as a 'bonus', yet it does not have a legal basis.

In comparison to other EU states, the situation in Poland does not appear optimistic and the level of employee ownership in large enterprises is substantially low, as is the dynamics of this development.

3. Research Method

The study was based on an online survey sent via e-mail. This is an ideal method due to the nature of the community analysed, the situational context and most of all the specificity of the issues examined. This method is based on respondents providing written answers. The drawback is the possibility of conducting the survey only with those who have access to the Internet. The elements for the sample were selected out of the listed companies, which had at least one out of three major financial participation programs, namely the share ownership, profit-sharing or stock-option scheme.

Respondents were provided with limited general information on who conducted the study, topic and purpose. Anonymity was guaranteed, especially if the subject was sensitive and required providing company-internal information.

It was assumed people whose answers are highly desired by the client filled in the surveys. The survey form was divided into three parts and contained 51 questions. The first part concerned information on the company, the second information on financial programs, and the third assessment of employee participation in the programs of EFP. A small number of questions were closed questions; the others were multiple-answer and multiple-choice questions.

The survey was prepared based on numerous similar surveys used by international companies and organizations to study the same problems (i.e. Slovenian and Dutch companies, CRANET data), yet their scope and analyses are broad-based. Two Slovenian surveys helped to prepare the survey for Polish companies: VPRAŠALNIK za MENEDŽERJE (the questionnaire for managerial staff) and VPRAŠALNIK za predstavnika SINDIKATA (the questionnaire for trade unions), to learn the different attitudes to EFP[3]. The general four-page 'Questionnaire for Survey complementing the CRANET data on employee financial participation' was also used to prepare questions for Polish companies. Some questions and study problems were taken from a Dutch report (Poutsma, 2006). The survey prepared for Polish companies was slightly modified to be suitable for Polish conditions. Each question had additional sub-clauses that described the precise analysed issues. The Polish survey was divided into three parts: general information about the company (activity of the company, employee structure, ownership structure, salaries, etc.), EFP programs implemented and offered in companies to different groups of employees (employee ownership plans, profit-sharing plans, stock options,

3 The author used these questionnaires with Slovenian colleague's permission.

percentage of employees covered by these programs, barriers and facilities to implement EFP programs, etc.), as well as employees opinions about EFP programs (economic results, worker cooperation, worker attitude, law regulations, etc.). The study was conducted on a sample of Polish companies listed on the Warsaw Stock Exchange. The total number of companies covered by the analysis was 645.

Companies that had at least one out of three major EFP programs, namely a share ownership, profit-sharing or stock-option scheme, were chosen for the sample. In order to single out companies with financial participation programs, the companies were contacted to identify if they had any such program.

Finally, 121 companies were chosen and sent the questionnaire via the Internet. Monitoring the return rate was difficult due to a high number of firms and frequent necessity to remind the companies to return the form. In many cases, the interviewers had to visit the company in order to help fill in the survey. The survey was primarily conducted from November 3rd 2010 to October 31st 2011, but was extended for some companies. Five interviewers collected information. Twenty-eight companies did not return their surveys. Before the start of the statistical analysis, those entities that provided incomplete data of more than 50 percent were removed from the survey. Consequently, further analyses were based on the information collected from 73 companies (response rate 60 percent). This was enough data to explore certain relationships in companies where any of the participatory programs were implemented.

4. *Preliminary Characteristics of the Results*

A statistical analysis of the collected data was conducted in several dimensions: economic perspective, structural indicators, as well as relationships between significant variables.

4.1 The company and employee structure

The first part, devoted to analysing the data, focused on the structure of companies as well as on a division of workers into four categories: the managerial personnel, the white-collar workers/specialists, the administrative/office personnel and the blue-collar workers. The described structure refers to the selected characteristics of the examined companies (Figure 1).

Figure 1. The structure of a company's main field of activity.

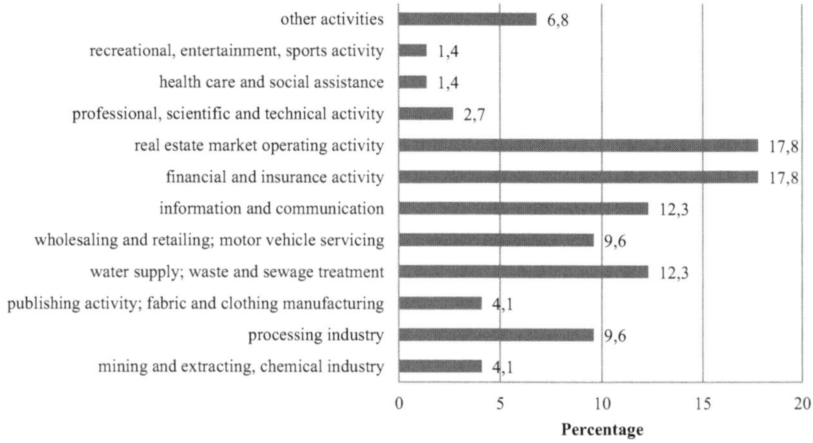

Source: Survey among Polish listed companies 2010/2011, own calculations.

Among the listed companies in which participation programs were implemented, the most popular were those operating in the field of real estate trading (17.8 percent) and in the financial and insurance sectors. Another large group included companies representing the following fields: information and communication and waste and sewage treatment (12.3 percent). There were 6.8 percent of companies whose activity could not be covered by any of the established categories. Every tenth company that took part in the survey operated in the field of wholesaling and retailing, as well as motor vehicle servicing and processing. The companies with the smallest number of representatives were those from the health care and social assistance sectors, as well as firms from the recreational, entertainment and sport industries.

The analysis of the number of employees in the companies show that the highest percentage of them employs over 250 people (35.6 percent), making them large enterprises. Companies that have between 51 and 250 employees represent 34.4 percent. The least represented were small companies employing between 10 and 50 people (30.1 percent).

The analysis of the structure of employees is also included in the study (Figure 2).

Figure 2. Employee structure in the surveyed companies (percentage) (N = 73)

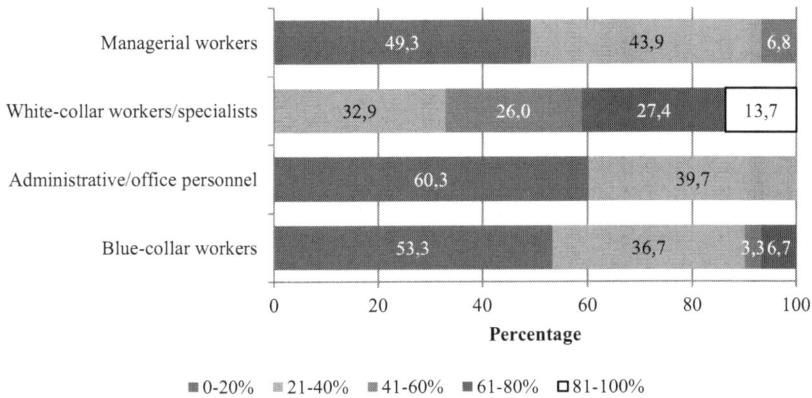

Source: Survey among Polish listed companies 2010/2011, own calculations.

According to company representatives (especially CEOs), it is clear that in every company the highest percentage is represented by white-collar workers/specialists. In every seventh company (13.7 percent), these workers represent at least 80 percent of the company, and more than two thirds (67.1 percent) claim the percentage of specialists is over 40 percent of all personnel. Sixty point three percent of respondents stated that the number of people represented by the administrative personnel in their company does not exceed 20 percent of all employed. In every second company, fewer than every fifth employee is a member of the management (less than 20 percent), and almost every fifteenth respondent (6.8 percent) declared that between 41 percent and 60 percent of all employed are members of the management (Figure 2).

Table 1 contains collective information on the major EFP programs offered to company workers.

Table 1 shows that the management is offered shares/stocks in the company (79.5 percent of firms) and stock/share options (30.1 percent). Cash-based profit sharing is offered to the management in every ninth company (11.0 percent). The white-collar workers/specialists who participate in share ownership in almost every fourth company (23.3 percent) are granted share/stock options in every eighth company (12.3 percent), and in every twelfth (8.2 percent) they participate in cash-based profit sharing. The administrative personnel may count on share/stock ownership in

Table 1. EFP programs offered to particular personnel groups (in percentage) (N=73)

Personnel group	Stock/share ownership		Cash-based profit sharing		Deferred profit sharing		Stock/share options		Pension schemes	
	yes	no	yes	no	yes	no	yes	no	yes	no
Managerial workers	79.5	20.5	11.0	89.0	0.0	100.0	30.1	69.9	0.0	100.0
White-collar workers/ specialists	23.3	76.7	8.2	91.8	0.0	100.0	12.3	87.7	0.0	100.0
Administra-tive/ office personnel	19.2	80.8	8.2	91.8	0.0	100.0	0.0	100.0	0.0	100.0
Blue-collar workers	0.0	100.0	0.0	100.0	0.0	100.0	0.0	100.0	0.0	100.0

Source: Survey among Polish listed companies 2010/2011, own calculations.

almost every fifth (19.2 percent) company, and in every twelfth (8.2 percent) for cash-based profit sharing.

No answer was received in regard to deferred profit-sharing and pension schemes. The absence of broad-based EFP programs in the surveyed companies confirms an opportunistic attitude of blue-collar employees, and that these schemes are offered to every personnel group in Poland except blue-collar workers, whereas in foreign enterprises they cover both high-level and low-level workers. It is reflected in the economic results of the companies and the relationships between the structure of employees and these results.

As is seen from the international studies, economic results are improved if the availability of programs for all employees is good (Braam & Poutsma, 2010). There are no such relationships in the analysed Polish companies. This agrees with the results of the international studies, in which only participation on the side of managerial workers had no impact on the economic results, or this influence was even negative (Braam & Poutsma, 2010).

The representatives of the companies were also asked to answer a question concerning the attitude of managerial workers to blue-collar worker[4] participation in ownership or profits of the company. In most cases, the management did not express similar views on this matter, or had

4 Blue-collar workers are employees at the lowest level of the company.

Figure 3. Declared changes in ownership structure in the analysed companies.

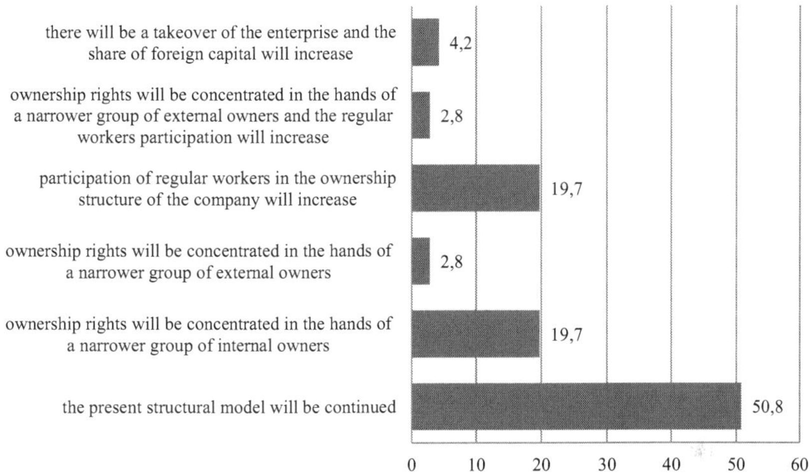

Source: Survey among Polish listed companies 2010/2011, own calculations.

negative opinions on allowing blue-collar workers to participate in EFP programs. From the analysis of the answers, it can be assumed that managerial personnel do almost nothing in order to maintain or increase blue-collar worker participation in the schemes (Pearson's C = 0.513). This would confirm almost absolute absence of blue-collar workers in these programs and limit them to other categories of employees. It is not optimistic information, bearing in mind a large percentage of blue-collar employees in companies. Such an approach may suggest that in spite of the official positive declarations, the unwillingness to share the power and profits in companies is still incredibly strong, and as a result of this, Polish companies with EFP programs have low positions among other European countries.

One of the questions asked to company representatives referred to planned changes in the ownership structure of the company that were to take place in following years (Figure 3).

Figure 3 shows that 50.8 percent of respondents will still follow the present model of the ownership structure. This may suggest that half of the companies were satisfied with the current situation. Every fifth respondent (19.7 percent) declared that the percentage of blue-collar workers in the company's structure would rise. The same percentage (19.7 percent) said that ownership would be in the hands of a narrower group of internal owners, which should be interpreted as a potential takeover of shares by a current owner. According to only 4.2 percent of respondents, there were attempts to take over the company and to increase the foreign capital. This may result in being more dependent on foreign entities or structural changes. Each of these options brings substantial alterations, which the answers imply are not desired by the companies. Only 2.8 percent of respondents stated that ownership will be in the hands of a narrower group of external owners or that ownership will be in possession of a narrower group of external owners and the percentage of blue-collar workers will be higher.

Respondents were also asked to answer a question on the influence of the increased percentage of blue-collar workers on the economic results of the companies.

The representatives of most listed companies claimed the increased percentage of blue-collar workers in the ownership structure of the company has positive influence on the economic results achieved by the company. It should be assumed that part of the answers might reflect the thoughts of respondents on EFP and not the actual situation in their company. It should be noted that in most of these companies, blue-collar workers have no share in the ownership structure, so the answer does not refer to their personal experience in the company. Moreover, it can be assumed that their knowledge on the matter is rather insufficient. Many of the questions refer to the subjective opinions of respondents. More than four fifths of respondents had the opinion that the results of the company were somewhat improving (59.8 percent) or definitely improving (20.8 percent). Among the interviewed people there were no negative answers in regard to the increased percentage of blue-collar workers in the ownership structure.

In spite of positive answers to a question concerning the relationships between the number of blue-collar workers possessing shares of the company and the economic results, in the case of an optimal ownership structure, according to respondents their share in the overall capital of the company should not be higher than 40 percent (82.2 percent). At the same time, the majority (57.5 percent) believe that in the best ownership structure, blue-collar workers ought to be in possession of less than 20 percent of shares. Twenty-four point seven percent of the interviewees declared that between 20-40 percent of the shares should be in the hands of blue-collar workers. Nobody found it optimal to have blue-collar workers owning more than 40 percent. Interestingly, 17.8 percent of company representatives were unable to clearly define an optimal share ownership structure of their company (Figure 4).

4.2. Marginal distributions of variables

This part focuses on the structure of the so-called marginal distributions of variables. They allow divisions to be made according to significant criteria and the relative frequencies of the emerging variants of an examined feature, expressed mostly as a percentage value.

Regarding the question of the method of distributing participation in profit sharing/share ownership, all entrepreneurs claimed the most important determinant is the position held, i.e. the personnel group. It depends whether it is a white-collar worker, administrative worker, office worker, low-level manager, senior manager, etc. It may be so due to the position of the people questioned, most of whom were managerial workers. Another important factor determining the method of distribution of company shares is job seniority – in the process of time one becomes more privileged. Only in over one third of the companies the level of remuneration and form of employment decides the way in which shares are distributed inside the company. In 62 percent of companies, respondents said the method of distribution does not depend on the form of employment. The level of remuneration reflects the dignity of a particular post: the higher the wages, the more profits the company gains – in this case 100 percent of respondents expressed their positive conviction. It must be noted that respondents could give more than one answer.

As commonly known, bonuses from profits or purchasing stocks of companies should reflect economic results. The question to identify the reflection of economic results was 'Does the payment from financial participation (stock or cash-based) relate to the general financial results of the firm?'

Seventy-one percent of respondents stated the money received from EFP (stock- or cash-based) is connected with general financial results of the company. However, this declaration was not later confirmed as justified in regard to the relevance of the relationships between the presence of EFP programs in companies and economic indicators. This means there is a positive relationship between these variables. It can be assumed that due

Figure 4. Distribution of stocks/shares among employees in the surveyed companies.

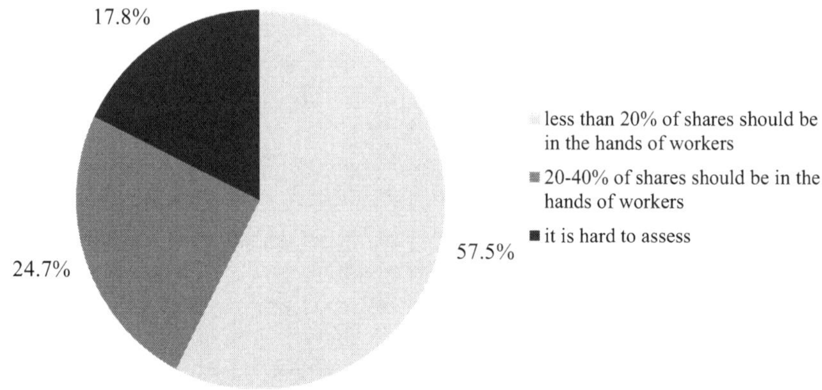

Source: Survey among Polish listed companies 2010/2011, own calculations.

to the introduced participation programs, the results of the company are improving.

According to the assumptions, EFP programs are advantageous for the company activity in which they were introduced. In the opinion of entrepreneurs motivating employees through additional financial incentives, apart from regular pay, this program is even more significant from the company's perspective, but not a person who makes use of this program. Additionally, respondents believed the national economy also benefits from EFP programs, which suggests that motivating the blue-collar worker is beneficial for all participants in the economic chain.

In turn, the company whose profits are rising is more willing to introduce and improve participation programs based on profits because it is financially possibly for it to do so and it can also allow a larger number of blue-collar employees to participate in the overall success (benefits apart from the standard remuneration are linked to a better situation of the company). Higher results make the shares more expensive; consequently, people involved in the company become richer. A result of the company becoming wealthier may be expansion focused on taking over companies whose financial situation is worse, leading to an increase in its market share. These relationships are complex and not always obvious, yet may occur.

Chairmen and directors of finance often ask themselves questions regarding whether all personnel groups should be motivated in the same way and whether blue-collar workers should be given the same rewards as managers. Considering the benefits from EFP, the answer is not obvious. It is difficult to choose incentives that would encourage better work because their impact varies in different personnel groups. This is why incentives should be differentiated. Such behaviour raises controversy and objections on the side of the employees, for example with low-level (administrative and specialist) or blue-collar workers, who feel aggrieved or underestimated in the case of different sizes of blocks of shares or the amount of a bonus. Here, respondents expressed their view that management is much more attached to the company, which results from the position held. It can be assumed that the higher the position, the stronger the attachment to the company. Decisive factors in this case are not only dependent on remuneration and prestige, but on EFP programs, which allow a higher risk for the decision-makers, which may pay off in the future. Low-level workers are less responsible for making decisions concerning the company (if they are decisive at all), which means they feel unnecessary. This is why they become less loyal to their enterprise, their attachment is weaker and they do not identify with the company as much as they should. A low salary also strengthens this attitude. In almost half of the companies, blue-collar workers do not earn more than 3,000 PLN per month, and in other companies their earnings do not exceed 2,000 PLN (author's study). Therefore, it is not surprising they do not express attachment to the company and are unwilling to cooperate.

Another question asked referred to defining factors that may influence realisation of each of three programs: share/stock ownership, share/stock options and profit sharing. The interactions have been classified as: barriers, facilitations and no effect.

For the first of the aforementioned programs, the crucial facilitations were as follows: tax incentives (79 percent of the companies), costs of social insurance (59 percent), employee interest (68 percent), owner interest (84 percent), owner decisions (62 percent) and company culture (66 percent). A serious barrier was presented by accountancy regulations (42 percent), the requirements concerning securities, as well as the level of knowledge of the program (38 percent). According to respondents, the greatest difficulty in realisation of a share ownership program was the presence of other incentive stimuli for the workers (72 percent). In the opinion of the same number of respondents, personnel structure (52 percent) and market conditions (52 percent) facilitate realisation of the program in the company. The second most popular participation scheme was a share/stock-option program. In this case, the factors that make its realisation easier include owner decisions (64 percent), company culture (59 percent), employee interest (50 percent) and tax incentives and costs of social insurance (44 percent). Regarding the factors considered as barriers to realisation of this program, the most frequently chosen are: the level of knowledge in this field (96 percent), the structure of the scheme and the accountancy regulations (both 68 percent) and program administration costs (44 percent). It appears that the structure of the program and unclear regulations are mostly the result of a lack of proper knowledge on the matter, which definitely discourages entrepreneurs from introducing these programs.

While analysing the factors that may exert influence on realisation of profit-sharing programs, despite a small percentage of respondents who declared this scheme had been or was introduced in the enterprise, the barriers are clear and visible. All respondents stated that the main factor preventing realisation of schemes is the costs of social insurance. On the other hand, in regard to factors facilitating realisation of this particular program, representatives of different companies pointed to several equal options:

- Level of interest and owner decisions,
- Company culture (perceived as a set of values that helps members of the organization understand what the attitude of the organization is, how it works, and what it considers to be important) (Kostera, 1996; Nogalski, 1998),
- International regulations,
- Company structure,
- Market conditions,
- Labour law and,
- Benefits that may be offered to workers who earn less.

Having examined the major programs and factors that have influence on their realisation in the company, in spite of the multitude of programs, a theme emerges. Determinates of barriers in the introduction of EFP schemes are the level of knowledge in the field of realisation of a particular scheme and accountancy regulations. Accountancy regulations are unclear or simply do not exist. However, there are more factors that can make realisation easier, including tax incentives, employee interest, owner reactions (interest and decisions), company culture and its ownership structure.

It must be noted that the majority of highlighted factors that facilitate realisation of a scheme are endogenic by nature. Before introduction of a program, the company should match its goals and needs and then provide the whole of personnel with proper training concerning introduction and realisation of the scheme. The aforementioned factors should be firmly considered only as declared expectations in this matter because the percentage of companies having participation schemes could have been higher if, for instance, the interest in their implementation had been more extensive or the tax incentives had been more stimulating for development of such schemes.

The analysis of the data concerning the form of stimulation and in what manner it influences the particular personnel group shows that the higher the position, the more interested workers are, not only in a financial reward, but also in having their share of ownership of the company (Figure 5a and 5b).

Figure 5a. The type of program as a stimulus for particular groups of personnel in the surveyed companies (participation in income – profit sharing) (N = 72).

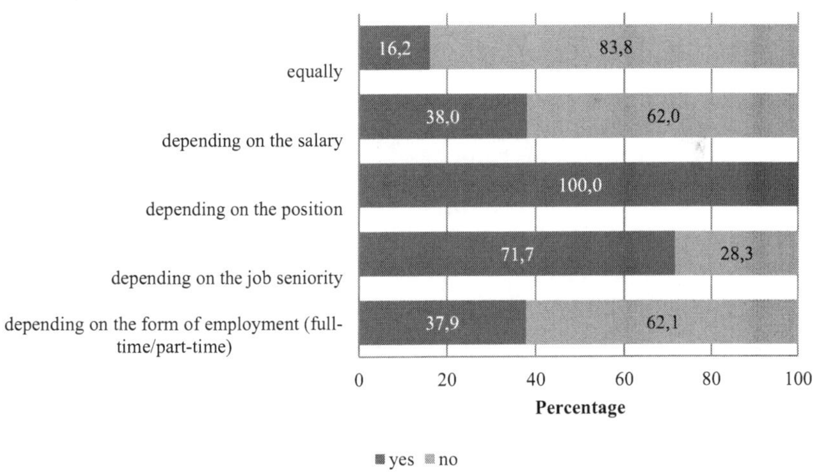

Source: Survey among Polish listed companies 2010/2011, own calculations.

Almost nine in ten representatives of management would decide on company shares, and only every fifth of them a cash reward. In regard to blue-collar workers, only 14.2 percent would choose company shares as a form of additional remuneration, in comparison to 89 percent of the examined companies, in which blue-collar workers would opt for profit sharing.

Figure 5b. The type of program as a stimulus for particular groups of personnel in the surveyed companies (participation in ownership).

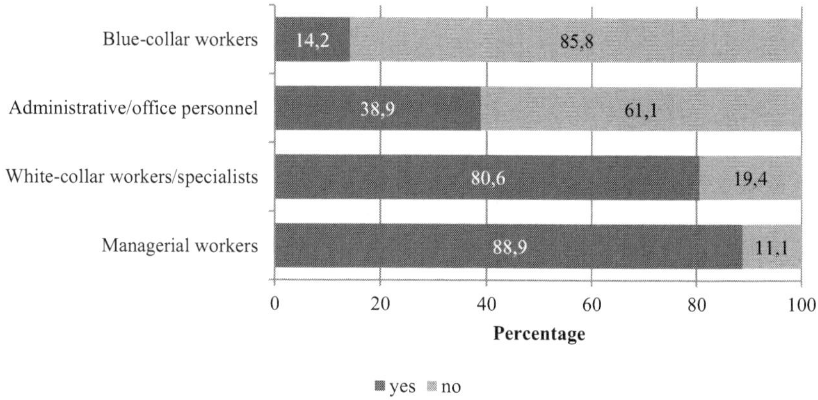

Source: Survey among Polish listed companies 2010/2011, own calculations.

This may mean that employees in Polish companies do not think ahead or see themselves as potential managers. According to the study, three-quarter of the administrative/office personnel, driven by a short-term desire to maximise their profits, expressed similar attitudes. White-collar workers, who in 70 percent of the companies were more interested in maximising their profits in the long run, had completely different attitudes.

5. *Management share in employee participation programs*

Another group of questions concerned the correlation between the percentage of managerial staff or of managerial staff and another group of personnel of Polish companies, covered by financial participation programs and, among others, such aspects as obtaining benefits, identification with the company and types of implemented programs (share ownership, profit sharing).[5]

5.1 The analysis of correlation between the selected characteristics of the companies

This part focuses on the relationships between the questions and describes in detail the level of the contingency coefficients, i.e. Pearson's C and Kramer's V, together with the accompanying levels of significance.

The analysis divides the division of enterprises into three groups. The first group includes companies in which up to 25 percent of the managerial personnel took part in participation programs. In the second group are firms in which the share of the managerial staff ranges from 25-75 percent, and the third group is represented by firms in which at least 75 percent of the management was covered by different programs.

At the beginning of the analysis it became apparent that in companies where the managerial staff was covered by an employee share ownership program, there was a directly proportional relationship between the payments resulting from using programs that contributed to achieving financial benefits for the company and the percentage of the management covered by such a scheme. Simultaneously, over 60 percent of all respondents declared that financial participation programs aimed at the managerial personnel are connected with the general results of the firm.

Investigating the relationships between the percentages of the managerial personnel covered by a scheme and their attitude toward their own company resulted in the answers in Table 2.

Table 2. Attachment of the managerial personnel to the company according to the percentage of this employee group covered by a share ownership program in percentage (N=49)

Attachment to the company	Employees covered by employee financial participation programs - Stock/ share ownership			Total
	100-75%	75-25%	25-0%	
Very high	53.1	26.5	6.1	85.7
High	0.0	0.0	14.3	14.3
Total	53.1	26.5	20.4	100.0

Source: Survey among Polish listed companies 2010/2011, own calculations.

5 All the investigated cases concern only statistically significant relationships, with a significance level $p<0.05$

A strong correlation has been observed (Kramer's V = 0.806) between the percentage of managerial personnel covered by a stock/share ownership program and their attachment to the company. Respondents taking part in the survey indicated the higher the number of managerial staff participating in a stock/share ownership program, the stronger the bonds with the company for which they work. This regularity is statistically significant. However, there were no significant relationships between the number of white-collar workers covered by the scheme and the strength of relationship between them and the company.

Another point to be analysed was the question of whether the year when participation was implemented had influenced the results, i.e. higher identification with the company, better relations among workers and increased entrepreneurship. The selected correlation is presented in Tables 3-5. A division into two periods was introduced – prior to 2004 and from 2005 to 2011.

Table 3. The influence of the time when a share ownership/profit-sharing program was implemented on the attitudes characterizing identification with the firm according to investigated companies in per cent (N=47)

Introduction of employee financial participation	Identification with the company - Stock/share ownership		Total
	Positive	No effect	
Prior to 2004	47.0	21.0	68.0
2005 to 2011	32.0	0.0	32.0
Total	79.0	21.0	100.0

Source: Survey among Polish listed companies 2010/2011, own calculations.

A detailed analysis of the results of using a share ownership program indicated a significant relationship between the scheme and the time when it was introduced in the company (Pearson's C = 0.335). In firms where the programs were introduced in 2005, all respondents expressed a positive opinion of the scheme's impact (stock/share ownership) on identifying oneself with the company. Among respondents who said that in their enterprises the programs were introduced before 2004, 47 percent shared a favourable belief in their positive influence, while others stated that implementation did not have any impact on identification with the company.

On one hand, this means the majority of programs were introduced in the first period, which does not foster optimism for the future of participation programs in Polish companies. On the other hand, programs implemented after 2004 are more effective, which might have been a result of companies being better prepared for the introduction by more efficient informative and promotional campaigns.

Table 4. The influence of the time when a share ownership/profit-sharing program was introduced on the relations between employees[6] in companies in percentage (N=47)

Introduction of employee financial participation	Relations between employees in the company - Stock/share ownership			Total
	Positive	No effect	Negative	
Prior to 2004	2.,3	23.4	23.4	68.1
2005 to 2011	19.1	12.8	0.0	31.9
Total	40.4	36.2	23.4	100.0

Source: Survey among Polish listed companies 2010/2011, own calculations.

The relations between the workers in companies, which implemented the schemes prior to 2004, are evaluated differently by various firms (Pearson's C = 0.367). The results show that 21-23.4 percent of the investigated companies mentioned the positive influence of the program, no influence or a negative impact on interpersonal relations, which means that on the basis of 23.4 percent of the firms in which the program had been introduced earlier, the scheme exerted a negative influence on relations between employees. This may stem from a disproportional distribution of the program among the employees. In firms that implemented a stock/share ownership programs after the year 2004, the situation looks completely different. In these companies, almost 20 percent of respondents indicated the positive impact of the scheme on relations between employees, while the others were of the opinion that relations did not change. This is indicative of a qualitative improvement in the functioning of the schemes, which contributes to better relations between employees.

Moreover, the programs have an impact on the way the employees think and also contribute to the adoption of more entrepreneurial attitudes. This phenomenon can be mostly observed among some of the managerial staff, though such an approach is becoming increasingly popular (Table 5).

6 Employees are all working members of an organization

Table 5. The influence of the time when a share ownership/profit-sharing scheme was introduced on entrepreneurial attitudes in the investigated companies in percentage (N=47)

Introduction of employee financial participation	Entrepreneurial attitudes and behaviours of employees - Stock/share ownership		Total
	Positive	No effect	
Prior to 2004	23.4	44.7	68.1
2005 to 2011	31.9	0.00	31.9
Total	55.3	44.7	100.0

Source: Survey among Polish listed companies 2010/2011, own calculations.

Strong, significant relationships have also been observed between the year of the scheme's introduction (stock/share ownership) and its influence on entrepreneurial attitudes and employee behaviours (Kramer's V = 0.615). Of the companies in which the scheme was introduced for the first time prior to 2004, almost 45 percent of respondents stated that it did not affect entrepreneurial attitudes and employee behaviours. If the programs were implemented in 2005 and later, all respondents (32 percent of the total number of companies) claimed there had been only positive results. Therefore, it should be stressed once again that the availability of programs should be increased because it would lead to improved results from their use. Respondents also gave favourable opinions about the influence of implementation of schemes on the growth of the company's value (Table 6).

Another effect, which has been correlated with the year of introducing a share ownership program in the enterprise, is the company's value. A moderately strong (Kramer's V = 0.558), significant relationship shows that when the program had been in operation since 2005, all respondents noticed its positive influence on the company's value. In cases where the interviewees indicated an earlier date of implementation (prior to 2004), only 28 percent of them mentioned a positive impact. The others thought introduction of a share ownership participation program did not exert any influence on the company's value. In general, about 60 percent of respondents recognised the positive influence of running an ownership scheme on the company's worth, which represents a considerable percentage of answers and gives hope that in the future these results will improve

Table 6. The influence of the time when a share ownership/profit-sharing scheme was introduced on the company's value in investigated firms in percentage (N=46)

Introduction of employee financial participation	Company's value - Stock/share ownership		Total
	Positive	No effect	
Prior to 2004	28.3	39.1	67.4
2005 to 2011	32.6	39.1	32.6
Total	60.9	39.1	100.0

Source: Survey among Polish listed companies 2010/2011, own calculations.

substantially[7]. However, it should also be noted that while it is difficult to attribute all the merits to the implemented financial schemes in companies, the representatives are aware of these relationships, which is undeniably a positive effect of the discussed process.

Considering the frequently antagonistic relations between the management and other workers (mostly blue-collar), respondents were asked a question on whether implementation of the scheme contributed to improving relations between these groups of personnel (Table 7).

Analysing the questionnaires displayed a moderately strong (Kramer's V = 0.565) relationship between the year when the program was launched and its influence on the relations between blue-collar workers and the management. Respondents from firms that started their stock/share ownership program from the year 2005 did not notice any difference between the impact of the scheme on the relations between blue-collar workers and

7 The positive influence of the programs on the company's value was also indicated by analysing the correlations between the groups of employees who have stocks/shares in the company and the opinion of the company's value within an ownership program (Kramer's V = 0.748; Pearson's C = 0.599). The conditional frequencies show that if the total workforce have 75 percent to 100 percent of stocks/shares, excluding blue-collar workers, and the management are in possession of zero percent to 25 percent of stocks/shares, stock/share ownership had a positive impact on the company's value (93 percent and 100 percent of the investigated firms, respectively). On this basis, it can be assumed that the more differentiated the participation level of employees covered by the program, the higher the percentage of the representatives who see a positive effect of the scheme in the form of increasing value of the company. Such opinions were rather rare in the cases where only the program, which may be surprising considering that their attitudes are characterised by long-term thinking and therefore aiming at the growth of the company's value in the long run, covered the management personnel.

Table 7. The influence of implementing a share ownership/profit-sharing program on the relations between workers and the management in the investigated companies in percentage (N=47)

Introduction of employee financial participation	The relations between workers and the management			Total
	Positive	No effect	Negative	
Prior to 2004	23.4	6.4	38.3	68.1
2005 to 2011	19.1	12.8	0	31.9
Total	42.5	19.2	38.3	100.0

Source: Survey among Polish listed companies 2010/2011, own calculations.

the relations between these workers and the management. These differences are noticeable in the case of firms in which the program was implemented earlier. Over half of the interviewees (56.2 percent) observed negative influence of the scheme on the relations between blue-collar employees and the management, and only one third noticed a positive impact on the relations between them. It appears that employee relations in firms which introduced the programs later seem to be more improved than in those companies where the schemes had been in operation for a longer time. This situation may be surprising because firms with greater experience in using participation programs should be characterised by a lower level of conflicts between these groups of personnel, but the study did not confirm this. Perhaps the above-mentioned promotional and educational campaign has made everyone aware that only mutual support and cooperation can contribute to the success of the program.

The analysis of the responses also showed mutual relationships between the percentage of the managerial personnel covered by a stock/share ownership program and the factors that may also affect implementation and realisation of the scheme. These factors were the level of employees' interest (Pearson's C = 0.541) and the level of owners' interest in a particular scheme (Pearson's C = 0.707). In firms where over three quarters of the management was covered by a stock/share ownership program, all respondents claimed that the interest level of both employees and owners has a significant influence on realisation of the program itself (54 percent of all the interviewees in this group of the managerial staff). Only in enterprises where less than 25 percent of the management is offered this ownership program did respondents think the level of interest on the part of owners hindered realisation of the scheme (15 percent of all respondents and 78 percent of companies in this group). Such a small percentage of managerial personnel participating in the program is a result of the low engagement of firm owners who are not interested in implementing the schemes and do not see any benefits. In the other two groups, the owners were much more interested in introduction of financial programs, possibly because the management personnel had a high or very high level of participation in these programs.

Interesting (though rather controversial) results were achieved when asking about the influence of legal regulations on realisation of ownership programs in companies. The previously mentioned lack of legislation and legal solutions regulating the preparation and implementation of financial participation programs may, on one hand, act to facilitate, or on the other hand, become a significant barrier to their realisation (Table 8).

Table 8. The legal framework as a factor affecting realization of financial programs in companies according to the percentage of managerial workers covered by share ownership programs (N=48)

Stocks/shares owned by managerial personnel (in %)	The legal framework as a factor affecting realisation of financial programs in companies according to the percentage of managerial workers covered by share ownership programs			Total
	Barrier	No effect	Facilitation	
100-75%	0	54.2	0	54.2
75-25%	0	10.4	16.7	27.1
25-0%	14.6	4.1	0	18.7
Total	14.6	68.7	16.7	100

Source: Survey among Polish listed companies 2010/2011, own calculations.

The results indicated strong and significant correlations (Pearson's C = 0.746). All respondents from firms where more than 75 percent of the management is covered by a stock/share ownership program declared that legal regulations do not affect realisation of the scheme. However, they are seen as a barrier by 77.8 percent of respondents in firms where less than 25 percent of the managerial personnel take part in the program. Over 61 percent of the interviewees representing companies in which 25-75 percent of top-level employees participate in the programs are of the opinion that the legal framework facilitates realisation of the scheme. It is difficult to completely agree with this, bearing in mind the aforementioned opinions on the need to devise suitable regulations which will clearly set out rules for the creation and implementation of financial participation programs and the resulting tax and insurance obligations. It is probable that companies with a low level of managerial personnel participating in these schemes encounter the largest number of unfavourable circumstances, which prevent them from developing the program. This does not have to be a legal framework. A high percentage of the management taking part in the programs may also stem from the dominant position of these employees in the personnel structure of the examined companies and the additional income from participation, which allows them to 'ignore' other factors limiting implementation of schemes while obtaining considerable benefits.

5.2 Other barriers and facilitations affecting EFP realization

The aim of the detailed analysis was to provide answers to, among others, the following questions:

- What type of personnel structure exerts influence on opinions concerning the effects of participation?
- What factors (considered as barriers and facilitations) influence the percentage of employees covered by a participation program, allowing for the employee structure and the type of program?

The analysis showed significant correlations between the percentage of the management in the company covered by a stock/share ownership program and other factors, which may affect its realisation. Therefore, it is advisable to list the most crucial of them:

- Regulations concerning accountancy (Pearson's C = 0.615). Over 61 percent of respondents representing companies in which 25-75 percent of the management is covered by the program think that accounting regulations facilitate realisation of the scheme. For more than three quarters of the interviewees in companies where less than 25 percent of the management is able to participate in the scheme and for over 46 percent of respondents from firms where more than 75 percent of the management is covered by the scheme they represent a barrier.
- Administration/bureaucracy (Pearson's C = 0.746). All respondents from firms in which over 75 percent of managerial staff take part in a share ownership program believe that this factor does not have any influence on realisation of the program. Administration/bureaucracy is

seen as an obstacle by 77.8 percent of respondents from firms where less than 25 percent of managerial personnel were covered by the scheme and over 60.0 percent of respondents representing companies in which 25 - 75 percent of top-level employees are offered the scheme say this factor makes introduction of the program easier.

- The level of knowledge about the programs (Pearson's C = 0.362). This aspect was not mentioned as facilitating realisation of the program. Four in ten interviewees think of this factor as a barrier to realisation of the scheme (40.0 percent), while the highest percentage was observed in firms in which less than 25 percent of the management is covered by the scheme (77.8 percent). At the same time, as many as 35.0 percent of companies in which 75-100 percent of the management take part in financial participation programs say the level of knowledge does not exert any influence on implementation and realisation of the program. This may be a group of companies in which the management has sufficient knowledge allowing them to administer these schemes, yet a large number of representatives think the opposite. It seems this opinion is crucial if one wants to adequately prepare the company for introduction of the program and achieve the necessary level of knowledge.
- The level of political support/interest from the government (Pearson's C = 0.578). Only respondents from companies with the highest percentage of management covered by the program consider this factor as a barrier to its realisation (35 percent), while almost two thirds of this group believe that it does not have any influence on introduction of the scheme. It can be assumed that the first group (75 - 100 percent) perceives the level of political interest as too low, and as such, treats this factor as a barrier hindering implementation of schemes.
- Corporate culture (Pearson's C = 0.597). Considering the impact of corporate culture on realisation of the program, the opinions vary. Although 68.8 percent of all the interviewees treat this factor as a form of facilitation, 61.5 percent of the companies' representatives, in which 25-75 percent of the management are covered by the program, believe that corporate culture is an obstacle to fulfilling the scheme. This factor is frequently mentioned by authors who work on, among other things, the conditions of implementing participation solutions as one of the major determinants facilitating or inhibiting fulfilment of programs.
- International regulations (Kramer's V = 0.734). According to the survey, these are not thought of as obstacles to realizing the program

and do not affect its implementation. This was more than expected because the vast majority of companies are domestic firms, functioning under national legal regulations. It can be supposed that international regulations are regarded as recommendations which can only be taken into account when introducing participation solutions and which, so far at least, have not been treated as mandatory regulations. Nevertheless, it is necessary to standardise the legislation governing financial participation programs.

- The company structure (Pearson's C = 0.536). More than half of respondents (54.2 percent) believe that a proper company structure may facilitate realisation of a stock/share ownership program, while other interviewees do not see the influence of company structure on implementation of the program (45.8 percent). However, it is possible to notice regularity – the higher the number of managerial personnel taking part in the schemes, the more of them perceived the structure of the company as a facilitating factor in realisation of the program. This may also be connected with personnel structure in the examined companies.
- Market conditions (Pearson's C = 0.536). Among firms with the highest percentage of management covered by the scheme, over 80 percent declared that market conditions make realisation of an ownership scheme easier. Consequently, once again there is a clear correlation – the more managerial personnel covered by the scheme, the higher the number of those who express a favourable opinion of the influence of market conditions on fulfilling the program.

Table 9 shows the relations between employees and the percentage of different personnel groups covered by an ownership program.

A strong correlation (Kramer's V = 0.783; Pearson's C = 0.742) occurred between employees who have stocks/shares in the company and the opinions on the relationships between employees in the company as a result of using a financial program. The conditional frequencies show that those groups in which management personnel have 75-100 percent and 25-75 percent of stocks/shares believe that stock/share ownership negatively affects relations between employees (83.3 percent and 9.1 percent of the companies in each group, respectively). This indicates the following type of correlation: The more varied the personnel structure covered by the scheme, the more visible influence this type of scheme has on interpersonal relations. However, it is quite astounding that there is a very high

Table 9. Opinion on the relation between employees in the company in comparison to the percentage of different personnel groups covered by an ownership program (N=48)

Personnel group	The relations between employees			Total
	Positive	No effect	Negative	
Only managerial personnel 75-100%	4.1	0.0	20.9	25.0
All personnel (except blue-collar) – 75-100%	27.1	2.1	0.0	29.2
Only managerial personnel 25-75%	6.2	14.6	2.1	22.9
Only managerial personnel 0-25%	2.1	16.7	0.0	18.8
Managerial personnel and white-collar workers	0.0	4.1	0.0	4.1
Total	39.5	37.5	23.0	100.0

Source: Survey among Polish listed companies 2010/2011, own calculations.

percentage of responses reporting the negative impact of programs on the relations between employees in the group of companies where 75-100 percent of the management was covered by the program. Apparently, the view of managerial personnel by other employee groups as a privileged group exclusively benefiting from introduction of the scheme exerts a negative influence on general relations and attitudes in the enterprise.

Summarising the results of this part leads to some observations about the influence of particular factors on implementation of financial participation programs in Polish companies. Considering the division of firms into groups with a defined percentage of the management covered by participation programs, a significant discrepancy is evident in the answers obtained; therefore, the results are not fully satisfactory and require additional questions in order to justify the choices made.

5.3 Benefits from EFP

In spite of not always positive interpersonal relations, ownership programs were shown to be beneficial in their influence on identification with the company, increased involvement, job satisfaction or a higher sense of security (Table 10).

Table 10. Opinions on the selected job aspects in the company in comparison to the percentage of different personnel groups covered by an ownership program in percentage (N=48)

Stocks/shares owned by:	Identification with the organization through internal involvement, direct participation, job satisfaction and security - Stock/Share ownership		Total
	Positive	No effect	
Only managerial personnel - 75-100%	20.8	4.2	25.0
All personnel (except blue-collar) - 75-100%	16.7	12.5	29.2
Only managerial personnel - 25-75%	4.2	18.7	22.9
Only managerial personnel - 0-25%	12.5	6.2	18.7
Managerial personnel and white-collar workers - 0-25%	0.0	4.2	4.2
Total	54.2	45.8	100.0

Source: Survey among Polish listed companies 2010/2011, own calculations.

There was a moderate correlation (Kramer's V = 0.517; Pearson's C = 0.459) between employees who have stocks/shares in the company and an opinion on one's own identification with the organization through increased inner involvement, direct participation, job satisfaction and a sense of security as part of a stock/share ownership program. The conditional frequencies indicate that respondents from the majority of companies in which the management has 25-75 percent of stocks/shares, and all the representatives in companies where managerial personnel and other workers have 0 percent to 25 percent of stocks/shares, think that having stocks/shares does not affect broadly defined identification and job satisfaction. Lower participation of the management in these groups probably had most impact on the distribution of answers, which may also mean that employees in many companies do not perceive such benefits. This could also be a result of insufficient preparation by firms when introducing participation programs, lack of information, the year of implementation etc. It is not possible to grasp all the relationships and reasons why such answers were given. The percentage of company representatives, who do not see any benefits (45.8 percent), is very high, which also is confirmed by the international study (Braam & Poutsma, 2010). A summary of the considerations on different aspects of efficient EFP programs can be made on the basis of an analysis of the answers displayed in Tables 11 and 12.

Table 11. Considering participation as a form of potential benefits for the national economy in comparison to the percentage of different personnel groups covered by a financial participation program in percentage (N=42)

Stocks/shares owned by:	Do you find financial participation beneficial for the national economy?		Total
	Yes	No	
Only managerial personnel - 75-100%	28.6	0.0	28.6
All personnel (except blue-collar) - 75-100%	14.3	0.0	14.3
Only managerial personnel - 25-75%	23.8	7.1	30.9
Only managerial personnel - 0-25%	7.1	14.3	21.4
Managerial personnel and white-collar workers - 0-25%	4.8	0.0	4.8
Total	78.6	21.4	100.0

Source: Survey among Polish listed companies 2010/2011, own calculations.

There is a strong correlation (Kramer's V = 0.773; Pearson's C = 0.530) between employees who have company stocks/shares and an opinion whether financial participation programs are beneficial to the national economy. The conditional frequencies show that over 78 percent of all respondents believe that these schemes exert a positive influence on the national economy, whereas, when management have 0-25 percent and 25-75 percent of stocks/shares there are negative opinions about the influence of participation programs on the national economy (14.3 percent and 7.1 percent of the surveyed people, respectively). These two groups stand for 21 percent of respondents who can see some dangers, which stem from introduction of the schemes. Those point of view are difficult to explain, but perhaps respondents take into consideration high expenditures on implementing such programs. However, this aspect requires the use of more profound focus on group interviews. Analysing the influence of financial participation programs in a microeconomic scope, i.e. especially on employees and companies using these programs, is rather positive (Table 12).

Table 12. Considering participation as a form of potential benefits for the members of particular organizations and institutions in comparison to the percentage of different personnel groups covered by an ownership program in percentage (N=39)

Stocks/shares owned by:	Do you find financial participation beneficial for the members of particular organisations and institutions?		Total
	Yes	No	
Only managerial personnel - 75-100%	0.0	5.1	5.1
All personnel (except blue-collar) - 75-100%	33.3	2.6	35.9
Only managerial personnel - 25-75%	18.0	12.8	30.8
Only managerial personnel - 0-25%	15.4	7.7	23.1
Managerial personnel and white-collar workers - 0-25%	5.1	0.0	5.1
Total	71.8	28.2	100.0

Source: Survey among Polish listed companies 2010/2011, own calculations.

A weaker correlation than in the case of the influence of participation on the economy exists for members of the organization (Kramer's V = 0.510). However, almost 72 percent of the interviewees confirm this positive relationship. It is mostly emphasized by companies in which everyone – except blue-collar workers - participates in the programs and have 75-100 percent of stocks/shares. As was mentioned earlier, this group seems to provide a good reflection of various opinions collected in the survey because of its diversity of employees, which, of course, does not mean that the views of representatives from other groups of companies should not be taken into account. Nevertheless, as many as 28 percent noted negative consequences of implementation of the program. It should be assumed that they stem from some of the aforementioned reasons, namely: insufficient preparations for realisation of the scheme, maybe even applying the wrong participation solution to a specific type of company, lack of information etc., which leads to organisational chaos (something that was also pointed out by respondents), a low level of involvement and absence of entrepreneurial attitudes resulting in weak economic benefits which are maybe too eagerly awaited after implementing the program in the firm. This can cause frustration and unjustified claims and lead to worsening relations between different groups of personnel.

However, it can be said for sure that the results, to a large extent, match the studies conducted in other EU countries and the US (Braam & Poutsma, 2010; Kruse, Freeman, & Blasi, 2010). Yet it ought to be stressed that it is necessary to draw appropriate conclusions allowing the preparation of a suitable political strategy, which will encourage different entities to apply participation solutions, including both specifically for individual companies and broadly defined conditions governing implementation of these solutions, relying on the experience of foreign countries. A significant role should be played by entrepreneurs convinced there is a need for implementation of such programs, which at the same time, must be connected with their belief in obtaining measurable benefits on these grounds. However, this requires changes in the way of thinking, among others, in the area of industrial relations and making necessary revaluations.

This is not an easy task due to, among other factors, a decrease in the number of companies with employee ownership as a proportion of the general number of privatised enterprises; it is not yet known whether a governmental support program of October 20th 2009 has changed anything. Such a point of view is based on several observations, i.e. the absence of legal solutions promoting the creation and functioning of employee-owned companies (it also, or maybe even mostly, concerns transnational companies), which can implement financial participation solutions, lack of support from the government, an indifferent attitude toward new challenges in the economy, worldwide tendencies in ownership changes, an absence of comprehensive solutions supporting the capital participation of employees in their own enterprises, the absence of more detailed information on the functioning of employee-owned companies in other countries, subsequent unwillingness to popularise this form of ownership and to introduce participation solutions though, of course, applying financial participation programs does not have to lead to setting up an employee-owned company.

However, it can be said that Polish company blue-collar workers would be interested in share ownership in their firms, yet the lack of longer tradition and not very favourable experience in the last few years do not guarantee the quick development of employee share ownership in Poland. This might stem from a too remote perspective on gaining profits for most employees, whereas the responsibility appears at the very beginning of introducing particular forms of participation programs, and from a too large discrepancy between the shareholders' goals in the enterprise.

6. Conclusions

Having conducted the analysis of factors that may exert an influence on realisation of particular programs, now the effects of introduction of all participation solutions is presented. The impact of the programs on the results varies from positive, negative and neutral. Considering the ownership of stocks/shares, the programs exert a positive influence on profitability and the opportunity to show the company's appreciation to workers (both 96 percent), work motivation and satisfaction (both 92 percent) and identification of oneself with the company (75 percent)[8]. On the other hand, in the opinion of respondents, the factors that may be influenced negatively by the program include relationships between workers and management (43 percent) and the workers themselves (24 percent). In regard to profit sharing, respondents had identical views.

The programs had a positive influence on most of the factors listed in the survey. There were no negative results given of implementing the scheme. Stock/share options is a program that has positive impacts on such attitudes as identifying oneself with the company, the opportunity to show that the company appreciates its workers, the value of the enterprise (100 percent), profitability, acquiring suitable employees, work motivation, enterprising attitudes and behaviour of the employees, identification with the organisation, direct participation, satisfaction with work and safety (95 percent)[9]. Other effects were also positive. From the point of view of interpersonal relations, the crucial problem resulting from introduction of the scheme seems to be a fear that relationships between workers themselves, and workers and management, may worsen. These social internal relations within the company should be taken into account when introducing the schemes and deciding on the benefits depending on the position held.

Having examined the major programs and factors that influence their realisation in the company, in spite of the multitude of programs, one theme emerges. Determinates of barriers in the introduction of EFP schemes are the level of knowledge in realisation of a particular scheme,

8 It is also indicated by Festing, Groening, Kabst, & Weber (1999) and Blasi, Kruse, & Bernstein (2003).

9 The direct, indirect and total effects that a variable has on other variables in the system were also determined by Bakan, Suseno, Pinnington, & Money (2004) and Braam & Poutsma (2010).

accountancy regulations or lack of tax incentives (Postlethwaite, 2004; Poutsma, 2001; Bulcke, 2000; Pérotin & Robinson, 2002). Accountancy regulations are unclear or simply do not exist. However, there are factors that can make realisation easier, including tax incentives, employee interest, owner reactions (interest and decisions), company culture and its ownership structure.

It must be noted that the majority of highlighted factors that facilitate realisation of a scheme are endogenic by nature. Before introduction of a program, the company should make the right choice in order to match its goals and needs and then provide all personnel with proper training concerning introduction and realisation of the scheme (European Economic and Social Committee, 2010). The aforementioned factors should be firmly considered only as declared expectations in this matter because the percentage of companies with participation schemes could have been higher if, for instance, the interest in their implementation had been more extensive or the tax incentives had been more stimulating for development of such schemes.

A result of analysis of the structure is the conclusion that EFP programs generally have a positive influence on the functioning of the enterprise. However, the effects are more social than economic. More rigorous statistical analysis carried out by the author did not yield satisfactory results. There are questions that need to be answered, for example: Why do so few companies operate EFP programs and why are they not broad-based?

Considering the statistical compilation of materials, it must be noted that the sample including 73 companies is too small to provide plausible statistical results. These results could be a generalization of the statistical measurement values achieved on this basis with regard to the population of enterprises in Poland that have introduced any form of EFP program. Regarding statistical values, one should consider structural indicators and contingency coefficients.

The purpose of this chapter was to present selected views on attitudes toward relationships between employee participation and company results. After many years of conducting empirical studies on the benefits from implementation of EFP plans, the information provided almost only by reports is insufficient to make a uniform decision concerning influence on the results (productivity) achieved by companies[10]. Acquiring the aforementioned opinion is additionally hindered by the lack of clear-cut data and to what extent the implemented participation schemes contribute to the change of financial results.

Previous theory and studies do not convincingly explain the relationship between EFP schemes and results achieved owing to their implementation, which only proves there is a need for further study in this field. In this case, an empirical approach should concentrate on qualitative and not quantitative research, which although broad-based, does not precisely identify the aforementioned relationships. Another conclusion that can be drawn is the necessity to conduct further study based on larger samples of companies, taking their business specificity and environment into account. Other aspects should also be taken into consideration, such as the type of introduced EFP schemes, because this decision may influence future results. Research should be started well before introduction of a scheme, as this would allow further comparisons and evaluation of the influence of a given scheme on productivity.

10 Most studies show positive effects of implementation of participation ownership solutions, as well as employee profit-sharing schemes. An example might be the analyses conducted by Kaarsemaker (2006), in which he showed that among 70 papers he studied, in 48 of them there is evidence of positive influence of schemes based on employee participation in ownership on economic results of companies, but only in 6 the issue of negative relationships (Kaarsemaker, 2006). Similar conclusions drawn by different authors dealing with this topic, especially solutions based on employee ownership, can be found, e.g. in a summarizing work by Kruse & Blasi (1997). These researchers claim there is no automatic or direct relationship between employee ownership and economic indicators (e.g. productivity). A great number of studies point to better or the same results achieved after introduction of participational solutions. However, only sporadically can there be found any information in the literature presenting negative relationships between employee participation in financial schemes and economic results (Kruse & Blasi, 1997).

References

Bakan, I., Suseno, Y., Pinnington, A., & Money, A. (2004). The influence of financial participation and participation in decision-making on employee job attitudes (pp. 587-616). *International Journal of Human Resource Management*, no. 15, 3 May.

Blasi, J.R., Kruse, D.L., & Bernstein, A. (2003). *In the Company of Owners*. New York: Basic Books.

Braam, G., & Poutsma, E. (2010). The Influence of Financial Participation on Company Performance. Evidence from a Dutch Longitudinal Panel. Institute for Management Research. Nijmegen School of Management. *Paper for the 15th World Congress of the International Association for the Economics of Participation (IAFEP)* (pp. 15-22). Université Panthéon-Assas, Paris II. 8 – 10 July.

Bulcke van den F. (2000). *A company perspective on financial participation in the European Union, Objectives and obstacles*. European Commission, Employment and Social Affairs, Series: Industrial Relations and Industrial Change.

Caramelli, M. (2010) *Employee Ownership and Corporate Performance: Towards Unlocking The Black Box*. Paper for the 15th World Congress of the International Association for the Economics of Participation (IAFEP). Université Panthéon-Assas, Paris II, 8 – 10 July.

European Economic and Social Committee (2010). SOC/371, *Employee financial participation in Europe* (pp. 3-4). A. Graf von Schwerin (rap.). Draft Opinion of the Section for Employment, Social Affairs and Citizenship on Employee financial participation in Europe (Own-initiative opinion). Brussels, 2 September.

Fakhfakh, F., & Pérotin, V. (2000). The effects of profit-sharing schemes on enterprise performance in France. *Economic Analysis*, *3*(2).

Fakhfakh, F., & Pérotin, V. (2002). France: Weitzman under State Paternalism? In M. Brown & J. S. Heywood (Eds.). *Paying for Performance. An International Comparison* (pp. 90-114). Armonk, NY: M.E. Sharpe.

Festing, M., Groening, Y., Kabst, R., & Weber, W. (1999). *Financial participation in Europe – Determinants and outcomes* (pp. 295-329). Economic and Industrial Democracy, 20(2).

Freeman, R.B., Blasi, J.R., Kruse, D.L., & Mackin, C. (2010). Creating a Bigger Pie? The Effects of Employee Ownership, Profit Sharing, and Stock Options on Workplace Performance. In D.L. Kruse, R.B. Freeman, J.R. Blasi (Eds.). *Shared Capitalism at Work.* Chicago: University of Chicago Press.

Frye, M.B. (2004). Equity-Based Compensation for Employees: Firm Performance and Determinants. *Journal of Financial Research*, *27*(1).

Gregoric, A. & Ivanjko, S. (2006). *Extended Country Report, Financial Participation of Employees in Slovenia*. Split/Berlin: Inter-University Centre.

Hashi, I., Lowitzsch, J., Uvalić, M., Vaughan-Whitehead, D. (2006). *Employee Financial Participation in the New EU Members and Candidate Countries: An Overview of the Developments in Legal and Economic Fields*. 13th Conference of the International Association for the Economics of Participation (IAFEP). Mondragon, July 13-15.

Jirjahn, U. (2002). The German experience with performance pay. In M. Brown & J.S. Heywood (Eds.). *Paying for Performance. An International Comparison.* Armonk NY: M.E. Sharpe.

Kaarsemaker, E. (2006). *Employee Ownership and Human Resource Management: a Theoretical and Empirical Treatise with a Digression on the Dutch Context* (p. 44). Ph.D. Dissertation. Nijmegen: Radboud University.

Kalmi, P., Pendleton, A., & Poutsma, E. (2004). *The Relationship between Financial Participation and Other Forms of Employee Participation: New Survey Evidence from Europe.* Helsinki School of Economics and HECER. Discussion Paper No. 3, April.

Kato, T. (2002). Financial participation and pay for performance in Japan. In M. Brown & J. S. Heywood (Eds.). *Paying for Performance. An International Comparison.* Armonk NY: M.E. Sharpe.

Kostera, M. (1996). *Postmodernism in management* (p. 56). Warsaw: Polish Economic Publishing House (PWE).

Kruse, D.L., & Blasi, J.R. (1997). Employee ownership, employee attitudes and firm performance: A review of the evidence (p. 143). In D. Lewin, D. J. B. Mitchell & M. A. Zaidi (Eds.). *The Human Resource Management Handbook*, Part 1. Greenwich, CT, USA: JAI Press.

Kruse, D.L., Freeman, R.B., & Blasi, J.R. (Eds.) (2010). *Shared Capitalism at Work.* Chicago: University of Chicago Press.

Long, R. J. (2002). Performance pay in Canada. In M. Brown & J. S. Heywood (Eds.). *Paying for Performance. An International Comparison.* Armonk NY: M.E. Sharpe.

Lowitzsch, J., Hashi, I., & Woodward, R. (2009). *The PEPPER IV Report: Benchmarking of Employee Participation in Profits and Enterprise Results in the Member and Candidate Countries of the European Union.* Berlin: Inter-University Centre Berlin/Split, Institute for Eastern European Studies, Free University of Berlin. October.

Mathieu, M. (2009). *Annual Economic Survey of Employee Ownership in European Countries 2008* (pp. 9-37). Brussels, May: European Federation of Employee Share Ownership.

Mathieu, M. (2010). *Annual Economic Survey of Employee Ownership in European Countries* (pp. 6-10). Brussels: European Federation of Employee Share Ownership.

Mathieu, M. (2013). *Annual Economic Survey of Employee Ownership in European Countries 2012* (pp. 34-41). Brussels: European Federation of Employee Share Ownership.

McCartney, J. (2004). *Financial participation in the EU: Indicators for benchmarking.* Luxembourg: European Foundation for the Improvement of Living and Working Conditions. Office for Official Publications of the European Communities.

Nogalski, B. (1998). *Organizational culture. A spirit of organization* (p. 105). Bydgoszcz: The Publishing House of the Organizational Advancement Center.

Pendleton, A. (1997). Characteristics of workplaces with financial participation: Evidence from the Workplace Industrial Relations Survey (pp. 103-119). *Industrial Relations Journal, (28)*2.

Pendleton, A., Poutsma, E. (2004). *Financial participation: The role of governments and social partners*. Luxembourg: Office for Official Publications of the European Communities.

Pérotin, V., & Robinson, A. (2002). *Employee Participation in Profit and Ownership: A Review of the Issues and Evidence* (pp. 2-3, 22-27). Leeds: Leeds University Business School, Maurice Keyworth Building.

Postlethwaite, R. (2004). *Financial participation for small and medium-sized enterprises: Barriers and potential solutions.* Dublin: European Foundation for the Improvement of Living and Working Conditions.

Poutsma, E. (2001). *Recent trends in employee financial participation in the European Union* (pp. 57-58). Luxembourg: European Foundation for the Improvement of Living and Working Conditions. Office for Official Publications of the European Communities.

Poutsma, E. (ed.) (2006). Changing patterns of employee financial participation in Europe. A survey among listed firms in Six European Member States. Final Report (pp. 1-40). Nijmegen: School of Management, January.

Robinson, A., & Wilson, N. (2001). *Employee participation, ownership and productivity: An empirical re-appraisal.* Leeds: Leeds University Business School, Mimeo.

Robinson, A.M., & Wilson, N. (2006). Employee financial participation and productivity: an empirical reappraisal. *British Journal of Industrial Relations*, *44*(1).

Shields, J. (2002). Performance related pay in Australia. In M. Brown & J. S. Heywood (Eds.). *Paying for Performance. An International Comparison.* Armonk NY: M.E. Sharpe.

Employee financial participation in Bulgaria

Spartak Keremidchiev[1]

Abstract

The development and initial spread of Employee Financial Participation (EFP) schemes in Bulgaria has been influenced by both the historical commitment to a strong cooperative movement and the specific circumstances accompanying the transition of the country to a market economy. To understand the evolution of EFP in Bulgaria a path dependency approach needs to be applied.

The goal of this chapter is to outline and disseminate the Bulgarian experience and learned lessons that arise from the development of various EFP tools and schemes. To this end, the chapter provides systemic overview of historical roots of EFP starting from the cooperative movement, then analyses the attempt to impose employee self-governance schemes in the late 80's of the 20th century. Chronologically, the following part of the chapter is devoted to the experience of application of Management and Employee Buyout (MEBO) schemes within the privatisation process of state owned enterprises in the late 90's of the 20th century. Current tools of EFP and their dissemination in the already dominant private sector of the Bulgarian economy are also taken into account. Mainly EFP in Bulgaria is envisaged as hands-on tool for keeping the motivation high and attracting well-qualified experts in the business. The last part of the chapter deals with the main findings and policy recommendations to facilitate application of EFP schemes in Bulgaria.

1. Background

The development of the Employee Financial Participation (EFP) in Bulgaria is ruled by historical trends coming from the cooperative move-

1 Spartak Keremidchiev: Economic Research Institute, Bulgarian Academy of Sciences, spartak@club2000.org

ment and socialist experiment with the collective ownership, as well as by the characteristics of transition to market economy, such as privatisation, establishment of private property regime and accession to the EU.

The working class in Bulgaria was considered to be the vanguard of the society during the socialist regime. In the Bulgarian case, in particular, this meant full employment policy, high guarantees against dismissals, and higher economic standard than the existing economic capacity. Workers with basic or lower level of education and qualification, in many cases, received higher wages than intermediate and senior managers of the enterprises. This system led to poor personnel motivation, low productivity and quality of goods and services. At the end of the socialism period it was obvious that the existing system needed to be changed.

Loss of power and social status of employees and workers, which started during the transition, indisputably implied a change of property. This process was impeded until 1997 by struggles for keeping the existing social privileges of the personnel. Schemes for preference employees and management participation in privatisation process were proposed as a way out of this situation. A scheme for mass privatisation which allowed all interested parties to participate in sharing the socialist property was developed. By this action it was predetermined that the main form of employee participation at that time will be ownership.

Other determining factors of EFP were the private sector and the relationship between principal-agent and personnel. The emerging private sector in the country led to high entrepreneurial risk because of the extremely unstable institutional and financial framework. This risk presumed high profits as well as quick bankrupt. Naturally, it was expected that high profits will be gained fully by the investors of capital. The problem with sharing this profit emerged later when private sector began to stabilise and human capital became a major factor for company success. Another way to develop the participation schemes were foreign investors who came to Bulgaria with a know-how that they applied. Bulgarian entrepreneurs learned from that know-how as well.

The Bulgarian accession to the European Union and the adoption of *acquis communautaire*, including requirements for employee participation[2], also encouraged the development and application of EFP schemes.

2 Following implementation of Directive 94/45/EC of 22 September 1994 on the establishment of a European Works Council or a procedure in Community-scale undertakings and Community-scale groups of undertakings for the purposes of

2. Historical determinants of EFP

2.1 Cooperative movement

The first cooperative society that set the basis for cooperative movement in Bulgaria was established in 1890 (Palazov, 1946). As precursors of cooperative forms on the territory of the present Republic of Bulgaria can be listed:

- The office for popular use, established by Midhat pasha in Danube and Edirne districts (Vilayets) in the period of Ottoman servitude;
- Associations, such as 'Anonymous Commercial Company Future', established in 1871 in Gabrovo, 'Happiness' – in 1876 in Gabrovo, Bulgarian Printing Company 'Providence' established in 1870 in Constantinople (present Istanbul), as well as other temporary associations that applied the Schulze-Delitsch principles for the popular offices.

After the Liberation of the country in 1879 the emphasis originally was put on studying and distributing foreign experience among business and administration. A strong catalyst for cooperative society's establishment was the Bulgarian Agriculture Bank, which started a more systematic educational work with the Bulgarian farmers in 1897. As a result, 147 cooperative societies with 11,224 members were registered in Bulgaria in 1906 (Palazov, 1946).

The second incentive for the development of cooperative movement was the adoption of the first Cooperative Law in 1907 and the establishment of the 'Central Union of Bulgarian Agriculture Cooperative Societies' during the same year. Following this tendency, the number of cooperative societies quickly increased to 604 at the beginning of 1909, of which 559 were credit cooperative societies (Palazov, 1946).

---

informing and consulting employees; Directive 2001/86/EC of 8 October 2001 supplementing the Statute for a European company with regard to the involvement of employees; Directive 2002/14/EC of the European Parliament and of the Council of 11 March 2002 establishing a general framework for informing and consulting employees in the European Community; Directive 2003/72/EC of 22 July 2003 supplementing the Statute for a European Cooperative Society with regard to the involvement of employees.

Passing different periods of cooperative development, the Bulgarian cooperatives counted 4114 in 1944, with 1,614,117 individual members (total population of the country – 7 million)[3] and 11,398 collective members (Palazov, 1946).

Popularity and scale of the cooperative organisation were so significant during that period that some liberal economists think that the cooperative movement had acquired a status of official state ideology and encouraged a mindset that had prevented liberal economic ideology development, thus becoming a precursor of socialism (Avramov, 2001). The words of St. Bochev, namely that while in other countries cooperative movement is considered as corrective to capitalism, in Bulgaria it was accepted as its alternative, are emblematic (Bochev, 1998).

During the socialism, the attitude towards cooperatives was not single-sided. According to the official ideology, cooperatives were considered a supplementary form to socialist property. Agriculture was an exception where cooperatives were used for forced integration of individual farmers by the accomplished forced land collectivisation (without nationalisation) during the 1950s.

Later, with abolishing of the ground rent, the 'voluntary' renouncing of stake payments, with the destruction of the cooperative democracy and imposing management staff from the nomenclature, the introduction of centralised system of planning and purchasing agriculture production, the agriculture cooperatives were depersonalized and practically functioned as typical state enterprises.

The other types of cooperative organisations working in the industry and crafts suffered similar faith. Their property was considered as socialist one, and those which continued to function were pushed into low-profit and were insignificant to the national economy production and activities.

2.2 Introducing workers' self-management during the socialism

Until the start of the democratic changes in the country in November 1989, the traditional economic paradigm on which the concept of planned economy was created was the so-called 'public property'. A thesis of

3 It has to be taken into account that one citizen could participate in several cooperatives.

'common public property' was born, according to which the cooperative and insignificant private property existing at that time should be transformed. With these formulations the opportunity to establish any forms of employee participation in the property was eliminated, because the 'public property' by default should belong equally to all citizens of the country. The role of the owner at that time was played by the state and party apparatus, while the personnel (i.e. the 'working people') were isolated from participation in property.

There were certain conditions for employee participation in the distribution of the economic results of the enterprises and in its management. From 1970 until 1986 the employee participation in the management was formal participation of the personnel's representatives in the Economic Council of the enterprises, while the General Assembly of the personnel had counselling functions.

In the mid-1980s, when partial attempts to change the mechanism of the central planning and management started, the idea of transferring the property to the labour collectives was introduced. In this way the material base for introducing workers' self-management in the enterprises was created. In its meaning the workers' self-management reminded of the Yugoslavian experience introduced in the 1950s.

In the process of creating contracts for transferring the property from the state to the labour collectives there was an attempt to determine the rights and obligations of the state, particularly the ministries and the personnel. The main right, which was formally transferred to the personnel, was the election of directors and the Economic Council of the enterprise. At a lower level (workshop, team and department) the employees had the right to elect themselves their superiors.

Legally, these norms were fixed by a newly adopted Labour Code in 1986, which became active in the beginning of 1987. However, along with the rights accumulated state debts and execution contracts, as well as other obligations coming from the centrally planned volumes of production and realisation were distributed and transferred to the personnel and enterprises. In fact, the whole campaign was administratively imposed on the enterprises and their personnel because they could neither negotiate the contract clauses of transferring property, nor refuse its signing. Gradually the experiment with the social self-management was depersonalised and ended ingloriously in late 1988. It was replaced by newly promoted ideas of introducing firm production organisation. The rights of the personnel to elect the management bodies were reduced to the opportunity to elect 49 per cent of the members of the Board of Managers, and the Board of Managers was electing the director of the enterprise. The lower management levels had the untouched clauses of the Labour Code for direct election of direct superiors by their subordinates.

In this way the idea of employee participation in ownership and management was compromised. Contrary to the official socialist ideology at that time, the personnel were very much estranged from ownership and management of the enterprise it worked in. The main reason for the quick revoke of the workers' self-management in the enterprises was its formal and centralised introduction, and that is why the disappointments of its application appeared very quickly.

In fact, even back then, the big question that was raised but not solved was who should be the owner of the enterprises. The attempt of the personnel to take these functions turned out unsuccessful. In reality the personnel was empowered with all the functions of owner except election rights, which were strongly controlled by the party apparatus. The planned distribution of resources remained, as well as the price control on the manufactured goods.

Enterprises continued to be managed in the same way as before these changes. The only significant difference was the election of superiors at the lower management levels. In some enterprises, by exception and despite the total control of the choice of supervisors by the party committees, the personnel managed to get rid of its unwanted managers. It was a paradox that due to the threat of the nomenclature in some sectors, such as foreign trade, the new rights of the personnel to directly choose the management of the enterprise were not allowed to be executed. The foreign trade companies continued to be managed by the old laws.

After the political changes in November 1989, Bulgaria started serious reforms in the trade and labour legislation. The socialist Labour Code was eliminated from its ideological bases. Also, the system of workers' self-management was liquidated at all management levels. In 1991 the Trade Law was adopted, which established the legal model of all traders and trade companies. It regulated also the procedures of electing management, supervisory and control bodies of the enterprises. According to the trade legislation, personnel representatives have a preserved place in these bodies. One and only exception concerned the limited liability companies and those with personnel of more than 50 people. A personnel representative in such companies has the right to participate in the General Assembly of partners.

From the short but instructive history of the workers' self-management during the administrative system we can draw some lessons:

- Firstly and most importantly, the industrial democracy is impossible in conditions of an administrative system. The election right has many dimensions, but it cannot be limited only to the production and electing managers of the enterprise, and not be present in the other public areas. There should be a choice and freedom of decision making concerning the production, as well as the realisation of the production and goods, prices and hiring personnel.
- Secondly, the free election of economic managers is incompatible with the principles of nomenclature and career development. This election was impossible in the administrative one-party system that existed until the end of 1989. The artificial imposing of elements of industrial democracy logically led to its antipode.
- Thirdly, the workers' self-management was hastily introduced without the necessary preparation. If there were enough studies, perhaps we could evaluate that, like in most cases of workers' self-management, the employees should not elect directly their superiors. They should do it indirectly – through their representatives in the management bodies. Such example is the then socialist Hungary. The scheme is similar also in the famous Mondragon cooperative corporation in Spain.

In conclusion, the introduction of the workers' self-management in the last years of the administrative system was a clear failure of those in power. That is why it was replaced with a system which was meant to introduce elements of market relations in the Bulgarian socialist economy. This hard failure compromised the idea of employee participation for years ahead. All future projects of using similar forms and schemes always received the unsuccessful experience of the past as a contra point.

3. EFP in the transition to a market economy

3.1 General attitudes

The transition to market economy in Bulgaria, with all its economic elements, was accepted unanimously by business and population. Referring to transition and employee participation, the following attitudes of the public were formed at the beginning of the 1990s[4]:

- The population's prevailing attitude was that of demanding developed market economies' living standard and at the same time preserving the socialist social safety. About 40 per cent of the population gave a positive answer to the question if the general direction of the economic changes was correct. The same number of respondents was negatively minded, while 20 per cent did not know or could not say. Over 73 per cent of the respondents considered that the liberalization positively affected the variety of goods on the market, but also over 80 per cent thought that this process had a negative impact on price dynamics (Keremidchiev et al., 1992). So, unlike Poland, Hungary and the Czech Republic, the public support of the reforms and the transition to a market economy was much weaker (see Hann & Laki, 1992; Kozak, 1991).
- Similar economic naivety was observed in the study of the attitude towards privatisation. About 90 per cent of the respondents thought that privatisation was necessary, but nearly half of all answers hinted that it should not be hurried on it. Half of the respondents expected positive impact of the privatisation on the economy. However, 56 per cent defended the statement that state enterprises might be as efficient as the private ones. About 60 per cent of the population considered that the reform could not be implemented without foreign investments and loans from international financial institutions. All the while, though, the prevailing opinion was that the state should 'limit price growth' – 73 per cent, 'define the salaries of the state sector employees'– 68 per cent, 'open new jobs' – 80 per cent, 'support financially the loosing enterprises' – 38 per cent (Keremidchiev et al., 1992).
- The settlement of employee buyout of enterprises was regarded as the main form of establishing private property. That privatisation technique had the most numerous supporters among the population. The public offering of shares ranked second for the population and first for the business elite. When asked directly with what amounts they would

4 Data from a national representative opinion poll. The poll took place in March 1992. It is representative for the population of the entire country. The sample size is 1,967 people aged 18 and over. For more details see Keremidchiev, Gradev & Stoyanov (1992).

participate in privatisation, almost 80 per cent of the respondents claimed they would not participate, and only about five per cent would invest significant personal funds (Keremidchiev et al., 1992).

Given the development of the cooperative movement, the sociological surveys in the country were made primarily with the objective to specify the intentions of the population for the future use of the restituted land. One of the studies was conducted by the Center for Studying of Democracy in March 1992 and covered 1967 respondents. The other study was led by the National Statistical Institute in January 1992 and covered 2300 respondents in the country. Those surveys specified that the amount of the expected restituted land was up to 1 ha for 44 per cent of the respondents and between 1.1 and 5 ha for 50 per cent of them. About one third of them were willing to be involved in agricultural cooperatives, while 17 per cent would like to cultivate the land on their own (Keremidchiev, Sp., Hristova, M., Popov, T., & Georgieva, M., 1993).

The lack of solid support for the economic reforms and egalitarianism in the population turned out to be a serious barrier to the reforming part of the Bulgarian elite. It had to find and suggest to the public such reforms, which would respond to the prevailing intentions in the society, but also to introduce market elements in the existing economic system.

3.2 EFP in the privatisation process

3.2.1 Mass privatisation process

Mass privatisation conducted in Bulgaria in the period from 1996 to 1998 was one of the possibilities for establishing employee ownership. The experience in the Czech Republic was used as a model of mass privatisation in Bulgaria. Investment vouchers were distributed to over three million people at the age over 18, for investment in 1,040 enterprises or in the purposely made private privatisation funds. Over 80 per cent of the investment vouchers were transferred to the 81 licensed privatisation funds. Up to ten per cent of the appointed capital of the enterprises for the mass privatisation was distributed free of charge among the personnel in accordance to their length of service.

The formal goals written in the mass privatisation program were as follows (Centre for Mass Privatisation [CMP], 1995):

- To ensure a turning-point in the privatisation process.
- To involve Bulgarian citizens in the process of property transformation and to reveal opportunities for participation in the management of the transformed property.
- To bring the long-term structural policy in line with the concrete goals of the current economic policy: recovery of the state budget, significant improvement in the state sector management, and clear national priorities in the field of investments.

Mass privatisation was expected to break the existing model of interests that was which blocking it, and with this to speed up considerably the transfer of assets from the state to the private sector (CMP, 1995). It was expected that mass privatisation would accelerate the establishment of the stock market and would stimulate the capital transactions as capital of billions BGN would emerge on the market and would be bought and sold. Finally, by mass privatisation it was envisaged to introduce the main elements of the corporate management in companies, which had to make their actions more dynamic and to contribute to their successful restructuring and adjustment to market economy conditions.

In addition to these main goals of mass privatisation some others were added: facilitating the creation of a middle class in the country, provision of fair and transparent transfer of property and decrease of privatisation abuse and fraud (CMP, 1995).

The management-employee ownership in Bulgaria that resulted from the mass privatisation was established by:

- The creation of privatisation funds in which capital and control were dominated by managers, and personnel were encouraged to invest their vouchers in these funds.
- Agreements between privatisation funds and managers of enterprises for taking control over these enterprises; relevant privatisation funds and their subsequent sale to the company of the managers (in rare cases with the employee participation).
- Direct investments of the investment vouchers allocated to the managers and personnel in their enterprises.

Examples of the first form are nine privatisation funds established by major state enterprises whose capital was included in the privatisation scheme, such as Albena PLC, Petrol PLC and Bulgartabac PLC. The second form used is known by the practice, but there is no quantitative data available. The scale of the third form can be illustrated by calculations (Georgiev & Keremidchiev, 1999) revealing that individual shareholders, possessing over 50 per cent of one enterprise, took control of over 64 companies (6.18 per cent of all enterprises participating in the mass privatisation scheme). The combination of individual shareholders and one privatisation fund that possessed over 50 per cent of an enterprise, took control of over 173 companies (16.71 per cent of all enterprises participating in the mass privatisation scheme).

This data shows the picture immediately after the end of the mass privatisation. The picture changed significantly very soon after that. The privatisation funds that were restricted from possessing more than 34 per cent of the capital of one enterprise, after the abolition of the restriction of trading with shares of enterprises of the mass privatisation, started to exchange or sell share packages among themselves. In enterprises with strategic interest, the privatisation funds used the method of capital increase in order to gain enough share for their independent management. In this way, the portion of the personnel and individual shareholders was seriously decreased.

As a result of mass privatisation, employee participation reached its peak immediately after the completion of this process. At that time employees possessed directly about seven to twelve per cent of the enterprise shares. However, after the beginning of the exchange of shares among privatisation funds and faith to conquer enterprises, the personnel lost its shares and the control was transferred to the managers and other owners.

3.2.2 Management and employee buyouts

The opportunities for preferential employee participation and the managers of enterprises have never been questioned in any part of the formation of the privatisation policy in Bulgaria. Initially in Bulgaria, in spite of the strong trade-union lobby, the privatisation policy represented in the adequate legislative framework envisaged only one preference for the employee and the managers. Similar to art. 24 of the Polish Law on privatisation (Ministry of Privatisation, 1992), the preference that in case of privatisation the workers in the enterprise could gain up to 20 per cent of the shares at half price was adopted. No other preferences were envisaged in the initial version of the law.

The first breakthrough in the implementation of the worker-manager privatisation in the legislative framework and policy was made in 1994. Amendments to the Law on privatisation introduced the concept of a Society for Employees and Managers Buyout (SEMB), rescheduling payment of its price for a period of up to ten years with one year grace period, 10 per cent initial payment of the selling price and accumulation at interest of the outstanding part of the price at half of the average annual base interest rate.

The second major amendment in accordance to the implementation of preferential regimes was made for the personnel and leaseholders of small companies and differentiated bodies whose balance sheet value of the fixed assets was up to ten million (old) BGN for industrial enterprises, and up to 5 million (old) BGN for commercial bodies by the date of submission of the privatisation proposal. They were permitted to buy the bodies, which lease without auction, at price equal to the assessment that they could pay in rescheduling scheme for a period up to six years for industrial bodies and up to five years for commercial bodies with primary payment, respectively, ten per cent and 30 per cent of the body assessment. Similarly to the SEMBs, the accumulation of interest for the leaseholders was accepted to be made on the outstanding part of the price at half of the base interest rate.

Some small but significant changes in the preference policy for the SEMBs were adopted in 1997 and 1998. It was recorded that in the SEMBs managers (in 1997) and inventors, which inventions are incorporated in the company could participate (in 1998). It was more important that the threshold for the recognition of a company as a SEMB fell from 50 to 20 per cent participation of the personnel of the enterprise for privatisation. At the same time, some restrictions were installed regarding the distribution of the SEMB capital, the type of the emitted shares, the securities to the price payment, etc., that did not put serious difficulties for the SEMBs. A very serious breakthrough in favour of the SEMBs was made by a legislative text that enabled them to cover completely the outstanding part of the price until the end of 2000 with compensatory papers for concluded transactions.

As a result of the changes in the preference policy to the SEMBs, the following types of preferences were revealed:

- Rescheduled payment over 10 years of the selling price of the enterprise ;
- One year grace period after signing the transaction;
- Low-interest credit of the SEMBs, since the accumulation of the interest of the outstanding part of the price is half of the base interest rate;
- Preferential buyout up to 20 per cent of the capital of the enterprise at half of the reached selling price to the personnel;
- Free acquisition up to 10 per cent of the capital of the enterprise by the personnel in mass privatisation;
- Direct buyout of small bodies at their assessment at rescheduled payment – according to art. 35 of the Law on privatisation;
- Use of investment vouchers for capital share in SEMBs with the following proportion: one voucher = one BGN;
- Use of investment vouchers for payment of the price of the privatisation transaction with the SEMB with the following proportion: one voucher = one BGN;
- Payment of 100 per cent of the outstanding part of the price by the end of 2000 with compensatory papers for already accomplished transactions with SEMBs.

In spite of this main preferential package for the SEMBs, there are other significant preferences, the most important of them being:

- The lack of sector and other restrictions for privatisation with SEMBs (excluding the so-called "objective-oriented privatisation" that was introduced in 1996). Such restrictions existed for the implementation of schemes for employees-management privatisation in most transition countries (Bornstein, 1997). Similar attempts for implementation were made in the preparatory bill for amendment to the Law on privatisation, proposed by the Council of Ministers in the National Assembly in 1996, but the influential lobbies managed to deflect the attempt to restrict employee-management privatisation to enterprises with balance sheet value of fixed assets of up to 70,000,000 (old) BGN;
- The participation of only 20 per cent of the enterprise personnel in SEMB, including the newly-appointed personnel who did not

contribute to the enterprise development, as well as pensioners who worked in the enterprise;
- The participation in SEMB of newly-appointed managers and members of the managing bodies of the sold company (Supervisory Board, Management Board, Board of Directors, controller) who hardly constitute to the preservation and development of the company capital.

The dynamics of introducing preferences for SEMB clearly outlines the tendencies in the privatisation policy in the meantime. After the first breakthrough for regulating preferences in 1994 they were nine and they preserved their number until 1997, followed by an increase to eleven. Equally important is the quality of the respective preferences, which after 1997 became quite high.

These preferences may be complemented by others, which prove to be in many cases crucial in favour of the SEMB due to the asymmetry of information they have and the situation displayed before the external buyer. This asymmetry is very important in all sectors of the economy, but it is fundamental for the privatisation of enterprises that were closed until recently for the public, such as military industry and foreign trade.

The shortened terms for carrying out the privatisation procedure, adopted in the middle of 1997, also put the buyers outside of SEMBs in weakened positions. The lack of open competition, when enterprises are sold, had a negative effect on the behaviour of the managers before the privatisation. In order to decrease the privatisation assessment, the managers literally tried to worsen the financial and economic condition of the enterprises. The participation of SEMBs in the privatisation gave ground to developing corruption practices. Inspired by their sacred aim – acquisition of the enterprises – the managers cunningly took advantage of all illegal or amoral tricks, such as:

- Trying to present inaccurate information about the condition of the enterprise or restricting the public information of the enterprise;
- Using the means of a state enterprise for payment of deposit and other costs of privatisation;
- Paying with state funds the fees of consultants who are seemingly hired for carrying out other services;
- Manipulating the assessment of the enterprise by handing out bribes to appraisers;
- Using the civil servants, who are hired in their managing bodies, for manipulating the privatisation procedure by putting restrictions, e.g.

preserving a point of activity, securing short term periods for turning in the offer, exerting pressure for change of privatisation contracts, receiving in-house information about competitive offers, etc.;
- Transferring the funds from the state enterprise to banks, which after that grant credit to them to buy the enterprise;
- Transferring the funds from the state enterprise to other companies, which after that give them back the funds to buy the enterprise;
- Obliging the personnel to participate in SEMB and forcing them to make constituent payments;
- Concentrating the power of SEMB in their hands and in that way depriving the petty stockholders of their rights of ownership in SEMB;
- Striving for changing the clauses of the privatisation contract in order to decrease their responsibilities for the price, investments, employment, etc. stipulated in the contract. Having priorities over the other buyers, with regards to the selling price of SEMBs until March 2000, when the rules for discounting of the proposed by SEMBs price was adopted in order to allow comparison of prices. According to calculations (Keremidchiev, 2001), the quantitative expression of the rescheduled payment in some cases reached 36 per cent priority in the price over the other candidates.

The sales to SEMBs in the privatisation process reached 1,436 out of 5,165 deals (28 per cent). If we add other sales that gave also preferences to employees (e.g. privatisation of separate part of enterprises), almost half of the conventional privatisation has been carried out through insiders.

The consequences of strongly subsidised sales to SEMBs were publicly disclosed after the establishment of the Agency for Post-Privatisation Control at the end of 2002. They consisted of delays or refusals of payment of the due amounts of the contracted price and investments. Apart from the fact that a lot of contracts had been changed towards reduction of the due payments, roughly 10 per cent of the SEMBs did not pay their rescheduled instalments in due time. The total losses of the unfulfillment of privatisation contracts were accounted to be one billion BGN. The Agency for post-privatisation control claimed 200 million BGN to incorrect buyers.

Another significant change is the concentration of ownership in the hands of managers. In the study on ownership, a breakdown revealed that out of 20 Bulgarian companies only three were not owned by their managers (Minchev, 2004).

The preferences for the personnel, connected to preferential partnership in the company buy-out by the SEMB, as well as preferential buyout of up to 20 per cent of the shares of the sold company, were eliminated with the adoption of the new Privatisation Law in 2002. The participation of SEMBs in acquisition of company ownership following the general procedures remained the only option. There are no data if that option was used after 2002.

3.2.3 Minority interest sales

In conventional privatisation the personnel has the rights to buy up to 20 per cent of its company's shares at half price reached on the sale of the main stock. There are no studies that indicate what part of the ownership has been privatised this way. Certainly, it could be argued that this part was not high and in practical terms fluctuated between four to five per cent. Arguments for that level were, on the one hand, the limitation imposed by the length of services and average salaries of employees. On the other hand, the personnel's doubts on new owners, the lack of liquidity of the Stock Exchange and limitation of reselling them within certain period after their acquisition discouraged the employees.

In the mass privatisation the preferred shares were distributed for free by applying the same algorithm for calculation. Through these shares about six per cent (out of ten per cent maximum) of the allocated mass privatisation scheme capital had been privatized.

Contemporary studies show a strong amnesia of the Bulgarian society regarding the attempts to be incorporated in the production ownership. According to the results of a national representative study (carried out in 2010), 9.8 per cent of the population states that they own or have owned shares of Bulgarian companies (Dimitrov, M., Keremidchiev Sp., Tchipev Pl., Bakardjieva, R., Daskalov, V. and Ivanova, N., 2014). Almost 86 per cent of the interviewed state with certainty that they have never owned such securities, and 4.4 per cent of the respondents do not know whether they have owned shares or not.

These subjective views strongly differ from the objective information concerning the privatisation carried out in the country. Through the mass privatisation over three million adult Bulgarian citizens received certain number of free bonds, which they could trade for shares of privatisation funds and state enterprises for such sale. This sums up to half of the adult population and over 37 per cent of the citizens in the country. If we add the participants with preferences in the cash privatisation and those who purchased shares at the stock exchange to this number, despite some double counting, the number of formal share owners should be many times bigger than the one stated by the respondents. The failure of the idea of developing a mass shareholding through privatisation is obvious.

In the same study 19 per cent of the people, who ever owned shares, state that they still have such asset in their portfolio (Dimitrov et al., 2014). This is two per cent of shareholders from the whole population of the country, or about 158,000 people, which is a substantial reduction by over 19 times.

4. Current state of EFP

4.1 Current attitude towards EFP

Information about the current attitude towards employee participation in ownership, financial results and management of the enterprises, can be obtained from the data of two studies, carried out in 2011 and 2013 among managers of respectively 120 and 131 large Bulgarian shareholding public and non-public enterprises (Dimitrov et al., 2014).

As a whole, the attitude of the interviewed managers towards employee participation in ownership, financial results and management of the enterprises is positive. It is especially strong in the first sociological study (Figure 1). Over 62 per cent of the managers support to fully support such participation. In the second study this share drops to 47 per cent. During both studies the share of negative attitude towards the employee participation increases from eleven to over 30 per cent (Figure 1). The share of balancers on this matter, which have chosen evaluation three in the scale from 1 (fully support) to 5 (don't fully support), drops by about five percentage points.

Figure 1. Attitude towards employee participation in ownership, financial results and management of the enterprises

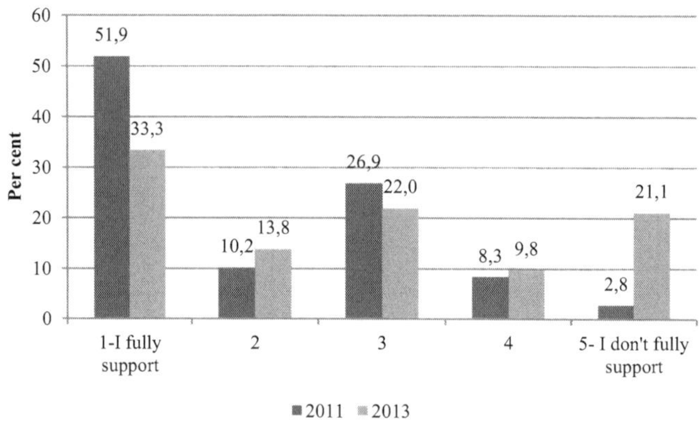

Source: Own calculations based on Dimitrov et al. (2014).[5]

Surveying the interest in acquiring ownership in the enterprises, where the managers and employees work, showed the following results. After high payment, second priority among managers is their interest in acquiring ownership of the enterprises. This interest accumulates highest priority for about 28 per cent to 29 per cent of the respondents in both studies (Figure 2). While in the first study the responses, placing this interest with lowest priority, are about 18 per cent, in the second study they increase to 44 per cent. It is on the account of the accumulation of the responses with average priority. In comparable plan, they decrease from 53 per cent (in the first study) to 28 per cent (in the second study) (Dimitrov et al., 2014). A possible explanation of this fact is that during the crisis the ownership of the enterprises has devaluated and it was no longer very attractive to acquire them.

The interest of the personnel in participation in ownership, financial results and management of the enterprise has the lowest priority among the tested three versions of responses. The preferences for higher payment and professional career are higher prioritised. Most responses classify this interest with lowest and average priority (Figure 3). However, for 23.7 per

5 Data provided from two surveys with managers of large public and non-public Bulgarian companies. The first survey was carried out in 2011 and covered 120 joint stock companies. The second survey one was carried out in 2013 and covered 131 joint stock companies (Dimitrov et al., 2014).

Figure 2. Managers' interest in acquiring ownership of the enterprise

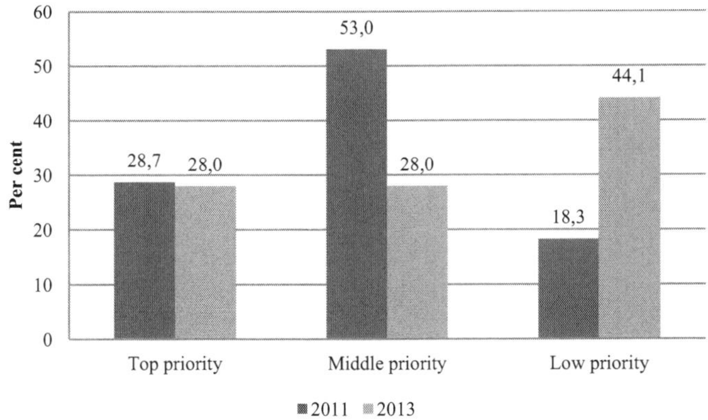

Source: Own calculations based on Dimitrov et al. (2014).

cent and 20 per cent of the responses, respectively in the first and second study, this interest is defined with the highest priority. In comparison between the two studies, it is noted that this interest loses its priority. The accumulation of responses moves from the right part of the scale to a lower priority. This is possibly due to worsened financial state and investment attractiveness of the enterprises in conditions of the crisis, as well as the end of the illusion for wider employee participation, executed in the process of privatisation of state enterprises in the country.

Figure 3. Personnel's interest in acquiring ownership of the enterprise

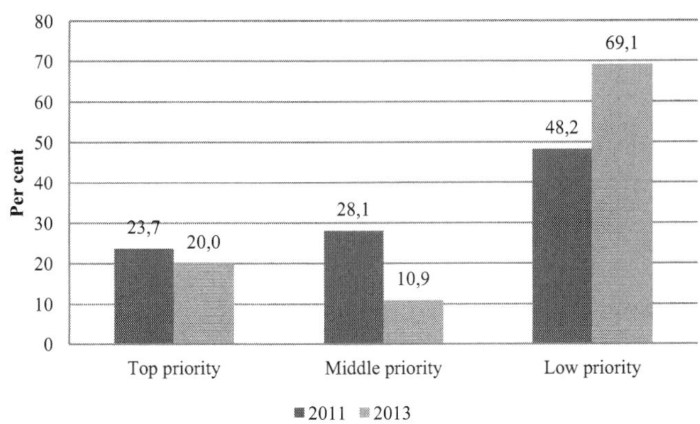

Source: Own calculations based on Dimitrov et al. (2014).

Concerning the question about determining the significance of the different groups of stakeholders to the success of the enterprise now and in five years, the internal stakeholders dominate (Figure 4). The first place is occupied by the managers. The personnel are on the third place after the shareholders. This evaluation imposes the use of attractive motivational systems for incorporating the managers and personnel to the goals of the enterprise, including through participation in its financial results in the near future.

Figure 4. Significance of groups of stakeholders for the success of the enterprise in the study in 2013. Note: The values of the figure come from the sums of the responses of the first three choices of the respondents.

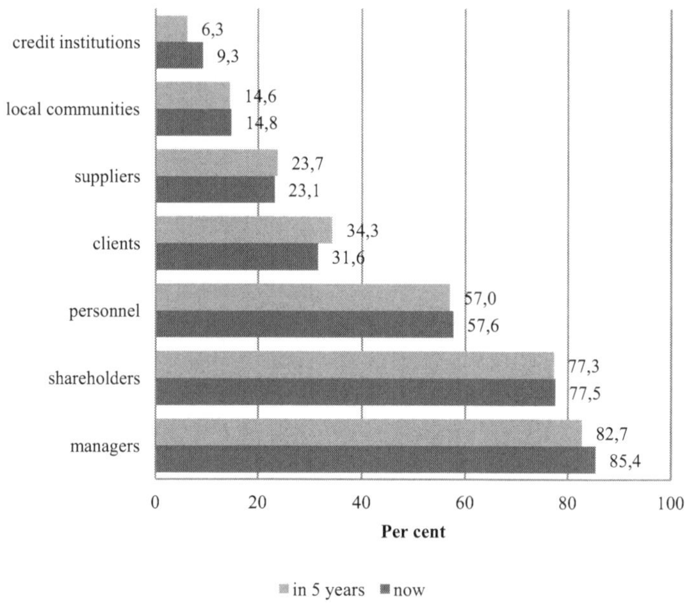

Source: Own calculations based on Dimitrov et al. (2014).

4.2 Distribution and practices of EFP

According to the European Company Survey (ECS), a survey of more than 27,000 human resource executives across Europe, conducted in 2013, 4.4 per cent of the companies in Bulgaria offer their employees stock-ownership schemes and 33.2 per cent offer some form of profit-sharing.

The European Working Conditions Survey (EWCS), a regular household survey, which in 2010 covered 43,816 randomly selected individuals in 34 countries, shows that 0.73 per cent of Bulgarian participants were taking part in employee stock ownership schemes, while 7.99 per cent of them were participating in profit-sharing.

Another study published in 2012 confirmed that Bulgaria is among the EU countries with lowest support of EFP. The EU countries are divided into four clusters: (1) UK, France, Slovenia, Finland, Spain and Ireland; (2) Denmark, Netherlands, Italy, Austria, Poland, Romania, and Belgium; (3) Germany, Hungary, Sweden, Greece, Lithuania, Malta, Portugal, Latvia, Czech Republic and Slovakia; and (4) Bulgaria, Cyprus and Estonia (Lowitzsch, 2012).

4.2.1 Employee stock ownership participation

Comparing Bulgaria with the Czech Republic, Hungary, Lithuania, Latvia and Greece, we find that it is among the lowest ranked countries by employee stock ownership (ESO) participation rates: under one per cent in 2010 (Figure 5). While in most EU countries this share increases in 2010, Bulgaria is one of the few countries where it decreases.

Nevertheless, there are Bulgarian enterprises, which develop and offer schemes for ESO participation. For instance, such are 'Mobiltel' JSC, 'Investor.BG', 'Automotor Corporation', 'Devin', 'CBA Asset Management', IT company 'Magic Solutions', 'Hewlett Packard', 'Elana Trading'. These firms use different schemes for transferring shares to the personnel.

One of the pioneers in this practice is the Bulgarian branch of 'Schneider Electric'. Most workers in the enterprise own shares, which are traded at the Paris Stock Exchange (Schneider Electric, 2015).

In 'Mobiltel' such scheme is active since the end of 2005. The leading managers of the firm can acquire options of the mother company 'Telecom Austria'. They buy the options at preferential conditions. The purchased options are traded at Vienna and New York Stock Exchanges. (Popova, 2007).

Figure 5. Proportion of employees participating in employee stock ownership (per cent)

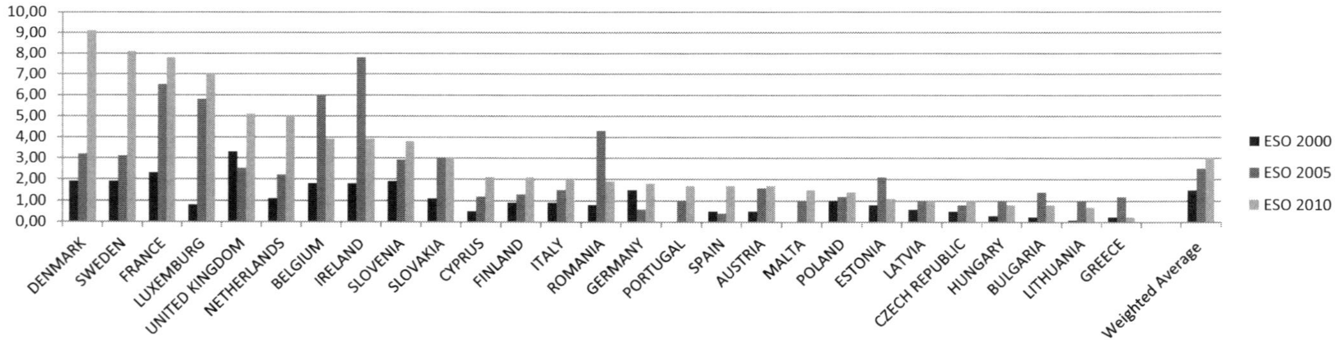

Source: European Working Conditions Survey, 2000, 2005 & 2010.

In the end of 2007 'Hewlett Packard' provided opportunity to all of its personnel in Bulgaria to buy shares of the mother company at preferential conditions (Popova, 2007). The Bulgarian branch of the company became the first in the region, which 'Hewlett Packard' included in its initiative. The company foresees to sell to its personnel worldwide a total of 355 million deferred certificate shares with a vote right at nominal price of 0.01 USD. The price of acquiring the shares by the personnel was 85 per cent of their market price at the purchase date. Every member of the personnel had the right to buy shares at total value of ten per cent of their monthly salary. Before 2007 only managers of the company had the opportunity to buy shares at preferential prices under the condition that good results are achieved. These shares can be traded at the New York Stock Exchange (NYSE), where the company is listed.

Similarly, in 2007 the company for bottling of mineral water "Devin" distributed 22,000 shares to 20 executives of the company, thereby rewarding them for the good results achieved the previous year (Popova, 2007).

According to company information of 'Automotor Corporation', twelve per cent of the firm's shares belong to the minority owners, as a result of an initiative few years ago to provide shares to the personnel (Automotor Corporation, 2014).

The public company 'Investor.BG' JSC, which in 2011 occupied the 31st place among the 50 fastest developing IT companies in Europe, planned the transfer of its shares to managers and employees even in 2005 (Popova, 2007). Such right was given to all members of the Board of Directors and employees who had been in the company for over a year. The shares were endowed conditionally through a contract between the company and the manager or employee. The factual transfer of shares' ownership was foreseen to happen for a period of three years after signing the contract, if the beneficiaries continue to work in the company. The minimal amount of the endowment per employee was 1,000 BGN for a calendar year, and the amount could be bigger depending on the merits and personal contribution of each one of them. Every beneficiary had the right of choosing between receiving the determined shares or their equivalent in BGN, discounted by 50 per cent if taken immediately.

'Elana Holding' also gives opportunity to its managers and key employees who have occupied the same position at two years to buy shares of the branches they work in (Popova, 2007). They pay 50 per cent of the market price, which is determined by exactly prescribed mechanism, and receive dividends like all other owners. The firm guarantees buying up of the securities at market price. The rights on the acquired shares are lost only if there is a disciplinary dismissal. According to firm's information, nine of totally 15 invited employees embraced this right.

In other Bulgarian companies the leading managers and employees receive stakes of the capital of the firm completely for free. Such practice is used in the career portal 'JobTiger' in order to stimulate some key employees. The specificity about these stakes is that if a person leaves the job, these stakes should be offered first to the other owners of the firm. Such scheme is applied in the IT firm 'Magic Solutions' Ltd. It gave as a present a stake of ten per cent to its technical director, since in a year he convinced the owners in his qualities. Unlike the first examples, in 'JobTiger' and 'Magic Solutions' to the managers are transferred not shares but stakes, since these companies are with limited liability (Popova, 2007).

In a wider plan, in Bulgaria and globally, the biggest employee participation in the ownership is in consulting firms, law firms, non-government and other similar organisations. At their registration these firms are created as partnerships, where the ownership is distributed between the partners working there. The newly hired personnel, after a successful integration in the company, receives the opportunity to gradually acquire certain stake in it, corresponding to his or her position. This stake is sold back if the person leaves the firm.

4.2.2 Participation in profit sharing

Concerning the distribution of schemes for employee participation in the profit, Bulgaria is also below the EU average level, but has been ascending (Figure 6). In 2010 about ten per cent of the employees participate in such schemes. However, other bonus schemes are widely distributed.

After 2005 the annual bonuses were widely spread not only in the production, but also in administration and services. They were paid mainly before New Year's holiday, sometimes before other national holidays as well. Most often they are differentiated and formed on the basis of receiving individual payment, which should reflect the contribution of each member of the personnel to the achievement of the enterprises' goals.

Figure 6. Proportion of employees participating in profit sharing schemes (percentage)

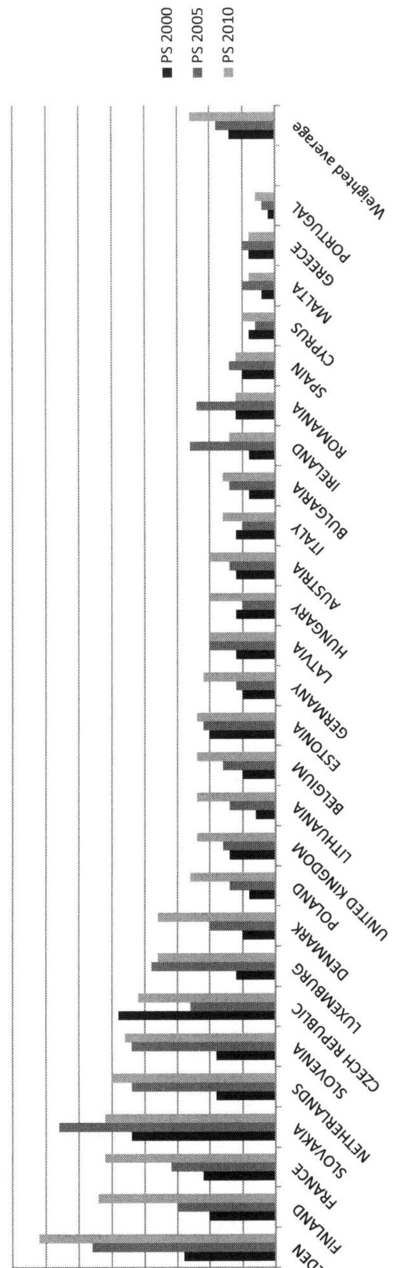

Source: European Working Conditions Survey, 2000, 2005 & 2010.

In the state administration and public institutions, such as schools (especially after applying the system of delegated budgets) and hospitals, there is also a wide spread practice among employees to receive annual bonus in the amount of one or more average monthly salary. These bonuses are known as a 13th salary. The bonus was formed depending on the budget savings and attracted funds from paid services provided to external clients. It can be different than the average or individual monthly salary. However, this practice ended in the beginning of the economic crisis and has not been renewed in the public sector yet.

More and more enterprises orient towards using systems of labour payment, where the main salary has a considerably low share, and the serious part of the labour payments is formed by *monthly or three-month bonuses for achieved* results. Thus, the payment system has two pillars. The first pillar is the main salary by labour contract, which is a function of the ranking of the relevant position in the Unified Jobs Classification. The second pillar in the payment system is the additional payment for individual performance, which is based on achieved individual and/or group results.

In the normative world this payment system is introduced through the Regulation on the Structure and Organisation of the Salary and is active since July 1st, 2007. Art. 13, line 1 states that the collective labour contract, the internal regulations on salary and/or individual labour contract can determine also other additional labour payments for:

- Achieved results from work – current, annual or for other period;
- Changes in labour conditions of temporary character, which lead to additional burnout, and in other conditions – detrimental to the employee's health;
- Participation in profit sharing;
- Other.

The study carried out by KPMG (2007) among state ministries and 58 large private companies from different sectors of the economy, gives a special view on the distribution of such schemes for participation in the financial results. The study shows the financial stimuli and bonuses have a leading role in motivating the employees and increasing their engagement in the company. The combination of their influence with non-financial stimuli increases the labour motivation of the personnel. Data show the most important factors for motivating the collective:

- Financial stimuli and bonuses – 31 per cent;
- Acknowledgement – 20.7 per cent;
- Career opportunities – 17.2 per cent;
- Looking for the employees' opinion – 13.8 per cent;
- Social gains – 8.6 per cent.

More than 80 per cent of the interviewed state that business results and success of the company mainly depend on the employee engagement, their professional skills, and motivation. That is why the managers of companies should study and take into consideration the influence of the needs, motives and attitudes of the employees and should contract more flexible schemes for employee participation in the financial results of the enterprise as part of the strategy for increasing the labour quality.

Nevertheless, as a reaction to the crisis, the managers of the Bulgarian enterprises place the measure of cutting back on bonus payment tied to company performance on third place, after measures of cutting back on recruiting and cutting back on company events (Strack, R., Caye, J.-M,. Thurner, R., & Hayen, P., 2009). Nevertheless, a study of Aon Hewitt discovered that the best employers in Bulgaria devote 18 per cent of salary fund for encouraging the employees to achieve initially set goals (Tcherkezova, 2013).

According to a study of the Bulgarian Industrial Capital Association, in Bulgaria in the end of 2013 over 57 per cent of the enterprises would give Christmas bonuses to their personnel (Bulgarian Industrial Capital Association, 2013). Almost all interviewed managers state that the bonuses are bound to the expected financial results of the firm for this year. 27 per cent of the firms would give a bonus of up to 100 BGN to every employee, 35 per cent – between 100 and 300 BGN, and 38 per cent – more than 300 BGN.

Study of the Bulgarian Industrial Association in 2013 shows similar results – 56 per cent of the firms would give Christmas bonuses to all employees (Dariknews.bg, 2013). 22 per cent of all 410 interviewed companies would not stimulate their employees, and ten per cent would encourage only some employees. 43 per cent of the firms would not change the size of the bonuses compared with 2012, while 30 per cent would give bigger bonuses, and 18 per cent would give smaller ones. Most of the managers (73 per cent) preferred financial stimuli and the other 27 per cent would give their employees presents and souvenirs.

Additionally to the bonuses, almost ten per cent of the enterprises would give food vouchers to their personnel (Markova, 2010). For 48 per cent of the employers a main condition for Christmas stimuli of the employees was the achieved financial results of the enterprise, and for 24 per cent of them it was the careful evaluation of the contribution of every employee. Almost half of the interviewed employers (47 per cent) were ready to give 20 per cent of the monthly salary as a Christmas bonus. 38 per cent would stimulate their employees with up to half of the monthly salary, and six per cent could give more than 100 per cent of the salary to their employees.

4.3 EFP in cooperatives

During the transition to market economy cooperatives went through difficult periods. They were considered by market reformists as a remnant from the past and an impediment to free entrepreneurship. Restitution had the most destructive impact on agricultural cooperatives. A land reform model for restitution of land to its former owners and their heirs was adopted, which led to liquidation of the existing cooperatives. The restitution affected cooperatives in other sectors of the economy, as well. After adopting a new Law for Cooperatives, they were compelled to re-register. Furthermore, the registration procedures were complicated. Serious restrictions concerning the work of credit cooperatives were introduced that in practice wiped them out from legal milieu.

The statistical data for the number of cooperatives show that their number increased from 18 in 1989 to 5,693 in 1997, representing 1.3 per cent of all registered companies (Table 1). More than half of them were agriculture cooperatives. Until 1993, when statistics reported cooperatives separately from private sector, about one to 1.5 per cent of all investments were made by them and about 2.5 per cent of industrial production was produced there (see Table 1).

The most powerful representative of the Bulgarian cooperatives is the Central Co-operative Union (CCU). So far the CCU embraces 33 regional co-operative unions and one branch union. The CCU incorporates 795 cooperatives with 146,000 cooperative members. Most of them are consumer cooperatives.

The second most important cooperative union is the National Union of Labor-Productive Cooperatives (NU of LPC). In 2014 its members are

251 cooperatives with over 14,000 cooperative members all over the country. They form 14 regional unions that compose the National Union. The NU of LPC consists also of 30 specialized cooperatives for people with disabilities, where 1,180 cooperative members work. NU of LPC is an associate of the daughter company of the group 'Cheque Dejeuner', France that issues food vouchers.

Table 1. Main data for cooperatives in transition period

	1989	1990	1991	1992	1993	1994	1997
Number of registered firms	1,534	3,491	30,660	202,250 *	368,703	454,963	447,714
Number of registered coops	18	23	1,676	1,722*	4,545	5,739	5,693
Per cent coops out of all registered firms	1.2	0.7	5.5	0.9*	1.2	1.3	1.3
Per cent industrial output made by coops	n.a.	2.5	2.8	1.7	2.4	n.a.	n.a.
Per cent investments made by coops	n.a.	1.5	1.5	1.1	1.2	n.a.	n.a.

Note. * By 12.02.1993. n.a. = not applicable
Source: National Statistical Institute.

A more detailed and current information can be acquired from the surveys of agricultural entities that are periodically carried out by the Ministry of Agriculture and Food. According to them, the dynamics of the number of agricultural cooperatives draws a curve, which is close to the normal distribution (Figure 7). After breaking the agriculture cooperatives inherited from the socialism, in 1992 347 new agricultural cooperatives were created. Gradually their number increased and reached its peak in the period from 1996 to 2000. At that time, the agricultural cooperatives were more than 3,100. After this period a fast drop of these organisations started. They reached 940 in 2010. Most of the agricultural cooperatives cultivated their available land by themselves. It should be noted that few of them did not cultivate land but rented it to private producers.

Figure 7. Dynamics of agricultural cooperatives and average size of cultivated land by them

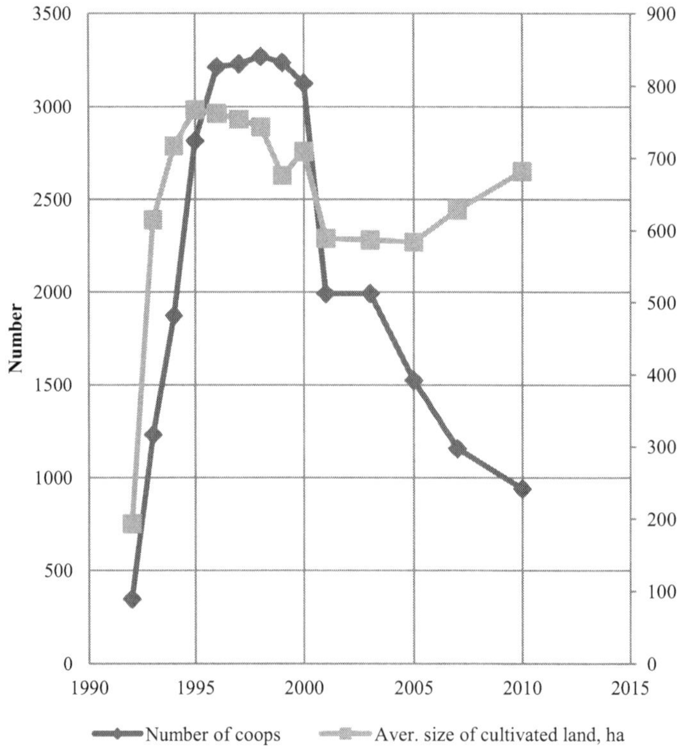

Source: Ministry of Agriculture and Food (2013).

The decrease of the number of agricultural cooperatives had a favourable impact on the size of the cultivated land. Starting from 193 ha in 1992, it reached 740 to 760 ha in the period from 1995 to 1998. In 2010 the average size of the cultivated land per cooperative was 682 ha.

The share of land cultivated by the agricultural cooperatives has a similar dynamics to the number of these business organisations (Figure 8). In the beginning of the transition it was 1.44 per cent of the total cultivated land. In 1995 it reached its first peak of almost 46 per cent of the cultivated land, and in 2000 to its highest value of 61.5 per cent. After that a gradual decrease started, and in 2010 the agricultural cooperatives cultivated 17.7 per cent of the whole cultivated land in the country.

Figure 8. Share of cultivated land by agricultural cooperatives

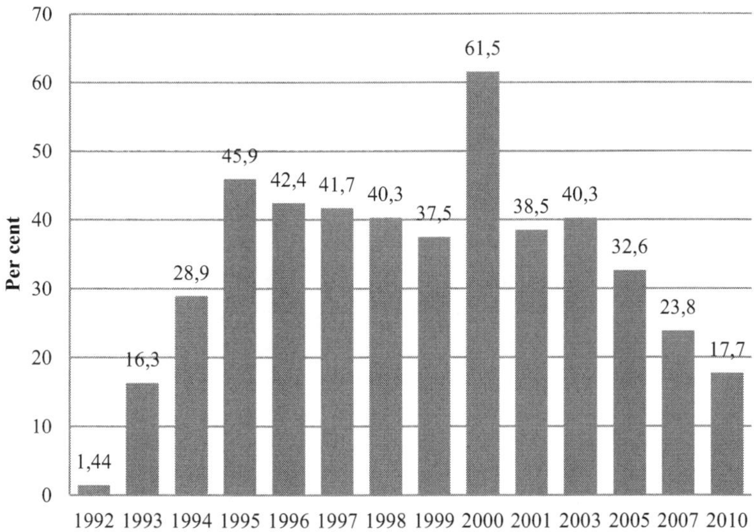

Source: Ministry of Agriculture and Food (2013).

Although by default the ownership of the cooperatives consists of the instalments of their members, in most cases the agricultural cooperatives use hired labour, and that is why they are not owned by their personnel. Most of the non-agricultural cooperatives are consumer ones, which also excludes them from the cases of EFP. In conclusion, in only few of the existing cooperatives in the country there is an employee participation in the ownership and their financial results.

5. Perspectives on development of the employee participation in Bulgaria

The legal framework for applying different forms and schemes for employee participation depends on the state policy. On one hand, it should facilitate and support the introduction of best practices concerning the employee participation. On the other hand, the state should set its internal legislation to a state, which should not hinder or limit the use of different forms and schemes of employee participation.

Social partners play a decisive role for the development of the EFP. The Bulgarian unions should clear their position concerning this participation. Still some unions consider it a mean for the management to ensure the employee loyalty, which leads to weaker influence of the unions. There are also concerns that the introduction of schemes for employee participation could have a negative impact on the process of contracting salaries and the flexible payment to reduce payments.

The schemes for employee participation are successful when they are introduced in partnership between the social partners. That is why the social dialogue is the most suitable mechanism for this and the collective contracting could be a very successful transmission of the decisions made.

Suitable information campaigns, exchange of experience, sharing fears and risks between the social partners, could set the bases of mutually beneficial and balanced development of the models and schemes for employee participation at branch, national and cross-national level. At national level the employers and union organisations should develop compensations for organisational, methodical and informational support to their members regarding the development and introduction of schemes for employee participation, suitable for the Bulgarian conditions.

The employee participation, especially in the financial results, should not be limited only to the employees in the business sector. The public administration sector also actively uses such methods for stimulating and motivating their employees. Particularly since the public administration sector started applying management methods that are introduced from the business sector, such as strategic planning, balanced scorecards, benchmarking, delegated budgets, programmed budget planning, it would be unforgivable if the personnel payment in the state administration would not be bound to achieving final and intermediate results and goals.

The employee participation in the ownership of the enterprises could be supported through the following measures:

- Improvement of the protection of the rights of the minority shareholders;
- Development and application by enterprises of schemes for employee participation in the General Assembly of shareholders, representation in the governing bodies, creation of guarantees for receiving dividends, electronic voting and authorizing, etc.;
- Introduction on the capital market of options on shares, free shares (Restricted Stock Units), preferred shares, including in the public companies;

- No tax on dividends from personnel shares;
- Introduction of pilot employee stock ownership scheme of state enterprises.

The employee participation in the financial results of the enterprises could be developed by:

- Using mechanisms of collective labour contracting for developing payment systems, which would be bound to the achieved results of the personnel;
- Creating stimuli for investing the bonuses of the personnel into company's shares;
- Pilot state enterprises to develop and apply schemes of employee participation in their financial results.

The experience of the other European countries and the US in creating and applying models of financial participation of the employees could serve as a starting point of the policy, which should be developed and applied in Bulgaria.

References

Automotor Corporation. (2014). *23 successful years of CITROËN in Bulgaria!* Retrieved from http://www.citroen.bg/wp-content/uploads/2014/06/Broshura-BG.pdf

Avramov, R. (2001). *The XXth Century Bulgarian Economy*. Sofia, Centre for Liberal Strategies (in Bulgarian).

Bochev, St. (1998). *Capitalism in Bulgaria*. Sofia, Foundation 'Bulgarian Science and Culture' (in Bulgarian).

Bornstein, M. (1997). Non-standard methods in the privatization strategies of the Czech Republic, Hungary and Poland. *Economics of Transition*, 5: 323–338.

Bulgarian Industrial Association. (2013). 57% of the firms in Bulgaria are going to distribute Christmas bonuses. Retrieved December 15, 2013, from http://bica-bg.org/admin/admin/upload/3803_media_monitoring_24.11.2014.pdf, (in Bulgarian).

Centre for Mass Privatisation. (1995). *Program for Privatisation through Investment Vouchers*. Sofia.

Council of Ministers. (2007). *Regulations on the structure and organisation of wages*. State Gazette, 07.01.2007 (in Bulgarian).

Dariknews.bg. (2013). More than half of the firms are going to give out Christmas bonuses to their employees. Retrieved December 13, 2013, from http://dariknews.bg/view_article.php?article_id=1185552 (in Bulgarian).

Dimitrov, M., Keremidchiev Sp., Tchipev Pl., Bakardjieva, R., Daskalov, V., & Ivanova, N. (2014). *Corporate Governance for XXIst century*. Sofia, ERI-BAS (in Bulgarian).

doi: 10.1111/j.1468-0351.1997.tb00020.x

EC. (2002). Communication on a framework for the promotion of EFP, COM (2002)0364.

European Foundation for the Improvement of Living and Working Conditions. (2012). *Fifth European survey on working conditions 2010*. Dublin.

European Foundation for the Improvement of Living and Working Conditions. (2007). *Fourth European survey on working conditions 2005*. Dublin.

European Foundation for the Improvement of Living and Working Conditions. (2001). *Third European survey on working conditions 2000*. Dublin.

Georgiev, Il., & Keremidchiev, Sp. (1999). *Corporate Governance of Privatised Companies*. Sofia, Bulgarian Association for Management Development and Entrepreneurship (in Bulgarian).

Hann, E., & Laki, M. (1992). The Hungarian Public on the Advance of Private Economy. Acta *Oeconomika*, 44: 191-200.

Keremidchiev, Sp. (2001). *Privatisation of the Bulgarian industry* (Doctoral dissertation).

Keremidchiev, Sp., Gradev, T., & Stoyanov, Al. (1992). *Public opinion and privatisation*. Sofia, CSD (in Bulgarian).

Keremidchiev, Sp., Hristova M., Popov, T., & Georgieva M. (1993). *Agrarian Reform and Agricultural Organisations*. Sofia, Foundation 'Agriculture' (in Bulgarian).

Kozak, M. (1991). Social Support for Privatisation in Poland. *Communist Economies and Economic Transformation*, 3 (2), 155-167.

KPMG. (2007). *The Organizational Survey*, Sofia.

Lowitzsch, J., & Hashi, Ir. (2012). *Employee Financial Participation in Companies' Proceeds*. Brussels, European Parliament.

Markova, Z. (2010, January 29). Voucher System. *Kapital press*. (in Bulgarian).

Minchev, V. (2004). Stakeholders in the Bulgarian public companies. *Ikonomika*, 2, 55-57 (in Bulgarian).

Ministry of Privatisation. (1992). *Law on privatisation of state – owned enterprises*. Warsaw.

National Statistical Institute. *Statistical Yearbook*, various issues. Sofia.

Palazov, Il. (1946). *Theory and practice of cooperative*. Svishtov, BCB (in Bulgarian).

Popova, Ek. (2007, August 3). To work for yourself. *Kapital Karieri* (in Bulgarian).

Popova, Ek. (2008, January 21). "Devin" distributed bonuses in the form of shares'. K*apital Karieri* (in Bulgarian).

Schneider Electric. (2015). *Benefits*. Retrieved from http://www.schneider-electric.bg/sites/bulgaria/bg/company/careers/your-career/benefits.page

Strack, R., Caye, J.-M,. Thurner, R., Hayen, P. (2009). *Creating People Advantage in Times of Crisis*. Boston, MA: Boston Consulting Group & European Association of People Management.

Tcherkezova, D. (2013, November 22). Our employees are important. *Kapital press*. (in Bulgarian).

Determinants of financial participation – two decades of Croatian practice

Nina Pološki Vokić, Maja Klindžić & Ivana Načinović Braje[1]

Abstract

The chapter presents the national context, trends and determinants of employee financial participation (EFP) in medium and large-sized organisations in Croatia. Transition and post-transition economies usually exhibit a low incidence of EFP schemes when compared to free market economies, and Croatia is no exception. Even though Croatia has inherited a long tradition of employee participation in the form of the unique self-management model, the current legal and fiscal framework is not supportive of EFP. Empirical findings based on the Cranfield Network on International Human Resource Management (CRANET) survey conducted in 2014 revealed that approximately only ten per cent of organisations in Croatia offer all EFP schemes (profit sharing, stock sharing and stock options) to all employees, and that on average, only around ten per cent of employees are given the opportunity to participate financially. Furthermore, the study identified stock options as the most present, and profit sharing as the least present EFP scheme in Croatia. Finally, after analysing 39 different determinants of EFP in the Croatian context, the establishment age, profitability, proportion of annual payroll costs spent on training, the human resource (HR) director's years of service for the organisation and the HR director's years of service in human resource management were found to be the primary determinants of EFP in Croatia.

---

1 Nina Pološki Vokić (corresponding author): Department of Organisation and Management, Faculty of Economics and Business, University of Zagreb, Croatia, email: npoloski@efzg.hr
Maja Klindžić: Department of Organisation and Management, Faculty of Economics and Business, University of Zagreb, Croatia, email: mklindzic@efzg.hr
Ivana Načinović Braje: Department of Organisation and Management, Faculty of Economics and Business, University of Zagreb, Croatia, email: inacinovic@efzg.hr

1. Introduction

It can be reasonably expected that employee participation (in different forms) is increasingly present in the modern world (Goić, 1999), as participation principles such as empowerment and transformational leadership are the only acceptable practices for today's workforce, increasingly composed of knowledge workers. As such, employee financial participation (EFP) is becoming part of the employment relationship of a rising number of employees in the industrialised world (e.g. Addison & Belfield, 2000; Poutsma, de Nijs & Poole, 2003). However, transition countries belong predominantly to the bottom 15 per cent in terms of their usage of EFP schemes (Poutsma & Ligthart, 2011), as a consequence of approximately only 20 years of human resource management (HRM) practices typical of free market economies[2].

This chapter presents the first comprehensive overview of the history, practice and determinants of EFP schemes in Croatia. It is interesting to discover whether organisations in Croatia have incorporated this 'typical form of "new" HRM' (Pendleton, 1997), and evaluate the relative importance of different EFP determinants in the Croatian context. In fact, the adoption of EFP is likely to vary, depending on a number of contextual factors (Poutsma, Ligthart & Schouteten, 2005). This debate is especially set in the context of national systems (e.g. Jones, Kalmi, Kato & Mäkinen, 2012; Poutsma & de Nijs, 2003), creating the impetus to conduct such research in the Croatian setting.

First, the Croatian EFP framework – foundations, practice of the last two decades, and the legal and fiscal support are presented. Next, the existing literature and research on EFP determinants are reviewed, in order to enable a better understanding of the relationship between contextual factors and EFP schemes. The main part of the chapter deals with EFP in Croatia at present, where the incidence of EFP in medium and large organisations in Croatia in 2014 was assessed using CRANET[3] methodology.

---

2 The transition process from a planned to a free market economy in former socialist European countries began in the 1990s.

3 The Cranfield Network on International Human Resource Management (CRANET), launched in 1989, is an established research collaboration of over 40 countries with a proven track record of collecting powerful, representative data on a continuing basis and undertaking rigorous analysis and disseminating high quality results in the area of human resource management (http://www.cranet.org/).

The determinants of EFP are analysed statistically as well. The chapter ends with arguments indicating the role of EFP schemes in organisations' competitiveness, with the aim of inspiring employers in Croatia to incentivise such schemes.

2. *Croatian financial participation framework*

2.1 *Foundations of financial participation in Croatia*

Croatia, the 28th European Union (EU) member state, declared independence from the former Yugoslavia and was established as an independent state on 25 June 1991. Its break-up with the former Yugoslavia was significant not only for national reasons, but also created a stimulus for transition to a market economy. The transition process that followed was hindered severely by the Croatian Homeland War (1991-1995); however, Croatian EFP history can be traced back almost two and a half decades.

Initially, Croatia had good prerequisites for the implementation of EFP, due to a long tradition of employee participation in the form of the Yugoslav model of self-management and the co-operative movement (Brnabić, Goić & Završak, 2006). The self-management model used in the former Yugoslavia was unique compared to other centrally planned economies in Eastern Europe (e.g. Gligorov, 1982; Milenkovitch, 1977). In essence, it was a model of total employee participation in both decision-making and financial results, while ownership was neither private nor public, but 'social' – it belonged to the organisations. Moreover, since enterprises were managed by their employees, there was a kind of 'collective ownership' without any right to individual claims. Similarly, co-operatives were managed by their members, who were obliged to combine their resources in co-operatives, from which point on they were considered collective property, although members could exercise some individual claims (Brnabić et al., 2006).

The foundations of the market economy in Croatia were laid by the last Yugoslav government under Prime Minister Marković, when the *Act on Social Capital* was introduced in 1989. This Act allowed the creation of private enterprises and made the privatisation of existing "social" enterprises possible, simultaneously favouring insiders – employees and managers – by giving them a special position in the process (the opportunity to buy a large amount of shares in their company at heavily discounted prices – as much as 70 per cent). The exact number of organisations that were privatised according to Marković's laws is unknown, but it remained relatively low. After Croatia gained independence, Marković's laws were suspended and then abolished in 1991 (Brnabić et al., 2006).

In 1991, when Croatia started the massive transition process of its entire economic system, the first issue was to define clear ownership, since the self-management model was no longer compatible with the market economy (Bendeković, 2000). However, employees in Croatia entered the transition process with two assumptions: (1) they were the workers who had created organisational assets and hence had the right to participate in the ownership or distribution of company assets, and (2) only those whose work created value had the right to participate in the distribution of financial results (profits) (Goić, 1999). These assumptions created a positive attitude towards EFP and formed a solid ideological foundation for its implementation.

The process of privatisation in Croatia had two phases: (1) transformation of social ownership into private and/or state ownership, and (2) privatisation of state ownership formed during the stage of ownership transformation (Bendeković, 2000). The legal framework for ownership transformation was amended in April 1991 when the *Act on Transformation of Enterprises in Social Ownership* was institutionalised, and later with the *Privatisation Act* adopted in March 1996.

The *Act on Transformation of Enterprises in Social Ownership* prescribed that ownership transformation into a joint stock company or limited liability company should be completed by 30 June 1992.[4] The part of the ownership that was not transformed was transferred to the Croatian Privatisation Fund (two-thirds) and the National Pension Fund (one-third).

The *Privatisation Act*, passed in March 1996, set rules for the privatisation of state-owned companies, whose ownership was transferred to the Croatian Privatisation Fund during the transformation phase. Transformation and privatisation laws were suspended when the *Act on Administration and Disposal of Property of the Republic of Croatia* was passed on 30 July 2013. The Act regulates the privatisation of the remaining state portfolio. However, it states explicitly that state-owned enterprises can be

---

4 This transformation excluded organisations of strategic national importance, infrastructure companies and financial sector companies.

privatised to a maximum of 25 per cent of total shares through the employee stock ownership plan (ESOP).

It should be emphasised that employees were considered an important part of the transformation phase, and therefore the *Transformation Act* regulated their rights. However, employee ownership rights were not prescribed by privatisation legislation between 1996 and 2013. The *Transformation Act* prescribed that employees and those previously employed in an organisation had the right to buy shares at a basic discount of 20 per cent, and an additional discount of one per cent for every year of employment within the company. However, no more than 50 per cent of the organisation's value could be sold at a discount. The maximum total value of shares which could be bought at a discount by a present or former employee was limited to 20,000 DEM[5], paid in cash or in instalments over five years (Bendeković, 2000).

Employee share ownership, as a consequence of employee buyout (EBO), accompanied by management buyout (MBO), was among the key methods of privatisation in Croatia and led to a strong employee position. Since ESOP at that time was unregulated and had no official definition, each organisation was free to develop its own version. Consequently, many schemes used at that time were called ESOP, although they did not have all the features of ESOP (Lowitzsch, Bormann, Hanisch, Menke, Roggemann & Spitsa, 2008). ESOPs were implemented autonomously in the most successful Croatian organisations (such as Zagrebačka banka and Pliva (Galetić & Rašić Krnjaković, 2004)), possibly due to the fact that they were attractive to employees. Another reason was that only high-performing organisations were able to support employees financially from their own resources (profits), or provide outside support (Goić, 1999).

Employee interest in participating in ownership was very strong. Eligible employees or former employees bought shares mostly up to the maximum amount allowed. Their possible reasons for investment were the expectation of financial returns, and the desire to have some influence in the organisation (Goić, 1999). Unfortunately, there was no requirement for

5 DEM is the abbreviation for the Deutsche Mark, the official German currency until the adoption of the Euro in 2002. Until the 1990s, the DEM was used in south-east European countries as a measure of value, a currency in international trade, and for savings. After the introduction of the market economy, the first Croatian national currency (the Croatian Dinar) was pegged to the DEM as a part of policies to control inflation and stabilise the economy.

employees to keep their shares, so many either did not finish paying for them, or sold them shortly afterwards (Galetić & Rašić Krnjaković, 2004). The full benefits of employee share ownership were therefore exploited only by a small number of employees. Nowadays, both trade unions and managers in organisations still eligible for privatisation, and those already privatised but with a high stake of state ownership, advocate greater employee involvement, such as ESOP, which is yet to be institutionalised.

2.2 Financial participation in Croatia from the 1990s to the present day

The presence of three types of EFP (profit sharing, stock sharing, and stock options) in Croatia in the last two decades is shown in Table 1, through the systematisation of all publicly available, empirical research into EFP conducted to date[6]. Research in the area of EFP in Croatia gained importance at the end of the 1990s, with the aim of measuring and explaining the effects of several phases of the privatisation process that took place in the early 1990s. Research was mainly initiated by academics, later by Eurofond, and recently, under the auspices of the CRANET network.

Profit sharing. At the end of the 1990s, the first research into EFP in Croatia revealed that 18.1 per cent of the organisations surveyed used profit sharing (Galetić, Tipurić & Juri, 2000). The first comprehensive research on HRM in Croatia followed in 2001, covering only large organisations, of which 22.0 per cent applied profit sharing schemes (Pološki, 2003). A repeated study revealed that 17.5 per cent of organisations with more than 200 employees applied profit sharing (Pološki Vokić & Vidović, 2008). More recent research conducted by Eurofond (2009, 2012) showed 5.0 per cent and 5.8 per cent of respondents reporting their participation in company profit distribution. Lower rates were reported compared with previous research, presumably because respondents were assessing their personal compensation packages, rather than the overall presence of a scheme in the organisation. Finally, according to a study

6 The studies analysed were conducted using different types of samples (representative of the Croatian economy or convenience samples), sizes of entities (mostly large organisations), sample sizes (from 41 up to 552 organisations, or up to 1,110 individuals in the sample), and ownership characteristics (e.g. only private companies).

conducted in 2012 using CRANET methodology, profit sharing schemes were used by 31.7 per cent of large organisations in Croatia (Pološki Vokić, 2014).

Table 1. Profit sharing, stock sharing and stock options in Croatia in the last two decades

Research	Year to which data refers	Sample size (no. of organisations)	Company size	EFP schemes (per cent of organisations using)		
				Profit sharing	Stock sharing	Stock options
Galetić et al. (2000)	1998	139	All sizes	18.1	0.0	6.6
Pološki (2003)	2002	42	500+	22.0	8.0	-
Tipurić (2003)	2003	55	100+	-	12.7	-
Tipurić (2004)	2003	552	All sizes	-	9.4	-
Galetić & Načinović (2006)	2004	63	All sizes	8.2	16.7	14.6
Pološki Vokić & Vidović (2008)	2005	81	200+	17.5	34.5	-
Pološki Vokić, Klindžić & Đaković (2008)	2006	98	All sizes	2.1	2.1	-
Second European Company Survey (Eurofond, 2009)	2009	NA (500 individuals)	Private companies 10+	5.0	4.0	-
Fifth European Working Conditions Survey (Eurofond, 2012)	2010	NA (1,100 individuals)	NA	5.8	1.8	-
CRANET survey (Pološki Vokić, 2014)	2012	41	500+	31.7	22.0	-

Note. NA = not available

Share ownership. By the end of the 1990s, 6.6 per cent of organisations in Croatia had used stock options, mostly as a part of CEO compensation payments (Galetić et al., 2000). A study conducted at the beginning of the new millennium revealed that 8.0 per cent of large organisations had applied some form of share ownership (Pološki, 2003). Two years later, extensive research covering all company sizes showed that 9.4 per cent of organisations had implemented some form of employee share ownership (Tipurić, 2004). Additionally, the same study revealed that large organisations in Croatia had implemented ESOPs more than small and medium companies. In 2005, 34.5 per cent of organisations employing more than 200 employees reported implementing share ownership schemes (Pološki

Vokić & Vidović, 2008). Eurofond studies conducted in the majority of European countries (Eurofond, 2009, 2012) revealed a low incidence of share schemes in Croatia, 4 per cent and 1.8 per cent respectively, again probably because respondents were reporting on their individual working conditions. This positioned Croatia in the lower third of European countries according to the incidence of share schemes. The last available study that dealt with EFP in Croatia showed that stock ownership had been used by 22.0 per cent of large organisations in Croatia (Pološki Vokić, 2014).

Overall, profit sharing and stock ownership in Croatia in the last two decades have been used mostly by large organisations in the private sector. The incidence of EFP schemes was low when compared with the EU average (Pološki Vokić, 2014), probably due to Croatia's relatively short history of using high-performance HRM practices in general, as well as EFP schemes.

2.3 Current legal and fiscal support of financial participation in Croatia

The development of EFP schemes across the EU is strongly influenced by national policies. A national context is shaped by the existing legal framework, taxation and social security issues, labour/employment laws, financial market regulations, social and cultural traditions, and EFP implementation costs (Lowitzsch et al., 2008). The main elements of the EFP legal and fiscal framework in Croatia are presented in Table 2.

Table 2. Main elements of the EFP legal and fiscal framework in Croatia

Dimension	Status
Existing legal framework	No current legislation explicitly covering EFP
Tax law	No tax relief for enterprises or employees on profit sharing No tax relief for enterprises or employees on share ownership schemes
Labour law	Labour law does not foresee the necessity of consulting and negotiating financial plans with trade unions, work councils or other employee representatives, or the necessity to provide employees with the relevant information.

Note. Based on: Zakon o porezu na dobit [Profit Tax Act] (2014a), Zakon o porezu na dohodak [Income Tax Act] (2014b) and Zakon o radu [Labour Act] (2014c)

The Croatian legal system does not regulate EFP and there is a clear lack of economic incentives for introducing PEPPER[7] schemes in Croatia. The introduction of ESOP legislation was announced long ago (e.g. Gregurek, 2001; Galetić & Rašić Krnjaković, 2004), but legislation to support it has never been passed. Furthermore, although tax incentives are not a prerequisite for EFP, they should also be considered, as they effectively promote the spread of EFP (Lowitzsch et al., 2008).

In the fiscal sense, employee earnings resulting from participating in financial results (profits) or exercising stock options are treated as income and are accordingly subject to taxation and other duties. Since company profits are taxed as well, this means double taxation. The only tax relief is applied to dividends based on ESOP. Although dividends exceeding the limit of HRK 12,000[8] have been subject to tax since 2012, the *Income Tax Act* (NN, 2012) explicitly states that if shares have been obtained through a recognised ESOP scheme, such dividends are exempt from income tax. Altogether, the existing legal context for the implementation of EFP is unfavourable. There seems to be little political support for EFP, as any practice that is in any way associated with the former self-management system is distrusted (e.g. Lowitzsch et al., 2008).

3. *Determinants of financial participation*

The success of EFP schemes may be dependent on different institutional, economic and social contexts in the countries concerned (e.g. Poutsma et al., 2003), as well as organisational and individual variables. Determinants of EFP can therefore be classified in three groups (as shown in Figure 1): (1) national contextual determinants, (2) internal company-specific determinants, and (3) determinants at the individual level.

---

7 PEEPER stands for the *Promotion of Employee Participation in Profits and Enterprise Results*, a European Commission (EC) initiative for the promotion of this phenomenon in Europe (Poutsma & de Nijs, 2003). It is interesting to note that the 2006 PEPPER III report and 2009 PEPPER IV report assessed the status of EFP in Croatia, i.e. the EC supported EFP in Croatia even before Croatia became a full member of the EU.

8 The kuna, abbreviated HRK, has been the official currency of Croatia since 1994. It is divided into 100 lipas.

Figure 1. Three groups of EFP determinants

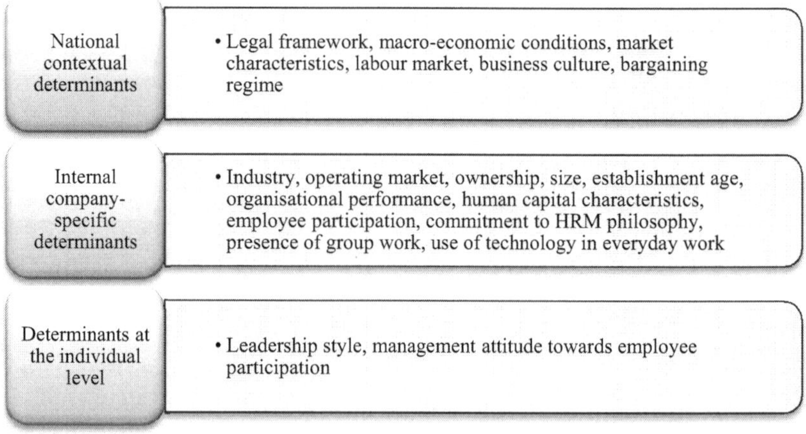

3.1 External contextual determinants

The development of EFP is directly (de)stimulated by the *legal framework* – EFP and taxation laws. In countries where EFP schemes are widespread, financial advantages are incorporated in the legal and fiscal framework. Legal/fiscal incentives can be provided for both employees and employers, including tax-free issues of shares/bonds to employees, tax-free allowances on distributed profits, or profitable changes to the taxation basis (Poutsma & de Nijs, 2003). For example, the European leaders in EFP in Europe are France, where profit sharing schemes are mandatory for organisations with more than 50 employees (Pérotin & Robinson, 2003), and the UK, with favourable tax treatment in the form of tax breaks for share ownership schemes (Jones et al., 2012; Poutsma & de Nijs, 2003). Researchers also report that the absence of a supportive legal framework is the reason for the low adoption of EFP schemes in many other EU countries (e.g. Darškuviené & Vazniokas, 2006; Fongwa, 2010; Jones et al., 2012; Poutsma & de Nijs, 2003; Remus, 1983).

Countries also differ in terms of the pervasive *business culture* which creates the EFP context for organisations. Shareholder-oriented organisations are more likely to adopt EFP schemes, because they are under less immediate pressure to display short term profitability, and can therefore afford to share some of the profits or shareholder value with employees, while organisations focusing narrowly on profit maximisation fail to provide EFP to a socially optimal degree (e.g. Blair, 1995; Levine, 1995). Researchers have shown that a general move towards shareholder value in European corporate governance has been a contributing factor to the increase of EFP schemes in Europe (Poutsma & de Nijs, 2003).

Economic theory suggests that EFP will be more widespread, all other factors being equal, in contexts where the economic risk is high and organisations want to transfer risk to employees (e.g. Darškuvienė & Vazniokas, 2006; Pendleton, 1997). In addition, *macro-economic conditions* influence the support of both governments and social partners for any proposal regarding EFP (Poutsma & de Nijs, 2003). Empirical findings confirm that in organisations affected by the crisis, EFP schemes are observed more often (Moeller & Bellmann, 2011). Furthermore, conditions on the capital market, such as the collapse of share values in some sectors in the EU, may have a negative impact on the development of EFP (e.g. Jones et al., 2012; Poutsma & de Nijs, 2003).

Various *market characteristics* are influential impetuses for the use of EFP. The *level of market dynamics*, as well as the *level of competition*, ranging from competitive to non-competitive markets, impacts the use of EFP schemes positively, due to the employee commitment these schemes cause (Poutsma & de Nijs, 2003). It can be deduced that EFP schemes are more present on growing markets. However, there is evidence that EFP schemes are also used as part of change management programmes in the case of declining markets (Pérotin & Robinson, 1998). In fact, profit sharing organisations were found to operate in declining industry sectors (Robinson & Wilson, 2006). Furthermore, a strong positive correlation was found between a high level of competition and cash profit sharing schemes (e.g. Drago & Heywood, 1995; Robinson & Wilson, 2006). However, some results suggest that workplaces with EFP record significantly lower levels of competition and higher levels of stability on product markets (e.g. Pendleton, 1997).

A deficit on *labour markets* tends to enhance the use of EFP, again due to increased employee commitment to the company, especially for groups of occupations such as qualified professionals in knowledge-intensive service industries (Poutsma & de Nijs, 2003).

Since profit sharing and share ownership are organisation-level phenomena, a positive relationship between decentralised *bargaining regimes* and the presence of EFP is expected (Poutsma & de Nijs, 2003). The incidence of share ownership plans was proven to be statistically significantly more prevalent in decentralised regimes; however there are no statistically significant differences between countries with decentralised and centralised regimes in the incidence of profit sharing plans (Kalmi, Pendleton & Poutsma, 2012).

3.2 Internal company-specific determinants

The adoption of EFP in different *industries* has been extensively researched. However, the results are not uniform. Although the industry concerned was not a predictor in many studies (e.g. Poutsma & de Nijs, 2003; Lavelle, Turner, Gunnigle & McDonnell, 2012), other researchers have shown that the greatest penetration of EFP schemes is in the finance sector, where half the companies have an all-employee scheme (e.g. Jones et al., 2012; Welz & Fernández-Macias, 2008). They are also found in the trade sector (e.g. Poutsma & de Nijs, 2003). The strongest argument for this is that companies operating in financial services are much more amenable to EFP schemes, given their knowledge and administrative experience of such schemes (Lavelle et al., 2012). The relationship between industry and EFPs could also be approached from the perspective of capital intensity. It is not surprising that the relationship between an organisation's *capital assets* and all-employee EFP schemes is very strong (Poole, 1988). Capital-intensive companies are more likely to have EFP schemes (e.g. D'Art & Turner, 2004; Kroumova & Sesil, 2006), although when industry was used as a proxy for capital intensity in one recent study, no support was found for the argument that capital-intensive companies are more likely to introduce EFP schemes (Lavelle et al., 2012). In addition, organisations operating in a more *technologically challenging environment* introduce profit sharing schemes more frequently, primarily to facilitate the adoption of new technology, because group-based incentives are more appropriate to changing patterns of work organisation (Cable & Wilson, 1990). In contrast, share ownership schemes are unlikely to be linked to the adoption of new production technology (Robinson & Wilson, 2006).

Profit sharing organisations appear to face highly competitive domestic markets, while organisations with share ownership are more internationally focused (Robinson & Wilson, 2006). Consequently, being present on the national or international *market* is also a determinant of profit-related pay and share ownership (Addision & Belfield, 2000).

One of the strongest predictors of EFP schemes is evidently *ownership structure*. Unlike *public companies*, *privately-owned companies* are more likely to have closed structures, and less likely to have EFP schemes in place (e.g. Kabst, Matiaske & Schmelter, 2006; Lavelle et al., 2012; Poole, 1988). EFP is expectedly rare in independent, *family-owned companies,* because families do not intend to share ownership of the firm with employees (since it comprises their family assets and savings, and in many ways supports their pensions) (Poutsma & de Nijs, 2003). In Europe, employee share ownership tends to be concentrated in large, publicly-listed companies (Poutsma & de Nijs, 2003), although smaller, privately-held companies in the US have tended to adopt it as well (NCEO, 1999). As for organisations mainly *owned by management*, they are also less likely to offer EFP (Jones et al., 2012). Additionally, one survey showed that organisations *owned by the state or co-operatives* have a likelihood of over 90 per cent of having EFP schemes (Jones et al., 2012). Concerning the differences between *publicly-listed* and *non-listed companies*, the evidence overwhelmingly points towards a positive relationship between publicly-listed companies and the presence of all types of EFP schemes (e.g. Kabst et al., 2006; Pendleton, Poutsma, van Ommeren & Brewster, 2001). For example, multi-national companies (MNCs) that trade their shares publicly are significantly more likely to have EFP schemes in place (Lavelle et al., 2012). Furthermore, concerning the 'nationality' of ownership, *domestic companies* are more likely to report these schemes (e.g. Pendleton, 1997; Poutsma & de Nijs, 2003). Finally, in the case of *single-* versus *multi-site companies,* the results are rather mixed, as findings imply that totally independent, single-site establishments do not tend to implement profit sharing (Poutsma & de Nijs, 2003), but that there is an insignificant relationship between having multiple-site establishments and EFP schemes as well (Jones et al., 2012).

Company size[9] is a determinant that has been extensively researched in the EFP context. Theoretical arguments that prevail in the literature give

9 Company size is mostly operationalised as the number of full time employees or equivalent, although size categories based on this particular criterion are not unified and vary in different countries and studies. For example, the EU recommendation (EU, 2003) is that companies that employ less than 50 employees are considered as small companies, those that employ up to 250 employees are labelled medium-sized companies, while those that employ more than 250 employees are usually regarded as large companies.

arguments in favour of a positive relationship between company size and EFP (e.g. Jones et al., 2012; Welz & Fernández-Macias, 2008), and especially share ownership (e.g. Pendleton, 1997; Poole, 1988; Poutsma & de Nijs, 2003; Robinson & Wilson, 2006). In fact, it has been argued that the problems typical of large organisations, such as high monitoring and coordination costs, or a wider social distance between employees and management (Pendleton et al., 2001), can be alleviated by the use of EFP schemes, as they encourage greater cooperation, information sharing and productivity (Lavelle et al., 2012). However, there are studies implying a negative relationship between establishment size and EFP presence (e.g. Bakan, Suseno, Pinnington & Money, 2004; Drago & Heywood, 1995). The contrary school of thought says that, as a result of the free-rider effect[10], the benefits accruing to employees from EFP schemes in large organisations are likely to be smaller (e.g. Fongwa, 2010; Oyer, 2004; Robinson & Wilson, 2006). Finally, there are studies implying that company size has no effect on EFP in general (e.g. Long, 2000; Robinson, 1997 after Pendleton, 1997), or on profit sharing specifically (e.g. Poutsma & de Nijs, 2003).

Many studies point towards the significance of *establishment age* for the adoption of EFP (e.g. Addision & Belfield, 2000; Poutsma et al., 2005). Profit sharing organisations appear to be older (Robinson & Wilson, 2006), probably due to the fact that they are unlikely to have made significant profits in the early years (Lavelle et al., 2012). For example, older MNCs are more likely to report EFP schemes, possibly as a revitalisation strategy (Pérotin & Robinson, 1998). However, some researchers report the opposite – that EFP schemes vary according to the different stages of a company's lifecycle, and that such schemes are much more likely to be found in new, growing organisations (e.g. Lavelle et al., 2012). Reasons for a higher incidence of EFP in younger establishments include a strong need for high employee commitment and performance to grow the organisation, the convenience of such reward types if the organisation is unable to ensure a steady income flow, as well as the fact that such rewards can be useful in retaining key employees and their knowl-

---

10 The 'free rider problem', arising from the fact that an individual may be able to obtain the benefits of a good without contributing to the cost, is discussed in a number of different contexts (Pasour, 1981). In the work context, it is generally considered that in large organisations, gains from the increase in productivity generated by one employee are shared among all employees (Fongwa, 2010).

edge (Pendleton et al., 2001). Notwithstanding these arguments, it has been also found that company age has little or no impact on the presence of EFP schemes (Pendleton et al., 2001).

EFP adoption can also be analysed in the context of *organisational performance*. In the case of *excellent* versus *companies in difficulties*, EFP has been viewed as an antecedent of performance (e.g. Darškuviené & Vazniokas, 2006; Fernie & Metcalf, 1995). Although it is reasonable to expect organisations adopting EFP to perform below average in terms of profitability and productivity, with sharing adopted to improve performance, evidence from France, Germany, Italy, the UK and the US implies that organisations adopting EFP tend to be better than average performers, suggesting that EFP is not widely adopted as a turnaround strategy by organisations in difficulties (Pendleton, 1997). More precisely, workplaces with both profit-related pay schemes and employee share ownership do better than average, whereas those with only one or the other do not (Addision & Belfield, 2000). Furthermore, the relationship between trends in *business volume* and EFP adoption is highly significant (Poole, 1988). In expanding companies experiencing an increase in business volume, managers will often promote these programmes, partly to attract and retain employees, but also thanks to financial ability to offer rewards of this type (Poole, 1988). *Organisational productivity* is another aspect of organisational performance which can be observed in relation to EFP. Both employee profit sharing schemes and share ownership have the potential to improve productivity (Robinson & Wilson, 2006). Profit sharing has been statistically linked to greater productivity (e.g. Fernie & Metcalf, 1995; Festing, Groening, Kabst & Weber, 1999), although no statistically significant effects on productivity (Robinson & Wilson, 2006), or only insignificant effects have also been found (Kalmi, Pendleton & Poutsma, 2005).

Many *human capital characteristics* have been found to correlate with the higher usage of EFP schemes, for example a higher *proportion of highly skilled/educated/qualified employees* (e.g. Addison & Belfield, 2000; Poutsma & de Nijs, 2003), a higher *proportion of white-collar employees* (e.g. Pendleton, 1997), a higher *proportion of high value human capital* (talents, key employees) (e.g. Frye 2004; Lavelle et al., 2012) and a higher *proportion of higher levels of staff* (managers and professionals) (e.g. Lavelle et al., 2012; Welz & Fernández-Macias, 2008). Such findings are in line with the emerging debate on attracting and motivating talents as vital HRM activities in the competitive 21st century, because of the impact of these employees on company success. However, contrary evidence is also found in the literature, for example predominantly low-skilled workforce employed in profit sharing organisations (Robinson & Wilson, 2006).

EFP and *direct employee participation* are found to coexist, as they are complementary and reinforce each other (e.g. Jones et al., 2012; Poole, 1988; Poutsma & de Nijs, 2003). In fact, increasing employee participation in isolated cases of decision-making may have negative effects, as employees gain access to strategic decisions and information, but lack the incentive to act in the best interests of shareholders (Ben-Ner & Jones, 1995). In other words, in organisations in which consultation, cooperation and information sharing are encouraged, there is a higher use of EFP schemes, as extensions of overall policies for stimulating employee involvement and pay-offs for direct participation (e.g. Pendleton, 1997; Poole, 1988; Poutsma & de Nijs, 2003). For example, influence on decision-making has been found to be a determinant of support for profit sharing (Bakan et al., 2004), while workplaces with share-based EFP schemes are clearly more participative than workplaces without EFP (Pendleton, 1997). Nevertheless, it should be mentioned that some studies have found mixed or insignificant relationships between the concepts (e.g. Jones et al., 2012; Kalmi et al., 2005).

Two dominant forms of *indirect employee participation* (staff associations and trade unions) impact EFP differently. Employee representation through *staff associations* is one of the predictors of EFP presence (e.g. Poole, 1988; Poutsma & de Nijs, 2003), although research on joint consultation committees (JCC) as the statistically insignificant variable is also found (e.g. Jones et al., 2012). On the other hand, EFP schemes are generally viewed as being at the expense of traditional forms of collective employee representation and undermining the position of *trade unions* (e.g. Pendleton, 1997; Poutsma & de Nijs, 2003). To be more precise, they may form a barrier to union-organised drives, or a management strategy to weaken and 'bypass' strong unions (e.g. Pendleton, 1997; Roche & Turner, 1998). In fact, unions are usually unsupportive of EFP schemes, since they aspire to stabilise and maximise base wages, because EFP has the apparent capacity to increase identification with the organisation and loyalty to the company rather than to the union, and because EFP encourages entrepreneurial attitudes, resulting in diminishing union membership and influence (e.g. Drago & Heywood, 1995; Lavelle et al., 2012; Pendleton, 1997; Poole, 1998). Consequently, EFP is expected to be applied less in organisations with a union presence, a substantial degree of unionisation (union density), and collective bargaining. However, empirical results in this area are mixed and contradictory. There is research confirming that organisations that recognise trade unions are less likely to have EFP schemes in place (e.g. Festing et al., 1999; Lavelle et al., 2012; Pendleton, 1997), but some evidence suggests a positive relationship between union presence/density and EFP (e.g. Kalmi et al., 2005; Kalmi et al., 2012; Poole, 1988). Finally, there are studies implying that industrial relations variables are statistically insignificant (e.g. Jones et al., 2012; Poutsma & de Nijs, 2003).

In the modern HRM literature, the use of EFP is recommended as one of the best HRM practices, since it is considered to be part of a high-performance work system (e.g. Pfeffer, 1994, 1998; Poutsma et al., 2003). Therefore, EFP schemes can be expected to be more present in organisations with a high *commitment to HRM philosophy*. Various high-performance HRM activities have been found to be complementary to EFP (e.g. Becker & Gerhart, 1996; Bloom & van Reenen, 2007; Jones et al., 2012; Wood, 1996), such as higher levels of median pay (Pendleton, 1997) and workplace training (Jones et al., 2012). A correlation can also be found between EFP schemes and the presence of a manager specialised in HRM (Pendleton, 1997), as the position indicates the importance assigned to human capital investment activities in the company.

By definition, EFP incentivises *group* rather than individual *performance* (McCartney, Croucher & Svetlik, 2005). Workplaces with team-based technologies, where it is difficult to measure individual effort, and intra-group cooperation is vital, might be perceived as suitable contexts for the introduction of EFP (for example, those with suggestion schemes, group consultation and interdependence of work tasks, quality circles, teamwork and self-managed teams) (e.g. Jones et al., 2012; Pendleton, 1997; Poutsma & de Nijs, 2003). However, there is empirical research that does not support teamwork variables as significant determinants of EFP (e.g. Kalmi et al., 2005).

Researchers have also discovered significantly negative relationships between the *presence of advanced automated technology* and share scheme workplaces, probably since it is more difficult to monitor individual workers in more technologically advanced workplaces (Pendleton, 1997). In addition, the use of *computers* has been found to be associated positively and significantly with EFP (Jones et al., 2012).

3.3 Determinants at the individual level

The consultative, participative *decision-making style* is stronger than the paternal, autocratic style in predicting the presence of EFP schemes (e.g. Poole, 1988). To be precise, there is a clear tendency for organisations in which management shares decision-making to have profit sharing or employee shareholding schemes (Poole, 1988).

The *positive attitude of managers towards* different forms of *employee participation* correlates with the existence of EFP schemes (especially profit sharing arrangements), since as with most HRM practices, a scheme's impact and implementation are successful when management adheres to it and is convinced of its function (e.g. Poutsma & de Nijs, 2003).

4. Presence and determinants of financial participation in Croatia today

4.1 Methodology

Research instrument. Data on the presence of EFP schemes in medium and large organisations[11] in Croatia in 2014 were obtained from the CRANET survey[12] conducted in 2014. The survey asked which of the three forms of EFP (profit sharing (PS), stock sharing (SS), and stock options (SO)) was offered to three categories of employees (managers, professionals without managerial responsibilities, and clerical and/or manual workers). It was also determined whether any of the EFP schemes

---

11 Classification of small, medium and large organisations in Croatia is defined by the *Accounting Act of Croatia* (NN, 1997). Small organisations are those that do not meet two of the following conditions: (1) total assets of HRK 32,500,000, (2) revenues of HRK 65,000,000, and (3) 50 or more employees on average during the business year. Medium organisations are those that do not satisfy two of the following conditions: (1) total assets of HRK 130,000,000, (2) revenues of HRK 260,000,000, and (3) 250 or more employees on average during the business year. Large organisations satisfy two of the conditions for medium enterprises.

12 The CRANET questionnaire collected numerous HRM indicators, as well as organisational data, grouped in seven areas: (1) HRM activities in the organisation, (2) recruitment and selection, (3) employee development, (4) compensations and benefits, (5) employee relations and internal communication, (6) organisational data, (7) personal data (about the person that completed the questionnaire).

was offered to all employees in a company, and whether there were organisations in the sample offering all three types of EFP to all categories of employees. For the purpose of assessing the determinants of EFP in Croatia, the statistical significance of 39 environmental, organisational and HRM indicators for 13 EFP indicators[13] was assessed. As the framework for collecting variables determining EFP occurrence was a CRANET questionnaire, a research instrument with an obvious HRM perspective, unfortunately not all the relevant determinants of EFP were taken into account. However, the research conducted was one of the first focusing on HRM practices related to EFP.

Sample. All organisations in Croatia with more than 200 employees were invited to participate in the survey. Out of around 500 organisations in this category[14], 110 returned a properly completed questionnaire, making a response rate of approximately 20 per cent and covering one-fifth of the entire category. The profile of the research sample presented in Table 3 shows that the organisations which participated in the survey were heterogeneous in size, industry and ownership. Medium (200 to 500 employees), wholesale and retail trade, and private sector organisations were over-sampled, but this corresponded with the category structure, implying no response bias and making the sample representative. Additionally, it should be mentioned that some public sector organisations, such as government agencies and infrastructure firms, were excluded from the analysis, because profit sharing or share schemes were not an option for them. As a result, 107 organisations from the sample were suitable for profit sharing analysis, and 80 organisations for share schemes analysis.

---

13 The 13 EFP indicators analysed were: (1) PS for managers, (2) PS for professionals, (3) PS for clerical/manual workers, (4) SS for managers, (5) SS for professionals, (6) SS for clerical/manual workers, (7) SO for managers, (8) SO for professionals, (9) SO for clerical/manual workers, (10) PS for all employees, (11) SS for all employees, (12) SO for all employees, and (13) all three types of EFP offered to all employees.

14 The list of Croatian organisations with more than 200 employees was obtained from the Croatian Chamber of Commerce web database, accessed on 15 February 2014.

Table 3. Profile of organisations in the sample

Indicator	Percentage of organisations
Size of organisation (no. of employees)	< 200 employees[15] – 7.3 per cent; 200-500 employees – 48.2 per cent; 500-1,000 employees – 25.4 per cent; >1,000 employees – 18.2 per cent; missing – 0.9 per cent
Main activity	Agriculture, hunting, forestry, fishing, mining and quarrying – 1.8 per cent; manufacture of food, beverages, textiles, wood and paper, coke and refined petroleum, and related products – 9.1 per cent; manufacture of chemicals, pharmaceuticals, and medicinal chemical products – 2.7 per cent; manufacture of basic metals and metal products, plastic and other non-metallic products – 7.3 per cent; manufacture of computer, electronic products, electrical equipment – 1.8 per cent; manufacture of machinery and equipment – 2.7 per cent; manufacture of transport equipment – 0.9 per cent; other manufacturing – 3.6 per cent; electricity, gas, steam, and water supply, waste management – 4.5 per cent; construction – 6.4 per cent; wholesale and retail trade – 17.3 per cent; transportation and storage – 2.7 per cent; accommodation and food service activities, publishing, broadcasting activities – 5.5 per cent; telecommunications, IT and other information services – 5.5 per cent; financial and insurance activities – 2.7 per cent; accounting, management, architecture, engineering, scientific research, and other administrative and support service activities – 0.9 per cent; public administration and compulsory social security – 2.7 per cent; other industry or services – 21.9 per cent
Ownership	Private sector – 67.3 per cent; public sector – 26.4 per cent; not for profit sector – 1.8 per cent; mixed sector – 3.6 per cent; missing – 0.9 per cent

Data collection and analysis. Questionnaires were sent to HR directors (the most senior HR managers in the organisations), as they are the most knowledgeable and informed respondents regarding HRM practices in their organisations[16]. Questionnaires were delivered both by electronic mail and post, with a brief covering letter explaining the purpose of the

15 There are organisations with fewer than (but close to) 200 employees in the sample, because some of the companies contacted had 200 employees at the time the database was accessed. These organisations were not removed from the study, as they once managed more than 200 employees (which is the focus of a global CRANET survey) and the practices they used to manage their employees had probably remained the same.

16 49.1 per cent of respondents who completed the questionnaire were HR directors themselves.

study. Respondents had the opportunity to remain anonymous by returning questionnaires by post, but only four organisations (3.7 per cent) used this option. Absolute and relative frequencies calculations, contingency tabulations, as well as χ^2 tests (the only appropriate method for analysing relationships since PS, SS and SO were dichotomous variables), using the Statistical Package for the Social Sciences (SPSS), were used for the data analysis.

4.2 Presence of financial participation

Figure 2 shows the availability of three EFP schemes analysed for the three categories of employees (clerical/manual workers – C/M, professionals – P, managers – M), average availability (calculated as a mean value of C/M, P and M data) and whether they are available to all employees in an organisation. In order to demonstrate how close/far from working in a high-performance work system employees in Croatia are, both private and public sector organisations were included in the analysis at this stage.

Figure 2. Percentage of organisations offering PS, SS and SO schemes (N = 110)

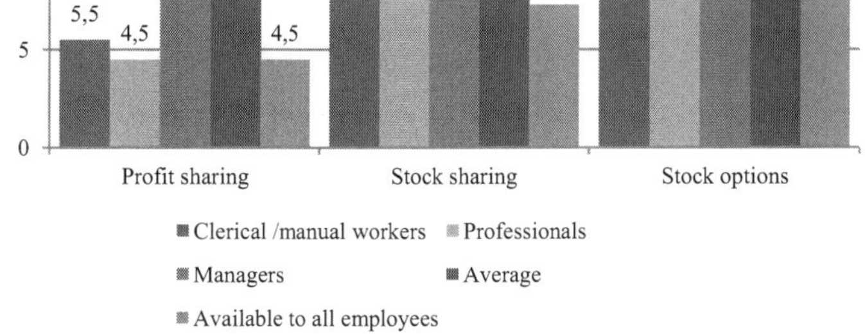

Note. Figure shows PF indicators in organisations which provided answers, meaning that missing data is treated as unoffered PF schemes.

As Figure 2 reveals, the EFP schemes analysed are not often used as a way to boost employee performance and involvement in Croatia, as on average only around ten per cent of the employees in the organisations in the sample are exposed to such practices. Moreover, all three types of EFP available to all employees are present in only two (1.8 per cent) privately owned companies in the sample.[17] However, it is interesting to notice that PS, usually the most implemented EFP scheme (see for example Addison & Belfield, 2000; Kalmi et al., 2012) is least present, while SO, usually the least implemented EFP scheme (see for example Poutsma & Ligthart, 2011) is most present. The first situation is probably a consequence of the economic crisis which is still impacting Croatia heavily, as during crisis times companies are generally reluctant to share their profits. The second is probably a reflection of the fact that many Croatian organisations still have the opportunity to grant shares to their employees, given that processes of transferring ownership into private hands are not yet complete, or companies are still using this option to consolidate their businesses. The relatively high incidence of SO could be attributed to the past (ownership transformation and privatisation years), when employee/ manager buyouts were popular.

However, it is interesting to examine the EFP practices of private companies in Croatia (shown in Figure 3), as they enjoy an appropriate context and should be interested in devising compensation packages in a stimulating way.

According to the latest available comparative EFP data (from the CRANET 2011 survey), profit sharing is on average present in 20.5 per cent of private organisations in post-transition countries[18], stock sharing in 17.3 per cent, and stock options in 15.5 per cent, while in the most developed countries[19], profit sharing is present in 44.0 per cent of cases, stock sharing in 25.1 per cent and stock options in 21.9 per cent (calculated using Poutsma & Ligthart, 2011). At the global level (post-transition, developed and developing countries), profit sharing is present in 36.1 per

17 Consequently, this EFP indicator is omitted from the inferential statistical analysis.

18 The following eight European post-transition countries were included in the analysis: Bulgaria, Hungary, Lithuania, Russia, Serbia, Slovakia, and Slovenia.

19 The following fifteen countries from among the world's most developed countries were included in the analysis: Australia, Austria, Belgium, Denmark, Finland, France, Germany, Iceland, Japan, Netherlands, Norway, Sweden, Switzerland, United Kingdom, and USA.

Figure 3. Percentage of private companies offering PS, SS and SO schemes (N = 74)

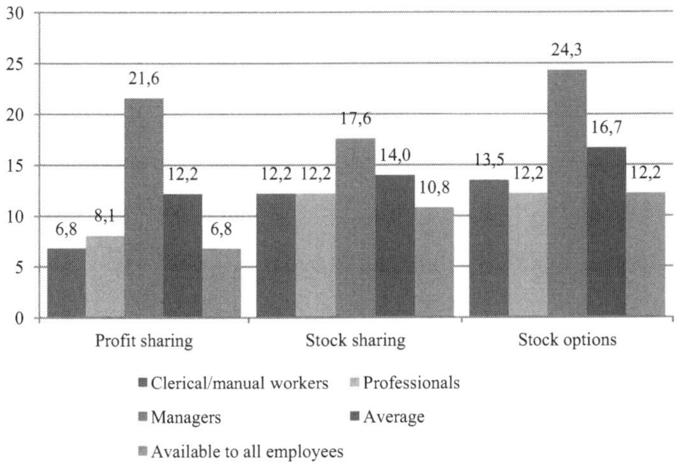

Note. Figure shows PF indicators in organisations which provided answers, meaning that missing data is treated as unoffered PF schemes.

cent of private companies, stock sharing in 23.6 per cent and stock options in 20.7 per cent (Poutsma & Ligthart, 2011). Looking at these data, it can be deduced that, from the PS and SS perspective, Croatia is a typical post-transition European country, as the presence of these EFP schemes (taking the highest individual percentage of presence indicating the availability of the scheme in the organisation) fully corresponds with the CRANET data for post-transition countries. However, looking at SO presence, the Croatian data exceed SO levels in the most developed countries in the CRANET sample. Again, this is probably due to the fact that the process of transferring ownership into private hands in many Croatian organisations is not yet complete, and the stock market is still developing in general. Therefore SO is used as a strategy for linking managers' efforts to the organisations' future.

4.3 Determinants of financial participation

Table 4 shows which of the 39 variables analysed, grouped in nine categories, could be labelled determinants of EFP in the Croatian context – those with a 0.1, 0.05 or 0.01 level of significance.

Table 4. Significant EFP determinants

	EFP determinants	Profit sharing				Stock sharing				Stock options			
		M	P	C/M	AE	M	P	C/M	AE	M	P	C/M	AE
	External contextual variables												
1.	Market trend (declining, static, growing)	0.056^{+}	0.096^{+}	0.100	0.162	0.244	0.450	0.421	0.691	0.162	0.170	0.074^{+}	0.091^{+}
	Company characteristics												
2.	Number of employees	0.339	0.329	0.329	0.315	0.316	0.311	0.311	0.317	0.397	0.424	0.432	0.451
3.	Industry	0.477	0.172	0.389	0.174	0.602	0.811	0.799	0.882	0.674	0.377	0.403	0.354
4.	Ownership	0.095^{+}	0.416	0.335	0.466	NA	NA	NA	NA	NA	NA	NA	NA
5.	Business owned or controlled primarily by one family	0.293	0.499	0.700	0.352	0.017*	0.211	0.221	0.075^{+}	0.016*	0.125	0.179	0.274
6.	Family owners involved in management	0.497	0.497	0.497	0.497	NC	0.684	0.684	NC	0.116	0.740	0.740	0.684
7.	Single or multi-site establishment	0.360	0.590	0.712	0.581	0.330	0.188	0.173	0.337	0.792	0.852	0.603	0.572
8.	Establishment age	0.510	0.045*	0.100	0.009**	0.066^{+}	0.010*	0.008**	0.004**	0.216	0.102	0.089^{+}	0.045*
9.	Main market(s) for products and services (from local to world-wide)	0.125	0.517	0.545	0.507	0.207	0.371	0.348	0.384	0.578	0.316	0.408	0.428
	Organisational performance												
10.	ROA	0.422	0.344	0.345	0.327	0.599	0.664	0.667	0.709	0.463	0.489	0.499	0.513
11.	ROE	0.384	0.410	0.410	0.661	0.520	0.664	0.667	0.543	0.553	0.616	0.636	0.653
12.	Rating of service quality	0.322	0.122	0.039*	0.202	0.710	0.838	0.825	0.565	0.418	0.786	0.874	0.888
13.	Rating of level of productivity	0.895	0.675	0.467	0.797	0.333	0.506	0.511	0.612	0.102	0.060^{+}	0.121	0.176
14.	Rating of profitability	0.218	0.363	0.506	0.581	0.006**	0.190	0.177	0.184	0.079^{+}	0.044*	0.015*	0.011*
15.	Rating of rate of innovation	0.811	0.193	0.297	0.173	0.972	0.515	0.516	0.549	0.321	0.376	0.440	0.435
16.	Rating of stock market performance	0.574	0.695	0.558	0.819	0.740	0.894	0.887	0.753	0.552	0.871	0.852	0.919
17.	Rating of environmental matters	0.935	0.619	0.617	0.634	0.412	0.188	0.188	0.138	0.774	0.644	0.772	0.787
	Human capital characteristics												
18.	Proportion of employees 25 years old and under	0.044*	0.030*	0.042*	0.074^{+}	0.841	0.492	0.496	0.457	0.421	0.375	0.427	0.422
19.	Proportion of employees 50 years old and over	0.176	0.657	0.006**	0.785	0.538	0.258	0.375	0.590	0.932	0.731	0.914	0.893
20.	Proportion of the workforce with higher education/ university qualifications	0.732	0.862	0.699	0.864	0.688	0.815	0.784	0.860	0.656	0.428	0.825	0.879
	HR department characteristics												

	EFP determinants	Profit sharing				Stock sharing				Stock options			
		M	P	C/M	AE	M	P	C/M	AE	M	P	C/M	AE
21.	Existence of independent HR department	0.139	0.157	0.122	0.171	0.171	0.346	0.357	0.507	0.045*	0.190	0.243	0.337
22.	Percentage of employees employed in HR department out of total number of employees	0.444	0.440	0.440	0.445	0.437	0.435	0.435	0.438	0.438	0.433	0.432	0.438
	HRM indicators												
23.	Percentage of operating costs accounted for by labour costs	0.346	0.119	0.119	0.056+	0.700	0.829	0.829	0.937	0.563	0.730	0.803	0.852
24.	Annual staff turnover (percentage)	0.189	0.714	0.714	0.862	0.079+	0.293	0.293	0.234	0.263	0.578	0.707	0.817
25.	Absenteeism (in days) per year	0.265	0.313	0.313	0.438	0.410	0.408	0.408	0.509	0.243	0.236	0.271	0.294
	HRM activities												
26.	Participation in project team work	0.800	0.861	0.532	0.847	0.815	0.337	0.314	0.454	0.509	0.474	0.366	0.399
27.	Proportion of the annual payroll spent on training	0.296	0.034*	0.002**	0.018*	0.228	0.050+	0.071+	0.021*	0.581	0.156	0.146	0.070+
28.	Days of training per year per manager	0.690	-	-	0.890	0.550	-	-	0.835	0.030*	-	-	0.421
29.	Days of training per year per professional	-	0.363	-	0.382	-	0.644	-	0.709	-	0.421	-	0.760
30.	Days of training per year per clerical/manual worker	-	-	0.282	0.696	-	-	0.662	0.319	-	-	0.112	0.147
	Indirect employee participation												
31.	Proportion of employees who are members of a trade union	0.978	0.875	0.875	0.845	0.421	0.403	0.403	0.358	0.232	0.341	0.342	0.320
32.	Extent to which trade unions influence organisation	0.189	0.205	0.386	0.271	0.025*	0.227	0.209	0.437	0.471	0.946	0.983	0.968
33.	Recognition of trade unions for the purpose of collective bargaining	0.896	0.460	0.901	0.451	0.009**	0.031*	0.028*	0.051+	0.337	0.377	0.422	0.469
34.	Existence of joint consultative committee or work council	0.076+	0.363	0.248	0.461	0.470	0.973	1.000	0.678	0.273	0.941	0.740	0.512
	HR director characteristics												
35.	Gender	0.257	0.048*	0.048*	0.065+	0.249	0.249	0.249	0.125	0.673	0.183	0.183	0.125
36.	Years of service in the organisation	0.569	0.195	0.195	0.110	0.093+	0.060+	0.060+	0.021*	0.312	0.092+	0.092+	0.054+
37.	Possession of a university degree	0.845	0.560	0.560	0.561	0.698	0.698	0.698	0.555	0.224	0.418	0.418	0.555
38.	Main academic field of the most advanced degree	0.680	0.911	0.911	0.894	0.392	0.303	0.303	0.551	0.098+	0.156	0.156	0.208
39.	Years of service in HRM	0.671	0.014*	0.014*	0.001**	0.163	0.083+	0.083+	0.087+	0.130	0.155	0.155	0.192

Note. M = managers; P = professionals; C/M = clerical/manual workers; AE = all employees; NA = not analysed as share schemes are not an option in the public sector; NC = not computed due to insufficient data
Significance level: <0.01 (**), <0.05 (*), <0.1 (+).

Table 4 shows that the foremost determinants of EFP in Croatia (variables found to be statistically significant for more than five out of twelve EFP indicators assessed) are establishment age, profitability (subjectively assessed), proportion of annual payroll costs spent on training, years of HR director's service for the organisation, and years of HR director's service in HRM. Other determinants of EFP schemes in Croatia identified are ownership (private vs. public), family ownership, service quality (subjectively assessed), productivity (subjectively assessed), proportion of employees 25 years old and under, proportion of employees 50 years old or over, existence of an independent HR department, percentage of operating costs accounted for by labour costs, annual staff turnover, days of training per year per manager, the extent to which trade unions influence organisation, the recognition of trade unions for the purpose of collective bargaining, the existence of a JCC or work council, the gender of the HR director, and the main academic field of the most advanced degree of the HR director.

In fact, looking at contingency tabulations (crosstabs), EFP schemes in Croatia are developed to a greater extent in older organisations, more profitable ones, organisations spending less on training, and those with a senior HR director in terms of service and experience in the HRM field. Additionally, EFP schemes are found more in organisations which are private but not family owned/controlled, those with higher service quality and productivity, those with fewer young and more older staff members, those with independent HR department, those with a higher proportion of labour costs in total operating costs, those with higher annual staff turnover, those providing more training days per year per manager, those with higher indirect employee participation (with more influential trade unions, recognised for the purpose of collective bargaining and with organised joint consultative committees (JCC) or work councils), and those with a male HR director with a social or behavioural sciences background.

From the specific EFP schemes perspective, the strongest determinants of profit sharing (significant for three or more out of four indicators) are the proportion of employees 25 years old and under (when fewer are present), the proportion of annual payroll costs spent on training (when less is spent), the HR director's gender (when male) and the HR director's years of service in the HRM area (when more experienced). The strongest determinants of stock sharing are the establishment age (when older), the proportion of annual payroll costs spent on training (when less is spent), the recognition of trade unions for the purpose of collective bargaining (when recognised), the HR director's years of service in the organisation (when longer) and the HR director's years of service in the HRM area (when more experienced). Lastly, the strongest determinants of stock options are profitability (when rated better than the competition's) and the HR director's years of service in the organisation (when longer).

The majority of the findings presented correspond with the prevailing theoretical conclusions elaborated previously. However, some of our findings are intriguing. For instance, although higher levels of workplace training have been found to be associated with higher levels of EFP (Jones et al., 2012), in our research, organisations providing less training reported offering EFP schemes more often. One possible explanation is that organisations providing EFP, and therefore apparently understanding the motivational effect of such practices, are those employing highly educated/qualified employees who do not need extensive additional training. The next, somewhat unexpected finding, although already revealed in some research (e.g. Kalmi et al., 2012; Poole, 1998), concerns the existence/influence of indirect employee representation (trade unions and JCC/work councils) in relation to the adoption of EFP schemes. The reasons for this finding are not entirely clear to academic circles (Kalmi et al., 2005), as unions traditionally do not show much interest in negotiating these issues in collective agreements (Jones et al., 2012). However, some authors report many unions accepting PEPPER, as it can contribute to a better ratio of value-added to production (e.g. Fongwa, 2010). In Croatia, the reason may also be that trade unions are more present and influential in older organisations (one of the main individual determinants of EFP according to our results).

Finally, since it is not elaborated in the contemporary literature, the findings are interesting regarding EFP schemes being more present in 'older' organisations (those with fewer employees under 25 and more employees older than 50 years of age), organisations which have an independent HR department, and organisations with a proficient HR director (one with considerable service and experience in HRM) and with a social/behavioural sciences background. These results have two things in common – maturity and a human resources focus. Organisations employing people with longer business experience, which has almost certainly taught them to appreciate a work environment oriented towards human resources (applying high performance work practices), can be expected to provide EFP schemes more often. The last interesting finding is that PS is significantly more present in enterprises with a male HR director, which may be explained by the more materialistic nature of men (Heim & Golant, 1993).

5. Conclusion

The conclusion deduced from the Croatian EFP framework description is that the development of EFP schemes in Croatia will continue to be slow, unless the government improves the legal and taxation context. The same is true for most of the newest EU countries, for example neighbouring Slovenia (McCartney et al., 2005) and Lithuania (Darškuviené & Vazniokas, 2006). At the moment, one consequence of the lack of legislation governing EFP in Croatia is the absence of EFP tax incentives for either employees or organisations. Accordingly, the Croatian government should introduce legislation designed to encourage EFP schemes, or even make them compulsory.

The conclusion that can be drawn from the empirical research conducted is that organisations in Croatia are not appropriating the motivational and performance benefits that can result from implementing EFP. Less than ten per cent of organisations in Croatia (4.5 per cent for PS, 7.3 per cent for SS and 9.1 per cent for SO) offer the three EFP schemes assessed to all their employees, and only around ten per cent of employees on average (8.5 per cent for PS, 9.7 per cent for SS and 12.4 per cent of SO) have the opportunity to participate in their organisations' financial gains. However, the research revealed that EFP schemes are adopted more in organisations where there is a higher level of employee representation through trade unions and other work associations, and where the HR director has a higher level of HRM competence. In other words, the two most influential groups of EFP determinants (see Table 4) were the HR director's characteristics (four out of five assessed were found significant), and indirect employee participation (three out of four assessed were found significant).

Finally, it should be stressed that the enormous benefits of EFP have been discussed theoretically and confirmed empirically, including a greater sense of responsibility and accountability for decisions taken (e.g. Bakan et al., 2004; Darškuviené & Vazniokas, 2006), increased employee productivity (e.g. Kalmi et al., 2005; Pendleton, 1997), increased cooperation/collaboration between individuals and prosperous teamwork (e.g. Fongwa, 2010; McCartney et al., 2005), greater employee motivation/

satisfaction (e.g. Darškuvienė & Vazniokas, 2006; McCartney et al., 2005; Remus, 1983), greater commitment and loyalty to the company (e.g. Bakan et al., 2004; Darškuvienė & Vazniokas, 2006; Fongwa, 2010), reductions in absenteeism, turnover, recruitment and training costs (e.g. Kalmi et al., 2005; McCartney et al., 2005; Pendleton, 1997; Poole, 1988), and obtaining the status of employer of choice (e.g, Lavelle et al., 2012), all resulting in an organisation's improved corporate performance (e.g. Addison & Belfield, 2000; Bakan et al., 2004; Pendleton, 1997; Robinson & Wilson, 2006). Consequently, the limited usage of EFP schemes among the largest and most successful organisations in Croatia is not rational from the business perspective. Outcomes would be multiplied if they supported EFP on a broader scale, as these practices offer a means of improving economic efficiency by increasing staff satisfaction and motivation.

References

Addison, J. T., & Belfield, C. R. (2000). The impact of financial participation and employee involvement on financial performance: A re-estimation using the 1998 WERS. *Scottish Journal of Political Economy*, *47*, 571-583.

Bakan, I., Suseno, Y., Pinnington, A., & Money, A. (2004). The influence of financial participation and participation in decision-making on employee job attitudes. *International journal of human resource management*, *15*, 587-616.

Becker, B., & Gerhart, B. (1996). The impact of human resource management on organisational performance: Progress and prospects. *Academy of Management Journal*, *39*, 779-801.

Ben-Ner, A., & Jones, D. C. (1995). Employee participation, ownership, and productivity: a theoretical framework. *Industrial Relations*, *34*, 532-554.

Bendeković, J. (2000). Privatisation in Croatia. *Ekonomski pregled*, *51*(1-2), 55-90.

Blair, M. (1995). *Ownership and Control: Rethinking Corporate Governance for the Twenty-First Century*. Washington, DC: Brookings.

Bloom, N., & van Reenen, J. (2007). Measuring and Explaining Management Practices across Firms and Countries. *Quarterly Journal of Economics*, *122*, 1351-1408.

Brnabić, R., Goić, S., & Završak, D. (2006). Extended country report – Financial participation of Employees in Croatia. In J. Lowitzsch (Ed.), *The PEPPER III Report: Promotion of Employee Participation in Profits and Enterprise Results in the New Member and Candidate Countries of the European Union* (pp. 111-124). Rome and Berlin: European Federation of Employee Share Ownership and International Association for Financial Participation.

Cable, J., & Wilson, N. (1990). Profit-Sharing and Productivity: Some Further Evidence. *Economic Journal*, *100*, 550-555.

CRANET, www.cranet.org

D'Art, D., & Turner, T. (2004). Profit Sharing, Firm Performance and Union Influence in Selected European Countries. *Personnel Review*, *33*, 335-350.

Darškuviené, V., & Vazniokas, P. (2006). Stock ownership as a form of employee and management financial participation: factors of development in Lithuania. *Organizaciju vadyba*, (38), 33-51.

Drago, R., & Heywood, J. S. (1995). The choice of payment schemes: Australian establishment data. *Industrial Relations*, *34*, 507-531.

EU (2003). EU recommendation 2003/361. *Official Journal of the European Union*, retrieved from: http://eur-lex.europa.eu/LexUriServ/LexUriServ.do?uri=OJ:L:2003:124: 0036:0041:EN:PDF

Eurofound (2009). *The Second European Company Survey*. Luxembourg: Publications Office of the European Union.

Eurofound (2012). *The Fifth European Working Conditions Survey*. Luxembourg: Publications Office of the European Union.

Fernie, S., & Metcalf, D. (1995). Participation, Contingent Pay, Representation and Workplace Performance: Evidence from Great Britain. *British Journal of Industrial Relations*, *33*, 379-415.

Festing, M., Groening, Y., Kabst, R., & Weber, W. (1999). Financial participation in Europe – Determinants and outcomes. *Economic and Industrial Democracy*, *20*, 295-329.

Fongwa, E. A. (2010). Financial Participation for Sustainable Business Development. *Journal of Business & Economics*, *2*, 228-244.

Frye, M. B. (2004). Equity-Based Compensation for Employees: Firm Performance and Determinants. *Journal of Financial Research*, *27*, 31-54.

Galetić, L., & Načinović, I. (2006). Compensation management in Croatian enterprises: an empirical study. *The Business Review Cambridge*, *5*, 204-212.

Galetić, L., & Rašić Krnjaković, S. (2004). Dioničarstvo zaposlenih u Hrvatskoj – stanje, mogućnosti i perspective [Employee stock ownership in Croatia – status, opportunities and perspectives]. *Ekonomski pregled*, *55*, 752-772.

Galetić, L., Tipurić, D, & Juri, B. (2000). Actual role and problems of compensation management in Croatian enterprises. *Journal for East European Management Studies*, *5*, 46-63.

Gligorov, K. (1982). The social and economic basis of socialist self-management in Yugoslavia. In R. Stojanović (Ed.), *The functioning of the Yugoslav Economy*, Armonk: M. E. Sharp.

Goić, S. (1999). Employees' Attitudes towards Employee Ownership and Financial Participation in Croatia: Experiences and Cases. *Journal of Business Ethics*, *21*, 145-155.

Gregurek, M. (2001). Stupanj i učinci privatizacije u Hrvatskoj [The level and effects of privatisation in Croatia]. *Ekonomski pregled*, *52*, 155-188.

Heim, P., & Golant, S. K. (1992). *Hardball for Women: Winning at the Game of Business*. New York: A Plume Book.

Jones, D. C., Kalmi, P., Kato, T., & Mäkinen, M. (2012). Financial participation in Finland: incidence and determinants. *The International Journal of Human Resource Management, 23*, 1570-1589.

Kabst, R., Matiaske, W., & Schmelter, A. (2006). Financial Participation in British, French and German Organisations: A Neoinstitutionalist Perspective. *Economic and Industrial Democracy, 27*, 565-585.

Kalmi, P., Pendleton, A., & Poutsma, E. (2005). Financial participation and performance in Europe. *Human Resource Management Journal, 15*(4), 54-67.

Kalmi, P., Pendleton, A., & Poutsma, E. (2012). Bargaining regimes, variable pay and financial participation: some survey evidence on pay determination. *The International Journal of Human Resource Management, 23*, 1643-1659.

Kroumova, M. K., & Sesil, J. C. (2006). Intellectual Capital, Monitoring, and Risk: What Predicts the Adoption of Employee Stock Options?. *Industrial Relations, 45*, 734-752.

Lavelle, J., Turner, T., Gunnigle, P., & McDonnell, A. (2012). The determinants of financial participation schemes within multinational companies in Ireland. *The International Journal of Human Resource Management, 23*, 1590-1610.

Levine, D. I. (1995). *Reinventing the Workplace: How Business and Employees Can Both Win*. Washington, DC: Brookings.

Long, R. J. (2000). Employee Profit Sharing: Consequences and Moderators. *Industrial Relations, 55*, 477-505.

Lowitzsch, J., Bormann, A., Hanisch, S., Menke, J. D., Roggemann, H., & Spitsa, N. (2008). *Financial participation for a new social Europe: A building block approach*. Rome and Berlin: European Federation of Employee Share Ownership and International Association for Financial Participation.

Milenkovitch, D. D. (1977). The Case of Yugoslavia. *American Economic Review, 67*, 50-60.

McCartney, J., Croucher, R., & Svetlik, I. (2005). *Financial participation in the EU: A benchmarking study of Slovenia*. Dublin: European Foundation for the Improvement of Living and Working Conditions.

Moeller, I., & Bellmann, L. (2011). Financial Participation During the Global Recession in Germany. *Proceedings of the 3rd European Reward Management Conference (RMC 2011)*. Brussels: EIASM.

NCEO (1999). *Employee Ownership and Corporate Performance*. Oakland, CA: National Center for Employee Ownership.

NN (2014a). *Zakon o porezu na dobit 143/14* [*Profit Tax Act*]. Zagreb: Narodne novine [Official Gazette]. Retrieved from Narodne novine Web site: http://www.zakon.hr/z/99/Zakon-o-porezu-na-dobit

NN (2012). *Zakon o porezu na dohodak 22/12* [*Income Tax Act*]. Zagreb: Narodne novine [Official Gazette]. Retrieved from Narodne novine Web site: http://narodne-novine.nn.hr/clanci/sluzbeni/2012_02_22_570.html

NN (2014b). *Zakon o porezu na dohodak 143/14* [*Income Tax Act*]. Zagreb: Narodne novine [Official Gazette]. Retrieved from Narodne novine Web site: http://www.zakon.hr/z/85/Zakon-o-porezu-na-dohodak

NN (1997). *Zakon o računovodstvu 109/97* [*Accounting Act of Croatia*]. Zagreb: Narodne novine [Official Gazette]. Retrieved from Narodne novine Web site: http://www.zakon.hr/z/118/Zakon-o-ra%C4%8Dunovodstvu

NN (2014c). *Zakon o radu 143/14* [*Labour Act*]. Zagreb: Narodne novine [Official Gazette]. Retrieved from Narodne novine Web site: http://www.zakon.hr/z/307/Zakon-o-radu

Oyer, P. (2004). Why do firms use incentives that have no incentive effects?. *Journal of Finance*, *59*, 1619-1649.

Pasour, E. C. (1981). The Free-Rider as a Basis for Government Action. *The Journal of Libertarian Studies*, *5*, 453-464.

Pendleton, A. (1997). Characteristics of workplaces with financial participation: evidence from the Workplace Industrial Relations Survey. *Industrial Relations Journal*, *28*, 103-119.

Pendleton, A., Poutsma, E., van Ommeren, J., & Brewster, C. (2001). *Employee Share Ownership and Profit Sharing in the European Union*. Dublin: European Foundation for the Improvement of Living and Working Conditions. Retrieved from Eurofond Web site: www.eurofound.europa.eu/pubdocs/2001/56/en/1/ef0156en.pdf

Pérotin, V., & Robinson, A. (1998). A Comparative Paper on Profit-Sharing and Productivity; Evidence from Britain, France, Germany and Italy. *Advances in the Economic Analysis of Participatory and Labour-Managed Firms*, *6*, 135-162.

Pérotin, V., & Robinson, A. (2002). Employee Participation of Profit and Ownership: A Review of Issues and Evidence. Retrieved from European Federation of Employee Share Ownership Web site: http://www.efesonline.org/LIBRARY/Employee%20Participation%20in%20Profit%20and%20Ownership%20P%E9rotin%2003.pdf

Pfeffer, J. (1994). *Competitive Advantage Through People – Unleashing the Power of the Work Force*. Boston, MA: Harvard Business School Press.

Pfeffer, J. (1998). *The Human Equation: Building Profits by Putting People First*. Boston, MA: Harvard Business School Press.

Pološki, N. (2003). *Kreiranje višekriterijskog modela za analizu doprinosa managementa ljudskih potencijala uspješnosti poduzeća [Creating a multi-criteria model for analysing HRM impact on organisational performance]*. Doctoral thesis. Zagreb: University of Zagreb, Faculty of Economics and Business.

Pološki Vokić, N. (2014.). Competitiveness and sustainability of HRM activities in Croatia – CRANET survey results. *Proceedings of Via Futuri 2014 International Conference on Sustainability, Competitiveness Urban and Regional Development – On the Crossroads of Theory and Empirical Research* (pp. 208-221). Pécs: Pécsi Tudományegyetem Közgazdaságtudományi Kar. 27-28 November, Pécs, Hungary

Pološki Vokić, N., Klindžić, M., & Đaković, M. (2008). Work Motivation of Highly-Educated Croatian Employees – What Should Managers and HR Experts Know?. *South East European Journal of Economics and Business*, *3*(1), 89-96.

Pološki Vokić, N., & Vidović, M. (2008). HRM as a Significant Factor for Achieving Competitiveness through People: The Croatian Case. *International Advances in Economic Research*, *14*, 303-315.

Poole, M. (1988). Factors Affecting the Development of Employee Financial Participation in Contemporary Britain: Evidence from a National Survey. *British Journal of Industrial Relations, 26*, 21-36.

Poutsma, E., & de Nijs, W. (2003). Broad-based employee financial participation in the European Union. *International Journal of Human Resource Management, 14*, 863-892.

Poutsma, E., de Nijs, W., & Poole, M. (2003). The global phenomenon of employee financial participation. *International Journal of Human Resource Management, 14*, 855-862.

Poutsma, E., & Ligthart, P. E. M. (2011). Compensation and benefits. In: *Cranet survey on comparative human resource management – International Executive Report 2011* (pp. 68-80). Cranfield: Cranet.

Poutsma, E., Ligthart, P. E. M., & Schouteten, R. (2005). Employee Share Schemes in Europe: The Influence of US Multinationals. *Management Revue, 16*, 99-122.

Remus, J. (1983). Financial participation of employees: An attempted classification and major trends. *International Labour Review, 122*, 1-21.

Robinson, A. M., & Wilson, N. (2006). Employee Financial Participation and Productivity: An Empirical Reappraisal. *British Journal of Industrial Relations, 44*, 31-50.

Roche, W., & Turner, T. (1998). Human Resource Management and Industrial Relations: Substitution, Dualism and Partnership. In: W. Roche, K. Monks & J. Walsh (Eds.), *Human Resource Strategies: Policy and Practice in Ireland.* Dublin: Oak Tree Press.

Tipurić, D. (2003). ESOP – izazovi i ograničenja za hrvatska poduzeća [ESOP – challenges and limitations for Croatian companies]. *Zbornik radova s tradicionalnog savjetovanja Hrvatskog društva ekonomista* (pp. 200-223). Zagreb: Inženjerski biro.

Tipurić, D. (2004). *ESOP i hrvatsko poduzeće [ESOP and the Croatian company].* Zagreb: Sinergija.

Welz, C., & Fernández-Macias, E. (2008). Financial Participation of Employees in the European Union: Much Ado about Nothing?. *European Journal of Industrial Relations, 14*, 479-496.

Wood, S. (1996). High Commitment management and payment systems. *Journal of Management Studies, 33*, 53-77.

Workers' risk attitude and financial participation

Rahma Daly, Marc-Arthur Diaye & Jean-Max Koskievic[1]

Abstract

The French '2010 Household Wealth Survey' includes an experimental module that makes it possible to measure risk aversion in an objective manner. Using a utility-free definition of risk attitudes, a worker will be risk averse if he chooses to have an amount $a > 0$ with certainty instead of playing a risky lottery L with an expected value that is strictly greater than a. Over this survey, we analyse workers' attitudes towards financial participation with respect to their attitudes towards risk. This analysis makes sense because economic theory predicts that on the one hand the less risk adverse the worker is, the more he will be attracted by financial participation; and on the other hand, firms prefer workers with low levels of risk aversion, all things being equal, because these workers can be paid a smaller risk premium. About 60 per cent of the 430 individuals in our data set are risk averse. Recall that economic theory predicts that the less risk averse an individual is, the more likely he is to accept financial participation. We apply two statistical methods to check for the existence of a link between financial participation and risk attitudes: a classification tree and logistic regression. We confirm (in accordance with economic theory) that the less risk averse an individual is, the more likely he is to agree to financial participation.

1 Rahma Daly (corresponding author): University of Evry Val d'Essonne (EPEE), Evry, France, email: rahma.daly@univ-evry.fr
Marc-Arthur Diaye: University of Evry Val d'Essonne (EPEE), Evry, France, email: marc-arthur.diaye@univ-evry.fr
Jean-Max Koskievic: ESG Management School, Paris, France, email: j.koskievic@psbedu.paris

1. Introduction

Financial participation is a key managerial tool for firms and has motivated a substantial body of literature. The documented determinants of financial participation include workers' risk attitudes (Kurtulus, Kruse & Blasi, 2011). Financial participation, irrespective of the design of such programme, always includes a random component and is therefore risky. For instance, according to Amar (2010), the amount of financial participation-related premiums distributed in France in 2008 represented a seven per cent decrease relative to 2007.

Economic theory predicts that the less risk adverse the worker is, the more he or she will be attracted by financial participation. Moreover, firms prefer workers with low levels of risk aversion, all things being equal, because these workers can be paid a smaller risk premium.

Our chapter is devoted to an analysis of the relationship between workers' attitudes towards risk and financial participation (profit sharing, employee stock and ownership plan - ESOP). This issue has been studied in the literature, not only with respect to financial participation but also for the general case of contingent pay. Cable and Judge (1994), using an experimental data set and three self-reported risk aversion scales (developed by Slovic, 1972; Drankoski & Judge, 1992) to demonstrate that risk aversion is inversely correlated with the likelihood that individuals will select contingent-pay over fixed-pay. Cadsby, Song and Tapon (2007), using an experimental data set and an objective measure of risk aversion, obtain the same result. Kurtulus et al. (2011) use an NBER-sponsored survey of approximately 40,000 workers and reach the same result. However, the latter study employed a self-reported risk aversion scale.

The purpose of our chapter is to complete the work of Kurtulus et al. (2011) by using both an official database and an objective measure of risk aversion. This is made possible by the existence of an official French statistical database called '*Enquête Patrimoine*', which includes a risk measurement component. Risk is objectively measured by making workers choose between a series of lotteries. Using a utility-free definition of risk attitudes, a worker will be risk averse if he chooses to have an amount $a > 0$ with certainty instead of playing a risky lottery L with an expected value that is strictly greater than a.

The remainder of the chapter is organised as follows. Section 1 includes a brief literature review on the theoretical relationship between risk attitudes and financial participation. In section 2, we present the database and the main variables. Section 3 addresses the empirical tests, and finally, section 4 concludes.

2. *What does theory say about financial participation and attitudes towards risk?*

The standard economic theory on profit sharing inaugurated by Weitzman (1984) predicts that a profit-sharing system can be expected to increase a worker's effort relative to that under a fixed wage system. Because the worker has a stake in the outcome, he will devote greater effort and produce more output. This result has given rise to an abundant body of theoretical and empirical literature (see Weitzman & Kruse, 1990, for a survey). However, all of these simple models omit certain aspects of reality, as they abstract from risk-bearing issues associated with financial participation that may expose workers to considerable income fluctuations that they would find undesirable.[2]

Blanchflower and Oswald (1987) argue that Weitzman's theory and the other models that focus on this topic fail to address the problem of risk allocation between workers and the firm in profit-sharing schemes, although empirical evidence suggests that firms' and employees' attitudes towards risk obviously constitute an important element in the formation of financial participation schemes. In a deterministic context, linking a worker's pay to his output is sensible because it will encourage the optimal level of effort, but what will the outcome be in the presence of risk? Intuitively, a higher degree of financial participation relative to a fixed base wage will elicit greater effort from the worker but will also expose him to greater risk. For example, Estrin, Grout and Wadhwani (1987) or Pissarides (1987) note that financial participation (e.g., profit sharing) would expose workers to considerable income fluctuations, which

2 Weitzman (1980) derives a formula for the optimal mix of a base wage and profit sharing, which is typically a complicated function that is inversely related to the degree of risk aversion. However, he concludes that explicitly modelling risk considerations does not per se eliminate the argument for profit sharing, though it likely entails a reduction in the degree of profit sharing to reduce the worker's exposure to risk. More important, he demonstrates that under standard assumptions, it is quite difficult to derive a corner solution in which the efficient pay contract involves only fixed wages and no profit sharing.

they would not desire, and give rise to a disincentive effect on worker effort.

This issue has been extensively examined in the theoretical literature under the heading of the well-known 'Principal-Agent' or 'Employer-Employee' problem. A basic assumption in most theoretical models is that the worker is risk averse, deriving greater utility from a fixed wage than from a variable wage of equal expected value (Holmstrom, 1979, Milgrom & Roberts, 1992). Focusing on the risk imposed by performance pay, the classic agency model involves a trade-off between incentives and insurance (Prendergast, 2000; Holt & Laury, 2002). While the firm can increase effort through performance pay, it must compensate risk-averse workers for the greater earnings risk such that the agent still receives his reservation utility. Thus, the classic agency model predicts that no relationship exists between risk attitudes and utility, even if workers receive a performance payment. However, workers who are highly risk averse will prefer to have lower compensation risk compared with those who are less risk averse. Therefore, an alignment of risk preferences and compensation risk is likely to lead to improved utility.

Based on these facts, it has been worthwhile to develop a theoretical framework that incorporates the risk attitudes of firms and workers into Weitzman's share economy to apply it and thus shed light on the role of sharing schemes in the presence of income fluctuations.

The efficiency wage theory (Chang, 2006) and sorting models literature (Cornelissen, Heywood, & Jirjahn, 2011) have recently pursued this approach. Chang (2006) establishes a theoretical model that combines remuneration from financial participation schemes and the shirking-type of efficiency wage theory proposed by Shapiro and Stiglitz (1984). Departing from the usual efficiency wage model, it allows both employees and the firm to be risk averse (see Hart, 1983), and employees exert effort according to the compensation they receive and the risk costs that they incur. Accordingly, firms can unilaterally set base wages and sharing coefficients to induce worker effort and diversify risks. Based on this model, Chang (2006) finds that the risk attitudes of firms and workers are the crucial elements in determining the workers' effort and the firms' choice of payment method. Specifically, if firms are risk neutral and workers are more risk averse, the fixed-wage system will prevail. Second, a higher sharing coefficient (the ratio of financial participation to an employee's total wage) is not necessarily a sufficient motivator to increase work effort, particularly when employees are more risk averse, because even if it creates a stronger incentive effect, it also exposes employees to a greater amount of income risk. Third, if firms are risk averse and workers are risk neutral, firms facing greater output fluctuation will increase their sharing ratio to diversify the risk among their workers but will decrease the base wage. If the firm is risk neutral and workers are risk averse, increased output fluctuations will increase the fixed base wage but have an ambiguous effect on the sharing coefficient.

While Shapiro and Stiglitz (1984) focuses on the relationship between the firm's and worker's risk tolerance, Cornelissen et al. (2011) extends the sorting models of Lazear (1986) and Booth and Franck (1999) by considering two sectors (a performance pay sector and a time rate sector) to account for the income risk associated with performance pay and allow for different risk attitudes across workers and abilities. While standard agency analyses are limited to risk-averse workers, their model allows for the presence of risk-neutral and risk-loving workers. Levine and Tyson (1990) have noted that because firms employing financial participation schemes will pay varying wages, risk-averse workers will tend to leave them for employment in other firms. In addition, assuming that financial participation replaces a share of basic wages, in a recession, remuneration in a financial participation firm may fall below that of its non-financial-participation competitors - which will tend to have greater recourse to lay-offs, redundancies and short-time work. The financial participation firm may then run the risk of losing its best staff to other firms, at which the levels of pay are temporarily higher. However, it is unclear how important this argument will be in practice.

Levine and Tyson (1990) predicts, first, that the more able and risk tolerant workers will sort themselves into performance pay schemes to capture rents and thereby increase their on-the-job satisfaction. Second, workers with greater risk aversion benefit to a lesser extent from working in the performance pay sector, all else being equal. If workers in the performance pay sector are risk averse, they will suffer from both a disutility of effort and a disutility resulting from income risk. If workers in the performance pay sector are risk loving, two opposing components remain, namely the disutility of effort and the utility of having an uncertain income. Thus workers in the performance pay sector receive a rent that decreases in their degree of risk aversion. These results obviously contrast with the classic agency model in which employers offer earnings that precisely compensate agents for their disutility of effort and their disutility of income risk. Because workers are typically assumed to be risk averse, a clear, negative relationship between performance pay and utility emerges after controlling for compensating earnings. Our approach accounts for the possibility that at least some workers may be risk loving (or at least less risk averse than others), implying an ambiguous relationship between performance pay and utility after controlling for earnings.

3. The Database and the main variables

3.1 The database

We use a survey called 'Enquête Patrimoine 2010' ('2010 Household Wealth Survey') designed by the French National Institute of Statistics (INSEE). This survey is administered every six years, and its purpose is to describe the wealth structure of French households (e.g., real estate, financial and professional assets, intangible assets).[3] The survey size is approximately 15,006 households and 35,729 individuals.

However, the '2010 Household Wealth Survey' also includes three sub-samples, respectively devoted to consumption habits, risk attitudes and immaterial wealth. In this chapter, we consider the sub-sample measuring risk attitudes. Note that the survey assesses risk attitudes in an objective manner through an experimental device. Namely, the individual reveals his attitude towards risk through his choice between lotteries $L1$ and $L2$, $L3$ and $L1$ and $L4$ and $L1$, where $L1 = (w, 1)$ is the degenerate lottery of obtaining his current wage w with certainty and $L2 = (2w, 0.5; \frac{2}{3}w, 0.5)$ is the lottery that awards twice the current wage of the individual with probability 0.5 and two-thirds of the current wage with probability 0.5, $L3 = (2w, 0.5; \frac{1}{2}w, 0.5)$, $L4 = (2w, 0.5; \frac{4}{5}w, 0.5)$.

The choices are sequential, and the individuals are first asked to choose between $L1$ and $L2$. Then, only individuals who chose $L2$ over $L1$ are asked to choose between $L3$ and $L1$. Individuals who chose $L1$ over $L2$ are asked to choose between $L1$ and $L4$. As $L1$ is a degenerate lottery, its certainty equivalent is equal to its mathematical expectation $E(L1) = w$. As a consequence, if we assume a Von-Neuman and Morgenstern setting, then individuals who choose $L1$ over $L2$ are more risk averse than individuals

3 http://www.insee.fr/en/methodes/default.asp?page=sources/ope-enquete-patrimoine.htm

who choose *L*2 over *L*1. In other words, *L*1 is the least risky lottery, followed by *L*4, then *L*2 and, finally, *L*3 (the most risky).

The sub-sample on risk attitude measurement initially includes 4,960 individuals. However, we restrict our attention to the 430 individuals who are (1) active; (2) full-time workers with permanent contracts; (3) employed in the private sector (agriculture and artisanal handicrafts are excluded); (4) not self-employed; (5) not managers; and (6) between 18 and 55 years old.

3.2 The main variables

Our dependent variable is a binary variable denoted '*FPART*' that is equal to one if the employee reported having a financial participation device (profit sharing, employee stock and ownership plan-ESOP) and 0 otherwise. Let us remind that three main mechanisms make up the French financial participation system: a mandatory[4] profit sharing called '*participation aux bénéfices*', a voluntary profit-sharing called '*intéressement*' and an ESOP called '*plan d'épargne entreprise*'. In our analysis, by profit sharing we mean the voluntary profit sharing.

The risk attitude variable (denoted '*RACCEPT*') is constructed based on the individuals' choices between the abovementioned lotteries. It takes the value 1 if the individual rejects both *L*2 and *L*4; *RACCEPT* = 2 if the individual does not choose *L*2 but chooses *L*4; *RACCEPT* = 3 if the individual chooses *L*2 but does not choose *L*3; and *RACCEPT* = 4 if the individual chooses both *L*2 and *L*3. Thus, the higher *RACCEPT* is, the less risk averse the individual is.

Because an individual's risk attitudes may depend on his wealth, we add wealth as a control variable. Finally, as explanatory variables, we consider the worker's gender, age, geographic zone, whether the worker is single and the number of dependent children.

Table 1 provides a complete definition of our variables, while tables 3 and 2 present a brief statistical summary of each variable. For instance, according to table 3, about 60 per cent of individuals in our data set are risk averse.

---

4 Mandatory for firms with a minimum of 50 employees, except for specific kinds of firms such as mutual funds and state-owned firms. This type of profit sharing is more close to a reserve fund.

Table 1. Definition of Variables

Variable	Description
FPART	Binary variable = 1 if the individual holds FP and 0 otherwise.
RACCEPT	Risk attitude variable. Takes four values, from 1 to 4. The lower the value, the more risk averse the individual.
LNETWEALTH	(log) Total net wealth in Euros (total gross wealth minus debts).
AGE	Continuous variable. Age of the individual.
SEX	Binary variable = 1 if female and 0 otherwise.
NOTSINGLE	Binary variable = 1 if the individual is not single and 0 otherwise.
NDEPCHILD	Number of dependent children.
DEPCHILD	Binary variable = 1 if the number of dependent children (NDEPCHILD) is > 0 and 0 otherwise.
GEOZONE	Binary variable = 1 the individual lives in Paris or the Paris region and 0 otherwise.

Table 2. Summary Statistics for Categorical Variables

Variable	Values	Frequency	Percent
RACCEPT	1	255	59.3
	2	88	20.47
	3	61	14.19
	4	26	6.05
FPART	0	286	66.51
	1	144	33.49
SEX	0	247	57.44
	1	183	42.56
NOTSINGLE	0	114	26.51
	1	316	73.49
NDEPCHILD	0	183	42.56
	1	112	26.05
	2	94	21.86
	3	34	7.91
	4	4	0.93
	5	2	0.47
	6	1	0.23
DEPCHILD	0	183	42.56
	1	247	57.44
GEOZONE	0	314	73.02
	1	116	26.98

Table 3. Summary Statistics for Real-Valued Variables

Variable	Mean	Std. Dev.	Min.	Max.
RACCEPT	1.67	0.93	1	4
LNETWEALTH	10.2	4.62	-10.19	15.41
AGE	40.32	9.01	18	55
NDEPCHILD	1.01	1.09	0	6

4. Empirical tests

Recall that economic theory predicts that the less risk averse an individual is, the more likely he is to accept financial participation. We apply two methods to assess this prediction.

4.1 Classification Tree Method

The first method permits us to check for the existence of a link between financial participation and risk attitudes. Specifically, we construct a classification tree for the variable *FPART* with respect to the abovementioned explanatory variables: risk attitude, net wealth, age, sex, whether the worker is single, the number of dependent children and the geographic zone. Recall that a classification tree, sometimes called a decision tree, is a (non-parametric) supervised learning method. The use of such a method in economic analysis is highly recommended by Varian (2014).

According to the decision tree, the first variable that explains the division of our sample into two parts with respect to whether a worker is compensated through financial participation (*FPART* = 1 or 0) is net wealth. The next variable is the risk attitude variable (*RACCEPT*). Specifically, there are two branches that are, respectively, applicable to 22 per cent and 48 per cent of our sample:

For individuals whose net wealth is higher than €278,392.50, risk attitudes do not play a role in the decision of whether to accept financial participation.

For individuals whose net wealth is between €21,971.50 and €278,392.50, risk attitudes play a role in the decision of whether to accept financial participation. For instance, according to the decision tree, highly risk-averse individuals (*RACCEPT* = 1) whose net wealth is between

€21,971.50 and €278,392.50 do not accept financial participation, whatever their other socio-demographic characteristics.

Figure 1. Decision tree of having financial participation

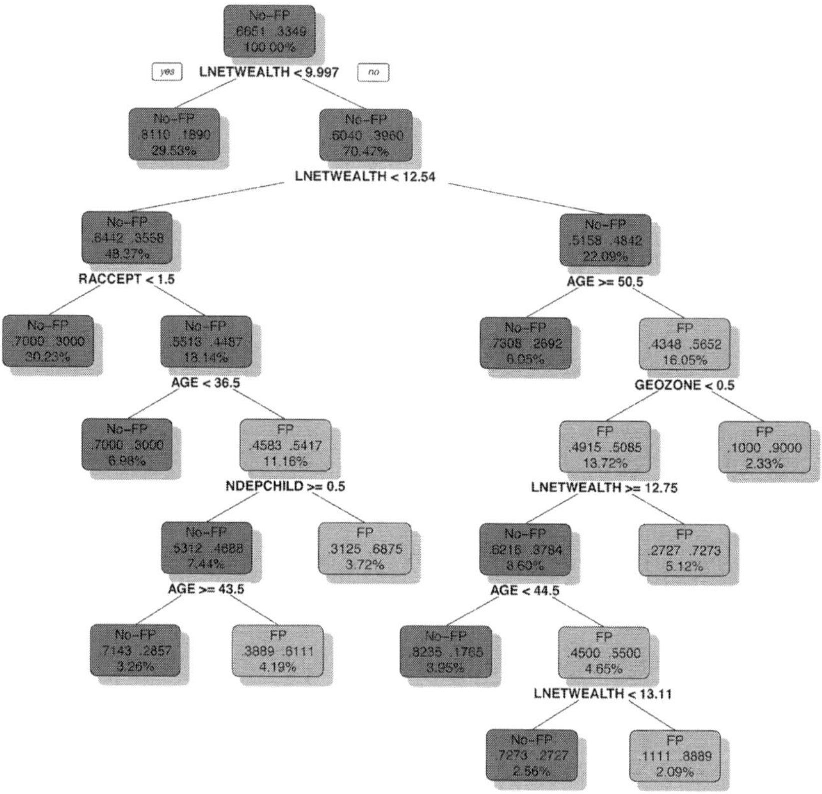

4.2 Logistic Regression Model

In the second method, we employ a logistic regression model (because the outcome variable FPART is binary). Specifically,

$$FPART = \begin{cases} 1 \text{ if } FPART^* = X'\beta + \varepsilon > 0 \\ 0 \text{ otherwise} \end{cases}$$

where $FPART^*$ is a latent variable and X and β are the matrix of explanatory variables and the vector of regression coefficients:

$X = (RACCEPT, LNETWEALTH, AGE, SEX, NOTSINGLE, DEPCHILD, GEOZONE)'$

$\beta = (\beta_0, \beta_1, \beta_2, \beta_{03}, \beta_4, \beta_5, \beta_6, \beta_7)'$

The results of the logistic regression of *FPART* are presented in table 4.

Table 4. Logistic Regression of the variable FPART

Analysis of Estimates					
Parameter	Reference Modality	Estimate	Standard Error	Wald Chi-Square	Pr>KhiSq
Intercept		-3.07***	0.63	23.78	<0.0001
RACCEPT		0.26**	0.11	5.48	0.02
LNETWEALTH		0.09**	0.03	6.17	0.01
AGE		0.02	0.01	2.54	0.11
SEX	0	-0.09	0.108	0.68	0.4
NOTSINGLE	0	0.15	0.13	1.29	0.25
DEPCHILD	0	-0.04	0.11	0.11	0.73
GEOZONE	0	-0.17	0.12	1.81	0.18
Wald Score	20.85		AIC	550.32	
Number of Observation		430			

Note. Significance level: * : $p < 0.1$ ** : $p < 0.05$ *** : $p < 0.01$

Note that *RACCEPT* has a positive effect on *FPART*. In other words (and in accordance with economic theory and Kurtulus et al. (2011)), the less risk averse an individual is, the more likely he is to agree to financial participation.

Net wealth (*LNETWEALTH*) also has a positive and significant effect on the probability of accepting financial participation. No other explanatory variables have a significant effect.

5. Conclusion

The implementation of financial participation schemes (profit sharing, ESOP) within firms depends on the workers' attitudes towards risk. The less risk adverse the worker is, the more likely it is that he or she will be attracted by financial participation. Moreover, firms will prefer workers with low levels of risk aversion, all things being equal, because they will pay the workers a lower risk premium. The purpose of this article is to test the link between workers' attitudes towards risk and financial participation, using an original French data set that provides us with an objective measure of risk aversion. Our paper contributes to the literature by asserting that attitudes towards risk are a key determinant of workers attitudes towards financial participation. This issue is important because economic theory predicts that firms that implementing financial participation schemes will prefer to hire workers with low levels of risk aversion to pay a lower risk premium. Thus, it may be the case that financial participation could be biased against some types of individuals. For instance, according to some studies (Agnew et al., 2008), women are more risk adverse than men. As a consequence, ceteris paribus, by hiring individuals with low levels of risk aversion, firms may hire more men than women.

References

Agnew, J.R., Anderson, L.R., Gerlach, J.R., Szykman, L.R. (2008). Who Chooses Annuities? An Experimental Investigation of the Role of Gender, Framing, and Defaults. *American Economic Review*, 98, 418-442.

Amar, E. (2010). Participation, Intéressement et Epargne salariale en 2008. Dares Analyses, No. 71.

Blanchflower, D.G., Oswald, A.J. (1987). Profit Sharing-Can It Work? *Oxford Economic Papers*, 39, 1-19.

Booth, A.L., Franck, J. (1999). Earnings, productivity, and performance-related pay. *Journal of Labor Economics*, 17, 447-463.

Cadsby, C.B., Song, F., Tapon, F. (2007). Sorting and Incentive Effects of Pay for Performance: An Experimental Investigation. *Academy of Management Journal*, 50(2), 387-405.

Cable, D.M., Judge, T.A. (1994). Pay Preferences and Job Search Decisions: A Person-Organization Fit Perspective. *Personnel Psychology*, 47, 317-348.

Chang, J.J. (2006). Profit Sharing, Risk Sharing, and Firm Size: Implications of Efficiency Wages. *Small Business Economics*, 27, 261-273.

Cornelissen, T., Heywood, J.S., Jirjahn, U. (2011). Performance pay, risk attitude and job satisfaction. *Labour Economics*, 18, 229-239.

Drankoski, R., Judge, T.A. (1992). *Employee pay satisfaction, pay attitudes, and pay preferences.* McLean, VA: Xerox Corporation.

Estrin, S., Grout, P., Wadhwani, S. (1987). Profit-Sharing and Employee Share Ownership. *Economic Policy*, 4, 13-62.

Hart, O.D. (1983). Optimal Labour Contracts Under Asymmetric Information: An Introduction. *Review of Economic Studies*, 50, 3-35.

Holmstrom, B. (1979). Moral Hazard and Observability. *Bell Journal of Economics*, 10(1), 74-91.

Holt, C.A., Laury, S.K. (2002). Risk Aversion and Incentive Effects. *American Economic Review*, 92(5), 1644-1655.

Kurtulus, F., Kruse, D., Blasi, J. (2011). Worker Attitudes Towards Employee Ownership, Profit Sharing and Variable Pay. *Advances in the Economic Analysis of Participatory and Labor-Managed Firms*, 12, 143-168.

Lazear, E.P. (1986). Salaries and piece rates. *Journal of Business*, 59, 405-431.

Levine, D., Tyson, L. (1990). Participation, productivity and the firm's environment. In: Blinder A.S. (Ed.), *Paying for Productivity: A look at the evidence.* Brookings Institution, Washington, D.C., 183-243.

Milgrom, P., Roberts, J. (1992). *Economics, Organization and Management.* Prentice Hall, New York.

Pissarides, C.A. (1987). Wages and Employment: A Framework for Analysis with Application to Three Policy Issues. *Economic Record*, 63, 301-312.

Prendergast, C. (2000). What trade-off of risk and incentives? American

Economic Review (Papers and Proceedings), 90, 421-425.

Shapiro, C., Stiglitz, J.E. (1984). Equilibrium Unemployment As a Worker Discipline Device. *American Economic Review*, 74, 433-444.

Slovic, P. (1972). Information processing, situation specificity, and the generality of risk taking behavior. *Journal of Personality and Social Psychology*, 22, 128-134.

Varian, H. (2014). Big Data: New Tricks for Econometrics. *Journal of Economic Perspectives*, 28, 2-28.

Weitzman, M.L. (1980). Efficient Incentive Contracts. *Quarterly Journal of Economics*, 94, 719-730.

Weitzman, M.L. (1984). *The Share Economy.* Harvard University Press, MA.

Weitzman, M.L., Kruse, D. (1990). Profit Sharing and Productivity. In: Blinder A.S. (Ed.), *Paying for Productivity: A look at the evidence.* Brookings Institution, Washington, D.C., 95-140.

Cooperatives: Direct and indirect forms of employee financial participation

Theresia Theurl & Sandra Maria Swoboda[1]

Abstract

This chapter examines the practice of employee financial participation (EFP) in cooperatives since they are characterized by their special ownership structure and their special form of owner control. The aim of cooperatives is rather to set incentives for owners than for dependent employees. Therefore direct EFP is not a predominant subject of cooperatives. However it is possible to use a cooperative as a means for participation in economic activities. Employees can be given the opportunity to participate through the complete acquisition of the operating results with other owners instead of only an additional participation in these results. This involvement in economic activities may have the effect of an indirect EFP. Thus, member value can be created, which consists of three components. In this chapter four different possibilities to involve employees in economic activities are illustrated by using examples of cooperatives in Germany. Firstly, cooperatives can be founded to realise special projects within an enterprise. Secondly, cooperatives can prevent staff of a former enterprise from an exit from the market. Thirdly, the foundation of a cooperative by employees of an enterprise can present a solution of business succession. Fourthly, self-employed persons can found a cooperative to enter into a market. The four options are complemented by an example illustrating the possibility of direct EFP by founding a cooperative.

1 Theresia Theurl (corresponding author): Institut für Genossenschaftswesen, Westfälische Wilhelms-Universität Münster, email: theresia.theurl@wiwi.uni-muenster.de
Sandra Maria Swoboda: Institut für Genossenschaftswesen, Westfälische Wilhelms-Universität Münster, email: sandra.swoboda@wiwi.uni-muenster.de

1. Introduction

Employee financial participation (EFP) in enterprises is practised in different forms and models. It involves a change of the property rights of an enterprise which transfers individual ownership functions to employees to varying degrees. Thus, it is obvious to ask how this is realised in cooperatives, because these are characterised by a special ownership structure and a special form of owner control. As in any other enterprise, direct EFP in cooperatives is, in principle, possible. In practice, however, it is a rare scheme compared to other legal forms of entrepreneurial activities. Furthermore, the special governance of cooperatives, however, offers further possibilities to involve employees in economic activities, which may have the effect of an indirect financial participation. These possibilities will also be discussed in this paper. Indeed, actual and potential employees of cooperatives may become owners with designated property rights. Before discussing specific cooperative participation models, the governance of cooperatives will be explained since it differs from that of other legal forms of enterprises. Section 2 outlines cooperative governance, while section 3 focuses on the decisive feature that –being the owners of the cooperatives – the cooperative members form its very core. It will be examined whether employees can actually be members (3.1), in which context this is actually realised in the cooperative practice, and which forms of employee participation are possible (3.2). Section 4 gives practical examples of the identified forms of direct and indirect EFP in cooperatives. Finally, section 5 provides an overview of existing restrictions as well as a short outlook.

2. Cooperative governance

In Germany, there are almost 8,000 cooperatives which belong to a total of 20 million members (their owners), and which have approximately 800,000 employees. Cooperatives worldwide provide jobs for 100 million employees. They are actively involved in various sectors of the economy and society (for empirical data on cooperatives see Deutscher Genossenschafts- und Raiffeisenverband e.V. [DGRV], 2014a). Today, cooperatives are mainly founded in those sectors of the economy and society which are subject to profoundly changed framework conditions offering measures and facilitating means to the individuals and enterprises affected to cope with these changed conditions (for the reasons and specific characteristics see Theurl & Schweinsberg, 2004). Cooperatives differ from all other forms of organisation and their legal structures in their special governance features which will be presented in the following (for an overview see Theurl, 2010).

2.1 Economic rents through the formation of an enterprise

The development of cooperatives as an institutional innovation as well as the foundation of each of these societies is motivated by microeconomic considerations and implemented on the basis of cooperation. As with any other cooperation, work within cooperatives is neither an end in itself nor an altruistic approach, but it follows microeconomic calculations. They examine whether the respective objectives can be realised by acting on an individual basis. If this is not the case, at least not to the desired extent, alternative courses of action must be sought which are based on cooperative strategies. These allow to achieve an economic rent through cooperation. This forms the basis for the foundation of an enterprise capitalised by the cooperation partners who buy shares of this enterprise. We can therefore state that the decision for a cooperation is based on individual calculations which compare the advantages to be expected with the disadvantages, each time discounted to the time of the decision. Cooperation costs arise mainly for decision finding, coordination and conflict solution activities and always include the assessment and evaluation of the evolving dependency on other members. The economic rent of cooperation corresponds to the cooperative member value from the (individual) cooperating partners' perspective. This rent is distributed to the individual cooperation partners (for the contents and structures of the cooperative member value and its theoretical foundation see Theurl, 2013a).

In their historical context, cooperatives were created more than one century and a half ago because there were no alternatives for an economic participation, neither in a productive nor in a consumptive way. The organisational answer[2] to this deficiency was and still is business activity as one form of self-help. The purpose of self-help is to organise or provide

2 All references to actual governance elements made in this paper are based on the German law as laid down in the German Act on Cooperatives (Genossenschaftsgesetz).

for an advance input for the actual economic or other activity of the cooperative partners. Thus, a concurrent organisational demand of the partners exists. The cooperating actors may be private individuals or companies, their cooperative activities may be of economic, cultural, sporting, social or other nature, and the cooperation may be permanent or intended for a long-term project. The crucial point is that this help is no state or private assistance, i.e. an external help, but a collective self-help realised in the form of an enterprise. Under company law, cooperatives are associations of persons based on the personal membership in a common organisation.

The fact that several persons or enterprises form a cooperative in order to create something together which would be impossible to achieve alone, is known to a wider public. 76.2 per cent of the German population share this view, while 80.7 per cent of them think it is good or very good that such a possibility for cooperation exists (Theurl & Wendler, 2011).

Cooperatives and groups of cooperatives are not non-profit organisations. They are subject to special requirements concerning the use of profits or surpluses gained from the cooperation as well as concerning the coverage of shortfalls. Profit making, too, is based on legally defined and not on arbitrary transactions. And the profits made are distributed following legal provisions and rules laid down in the statutes.

2.2 Added value in networks

Cooperative enterprises implement a complex principal-agent relation with several overlapping delegation relations and many principals, frequently thousands. The cooperation corresponds to an organisational structure characterised by the interaction of centralised and decentralised actors within structures based on the division of labour. The decentralised actors, i.e. the members, as the principals delegate joint tasks to their agent. This agent is the actor at the central level, i.e. the joint enterprise with its management. Independent of the size, complexity and specific details, the interaction involves actors who differ in their capabilities, competences and tasks, altogether covering an entire value creation chain (Theurl, 2013b).

The strength of the actors of the decentralised level is that they contribute individual and local information on the specific demands of their common organisation, thus providing for a decentralised anchoring of this organisation as well as for a direct contact to the customers. Thus, communication advantages and individualised solutions can be developed. In contrast to hierarchically organised enterprises like, for example, public limited companies with branches at the decentralised level, cooperatives make market research regarding the demands and preferences of the customers an inherent part of the creation of value and its associated communication activities.

In order to start activities on competitive markets or to become or remain competitive, economies of scale and economies of scope as well as economies of risk, competence and knowledge advantages must be identified and used. The activities of a central actor create these positive effects for the benefit of the decentralised members. The special combination of these two levels of activity does not only show the network-like structure of cooperatives but it also lays the foundation for the mutual control relationships which are typical of cooperative governance. To prevent the members from causing negative external effects on the collective, they permit control and behavioural regulations by the centralised level. In return, they exercise control rights over the management via the bodies intended for this purpose (Kräkel, 1999). One feature of cooperative governance is that it allows to combine the advantages of being big and being small, to join the decentralised level with the centralised level, and to realise dependency and autonomy, simultaneously.

2.3 Simultaneous suppliers and customers

In cooperatives, members have multiple functions. They are not just owners and thus decision makers and financiers, but at the same time also customers and suppliers (in more detail and in context see Theurl, 2012). In short: Those who own the joint enterprise, who take the decisions setting the strategic course, and who are affected both by profits and losses, those are also the persons who demand the jointly organised goods and services. With restrictions, Article 8 of the German Cooperatives Act allows to have a few investing members (Federal Ministry of Justice and Consumer Protection, 2014). Such members do not make use of the goods and services of the cooperatives. This can also take place through the normative power of the current practice.

The double-hatted function of the members leads to particularities with regard to owner control and business strategy, which result in an extraordinary consistency of incentives and which can cause a cooperative to be understood also as a club which organises club goods (Theurl, 2013d). Based on legal provisions, the only purpose is to create values for the members by supporting their activities and meeting their demands. 81 per cent of the Germans know that cooperatives have to act to the benefit of their members, and 83.6 per cent think this is good or very good (Theurl & Wendler, 2011). If the relationships outlined here are translated into today's diction of strategic management, the creation of a cooperative owner value – a member value – from the point of view of the members has to stand in the focus of the cooperative's actions.

2.4 Values for the members, not for the investors

The orientation of a cooperative towards the member value represents a value-oriented corporate governance concept. The advantages which this concept provides for the members can be exploited without having to accept the disadvantages of a short-term shareholder value strategy. Such a strategy tries to maximise the value of the enterprise for its owners - who understand themselves as investors - through the transaction with the customers. The member value strategy determines the value of the cooperative for the members through the transaction of with its members (for all details see Theurl, 2013a).

Both the shareholder value strategy and the member value strategy are based on the concept of a long-term value orientation which, as a prerequisite for business success, calls for the orientation of all activities towards this precondition (for the development of this concept and the exploration of the consequences see Theurl, 2002). In the economic practice, business activities are valued in two different ways. An ex-ante valuation is realised by the management to determine the effects of its decisions concerning the long-term value of the enterprise from the point of view of the owners. This applies both to public companies and cooperatives. The decisive difference is the ex-post valuation which is performed whenever equity is demanded on the financial market. Before they provide their capital, suppliers of equity evaluate the activities of the management and compare these activities with existing alternatives. The results of their evaluation are reflected in the conditions on which equity is provided, i.e. in the stock price.

Financial markets have numerous imperfections. Obvious imperfections are a lack of information, a short horizon of activities, herd behaviour, overvaluation caused by speculation and subsequent corrections. As soon as an enterprise is dependent on investors from such an environment, the interests and preferences of these investors have to be taken into account, too. In a competition for equity, this can result in wrong business decisions because the focus is laid on the interests of the investors. Considerations mainly geared to the short term as they are predominant on the financial market are then transferred to the enterprises. This is associated with the fact that the intended long-term value orientation is undermined. Furthermore, legitimate rights and interests of stakeholders may be ignored. These may be the demanders of the goods and services of an enterprise, but also the employees. This can lead to the situation that enterprises are driven by the financial market. This, in turn, involves the consequences of a short-term and short-sighted behaviour of the management, which a strict shareholder value strategy is frequently accused of. This accusation does not refer to the orientation towards the value of the enterprise, but to the consequences of the gap between the ex-ante and the ex-post valuation. The developments described can only occur if an enterprise is fully or partially financed via the financial market. Cooperatives are denied access to the financial market by law.

2.5 Member value of cooperatives

While the owner value of a listed company – the shareholder value –flows to the investors one-dimensionally, i.e. in the form of a dividend and/or rising stock prices, the owner value of a cooperative consists of three components: a direct component, an indirect component and a sustainable component.

The direct member value is based on the transactions between the members and the cooperative. It develops through the relation of the jointly organised services with the defined standards and the agreed conditions. These services support the members in their own activities by meeting those demands which cannot be managed on an individual basis and which thus have to be organised jointly.

The indirect member value arises from the members' owner function who are financing the enterprise with equity or who make other contributions to provide the financial basis for the fulfilment of the joint tasks. The indirect member value is thus composed of the return of the equity and of a payout in the form of dividends, if paid. In the case of cooperatives, this is to be laid down in the statutes. The second element of the indirect member value is constituted by the rights of decision and the rights to coordinate which are associated with the ownership. One peculiarity of cooperative property rights is that every member is entitled to bring one vote into the decision-making process, notwithstanding his share in the capital. This feature especially embodies the right of participation at the general meeting as well as all rights of control. All studies have shown that members generally consider the indirect member value to be less important than the other two components (see the two empirical studies: Böttiger, 2009, for housing associations, and Tschöpel, 2013, for cooperative banks).

The sustainable member value corresponds to the investment relationship and to the long-term elements of the service and ownership functions. It represents a benefit taking the shape of an economic option for the members offered through the future existence and efficiency of the cooperative. This benefit arises through investments in products, processes and institutions. Such an economic option can be operationalised with the current investments and the currently unused components of the jointly realised profit or surplus which are allocated to the reserves, i.e. the overall accumulated profit components.

The three components of the member value are like communicating vessels, they are interdependent. For example, the pay-out of dividends and the value of the current output volume limit the possibilities to build up additional equity through reserves. On the other hand, planned large investments limit the possibilities to pay out dividends. Because cooperatives have no access to the financial market (for equity), it is impossible to spend more than the values that have been generated in the past. And these values are exclusively created to the benefit of the members, now and in the future. They are not withdrawn from the cooperative because there are no means to do so.

2.6 Cooperative owner control

The strategic orientation of cooperative enterprises as described above results in important consequences. Since cooperatives' shares are not traded on the financial market because they are not admitted to trading, there is no ex-post assessment. This has far-reaching consequences: Cooperatives are thus anchored in the real economy in such way that business decisions cannot be impeded by direct influences of the financial market, and cooperatives cannot be subject to a hostile takeover. As a result, however, the management is not disciplined by the investors, which at the first glance might look like a disadvantage of co-operative governance. To this, however, one can object that the management is disciplined through other mechanisms. These include the competition on the goods, labour and manager markets to which cooperatives are exposed as well. Further, disciplining takes place by the members via the designated decision-making channels, the exertion of the rights of control, and – in the case of debt financing – by the creditors (for more detail see Theurl, 2013a).

Another consequence is the limitation concerning the acquisition of equity on the financial markets, because the latter is not available to cooperatives at all or just to a very limited extent. This restriction, too, could be regarded as a disadvantage. The consequence, however, is that equity can only be procured from the members. This means that the management is continuously compelled to convince the members of the quality of the planned investment projects and of the goods and services offered. A fundamental prerequisite for the establishment of reserves and further investments is a solid economic performance, as well as profits or surpluses which will remain in the enterprise. This applies in a similar way for debt financing. Thus, the particularities of cooperatives' internal financing and procurement of equity require a good member value management.

Finally, member value orientation has a third consequence. It provides cooperatives with the possibility of a long-term orientation right from the start. Such a long-term orientation is part of the strategy derived from cooperative governance and is reflected in the weighting of the individual member value components. These components are not weighted on the basis of determinants of the financial market, but by the decision of the members who are interested in their relationship with the cooperative. It is not possible to reduce the cooperative's capital by increasing the dividends on cooperative shares, which would weaken the sustainable component, i.e. the available investment budget. This aspect is a clear advantage of co-operative governance (for the sustainability inherent in cooperative governance see Theurl, 2013b).

The German public is aware of the fact that cooperatives follow long-term strategies. 66.7 per cent of the German population know this, and 75.5 per cent think this is good or very good. That a large portion of the profits are re-invested in the cooperative is known to 58.7 per cent of

Germans, and 73.8 per cent of them think this is good or very good (Theurl & Wendler, 2011).

2.7 General economic and social collateral effects

Microeconomic decisions on the foundation of a cooperative are based on the intention to create values through cooperation which otherwise could not be created, as well as on a special form of cooperation.

2.7.1 Upgrading of business locations

It has been shown, however, that successful cooperatives produce general economic and also social effects, in addition to the microeconomic effects (for details on the effects of a strictly micro-economic concept of cooperatives see Theurl, 2013b). These effects represent added values and incomes which would otherwise not be created, and they create additional jobs and training places as well as an increased tax revenue. In addition, cooperatives are able to create and maintain infrastructures and to stabilise their environment overall, not just from an economic point of view. This means that business locations and living spaces are upgraded, thus allowing to maintain or produce (usually local or regional) economic cycles. It is important to note that no activities are replaced or pushed out but that, on the contrary, activities are generated which otherwise would not evolve. The effects mentioned are additional effects. The generation of such effects is neither an isolated purpose of microeconomic calculations nor is it required by any economic policy.

2.7.2 Correction of market failures

In addition, cooperatives are suitable to correct malfunctioning markets and insufficient market results. In market economies, information asymmetries, external effects, public goods, subadditive cost structures with natural monopolies as well as adjustment shortcomings represent the most important reasons for government regulatory and economic interventions. In most market economies, undesired market results are also corrected by the government's economic policy. The following sections can just give a short description of these aspects (for more details see Theurl, 2013c).

Cooperatives were developed because persons without any perspectives took the initiative to establish a livelihood. By interaction with others, these societies facilitated an entry into the market and thus an economic participation. Here, current approaches to cooperative self-help can be recognised as an alternative or an addition to government transfers, e.g. health, care and old age provisions organised and financed by the state. Numerous examples have already emerged in this sector, for example in the form of social cooperatives or family cooperatives.

The local or regional activity range of cooperatives allows them a superior management of information asymmetries. This results in information procurement and monitoring cost advantages, which becomes visible already in the selection of the members of a cooperative as well as in the monitoring of their activities and those of the management. Cooperative banks and cooperative wineries are just two of many examples clearly proving the efficiency of such information advantages. The mutual control which is characteristic for cooperatives is based on a combination of control rights delegated by the members to the cooperative with owner control. The regional activity range makes it easier for the members to monitor the management and protects the latter against transactions with high information demands. But the activities of the members, too, can be monitored with comparatively low information and control costs. The use of regional information pools positively influences transaction costs and the internal confidence of the actors in the cooperative. The described effects became very obvious in the superior performance of the Cooperative Financial Network in the course of the global crisis of the financial markets over the last few years. Here, too, the general economic effects are obvious, because cooperatives are not just information pools but also pools for the joint management of risks.

In addition, cooperatives can internalise external effects when originators and those affected become members. As a result, a private solution for such a market failure becomes possible. On the other hand, a cooperative organisation must be capable of offering a solution for non-excludability and non-rivalry. The first requirement can be met via the legally regulated membership modalities, while the extent of the non-rivalry can help to gain information on the activity range and the involvement of the members.

Today, cooperative solutions are frequently discussed when it comes to the organisation of global public goods. Taking into account that hardly any viable government solutions are beginning to emerge and that NGOs and citizen groups are increasingly addressing this issue, an investigation of cooperative solutions and activities seems rather obvious. This may include climate and environment-related goals or the stability of the financial market. The foundation of global cooperatives might be a possible conceptual model just as the foundation or use of local co-operatives which provide for the local supply of global public goods. Cooperatives cannot only facilitate the implementation, but also the transfer of the knowledge on global goods, just like development partnerships can lead to the provisioning of global public goods through the transfer of cooperative know-how. Nations, citizens, NPOs or enterprises as well as combinations thereof form the member group in such models (for the co-operative solutions concerning the supply of public goods see Theurl, 2012).

Natural monopolies are the organisational answer to subadditive cost structures which are either organised or regulated by the state. Today, network industries are of special importance. They are characterised by natural monopolies in the value-added chains which are upstream and/or downstream of competitive sectors. The services of such natural monopolies represent an intermediate input necessary for wide range of goods and services offered to customers. Recently, private solutions in the form of cooperatives have emerged as alternatives to government organisation or regulation. Infrastructure cooperatives could be organised, for example, for the management of regional motorway networks, railroad networks or airports. The members of these cooperatives might either be the users or, in the case of network infrastructures, the purchasers of these services which represent an intermediate input that can be used to offer transport services etc. to customers. Already today, some co-operative network companies of the energy sector are cooperating with municipal utilities, while a considerable potential still remains dormant. Energy cooperatives, too, have become very important.

2.7.3 Easing of adaptation processes

Particularly in phases of major changes which require adaptations and new strategies, cooperatives can exploit their relative strengths. This has been true ever since they were developed and becomes visible also in today's newly founded cooperatives which represent an answer to new challenges. The special characteristics of cooperative governance facilitate such answers which can be adapted to the specific demands of the members and which then form the purpose of the individual cooperative. A cooperative answer suggests itself if alternatives are not available or do not meet the preferences of the actors, maybe because dependencies are to be avoided or because a sound economic base is to be established. Cooperatives therefore also offer an opportunity to absorb or mitigate adaptation deficiencies which occur in the course of economic changes. In addition, it turned out that cooperatives are organisations well suitable for the decentralised realisation of economic policy provisions, again, to the benefit of the microeconomic interest of the individuals. This relationship is particularly strong between the German energy transition and energy cooperatives.

2.7.4 Facilitating an economic participation

Cooperatives that have developed due to microeconomic considerations usually have positive macroeconomic effects which, however, are never the cause for the foundation of these cooperatives. Rather, these effects are collateral effects which were not intended. Thus, cooperatives assume a direct or indirect social responsibility. They are based on a long-term and sustainable strategy right from the start and can therefore provide for stabilising effects. Another source of the social responsibility of cooperatives arises from a base effect which can be achieved through their foundation. Examples of such constellations are the co-operative organisation of new markets and value-added chains as well as the development of new problem solutions, the closing of supply gaps in areas from which the government retreats, and the compensation for a lack of local supply. The foundation of cooperatives then forms the nucleus for the development of a new economic basis for a location as well as for economic cycles in regions. At that point, many citizen cooperatives, too, are entering this field today. Such cooperatives are founded by people who are endeavouring in their own interest to maintain or create infrastructures in the areas of social welfare, culture and sports as well as traffic and local supply. As a consequence direct and more frequently indirect sources of income as well as jobs are created for people. It is easy to recognise that such processes create effects going far beyond those microeconomic benefits. This is true even more if groups of the society who have no other options take the initiative or are positively affected. In such an environment, economic and social participation is made possible only through cooperative activities.

3. Members in the core of cooperatives

Experience has shown that the core of cooperatives is formed by their members acting as owners and users. They finance the enterprise, they make use of its services directly and or indirectly[3], they decide on new strategies, they generate benefit, and they obtain a co-operative return (member value) through various channels. Just like any other enterprise, cooperatives, too, generate an added value through the combination of different production factors, which also includes human capital. The distinction between management and staff leads to a prominent peculiarity: The executive boards and the supervisory boards must be members of the cooperative. In cooperatives, too, employees are employed on the basis of employment contracts which, among other things, determine the amount and form of their payment. With respect to the subject of this paper we now have to ask how employees can achieve a financial participation in the enterprise, i.e. in the cooperative.

3.1 Personnel as members

Because of the peculiar ownership constellation of cooperatives, this question arises in a special way: It is not just the usual instruments of the participation of employees in the capital and the success of the enterprise which have to be taken account of, but it is also necessary to consider the possibility that employees become members or that, right from the start, the cooperative is founded by personnel who buy or take this enterprise over from the former owners. And cooperatives might also be founded right from the start by persons who intend to become members of a staff working of a joint enterprise. In such a founding constellation, cooperative

---

3 An indirect use of services takes place when the member value of a cooperative is generated for its members through the realisation of a defined project with the intended effects, for example on the environmental sector or concerning the survival of the site, the enhancement of the region, etc.

relationships have a special character. For its members, the cooperative provides the service of a direct generation of jobs and of offering a possibility to earn income. The cooperative return is thus created through joint production. The personnel are simultaneously owners, and they become entrepreneurs, as well. Their economic activities take place directly in the cooperative and not in another enterprise. Such cooperatives – which were more important in the early days of the cooperative movement than they are today – are also known as workers' cooperatives. At present, this founding constellation is popular among free-lancers. Working within a cooperative allows them to take on larger and more complex orders. Frequently, this is the only way to enter the market. In this case, those persons are no employees but they generate an added value, in addition to their tasks as owners. This is accompanied by a reduction of the division of labour in the enterprise, i.e. by the withdrawal of the diversification of the tasks to be performed. In this constellation, personnel acting as members can generate the member value, which is made available to them.

3.2 Basic models of EFP in cooperatives

When we summarise these first considerations, two basic models of EFP in cooperatives are feasible.

3.2.1 Direct form of EFP

Within the scope of the first model, employees of cooperatives can participate in the profit of these companies on the basis of the applicable statutory regulations if the members agree so and can find solutions complying with the Act on Cooperatives.[4] For the purpose of this chapter, this is

4 For an EU-wide overview also see http://de.worker-participation.eu/. For the individual member states, there are hardly any special regulations concerning the financial participation of employees in cooperatives. Corresponding regulations are either included in the national acts on cooperatives or they do not exist at all because it is not intended to create peculiar features specific to this legal form. Neither do the German statutory regulations concerning the financial participation of employees (*'Mitarbeiterbeteiligungsgesetz'*) include provisions specific to coop-

understood as a direct form of the financial participation of personnel. In this case, the personnel remain employees of the cooperative, and this is the predominant relationship. One part of the member value is used to increase the pay for the employees. This means a redistribution of the member value takes place, because part of the cooperative return is paid out to the employees. For this reason, institutionalisations compatible with cooperatives and in compliance with the German Act on Cooperatives have to be found and agreed by the members as the owners of these societies, because the member value paid out to them is reduced. Further, the participation instrument must meet strict requirements. In particular, it must fulfil a purpose which is not exclusively capital-oriented. So far, such a model has rarely been translated into the cooperative practice. An example is given in section 4.1.

3.2.2 Indirect forms of EFP

With a second model, however, personnel can completely become owners, and thus entrepreneurs, by becoming members of the cooperative for which they are working[5], or by becoming members of a cooperative which stands in close relationship to their employer. For the purpose of this chapter, this constellation is understood as an indirect form of financial participation. The employees achieve a member value generated from their function as owners of the cooperative. This can take place via four different constellations:

First, employees can – as far as this is not precluded by the statutes – become members of their cooperative while they remain employed by it.[6] In this case, their dependent activity will be in the foreground. However, they are additionally paid out part of the member value. This situation will not be discussed any further in the following. The feature peculiar to this situation is that persons obtain values from their activity as co-owners in

eratives nor does the German Act on Cooperatives (Genossenschaftsgesetz) contain such special regulations.

5 This constellation is described in section 4.1. Of course, staff members of cooperatives may be members of other unrelated cooperatives. This, however, does not represent a EFP.

6 In turn, members may also become employees. Self-explaining examples are housing cooperatives and banking cooperatives.

their employing cooperative, in addition to their salary from their dependent activity. A correlation between these two activities arises through the level of effort within the scope of the dependent activity of the respective person, which can influence the amount of the member value. This constellation is regarded an indirect form of the financial participation of personnel for the very reason that it does not aim at the participation of personnel. It is an instrument intended either to make communication with the members easier or to gain additional equity.[7]

Second, staff members of an enterprise – independent of its legal form – may found a cooperative which is oriented towards a certain purpose, e.g. within the scope of energy supply or of social projects, and essentially remain employees of their enterprise. Such employees thus start a secondary activity which, and this is the special feature, is usually closely linked to the original enterprise. The employees are then owners of the cooperative, and they become entrepreneurs, as well. In practice, they are frequently supported by their employers in the form of leaves, know-how, premises and buildings, start-up capital, etc. By supporting the foundation of cooperatives, the employing enterprise frequently demonstrates its social commitment like, for example, for the environment, the fostering of the use of energy from renewable resources, or for the site. Independent of this, the enterprise can become a customer of the cooperative, as this is sometimes the case with outsourced energy cooperatives. An example is given in section 4.2. If the employing enterprise is a cooperative itself, this model can become very similar to a direct participation of employees and can be shaped to a real participation instrument which then has a clearly defined purpose.

Third, employees of a non-cooperative enterprise can buy this enterprise and continue to operate it as a cooperative. In this case, however, they are no longer employees but become entrepreneurs. This is referred to as an employee buy-out. Such a buy-out is frequently taken into consideration in the case of corporate crises and, in some individual cases, is also put into practice. It also serves as a model for the organisation of the succession of enterprises. Two examples are given in the sections 4.3 and 4.4.

Fourth, persons not yet working or employed in an enterprise can become founders, i.e. they can found a cooperative and carry on their

7 De facto this is usually a matter of an 'expensive equity'.

future economic activity within the cooperative. In this case they are employees and entrepreneurs at the same time. Different starting conditions are possible and can also be found in practice. In some cases, for example, the reason might be the start of a career, or the return to work after a period of unemployment or a family-related absence from the labour market. In addition, cooperatives are founded by – usually freelance – persons in order to reach the minimum size for an entry into the market. Section 4.5 gives an example from the cooperative practice.

The identified indirect forms of EFP differ in the combination of the incomes flowing to the participants. The latter two forms are focussing on the achievement of a member value, while the first two concentrate on the pay for the dependent activity and the member value is just a supplementary aspect.

4. Examples from cooperative practice

When taking a closer look at the cooperative practice, it suggests itself to look at the different forms of the financial participation of personnel on the basis of the constellations described above. In practice, models of a direct financial participation are realised where cooperatives are founding a cooperative of their own. The only purpose of this cooperative is the financial participation of the staff (Model 1: The foundation of cooperatives as an instrument of EFP). All other models (2 to 5) refer to an indirect form of EFP. Further, employees of an enterprise are founding cooperatives to achieve special goals which, however, are not primarily focused on the earning of income in their enterprise (Model 2: The foundation of cooperatives for the purpose of the realisation of special projects).

Employees become members when all or some of them continue to operate the enterprise for which they are working as a cooperative because a company crisis and the resulting insolvency or the exit from the market is to be prevented (Model 3: The foundation of cooperatives to prevent an exit from the market). Employees also become members when all or some of them continue to operate the enterprise for which they are working as a cooperative because there is no successor for this enterprise (Model 4: The foundation of cooperatives for the purpose of business succession). Further, persons may found a cooperative to exert economic activities for the purpose of earning income (Model 5: The foundation of cooperatives for the purpose of an entry into the market).

The following will give examples of the forms described above, including the constituent characteristics. These examples are simultaneously giving an impression of the extraordinary variety of cooperative activities which exists beyond EFP.

4.1 The foundation of cooperatives as an instrument of EFP[8]

The NOWEDA Mitarbeiter eG was founded in 2010 and is member of the NOWEDA eG, which is the cooperative of self-employed pharmacists. It can bring only one vote into the NOWEDA eG. Already in the previous years, the employees of the NOWEDA eG, which also include non-pharmacists, received voluntary extra payments and additionally had the option to make use of their own pension fund or of capital accumulation benefits (Fähndrich, 2011). Because only pharmacists can become members of the NOWEDA eG, however, the NOWEDA Mitarbeiter eG was established, explicitly with the aim to participate the complete staff in the success of the NOWEDA eG. This is thus a direct form of EFP. In addition, the NOWEDA Mitarbeiter eG is intended to support the old age pension scheme for the staff.

The legal form of a cooperative was chosen because the NOWEDA eG itself is a very successful cooperative with a long tradition and therefore has an affinity to cooperatives. This way, the NOWEDA Familiengenossenschaft (family co-operative) was founded, in addition to the NOWEDA Mitarbeiter eG. The official reason for the selection of this legal form is that persons can enter and exit a cooperative without major formalities and that the cooperative can provide for safety, stability and trustworthiness due to the annual review performed by a cooperative auditing association.

In 2014, the NOWEDA Mitarbeiter eG had 1,040 members. To become a member, one has to buy at least one share of €500. The longer a member has been employed by the NOWEDA eG, the more shares he can buy (Fähndrich, 2011). However, the amount is limited to a maximum of €50,000 after 20 years of employment. The management board of the NOWEDA Mitarbeiter eG consists of two members, one of which is also

8 This case study is based on the written information given by Lothar Breimann, NOWEDA eG.

member of the NOWEDA eG while the other is active on the business administration and taxes department. Furthermore, the members of the supervisory board of the NOWEDA Mitarbeiter eG are also members of the management board of the NOWEDA eG. Because the NOWEDA eG and the NOWEDA Mitarbeiter eG are headed by the same persons, the law regards the combination of these two cooperatives as a so-called 'Gleichordnungskonzern', i.e. two horizontally organised enterprises.

The foundation of the NOWEDA Mitarbeiter eG involved some challenges. For example, the NOWEDA Mitarbeiter eG was originally intended to be a pure capital investment cooperative. However, because capital investment cooperatives do not involve any economic business and are therefore not allowed according to the German Act on Co-operatives, a service had to be found which is financed by the cooperative. For this reason, the cooperative accounts for the follow-on and advanced training activities of the staff (Fähndrich, 2011). Further, capital investor protection law required written information on the risks. But even following the foundation there were still some challenges remaining. For example, there is a double tax on the dividend because the latter is paid out by the NOWEDA eG and then by the NOWEDA Mitarbeiter eG to its employee members. In addition, there are always some employees who need their invested capital within short term and want to withdraw it, so that regulations concerning a transfer without a period of notice had to be introduced.

The member value of the NOWEDA Mitarbeiter eG flows to the members through the known channels. The indirect member value for the employees corresponds to the interest return of the shares in the employee cooperative (property right). At the same time, the employees gain influence on the determination on the amount of the interests (right of participation). The direct member value is based on the general decision concerning the financial participation in the NOWEDA eG. The hedging through the foundation of an additional cooperative for this purpose represents the sustainable member value.

The employee cooperative is well accepted by the employees. During the first weeks after the foundation, €1.65 million were invested. Meanwhile more than one third of all employees are holding shares of the NOWEDA Mitarbeiter eG. For the future this is expected to increase to one half (Fähndrich, 2011). Some larger cooperative groups of the trade sector, too, have developed similar models of the financial participation of employees. Still, they are not very widespread yet.

Table 1. Overview of the NOWEDA Mitarbeiter eG

Name:	NOWEDA Mitarbeiter eG
Location:	Essen
Sector:	Pharmaceutics
Founded in:	2010
Members:	1,040 employees of the NOWEDA eG
Philosophy:	Participation of employees in the success of the enterprise

4.2 The foundation of cooperatives for the purpose of realising special projects

The 'Volkswagen Belegschaftsgenossenschaft für regenerative Energien am Standort Emden eG' (Volkswagen staff cooperative for regenerative energy in Emden), referred to as 'staff cooperative' in the following, was founded by Volkswagen employees in Emden in 2008 and involves the production of solar electricity on the premises of the Volkswagen plant (Clausen, 2014). The idea of installing renewable energy systems on the premises of the Volkswagen plant evolved already at the beginning of the nineties, when there were considerations to participate the staff in wind turbines on the Volkswagen plant. However, these considerations were not put into practice at that time. It was not until the reform of the Act on Cooperatives and the rapid development of photovoltaic technologies that good preconditions had been established to found a staff cooperative in 2008 (DGRV, 2014b). With this staff cooperative, the employees of Volkswagen in Emden hope to be able to offer a CO_2-neutral production in the future. On the roof of a production hall, 2,300 solar modules with a total surface area of 3,000 m² were installed which produce 350 megawatt hours of electric power per year (Volkswagen AG, 2011). The legal form of a cooperative was chosen because the members were convinced of the 'one-voice' principle. This is important because not just the staff but also persons from the management are members of the staff cooperative. This way, the initiators emphasise that the foundation of the staff cooperative has strengthened the cohesion within the employing company and has increased the identification of the staff with Volkswagen. This, in turn, improved the internal communication between the Volkswagen company and its employees (DGRV, 2014b).

In 2014, 227 Volkswagen employees were participants in the staff cooperative, while 99 per cent of the members are employed at the Emden site and the remaining percent is working in the Volkswagen plant in Wolfsburg ('Netzwerk Energiewende jetzt', 2014). In addition, members have the option to have their parents, children or brothers and sisters join the cooperative. This results in the fact that whole families are members of the cooperative, in addition to individual members who still represent the majority (Clausen, 2014). Participation in the cooperative requires to buy a share of at least €250. The maximum investment permitted is €10,000 ('Netzwerk Energiewende jetzt', 2014). The roofs of the production halls on the Volkswagen plant are required for the production of solar power. These halls are provided by the Volkswagen AG for 25 years for a token annual rent of €1 ('Netzwerk Energiewende jetzt', 2014). The total investment sum amounts to €1,340,000. 39 per cent of this sum are covered by equity (Clausen, 2014). Originally, the dividend was promised to reach at least five per cent in the first year. This value was reached also in the following years (DGRV, 2014b).

The project group established for the preparation of the staff cooperative consisted of the works council as the initiator as well as of staff members of the factory planning, personnel, and factory engineering departments. At the beginning, however, there were doubts whether the project could actually be run economically. For this reason, the business representatives of Volkswagen temporarily distanced themselves from the project before it finally was planned and realised (Clausen, 2014).

The foundation of a staff cooperative is based on a complex motivation which, on the staff level, is largely borne by the indirect member value component. Those VW employees who became members of the cooperative invested their own capital to finance the production of solar power. In return, they receive a dividend of five per cent. The political objectives of the energy transition and their regulatory implementation allow for a corresponding interest return, which makes the model viable also in the long term. The direct member value is proportional to the staff's support of the goals of the promotion of electricity produced from renewable energy sources. But the employing company, too, will take advantage from its Corporate Social Responsibility policy. In addition, there are macroeconomic and social effects.

The staff cooperative described above is regarded as a model of a successful initiative and serves as an example for other staff cooperatives. The production of solar power cuts down the release of CO_2 by more than 187 tons, which corresponds to the consumption of one hundred four-person households. The help of the staff cooperative made it possible to install an additional solar system on the roof of another production hall. This solar system produces 243 megawatt hours of energy and reduces the release of CO_2 by more than 124 tons (Volkswagen AG, 2011). In 2010, the staff cooperative was awarded the German Solar Prize by the German Solar Industry Association (Bundesverband der Solarwirtschaft) (Clausen, 2014).

This form of EFP, too, is an indirect one because there is no participation in the operating results of the Volkswagen plant. However, there are first signs of it because resources of the plant are utilized.[9] However, this staff cooperative model, which is not very widespread yet and which is mainly realised in the form of energy cooperatives, can be developed further and be made available to family cooperatives, for example. Within the scope of such family cooperatives it would be possible to organise nursing and care services within the scope of cooperatives founded by companies and/or the staff and to provide these services to employees. The financing and clearing could be combined with models of a financial participation of employees. So far, however, such considerations are just at the outset, at best.

Table 2. Overview of the 'Volkswagen Belegschaftsgenossenschaft für regenerative Energien am Standort Emden eG'

Name:	Volkswagen Belegschaftsgenossenschaft für regenerative Energien am Standort Emden eG
Location:	Emden
Sector:	Renewable energies
Founded in:	2008
Members:	227 employees of Volkswagen
Philosophy:	Blue Factory

4.3 The foundation of cooperatives to prevent an exit from the market

The TowerByte eG is a virtual corporate network institutionalised in the form of an e-commerce cooperative. This network was founded in Jena in the year 2003 by then seven enterprises with a total of 16 staff members.

9 This leads to interesting questions concerning the distribution of the operating results to members and non-members of the staff cooperative. However, these issues cannot be investigated further here.

Already at the time of its foundation, this network specialised on e-commerce. In 2005, it was entered into the register of cooperatives (Allert, 2008). The reason for the foundation of the cooperative was the bursting of the dotcom bubble in the year 2000. At this time, the Intershop Communications AG was a pioneer in the new economy. In the course of the economic problems following on this sector, however, they had to lay-off staff (DGRV, 2014c). In response to their dismissal, former staff members founded their own software companies. However, they faced major problems in renting business and office rooms, because the newly established enterprises could offer neither reputation nor a convincing evidence for their creditworthiness (Münster, 2013). To be able to find suitable office rooms for their enterprises nonetheless, they founded the TowerByte eG. Originally, the purpose of this cooperative was to rent suitable business and office rooms for the individual entrepreneurs. From that time on, the individual enterprises did no longer act as single tenants but as one large company.

The purpose of founding this cooperative was and still is to support young enterprises and start-ups in their entry into the e-economy. The TowerByte eG achieves this goal primarily by making use of scale and competence effects. This way, the cooperative can organise the technical infrastructure and the renting of office rooms at favourable conditions. At the same time, it aims at the joint realisation of major projects within a corporate network (Allert, 2008). This facilitates an entry into the market which would otherwise not be possible. In addition, complementary core competences of the members may be used for this purpose, too. The legal form of a cooperative was chosen by the member firms because it allows to retain the flexibility of each individual firm while simultaneously benefitting from the economies of scale and complementarity advantages evolving from the corporate network (Münster, 2013). For example, it was important to the member firms not to see their freedom and innovation being limited by the virtual corporate network. At the same time, this corporate network was intended to provide a framework allowing the firms to make joint use of the resources and the infrastructure (TowerByte eG, 2014). This way, the member firms can specialise on a certain sector within the cooperative while still keeping an overview of e-commerce developments through mutual professional exchange. The best possible use of the resources available within the cooperative is supported by the individual member firms' focus on their respective core competences (Allert, 2008).

At present, the TowerByte eG includes 24 member firms with a total of 350 staff members who are specialised in different areas. All member firms are residing in the JenTower in Jena. This allows the cooperative to make joint use of the resources and the infrastructure (TowerByte eG, 2014). By founding this cooperative, the individual entrepreneurs transformed their employee relationship into an ownership relationship, thus providing for additional jobs. Their status as entrepreneurs entitles them to the member value. They obtain this value on the direct way by utilising economies of scale, scope and risk. Before, the individual software firms were not sufficiently large to be able to organise the technical infrastructure or suitable office rooms and, especially, larger orders. The results of the cooperative service relationship are thus obvious. The sustainable member value is the result of the good starting position which the cooperative and its member firms have managed to establish on their market sector, which proves their good prospects for the future. The indirect member value arises not only through the property right but especially through the participation in decisions concerning new strategies of the cooperative, which is a very important aspect for the member firms (Münster, 2013).

The success of this cooperative is supported by the fact that numerous companies which were not founded by former Intershop employees show great interest in becoming members of this cooperative. For this reason, the cooperative does not only grow fast but it also serves as a model for the foundation of further cooperatives. In Leipzig, for example, another e-commerce cooperative – the E-Commerce Genossenschaft eG – has already been founded; it consists of nine member firms (E-Commerce Genossenschaft eG, 2014). Further, the TowerByte eG founded the Tower-Venture eG, which is intended to support new technology-oriented companies in financing themselves. This way, companies settle in Jena, providing for new jobs in this region. At the same time, Jena confirms its good reputation as an e-commerce site. Already today, the town is referred to as 'Saalicon Valley' (TowerByte eG, 2014). To sum it up, there are obvious macroeconomic and social collateral effects which have emerged on the basis of the microeconomic decision to found such a cooperative. The financial participation of the staff, however, is an indirect one because it involves the transformation of dependent workers into owners with all the property rights associated with this, implemented in the form of a cooperative.

Table 3. Overview of the TowerByte eG

Name:	TowerByte eG
Location:	Jena
Sector:	Software and e-commerce
Founded in:	2003 (registered: 2005)
Members:	24 member firms
Philosophy:	Expert knowledge and dedication under one roof

4.4 The foundation of cooperatives for the purpose of business succession

The 'Planergemeinschaft Kohlbrenner eG' is a cooperative enterprise focusing on the urban and regional development planning in and around Berlin. This cooperative emerged from the city planning office 'Kohlbrenner'. In 2006, its 64 year old owner was looking for a successor among his employees for age reasons. However, he did not find anybody willing to take over the company all on his own (Wieg, 2013). For this reason, the staff of the city planning office founded a cooperative with the aim to ensure the further existence of the enterprise. In April 2012, the staff of the enterprise took over the business (Planergemeinschaft, 2014a). In addition to the legal form of a cooperative, the staff had examined the KG (Kommanditgesellschaft as a limited partnership) and the OHG (Offene Handelsgesellschaft as a general partnership) as a possible future legal form of the city planning office. In the end, however, they chose the cooperative because they found the processes and structures of the city planning office to fit in best with the principle of democracy which (one man, one vote), in turn, they regarded to be best reflected by the legal form of a cooperative (Wieg, 2013). They assumed that the work of the city planning office, which is characterised by an equal cooperation among different specialists of various fields, corresponds best with cooperative governance (Wieg, 2013). At the same time it was emphasised that the hierarchical levels in the city planning office were not explicitly regarded as such by the staff members (Kohrs, 2012).

The Planergemeinschaft Kohlbrenner eG is headed by four persons who are also employees of the city planning office (Planergemeinschaft, 2014a). In addition, the former owner is still active in the enterprise and is a member of the Planergemeinschaft Kohlbrenner eG, too (Planergemeinschaft, 2014b). At the beginning, eight of the then 20 employees were prepared to participate in the city planning office (Wieg, 2013). Meanwhile, 17 of the 24 staff members are owners of the cooperative. They are holding between two and eight shares in the enterprise (DGRV, 2014d). To participate in the cooperative, at least two shares of €1,250 have to be bought (Wieg, 2013). With respect to the price, the staff members have agreed with the owner of the office that it will depend on the success of the enterprise: First, the holder receives a one-off payment and is given a share in the profits of the planning office for the following five years. This means that the holder is paid 20 per cent of the profit during the first three years and ten per cent in the fourth year. In the fifth year, the profit sharing is reduced to five per cent (Wieg, 2013). This represents a complex model of the distribution of the member value and the combination of the income from a dependent activity and the income as an entrepreneur.

Finding a compromise regarding the purchase price was the greatest challenge during the foundation of the cooperative. The opinions of the staff members and the owner concerning the price differed by the factor ten, which resulted in difficult negotiations. These negotiations continued for two and a half years without being able to come to an agreement. Following this, the negotiations were suspended for one year. After three employees had quit their job, however, the remaining ones were increasingly willing to find a joint solution to ensure the further existence of the city planning office. The negotiations were resumed again, and indeed a solution was found. This solution was also to be attributed to the work of a mediator who supported the two parties in the second half of their negotiations. To the opinion of the negotiating partners, this institutional procedure was of special importance because the employees were negotiating with the owner who, however, was still their superior at the same time (Wieg 2013).

With the foundation of the cooperative, the employees of the city planning office transformed their dependent employment salary into a member value. The direct benefit of this member value arises through the further existence of the enterprise as well as the possibility to use the infrastructures and the customer relationships. The sustainable component consists of the option benefit to have a job and an income also in the future. The indirect component is ensured through the interest return of the shares and the desired participation in all strategic decisions concerning the enterprise.

Concerning the cooperative, the response of the customers, too, was positive because some of them had already started to worry about the future of the city planning office and their business relations. After the cooperative had been founded, the city planning office received some inquiries by other offices which were also interested in the cooperative model for their own enterprise (Wieg, 2013). Here, too, are effects extending beyond the former employees concerned.

Table 4. Overview of the Planergemeinschaft Kohlbrenner eG

Name:	Planergemeinschaft Kohlbrenner eG
Location:	Berlin
Sector:	Architects/city planning
Founded in:	2012
Members:	17 members
Philosophy:	Designing public spaces in such a way that they also serve as a place for people to stay and not just as traffic areas.

4.5 The foundation of cooperatives for the purpose of entering into the market

The IT co-operative '7-it Informations-Management & Services eG', in the following referred to as '7-it eG' for short, is a virtual enterprise which acts as an IT service provider for small and medium-sized enterprises located in Munich. The name '7-it eG' originates from the seven IT experts who founded the cooperative in 2002 (7-it, 2014). The cooperative was mainly founded because self-employed IT experts found it difficult to become established in their sector since many customers prefer a relationship with larger enterprises (Ernst, 2012). For this reason the cooperative aims at providing self-employed IT experts with a network through which they can obtain larger and more interesting orders which otherwise would not be awarded to individual persons. However, the IT experts are not depending on this network. They keep their autonomy and can procure and process orders independent of their cooperative. The network does not just offer IT experts the possibility to deal with orders collectively but also the opportunity of a professional and social exchange as well as support by other IT experts within the enterprise (Im Einsatz für die eG, 2011). In addition, the IT cooperative seeks to concentrate the procurement of goods and services and to get better prices through economies of scale (Härtel, 2005).

There are several reasons for which the virtual enterprise chose the legal form of the cooperative: For example, the IT experts concerned wanted to keep both the foundation expenses and the liability risk as low as possible (Ernst, 2012). At the same time, most of the IT experts had been self-employed for many years and therefore wanted to retain their independence also after the virtual enterprise had been established (Härtel, 2007a). The legal form of the cooperative allows combining these two aspects: It allows the IT experts to make use of the economies of scale of the virtual enterprise without losing their independence. This also means that the IT experts can decide all by themselves whether to continue to take care of their current customers autonomously or to bring them into the co-operative. At the same time, the members of the IT co-operative are liable exclusively with their capital contribution (i.e. their cooperative shares) and not with all of their personal assets, so that the business assets remain separate from the private assets. This means a limited liability risk for the individual members, which is a great advantage of the legal form of the cooperative (Härtel, 2007a).

The members of the cooperative increased from seven in the year 2002 to 23 in 2014. All those members are IT experts who have specialised in the areas of IT organisation, IT system technology, software development or the internet (7-it, 2014). The special feature of this cooperative is that each member has his/her own office. In contrast, the 7-it eG has no office rooms of its own and no permanent employees. This minimises the fixed costs of the cooperative (Ernst, 2012). The foundation of the cooperative required a time of 300 working days. The costs of the foundation amounted to approximately €8,000, and had to be borne by the founding members (Härtel, 2005, p. 13). To cover the costs incurred today and to build up reserves, the cooperative receives a certain percentage of the turnover for each order which is transacted through it. At the beginning this percentage was five per cent. Since 2006, ten per cent of the turnover is paid to the 7-it eG. Further, new members have to pay an 'entry fee' of €1,000, in addition to their capital contribution. This fee is intended to cover the foundation expenses of the 7-it eG (Härtel, 2007b).

The selection of new members constitutes a major challenge for the cooperative. For example, it is important to the existing members that new partners are harmonising among each other and fit in well with the old members, to ensure smooth cooperation within the cooperative. This also requires that the way of working and the business practices of the individual members do not differ too far. For this reason, the 7-it eG checks in a joint project whether a potential new member actually fits into the cooperative, before admitting him/her as a new member (Härtel, 2007a).

Concerning the actual institutionalisation, the two examples given above may differ just marginally from the foundation model described in section 4.3. The reasons for and the way towards the foundation of a cooperative are different, however. In the case of the TowerByte eG, a business crisis and thus self-help was standing in the foreground in order to prevent individual actors from exiting the market. In contrast to this, the 7-it eG was founded to facilitate an entry into the market. This concerns actors who become suppliers for the first time (newcomers) or who can no longer ensure the competitiveness of their self-employed activity due to changed framework conditions and therefore become members of the cooperative. Overlapping foundation or entry motivations are possible only in the case of this group of actors.

Here, too, the member value for the members of the virtual enterprise 7-it eG is composed of three elements: First, there is the direct member value in the form of a service relationship. The IT experts are integrated into a network which allows them to deal with orders which otherwise would not be awarded to individual persons. They can retain their autonomy while still taking advantage of the jointly organised services of the enterprise network. This also ensures a sustainable basis for their self-employed activity (sustainable member value) and allows them to take influence on decisions concerning the development of the network (indirect member value).

The foundation of the 7-it eG is considered a success both by the trade and the members. A survey among the members of the virtual enterprise shows that the membership of the IT experts in this enterprise gives them a chance to get hold of orders which they otherwise would not obtain as self-employed IT experts (Härtel, 2007a). In the year 2012, the turnover of the cooperative was in the upper six-digit range, with the members expecting a further rise for the future (Ernst, 2012). There are numerous other examples of the foundation of cooperatives for the purpose of a market entry, mainly by free-lance actors like, for example, artists (e.g. the 'Berliner Künstlergenossenschaft eG', 2014), media service providers (e.g. 'mediaPolis', 2014), creative economy providers (e.g. 'the seed eG, 2014'), or by craftsmen (e.g. the 'Handwerkergenossenschaft die dichter eG', 2014, or the 'Roter Hahn eG', 2014).

Table 5. Overview of the 7-it Informations-Management & Services eG

Name:	7-it Informations-Management & Services eG
Location:	Munich
Sector:	Information and communications technology
Founded in:	2002
Members:	23 IT experts
Philosophy:	High IT competence at fair prices

5. *Restrictions and perspectives*

Cooperatives represent a cooperation and participation model directed at providing individual persons with the possibility to become economically active as entrepreneurs and owners. This forms the basis of their special governance which they made an institutional innovation at the time of its emergence. Today, too, a cooperative is founded as a form of self-help with the aim to establish or support an economic basis for self-employed persons. The primary purpose of cooperatives is thus to promote enterprises and not staff members; their performance and pay are institutionalised via corresponding contracts. The aim is rather to set incentives for owners instead of dependent employees. Economic participation is thus not intended to be achieved through an additional participation in the operating results of an enterprise but through the complete acquisition of these results, also by the other owners. This is the main reason why the financial participation of staff members is not one of the predominant subjects of cooperatives. In addition, cooperatives are medium-sized enterprises which exist especially in the form of smaller companies. Models of a direct financial participation of staff members are discussed and implemented especially by larger cooperative groups.

But much more important and more extensively used in cooperatives are indirect forms of the financial participation which arise from the opportunity or the necessity for employees (together with their partners) to become owners of their own cooperative, thus becoming more than just employees, i.e. they become cooperative entrepreneurs in addition to their dependent activity. The latter may not represent a financial participation of employees, but it might generate an additional income. At least, however, it generates a member value. There are strong indications that such indirect models of a financial participation will become more important in the future because the economic and social framework conditions have proven to be promoting cooperatives. With the foundation of even more cooperatives, alternatives to dependent activities, too, will increasingly move into the focus.

There are several developments pointing into this direction. First, employment contracts are increasingly diversified and also include self-employment elements. Second, the developments on the information and communication technology sector have resulted in changed value-added models which are suggesting network structures. Third, project-oriented economic activities are emerging which are pushing long-term employment contracts into the background and are fostering free-lance activities instead. Fourth, the demographic developments involve extraordinary challenges which suggests cooperative solutions in many areas.

If these developments are taken into account, the subject of EFP through cooperatives must be reformulated, too. In the face of these circumstances, the question is how cooperatives can contribute to come to a more equitable distribution of incomes, while 'equitable' will have to be measured against the contribution of the individual actors to an added value. EFP in its current form involves concessions to the employers. Such concessions are usually negotiated by the state as an agent of the employees, are laid down in participation acts ('Beteiligungsgesetze'), and become agreeable through fiscal incentives. Cooperatives, however, do not only give incentives for business activities but they also promote the willingness to take responsibility for economic activities, facilitate an economic participation, and provide for an adequate return for the willingness to take economic risks.

References

7-it (2014). *Die Genossenschaft.* Available at: http://www.7-it.de/genossenschaft/-7-it.html [12.12.2014].

Allert, W. (2008). *Das kleine Wirtschaftswunder aus dem Intershop-Tower.* Dialog, 10, p. 26-27. Available at: http://www.towerbyte.de/pressespiegel/0809_DZ_magazin_MGV_TowerByte.pdf [12.12.2014].

Berliner Künstlergenossenschaft eG (2014). Über uns. Available under: http://www.berliner-kuenstlergenossenschaft.de/page1.php [12.12.2014].

Böttiger, J-M. (2009). MemberValue für Wohnungsbaugenossenschaften. Ein Ansatz zur Operationalisierung des MemberValues für Wohnungsbaugenossenschaften und Handlungsempfehlungen für ein MemberValue-Management. Aachen: Shaker.

Clausen, J. (2014). *Belegschaftsgenossenschaften zur Förderung der Energiewende.* Available at: http://www.eneebler.de/wp-content/uploads/2014/03/Leitfaden_Belegschaftsgenossenschaften_Energiewende.pdf [12.12.2014].

Deutscher Genossenschafts- und Raiffeisenverband e.V. (2014a). *Genossenschaften in Deutschland.* Available at: http://www.genossenschaften.de/ [12.12.2014].

Deutscher Genossenschafts- und Raiffeisenverband e.V. (2014b). *Portraits junger Genossenschaften - Volkswagen Belegeschaftsgenossenschaft für regenerative Energien am Standort Emden eG.* Available at: http://www.genossenschaften.de/volkswagen-belegeschaftsgenossenschaft-f-r-regenerative-energien-am-standort-emden-eg [12.12.2014].

Deutscher Genossenschafts- und Raiffeisenverband e.V. (2014c). *Portraits junger Genossenschaften – TowerByte eG, Jena.* Available at: http://www.genossenschaften.de/towerbyte-eg-jena [12.12.2014].

Deutscher Genossenschafts- und Raiffeisenverband e.V. (2014d). *Portraits junger Genossenschaften – Planergemeinschaft Kohlbrenner eG, Berlin.* Available at: http://www.genossenschaften.de/planergemeinschaft-kohlbrenner-eg-berlin [12.12.2014].

E-Commerce Genossenschaft eG (2014). *Die E-Commerce Genossenschaft.* Available at: http://www.e-commerce-genossenschaft.de/ [12.12.2014].

Ernst, E. (2012). *Besser gemeinsam.* Wirtschaft – Das IHK-Magazin für München und Oberbayern,10, p. 52-54. Available at: http://www.7-it.de/dokumente/upload/8f311_ihk_magazin_10_2012.pdf [12.12.2014].

Fähndrich, C. (2011). *„Das Wir-Gefühl stärken".* Genossenschaftsblatt für Rheinland und Westfalen, 2, p. 40. Available at: http://www.rwgv.de/_downloads/Genossenschaftsblatt/NEU-FINAL-RWGV-11.244-genoblatt.pdf [12.12.2014].

Handwerkergenossenschaft die dichter eG (2014). *Handwerkergenossenschaft die dichter eG.* Available at: http://www.die-dichter.com/ [12.12.2014].

Härtel, H. (2007a). *Autonomie und Bindung: IT-Genossenschaften als Zusammenschluss Selbständiger.* Contraste, 12, p. 7. Available at: http://www.7-it.de/dokumente/upload/b87c7_selbststaendigen-genossenschaften.pdf [12.12.2014].

Härtel, H. (2007b). *Verbindliche Rollenaufteilung: Grundlage professioneller Auftragsabwicklung.* Contraste, 12, p. 8. Available at: http://www.7-it.de/dokumente/upload/b87c7_selbststaendigen-genossenschaften.pdf [12.12.2014].

Härtel, H. (2005). *Genossenschaften – eine vergessene Alternative?* Available at: http://www.7-it.de/dokumente/upload/6583e_vortragsunterlagen_genossenschaften.pdf [12.12.2014].

Im Einsatz für die eG (2011). Profil, 9, p. 41. Available at: http://www.7-it.de/dokumente/upload/d359f_profil_artikel_09_2011.pdf [12.12.2014].

Kohrs, J. (2012). *Mediatoren der Veränderung - Die Planergemeinschaft Kohlbrenner hat sich als Genossenschaft neu erfunden.* Morgenpost, 25.06.2012. Available at: http://www.planergemeinschaft.de/article/presseresonanz-auf-genossenschaftsgr%C3%BCndung [12.12.2014].

Kräkel, M. (1999). Organisation und Management. Tübingen: Mohr Siebeck.

mediaPolis (2014). *Sieben auf einen Streich! – Startschuss für Agentur-Genossenschaft.* Available at: http://www.mediapolis.de/sieben-auf-einen-streich-startschuss-fuer-agentur-genossenschaft/ [12.12.2014].

Münster, T. (2013). *Bürokratische Hürden bremsen Gründungsboom der Genossenschaften aus.* Available at: http://www.impulse.de/management/genossenschaften-der-gru%CC%88ndungsboom-wird-durch-bu%CC%88rokratische-hu%CC %88rden-gebremst [12.12.2014].

Netzwerk Energiewende jetzt (2014). Volkswagen Belegschaftsgenossenschaft für regenerative Energien am Standort Emden eG. Available at: http:// www.energiegenossenschaften-gruenden.de/82.html? &cHash=0173280393c6b9737c29c07345fe4c14&tx_egg_pi1[action]=detail&tx_egg_pi1[energy_association]=227&tx_egg_pi1[region]=79&tx_egg_pi1[searchGs]=on [12.12.2014].

Planergemeinschaft (2014a). *Planergemeinschaft. Interdisziplinär, erfahren, engagiert.* Available at: http://www.planergemeinschaft.de/planergemeinschaft-interdisziplin %C3%A4r-erfahren-engagiert [12.12.2014].

Planergemeinschaft (2014b). *Urs Kohlbrenner.* Available at: http://www.planergemeinschaft.de/person/urs-kohlbrenner [12.12.2014].

Roter Hahn eG (2014). Available under: http://www.der-rote-hahn.de/ [12.12.2014].

the seed eG (2014). *Über uns.* Available at: http://communications.theseed.de/ueber-uns/ [12.12.2014].

Theurl, T. (2013a). Genossenschaftliches MemberValue-Management. In M. Gmür, R. Schauer & L. Theuvsen (ed.), *Performance Management in Nonprofit-Organisationen* (p. 316-325). Bern: Haupt Verlag.

Theurl, T. (2013b). Genossenschaften 2012: Einzelwirtschaftliches Fundament, Gesamtwirtschaftlicher Erfolg, Gesellschaftliche Werte. In J. Brazda, M. Dellinger & D. Rößl (ed.), *Genossenschaften im Fokus einer neuen Wirtschaftspolitik, Subvol. 1* (p. 23-44). Münster: LIT Verlag.

Theurl, T. (2013c). Gesellschaftliche Verantwortung von Genossenschaften durch MemberValue-Strategien, In: *Zeitschrift für das gesamte Genossenschaftswesen*, Vol. 63 (2), p. 81-94.

Theurl, T. (2013d). Das ordnungspolitische Profil von Genossenschaften. In I. Pies (ed.), *Das weite Feld der Ökonomik. Volume 98. Schriften zu Ordnungsfragen der Wirtschaft* (p. 185-191). Stuttgart: Lucius & Lucius.

Theurl, T. (2012). Genossenschaftliche Organisation globaler öffentlicher Güter. In M. Maring (ed.), *Globale öffentliche Güter in interdisziplinären Perspektiven* (p. 215-233). Karlsruhe: KIT Scientific Publishing.

Theurl, T. (2010). Genossenschaftliche Kooperationen. In D. Ahlert & M. Ahlert (ed.), *Handbuch Franchising und Cooperation* (p. 71-105). Frankfurt/Main: Deutscher Fachverlag.

Theurl, T. (2002). "Shareholder Value" und "genossenschaftlicher Förderauftrag" - Zwei unvereinbare strategische Ausrichtungen? In T. Theurl & R. Greve (ed.), *Vom Modell zur Umsetzung - Strategische Herausforderungen für Genossenschaften* (p. 51-91). Aachen: Shaker.

Theurl, T. & Schweinsberg, A. (2004). Neue kooperative Ökonomie. Moderne genossenschaftliche Governancestrukturen. Tübingen: Mohr Siebeck.

Theurl, T. & Wendler, C. (2011). *Was weiß Deutschland über Genossenschaften.* Aachen: Shaker.

TowerByte eG (2014). *Über die TowerByte eG*. Available at: http://www.towerbyte.de/ueber_uns.php [12.12.2014].

Tschöpel, M. (2013). Die MemberValue-Strategie von Genossenschaftsbanken. Die Operationalisierung des MemberValue und Implikationen für das Management von genossenschaftlichen Primärbanken. Aachen: Shaker.

Volkswagen AG (2011). *Die nachhaltige Fabrik – Ein ökologischer Spaziergang durch das Werk Emden / Sonne, Wind und Biomasse.* Available at: http://autogramm.volkswagen.de/05_11/standorte/standorte_06.html [12.12.2014].

Wieg, A. (2013). *Nachfolgen planen.* Genossenschaften für den Mittelstand – Größenvorteile nutzen, Spielräume erweitern, Selbstständigkeit sichern. P. 32-35. Available at: http://www.genossenschaften.de/sites/default/files/Gr%C3%BCnderfibel_Genossenschaften%20f%C3%BCr%20den%20Mittelstand.pdf [12.12.2014].